G000074986

REFORMING BRITAIN

New Labour, New Constitution?

REFORMING BRITAIN

New Labour, New Constitution?

JOHN MORRISON

REUTERS

Published by **Pearson Education**

London / New York / San Francisco / Toronto / Sydney / Tokyo / Singapore
Hong Kong / Cape Town / Madrid / Amsterdam / Munich / Paris / Milan

PEARSON EDUCATION LIMITED

Head Office:
Edinburgh Gate
Harlow CM20 2JE
England
Tel: +44 (0)1279 623623
Fax: +44 (0)1279 431059

London Office:
128 Long Acre
London WC2E 9AN
Tel: +44 (0)20 7447 2000
Fax: +44 (0)20 7240 5771
Website: www.business-minds.com

_____

First published in Great Britain 2001

ISBN 1 903 68403 X

British Library Cataloguing in Publication Data
A CIP catalogue record for this book can be obtained from the British Library

10 9 8 7 6 5 4 3 2 1

Typeset by Pantek Arts Ltd, Maidstone, Kent.
Printed and bound in Great Britain by Biddles Ltd of Guildford and King's Lynn.

The Publishers' policy is to use paper manufactured from sustainable forests.

ABOUT THE AUTHOR

JOHN MORRISON studied Modern Languages at Oxford and joined Reuters as a journalist in 1971. His career as a foreign correspondent took him to the Soviet Union, France, The Netherlands, Austria, Southern Africa and post-communist Russia and Ukraine. He spent 1990–91 as a Fellow of the Russian Research Center at Harvard University and wrote *Boris Yeltsin: From Bolshevik to Democrat*, the first biography of the Russian leader in any language, described by the *Los Angeles Times* as 'an incisive analysis of the tumultuous events in the Soviet Union since 1985'. From 1997–99 he was Chief Political Correspondent for Reuters at Westminster. He is now a freelance author and lives in Kent.

This book is dedicated to the memory of my parents

Jim and Muriel Morrison

CONTENTS

FOREWORD
by Michael Brunson, former ITN Political Editor

SHORTLY AFTER 10 PM ON THE night of 1 May 1997, Jonathan Dimbleby and I, as co-presenters of ITV's General Election results programme, were discussing the astonishing findings of the exit poll we had just made public. The poll showed that Labour was about to win a landslide victory of far greater proportions than either the party itself or the political commentators had dared to contemplate.

Jonathan asked me for my reaction to it. I said that if our predictions were confirmed, we were about to witness a truly decisive moment in British political history. I went on to explain why. The new government would command the sort of majority that would give it the confidence to carry through its promise of radical reform. Above all, such a majority made it certain that the new administration would implement one major programme of reform above all – its proposals for far-reaching constitutional change.

The Labour party's plans for devolution – effectively the redrawing of the political map of Britain – and the effect those plans would have on the future of the United Kingdom as a whole, had been an important election issue. As the campaign drew to a close, one of John Major's last acts as prime minister and leader of the Conservative party had been to highlight what he saw as the terrible dangers of devolution. Standing outside the Houses of Parliament, and with Big Ben symbolically chiming behind him, he declared that 'there are just 24 hours left to save the Union'. What Labour was planning to do was, in Tory eyes, that serious – no less, they said, than the destruction of the UK as we knew it.

Mr Major's dire predictions of the immediate break-up of the Union may not have come to pass thus far, though there are many who still believe that the worst is yet to come. Nonetheless, a great deal of change has already taken place. In this book, John Morrison sets out with great clarity how Labour formed its ideas for radical change. He describes how Tony Blair and his ministers tackled the job of implementing them, and how those reforms, piecemeal though they may be thus far, are already affecting every corner, not just of government but of public life in Britain.

The book draws together evidence from those who have been closely involved in what became, in the event, a somewhat haphazard process, and from those whose job it is to be professional watchers of political and constitutional change. Long hours of personal interviews with the principal players, together with other contributions from a great variety of writers and commentators, have been sifted, edited and brought together in a narrative framework. In some of that testimony, people like Home Secretary Jack Straw and the Liberal Democrat leader Paddy Ashdown take a step back. They set out, for the first time, their considered views on just how Tony Blair and his government have tackled the biggest programme of reforming our political institutions for a century.

I am delighted to see that the author pays due regard to something in which I had a personal hand. The government's decision to make citizenship education part of the National Curriculum, following the recommendations of the Crick Committee of which I was a member, may not be the most monumental of those it has taken, but it is, in my view, one of the most important. I believe that extending the teaching of citizenship to English and Welsh schools (it's long been taught in Scotland) will have far-reaching consequences. In the long term, it will increase our national political literacy. In the short term, I very much hope that it will help to reduce the distaste and cynicism about politics and government that so many young people presently feel.

But, as constitutional change continues, everyone, and not just the younger generation, is going to need a touch of citizenship education. In every way, therefore, this is a timely book. After the initial excitement of the referendums on devolution, and the establishment of the Scottish Parliament, the Welsh Assembly, together with the new arrangements in London, and the changes to the House of Lords, constitutional change has become the slow burn of the Blair administration. This book repeatedly emphasizes, for example, that after devolution in Scotland and Wales, change must follow in England. There is, too, the unfinished business of the reform of the House of Lords, and the constitutional consequences that *will* arise, whatever Gordon Brown says now, if Britain joins the Single European Currency.

Constitutional reform will always come and go in the headlines as more traditional issues such as the management of the economy and the state of our schools and hospitals reassert themselves. But, headlines or not, the reform process is inexorably under way, and cannot now be checked. It is beginning to touch all our lives, and we need to understand how and why. This book, the first comprehensive overview of the process, is a valuable aid to our doing so.

PREFACE AND ACKNOWLEDGEMENTS

THE LABOUR CABINET LED BY TONY BLAIR has done more than govern Britain. It has begun reforming *the way* it is governed. Constitutional change has been far-reaching, but largely unexplained. Because we are almost the only country in the world without a written constitution, it is often hard to see the dividing line between continuity and change. Since May 1997 the traditional orthodoxy about how Britain is governed has been called into question by a historic sequence of reforms, but there has been no new narrative to take its place. My ambition has been to fill that gap, not just for experts but for everyone who has a vote.

Most books about British politics by journalists are described as the work of 'Westminster insiders'. My vantage point is slightly different. I began reporting British politics in 1997, after a quarter of a century as a foreign correspondent. I believe that, instead of looking out at Britain from the Palace of Westminster, it can be helpful to stand back and look at our political system from the outside. A bit of distance can add perspective to the picture.

Before getting to know the Blair government as Chief Political Correspondent for Reuters, my relationship with British politics was partly determined by the fact that for six successive general elections, I was abroad and unable to vote. When Edward Heath became prime minister in 1970 I was a student in Paris, moving on to live and work in Moscow, Vienna, The Hague, Moscow (again), Paris, Harare and Boston. When I returned in 1991, the Thatcher revolution had come and gone, and John Major was in 10 Downing Street.

Under Brezhnev I read a lot of *Pravda*, counted the Soviet politburo as they lined up on the mausoleum in Red Square, and met discreetly with dissidents on park benches. Under Yeltsin, 20 years later, I watched tanks shell the Russian parliament. In between I covered France's first experiment in political *cohabitation* of a leftwing president and a rightwing prime minister. I was in The Hague when the Dutch political parties spent five months wrangling over the shape of their new coalition (and nobody cared). I was in Kiev when Ukraine voted for independence from the Soviet Union. And

I reported on election campaigns and party congresses under various political regimes, pleasant and unpleasant, from Austria to Zimbabwe. I hope my outsider's perspective on how the British 'do politics' has been informed by watching other people do it elsewhere. Living and working for long periods in countries where human rights were a bad joke and democracy was a sham has given me a strong belief in the importance of both, and a lifelong suspicion of institutions which claim a monopoly of political power and wisdom. I also learned that it is good to think the unthinkable, because political systems are more fragile than they look. Sometimes a dose of democracy can prove fatal. I left Moscow in 1983 thinking the Soviet Union, if not exactly permanent, would probably outlast my journalistic career. A few years later I was back again, watching it collapse after a bare five years of Mikhail Gorbachev's *perestroika* reforms, with nobody lifting a finger to defend it.

When I finally began reporting the politics of my own country, as a recycled Kremlinologist, I stumbled on something unfamiliar. Everywhere else had a political rulebook, even if politicians ignored it. In most of the Reuters offices where I had worked, somewhere at the back of a bookshelf there was a tattered copy of the national constitution. But in Britain, nobody had ever written down the rules of the political game in one place. The only place I had seen which relied on mysterious tribal conventions in the same way as Westminster and Whitehall was the royal kraal in Swaziland.

So this book is the product of my curiosity; in a period of unprecedented constitutional change, I have tried to ask that old journalistic question: 'What's going on here?'. If I have felt something of an outsider at Westminster, then so have millions of others, the ones the Labour government has dubbed, in Charles Falconer's memorable phrase, *ordinary people*. My project has been to sketch a preliminary map of the constitutional reforms that Labour has set in motion, and the ones it has quietly avoided or overlooked. This is a book about a British version of *perestroika*, about the *re-forming* of Britain since 1997. It is not another book about the demise of British identity, a subject covered in admirable fashion by other authors. Inevitably, it deals more with government than the governed, more with the state than with its citizens. 'We must not let daylight in upon magic,' warned that Victorian constitutional sage Walter Bagehot. My starting point is the opposite: to shed a little daylight (what Gorbachev used to call *glasnost*) on Tony Blair and his government. If the answers to the questions I ask do not always emerge with certainty, it is because constitutional reforms take years before their final significance becomes clear. In the oft-repeated phrase of former Secretary of State for Wales Ron Davies, we are dealing with a process rather than an event. Starting from a position broadly sympathetic to constitutional reform, I have tried to be fair. In the best traditions of the European Convention on Human Rights I have treated all politicians as innocent until proved guilty, at least until the final chapter.

My approach has been to illuminate my subject matter by quoting a cross-section of informed views rather than just my own. I conducted more than 50 hours of on-the-record taped interviews with politicians and academic experts. Quotes in the text whose source is not otherwise identified come from these interviews. In referring to life peers I have generally used the names by which they are best known, for example, Douglas Hurd rather than Lord Hurd. Hereditary peers and Law Lords are, however, mostly referred to by their titles.

I would like to thank all those in Westminster, Edinburgh and Cardiff who found time in their busy diaries to see me, particularly present and past government ministers. Those who could not find the time will discover in some cases that their silence has brought its own rewards. Inevitably, on such a broad subject, I have drawn many insights from the writings of others. These are listed in the bibliography. I have also been helped by many politicians, journalists and academics who have given me the benefit of their advice in less formal ways. These include Peter Hennessy, Robert Hazell, Peter Riddell, Meg Russell, Michelle Mitchell, Pam Giddy and her colleagues at Charter88, Vernon Bogdanor, Greg Power of the Hansard Society, John Tomaney, John Adams and Maurice Frankel. I am particularly grateful to Dominic Hilton for allowing me to quote from his unpublished Oxford University master's thesis on Labour's constitutional policymaking before 1997. Among lobby correspondents at Westminster I owe a special debt to my former colleagues Mike Peacock, Dominic Evans, Edna Fernandes and Susan Cornwell of Reuters for their help.

I would like to thank my son Alexander for preparing most of the bibliography, and my wife Penny for reading the manuscript. I hope that they and my other son Nicholas have forgiven me my failure to concentrate on other matters during the writing of this book. I would like to thank my former employer, Reuters, for the opportunity to write this book. Izabel Grindal and Elaine Herlihy of Reuters helped get this project started. Martin Drewe, Vivienne Church and Linda Dhondy of Pearson Education helped get it finished. Needless to say, any errors are entirely mine.

1

FROM BAGEHOT TO BLAIR

'In the United Kingdom, alas, we do not plan our constitutional changes. We drift, or we walk crablike, along the path of constitutional change'
– Donald Anderson MP

'Most of the senior ministers involved in constitutional reform either don't believe in it, aren't interested in it, or don't understand it'
– Whitehall insider, quoted by Professor Peter Hennessy

'We are the anorak brigade' – Oona King MP

OWN UP. ADMIT IT. YOU'VE SEEN their type before. Nothing personal, mind, but you'd rather not sit next to one on a long train journey, or be trapped in a long conversation with one in the pub.

Constitutional reformers, that's who I mean. You know the sort. Hanging around party conferences with a bag of leaflets and scribbling with green ink in a notebook. They'd rather spend an evening at the Electoral Reform Society than go to a football match. Middle-class trainspotters, the sort who fix you with a beady stare, pin you against the bar for an hour and harangue you about the difference between the alternative vote and the single transferable vote.

Labour MP Oona King has watched people's eyes glazing over and recognizes the symptoms:

It's associated with anoraks, isn't it? We are the anorak brigade. It's associated with people who think electoral reform is, well … it's things you don't understand, it's AV, it's STV, it's probably the human genome project, things that you haven't quite got a grip on, so people shy away from it.[1]

Most Labour politicians (Oona King is one of the exceptions) take the view that if the voters aren't that interested in constitutional questions, there is no great reason why they should be either. Sensible MPs who want to get re-elected stick to bread-and-butter issues. Constitutional reform 'doesn't play down at the Dog and Duck', say the experts with a shake of the head. It's an issue for the chattering classes, for *student unions* (pronounced with special venom) and for people who have nothing better to whinge about. Democracy? On working-class housing estates in Doncaster, the voters have got more important things to worry about – jobs, schools, hospitals. These are the things for which a Labour government should save its time and energy.

The alternative view is that the issue is fundamental. Leave aside the anorak words *constitutional reform* for the time being, and think about democracy and citizenship. Oona King, who represents one of Britain's most deprived areas, Bethnal Green and Bow, believes inner-city London is suffering a 'crisis of democracy', not just social exclusion but political exclusion, with apathy and low turnouts. Under the existing first-past-the-post electoral system, safe seats like hers simply do not count. Elections are won and lost in 100 or so marginal constituencies somewhere in the suburbs of Middle England. Elsewhere politicians ignore the voters and so the voters ignore them. 'And you might think that's not a bad thing if you didn't have a little bee in your bonnet about democracy.'

> 66 Elections are won and lost in 100 or so marginal constituencies somewhere in the suburbs of Middle England. Elsewhere politicians ignore the voters and so the voters ignore them. 99

YOU DON'T HAVE TO WEAR AN ANORAK

So it is not for the Hampstead chattering classes that constitutional reform is vitally needed, but for the people at the bottom of the heap. Ask voters if they care how decisions are made that affect their lives, and they will say yes. Who decides how much interest you pay on a mortgage, on the route of a bypass, on the closure of a maternity ward, on the level of your council tax? Should you have the right to stage a sit-in protest in the middle of the road? Can you go to court if your child is excluded from school? Can you find out whether those electricity power lines behind your house are really safe? These may not look like constitutional questions, but they all involve the relationship between the citizen and the state. You don't have to wear an anorak to understand them.

Tony Blair has managed at different times to espouse both of these positions. In 1996, well before he entered Downing Street, he appeared to put constitutional reform near the top of his agenda, proclaiming: 'This issue of government is not one for the "chattering classes" – consigned dismissively to the inside pages of the broadsheets. It touches the vitals of the nation.' At other times, he has appeared totally uninterested.

I hope this book will show that constitutional reform, while sometimes complex and contradictory, is a lot simpler than the human genome project. Some of the time, it can even be interesting. Essentially, it is about political power and the rules that govern how it is exercised; it is also about who we are and where we belong. An extraordinary amount has happened, much of it irreversible, since 1 May 1997. The United Kingdom is no longer a unitary state; it has created a Scottish parliament, a Welsh assembly, and a Northern Ireland assembly; there has been groundbreaking legislation on human rights which will mean a historic change in the relationship between the courts and parliament; nine-tenths of the hereditary peers have been expelled from the House of Lords; we have a freedom of information law, hugely complex new rules on party funding, and a new impartial body to supervise elections and referendums. Taken together, these are the biggest changes in constitutional arrangements for more than a century, possibly since the Glorious Revolution of 1688 and the Act of Union with Scotland of 1707.

But here is the first of many paradoxes. From a government that is frequently accused of being obsessed with presentation, there has been little or no explanation of how these reforms fit together. The old British constitution has slipped its anchor and is floating away downstream, but the captain on the bridge has failed to indicate the final destination. In the view of one political scientist, he even appears to be asleep on the bridge.

A JIGSAW WITH MISSING PIECES

Here is a second paradox. While large areas of the British constitution have been subject to reform, others have remained curiously untouched by the magic wand of Blairite modernization. These include the electoral system for the House of Commons, the monarchy and the senior judiciary. Some reforms, such as freedom of information, have been more limited than promised; others, like the reform of political finance, have gone further; and some have been missing altogether. Overall, the impression is of a jigsaw with missing pieces.

What is lacking is a strong democratic narrative that would link everything from devolution to the European Union, from the monarchy to electoral reform, from human rights to citizenship education and beyond. What evidence we have suggests that people like the taste of constitutional reform and want more, but are losing faith in Labour's ability to deliver it. A remarkable 'State of the Nation' poll conducted by ICM Research for the Joseph Rowntree Reform Trust in November 2000 showed big majorities for fixed parliamentary terms, a written constitution, freedom

> 66 What evidence we have suggests that people like the taste of constitutional reform and want more, but are losing faith in Labour's ability to deliver it. 99

of information, referendums on electoral reform and regional assemblies, a largely elected House of Lords, greater decentralization of power, an expanded Bill of Rights, and for proportional voting for parliament and local government. But the trust in government which Labour promised to restore in 1997 was woefully absent. Large majorities said they did not trust ministers to tell them the truth about such issues as genetically modified crops, nuclear safety and British beef. Most people saw sleaze, cronyism, media manipulation and government favouritism towards business as major problems, and 54 per cent believed the country was getting less democratic. One of the survey authors, academic Stuart Weir, commented: 'Faith in the way we are governed, which grew after 1997, is falling away again. Blair has failed to restore trust in British democracy and to bring government closer to the people. Overall, the public now take much the same view of government and the governing system as they did under John Major.'[2]

This book examines both the complete and the incomplete parts of the jigsaw, beginning with a brief look at the conventional wisdom about the constitution, summed up by the Scottish writer Tom Nairn as 'a realm of quasi-legal necromancy' performed on a mist-shrouded plateau by a special breed of academic shamans.[3] We shall then travel down what Nairn describes as the ancient goat-track leading to Westminster to look at Labour's constitutional policies before its election victory on 1 May 1997. The next two chapters deal with devolution, firstly in Scotland and Wales and secondly in England, one of the missing pieces of the jigsaw. We then move on to the unfinished reform of the House of Lords and the largely unreported story of how a simple proposal to outlaw foreign donations to the Conservative party has mushroomed into a complicated new legal framework to regulate political funding, elections and referendums. Reform of the voting system for Westminster, another missing jigsaw piece, is the subject of a separate chapter, followed by an analysis of how the Blair government has managed Whitehall and how its initial enthusiasm for freedom of information faded. The Human Rights Act is explained in the following chapter, which uses policy towards China as a case study of Labour's difficulty in steering a straight course over human rights. Next comes a look at the higher judiciary and the role of the Lord Chancellor, a constitutional protected zone where reform has been largely avoided. We move on to examine the increasingly dysfunctional and marginalized House of Commons. The penultimate chapter looks at three related constitutional issues – citizenship, the role of the monarchy, and the British relationship with the European Union. Finally, there is an attempt to draw up an overall verdict on Labour's constitutional reforms and look more closely at Tony Blair's governing style and his 'Third Way' ideas.

The unique quality of Blair, identified early on by David Marquand, Principal of Mansfield College Oxford, has been his combination of pluralism and control freakery, his apparent willingness to share power and his simultaneous desire to hang on to it.[4] The contradiction can best be understood by the transition from policymaking in opposition to policymaking in government. One of the threads I shall trace is the way Labour's ideas originated in the wasteland of opposition and underwent a metamorphosis as government approached. The constitutional writer Ferdinand Mount once described proposals for constitutional reform as 'the poetry of the politically impotent'. Constitutions tend to limit the power of government, and proposals for reform inevitably lose their attractiveness when opposition politicians move within sight of power. Long before election day, they naturally start to favour ideas that will make their lives easier over ones that will make them more difficult. This is a tendency of all governments, but one particularly characteristic of Tony Blair's. The deepest and most far-reaching of the reforms carried out since 1997 were rooted in commitments inherited by Blair from his predecessors Neil Kinnock and John Smith. Since Blair succeeded John Smith in 1994, party policy has gradually moved from *democratization* to the more ambiguous concept of *modernization*, a shift of the tiller which has set the Labour constitutional project on a very different course.

A RISKY BUSINESS

Perhaps we should not be too surprised by this change of heart. For governments, constitutional reform can be a risky and thankless business. Ungrateful voters can frustrate the most generous and democratic of governments by using the freedom of the ballot box to vote for someone else. Changing the constitutional rules may seem hugely important to a political party in opposition, but in government inertia takes over. The system seems to work after all. If our side has won power according to the existing rules, then surely they can't be quite so bad? A party which concentrates too much on constitutional reform risks appearing like a cricket team that can neither bowl nor bat successfully but is always complaining to the umpire or seeking a change in the rules of the game. The unwritten nature of the United Kingdom constitution, with its back-of-the-envelope improvizations and its clubby reliance on convention, encourages an insider's mentality which gets more pervasive the longer a party remains in government. What can those people on the outside understand about what happens inside the complex machine of government? If it ain't broke, don't fix it. And above all, let's not make our lives more difficult than they are already.

We have to realize that governments do not undertake constitutional reform to get good reviews from high-minded journalists, academics and anorak-wearers who write in green ink. They do it either because they see a political advantage, or because they have no choice, as Ferdinand Mount describes:

It is an ever-recurring fact of history that constitutions are made, amended and broken, not by the play of rational arguments deployed by clever young men in research institutes but by the harsh clash and grinding of the tectonic plates of power. It is the political struggle rather than the pursuit of good government which ultimately decides rulers and ruling classes whether or not to drive through or give in to proposals for reform; and it is the balance of the arguments which dictates which side is to prevail.[5]

It means setting sail across uncharted waters for an unknown destination. Will the ship return safely to port in time for the next election? Or will it be lost with all hands, sent to the bottom by a sudden nationalist squall or a legal reef? All around the young ship's captain there are old sea-dogs who shake their heads and remember past voyages which came to grief. For a Labour prime minister like Tony Blair, there is the example of how James Callaghan's government wrestled unsuccessfully with Scottish and Welsh devolution in the late 1970s. The voyage ended in shipwreck on the rocks of a lost referendum and brought Labour 18 years on the desert island of opposition.

DAYLIGHT AND MAGIC

In the absence of a written text, most books on the constitution begin with the mid-Victorian pundit Walter Bagehot, and this one is no exception. It was Bagehot, analyzing what he called the *English* rather than the British constitution, who warned against letting daylight in upon magic. Bagehot was in fact referring cynically to the magic of the monarchy, which he identified as part of the 'dignified' elements of the constitution in contrast to the 'efficient' elements that did the real business of running the country. 'England is the type of deferential countries', he noted with approval in the 1860s. 'The English constitution in its palpable form is this – the mass of the people yield obedience to a select few.' The 'real rulers' of the country were not at the front of the procession in a gilded coach but travelled in rather ordinary second-rate carriages further back down the line. 'The Queen is only at the head of the dignified part of the constitution. The prime minister is at the head of the efficient part.' Behind the foreground pantomime of monarchy, devised to fool the unwashed masses with a glittering display of crowns, sceptres, gilded carriages and men in tights, was parliamentary government, a uniquely modern, practical and useful system of centralized rule through the cabinet, 'a board of control chosen by the legislature'. This is the core of Bagehot's argument: 'The efficient secret of the English constitution may be described as the close union, the nearly complete fusion, of the executive and legislative powers.' He set out to prove that this was superior to an American-style division of powers and that there was no need for external checks and balances on the power of Westminster government. Described by Ferdinand Mount as the first of the great constitutional simplifiers, Bagehot revels in reconciling apparent opposites: 'A Republic has insinuated itself beneath the folds of a Monarchy.'

One can imagine him, having settled that question once and for all, hailing a hansom cab in Whitehall, on his way to demolish a large plateful of mutton chops somewhere along the Strand. His famous analysis is factually wrong and incomplete at many points. He airily dismisses the idea that the monarch might wield real political influence over a change of government as equivalent to 'a volcanic eruption in Primrose Hill'. But historians now know that Queen Victoria was far from the political cipher he imagined her to be. His view is largely limited to Westminster, he ignores whole areas of what today would be considered part of the constitution, such as the role of the judiciary, and he avoids any discussion of Ireland, Scotland and Wales, or the governance of the British Empire.

Bagehot's cheeky aphorisms, such as his description of the Queen and the Prince of Wales as 'a retired widow and an unemployed youth', have such a contemporary ring that it comes as a shock to find how remote he is from our ideas of democracy and citizenship, based on equality and universal suffrage. Writing before the extension of the franchise in 1867, he explicitly rejected the idea of the workers getting the vote: 'If you once permit the ignorant class to begin to rule you may bid farewell to deference for ever.' He mocked 'ultra-democratic' calls for universal suffrage:

Upon this theory each man is to have one twelve-millionth share in electing a parliament; the rich and the wise are not to have, by explicit law, more votes than the poor and stupid; nor are any latent contrivances to give them an influence equivalent to more votes.

Under such a system, he declared confidently, parliament would not work. 'I do not consider the exclusion of the working classes from effectual representation as a defect in this aspect of our parliamentary representation.'

Some of his observations of Westminster, however, are as true today as when he made them. Universal suffrage has been added on to the system that Bagehot knew without fundamentally changing it. The socialist writer R.H. Tawney once said that Britain accepted democracy as a convenience, rather like an improved system of telephones, and went to the ballot box touching her hat. Here is Professor Vernon Bogdanor's unvarnished definition of how the Westminster model functions today:

The defining feature of the British system of government is the concentration of power at the centre and the absence of checks or balances on the executive. The British constitution can be defined in eight words: 'What the Queen in parliament enacts is law.'[6]

Today Bagehot would be mystified by the electronic pagers used by MPs but he would see them as proof of his argument that 'party is of the essence' to the organization of the House of Commons. He would be puzzled by the decline of the importance of the Commons chamber, no longer fulfilling its role as 'the great scene of debate, the great engine of popular instruction and political controversy'. He would no doubt appreciate among the 'curious oddities' of the constitution some new ones – hereditary peers being given a new lease of life by being allowed to elect each other to seats in the House of Lords, and advertisements in the newspapers to select 'people's peers' to sit alongside them. Bagehot, despite his fear of the 'ignorant multitude', was not part of what Tony Blair would call the forces of conservatism. Instead he was a modernizer, seeing government as a sophisticated conjuring trick. Let in too much daylight and the Victorian magic lantern loses its power.

Bagehot described how idealists become pragmatists as they move from opposition to government: '... the air of Downing Street brings certain ideas to those who live there, and ... the hard, compact prejudices of opposition are soon melted and mitigated in the great gulf stream of affairs.' He described the judicial functions of the House of Lords as 'a matter of accident' which no theorist would ever invent; and he saw the multiple roles of the Lord Chancellor as 'a heap of anomalies'. It is hardly fair to expect him to have anticipated the late 19th-century rise of the two-party system, which replaced the more fluid system of shifting Commons majorities that he knew. Nonetheless, Bagehot's defence of the Westminster model of parliamentary government, unrestrained by a written constitution or checks and balances, is essentially the same as that offered today by its dwindling band of supporters. In contrast to the American constitution, the British model 'has only one authority for all sorts of matters', he argues. Parliament, when freshly elected, 'is absolute, it can rule as it likes and decide as it likes'.

APPEARANCE AND REALITY

Despite his shortcomings, there is a key insight in Bagehot that prevented his book from being forgotten: he understood the importance of the gap between appearance and reality in the way Britain is governed. What is more, he approved of it, revelling in the way the system conspired to pull the wool over the eyes of the mob, leaving the elite to rule unhindered and keeping the 'charmed spectacle' separate from the reality of politics:

The poorer and more ignorant classes – those who would most feel excitement, who would most be misled by excitement – really believe that the Queen governs. You could not explain to them the recondite difference between 'reigning' and 'governing'. The words necessary to express it do not exist in their dialect; the ideas necessary to comprehend it do not exist in their minds.

The unnerving thing about Bagehot's *English Constitution* is that it singles out what we see as defects in the Westminster system of government, only to praise them as its essential pillars. As Professor Bogdanor points out: 'The British constitution, as it is at present, knows nothing of the people. If parliament is sovereign, then the people cannot be.'[7] This is exactly what Bagehot so admires. Faced with a choice between efficiency and transparency, he opts immediately for the former. A lack of separation of powers, a lack of checks and balances and a lack of popular sovereignty, democracy and decentralization are in his book not faults but virtues. What we would call political exclusion is for him a sign of modern and effective government. We can draw a straight line from Bagehot to the system of 'elective dictatorship' which a Conservative Lord Chancellor, Lord Hailsham, complained about in a famous speech in 1976. There are echoes of Bagehot's pragmatic managerial view of government in Tony Blair's modernizing rhetoric, with its stress on 'what counts is what works'.

> ❝What we would call political exclusion is for him a sign of modern and effective government.❞

Bagehot's stress on the gap between image and reality reminds us that politics is an art, not a science. A magician's cloak and wand are more useful than an anorak. Constitutions and political systems are not always a matter of strict rationality, however infuriating that might seem. This is because they work through a mixture of custom and tradition, none the less meaningful for sometimes being deliberately invented. Some of these are international, transcending borders. Going to the polling station to put a cross on a ballot paper is an act that has meaning on more than one level; it is rational, but it also carries a weight of ceremonial and symbolic meaning.

Bagehot divided the British constitution neatly between its dignified and its efficient parts, but the division is less clear-cut than he imagined. Symbols and ceremonies, flags and wigs and crowns are also 'efficient' in a way that Bagehot, writing before the birth of modern anthropology, did not appreciate. Just think of the Scottish saltire or the Welsh red dragon, or the symbolic importance of Big Ben, or the shape of the Commons chamber. I have deliberately left Northern Ireland off the list. In other words, there is more to mumbo-jumbo, whether royal or parliamentary, than just mumbo-jumbo. Not everything that is important can be written down. When Britons leave the Christmas table to switch on the Queen's annual broadcast on television, or when they decide not to bother, they are also performing a constitutional act. A constitution is only a word for a highly complex set of rules governing relationships, many of which are the product of historical accidents. In the words of Tom Nairn, 'Constitutional arrangements are not just bits of institutional machinery, they are meant to secure the popularity, prestige and standing of the state responsible for them.'[8]

Constitutional reform therefore involves more than just the search for logic and rationality, still less the simple substitution of modernity for tradition. New institutions use new rituals and symbols which both reflect past social and political changes and help in turn to shape future changes. The Scottish Parliament's semicircular chamber was deliberately designed to be different from the House of Commons in order to reflect a different type of politics. Constitutional reform therefore involves not just peeling away tradition but actively inventing it, as the Victorians of Bagehot's generation perhaps understood better than we do today.

INVISIBLE INK

It is the unique unwritten nature of the United Kingdom's constitution that gives the debate on reforming it a special quality. Israel is the only other country with no written constitution. The traditional case for this exceptional state of affairs is that 'our arrangements are flexible, evolving, fluid, alive; theirs are rigid, static, ossified, dead and unable to respond to change'.[9] The argument against is familiar to any reader of Tom Paine's *Rights of Man*, written in 1792 as a polemic against Edmund Burke. Paine contrasted Britain's absence of a written set of rules for the political system with the newly forged American constitution, which not only politicians but ordinary people carried in their pockets: 'It was the political bible of the state. Scarcely a family was without it.' Go to the National Archives in Washington and you can see Americans queuing every day to look at the faded original document. Writing in 1999 in *Bring Home the Revolution*, *Guardian* political columnist Jonathan Freedland could see little progress here in the two centuries since Paine:

The superstitious nonsense of a constitution written in invisible ink, which so incensed Paine, is still with us, exerting the same effect now as it did then – casting government as the exclusive preserve of a set of initiates rather than of the people.

Freedland's invisible ink metaphor is only partly right. A letter written in real invisible ink can be read with the right chemical treatment, but the British constitution remains a puzzle even to the magic circle of its initiates. It means pretty much whatever you want it to mean. As political scientist Michael Foley describes it: 'In Britain, the controlling premise has been one of a working constitution, whose existence is verified, rather than thrown into doubt, by its characteristic flexibility. The British constitution has no pretence to pure forms, immutability and precision. Its defining condition and chief virtue is one of evolutionary change.'[10] Politicians can spend their entire careers in the House of Commons without thinking too hard about the constitution at all; its very familiarity makes it easy not to notice it, just like the Gothic tiled floors and wooden panelling of the Palace of Westminster or the uniformed policeman at its gate. But behind the floors and panelling there is what Professor Peter Hennessy has described as the 'hidden wiring', the web of understandings and secret rules underpinning what Bagehot called the efficient parts of the constitution. Gladstone said that the British constitution 'presumes, more boldly than any other, the good faith of those who work in it'. This much-quoted statement has held valid for more than a century, but over the past decade or two, things have begun to change. The gentlemen's conventions of government, which depended on 'the lift of an eyebrow or the unanswered question', have increasingly been replaced by public codes of practice in a process of 'constitutionalization'.

It is important to understand that this process predates the Labour government of 1997 and will continue after it has gone; it reflects a change in political culture that goes beyond the manifesto commitments and programme of a single government, and is best illustrated by the publication in 1992 of the previously secret *Questions of Procedure for Ministers*, now known more formally as the *Ministerial Code*. Controls on party funding and the establishment of an Electoral Commission with all-party backing represent further moves down the same road. In the view of many politicians and political scientists, it means the United Kingdom is moving away from exceptionalism and closer to the international norm in which constitutions are written down.

THE WESTMINSTER MODEL

Later in this book a constant reference point will be the traditional Westminster model of government, which owes quite a lot to Bagehot, but even more to his successor, the Oxford law professor Albert Venn

Dicey, whose *Introduction to the Study of the Law of the Constitution* was uniquely influential over several generations from its first edition in 1885. Dicey was a staunch opponent of Irish Home Rule, arguing that any form of federalism would spell the end of British parliamentary government. Ferdinand Mount highlights the quasi-religious intensity of his beliefs in such extracts as this:

Under all the formality, the antiquarianism, the shams of the British constitution, there lies an element of power which has been the true source of its life and growth. This secret source of strength is the absolute omnipotence, the sovereignty of parliament.

There were major inconsistencies in Dicey's thought, which led him to ignore parliamentary sovereignty and argue the case for a referendum or even for armed insurrection to prevent what he saw as the ultimate disaster of Irish Home Rule. As Mount observes:

It seems extraordinary that such an erratic and violent thinker could ever have achieved such monumental status as a constitutional authority.[11]

Dicey had little time for the protection of minorities and even less for the political rights of women, whom he found unfit to have the vote. The fact remains that his central idea of parliamentary sovereignty still holds sway, as Michael Foley describes:

His interpretation became the classic depiction of the British constitution. It has been criticized. It has been dented. And yet Dicey's construction remains the classic statement and one that still dominates the literature today. The important point to grasp about Dicey is not so much the content of his work as the effect that it has had on British politics. It rendered the constitution a neutral subject and therefore a non-issue. Dicey induced a state of unparalleled constitutional narcosis into the British state.[12]

Parliamentary sovereignty in the Diceyan sense – what Mount calls 'parliamentary monotheism' – is still the operating code at Westminster. In the words of Professor Robert Hazell of the London University Constitution Unit: 'No constitutional textbook now seeks to uphold the doctrine of parliamentary sovereignty as expounded by Dicey; but in the minds of politicians, the doctrine lives on.' This illustrates perfectly Bagehot's insight that each generation describes the constitution using words and concepts transmitted from the past:

When a great entity like the British constitution has continued in connected outward sameness, but hidden inner change, for many ages, every generation inherits a series of inapt words – of maxims once true, but of which the truth is ceasing or has ceased. As a man's family go on muttering in his maturity incorrect phrases derived from a just observation of his early youth, so, in the full activity of an historical constitution, its subjects repeat phrases true in the time of their fathers, and inculcated by those fathers, but now true no longer. Or, if I may say so, an ancient and ever-altering constitution is like an old man who still wears with attached fondness clothes in the fashion of his youth: what you see of him is the same; what you do not see is wholly altered.

Despite what appears by international standards to be a record of extraordinary continuity in its forms of government since the days of Bagehot and Dicey, the United Kingdom constitution has in fact undergone significant change over the last century or two. Reform has often been hard to read because it has been slow and incomplete, and outward forms have been preserved. The biggest shift has been the advance of universal suffrage, which arrived more slowly than in many other European states and was not accompanied by any general overhaul of the constitution. It took a century from the Great Reform Bill of 1832 until all adult women had the vote. Multiple voting was only abolished finally by the Labour government after the Second World War. The Edwardian era saw a bitterly fought confrontation over the House of Lords, ending in a partial reform under which the hereditary upper chamber survived but lost some of its powers. The expulsion of hereditary peers from parliament seemed only a matter of time, but did not happen until nine decades later. Half a century of argument over Irish Home Rule ended in the partition of Ireland after the First World War, a period of constitutional ferment when proportional representation and devolution for Scotland and Wales also came close to being implemented. Two world wars and the creation of a welfare state saw a huge expansion in the role and complexity of government. But for most of this period the Westminster model, centred on the sovereignty of parliament, was not a major subject of debate. Its superiority to foreign models was generally taken as read and was not seriously questioned or analyzed.

A GROWING MALAISE

Since the 1970s, however, a number of factors have combined to push constitutional reform up the political agenda. Although the fears expressed in that turbulent decade that Britain was becoming 'ungovernable' have receded, unease over the constitution has not. There has been no sudden crisis to trigger demands for change, rather a continuing malaise. The old certainties have been undermined by a long list of factors. These have included the decay of the two-party system which dominated the first two decades after the Second World War; the decline of class-based politics, and the rise of nationalist parties in Scotland and Wales; the Northern Ireland conflict, beginning in the late 1960s; the erosion of parliamentary sovereignty following membership of the European Community from 1973; the rise in the practice of judicial review of government decisions in the courts; the effect of repeated judgments against the UK in the European Court of Human Rights in Strasbourg; a general decline in political participation, with falling voter turnouts and declining party memberships; the determination of Margaret Thatcher to smash what she saw as a cosy consensus at the centre of British politics; the emergence of a multi-ethnic, multi-cultural, less deferential and more secular society; a weakening of British identity and of respect for the monarchy.

Meanwhile, the international environment has also changed, with economic globalization and the weakening of the traditional idea of the sovereign nation state. The end of the Cold War, the collapse of the communist system and the emergence of new states in Eastern Europe and the former Soviet Union have underlined the fact that political structures do not remain frozen in time for ever. As Professor Vernon Bogdanor has pointed out, none of the new democracies in the East has been tempted to adopt the Westminster model. Over the past decade, the move towards closer political integration in the European Union has given a special urgency to the British constitutional debate. How can a United Kingdom with no written constitution of its own reconcile national sovereignty and parliamentary supremacy with the daily reality of power sharing in Brussels?

> **❝ None of the new democracies in the East has been tempted to adopt the Westminster model. ❞**

The general feeling of constitutional unease at the end of the Thatcher period was summed up in 1992 by the distinguished judge Lord Scarman in a lecture to Charter88, an organization which at the time was beginning to wield considerable influence on the Labour party. He called for a fully written constitution, rather than just improved checks and balances, and a degree of entrenchment for basic rights. Scarman argued for legal limits on the power of the executive and of parliament, adoption of the decentralizing principle of subsidiarity, and a judiciary with powers to protect the constitution.

Today our constitution is not 'unwritten' but hidden and difficult to find. Much of it is, of course, in writing in the sense that it is published and available to all who wish to read it. The 1688 settlement is incorporated into our statute law: but how many of us read Acts of Parliament? ... The citizen lacks a constitution which he can read and understand and which enables him, if need be, to claim a right which he can enforce.

Scarman examined the Glorious Revolution bargain of 1688, which he described as 'a set of genuine checks and balances in restraint of power'.

They were political in character, but none the less effective so long as the partnership of the Crown in parliament was a partnership of equals. But over the years since 1688 first the Crown and later the House of Lords lost the power effectively to stop the House of Commons ... The loss of this power may be familiar. But the reason for it is still not fully understood. I can put my argument in three short propositions: 1) Britain had a genuine system of checks and balances after 1688. 2) The Commons gained power at the expense of the monarchy and Lords, especially after it extended its franchise. The more democratically based the House of Commons became, the more it was able to usurp the power of the others. Now the modern party system has created a single centre of power that controls both the executive and legislature. 3) Thus the democratization of a part has threatened the constitutional settlement as a whole; indeed, the concentration of power in the Commons has capsized the old system of checks and balances.[13]

Scarman's bleak conclusion was that all that remained of the 1688 checks and balances was the political process within parliament, and the periodic requirement of a general election. Defenceless and unrepresented groups were particularly at risk, and citizens who wanted to use the European Convention on Human Rights faced an 'expensive and exhausting' journey to Strasbourg because it was not incorporated into United Kingdom law. To remove this 'monstrous burden' Scarman called for a Bill of Rights enforceable in the courts as part of a written constitution, to respond to the age-old 'need to keep government in order'.

Scarman's historical critique of the way the Westminster model has evolved forms a good starting point from which to measure Labour's constitutional reforms. Anthony Barnett, a founder of Charter88, believes they are so fundamental that they will eventually lead to the end of the 1688 settlement. Others see the reforms as timid and minimalist, and designed to prop up the traditional status quo. It is quite possible that each of these interpretations is right. Only history will give us the final answers, but it is time to start asking the questions.

NOTES

[1] From remarks to a fringe meeting of the electoral reform group Make Votes Count at Labour's 2000 annual conference in Brighton.

[2] *New Statesman*, 20 November 2000.

[3] Nairn, Tom (1994) *The Enchanted Glass. Britain and its Monarchy*, London, Vintage, p 362.

[4] Marquand, David (1998) 'The Blair Paradox' in *Prospect* magazine, May.

[5] Mount, Ferdinand (1993) *The British Constitution Now*, London, Mandarin, p 2.

[6] Bogdanor, Vernon (1997) *Power and the People. A Guide to Constitutional Reform*, London, Victor Gollancz, p 11.

[7] Bogdanor, op. cit., p 15.

[8] Evidence to House of Commons Scottish Affairs Committee, 24 June 1998.

[9] Mount, op. cit., p 10.

[10] Foley, Michael (2000) *Isaac Newton meets Peter Mandelson: British Politics on the Turn*, Millennium Public Lecture, University of Wales, Aberystwyth.

[11] Mount, op. cit., p 56.

[12] Foley, op. cit.

[13] Scarman, Lord (1992) *Why Britain needs a Written Constitution*, London Charter88 Trust.

2

THE STATUS QUO PARTY

'Whiners, whingers and wankers'
– Neil Kinnock on constitutional reformers (attributed)

'Too many parliamentary colleagues still think pluralism is a lung disease'
– Graham Allen MP

IT IS A PARADOX THAT THE United Kingdom's biggest constitutional changes in a century have been introduced by a party that for most of its existence has been anxious not to disturb the constitutional status quo. Labour, despite its efforts to pretend otherwise, has most of the time been a conservative and often backward-looking party. Just as in Holland even the Catholics are reputed to be Calvinist, in Labour ranks even radicals such as Tony Benn often seem to be looking back to the 17th century for inspiration. Benn has proposed a 'Commonwealth of Britain Act' with a Cromwellian flavour, but such ideas have traditionally failed to find favour in the party as a whole. For most of its history, the party has shared an unspoken consensus with the Conservatives on constitutional matters, shunning innovation. When in 1945 Winston Churchill proposed a referendum to extend the life of parliament until after the defeat of Japan, Labour leader Clement Attlee demurred, opposing 'a device so alien to all our traditions as the referendum, which has only too often been the instrument of Nazism and Fascism'.

A simple answer to the question of why the 1997 Labour government broke with this tradition would be to ascribe all the changes to the election of Tony Blair in 1994 and assume that constitutional reform was added to the New Labour mixture to distinguish it from the previous product, as a unique selling proposition to replace Old Labour's socialism. As I hope to show in this chapter, this explanation is almost entirely wrong, and as far as I am aware Blair himself has never made such a claim. Before he became leader Labour had committed itself to a range of constitutional changes, an agenda which he was to inherit and which he changed in several aspects before the 1997 general election. Reconstructing Labour's policymaking in opposition is therefore something in the nature of an archaeological dig through different strata. The account which follows does not pretend to be exhaustive, but will excavate enough of the site to provide an outline.

KEIR HARDIE RETURNS

One of the more bizarre moments of Labour's 1999 conference in Bournemouth was when a familiar-looking figure strode on to the platform disguised in a deerstalker hat and false whiskers. Keir Hardie quickly revealed himself to be Tom Sawyer, the party's former general secretary, who was highlighting the party's 100th anniversary. Hardie is a useful figure for supporters of constitutional reform, for it was in Labour's early years that the party was most committed to devolution (then called Home Rule) and to changing the voting system for parliament. Developing in opposition under the shadow of the Liberals, Labour wrestled with questions of constitutional reform, democracy, syndicalism and state power for the first quarter of the 20th century. By the time Labour had supplanted the Liberals as the main alternative to Conservative rule in the 1920s, the dominant strain of ideas in the party was the Fabianism of Sidney and Beatrice Webb. In the words of one historian:

In contrast to the revolutionary politics of Marx ... the Fabians sought to show that socialism was perfectly compatible with British political institutions and modes of behaviour. They were strict constitutionalists who looked on parliament and the civil service as an adequate means of achieving socialism, especially after their limited constitutional demands for the extension of the franchise, payment of MPs and reform of the House of Lords had been granted.

Where Marx had called for the existing state machinery to be replaced with a very different type of state, the Fabians identified socialism with the extension of the existing British state – with its monarch, parliament, courts and military.[1]

With Ramsay MacDonald leading the party and the Webbs shaping its ideas, support for Home Rule and electoral reform fell away, to be replaced by a belief in a strong centralized state and 'the inevitability of gradualness'. Too much democracy might get in the way of the rule of experts:

In Fabian eyes, the civil servant was to be the real governor of a socialist Britain, with representative democracy acting as a mere check on the administrators.[2]

This was the bureaucratic ideal that led the Webbs to their rosy view of Stalin's Russia, which they praised to the skies in *Soviet Communism: A New Civilisation*, published in the 1930s just as the dictator's purges were getting into their stride. This monumental (1,000 pages) compendium of idiocy is now largely forgotten, though some of its attitudes still linger on in the Labour party.

A PARTY OF POWER

Labour's formation of a minority government in 1924 was a turning point in its acceptance of the constitutional status quo, in particular the electoral system, which had delivered it near-absolute power. In the words of Dominic Hilton:

It would from now on seek to obtain and then hold on to the power at the centre of the traditional constitution. A philosophy of power seeking and wielding, not power sharing, came to dominate the party's thinking … In a sense, a *lack* of argument on the most fundamental issues has nurtured a confusion about which way Labour's constitutional blood flows.[3]

Labour, in Vernon Bogdanor's pithy phrase, was now more concerned with capturing the British state than reforming it.

Lacking a detailed and coherent philosophy of the state, Labour was particularly receptive to pragmatic considerations. The party's experience in government persuaded it of the merits of the traditional procedures and institutions of the British state.[4]

It saw the flexibility of the unwritten constitution as an advantage, believing that to impose checks and balances to protect civil liberties would only serve to undermine its economic and social goals. Judges were seen as the class enemy. Power sharing with other parties, a necessity in the party's early years, became anathema after Ramsay MacDonald's betrayal in 1931 to form a National Government with the Conservatives. The party found its belief in first-past-the-post elections vindicated by the huge majority with which the Attlee government came to power in 1945. It was essentially a centralizing philosophy of government in which regional variations in public services were to be ironed out and the man in Whitehall really did know best. Labour's view of parliament was essentially unicameral, and the Attlee government's only constitutional reform was a minor change to the 1911 Parliament Act to speed the passage of its legislation through the House of Lords.

> 66 It was essentially a centralizing philosophy of government in which regional variations in public services were to be ironed out and the man in Whitehall really did know best. 99

> ... the 1949 Parliament Act can hardly be interpreted as part of a long-term strategy of institutional reform. It was a pragmatic response to the problems posed by the passage of the Iron and Steel Bill and reflected Labour's most persistent characteristic: an unwillingness to think and act on institutional matters except when obliged to by political circumstance.[5]

Class politics on a national scale had replaced the territorial politics of Keir Hardie's Britain and in what appeared to have become a two-party system the case for electoral reform was no longer relevant. During Labour's 13-year spell in opposition from 1951 the party's left and right wings argued furiously over a wide range of issues, but constitutional reform was not among them.

NATIONALISM STIRS UNDER WILSON

It was not until the Labour governments of 1964–70 led by Harold Wilson that constitutional reform stirred as an issue. An attempt to reform the House of Lords by taking away the voting rights of hereditary peers was blocked in the Commons in 1969 by a filibustering alliance of right and left led by Enoch Powell and Michael Foot. Far more significant for the future course of Labour policies was the by-election victory in 1967 of the Scottish National party (SNP) candidate Winnie Ewing in the safe Labour seat of Hamilton, which in the words of Labour MP Tam Dalyell 'went off like an electoral atom bomb in the Labour establishment'. In the previous year the Welsh nationalist party Plaid Cymru had won its first by-election in Carmarthen. From that moment, the need to counter the electoral threat from nationalism was to drive Labour policy in fits and starts towards the creation of assemblies in Edinburgh and Cardiff, which finally took place three decades later.

For most of that period devolution was a divisive issue in which the electoral interests of the Labour party, rather than high constitutional principles, were uppermost in the minds of most of those involved. The party's internal rows over devolution led indirectly to the collapse of the government of James Callaghan in 1979 and to Labour's 18 years in opposition. Although pro-devolutionists have won the argument, many of the tensions of that period are still alive within the party, notably an undercurrent of resentment among English MPs at what they see as favourable treatment given to the Scots.

THE FAILURE OF DEVOLUTION IN THE 1970s

Harold Wilson's government set up a Royal Commission on the Constitution in 1969 which reported in 1973. Its recommendation of assemblies for Scotland and Wales was opposed by the Labour party in Scotland. Further nationalist gains such as Margo Macdonald's by-election win in Govan in 1973 persuaded Wilson to press ahead despite internal divisions when Labour returned to power the following year. After long parliamentary guerrilla warfare, devolution bills for Scotland and Wales finally passed in 1978 and referendums were held on 1 March 1979.

In Scotland, the 'yes' votes won a majority, although more than 36 per cent of voters failed to turn out. But the 'yes' camp failed to clear the hurdle of 40 per cent of the electorate that Labour MPs opposed to devolution had imposed in the Commons. In Wales, the result was a disaster for devolution, with the assembly plan rejected by a huge majority of four to one. The outcome triggered the withdrawal of SNP support from Callaghan's minority government and a general election in which the Conservatives under Margaret Thatcher returned to power.

Two decades later, on 26 November 1998, Jack Straw summed it up in a speech to Charter88: 'Here was a weak government attempting to push through constitutional change and failing above all because it lacked a clear majority, and because it was wracked by divisions so serious as to trigger the SDP split within 20 months of our loss of office. If nothing else, the Labour party's history tells us that division and drift are the enemies of radical political change, not its friends.'

THE SWING TO THE LEFT

The ignominious end to Labour's period in office under Wilson and Callaghan, who occupied 10 Downing Street for 11 of the 15 years between 1964 and 1979, helped push the party into a leftward spiral and led to the formation of the breakaway Social Democratic party (SDP), whose alliance with the Liberals narrowly failed to drive Labour into third place in the general election of 1983. Although the party failed to supplant Labour as the main opposition to the Conservatives, the rise of the SDP-Liberal Alliance, later to become the Liberal Democrats, helped pave the way for the emergence of New Labour and the constitutional reforms of Tony Blair's government.

The overall failure of the Wilson and Callaghan governments led New Left thinkers to challenge the party's traditional view of the British state as a neutral instrument. Some Labour politicians blamed a reactionary civil service for frustrating the party's socialist ambitions. But instead of creative constitutional thinking, the left's priority was the struggle for power within the Labour party over whether activists could tie the leadership to socialist policies. Within parliament, this led to a contradictory approach. Rather than strengthen all-party scrutiny by backbenchers through Select Committees, Labour activists sought a strengthening of party control by making every MP 'a transmission belt from the party to the government machine'.[6] As far back as 1970, Michael Foot, a leftwinger and parliamentary traditionalist, had opposed the growth of Select Committees on the grounds that they would produce consensus and blur the clash of class politics. Committees, in the view of leftwingers such as Tony Benn and Brian Sedgemore, were there to assist Labour activists in preventing ideological betrayal by Labour cabinets, rather than to contribute to a more pluralistic political system.

Labour's thinking on the role of the state had advanced since the 1960s but had failed to grapple with many crucial issues. In particular it had failed to debate electoral reform and the distorting effects of first-past-the-post.[7] By 1977 Labour was committed not to reform of the House of Lords but to its abolition, a pledge which Callaghan struck out of the 1979 election manifesto, infuriating the left, which ensured that the promise was reinstated in 1983. As Barry Jones and Michael Keating concluded two years later: 'Once again, the party has failed to make clear whether it believes in powerful, centralized government or a pluralist dispersal of power.' This comment, as we shall see, remains valid 15 years later as the Blair government wrestles with Lords reform. The contradiction between Labour's desire to remove obstacles in its path and its desire to introduce more democratic and participative mechanisms is just as alive now as it was in 1985.

EUROPE DIVIDES LABOUR

Another constitutional legacy from the 1970s that is highly relevant to Labour's present debates is United Kingdom membership of the European Community. Although it was negotiated by the Conservative government of Edward Heath and took effect in 1973, it was Labour that was torn apart by the issue. Harold Wilson, trying desperately to keep his party from splitting in two, introduced the constitutional innovation of the referendum to British politics in 1975 when he asked the voters to support continued membership but allowed some of his ministers to oppose it. This simultaneously called into question two of the well-worn conventions on which the British constitution rested – the ultimate sovereignty of parliament, and cabinet collective responsibility.

One of the two principal arguments put forward by Labour opponents of the EC such as Neil Kinnock – that membership would prevent the introduction of socialist policies – is now dead and buried. Under Margaret Thatcher, Labour was slowly converted to the opposite belief, that Europe's social welfare model represented a defence against Conservative free markets. The other principal argument from 1975, over sovereignty, has taken on a new lease of life with the Maastricht and Amsterdam Treaties, the new European Union, and the prospect of the UK joining the single currency after a referendum. As Jones and Keating noted in analyzing Labour's attitude to the 1975 referendum, the party was fundamentally divided over the ultimate location of sovereignty within the British state. Parliamentary sovereignty and popular sovereignty are often mentioned in the same breath, but are not the same thing. While the party now appears far more united on Europe than 25 years ago, the current stress on 'five economic tests' for adopting the euro and the reluctance to discuss issues of principle have echoes of Harold Wilson's insistence on discussing the 'terms' of membership rather than constitutional principles. Those with even longer memories will recall that Wilson's predecessor, Hugh Gaitskell, once set 'five conditions' for membership. The flavour of political fudge over Europe has changed little in 40 years.

> 66 Parliamentary sovereignty and popular sovereignty are often mentioned in the same breath, but are not the same thing. 99

BLAIR ELECTED AS LABOUR HITS THE FLOOR

With the departure of Michael Foot as leader after the disastrous 1983 general election and the arrival of Tony Blair in parliament we enter modern times. Labour's recovery from the nadir of its electoral fortunes to a landslide victory under Blair took 14 years. As Dominic Hilton describes it, during the long years in opposition Labour's commitments were 'proposed, adopted, watered down, sensationalized, dropped, re-proposed, re-adopted and repackaged'. Credit for introducing new policies has to be shared between Neil Kinnock, John Smith and Tony Blair, but the real architect of change was Margaret Thatcher, a view encapsulated by Tony Wright:

In this sense it is Mrs Thatcher who perhaps has the best claim to be regarded as the real architect of constitutional reform in Britain. She provided an object-lesson in the nature of power in Britain's 'flexible' constitution and, at the same time, a crash course of constitutional education for the Labour party.[8]

Thatcher changed the terms of the debate about constitutional reform by demonstrating how few limits the Westminster system imposed on a government that was not bothered by longstanding conventions. Paradoxically, Thatcher was a conservative in strictly constitutional terms; her arrival put an end to her party's flirtations with Scottish devolution and electoral reform under Heath. But her assault on local government, including the poll tax and the abolition of the Labour-controlled Greater London Council, her changes to the civil service, her curbs on trade unions, and her privatization of state industries brought irreversible shifts in the way the country was governed.

It was not until after a third successive election defeat in 1987 that major changes in Labour thinking began. For the first time the party became concerned about the lack of accountability of the executive, and the absence of any mechanism of constitutional entrenchment. Labour even began to show a grudging appreciation of the value of the House of Lords as a check and balance on an over-mighty executive. Perhaps even judges, notorious for their reactionary views, might have a role in curbing government? And perhaps there was a case after all for proportional representation (PR) rather than the winner-takes-all system of first-past-the-post. In gloomier moments, the party began to wonder if it would ever win power again.

Resentment of Thatcherism was particularly strong in Scotland, where the Conservative tide had largely been held back in 1983. The 41 remaining Scottish MPs formed a quarter of Labour's Commons strength, giving them a bigger influence than usual in the party's councils. By the late 1980s Labour and the Liberal Democrat MPs in Scotland had signed a 'Claim of Right' proclaiming Scottish popular sovereignty and were taking part in a constitutional convention to renew the drive for a Scottish parliament. This process effectively meant that policymaking was now taking place in a forum which the party leadership could not entirely control. Irrespective of the outcome, the convention process left deep marks, encouraging a more pluralist, less tribalist approach to politics. By 1990 it was clear that Labour would have to accept some kind of proportional representation if a Scottish parliament was to be a credible project.

All Labour's policies were now up for review and by 1990 the party was also endorsing an elected second chamber, new regional authorities, a Freedom of Information Bill and a Ministry of Legal Administration that would take over most of the functions of the Lord Chancellor.

CHARTER88 EMERGES

This was the period when the party first began to be influenced by Charter88, formed in 1988 as a pressure group for constitutional change with the ultimate goal of a written constitution. Anthony Barnett, one of the group's founders, recalls that Kinnock was alleged to have initially described the organization as 'whiners, whingers and wankers'. Four years later he publicly signed up to support it.[9] Barnett is careful not to overestimate Charter88's influence but says 'the more intelligent members of the Labour party', including Mo Mowlam, began thinking about the constitutional agenda as a whole. Some individual aspects of the Charter88 agenda were already Labour policy, but the party had never put them together in a synthetic way.

According to Barnett, the real momentum for fresh thinking in Labour came from Scotland:

Scotland was the driver of all these things. Scotland was rooted in electoral politics. They had to go for a Scottish parliament if they were to hold back the SNP and if they were not going to divide completely internally. In Scotland Thatcher had generated a protective device for Old Labour. A lot of people in the Scottish Labour party wanting to protect the Labour experience came round to a Scottish parliament as a way of protecting Scotland from Thatcherism. It wasn't just electoral fear, it was also positive meditation on the Thatcher experience that led them to call for a Scottish parliament. Once committed to that, the taboos surrounding the whole constitutional agenda were broken. This was a crucial issue and Charter88 was not responsible for it. Scotland was a real driver for breaking the taboo on constitutional reform – you couldn't take the standard classic British position which is: 'It works, it's not broken old chap, why fiddle around with it, it's the best in the world.'

Kinnock, who had strongly opposed devolution in the late 1970s, began to change his mind on this issue and on electoral reform. His deputy Roy Hattersley was far less enthusiastic, expressing in the *Guardian* the traditional Labour view that government invariably knew best:

True liberty requires action from the government. At best, a written constitution diminishes the importance of positive freedom – government action to enable more and more people to do and enjoy those things worth doing and enjoying. At worst, it actually prevents or inhibits that action from being taken.[10]

By the 1992 election Hattersley too had reluctantly moved to articulating the party's demands for a 'Charter of Rights'. Hilton points out that this radical-sounding package in fact was very different from the Charter88 agenda and masked the shadow Home Secretary's opposition to electoral reform for the Commons and to a binding Bill of Rights, which he saw as taking power from parliament and giving it to unelected judges.

Despite these internal tensions, Labour's rhetoric on constitutional matters moved up several notches. At the last party conference before the 1992 general election, Jo Richardson, a member of the party's National Executive Committee (NEC), declared: 'We are going to undertake the most radical programme of constitutional reform Britain has seen since *we* chopped Charles I's head off.'[11]

As Pam Giddy, the head of Charter88, recalls:

There were two sets of groups in Labour who were interested in democracy. There was the left who were interested for their own reasons; they believed that what the state *was* was as important as what the state *did*. Then the people on the right who wanted to modernize the party. The whole internal debate about modernizing Labour's internal mechanisms grew at the same time. I remember when Hattersley was shadow Home Secretary he was very against the whole Charter agenda, but he had to introduce the Charter of Rights. Even he, running up to 1992, had to accept that these issues had to be addressed.

The party gave constitutional reform a high profile in its 1992 general election campaign, promising a Charter of Rights, a Freedom of Information Act, a Scottish parliament elected under proportional representation, a Greater London Assembly, regional government in England, an elected House of Lords and an end to misuse of prerogative powers to bypass parliament. But the campaign partially misfired. In the run-up to the election, Labour associated itself closely with 'Democracy Day', a series of more than 100 nationwide meetings organized by Charter88. As polls began to predict a hung parliament and a possible coalition between Labour and the Liberal Democrats, Kinnock came under pressure in a television interview to take a clear stand for or against proportional representation, and clumsily refused. As Anthony Barnett recalls:

The press moved independently on this issue to press Labour and they screwed up in their answers. Kinnock mishandled it. Then Major stood up and said: 'The Union is in danger.' It influenced votes. Hattersley blamed Charter88 for the defeat, but I don't believe I have that degree of influence. Labour was divided and we had increased that division by forcing the issue on the agenda. It increased the impression among the public that these guys didn't know what they were doing.

Pam Giddy believes that Kinnock became a genuine convert to constitutional reform and was comfortable with it, but was never fully confident of taking the party with him. After the 1992 defeat and the replacement of Kinnock by John Smith, the leadership became even more strongly committed to constitutional change. The memory of the party's difficulties over constitutional reform in 1992 undoubtedly contributed to the party's caution over the issue five years later, when Tony Blair's 'safety first' campaign played down the party's commitments.

ELECTORAL REFORM MOVES UP THE AGENDA

A key decision in 1990 was to create a working party on electoral systems headed by Raymond Plant, a political philosopher from Southampton University. The group's remit was technical – to devise suitable voting systems for the new bodies in Scotland, Wales and else-where to which the party was now committed. In the view of Plant (now Lord Plant), there was a general mood in the party to look at electoral reform, but the leadership's original intention had been to leave the trickiest issue, electoral reform for the House of Commons, out of the working party's remit:

Kinnock and Smith both felt strongly that if you were going to have a Scottish parliament you really had to go into the election with proposals about the electoral system, because if you were to go into an election with a proposal for a Scottish parliament on first-past-the-post, there wouldn't be much support. It would be like creating a one-party state with Labour winning a huge swathe of seats. I remember John Smith saying it would make a Scottish parliament like Strathclyde Regional Council writ large … Then the big thing occurred at the party conference. The idea had been to set up a committee to look at the electoral system for new institutions – Scottish Parliament, Welsh Assembly, Greater London Authority, elected House of Lords, and the European Parliament. So the NEC went to conference, where of course the people on the floor voted to extend its remit to the House of Commons, which caused a certain amount of consternation … Kinnock was actually in favour of this but couldn't really say so. Hattersley, of course, was vehemently opposed to it. They were very wrong-footed by the conference.

The other motive behind the creation of the working party was to help the party negotiate the 1992 election without open splits emerging over electoral reform. Plant recalls:

We were told not to report except on Scotland before the 1992 election because it would be too divisive. The fact that we didn't report led to Kinnock's dreadful evening. That was their fault. We could have reported six months previously but we were told not to.

The working group continued after the loss of the election and the replacement of Kinnock by John Smith. A month or two later at the 1992 party conference, Smith called Plant in:

He wanted to know what we were up to. I said I thought we would be recommending the additional member system for the House of Commons. I thought there was a clear majority against first-past-the-post and a clear though small majority in favour of AMS. He was very disconcerted by that. All of this took place in a room at the Labour party conference. He said he wanted to get back to me. We then had another couple of conversations. The final conversation before we reported was very much: 'Well, look, I don't think you should make any recommendations at all about the House of Commmons. I think you would do a great service by just rehearsing the arguments for or against.' I thought this was hopeless really. There was a definite majority against first-past-the-post. We had worked at it for two years and I thought there ought to be the opportunity for that majority to express itself. And secondly, we collectively and I individually would look very foolish if after two years of work all we were able to do was rehearse the arguments we knew when we started. So I said I wasn't really prepared to do that.

Not only Plant but a number of other figures in the Labour party were keen to prevent Smith rejecting proportional representation for Westminster outright, a move which would have ended cooperation with the Liberal Democrats and caused a big internal row. The working group had clearly come out against first-past-the-post but support for the proportional alternative, AMS, was becoming shaky.[12] Plant believes Smith had appealed to some members to change their minds: 'I think he felt it was a step too far, too proportional and would affect the constituency link. One or two people on the committee changed their view.'

Finally seeking to avoid deadlock, Plant switched his support to the non-proportional supplementary vote (SV) system instead.[13] But behind the scenes Smith had been persuaded to seek a different way out. Anthony Barnett believes Charter88's role was critical in bringing this about. 'We mounted a very intense, close, hand-to-hand lobby.' Through a number of channels Smith was urged to look at how the New Zealand government had held a referendum on electoral reform. The justification was that the electorate, not MPs, should have the final say because members of parliament had a vested interest in preventing any change in the system under which they had been elected. Raymond Plant had also written to him recommending the New Zealand solution, but when Smith endorsed the idea publicly, it came as a surprise.

"WELL, MAYBE IT'S WORTH A TRY."

John Smith, Robin Cook and Margaret Beckett consider the case for proportional representation as a means of ending 14 years of Conservative rule. Copyright © Daily Telegraph, 1993.

We then reported to the NEC and I had no idea what I was letting myself in for. A general discussion was about to take place and Tony Benn was sitting exactly opposite me chafing at the bit to get in. The chairman of the NEC said the leader wants to make a point before the discussion starts. So John fished in his pocket and produced a press statement and said, this is being released to the press, as I read it. It said, thank you for all you have done, etcetera, interesting report. He said he could not personally support the recommendations on the House of Commons, but he thought … where there was a split of opinion about something as fundamental as this, it was wrong for MPs to decide, and it should go to a referendum.

This was the origin of Labour's still unfulfilled pledge to hold a referendum on the voting system, one of the major legacies John Smith left to his successor when he died in 1994. Murray Elder (now Lord Elder), who was one of Smith's closest aides, says 'John wasn't a fan of PR' and would have continued to support first-past-the-post at Westminster, but his commitment to a referendum was deeply felt and not just a political fudge:

John believed profoundly however that the people who should decide whether or not there was PR were the people rather than the government. I remember a day when Major in the House made some dismissive comment about this electoral system being perfectly all right, and when John came out of the chamber and met up with me, John was fizzing away, saying: 'That's exactly why it's wrong for people like Major who's got in with that kind of majority to decide whether or not it is the right system. It's not up to him, it's up to the people to decide.'

SMITH BRINGS NEW URGENCY

John Smith brought constitutional reform to the centre of Labour's agenda and gave it an urgency that neither his predecessor nor his successor did. His short spell as leader was the high point of the constitutional reform lobby's influence over Labour. Tony Blair was shadow Home Secretary, with an ardent reformer, Graham Allen, as his deputy responsible for constitutional affairs. Gordon Brown, an open advocate of a written constitution, was also an influential member of Smith's team. Brown delivered an impressive lecture on 'Constitutional change and the future of Britain' to a Charter88 forum

> ❝ His short spell as leader was the high point of the constitutional reform lobby's influence over Labour. ❞

in March 1992, a few weeks before the general election. Unlike most politicians, Brown showed intellectual depth in making the case for extending the Scottish idea of sovereignty of the people to replace 'old-fashioned and unacceptable ideas of Crown sovereignty' throughout Britain. Tying economic and constitutional arguments together in a way that most Labour politicians have found difficult, Brown's speech was a forerunner of the 'third way' doctrine that emerged as part of the New Labour project. He argued that Britain's unwritten constitution contained an implicit idea of 'leaders and led' which made the liberation and empowerment of equal citizens impossible. 'A modern constitution is essential to protect individuals against the state and to empower them within an interdependent community.' It would be interesting to speculate whether Labour's constitutional policy would have retained greater intellectual coherence if Brown had opted to oversee this policy area rather than the economy after 1994.

In 'A Citizen's Democracy', a speech to Charter88 on 1 March 1993, Smith said he had once believed in the mysteries of the British constitution, but his experience over the past decade had caused him to change his mind quite fundamentally.

It used to be said that the subject of constitutional reform was of interest to no one but the so-called chattering classes. Critics considered it a distraction from the bread-and-butter issues that matter to most voters. But in this atmosphere of decline and gloom, it is abundantly clear that people across the nation do care deeply about the way they are governed, and they feel angry and frustrated with a system that isn't working. So our crumbling constitution can no longer be dismissed as a side-show. It is at the heart of what is wrong with our country. People care, and they want change. Indeed, the more we scrutinize the way in which we are governed and the lack of legal rights at our disposal, the more clear it becomes that our present democratic process is both anachronistic and inadequate.

> 66 Our crumbling constitution can no longer be dismissed as a side-show. 99

Smith attacked the 'relentless centralization' of Conservative governments which had removed power from local authorities and placed it in the hands of the executive or of central government agencies. His remedy was a revival of local government, and a new framework of four levels – municipal, regional, national and European. This would include a new tier of government not just for Scotland and Wales but for the regions of England, to cover areas of policy such as health, education, employment, transport, planning and industrial development. Although he did not use the word, Smith's vision came close to the federalist ideas of the Liberal Democrats. His other commitments were to incorporate the European Convention on Human Rights into British law, to a Human Rights Commission and a justice ministry, to a Freedom of Information Act to 'blow the cobwebs of secrecy away from government', to an annual pre-budget report that would open up economic policymaking, and to an expansion of consumer rights and corporate disclosure. He had little to say about parliament in the speech, but in a debate afterwards he endorsed Lord Hailsham's famous 1976 criticism of 'elective dictatorship' at Westminster. 'Parliament is weak in this country. I've been in it for 22 years, and I think it's got weaker every single year I've been in it. We just don't check the executive properly in our system.'

BLAIR PROMISES A REVOLUTION

❝It was not only reform that was on offer but revolution.❞

The Labour conference of 1993, the year before Smith's death from a heart attack, marked the apogee of Labour's rhetoric on constitutional reform. It was not only reform that was on offer but revolution. Tony Blair spoke of 'a revolution in democratic accountability and control, to redistribute power from government to people – not the state governing the people, but enabling the people to govern themselves'. Blair drew ambitious historical parallels:

Today we pledge ourselves to a task as great as any undertaken by any Labour government in the past, as far-reaching in its effects as the Reform Acts of the last century, as important in its impact on the lives of people of this country as universal suffrage. We cannot renew our country, its community or its citizenship unless we first renew its democracy. Our purpose today is not a change in the management of our system; it is to change the system itself.

Pam Giddy recalls listening to Blair's speech with enthusiasm:

I remember sitting there ticking all the little boxes, thinking, this is fantastic, this is our agenda. But it never won the hearts of Labour activists. Exploring that is interesting when you look at what has happened since they got into power. They took on board that whole agenda, it was in the manifesto. But they never tried to link it to the issues that the activists were most concerned with, health, education and so on. There was a sense that Labour was really about those issues and this was just a kind of froth on the side.

Behind the rhetoric on constitutional reform there was a lengthy policy statement from the NEC, entitled 'A New Agenda for Democracy'.[14] This provides a useful benchmark for considering how Labour's constitutional agenda evolved between Smith's death and the 1997 election campaign.

LABOUR'S 1993 CONSTITUTIONAL PLAN

The 1993 plan began by describing the constitution as an issue not just for academics but one in which all the people have a direct interest. 'It is about power; where it is located and how it is made accountable.' The absence of a written constitution was described as 'not in itself an issue of vital significance' although it meant the task of putting the constitution into words had not been confronted. This would have involved 'concentrating the national mind' on hard decisions – a revealing phrase which spoke volumes about the lack of intellectual appetite in Labour for grappling with such sticky questions. 'The result is a constitution urgently in need of radical change and modernization.' Labour's goal was to establish a modern notion of citizenship setting new rules for the bargain between the individual and society. Collective action would serve the goal of advancing individual freedom. 'Our aim is to create a revitalized democracy which protects the fundamental rights of the citizen from the abuse of power, which proposes the substantial devolution of central government authority, and which insists that the legitimacy of government rests on it being both open and accountable to the people it serves.'

Labour's thinking bore the scars of more than a decade of Thatcherism: 'Today, the executive is immensely powerful. Parliament is easily overwhelmed. The ability of the ordinary citizen to challenge the executive is tightly limited. The UK has one of the most centralized systems of government in Europe.' The Conservatives had massively increased centralization, curtailed the power of bodies such as local government which might restrain it, and transferred power to unelected quangos. 'We are a deeply secretive society, without even minimal legislation on freedom of information.' The legal system was 'hopelessly out of date' and dominated by vested interests and the European Union's power was not subject to proper scrutiny. 'The result is that our democracy is profoundly flawed.' Change would not just mean increasing central government intervention:

'Government itself is a powerful interest that requires to be checked and controlled.' This in turn required a new constitutional settlement that 'fundamentally redresses power in favour of the citizen from the state'.

Without addressing directly the issue of parliamentary sovereignty, the document implied that it would be downgraded. Instead there would be a diversity of political institutions, each with their independence guaranteed from central government. There would be new constitutional checks and balances to hold the executive to proper account and to 'reflect the more pluralist, more decentralized, more devolved government which the people of our country want to see'. Constitutional reform was not an isolated project but part of a wider framework of ideas which included a more active notion of citizenship that would help to release economic potential. 'We hope, too, that we can lay to rest the notion that this is just an issue for what are dismissively called "the chattering classes".'

The main proposals were:

- an all-party commission to draft an entrenched Bill of Rights, going beyond the first stage of incorporation into British law of the European Convention on Human Rights (ECHR). This would give judges the power to override existing legislation, though parliament would have the final say. Human rights appeals would be judged by a court including extra lay members – a provision clearly reflecting the party's historic suspicion of the judiciary. Incorporation of the ECHR was described as a first step and not a substitute for a home-grown and entrenched Bill of Rights;

- a Freedom of Information Act, employee and trade union rights, official secrets reform and proper scrutiny of the security services, a Data Protection Act;

- reform of the royal prerogative to reduce the executive's ability to declare war and sign treaties without reference to parliament; this was described as the area of Labour's greatest concern, where 'massive power is exercised by executive decree without accountability to parliament and sometimes without its knowledge';

- devolution to Scotland and Wales and to regional councils in England, which would take control from Whitehall over health, education, employment, transport, planning and industrial development;

- a reform of electoral law, an independent electoral commission;

■ greater accountability and subsidiarity all round and a Greater London Authority for the capital;

■ a reform of parliament which would strengthen the independence of committees from the Whips and change the Commons hours; patronage would be reduced by making all major public appointments subject to scrutiny by parliamentary committees;

■ abolition of the House of Lords and its replacement by an elected second chamber which would check the power of the Commons; as a first step, hereditary peers would lose their right to sit and vote;

■ a Ministry of Justice and a new system for appointing judges.

The policy document said these pledges did not amount in themselves to a written constitution, but were nonetheless a significant step in that direction and 'we leave open the question of whether, at a later stage, we make progress to formal codification'.

THE MEANING OF SMITH'S 'CONSTITUTIONAL SETTLEMENT'

Anthony Barnett believes that by arguing for a new 'constitutional settlement' Smith was accepting the logic of a written constitution, even if he avoided using the words:

Smith would have gone for a codified constitution. He knew what it meant and it was his tradition, and once he started he would have gone the distance ... He understood that to call for a written constitution just like that was to use words for which the country wasn't prepared. A new constitutional settlement is a written constitution. If he had meant unwritten, he would have said so.

However, Murray Elder believes this represents more what Barnett might have hoped, rather than what Smith actually intended.

Those who worked with Smith describe him as partly an old-fashioned centralizer, but a man whose radical attitude to constitutional orthodoxy reflected his education in the continental tradition of Scots law. He was also anti-London in the sense of being a man from the periphery.

Elder believes Smith might not have implemented all parts of this package. In particular he might have held back on the creation of a Ministry of Justice, which would have made it impossible for him to appoint Derry Irvine, his close friend from student days at Glasgow University, as Lord Chancellor:

I think it is wrong to say he would have gone for that. I don't think he had ruled it out. He always had in mind that Derry would be his Lord Chancellor. That was something to be looked at and negotiated. I don't think he ruled it out but I don't think he was committed to that.

Elder is not certain that Smith was totally wedded to an elected House of Lords either, though he was committed to a two-stage reform in which the hereditary peers would be removed first:

John fundamentally believed the Commons was paramount, and the moment you have an elected second chamber you get into areas of some difficulty as to which is more legitimate. And in that sense I don't think he regarded an elected second chamber, because it would have challenged the dominance of the Commons, as being the way forward.

Anthony Barnett believes that had he lived on to win the 1997 election, Smith would have raised the profile of constitutional issues by immediately introducing a one-clause Bill to parliament, abolishing the voting rights of hereditary peers.

He would have electrified the country by doing that, he would have set the issue on fire … He wanted the issue to be hot. Smith would have democratized it in an instant. Then the whole question of what do we do next would have come on to the agenda.

After he succeeded Smith as leader in 1994, Blair's rhetoric on constitutional issues continued to sound radical, though some notes of caution crept in. Gradually the word 'modernization' began to occur more often while 'democracy' became less frequent. There were other signs of a more cautious agenda. The radical Graham Allen lost his role as spokesman on constitutional affairs and was replaced by the far less enthusiastic Kim Howells, a Welsh MP who was cool to devolution. Constitutional issues were now mostly in the hands of Jack Straw, known as a statist rather than a libertarian reformer. In *The Guardian*, Hugo Young, writing in December 1994, asked: 'Is the clammy hand of centralism already beckoning?'

Labour's caution increased as it got closer to the election and became more preoccupied with bomb-proofing its campaign against Tory attacks. It was also beginning to think seriously about how it would operate in government. Plans for a home-grown Bill of Rights were quietly shelved, though incorporation of the ECHR survived and was carefully prepared in opposition under the leadership of Derry Irvine. The idea of an overhaul of the government's prerogative powers also dropped off the agenda. There was less and less talk of the over-mighty executive having its wings clipped; the appetite for strengthening the powers of parliamentary committees also faded; regional government for England was hedged around with conditions; and the commitment to an elected second chamber became more fuzzy.

I asked Jack Straw how much notice the party had taken of pressure groups such as Charter88 and Democratic Audit in this period. His reply was: 'Lots, loads.' But he confirmed that Labour's approach changed under Blair as the prospect of an election victory became firmer:

There is a fundamental distinction to make in policy development between pre-May '94 and post-May '94, when John Smith died. I am not saying John would not have done this, but once Tony had been elected and confirmed, from then on it became fairly clear that unless we were really stupid we would form the government and therefore the policy process changed radically, from putting out manifestos, campaigning documents, to developing policy that could be implemented with the edges round it in government. The nature of the documents and the nature of the process changed quite markedly. It was very striking for all involved. So it moved from wish lists which were not particularly joined up, where often people had been driven by pressure groups in some areas. I was education spokesman between 1987 and 1992, and if you weren't driven by pressure groups – in the education case the teacher unions, particularly the NUT – they gave you a hard time.

TRADITIONAL CENTRALISM IN A MODERN SETTING?

In January 1995, after his sacking, Graham Allen (subsequently to be placed by Blair in the Trappist cell of the Labour Whips' office) wrote a pamphlet expressing fears that John Smith's constitutional legacy might be eroded. In *Reinventing Democracy: Labour's mission for the new century*, which was dedicated to Smith's memory, Allen wrote: 'The fear is that without the personal impetus supplied by John Smith, both the witting and the unthinking centralists will halt the process of policy development on democracy, or even quietly inter existing commitments.' In a parody of New Labour jargon, he warned that 'traditional centralism in a modern setting' was not enough and reform had to be based on a conscious philosophy rather than a centrally imposed shopping list. Centralizers had controlled the Labour party since its inception, he wrote, arguing instead for a greater separation of powers and 'a pluralist democracy of many competing, sovereign political institutions checking and balancing the executive'. Allen argued that the real struggle in the Labour party was not between left and right or between modernity and tradition, but between centralizers and pluralists. With the death of John Smith the Labour party's relatively few pluralists had lost their champion. 'The absence or implementation of pluralism will be the defining issue for the next Labour government. It will decide whether Labour administers government or changes government for good in its first term in office.' Labour should commit itself to 'unfudgeable' reforms and resist the temptation to hang on to centralized powers when it came to office.

Reading Allen's denunciation of the unchecked powers of the executive 'that would make a Stalin salivate' and of the House of Commons as 'the most sophisticated political prison in the world', it is not hard to see why Blair wanted someone less outspoken in charge of constitutional matters as the election approached. Allen's most radical suggestion was to send in the electricians and carpenters to reshape the Commons chamber into a continental-style semi-circle, symbolizing the birth of a new kind of politics.

> 66 It is not hard to see why Blair wanted someone less outspoken in charge of constitutional matters as the election approached. 99

Anthony Barnett speculates that the influence on Blair of his close advisers Peter Mandelson and Alastair Campbell helped make him more cautious on constitutional reform:

I think they sat around and discussed what to do. They decided these issues were not important, they thought they were crap, but they saw there were commitments made by Blair, and the thing they had to establish was the credibility of Blair's image. The damage it would do to his credibility was greater than any damage it would do to Britain or his government if they carried it out. They committed themselves to these reforms because they thought it was unimportant and they could get away with it. The all-important thing was his credibility. Having committed himself, he couldn't go back on it.

Tam Dalyell tells a revealing story of a meeting with Blair not long after he succeeded Smith. 'I think Tony Blair perceived at an early stage, shortly after he became leader of the Labour party, the difficulties and abysses of devolution. When I went to see him at his request on this topic, in 1995, he rang (*sic*) his hands and said, "Well, what do you expect me to do about it, now?" and the truth was that I suppose I could expect an incoming leader to do little else than go along with the policy.'[15]

Matthew Taylor, now head of the centre-left think tank IPPR, was the Labour party's director of policy in 1996–97, though he freely admits his job was to deliver policy rather than make it. He believes Blair was not in a position to change much of the agenda he inherited from John Smith, and so made the best of it. This applied in particular to the plans for a Scottish parliament, which had been the subject of such lengthy negotiation in the Scottish constitutional convention that Blair had little room for manoeuvre:

I don't think one will ever know what the New Labour constitutional agenda would have been, had Blair had the capacity to invent it from scratch. We will never know the answer to that, partly because people won't tell us the truth and partly because people rationalize it. If you are saddled with a policy and you know you can't get rid of it then you may as well start believing in it. So I think Blair genuinely does believe in devolution. Whether his commitment would have been so great if he had been able to stand back and think, I am going to win this general election by a mile, is this what I want to see as being a priority? That I think is a different question. Had Labour not had a commitment to devolution and won the election, an awful lot of momentum behind devolution would have disappeared in Scotland, because a lot of the momentum in Scotland was a reaction to the fact that a country that voted Labour was ruled by a Conservative government. So you can play some very interesting counterfactual history games.

BLAIR INSISTS ON REFERENDUMS IN SCOTLAND AND WALES

There was only one point at which Blair risked a major row in his own ranks over devolution. This was his decision in the summer of 1996 that Labour would only go ahead with devolution in Scotland and Wales if there was prior approval in referendums. There were mutterings of betrayal in the Scottish press, howls of anguish from many in the Scottish Labour party, and a couple of resignations. It took weeks of concerted arm-twisting before the Scottish Labour party executive endorsed the idea. But many of those who had doubts at the time acknowledge now that the decision, however awkward in the short term, was eventually proved correct.

The referendum victories in September 1997 – overwhelming in Scotland, extremely narrow in Wales – defused the risk of a long Conservative filibuster over the devolution bills which might have disrupted other elements of the government's legislative programme. Murray Elder argues that the double-barrelled referendum in Scotland (the second question concerned tax-raising powers) killed stone dead the Conservative attacks on Labour's planned 'tartan tax': 'I think that referendum gave the whole settlement an authority it would not otherwise have had. It was absolutely the right decision to have taken. I don't think Tony ever got as much credit as he should have done.'

To save appearances, shadow Scottish Secretary George Robertson presented the decision as his own, but it was an open secret at the time that the word had come from Labour party headquarters in London. The U-turn was inelegant; for a few days Labour was even committed to a third referendum question on whether tax powers, if approved, should actually be used. This suggestion lasted a week but was laughed out of court and finally dropped.

> ❝ It was an open secret at the time that the word had come from Labour party headquarters in London. ❞

Why did Blair insist on the referendum? One explanation may be that he was heeding advice from the London-based Constitution Unit, a small but influential body set up in 1995 at University College London to solve some of the difficult nitty-gritty questions connected with constitutional reform. It was headed not by an ivory-tower academic but by Robert Hazell, a former Home Office civil servant and lawyer. Unlike Charter88, the Constitution Unit saw itself not as a campaigning lobby group but as a group of expert problem solvers who just happened to be in Bloomsbury rather than in Whitehall.

Most of the real political decisions about the new Scottish Parliament had been taken within the Scottish constitutional convention, whose final report came out in 1995, largely the product of negotiations between Labour and the Liberal Democrats. The SNP had boycotted the convention, as had the Scottish Conservatives, both attacking the proposed parliament for different reasons. But there was a large amount of work to do to turn the Scottish plan into workable legislation. Hazell believes the Constitution Unit helped Labour make a very important technical change to its proposed Scotland Bill; rather than listing all the responsibilities of the new parliament and executive, as had been the case in the ill-fated 1978 legislation, it listed instead the reserved powers that would remain at Westminster.

The Constitution Unit's lengthy reports on how to legislate for Scottish and Welsh devolution were passed to the Labour leadership in draft in June 1996, before they were made public. 'It was the best way to get them to read them,' Hazell notes drily. He also attributes to the unit Labour's change of policy on the devolution referendums.

In 1979 the people of Wales voted four to one against the proposals in the Wales Act 1978. The government had expended enormous amounts of political capital and parliamentary time in getting that Act onto the statute book. It seemed to me that next time round, instead of having a referendum after putting the legislation through parliament, it would be sensible to ask the people first.

Within two days of publication of the unit's report in June 1996, Labour policy had changed, with Tony Blair announcing pre-legislative referendums in Scotland and Wales. 'I can't prove it but I am pretty sure we had an influence there. It was too much of a coincidence, to change their policy just at the time our devolution reports were published.' Murray Elder remembers it differently, arguing that it would be absurd to imagine the Labour leadership changing policy so fast on the basis of an outside report.

Blair's fullest speech on constitutional matters as leader was his John Smith Memorial Lecture on 7 February 1996. It should be remembered that by this time Blair had already gone far beyond Smith's legacy in other fields, especially the internal modernization of the Labour party. According to Raymond Plant, Blair saw the debate about electoral reform for the House of Commons as a distraction from the task of modernizing the Labour party:

Part of Blair's project for the Labour party has been to make it internally more pluralistic and to widen its value basis to appeal to a wider cross-section of the electorate. In some way he may have believed that a preoccupation with electoral reform could have stood in direct opposition to this, namely a concern to secure an electoral system under which older and unreformed Labour would be able to do well, even though it would mean coalition government. Electoral reform therefore could almost be seen as providing an incentive not to modernize but to seek an electoral system under which Labour could gain at least a share of power on its less radically modernized policies and values.[16]

Blair's drive to capture the vital votes of middle England by persuading *Daily Mail* readers that New Labour was a different creature from Old Labour was based on his successful campaign to rewrite Clause Four of the party's constitution, its commitment to public ownership. Meanwhile, Gordon Brown was expunging the last traces of old-fashioned tax-and-spend socialism from Labour's message. But on constitutional matters the radicalism of Smith's approach was being toned down. Murray Elder says 'John was genuinely committed and radical on constitutional change, I would say more than Tony Blair. There are no doubt areas where Tony was prepared to do more, but on the constitution, he was the less radical.'

Dominic Hilton sees the Blair approach as one of 'disaggregation' of policy, so that Smith's package of reforms was broken down into separate and discrete issues. 'By 1995, the inexorable slide towards the lessened agenda of 1997 was fully under way.' There was no more talk of revolution: 'Reform, under Blair, became a necessary plugging of the holes in the ancient constitutional ship upon which Labour were passengers.'[17]

BLAIR AND SMITH'S 'UNFINISHED BUSINESS'

Blair's John Smith Memorial Lecture[18] can be read two ways – as a rousing pledge to carry out his predecessor's unfinished agenda, or as a cautious retreat. The rhetoric at the beginning supports the first interpretation, the fine print later on the second. Blair began by quoting the call in Smith's 1993 Charter88 lecture for 'a fundamental shift in the balance of power between the citizen and the state – a shift away from an overpowering state to a citizens' democracy where people have rights and powers and where they are served by accountable and responsive government'. This was 'his unfinished business which we must now finish,' Blair declared, echoing Smith by adding: 'The issue of government is not one for the "chattering classes" – consigned dismissively to the inside pages of the broadsheets. It touches the vitals of the nation.' The

Tony Blair's style as Labour leader in opposition evokes comparisons with Rigaud's portrait of Louis XIV. Copyright © Steve Bell, 1996.

uncompromising critical tone continued: 'The citizen feels remote from power because he or she is remote from power. Britain is *the* most centralized government of any large state in the Western world.'

When it came to laying out New Labour's remedies, however, Blair's message was more cautious. For local government, he had little to offer apart from the end of 'crude rate-capping' and a new strategic authority for London. He also floated the idea of directly elected mayors. For the English regions, the firm pledge of a new tier of government had become heavily diluted with a reminder that support for such elected bodies varied across the country. Defending Labour's devolution policy for Scotland and Wales, Blair introduced a curious argument which revealed that his thinking on the nature of democracy was a world away from that of John Smith. Devolution, he argued, was analogous to the decentralization of a business:

In today's economy, successful companies devolve decision making to their autonomous units, they allow for regional variations, and in doing so they get much more from the people who work for them. Of course, the centre still decides on the core functions and sets out the broad company strategy, but the trend is increasingly to give managers on the ground the freedom to decide how to implement its goals.

Blair renewed the commitment to a Freedom of Information Act, linking it to the idea of a code of citizens' rights which would guarantee the rights of individuals to basic freedoms and opportunities. Because codes are by definition not legally enforceable, this amounted to a significant retreat from Labour's promise of a statutory Bill of Rights. However, Blair reaffirmed that Labour would incorporate the ECHR into British law.

When Blair came to deal with parliament, it was clear that the Commons – getting weaker every year in the view of John Smith – would escape major changes. He made no mention of strengthening parliamentary committees, or of scrutinizing appointments, let alone overhauling the royal prerogative. Legislative procedures should be updated in order to make parliament more effective, Blair argued: 'And it does not help produce good government when almost every change in every clause of a Bill is interpreted as a defeat for the government.' Much harsher language was evident when Blair turned to make a lengthy attack on hereditary peers, describing them as mostly 'Tory voting-fodder'. But the tough language masked a significant watering down of Labour's 1993 commitment to an elected second chamber that would replace the House of Lords.

Blair made it clear that life peers would remain in place, thus ruling out the creation of a completely new institution. 'We have always favoured an elected second chamber,' he added – hardly an accurate summary of Labour's past policies. If there was to be an elected chamber, then the gates of patronage should not be closed altogether: '... provision could also be made for people of a particularly distinguished position or record.' Blair rejected the idea that a reformed House of Lords stripped of hereditaries would be 'an unelected quango', arguing that there was scope to make the Lords 'a genuine body of the distinguished and meritorious – with a better, more open and independent means of establishing membership – and then debate how we incorporate democratic accountability'. This passage, though little noticed at the time, clearly pointed the way to scrapping the commitment to an elected second chamber and signalled Blair's preference for a mainly appointed House of Lords. Delivering the detailed plan for this undemocratic hybrid was to be the work of the Wakeham commission in 1999.

Blair made it clear he was still unconvinced by the arguments for proportional representation: 'I do not dismiss such arguments. But in truth I have never been persuaded that under proportional representation we can avoid a situation where small parties end up wielding disproportionate power.' His final rhetorical flourish was a quotation from Thomas Jefferson and a promise of 'a journey of national renewal which creates a new young Britain – a young, self-confident and successful country which uses the talents of all its citizens and gives them a stake in the future.'

There was no clear pledge to reverse the centralization of power, and no mention of elective dictatorship. Nonetheless, Blair's speech was seen by those sympathetic to constitutional change as very significant. Andrew Marr commented that Blair's speech threw the question of reforming Britain into the centre of British politics. 'No one can be in any doubt of the magnitude of the changes to which Tony Blair has committed Labour ... These are words that cannot be eaten.' Others commented on the success of Charter88 in lobbying the Labour party. In fact, as the election approached, some people at the heart of New Labour were worried that the party would be too closely identified with constitutional reform rather than the 'doorstep' issues of education and health. Matthew Taylor, who was at the heart of Labour's campaign, describes the process he saw from inside Millbank in the run-up to 1997:

My sense would be that if the constitutional agenda became less significant, it was less to do with a change of heart and more to do with the fact they did not want the government to be caricatured as a government more obsessed with constitutional nerdling than it was with improving schools and hospitals. They were acutely aware of Clinton's problems with gay servicemen and the last thing Labour wanted to do was get into a situation where it seemed that the agenda they had was an agenda of no salience. As you know from opinion polls, the whole constitutional agenda is very very low salience … The golden rule of British politics is, the government is in favour of centralization and the opposition is in favour of decentralization. Regardless of what parties they belong to.

One pre-election book which was full of clues to how Labour would actually behave in power was *The Blair Revolution* by Peter Mandelson and Roger Liddle, a former SDP member who became Blair's European policy adviser in Downing Street. The book said there was no need for 'high theory or fancy schemes of constitutional reform' and dismissed the debate on electoral reform as mostly motivated by partisan interests. The authors wrote that constitutional reform lobbyists such as Charter88 'must appreciate that constitutional reform is not Labour's sole concern' and did not constitute a panacea. Steady piecemeal reform was the answer rather than a 'Big Bang' reform package.

'THE UNION IS IN DANGER'

Throughout the election campaign Labour played down constitutional issues while the Conservatives did their best to scare the voters with attacks on 'the yapping dogs of Welsh and Scottish separatism' and warnings that the Union was in danger. In the words of John Major, constitutional reform would 'unstitch our way of life'. At the last Conservative conference before the election, Scottish Secretary Michael Forsyth spoke of the 'mortal danger' posed by devolution and condemned the 'constitution-mongers' of Charter88. 'There is no such thing as Scottish devolution – there is only British dissolution,' Forsyth declared, winding up to a climax in which he invoked the Almighty on behalf of the status quo: 'God has smiled on this island … Ours is the mother of parliaments, evolved over a thousand years. Our monarchy, even more ancient, consecrates the compact between accountable government and a free people, even as it cements the bonds between the nations of the United Kingdom.'

THE 'PARISH COUNCIL' GAFFE

Blair's stickiest campaign moment on constitutional issues came on a visit to Scotland. Despite his Fettes education and Scottish family connections through his father, Blair has often seemed curiously deaf to the totems and taboos of political discourse north of the border, and ill at ease with Scottish audiences, even those of his own party supporters. Blair talking to the Scots has always reminded me of Gorbachev talking to the Ukrainians in his inability to comprehend their feelings about national identity and sovereignty.

In an interview with *The Scotsman*, Blair compared the revenue-raising powers of the Scottish Parliament to those of 'the smallest English parish council' and added for good measure: 'Sovereignty rests with me as an English MP and that's the way it will stay.' The remarks were seized on by the Scottish Nationalists, whose leader Alex Salmond complained: 'God tells Blair and King Tony then tells Scotland.' Veteran Scottish Liberal Democrat Sir David Steel, who was later to become Presiding Officer of the Scottish Parliament, commented acidly that Blair needed a history lesson, ascribing his remarks to ignorance rather than a change of policy: 'On the supremacy of the Crown-in-Parliament at Westminster, the Labour leader was absolutely correct in English law, but in Scotland, sovereignty has always rested with the people.'[19]

THE COOK-MACLENNAN AGREEMENT

Rather as an insurance policy for both sides in case of a narrow election result and a hung parliament, Labour and the Liberal Democrats decided to negotiate a joint policy document on constitutional reform, which emerged in March 1997. This stopped well short of any coalition pact and each party subsequently unveiled its own separate manifesto. But the six-month negotiation process under Robin Cook and Robert Maclennan was important in shaping what happened after the election.[20] Maclennan recalls that at the outset the Liberal Democrats wanted a more coherent, integrated package of constitutional reform than Labour was planning to deliver:

Our thinking had been very largely crystallized and we had a global programme for the reform of the British constitution, even up to and including steps to consolidate different measures within a framework of a written constitution. Labour had a number of discrete policies on the constitution, to which they were committed in greater or lesser degree, notably on Scottish devolution. For the rest, although there had been statements from time to time on freedom of information, there was, I think, no sense of it all being an overall constitutional package for the modernization of Britain's governance ... We focused on how to bring these discrete matters together into a package that could be jointly presented by the two parties to the country in the election in manifestos where these matters were the same. We both took the view that constitutional changes impacted on each other, and more widely than was often recognized, and it was wrong to think of them as entirely discrete measures. We saw there was a case for presenting the whole package as having a major political purpose which went beyond the accumulation of these reforms, but which was really to do with empowering the British citizen and redressing the imbalance between the executive and the legislature and the excessive centralization of British government.

Much of the talking took place in bilateral meetings between Cook and Maclennan, who had come to the Liberal Democrats via the breakaway SDP and had served as a junior minister under Wilson and Callaghan. Blair's choice of Cook, a longstanding supporter of constitutional reform, rather than a less enthusiastic figure such as Jack Straw or John Prescott, ensured that the negotiation had a good chance of success.[21] The final report of what was grandly dubbed the Joint Consultative Committee on Constitutional Reform proclaimed: 'If this programme is enacted, Britain's democracy will have been transformed.'

On many issues, such as the new Scottish Parliament, there was no need to break new ground; on others, such as the plans for a Human Rights Act to incorporate the ECHR, detailed preparation got under way to enable an early start to legislation; on regional government for England the outcome was vague; on electoral reform, the parties agreed that the referendum first proposed by John Smith should give a straight choice between two systems, first-past-the-post and 'one specific proportional alternative'; a commission on voting systems for Westminster would be set up to recommend such an alternative; on freedom of information, little or no detailed preparatory work was done, an omission which proved costly once Labour entered government; reform of the Lords would be a two-stage process, with the hereditary peers being expelled first and a second stage coming later.

The Liberal Democrats acquiesced in the downgrading of plans for regional government in England, agreeing these would have to wait until after devolution for Scotland and Wales, which would take priority.

Labour's manifesto differed only in minor details from the Cook-Maclennan package. It described government not so much as undemocratic or unaccountable but as 'centralized, inefficient and bureaucratic', adding: 'There is unquestionably a national crisis of confidence in our political system, to which Labour will respond in a measured and sensible way.' It subjected the idea of regional assemblies in England to extraordinarily tight conditions, saying they would only come about where clear popular consent was established, where no extra costs were involved, and only where a unitary system of local government was already in place. London was promised a mayor as well as a strategic authority. The manifesto stressed the role of 'a sovereign Westminster parliament' and insisted Labour's devolution plans did not involve any kind of federation. The House of Lords, after removal of hereditary peers, would eventually be made more democratic and representative but with its powers unaltered. To reassure royalist sentiments in Middle England, it added: 'We have no plans to replace the monarchy.' The horses were not to be frightened.

As the remaining chapters of this book will show, Labour broadly stuck to the programme outlined in its manifesto after its general election victory. Judged by the broad sweep of Labour's history, it was still an ambitious programme, though Dominic Hilton describes the 1997 commitments as 'minimal in nature'. His view is that the Smith period was something of an anomaly and that under Blair the party has resumed the constitutional conservatism that has marked most of its first 100 years. This interpretation, of Blair's New Labour coming to the rescue of the British *ancien regime*, is broadly that of Anthony Barnett and Tom Nairn. Hilton's verdict is that Blair 'stole the clothes of reform but castrated the policy'.

Robert Maclennan inclines to the view that Blair's constitutional pledges were prompted less by a belief in democracy and more by his need to bring liberal intellectual opinion into the Labour tent:

I think he came to these issues only because he recognized that the *bien-pensants* in Britain – and that was a constituency in which he was interested when he was looking to become prime minister – had an agenda for reform that had united a lot of people from a lot of different quarters of the political spectrum. The language they used about modernizing governance to some extent reflected the language he was using, though his objectives were somewhat different. And I think he thought to bring them under his tent by giving a degree of priority to the agenda which was theirs.

I think added to that was his understanding of the fact that not only was the John Smith commitment to the unfinished business in Scotland one that he should not depart from, it was one that he *could* not depart from without Scots looking for secession. So there was an element of political necessity reinforcing his judgement that a move had to be made there. That could be justified not only in terms of buying off the Scots, who were becoming increasingly restive, but in terms of a philosophy of decentralization to which I think he paid lip service. I do not think he instinctively is a decentralist. But certainly in speaking to the Charter88 organization prior to the election, he used the language which was designed to appeal to that section of public opinion.

In the long run, precise motivation in politics is secondary; whether Blair promised constitutional reform because of a deeply held belief or because of electoral considerations is less relevant than what he actually achieved. However, it is important to register the fact that in the three years he spent as Labour leader in opposition, Blair significantly thinned out the constitutional agenda he had inherited from John Smith. Although many of the individual items remained, the central commitment to a revolutionary change in the way the country was governed was quietly dropped.

THE COOK-MACLENNAN AGREEMENT

Human rights

Incorporation of the ECHR into British law would be done in a Human Rights Act which would not affect the sovereign powers of parliament. No special courts would be set up. A joint committee of the Commons and the Lords would monitor the Act and scrutinize legislation, and a Human Rights Commissioner or Commission would be able to bring proceedings under the Act.

Freedom of information

A Freedom of Information Act with independent machinery to 'shift the balance decisively in favour of the presumption that government information should be publicly available unless there is a justifiable reason not to do so'.

Scotland

A Scottish parliament to be elected by the additional member system with powers to handle the business currently managed by the Scottish Office. Revenue by block grant from London, with the Scottish parliament able to raise its own extra revenue within a defined limit. Both parties to campaign for a 'yes' in the referendum.

Wales and English regions

An assembly for Wales to be elected by the additional member system. Indirectly elected regional chambers for England to be followed by directly elected assemblies only after approval in local referendums. An elected authority for London.

Electoral systems

Proportional systems agreed for Wales and Scotland, a referendum on voting for Westminster to be held in the lifetime of the new parliament, with a straight choice between the status quo and one proportional alternative; a commission to be set up to recommend which proportional alternative would command consensus among supporters of PR; elections to the European Parliament to be held by a proportional system of regional lists.

Commons

Better use of parliamentary time, more pre-legislative scrutiny, a change in Prime Minister's Question Time 'to make it a more genuine and serious means of

▶

holding the government to account'; better scrutiny of EU legislation, an enhanced role for select committees; establishment of a Modernization Committee.

Lords

A first-stage reform to remove hereditary peers; a new mechanism to nominate cross-benchers; some hereditary peers to be given life peerages; life peers to be preserved but allowed to retire voluntarily; no party to seek a majority; party numbers to reflect more accurately the result of the previous general election; a joint committee of both houses to work out proposals for 'a democratic and representative second chamber'.

Other matters

An independent statistics service; a Civil Service Act; greater openness in appointments to quangos; an early declaration by government on constitutional reform outlining its proposals for a more open and modern democracy.

NOTES

[1] Foote, Geoffrey (1997) *The Labour Party's Political Thought. A history*, London, Macmillan, 3rd edition, p 29.

[2] Foote, op. cit., p 30.

[3] Hilton, Dominic (2000) 'How did the British Labour Party Come to Adopt the Proposals for Constitutional Reform as Described in its 1997 General Election Manifesto?', University of Oxford unpublished M.Phil thesis.

[4] Jones, Barry and Keating, Michael (1985) *Labour and the British State*, Oxford University Press, p 53.

[5] Jones and Keating, op. cit., p 55.

[6] Jones and Keating, op. cit., p 156.

[7] Although it is now taken for granted that the ideas of New Labour have nothing in common with the leftwing doctrines of Tony Benn and the early 1980s, there are in fact some similarities which both sides do their best to play down. These are ideas which have survived intact into the New Labour project. The instrumentalist attitude to parliament as a device for implementing party policy rather than as an institution in its own right is common to both Benn and Blair. Blair has used the memory of Labour's internecine quarrels of the early 1980s to keep a tight rein on backbenchers through the Whips, in the process reducing the risk of independent scrutiny. There is something very Bennite in Blair's repeated reminders to would-be rebels that they were elected on the party manifesto, not because of their own ideas. One can trace a straight line from Michael Foot's opposition to Select Committees in 1970 because they would lead to consensus

politics, to Margaret Beckett's dismissal of the Liaison Committee report calling for greater independence in appointments to committees in 2000.

[8] Wright, Tony (ed.) (2000) *The British Political Process: an introduction*, London, Routledge, p 333.

[9] Kinnock always denied uttering these comments. Barnett gave me the following account of how he believes they became public: 'The source of the quote was Anthony Howard in a diary he wrote in *The Spectator*. His source was Roy Hattersley. Hattersley was a real opponent of Charter88 ... My guess is, Hattersley said: "These people are just fashionable so-and-sos." Neil in his way said: "Oh, you mean they are just whiners, whingers and wankers?" without making a public statement, and Hattersley, wanting to crush the Charter, then leaked that, as the voice of Kinnock, to Howard.'

[10] Quoted in Hilton, op. cit.

[11] Quoted in Hilton, op. cit.

[12] Plant gives a full account of this in Blackburn and Plant, op. cit.

[13] For an explanation of voting systems, see Chapter 7.

[14] Reproduced as an appendix in Blackburn, Robert and Plant, Raymond (eds) (1999) *Constitutional Reform. The Labour government's constitutional reform agenda*, London, Longman.

[15] Sutherland, Keith (ed.) (2000) *The Rape of the Constitution?* Exeter, Imprint Academic, p 258.

[16] Blackburn and Plant, op. cit., p 71. Plant's understanding of Blair's views is by necessity speculative; despite having led the party's study of electoral systems, he has never been consulted by Blair since he became party leader.

[17] Hilton, op. cit.

[18] Reprinted in Blair, Tony (1996) *New Britain. My vision of a young country*, London, Fourth Estate.

[19] Steel was referring to a famous 1953 court judgment by Lord Cooper which stated: 'The principle of the unlimited sovereignty of parliament is a distinctively English principle which has no counterpart in Scottish constitutional law.'

[20] Reproduced as an appendix in Blackburn and Plant, op. cit.

[21] Raymond Plant, also on the committee, recalls Straw as 'not engaging with the issues at all ... he turned up'.

3

A SCOTTISH AND WELSH MYSTERY TOUR

'I recall the fine story of a Welsh mystery tour by bus from Cwmrhydyceirw in my constituency. There was a sweep about where the tour would end, and it is said that the driver won. The people of Wales are driving this mystery tour. They will decide the pace and the direction, and I have confidence in our people' – Donald Anderson MP

'In short, devolution is a response to nationalist success' – Professor John Curtice

'Devolution is a process, not an event' – Ron Davies

IT WAS ON 9 FEBRUARY 2000, the day his protégé Alun Michael was forced out of office by the National Assembly for Wales in Cardiff, that Tony Blair discovered he was no longer in the driving seat of the devolution mystery tour. Alun Michael's eclipse after less than nine months holding the Soviet-style title of First Secretary came at a moment of maximum embarrassment for Blair, coinciding with the Wednesday afternoon Westminster ritual of Prime Minister's Questions. Blair had been on his feet in the Commons facing William Hague for several minutes when Michael, facing a motion of no confidence, suddenly broke off his speech in the Assembly chamber at Cardiff Bay to fish out of his pocket a letter of resignation which he handed to the Presiding Officer, Dafydd Elis Thomas. Watching from the press seats at the back of the chamber, I could see that Elis Thomas, a Plaid Cymru veteran, was as surprised as I was. Angry at the lack of any prior warning, he upset Michael's tactical

Tony Blair badly singed by the breath of the Welsh dragon. On the previous day his personal choice as First Secretary of Wales, Alun Michael, was forced to resign. Copyright © Peter Brookes, 2000.

survival plan by refusing to read the letter or cancel the imminent vote of no confidence tabled by the three opposition parties. The vote went ahead over Labour protests and Michael's fate was sealed. Nobody managed to tell Blair what was happening in Cardiff. By the end of Prime Minister's Questions, he was left forlornly defending a Welsh First Secretary who was no longer in office to a barrage of jeers from Conservative MPs, alerted by pager.

DEVOLUTION AND THE THIRD WAY

Devolution, like many of Blair's policies, is a balancing act, combining opposing elements to produce a 'third way' synthesis. Blair's approach to devolution combines traditional unionism, emphasizing the unity of the United Kingdom and the sovereignty of the Westminster parliament, with the promise of a radical shift of power away from the centre. He believes in the maxim of Enoch Powell, 'power devolved is power retained'. In the Blairite vision, power can safely be devolved from Westminster to Edinburgh and Cardiff because the Labour party, through its Scottish and Welsh 'managers on the ground', will be there to keep control of the process.

Northern Ireland, of course, is different because the Labour party, like other UK parties, is no more than a spectator of the province's tug-of-war between local political forces. To argue this is not to deny the huge significance of the Northern Ireland settlement for the future of United Kingdom statehood; but it lacks the party-political dimension that is crucial to the dynamics of devolution in Scotland and Wales. Unlike Scotland and Wales, Northern Ireland is not a reservoir of electoral strength for Labour at Westminster.

> 66 Labour sees Irish nationalism with a benevolent eye while treating Scottish and Welsh nationalism as illegitimate. 99

This explains why Labour sees Irish nationalism with a benevolent eye while treating Scottish and Welsh nationalism as illegitimate. In Northern Ireland, the 'politics of identity' is the basis of the Belfast Agreement and the new settlement. But the same 'narrow politics of identity' is held up to scorn by Blair in Wales and Scotland as an outdated 19th-century concept. 'For it is inherent to the politics of nationalism that the trappings of a 19th-century nation state – from armies to currencies – must take precedence over the needs of social justice.'[1] In its place, Blair proposes a concept of 'shared British values' around such unlikely totems as the National Health Service. Popular sovereignty and self-determination, the principles that underpin the Northern Ireland settlement, are not regarded as applicable in Scotland and Wales. As Professor Kevin Morgan and Geoff Mungham of Cardiff University point out, the 'modernizing' view is 'that territorial attachments are cultural residues of a pre-modern or pre-capitalist age, primordial attributes which, in the fullness of time, would be dissolved by the gastric juices of modernization'.[2]

Labour has displayed uneasiness not just about nationalism but also about regionalism, preferring to see a territorial approach to politics as backward. The temptation of centralism to which New Labour often succumbs is rooted not so much in the old Bevanite priority of class politics as in its new managerial ideology and its preoccupation with globalization and branding. The result has been ambivalence at the heart of Labour's devolution project, which helps explain why the party may not be the principal beneficiary of the huge constitutional changes it has wrought.

THE LEGACY OF THATCHER

Thatcherism never conquered Scotland, as the lady herself acknowledged in her memoirs.[3] She blamed council housing, the Scottish dependency culture, the grip of patronage and the obstructive tendency of her Scottish ministers such as Malcolm Rifkind to court popularity north of the border by standing up to Whitehall. The result, she ruefully admitted, was that 'there was no Tartan Thatcherite Revolution'. She concluded that the balance sheet of Thatcherism in Scotland was lopsided – economically positive but politically negative. 'Some part of this unpopularity must be attributed to the national question on which the Tories are seen as an English party and on which I myself was apparently seen as a quintessential English figure.' Thatcher dismissed the idea of 'wearing tartan camouflage' to woo the Scots and gave them up as a bad job, acknowledging after she left office that they have 'an undoubted right to self-determination' and should they opt for independence 'no English party or politician would stand in their way'. Devolution was something different; the Scots had the right to secede from the Union of 1707 but had no right to a devolved parliament unless the English approved. Thatcher's successor, John Major, argued vehemently that devolution would lead inevitably to the breakup of the United Kingdom.

66 The case for a Scottish parliament within the Labour party was that it would 'kill nationalism stone dead'. 99

Labour's counter-argument was that only through devolution could the breakup be avoided. The case for a Scottish parliament within the Labour party was that it would 'kill nationalism stone dead'. By delivering a Scottish parliament and making it work, Labour would definitively dish the Scottish National party's electoral fortunes. The result of the 1997 general election appeared to cement Labour's position as the dominant party in Scotland, giving it 56 out of 72 Westminster seats and eliminating the Conservatives. The scale of Labour's victory, however, meant that it inherited from the Conservatives the mantle of being the main unionist party. The presence of so many high-profile Scots in Blair's cabinet – Gordon Brown, Robin Cook, Alistair Darling – means the party will never be seen as 'English' in the same way as Thatcher's Conservatives. But it still has to perform a difficult balancing act between London and Edinburgh.

HORSES FOR COURSES BUT NO WHITE PAPER

When Labour took office there were many who urged the government to set out its overall views on constitutional reform in a White Paper before beginning its legislative programme. Robert Hazell of the Constitution Unit was among those who encouraged the government to 'set out its stall', but he was unsuccessful. According to Murray Elder, the idea of a White Paper was 'never a runner' because of the risk that it might fatally delay the devolution Bill for Scotland, whose supporters had long feared that their project might become entangled in other constitutional reforms. Blair appears to have decided well before the election to let each Whitehall department take charge of its own constitutional reforms, rather than appoint a single minister.

Robert Maclennan agrees with the decision not to name a constitutional supremo, believing it was better to spread the business around Whitehall. 'I favoured having it spread around the departments and given a degree of priority by those departments, also enabling a number of important ministers within the government to sign up to a constitutional package as part of their agenda.'

Delegating all constitutional reforms to one ministry, probably the Cabinet Office, would have seriously reduced the amount of legislative time available. As things turned out, the government succeeded in passing the Scotland Act, the Government of Wales Act and the Human Rights Act in its first session. The argument was 'horses for courses' but the risk was that different reforms might not fit together. The Scottish and Welsh Bills were the responsibility of Secretary of State for Scotland Donald Dewar and his Welsh counterpart Ron Davies.

GRIT IN THE OYSTER

To a large extent, the Scottish blueprint was ready, thanks to the work of the Scottish Constitutional Convention and negotiations in Scotland between Labour and the Liberal Democrats. Major changes to the plan would have been politically impossible after years of public debate and negotiation with people outside the party. Devolution, described by John Smith as 'the settled will of the Scottish people', could not be watered down too much because too many toes would be trodden on. If Blair needed any reminder of this, he had only to recall the painful impact on the party in Scotland of his tactical about-turn over the need for a referendum the previous year and his careless comparison of the parliament to an English parish council. While in the 1970s devolution was largely a 'not invented here' policy for the Scottish Labour party, forced on it from London, in 1997 it was the opposite – a home-grown formula in which the party's national leadership had played a secondary role.

> 66 Devolution, described by John Smith as 'the settled will of the Scottish people', could not be watered down too much because too many toes would be trodden on. 99

THE CLAIM OF RIGHT

The Scottish Constitutional Convention had long completed its work by the time of the 1997 election. Born in the wake of the collapse of Labour's devolution project in 1979, the Campaign for a Scottish Assembly's Constitutional Steering Committee in July 1988 published *A Claim of Right for Scotland*. This declaration was largely drafted by Jim Ross, a retired Scottish Office civil servant, but its uncompromising tone was hardly that of bland civil service prose. It came close to declaring the rule of the Thatcher government over Scotland to be illegitimate, saying that parliamentary government under the existing constitution had failed Scotland. Looking back to the 1707 Act of Union and to Claims of Right in 1689 and 1842, it robustly condemned the 'English Constitution' as an illusion of democracy. 'The United Kingdom is a political artefact put together at English insistence.'

Crucially, however, it did not argue that independence was the only solution. Instead, it proposed a constitutional convention by which Scots would start the reform of their own government, rather than waiting for action from London. 'They have the opportunity, in the process, to start the reform of the English constitution, to serve as the grit in the oyster which produces the pearl.' Labour's support for a constitutional convention was by no means guaranteed, but the impact of the introduction of the poll tax in Scotland and the shock loss of Glasgow Govan to the SNP in a by-election in November 1988 helped push the party into saying yes. As Brian Taylor puts it, 'Labour leaders had to swallow hard before pursuing this road to reform.'[4]

Labour's overwhelming strength in numbers of MPs and other elected officials ensured it would dominate the proceedings. Donald Dewar was instrumental in leading Labour into the convention. Dewar, even before the Govan by-election, made it clear in a speech in Stirling that Labour would take part. Murray Elder recalls: 'Donald had decided that while there would be risks, it would be right to take them. A lot of fast thinking on our feet would be needed … He also had an eye, even then, to the need to have a broader base of support for devolution than was the case in 1978.' The Liberal Democrats joined, while the Conservative party unsurprisingly stayed out. After inconclusive talks, the SNP also backed out, complaining the convention was rigged, a decision that gave Labour the chance to marginalize its deadly rival. 'Labour's objective, plainly, was to make it very difficult if not impossible for the SNP to join.'[5] The SNP's decision, described by the nationalist intellectual Tom Nairn as 'sectarian infantilism', left it sniping from the sidelines at the plans for what it dismissed as 'Labour's pretend parliament'. Not until the referendum campaign of September 1997 did the SNP manage to detach itself from the hook on which it had impaled itself and support a devolved parliament as a stepping stone to independence.

The convention's first report in 1990 was couched in the militant spirit of the Claim of Right:

Indeed, though it was a devolutionist body, its thinking was nationalist in the sense that it was solely concerned with Scottish needs and desires. At its heart was a fundamental contradiction: its members were overwhelmingly supporters of a reformed Union, yet they had all signed up to the nationalist doctrine of popular sovereignty and rejected parliamentary sovereignty.[6]

It was followed by a second report in 1995, less economically dirigiste but more detailed on the composition of the parliament.

The period after the 1992 election was marked by far more sophisticated and serious thinking about Scottish devolution than in the preceding 13 years. At the same time as the Constitutional Commission established by the convention was meeting, thinking within the Labour party was developing independently. Labour policymaking was subsumed within its electoral strategy.[7]

The size of the parliament was eventually agreed at 129 members, 73 to be elected in constituencies and the remainder by a proportional 'top-up' procedure. This additional member system makes it hard for any single party to win an overall majority in a four-party system. Labour's willingness to accept this was dictated partly by the need for a deal with the Liberal Democrats, and partly because it realized a proportional system would make it equally difficult for the SNP to win power. Brian Taylor, the BBC Scotland Political Editor, asked Labour's Scottish General Secretary Jack McConnell much later if this was the reason for the precise choice of electoral system. McConnell replied: 'Correct.'[8]

The story of the convention is important because it illustrates how theoretical constitution building inevitably becomes entangled with party politics; it laid the groundwork for a coalition between Labour and the Liberal Democrats when the Scottish Parliament began work in 1999. This process had no parallel in Wales, where bitter infighting in Labour ranks effectively ruled out any cross-party cooperation. The convention's other significance was that once Blair had accepted its 1995 blueprint, the Labour party effectively had the essentials of its Scotland White Paper.

While the newly minted government pushed through early legislation for the Scottish and Welsh referendums scheduled for September 1997, a cabinet committee prepared the White Paper on which the subsequent detailed legislation of the Scotland Act would be based. Dewar needed Blair's backing to fend off a serious attempt to unpick key details of the plan he had worked out with the Liberal Democrats, such as the proportional voting system.[9] Dewar had to win a series of arguments to safeguard elements that he had agreed with the Scots but which were opposed by other ministers such as Home Secretary Jack Straw, a long-standing foe of PR, who reportedly felt early drafts of the White Paper were 'too Braveheartish'. Blair insisted on watertight references to the sovereignty of the Westminster parliament and to a network of 'good behaviour' agreements between London and the devolved administrations, to be known as concordats. He also insisted on a future cut in the over-representation of Scotland in the Commons, paving the way for an eventual reduction in the number of Scottish MPs from 72 to 57 or 58.

In the view of Scottish Liberal Democrat Andy Miles, the convention, taking the Claim of Right as its starting point, marked the high water mark of Labour's commitment to Home Rule and the White Paper was a partial retreat.[10] Murray Elder, who was an adviser to Dewar, describes the DSWR[11] cabinet committee chaired by the Lord Chancellor Derry Irvine as 'hard-fought and lengthy' but no more so than Dewar expected:

I think it was quite right that the other departments took a very long hard look at the consequences for their own powers and authority. I think we got almost without exception the settlement we would have wanted. I think ironically, although it is almost impossible to get people to believe this, one of the reasons we got that was that intellectually Donald convinced Derry that he was right. And although people continue to write about how Donald and Derry never spoke to each other,[12] the closeness of their work on DSWR signed and sealed the deal that we got. It was not uncommon for Donald to come off the sleeper on a Monday morning and go straight to a private breakfast with Derry to discuss how they were going to handle that week.

SCOTLAND – THE KEY FACTS

The general election

Labour won 56 of the 72 Scottish seats in the House of Commons on 1 May 1997. The Conservatives were wiped out, while the Liberal Democrats won 10 and the SNP six.

The referendum

Scottish voters approved the idea of a Scottish parliament by a three-to-one majority in a referendum on 11 September 1997. The SNP joined Labour and the Liberal Democrats in campaigning for a 'yes' vote. On a 60.4 per cent turnout, 74.3 per cent voted in favour of the parliament and 63.5 per cent for it to have the power to vary income tax.

The Scotland Act

Published in December 1997, the Act became law on 19 November 1998. It set up a single-chamber parliament with 129 members, 73 of them elected by first-past-the-post from Westminster constituencies. The Orkney and Shetland seat was divided into two. The remaining 56 seats are elected from eight regions under the proportional additional member system. The parliament sits for a fixed four-year term, though it can be dissolved earlier by a two-thirds vote of all members, or in the event of a prolonged deadlock. The parliament has law-making powers in all areas not reserved to Westminster, whose general power to make laws for Scotland is unaffected. The main powers are agriculture, economic development, law and order, education, the environment, health, local government, social work, and transport. Funding comes in a block grant from the UK government, though the parliament can vary the income tax rate by up to 3 per cent. Reserved matters include the constitution and the Crown, registration and funding of political parties, foreign affairs and defence, the civil service, fiscal, economic and monetary policy, some aspects of home affairs including immigration, extradition and gambling, most trade, energy and industry matters, social security, abortion and broadcasting.

The Scottish election

In the election on 6 May 1999, Labour won 56 seats, the SNP 35, the Conservatives 18, the Liberal Democrats 17, with the Greens, the Scottish Socialist party and the rebel Labour MP Denis Canavan winning one each. Labour lost a by-election in Ayr to the Conservatives in March 2000.

The executive

Labour and the Liberal Democrats formed a coalition with Donald Dewar as First Minister and Jim Wallace as his deputy holding the Justice portfolio. Another Liberal Democrat, Ross Finnie, became Rural Affairs minister, while Labour held the remaining cabinet posts. When Dewar died suddenly in October 2000, Henry McLeish became First Minister.

SCOTLAND FORWARD

If any questions remained about whether the SNP would call for a 'yes' vote in the September referendum, they quickly evaporated, with Alex Salmond's party itching to give its support despite its boycott of the constitutional convention. For Labour, with bad memories of the 1970's failed referendum, SNP support for a 'yes' vote was important. With three of the four main parties campaigning under the 'Scotland Forward' slogan and only the Conservatives against, a 'yes' vote was not in doubt, but its size remained in the balance. The outcome on a turnout of 60.4 per cent was 74.3 per cent for the parliament, with 63.5 per cent voting for tax-raising powers. Only two regions – Orkney and Dumfries and Galloway – opposed the tax powers.

When the Scotland Bill began its long journey through parliament in December 1997 it was clear that Blair's decision to hold a referendum first had been far-sighted, despite the turmoil it caused. As Scottish Liberal Democrat leader Jim Wallace acknowledged, the referendum had politically if not legally entrenched the existence of the parliament, making it virtually impossible for any Westminster government to abolish it. The referendum also removed the threat of all-out filibustering by the Conservative opposition, which might otherwise have used its majority in the Lords to block the bill. While the SNP quibbled in the Commons over the extent of the powers still reserved to Westminster, the Conservatives made it clear that they accepted the reality of the new parliament while shaking their heads and predicting doom around the corner.

Conservative spokesman Michael Ancram described the final text as a mess and predicted that 'for many years it will be a dripping roast for lawyers on both sides of the border'. He said the Bill raised an unacceptable constitutional imbalance in the United Kingdom, and accused the government of creating 'a flaw so fundamental and an irritant so pervasive that it remains a ticking time-bomb within their devolutionary reforms'. The Conservative attack centred on the so-called 'West Lothian question', named by Enoch Powell after the one-time constituency of Labour's veteran MP Tam Dalyell, a lonely if widely respected figure at

> ❝ Dalyell described devolution as a motorway without an exit, which would lead inevitably to independence. ❞

Westminster whose implacable anti-devolution views have remained the same since the 1970s. In the debates on the Scotland Bill, Dalyell described devolution as a motorway without an exit, which would lead inevitably to independence. He warned of a backlash from 'the slow candle of English nationalism', pointing out that the long-term problem posed by the Bill for government at Westminster was masked by Labour's short-term 179-seat majority. Why, he asked, should Scottish MPs continue to vote on English domestic matters such as health and education when English MPs would no longer be able to vote on such matters in Scotland?

The West Lothian question was one of several to which Labour preferred not to give a clear response during the passage of the Bill. As in all political compromises, the final version contained ambiguities. Despite its references to the sovereignty of the United Kingdom parliament, there was no doubt that for most Scots, including Donald Dewar, the Scotland Act embodied Scottish popular sovereignty as asserted in the Claim of Right. Labour appeared hesitant and even half-hearted in proclaiming the constitutional implications of the new parliament it had created; in the run-up to the 1999 elections, the political initiative appeared to pass to Alex Salmond's SNP, which had for many years accused Labour of being 'unable to deliver a pizza, let alone a parliament'. Far from rolling over stone dead as George Robertson had predicted at the Scottish Labour party's 1998 conference, the SNP began to outpace Labour in the polls. The official answer from the Labour party was to try to minimize

Donald Dewar has to compromise over student tuition fees with Liberal Democrat leader Jim Wallace as the price of forming a coalition after the election of the Scottish Parliament. Copyright © Dave Brown, 1999.

discussion of constitutional questions and concentrate on bread-and-butter issues such as health and education as the core themes of the election campaign. There were moments when this strategy and Dewar's determinedly uncharismatic leadership looked likely to lead to disaster at the polls. At one stage in 1998 a poll showed the SNP about to win 57 of the parliament seats to Labour's 47. But the final election outcome turned out better than Labour had feared, possibly because of a risky SNP pledge to deprive Scottish taxpayers of a one penny income tax cut announced by Chancellor of the Exchequer Gordon Brown. The result left Labour with the lion's share of first-past-the-post constituency seats, leaving the SNP dependent on seats in the regional lists. Labour had no overall majority but was well placed as the largest party to form a coalition with Jim Wallace's Liberal Democrats.

With very few exceptions, the results of the first-past-the-post voting for constituency seats followed the 1997 Westminster pattern, but as Professor John Curtice of Strathclyde University noted, this disguised a revolution in Scotland's voting habits: 'It has been turned from a nation of safe seats into a country of marginals.'[13] With the SNP emerging clearly as the second-placed party, the election had given the lie to the idea that Scotland would always be natural Labour territory. Curtice described Labour's 34 per cent share of the list vote as deeply disappointing. For many in the party, the failure to win an outright majority proved that the introduction of proportional representation was a fatal mistake.

A PARLIAMENT CONVENED – OR RECONVENED

The biggest change in the constitutional framework of the United Kingdom since the partition of Ireland some 80 years earlier became a reality on 12 May 1999. It was five years since the death of John Smith. In the General Assembly building of the Church of Scotland, on the Mound at the foot of Edinburgh castle, the 129 members of the new Scottish Parliament (MSPs) gathered in their temporary home to swear or affirm allegiance under standing orders laid down by Westminster. After the oath-taking ceremony there was a moment of grandmotherly scene-stealing from the Parliament's oldest member, 69-year-old Winnie Ewing of the SNP. Before the election of Sir David Steel as Presiding Officer, the veteran nationalist took advantage of her status in the chair to make a short speech: 'I want to begin with the words that I have always wanted either to say or to hear someone else say: the Scottish Parliament, which adjourned on the 25th day of March 1707, is hereby reconvened.'

The applause for Ewing was not universal. Commentator Gerry Hassan, reflecting the Blairite modernizing view, wrote that the new parliament had nothing in common with the old 'feudal' one dissolved at the time of the Act of Union nearly 300 years earlier. 'She (Ewing) sees Scotland 1707–1999 as some kind of inter-parliamentary spasm, before "normal" service was resumed. Her case is based on restoring what was wrongly taken or "stolen" from Scotland: its ancient, independent parliament – an essentialist and outdated nationalist viewpoint, for which modern nationalists should have no time.'[14]

AN INFORMAL PARLIAMENT

When the Scottish Parliament held its formal opening ceremony on 1 July Blair was absent, detained by talks in Northern Ireland. There was a mixture of pageantry and informality which signalled that despite the presence in the gallery of Commons Speaker Betty Boothroyd, the ways of Westminster had been left behind. Walter Bagehot would probably not have approved. Outside in the streets there was the kind of popular show he would have found familiar: an open horse-drawn carriage for the Queen, with military bands and a procession up the Royal Mile from Holyrood Palace. But inside the mood was cheerful and informal, from the moment the Queen entered with Sir David Steel and Donald Dewar, past the grim and disapproving statue of the 16th-century Calvinist John Knox. The atmosphere was more Scottish fish tea than British state occasion. The Queen left her silk gowns and tiaras at home and wore a blue suit and an alarming hat spiked with feathers. The crown worn by Mary Queen of Scots in the 16th century was borne on a cushion by a kilted aristocrat, Lord James Douglas-Hamilton, accompanied by three gaudily dressed heralds. Otherwise the Victorian costume drama of the annual state opening at Westminster was avoided. Also mercifully banished from the chamber was the Scottish-baronial tartanry of George IV's famous visit to Edinburgh, choreographed by Sir Walter Scott. The ceremonies began with a joke by Sir David Steel about Prince Charles' interest in architecture and ended with a unique moment which would have been inconceivable at Westminster as folk singer Sheena Wellington sang Robert Burns' 'A man's a man for a'that'. Bagehot, no admirer of democracy, might have pursed his lips as the new MSPs joined in this assault on rank and privilege.

> 66 The atmosphere was more Scottish fish tea than British state occasion. The Queen left her silk gowns and tiaras at home and wore a blue suit and an alarming hat spiked with feathers. 99

DOWNHILL FROM THE MOUND?

In the view of large sections of the Scottish press, the story of the Scottish Parliament has been downhill all the way since then, to the point where its first anniversary passed unmarked, for fear of provoking tabloid scorn. 'What kind of family doesn't celebrate its child's first birthday? What kind of country doesn't commemorate the return of its parliament after 300 years? What kind of parliament is so cringingly apologetic that it can't bring itself to celebrate the anniversary of its own creation?' asked Iain Macwhirter in *The Herald.*

Dewar's coalition was plagued by controversy over a wide range of issues, most of them reflecting political inexperience and a lack of cabinet teamwork. As he told the Labour party conference in Brighton in September 2000, 'It has ... been a sharp learning curve – indeed so sharp that it has at times been the political equivalent of abseiling.' Expectations of a 'new politics' in which adversarial point-scoring would be replaced by the rational civic wisdom of the 18th-century Scottish Enlightenment proved to be wide of the mark. Dewar told me the constitutional convention's idea of a body less confrontational and more consensus-based than Westminster had not turned into a reality:

What we've got is an opposition which plays the Westminster game with great skill and energy and is extremely confrontational. So that makes life very difficult for us, largely because enormous power has been given to the committees. I sometimes have great difficulty explaining to people that as backbenchers they have more power than anyone ever dreamt of at Westminster. And it is really a remarkable obstacle course for the executive. Basically if you have got a substantial majority at Westminster you can forget about the House, within limits. But we have constantly on a daily basis to reconcile different points of view, and try to make sure that committees are not taking off on trips of their own, which they are perfectly entitled to do, but which obviously is a very real complication of the executive's life.

Dewar acknowledged that he had failed to anticipate quite how much power the committees and individual backbenchers would have in a situation where the executive lacked an overall majority:

The fact that there is no control over private members' bills is an enormous hazard because it means that at any time someone can pop up with a Bill, and maybe on the right popular subject it will have very substantial support. And this may suddenly become a very real legislative option in the middle of your programme. As you know, no private member's bill moves half an inch at Westminster if the Whips dislike it. We have no blocking mechanisms like that. Now that is something we should be proud of, but I have to tell you it makes life more difficult ... We have to fight our programme through in a way that may be good for us, but is very time-consuming.

The parliament's reputation has suffered, and may well continue to suffer, from the spiralling costs of its new building at Holyrood. But the fact that the executive has frequently appeared to be on the back foot over policy issues should not cloud the judgement on whether devolution itself is a success or a failure. 'The essential problem with the media coverage of Holyrood has been an inability to distinguish between the fortunes of the Scottish Parliament and the fortunes of the Labour-led administration,' says Macwhirter.[15] As another Scottish journalist put it, 'One way of interpreting recent poll results is that while people in Scotland show scant respect for their politicians, they want them in a forum where they can be disrespected properly.'[16]

The point is that even those like Cardinal Thomas Winning who denounce the parliament as an 'utter failure' because they do not like its policies have not suggested abolishing it. Devolution as such is no longer a matter of controversy or debate in Scotland and the settlement so far appears to be working – a verdict which is more difficult to pronounce in Wales. As Macwhirter puts it: 'Instead of girning (complaining) about Westminster, Scots are now girning about the Scottish Parliament.'[17]

> **❝ Even those like Cardinal Thomas Winning who denounce the parliament as an 'utter failure' because they do not like its policies have not suggested abolishing it. ❞**

Moderate Conservatives such as Malcolm Rifkind and Douglas Hurd now acknowledge that their party's long opposition to Scottish devolution was a mistake. Hurd told me:

Devolution is a big thing, one has to accept that. Where Scotland was concerned, an inevitable thing. We should have done it in the 1970 government and Scotland would be in a healthier state if we had done it, and the Tory party there certainly would be. We didn't do that, that was an error, and I think they were right to create that.

WAIT FOR HISTORY, SAYS BLAIR

When Blair finally visited the Edinburgh parliament in March 2000, more than eight months after its opening, he chose to avoid controversy by focusing his speech not on the parliament itself but on the international fight against drugs. But he also took a swipe at the Scottish press for 'corrosive' cynicism about the parliament and gave a robust defence of devolution:

You do not judge these changes in days or months, or even a short space of years. You judge them in the broad sweep of history. There is a historical movement away from centralized government. As democracy matures, so does the desire of the electorate for decisions to be taken closer to them. So does the desire for diversity. When people point to differences in devolved policy and ask me, 'Isn't this a problem?', my response is that it is devolution. Not an accident, but the intention. Other people say it represents the end of Britain. The truth is quite the opposite. Our identity as Britain is a matter of our values and our interests. It is not about fossilizing institutions and refusing to change them. Indeed it would be failure to modernize that would lead to the end of Britain. That is why we are bringing our constitution up to date. To make sure that it does give effect to our continuing values in fast-changing circumstances.

The historical verdict to which Blair was referring on the robustness of the Scottish Parliament as an institution will have to wait until it is tested by different parties holding power in London and Edinburgh. Such a test may come as early as 2003, should the SNP replace Labour as the largest party and form a government in Edinburgh, or it may not happen for many years. There is a useful parallel across the Channel in France, where the viability of de Gaulle's 1958 Fifth Republic constitution was not truly tested until long after the general's death. It was not until 1986 that François Mitterrand became the first president to lose his majority in the National Assembly. Widespread predictions of constitutional deadlock or chaos failed to materialize, and the outcome was 'cohabitation' between a president from one political camp and a prime minister from another. Uncomfortable, but hardly unworkable, cohabitation has now become virtually routine in France under the duopoly of Jacques Chirac and Lionel Jospin. The French constitution, previously seen as a framework for untrammelled presidential power, has turned out to be flexible enough to facilitate power sharing and parliamentary government instead. The final result can be seen as a success for de Gaulle's blueprint, though hardly the one he intended.

So in hazarding a guess as to whether devolution will succeed or fail, a clear line must be drawn between institutions and the parties and individuals that temporarily control them; a defeat in 2003 or a subsequent Scottish election for Labour will not necessarily mean that the Edinburgh parliament itself is a failure – although it may look that way to many inside the Labour party. Alternation of control between different parties is a sign of health rather than decay, and most Scottish Labour politicians now recognize that the SNP will probably win power at some point. The only failure will be that of Labour politicians who saw devolution not as an end in itself but as an electoral strategy to contain the rise of nationalism.

When I interviewed Donald Dewar in Brighton during the Labour party conference two weeks before his death, I broached the tricky subject of Labour losing the next Scottish election by asking if the settlement had been deliberately designed to cope with different parties holding power in London and Edinburgh. He replied: 'I hope not' but quickly added:

Well, it's a democratic process, you can't rule out that possibility. Almost inevitably, you are going to have a coalition. It is going to be very difficult for any of the major parties to get a majority of their own. That is a very substantial discipline on all the main parties to try to find common ground.

Dewar insisted that coalition government as such had not been responsible for the executive's bumpy ride in the first 18 months:

There has been no difficulty in working out a partnership agreement, largely on social policy areas. I think the Liberals have adapted well to the realities of government. Jim Wallace and Ross Finnie have been outstandingly effective. They have quickly learned. I think it is far more difficult for Liberal backbenchers … having been used to the freedom of permanent opposition.

If the Liberal Democrats play their cards right, they could gain a quasi-permanent place in Scottish government as junior coalition partner. But some in the Scottish Labour party would dearly love to abandon the new voting system in favour of first-past-the-post, according to Norman

Godman, Yorkshire-born Labour MP for a Scottish seat and married to a member of the Edinburgh parliament:

Where the Scottish group of Labour MPs is concerned I reckon many of them are saying that we have gone too far, that electoral reform doesn't work, that coalition government doesn't work. One colleague said we should go back to the first-past-the-post system. There is no way we can do that in Scotland. That was a *cri de coeur*, he was voicing his angst over the mistakes that appear to have been made by this Scottish government. Ours is a small country, five and a half million people. It now has its own administration. If Labour loses seats at the next election to the Scottish Parliament we may well see then a coalition of Liberal Democrats and SNP. Providing they didn't do anything daft I think the majority of people in Scotland would say, let's wait and see what they are about, what they are going to do.

LABOUR IN POWER

After more than a year of coalition with the Liberal Democrats, the party's long-term problems in Scotland appeared to go deeper than the collapse of inflated expectations about the power of the new parliament to change lives. The acrimonious controversy over the repeal of Section 28 (Clause 2A in Scotland), barring the promotion of homosexuality in schools, hit the party's self-confidence in the face of media attacks and a referendum campaign by millionaire Brian Souter. The Section 28 row eventually passed, but as Professor John Curtice of Strathclyde University found, voters were not convinced that in a crunch, Labour would stand up for Scotland's interests. Only 8 per cent of voters, including just 15 per cent of those voting Labour in Westminster elections, would always trust the party to work in Scotland's interests. The equivalent figure for the SNP was one in four.[18] Survey evidence suggested that the challenge was 'to convince voters that Scottish Labour ministers' first loyalty is to Edinburgh, not London'.

As long as Dewar remained in charge, serious conflict with the Blair government in London was unlikely. But Dewar was sidelined for several months after undergoing heart surgery in the summer of 2000, leaving Jim Wallace as acting First Minister. In early October the man who was father of the new parliament collapsed in Edinburgh and died of a brain haemorrhage. Tall and gangling, with a dyspeptic wit, Dewar had been a

unique asset for the Scottish Labour party in Scotland, not least because
of his close and easy relationship with Tony Blair. It would have been
hard to imagine any other politician teasing Blair in the Edinburgh parliament by comparing his visit to that of the soon-to-be-beheaded
monarch Charles I.

Dewar's successor, chosen under an abbreviated procedure that avoided
a full electoral college, was Henry McLeish, who narrowly beat off a
challenge from Jack McConnell. McLeish, a former professional foot-
baller, would not have been Dewar's choice to succeed him, but his
experience as a Westminster MP and a minister gave him the reputation
of having a safe pair of hands. Tony Blair kept well out of the contest,
although Gordon Brown was reported to have thrown his weight behind
McLeish. The new First Minister, it soon became clear, was keen to lay
down a distinctive Scottish course, paying less heed than Dewar to keeping in step with London. Not only did he improve relations with
previously marginalized leftwingers in the party, but he also promised
teachers in Scotland a higher pay award than their English counterparts,
and announced a more generous policy on care for the elderly.

Conclusive proof that the Dewar era of harmony between London and
Edinburgh was well and truly over came in January 2001 with an extraordinary public spat between McLeish's team and the Labour
government in London. A clumsy attempt to rebrand the Scottish executive as the Scottish government without consulting Downing Street
provoked a vitriolic backlash against McLeish in London. Renaming the
executive, the word deliberately chosen by Dewar and enshrined in the
Scotland Act, was 'never an option and never a plan', according to Blair's
spokesman. 'They can call themselves the White Heather Club if they
want, but they will never be the Scottish government,' was the off-the-
record putdown of one senior Labour figure at Westminster, reported by
The Scotsman.

The irritation with McLeish among Scottish Labour MPs was palpable,
though as commentator Iain Macwhirter pointed out in The Herald on
14 January, the Scottish First Minister was likely to have the last laugh
because his job security depended on keeping his friends in the Scottish
Parliament, not at Westminster: 'This is the important factor his Labour
detractors have failed to grasp. The logic of his situation will force Henry
McLeish down a more "autonomous" road, whether he likes it or not.
The lesson of the week is that when the First Minister stands up for himself he strengthens his position. He will win no plaudits for toadying to

London and he has no future at Westminster anyway.' McLeish, in other words, would only benefit in the eyes of Scottish voters from proving that he was rather more than Tony Blair's 'manager on the ground'. Though there would be no formal change of name, it was clear that the term 'Scottish government' would continue to be used. Tony Blair and Gordon Brown might well watch events in Edinburgh with growing irritation, but would find it hard to intervene. The Scottish Office in London, now renamed the Scotland Office, remains in existence with two ministers and a Law Officer, but though the Secretary of State still has a seat in cabinet, the role is much reduced. Junior minister Brian Wilson, deputy to John Reid until January 2001, told me the transfer of powers to Edinburgh left the office in the elegant Whitehall surroundings of Dover House 'a bit like the Marie Celeste'. With no clearly defined role, the Scotland Office now 'freelances' around Whitehall, trying to be creative in looking after Scottish interests and relying on the goodwill of other departments. Behind the scenes, even before Dewar's death, the new executive in Edinburgh was doing its best to marginalize its role.[19] The current arrangements, relying on concordats and a Joint Ministerial Committee, are fragile because they have no legal force and have not been approved by either parliament. 'If you had an SNP government, the whole game would change completely,' said one civil servant. 'We could have Labour in power in Scotland and the Tories in London – that would be pretty difficult. It would be a real challenge to keep the whole show on the road. Of course, it is designed to operate which ever party is in power, but I really wonder about that.'

STABLE BUT NOT STATIC

The Presiding Officer of the new parliament is Sir David Steel, one of a select group with experience of both Westminster chambers, having sat in the Lords as well as the Commons. He sees the situation as 'stable but not static', although he predicts tensions when power changes hands, as it eventually will. He acknowledges that there is a potential conflict between Blair's insistence on sovereignty at Westminster and the view, expressed in the Claim of Right, that the Scottish people are sovereign. 'I stand very firmly by the sovereignty of the Scottish people and I reckon that was recognized in the referendum. The deal we have is the expression of that sovereignty. But the constitutional framework is a matter of 'power devolved, power retained'. The theory is that the whole thing could be abandoned by Westminster. Would that ever be in accordance with the will of the Scottish people? Answer – no. Therefore I don't think it should ever happen. You've got two conflicting constitutional theories side by side with each other and at the moment we are making it work.'

Other potential problems include the future of the so-called Barnett formula governing the size of the block grant to Scotland, which historically gives it higher expenditure per head than England and Wales. 'I think there are serious debates to come on financing, on the Barnett formula,' Steel predicts. This formula, named after Joel Barnett, Labour Chief Secretary to the Treasury in the 1970s, was invented to avoid annual haggling over the Scottish and Welsh budgets. Although its effect is supposed to become less significant with time, it provides both devolved administrations with a hefty slice of per capita funding over and above that granted to England. Its continuation is bitterly opposed in some English regions where incomes are lower than in Scotland. But any proposal to review it with a fresh assessment of spending needs in Scotland would be certain to provoke a row between Edinburgh and London. The alternative of allowing Scotland to raise its own taxes and keep the revenue, thus avoiding the control of the Treasury, was never on the agenda. The result is that all funding for what is known as the 'Scottish block' depends on London.

Dewar told me that the Barnett formula 'will always be controversial' but that English regions, instead of looking enviously at Scotland, should be complaining instead about the inequalities in England itself:

If you really want to help Tyneside and Merseyside and Cumbria, you have got to redistribute money from the South. That will be the first push from our end. It isn't a matter of Scotland's allocation. We have got to look at the allocations for other parts of the United Kingdom. That is the only fair way. You cannot solve their problems by raiding our budget.

There will certainly be friction if Westminster insists in a few years' time on enforcing a cut in the Scottish Parliament's 129 seats to reflect the planned reduction in Scottish constituencies at Westminster. This is an issue that goes to the root of the arguments about sovereignty, and Dewar trod round it with extreme care:

That's a matter for discussion and debate. I wouldn't like to predict what exactly it will be. But I get the impression that this isn't a closed issue and there will be some very constructive debate north and south of the border on this.

THE SENSIBLE PARTY

For the SNP, the arrival of the parliament in Edinburgh has provided an invaluable platform for learning the arts of government. In the words of senior party figure Mike Russell: 'The SNP is learning to be a parliamentary party, to work within a parliamentary system of governance and learn the role of opposition.' He indirectly confirms Kirsty Milne's judgement In *The Scotsman* that 'the Scottish Nationalists have become the sensible party'.

For a party that had relied entirely on a handful of members at Westminster with no prominent role, the shift in status to a potential party of government in 1999 was a quantum leap. 'For all of its history until last May, the SNP was an extra-parliamentary party. At the height of its parliamentary representation it had 11 members out of 650 at Westminster.' Russell describes its role as 'learning the role of government as well, probing the cracks, finding out where the problems are, consciously squirrelling away the issues that they want to address in government'.

Past SNP predictions that devolution would be a sham have been quietly forgotten, as have Labour's warnings that the SNP would be out to wreck the parliament. Both sides have had to swallow their election rhetoric. There is no question that the SNP remains committed to independence as its ultimate goal, but the party leadership has chosen to ignore grumbling from fundamentalists in its ranks and make devolution work. Despite sniping from figures such as former leader Gordon Wilson, the party under Alex Salmond moved away from its longstanding strategy of reaching independence by winning a majority of Scottish seats at Westminster, followed by negotiations with the UK government and a referendum to endorse the deal. Now the idea is to win a majority in the devolved parliament in 2003 and then organize a referendum leading to independence by 2007. Under Salmond's successor, John Swinney, this gradualist policy looks set to continue. 'For the first time ever the Scottish Parliament gives you structure and a defined timescale to achieve that referendum. Because if the SNP wins the election in 2003 with that in its programme, it will hold that referendum.' Russell makes clear the SNP will not agree to be bound by the memorandum of understanding and the concordats negotiated with Whitehall as a book of rules for relations between the two governments.

Asked if the devolved settlement is stable, Russell says it is not, but adds: 'You shouldn't assume that the opposite of stability is instability. The opposite of stability might be dynamism.' The current deal is far from satisfactory from a nationalist point of view, but the limited powers transferred to Edinburgh can be used for the good of the people of Scotland. 'The democratic energy released by having this institution should not be underrated,' Russell says, describing it as a dynamic process under which the parliament will acquire more powers. He dismisses the idea that a successful parliament will put independence off the agenda. 'It is more fair to say that if the Scottish Parliament works well, people will be much more comfortable and confident in the Scottish Parliament having more powers and being an independent body.'

INDEPENDENCE BY 2007?

In theory, a referendum on independence can only be called by Westminster because the constitution is a reserved issue, although the Scottish Parliament might be able to organize some kind of consultative poll. In practice, however, it is hard to see any Westminster government rejecting the idea of a referendum on Scotland's future when the principle of such a vote was conceded in 1997. Brian Wilson, no friend of the SNP, says: 'My simple view is that if a majority of people in Scotland want independence, they will have it. At the end of the day the SNP's problem is that the Scottish people will not vote for something they do not want.'

Polls among Scottish voters point to solid support for independence running at between one-quarter and one-third of the electorate, sometimes higher depending on the question asked. Support is higher among young people – something that the SNP interprets as a sign that the tide is running its way. Surveys also show a rise in those professing a Scottish identity and a corresponding fall in British identity, but one should perhaps be wary of assuming that such findings automatically point towards independence. Surveys also show that relatively few British voters identify with Europe, but this does not mean that they necessarily support withdrawal from the European Union.

In Scotland, British identity may be, in the words of journalist Joyce McMillan, 'currently dead in the water both as a moral value and as a style item', but that does not mean it is quite as doomed as the SNP believes. Unlike Northern Ireland, where identity tends to be exclusively Irish or exclusively British, Scottish identity for many people has a British component. Tom Nairn has argued this point, questioning the SNP's Scottish-only view of identity: 'After all, the Scots and Welsh invented "Britain" and retain a (sometimes unwittingly) large stake in the notion, while the English rarely view it as more than a tiresome if necessary overcoat.'[20]

SCOTS FEEL IRRITATION, NOT OPPRESSION

Former Scottish Secretary and Foreign Secretary Sir Malcolm Rifkind, one of the most prominent casualties of the Conservative wipeout in May 1997, when he lost his Edinburgh Pentlands seat, believes Scottish voters are not ready to back independence in the foreseeable future or give the SNP an outright majority. He sees an SNP-led administration in Edinburgh as quite likely but adds: 'All the evidence suggests something like 75 per cent of Scots would vote against independence.' He warns against over-dramatizing the rise of the SNP, insisting that the Scots have never been oppressed by the English, merely irritated by them. 'Irritation is not the stuff of which martyrs are made. We don't produce Mandelas or Gandhis, we produce Alex Salmond.'

Rifkind, who as Scottish Secretary irritated Margaret Thatcher repeatedly by his inability to force her values on his fellow Scots, is unusual among Conservatives in showing sympathy for the idea of 'some kind of quasi-federal system for the UK'. He now believes the Scottish Parliament is essentially stable, though he describes its total dependence on London for finance as unhealthy and uncomfortable. He acknowledges the West Lothian argument but does not expect a huge battle over sovereignty. 'I think too much can be read into these fine theoretical distinctions.' More of a problem, in his view, is the Labour party's unresolved desire to control the affairs of its Scottish branch directly from London, including policies and candidate selection.

'LONDON LABOUR' TAG IS A HANDICAP

John Curtice's survey evidence from the 1999 election appears to back up Rifkind's analysis of Labour's problem. There are many in the party's Scottish ranks who are fed up with being pilloried by the SNP as 'London Labour' and would like more autonomy from London to reflect the reality of devolution. This unresolved tension between the Millbank view and the Scottish heartlands was reflected in an article in *The Guardian* in May 1999 by Matthew Taylor of the IPPR, who until a few months earlier had been assistant general secretary of the Labour party.

Taylor's article was a shot across the Scottish party's bows from London, attacking those who saw no role for the national leadership in what the party did north of the border on such issues as student tuition fees. 'This is to confuse national devolution with internal party decision making,' Taylor argued; while policies could differ, Labour had to have 'a single set of values, principles and core policies regardless of where it operates'. Devolution means the people of Scotland and Wales have the right to elect their own government, 'not to redesign the political platform of each party', he reminded the Scots:

The British Labour party has every reason to have a stake in the policies and practices of Scottish and Welsh Labour. It is a question of branding. The emergence of a Scottish Labour brand very different to that of Wales and England would undermine the credibility and coherence of British Labour as a whole. And this is the brand that will be on offer to the electorate in the next general election … Some in Labour's Scottish ranks appear to feel that having been carried to power on the shoulders of the British party, they can now dispense with its services. Their argument threatens not just the integrity of the Union but denies 100 years of Labour history.

While Taylor was not writing on behalf of the Labour party, there can be no doubt that his article reflected the Blairite view of Labour as a single national brand. When I asked Taylor a year later about his article, he was emphatic that his views had not changed despite what he called 'complete hysteria in Scotland' when they appeared:

What I said was a reaction to seeing Malcolm Chisholm on TV the weekend after the Scottish elections saying, devolution has now happened, it's up to us what we do. A political party that operates in a devolved or federal system has to reconcile on the one hand the devolutionary principle and on the other the principle that the party has to stand for broadly similar things wherever it operates, otherwise a political party becomes a franchise operation. It got me into a lot of trouble in Scotland, but I hold by every word of it. It is childish to suggest that when you have got devolution, the Labour party in Scotland can just go off and stand for anything it wants to … Not having tuition fees in Scotland does have a big knock-on effect for the English higher education system. So it was perfectly legitimate to engage in a discourse about Labour's position on that. To suggest that it was nothing to do with British ministers was bollocks.

THE SLIPPERY SLOPE

Most of the views I have quoted in this chapter have been relatively sanguine about the stability of the Scottish devolution settlement; the consensus for the medium term is that the present structure will probably work even if, as seems likely, the SNP gets its turn to lead a Holyrood government. But the chances of the SNP persuading a majority of Scottish voters to back independence in a referendum in the medium term are small.

However, not everyone shares this conventional wisdom, and in a longer-term perspective the outlook is less certain. There are staunch anti-devolutionists such as Tam Dalyell who believe Scottish independence is sooner or later inevitable. This is also the view of maverick nationalist intellectual Tom Nairn, who first predicted the breakup of Britain in the 1970s. In his view, the 1997 referendum was in effect a statement of self-determination by Scotland which has led to 'a kind of constitution-less semi-statehood' for the country. 'A dissolution of the old multi-national state is indeed under way, and there is now almost no one who believes otherwise.'[21] Nairn believes that the Blair government 'has reformed the ancient order just sufficiently to ensure its collapse. It has rendered it irretrievably unstable.'[22]

Scotland, he believes, is halfway to a real constitutional settlement in which it will fully recover the independence it lost in 1707. Devolution is merely 'a flightless bird ... now best abandoned to its fate'.[23]

Nairn believes the poor image of the Scottish Parliament stems from its lack of ambition, from Dewar's undramatic strategy of 'bedding down' the institution, which leads to '... a distinctive border here, or an admirable shrubbery there, but only as elements in the overall grand design of British modernity'.[24] He sees Blair trying vainly to breathe new life into the doomed British state with his New Labour branding. 'The Blair project ... is a continuation of the management of decline under extremely new and vigorous management ... Because of the challenge of the nationalists in Scotland, Home Rule became an essential part of the Labour agenda. Even the people most resolutely opposed to it before came to accept it. So when they had their stunning electoral victory, they had to do it. They tried to modify it and downscale it a bit. But they failed, and they had to live with the consequences, however much they have come to regret them.'[25]

RED DRAGONS AND RED FLAGS

In the great devolution mystery tour, Wales has had a bumpier ride than Scotland since 1997. Kevin Morgan and Geoff Mungham summed up the situation on the eve of Alun Michael's resignation:

Within two years of coming to power, however, New Labour had scaled the heights and plumbed the depths in Wales, its premier electoral heartland in the UK. Having delivered on its election pledge to create a Welsh Assembly after a referendum, it quickly squandered all the political capital it had painstakingly acquired by employing shamefully undemocratic tactics to decide the Labour leadership in Wales, tactics which demeaned and affronted the new era of democratic devolution and precipitated the worst crisis in the history of the Wales Labour party.[26]

The trigger for what became a chapter of accidents was the downfall of Ron Davies as Welsh Secretary six months before the 1999 elections to the new Assembly of which he was the architect. It is tempting to speculate how much of the subsequent series of events – the imposition of Alun Michael, Labour's failure to win an overall majority, and the replacement of Michael by Rhodri Morgan in February 2000 – might have been avoided if Davies had stayed at home to watch television rather than going for his fatal late October walk on Clapham Common. It is arguable that with Davies continuing in charge, the first year of devolution would have more resembled the course of events in Scotland. However, a closer look at what happened in Wales suggests that the Davies affair merely accelerated the emergence of some of the fault lines and contradictions inherent in the Labour party's handling of the Welsh devolution settlement.

'FOR WALES, SEE ENGLAND'

Although Wales and Scotland have always been bracketed together, the run-up to devolution was different, as was the historical background. Scotland's existence as a separate nation within the United Kingdom has been buttressed by the guarantees it retained under the Act of Union of a national church and a separate legal system, and by its developed system of governmental and civic institutions. While lacking a parliament, Scotland retained a residual kind of statehood based on its voluntary incorporation in the union state of Great Britain. By contrast, the complete absorption of Wales into England in 1536 and the relative absence of distinctive institutions until recently has made devolution there a matter not so much of state building as of nation building.

The Welsh Office dates only from 1964, some 80 years later than the Scottish Office, and the plethora of unelected quangos which help to run the country were mostly set up by Conservative governments in the 1980s and 1990s. The Assembly's 'National' label is no accident – its architects see it as a focus for bringing together a nation divided not only as in Scotland between rural and urban interests, but by widely differing degrees of assimilation into English culture. 'For Wales, see England', as the ninth edition of *Encyclopaedia Britannica* so unhappily put it, summing up the identity confusion of a nation with precious few institutions to call its own.

According to John Osmond of the Institute of Welsh Affairs, the creation of the National Assembly for Wales means building the whole arch, not just adding the keystone. He believes the National Assembly will gradually change the present situation in which '… most Welsh people do not see themselves as belonging to a country that provides them with a clear sense of who and where they are'. British identity remains strong, while Welsh identity, traditionally linked to language and culture, divides the country as much as it unites, reflecting regional patterns. It is this sense of incomplete Welsh nationhood that underlines Ron Davies' oft-repeated mantra that devolution is 'a process rather than an event' – a formula which has never found much favour in Downing Street. Blair's view is that new institutions 'do not necessarily create new feelings. They can just give longheld feelings new – and often better – expression'. Davies believes the opposite – that new institutions shape new mentalities, a view with which academic specialists on nationalism and national identity would certainly agree.[27]

LABOUR'S ONE-PARTY STATE

Labour's efforts to bring about devolution in Wales have been haunted by the memory of the 1979 referendum in which, on a turnout of 58.3 per cent, only 11.8 per cent of the electorate voted for an Assembly, while 46.5 per cent voted against. The campaign produced a split in the party which Alun Michael described to me as 'not just a chasm – it was continental in its nature'. The defeat for devolution was far more decisive than in Scotland, where a majority voted in favour but failed to

WALES – THE KEY FACTS

The general election

In May 1997 Labour won 34 of the 40 Welsh seats, leaving Plaid Cymru (The Party of Wales) with four and the Liberal Democrats with two. Labour's share of the vote was 54.7 per cent to 9.9 per cent for Plaid Cymru. As in Scotland, the Conservatives were wiped out.

The referendum

Voters in Wales approved the plan for a Welsh Assembly on 18 September 1997 by the narrowest of margins on a low turnout of 50.1 per cent. The margin was less than 7,000 votes, with 50.3 per cent voting 'yes'.

The Government of Wales Act

Published in November 1997, this Act became law on 31 July 1998. It created a 60-member Assembly with no powers to pass primary legislation or to vary taxes. Forty members are elected by first-past-the-post from Westminster constituencies and 20 from five electoral regions under the same additional member system as in Scotland. Unlike the Scottish Parliament, the Welsh Assembly is a hybrid creation with some of the characteristics of a local authority. It is a body corporate with a committee structure and a First Secretary heading a cabinet. The Secretary of State for Wales remains as part of the Westminster government and has the right to attend and participate in any Assembly proceedings. All expenditure comes from Westminster in a block grant. The initial powers of the Assembly cover agriculture and food, economic development, culture, education, health, transport, housing, industry, local government, tourism, social services, planning and the Welsh language.

The Ron Davies affair

The sudden resignation of Secretary of State for Wales Ron Davies, architect of the Assembly, on 27 October 1998 had far-reaching effects. Robbed after a mysterious nocturnal incident on Clapham Common, Davies resigned from the government but kept his Commons seat and ran successfully for the Assembly. Tony Blair's decision to pick Alun Michael as Welsh Secretary and subsequently to back him as Labour's candidate for First Secretary in the Assembly elections sent the party into turmoil. Michael won a bitter battle for the nomination against Rhodri Morgan, who was the clear choice of the Welsh party, thanks to the block votes of trade unions in an electoral college.

The Assembly election

Labour, demoralized by internal feuding, failed to win an overall majority on 6 May 1999, finishing with 28 seats to 17 for Plaid Cymru, nine for the Conservatives and six for the Liberal Democrats. Alun Michael formed a minority administration.

Michael's resignation

Michael was forced to resign on 9 February 2000 just before losing a vote of no confidence in his handling of the issue of European Union funding. Rhodri Morgan took over as First Secretary and Labour leader in Wales.

The coalition

After secret discussions, Morgan and Liberal Democrat leader Mike German announced a coalition agreement in October 2000 giving the smaller party two cabinet seats and making German deputy head of the executive.

clear the hurdle of 40 per cent support from the electorate as a whole. The return to devolution for Wales was approached with what J. Barry Jones of Cardiff University described as 'exaggerated stealth'.[28] The Labour party in Wales 'tried to smuggle an Assembly into being as part of its proposals for local government reform'.[29]

A further difference from Scotland in the run-up to 1997 was the absence of any cross-party forum or constitutional convention which would have given the tribalists of Welsh Labour the habit of cooperating with other parties. There was no Welsh equivalent to the Scottish Claim of Right, a public nailing of colours to the mast. The party in opposition, deeply divided over devolution, rejected an offer from Plaid Cymru of a Scottish-style convention. The party executive in Wales 'tried repeatedly to strangle' the all-party Campaign for a Welsh Assembly and censured MPs who flirted with it.[30] The lack of experience of cross-party cooperation hampered the campaign for a 'yes' vote in the referendum in September 1997, and became a critical factor when Labour unexpectedly failed to win an outright majority of seats in May 1999 and formed a minority government. While devolution in Scotland could be said to be the settled will of the Scottish people, this was far from the case in Wales, as the narrow referendum result indicated. It could not even be said to be the settled will of the Labour party in Wales, given the strength of the anti-devolution tradition, which Ron Davies describes as the 'red flag' as opposed to the 'red dragon' school of Labour politics:

Scotland had its separate legal and institutional framework, a strong and confident national identity, a convention, giving effect to what already existed. Wales was quite different, it didn't have all these qualities, neither the same identity nor the same cross-party agreement, and we had memories of 1979. We were very fortunate to have John Smith and his very strong commitment, enabling us to follow in the slipstream after Scotland.[31]

This was the reason why Davies was so insistent on the need for an 'inclusive' approach, to broaden support for the Assembly and make sure it was not just a Labour-only venture. Because of Labour's long hegemony in Wales, longer even than in Scotland where a now-forgotten unionist tradition among the Protestant working class boosted the Conservative vote until well into the 1950s, it believed in what Morgan and Mungham call 'one-partyism':

The ideology of one-partyism, born of prolonged electoral dominance, pervades the Wales Labour party and this is what sustains the belief that Labour has no need to forge pacts or alliances with others, be they political parties or social movements.[32]

The goal of Ron Davies, only partially achieved, was to get away from the winner-takes-all ethos of Westminster and of Labour-dominated local politics. Like the Scottish Parliament, the Welsh Assembly was to be elected partly by proportional representation. But unlike its Scottish counterpart, it was not to be a fully fledged legislature with the power to pass laws. The Assembly was initially designed to be more like a local authority than a parliament; it was to be a 'body corporate', with a system of powerful committees whose secretaries would take responsibility for policy. This scheme was heavily amended during the passage through parliament of the Government of Wales Bill, delivering a hybrid structure in which the body corporate and the committees were retained but an executive cabinet was added.

In March 1998, the government responded to advice from its own National Assembly Advisory Group and from a pro-devolution Conservative peer, Wyn Roberts, to change the Bill. The First Secretary would now have the right to pick his own cabinet, though the powerful committee structure would remain. The government also backed down by dropping a bizarre clause that would have subjected Assembly members to the Official Secrets Act, opening up the prospect that they might be sent to prison for revealing unauthorized information. Richard Shepherd, a Conservative backbencher with a keen interest in civil liberties, got the provision dropped, but its original presence in the Bill was hardly an advertisement for the government's understanding of constitutional issues or the work of its cabinet committees. 'If there had been no other reason, this constitutional nonsense marked the death knell of the local government committee model.'[33]

As Morgan and Mungham make clear, the real problem was that the original pluralist project was undermined by a potent combination of the old mindset of the one-party state in Wales, hostile to devolution and pluralism, and the new culture of control in Millbank and Downing Street. The result was symbolized by the choice of the curious title of First Secretary, hitherto favoured by Soviet apparatchiks, for the head of the new executive. The appellation suggested Wales was a one-party state somewhere on the banks of the Volga. It would be nice to think the choice was a postmodern ironic tribute to the *Animal Farm* nature of Welsh Labour politics, but according to those in the know, it was an Englishman, Jack Straw, who insisted on forcing a vote in a cabinet committee on this issue to block the possibility that Wales might get ideas above its station and appoint ministers.

> 66 The appellation suggested Wales was a one-party state somewhere on the banks of the Volga. 99

However, the Soviet-style terminology did not survive the year 2000. When he formed a coalition with the Liberal Democrats and carried out a cabinet reshuffle, Rhodri Morgan announced that he would henceforth be known as First Minister on the Scottish pattern, with the Assembly Secretaries also changing their titles. It was significant that this unilateral rewriting of the Government of Wales Act, a symbolic shift towards a more parliamentary model in Cardiff, was accepted without demur by Whitehall.

DAVIES AND THE UPHILL STRUGGLE

Ron Davies, speaking frankly about Labour's mistakes in a lecture to the Institute of Welsh Affairs in February 1999, recalled how the party had for years been ambivalent about the whole issue of Welsh identity, seeing it as part of the nationalists' agenda. 'The hostility of sections of the Labour movement towards the notion of identity has been a constant theme throughout Labour history.' There was a pro-devolution tradition in the Welsh Labour party but it was a minority one, said Davies, recalling that he had personally been accused of 'going native'.

Davies faced an uphill struggle in getting 'inclusive' politics – in uncoded language, proportional representation and the cross-party cooperation that went with it – accepted in Labour's Welsh heartlands. Davies was originally appointed shadow Welsh Secretary in 1992 by John Smith, with the brief to develop devolution policies for Wales to match the line the party was pursuing in Scotland. But his task in getting this concept off the ground was far more difficult than that of his Scottish counterparts. Despite his position in the Labour shadow cabinet, first under Smith and then under Tony Blair, Davies was an outsider for the trade union-dominated Welsh party executive. Nor was he ever close to Blair and his team, who had little interest in Wales. When I asked him about his experience of working with Blair, Davies replied:

He had inherited devolution from John Smith and recognized that it was a commitment that he had to deliver on. There was no great enthusiasm. He always took the minimalist view, I think. But he was fully cooperative and I never had any difficulty with him.

Davies' task was handicapped by nervousness in the New Labour project in London about the risk of talking too much about devolution in the run-up to the 1997 election campaign. Things were not helped by the fact that Kim Howells, the constitutional affairs spokesman appointed by Blair to Jack Straw's shadow Home Office team, opposed devolution altogether. Davies lost the battle to give the Assembly primary legislative powers: 'There was not a cat in hell's chance of getting more through the Labour party in Wales or in London,' he recalled.[34] But he eventually won the case for proportional representation using the same additional member system as in Scotland. This too was controversial, as Alun Michael told me:

This system was deeply, deeply divisive within the Labour party and I think an argument that wasn't well handled. I am sure that there was a majority against it but it was steamrollered through, not as has been suggested by Tony Blair and Number 10, but actually by Ron Davies, believing that was the way to go. I argued with him quite passionately in private when I was chair of the group of Welsh Labour MPs but that was the way he was determined to go.

The size of the Assembly was kept back to 60 members instead of the 100 Davies had wanted. Davies admitted that the Assembly, while stronger than he had dared hope in 1995, was the product of 'an uneasy compromise from an internalized debate between pro- and anti-devolution elements within the Labour party'.[35] With only one-third of the seats to be decided on a list system, significantly fewer than in Scotland, Labour fully expected to win a majority.

WHAT WELSH MODEL?

Davies now pours scorn on the idea that there was ever a carefully thought-out 'Welsh model' as part of a devolution master plan by the Blair government. He told a seminar in London in July 2000:

That is not how it happened … None of them was thought through at the time. Devolution was politically driven rather than being part of any master plan. We have a government that is determined to retain control of affairs, standardizing and centralizing public life. It was politically driven from the periphery.

According to Davies, the 'red dragon' pro-devolution wing of the Welsh Labour party got on top in the 1990s, but it still had to compromise with its opponents to avoid an open split in the party, as had happened in 1979: 'It was a straightforward political compromise between two elements.' The final outcome was a scaled-back version of devolution which was 'the minimum necessary to keep Plaid Cymru on board'. Unlike Scotland, where only the reserved powers remaining at Westminster were listed, the Government of Wales Bill gave the Assembly the same powers as were held by the Secretary of State for Wales, a formula that led to confusion. Davies admits that the legislation was far from perfect at the point where parliamentary time for further revision ran out: 'We decided to streamline the whole process, otherwise we would still be arguing three years later. So we drew the line … In retrospect, we made a lot of mistakes with the Act.'[36]

Alun Michael told me he was the victim not only of party infighting but of 'many flaws' in the settlement which were the fault of others, including Ron Davies:

One of the great ironies is that my predecessor has been referred to as the architect of devolution. Well, I think, having looked at the design of the building, I would keep quiet about that if I were him.

He argues that many of the mistakes in the legislation were avoidable and blames Davies for changing his mind on crucial issues such as the cabinet system at a late stage. The combination of a minority government and a powerful committee system led to a lack of clear lines of authority and 'a muddle that hadn't been thought through'.

FOR WALES, SEE SCOTLAND

All hope that the Welsh Labour party might have a smooth run-up to the general election in 1997 was destroyed, as in Scotland, by Blair's U-turn on a pre-legislative referendum. 'The referendum was driven solely by the Scottish tax issue, which was irrelevant to Wales, but Wales was dragged along on Scotland's coat tails, much as it had been in 1979.'[37] Blair's comparison of the Scottish Parliament's tax powers to those of an English parish council did not help. By implication, the Welsh Assembly, with no tax-raising powers, would be weaker than a parish council.

The party's success in winning 34 of the 40 Welsh seats at Westminster masked its continuing internal divisions. These continued with a bad-tempered contest between Ron Davies and Rhodri Morgan to be the party's candidate for First Secretary, a farcical dispute over where the new Assembly should be sited, and another internal row over the 'twinning' of Assembly constituencies as a way of getting more women candidates on the ballot. The selection of candidates for the Assembly produced more bitterness and conflict as some able pro-devolution candidates claimed they were dropped for no clear reason. The party was also distracted by a series of scandals in local government. After the general election, campaign planning for a 'yes' vote in the referendum got under way several months late, but was handicapped by apathy and disorganization within the Labour party, personal rivalries and continuing disputes with Millbank, which regarded Wales as a sideshow in the larger Blair 'project'. Tony Blair's pollster Philip Gould came to Wales and found 'emotional resistance' to the idea of the Assembly among his focus groups, and low awareness of what was at stake. The result was that the 'no' campaign, 'ramshackle, poorly staffed and cash-starved', came within a whisker of victory in the referendum.[38]

THE ONE-LEGGED DUCK

All these issues would have been enough for the Labour party in Wales to cope with, without Davies' dramatic resignation in October 1998, just six months before the Assembly elections. Even then, the damage might have been limited had it not been for Blair's insistence on intervening forcibly in the choice of his successor. Blair seems to have assumed that because of his unquestioned right to bring Alun Michael into his cabinet as Welsh Secretary, he could anoint him without further problems as party leader in Wales and candidate for First Secretary. Nobody bothered to think what Labour party members or voters in Wales might prefer. This proved a disastrous miscalculation when it quickly emerged that most of the Welsh party favoured Rhodri Morgan instead, though leading trade union figures and executive members were determined to block him. The resulting factional struggle was chronicled in all its poisonous awfulness by the off-message Labour MP Paul Flynn in his entertaining paperback *Dragons Led by Poodles*.

66 Nobody bothered to think what Labour party members or voters in Wales might prefer. 99

Morgan, who had narrowly lost to Ron Davies a few weeks earlier in a ballot, announced his fresh candidacy to lead Labour in the Assembly in his hallmark style: 'Does a one-legged duck swim in circles?' Morgan, while often flippant and off-message, was far from a militant rebel or an Old Labour dinosaur. A former academic and civil servant who chaired the Public Administration Committee in the Commons, the shockheaded former opposition spokesman had been passed over in 1997 for a job in Blair's government for unexplained reasons. According to Flynn, Blair had once stayed in the Morgan household in Wales during a pre-1997 campaign tour and been disturbed not only by its untidiness but by an elderly relative who mistook him for Lionel Blair, the dancer.

With Blair's public backing, Alun Michael, who before he became Welsh Secretary was a junior Home Office minister and had not been planning to stand for an Assembly seat at all, entered the race. Michael acknowledges he went into the contest with his eyes open and was not surprised by the bitterness of the campaign. In his view there was an inevitability about the poisonous atmosphere, given what had gone before.

Blair visited Wales three times to support Michael, declaring: 'I make no apologies for being a strong supporter of Alun Michael. I think he is a great guy.' Morgan was painted as a crypto-nationalist by his opponents. I asked Michael if with hindsight he regretted that Blair had intervened so strongly on his behalf:

I think one thing that I regret is the lies that were around about the way in which my decision to stand was taken. I can only describe them as lies because they were a complete invention. I decided that I should stand for the Assembly and told the Prime Minister that was my conclusion, and he then said that he respected and understood my decision and would support me in following through. I think as he has acknowledged, allowing the appearance that he was favouring one candidate over another caused problems. It actually caused more problems for me than for Rhodri. I think he felt as he has done in other contests, that in the sense of feeling that devolution was important and the success of the new institution was important, it would be dishonest not to say what his view was. He had, after all, had both Rhodri and myself at different times working in his team. Rhodri had been in his team on energy, I had been a member of his team in home affairs, and I can't say I was disappointed in the judgement that he made about which of us would make a better leader for Wales. The problem was, his expressing that opinion was somehow translated into being an exercise in control freakery. And I think he thought that many people would respect his judgement, rather than it turning out to be a negative … My view was that it wouldn't be terribly helpful for an intervention that would seem to be London-based. But I can't say I was disappointed to have the Prime Minister supporting me and saying, I think this guy can deliver the goods.

I think Tony's interventions were for the best of motives. Firstly, I'd been his deputy, he is a friend of mine, I think he expressed an opinion and provided support as a friend and a colleague would. I think he exercised a judgement. He can judge whether that is right or wrong. But I think he mistook the atmosphere in Wales and its difference from the atmosphere in Scotland. He's acknowledged that.

In the end Michael narrowly triumphed in the three-section party electoral college, losing heavily by nearly two to one to Morgan in the ballot of members but winning thanks to the votes of MPs and trade unions, many of whom did not bother to ballot their members. It was this deliberate departure from the OMOV (one member one vote) reforms introduced under John Smith and the return to the worst days of union vote fixing that appalled Flynn and many others in the party. 'We burbled pious platitudes. The truth was forbidden. Thinking was treacherous. Our minds were glued shut. That night, the Labour party in Wales was ashamed of itself. We were preparing our own catastrophe.'[39]

As both the MP Paul Flynn and the academics Morgan and Mungham make clear in their accounts of the truly Orwellian leadership election, it is important to remember that the party fix to get Michael elected was not just the work of Millbank; the biggest role was played by the trade unions and the executive of the Welsh Labour party.

A DISASTER FOR LABOUR

The Assembly election was by historical standards a disaster for Labour, given its dominance of the political scene in Wales. It gave Labour only 28 out of the 60 seats, while Plaid Cymru soared into a strong second place with 17. At the general election two years earlier, of the 40 seats at stake Labour had won 34 and the nationalists only four. Worst of all for Labour, Plaid Cymru, styling itself as 'The Party of Wales' to appeal outside its traditional Welsh-speaking heartland, emerged triumphant in Llanelli, Islwyn and the Rhondda, traditional Labour strongholds.

❝The smell of an electoral stitch-up was deeply damaging to the party's reputation and by extension to the whole Assembly project.❞

There was plentiful evidence that Labour voters were angered by the sidelining of Morgan and stayed away, or voted for the nationalists. The smell of an electoral stitch-up was deeply damaging to the party's reputation and by extension to the whole Assembly project. It was hard to envisage a party so riven by internal tension and so contemptuous of democracy giving clear and effective leadership to the new devolved body and launching an era of 'new politics' in Wales. The result was a huge setback for the pluralist culture that Davies had tried to build into the design of devolution. Labour, unexpectedly thrust into the role of a minority, lacked the confidence to respond to voter surveys suggesting the electorate wanted a coalition.

LONDON'S MAN IN WALES

Alun Michael sees 'a lot that was inevitable' in what happened to him. 'I think the problem was, I inherited a situation which was where it was.' But if he had been a different sort of person, he might have been able to overcome the handicaps. Michael's nine months as First Secretary were not a success. Ultra-cautious in taking any initiative that could be seen as departing from policy laid down in London, he left Assembly members unhappy at the way they were deprived of information in what was supposed to be a collegiate body. He proved reluctant to delegate decisions to his fellow cabinet members, showing what Morgan and Mungham describe as an 'anally retentive management style'. As Paul Flynn notes, the Welsh are so keen on committees that the definition of a deprived person in Wales is someone who is not a member of one. So when Alun Michael frequently ignored the supposedly powerful Assembly committees, the result was deadlock and frustration.

Morgan became a loyal member of Michael's team. By November, Liberal Democrat leader Mike German was complaining: 'We have a car on the road but the handbrake is still on.' Relations between Michael and the Presiding Officer, Dafydd Elis Thomas, became increasingly frosty. When the Assembly passed a motion of no confidence in Agriculture Secretary Christine Gwyther, Michael ignored it. He seemed unsure whether devolution was a process or an event, hedging his bets by describing it as both 'settled' and 'dynamic'.

Ron Davies, seen as increasingly close to Plaid Cymru, complained that while the structures for cooperation were in place, the political culture to deliver it was missing. In a hard-hitting lecture to the Institute of Welsh Affairs on 19 January 2000 he made a thinly veiled attack on Michael's leadership, describing his administration as 'vulnerable and uncertain' and criticizing the lack of meaningful consultation. 'We cannot go on the way we are,' Davies said. 'It's neither responsible nor realistic for Labour to assume or expect continuing cooperation on the one hand while on the other refusing to acknowledge the legitimate expectations of Plaid, the Liberal Democrats and the Conservative party, who between them command a majority in the Assembly. The Labour party didn't win a majority on May 6th and we shouldn't confuse minority control with a mandate to govern.' In another dig at Michael, he said Labour had to make it clear that it viewed the Assembly as the Cardiff headquarters of Welsh government, 'not the Cardiff branch office of the London headquarters'.

Michael told me the other parties in the Assembly were to blame for his problems: 'Plaid Cymru want on the one hand to have the greatest influence on everything that comes out of the Assembly, but on the other hand, not to be identified with or responsible for anything, because they want to take an oppositional approach when it comes to the elections. So they want to have their cake and eat it.'

MICHAEL FALLS AFTER LABOUR SUPPORT DRAINS AWAY

The pretext that led to Michael's fall in February was his failure to obtain firm guarantees of matched funding from Whitehall for European Union structural aid funds for Wales, an issue on which the three opposition parties could unite in voting no confidence. Michael dismissed it as a phoney issue, but the truth was that support for him in the Labour group was ebbing away. John Marek, the member for Wrexham, publicly criticized his ultra-loyalty to Downing Street and called for him to be loyal to Wales instead. Michael's chances of remaining in office were not helped by Labour's lamentable performance in a Westminster by-election at Ceredigion in early February in which its candidate limped in fourth behind the despised Conservatives. As Jon Owen Jones MP put it: 'We have to accept that Alun's leadership in the Assembly has been unpopular and that the root of this unpopularity is the widely perceived unfairness of his election.'[40]

Michael appears to have believed until the last moment that he would be able to resign and bounce back with the support of the Labour group in the Assembly, rather like John Major when he resigned the leadership of the Conservative party. Instead, Labour members switched their support to Morgan, who became acting First Secretary and a few days later Labour leader. Michael, embittered by what he considered a stab in the back, resigned his Assembly seat to resume his career at Westminster. Downing Street accepted the return of the unwanted Rhodri Morgan with as good a grace as possible, praising him for his loyalty. What Tony Blair thought privately was unrecorded, though he was reported to have made strenuous efforts to save Michael by asking Liberal Democrat party leader Charles Kennedy to lean on his Welsh colleagues not to support the motion of no confidence. But Michael's real problems were with his own party, as the Institute of Welsh Affairs (IWA) described it:

The melodrama surrounding the resignation of Michael and the succession of Rhodri Morgan as First Secretary was quickly recognized as a defining moment in

Welsh politics … But more fundamentally perhaps, it registered a shift in the underlying political culture of Wales. A threshold was crossed. This was not just in terms of opposition against what was seen as imposition of London rule; the vote marked a significant change inside Welsh politics as well. The internal change was most clearly exposed within the Labour group in the Assembly. In the last resort Alun Michael's position became unsustainable because he lost the confidence of a large majority of his own side.

In the words of John Osmond of the Institute of Welsh Affairs, the fall of Michael and the rise of Morgan was a victory for the 'maximalists' over the 'minimalists' in Labour's long-running feud over devolution. 'The maximalists came out on top last night,' Osmond told me the day after Michael's demise. 'The interesting thing will be whether they can sustain the momentum.'

A NEW BROOM

Morgan's first few weeks in office brought a rapid change in style that was welcomed by the other parties. Dafydd Wigley told me a few weeks into the new regime:

I think the most stark change since Rhodri Morgan came and Alun Michael went is that you see people smiling all over the place. It was as if there was a new dawn. Things had got so uptight in the Alun Michael era that people thought, with Rhodri Morgan there is going to be a more relaxed approach. There were instances during Alun Michael's time that horrified me in many ways – the way in which he would not let ministers in his own cabinet, secretaries in his own cabinet, reply to letters that I and colleagues were writing through to them. I would get a reply from Alun Michael replying to a letter I had sent to Peter Law, the Environment Secretary, for example. There was an occasion when Rhodri Morgan had a request from me for a meeting to discuss industrial policy, a totally practical meeting about developments in my constituency. I had to wait for several weeks and when I phoned up to ask what on earth was happening, I was told by a very embarrassed secretary in his office: 'Mr Morgan can't meet you without Mr Michael's permission.' Now that sort of control freakery was getting at everybody and it couldn't continue. However Rhodri Morgan's government works out, at least he seems to be willing to delegate powers and be willing to let ministers get on with doing their own job. It's a step in the right direction.

John Osmond singled out the 'startling' symbolic importance of remarks the new First Secretary made in April at the opening of an exhibition of the Pennal letter at the National Library of Wales. This document, written on goatskin parchment in Latin, was an appeal written in 1406 by Owain Glyndwr to the King of France. Morgan gave the event a nationalist 'red dragon' slant which would have been inconceivable under Alun Michael:

Owain Glyndwr was setting out his vision for Wales as a nation – a nation with a future national existence set in a European context and not solely bound up with its nearest neighbour, England. His vision included a nation with organized institutions including universities in the north and south where young people could be trained to run the institutions of the state.

Morgan has further departed from the ways of his predecessor by publishing minutes of Cabinet meetings with a six-week built-in delay, signalling a new era of Welsh *glasnost* and *perestroika*. He gave a remarkably frank off-the-cuff lecture to the IWA a few days after taking office, in which he thought aloud about the problems shown up by the Michael debacle, both within the Labour party and in the Assembly settlement.[41] The events of February did not mean that the devolution settlement in Wales was deeply flawed, he argued. 'Devolution is very clearly on the rails. It's just got a hiccup. It needs to be given time to grow and develop ... you wouldn't expect a lusty little infant eight months old to show maturity.'

However, he did draw attention to some institutional weaknesses, including the hybrid structure of the Assembly, which made it a county council with an executive cabinet tacked on. Another lesson he drew was that it was too easy for opposition parties to combine and depose the First Secretary without provoking the risk of a fresh election. 'The Welsh Assembly with its present rules could dispense "instant regicide" as quickly as the electric kettle in your kitchen could dispense instant coffee. It could occur weekly, so that all 60 members of the Assembly could finish up having a turn at being First Secretary in the space of two or three years.'

Morgan said that unlike in Scotland, Labour in Wales had been unprepared for the lack of a majority and had not planned for a coalition.

'Therefore nobody really gave thought to how these things were going to work when you put them together.' However, he made it clear that he did not want to give up adversarial politics altogether: 'Cosy consensus has no appeal for me whatsoever. I think to a degree the public expect honest disagreement to be honestly exposed by responsible debate.' Morgan, clearly thinking ahead to the possibility of a coalition, made it clear that Labour could no longer afford to ignore the other parties, going on to identify a lot of common ground between the three non-Conservative parties that would lead to shifting alliances over the next 20 or 30 years. Among the possibilities he raised was an understanding between Labour and Plaid Cymru, with or without the Liberal Democrats. Morgan recalled that it was abstention by Plaid Cymru that had allowed Labour to win approval for its budget and for several other important measures. He also acknowledged that Plaid Cymru, unlike the SNP, had once urged Labour to set up a constitutional convention for Wales. 'Now in Wales, if we had offered it, Plaid would have played a very major and presumably quite constructive role because they are not oppositionist in the same sense and to the same degree as the SNP are.'

DON'T BLAME THE DRIVER

Some of the weaknesses in the Welsh devolution settlement were pre-dicted by experts long ago. As Professor Robert Hazell of the Constitution Unit at London University noted before the Assembly was elected, the Welsh scheme was 'unstable and liable to change'. The lack of primary legislative powers means that to change the law affecting Wales, the First Secretary and the Assembly are dependent on the time and energy of the UK government, with its control of scarce parliamen-tary time at Westminster. 'An Assembly with executive powers only risks incurring the worst of both worlds. It will create high hopes in Wales of independent action which the Assembly may not be able to fulfil; but will be a permanent supplicant in Whitehall, leading to continuous ten-sion between London and Cardiff.'[42] If the same party is in control in Cardiff and in London, the cooperation may be forthcoming; if different parties are in charge, few would bet heavily on the chances of a Labour government in London squeezing other items out of its legislative pro-gramme to accommodate a Plaid Cymru-led executive in Cardiff. There would be the same problem with a Labour regime in Wales and a Conservative one in London. It is worth noting that according to Vernon Bogdanor's calculations, the political complexion of the government in power in London has been different from the majority in Wales for two-thirds of the time since 1868.

The question of the lack of legislative powers is unlikely to go away, and could be a big issue after the next Assembly elections in 2003. The architect of devolution, Ron Davies, says the asymmetrical arrangement under which Scotland and Northern Ireland have powers that Wales does not now looks distinctly untenable. 'As the comparisons are made, the case for parity will emerge,' he says.[43] He points out that even the Conservatives, the most hostile to devolution in the past, are now calling for the Assembly to get wider powers. He believes there is scope for a cross-party consensus to emerge in the Assembly which would enable a joint approach to Westminster which would 'carry very heavily ... the case then would be overwhelming'.[44]

The Assembly will be bound to want to pursue policies in local government, health and education which will exceed the powers available under secondary legislation. Dafydd Elis Thomas believes there is a clear majority in the Assembly for acquiring primary legislative powers. The 1998 Government of Wales Act had 'elevated piecemeal development to an art form,' he said in a lecture on 2 March 2000. 'We are at the beginning of the end of the old constitution ... We have the least that could be established at the time. We shouldn't say that a political fix is a national constitution. It is time we looked for more.' Elis Thomas has suggested the Assembly parties should jointly draft a Bill granting full legislative powers and present it to the Secretary of State for Wales to promote at Westminster.

Because of the nature of the Welsh settlement, Welsh Secretary Paul Murphy remains a key player in representing the Cardiff cabinet in Whitehall, negotiating with other departments over how they frame their legislation. As Jones and Balsom conclude: 'It would be a serious error to presume that devolution has made the Welsh Secretary of State redundant.'[45]

Morgan has made it clear on several occasions that he also favours giving the Assembly primary legislative powers, but has described this as 'something for the medium to long term'. In his February lecture he said he now felt it would be a mistake to rush ahead too fast. 'If they start hollering on the street corners ... for more legislative powers for the Welsh Assembly, because we made such brilliant creative use of the powers that we have already got, I'll be there to try to respond to that.' Speaking to the Welsh Labour conference a few weeks later, Morgan fended off pressure for immediate change by saying the Assembly had to grow organically and be given time. 'Devolution needs room to breathe,' he argued. 'If we let that happen, it will be perfectly natural for the National Assembly to grow in status and authority with the fullhearted support and consent of the people of Wales.'

Dafydd Wigley told me that after a year of operation, the Assembly had problems not just with its lack of legislative powers but with its internal structure:

The model of devolution started off as being a committee system and had a cabinet system grafted on to it ... That problem comes particularly to light when you have a minority regime. That, in a way, is a searchlight that highlights the cracks. If you had a majority regime then that majority could always get its way in committee, and therefore the policy being adopted by committee would correspond to the policy being advocated by the minister or secretary. If, however, you have an anti-government majority on the committees, you will often get policies emanating from the committees that are directly contrary to what the secretary wants to do. Therefore, to what extent is the secretary bound by a committee decision, and indeed to what extent is the cabinet bound by an Assembly decision? That has caused considerable controversy.

For Plaid Cymru, the choice is clear – a move to a system more like the Scottish Parliament, in which there is a clear division between government and opposition. Wigley also believes the Assembly with its 60 members is proving too small and should be increased to 80: 'People are stretched in all directions,' he says.

Another problem in making the Assembly meaningful to the people of Wales is that its technocratic diet of secondary legislation is not conducive to real political argument, what Rhodri Morgan calls the 'blood and thunder of debate'. Speaking to the Labour party journal *Progress*, he recalled signing the Sheep and Goats Identification Order (Wales) 2000: 'I know you have to separate the sheep from the goats! But that's the perfect example of the problem that you have. Secondary legislation is absolutely essential to the efficient functioning of, say, public health or animal health regulations on this, that or the other. But it's not a showcase for a new democracy.'

In July 2000, Morgan announced a four-party review of the Assembly's operations, to be chaired by the Presiding Officer and to last a year. Dafydd Elis Thomas, speaking to the Institute of Welsh Politics in Aberystwyth shortly before the announcement, made clear where he saw the weaknesses:

The current basis of the Assembly's power displays no constitutional logic, but was based entirely on the political processes of the gradual acquisition of powers within the office of the Secretary of State for Wales. Devolving 'secondary legislation' as a category makes no constitutional sense, because it is itself legislatively various.

While the Scottish Parliament was given clear responsibility for subject areas, the Welsh Assembly had to pick its way through Westminster legislation to work out which powers, if any, it could exercise. The result lacked any logical basis, he complained. However, even Plaid Cymru members of the Assembly recognize that it may take years before the resources and drafting skills are available in Cardiff to permit it to take over responsibility for primary legislation. 'We cannot lay claim or plan for legislative devolution until we have mastered executive devolution and pushed at its boundary. In ten years' time, with a significant increase in staff, we may have accumulated enough legislative experience to be able to claim the expertise possessed by Scotland to successfully operate legislative devolution. At present, we cannot make such claims.'[46]

A PACT WITH THE LIBERAL DEMOCRATS

Eight months after taking over from Alun Michael, Rhodri Morgan drew the inevitable consequences of Labour's minority position in the Assembly and signed a coalition agreement with the Liberal Democrats' leader Michael German. The 'partnership programme' – the word coalition was avoided – guaranteed the smaller party the job of deputy First Secretary on the Scottish pattern, and a second cabinet post. The deal was not one that Alun Michael would ever have contemplated. It set out a joint programme for government until the next Assembly elections in 2003, including a review of the case for electoral reform in local government. It also promised an independent commission to look at the powers and electoral arrangements of the Assembly itself, which would look at 'the extension of proportionality in the composition of the Assembly, and of the relevant competencies devolved'. This review would be published in the first year after the next Welsh elections in 2003, after which the Assembly would ask the government in Westminster to bring forward primary legislation if needed.

One clear advantage for Labour in giving the commission such an extended remit would be to take the issue of primary legislative powers out of the 2003 election campaign. The deal included other elements which appeared likely to raise eyebrows in Downing Street – a promise to move towards 'an increasingly independent and Welsh-based civil service' and a Welsh Bill of citizenship rights.

Under Morgan, Labour's fortunes look to be on the mend, thanks in part to a generous settlement for Wales in Gordon Brown's July 2000 spending review, which gave Cardiff extra money to match the European Union Objective One funds promised to Wales. Labour has now rebranded itself as *Welsh Labour – the true party of Wales*. Morgan, who is sympathetic to electoral reform for Westminster and supports a written constitution for the UK, is a politician who thinks in the long term. He told a fringe meeting of electoral reform campaigners at the September 2000 Labour party conference that the choice of proportional representation in Wales would inevitably mean the party would not win an outright majority in every election:

People say: 'You are fools, you could have had an easy majority, 27 seats out of 40.' We didn't want to make it too easy for ourselves. Over 20 years, five or six elections, Labour would win some of them, there would be an anti-Labour majority in the others, all according to how Labour was able to relate to the electorate. When Labour was doing badly, you would have no majority. In 1999 we were not doing well, we did not get a majority. I hope that in 2003 we will get a majority. Maybe in 2007 we won't. But if you have a system where regardless of what you deserve you still win a majority, you know all the perils of single-party rule, all the temptations of continuous power, and we will be prey to all of those temptations. Over the run of 20 years it will be much more positive. It doesn't make government impossible. You have to compromise with at least one minority party.

Although the coalition deal with the Liberal Democrats was criticized by some in both parties, it appeared likely to secure Labour a breathing space and a period of greater stability, while allowing Plaid Cymru to present itself clearly as a party of opposition. It is worth noting that while Morgan has often sounded conciliatory to the nationalists, Welsh Secretary Paul Murphy has attacked them as dangerous separatists and 'daffodil Tories' who are never to be trusted. The risk for the nationalists in engineering Alun Michael's dismissal was that they might harm their own electoral chances by replacing him with a Labour leader who carried greater electoral appeal. Dafydd Wigley, speaking to me a few weeks before he stood down for health reasons and was replaced by Ieuan Wyn Jones, acknowledged that there were those in his own party who felt it was a mistake to topple Alun Michael, seeing him as Plaid Cymru's secret weapon:

We have had a lot of questioning on that theme, including a lot of questioning among our own members and in our own National Council. It's a fair question. I think the decision we came to was that the Assembly could not carry on as it was, that the whole structure would be brought into disrepute unless there was an easing up on the whole thing, and power was shared out and decisions taken more quickly. So we didn't see the status quo as an option. We came to the conclusion that if Rhodri Morgan is a tremendous success, that is probably good for the Assembly itself, and good for Wales, and the institution will get its foundations right and grow. But if it is not a success, then they have played that card and do not have it left to play before the election. They could have held it back to six months before an election to see what the true value of Rhodri Morgan was. So we have flushed that card out, and we are happy to live with the consequences. I would be happy to see the Labour government a success. I would be happier to see that than to see it a dismal failure, with the well-being of Wales suffering in consequence.

In opposition, Plaid Cymru will now find it easier to escape responsibility for Assembly decisions it has been unable to influence; Wigley told me he wanted the voters to see a clear distinction between the Assembly as a body and its executive leadership:

There is a misconception not only among the ordinary punters, the voters and the person in the street, but also in the media in Wales, where time after time there are reports which say, the Assembly has decided this, the Assembly has decided that, when in fact they haven't been Assembly decisions at all. They have been decisions by government … If you don't get a differentiation between the government and the elected body of the Assembly, then it becomes very difficult to pin responsibility. That makes it very difficult then at a time of an election for the voters to realize that there is an alternative. It is like blaming the House of Commons for everything the government does, as if the institution of the House of Commons is at fault for government policy.

A BLAIR *MEA CULPA?*

Meanwhile, Tony Blair has now acknowledged that his attempt to block Morgan was a mistake. In a rare *mea culpa*, he told *The Observer* on a visit to Wales a few weeks after Michael's fall: 'I got that judgement wrong … You've got to exercise discretion. You've got to know the battles to fight and the battles not to fight.' Blair seems to have at last accepted that the Welsh Labour party can no longer be run in the old way. 'Essentially, you have got to let go of it with devolution,' he acknowledged.

Dafydd Wigley believes Blair's experiences in Wales have taught him lessons the hard way:

I am sure he regrets having parachuted Alun Michael in the way he did. It was unfair on Alun Michael, apart from anything else. He was put to do a job without having had time to prepare for it. He had to fight an internal election at a time when he should have been fighting an external campaign. He came into power without having had a programme ready to implement and he was seen as the messenger from Downing Street. It was unfair on him. I think Tony Blair and people around him should have seen that you can't do that, and then to repeat that with variations with Ken Livingstone – it does call certain things into question. Having said that, one has to pay tribute. Blair did set up the Assembly; it wasn't the model that we wanted, but it was a step that we regarded as worthwhile in its own right.

However, there are legitimate doubts as to whether Blair has really learned all the right lessons from his mistakes in Wales. A year after the stitch-up which secured Alun Michael victory in an electoral college, exactly the same methods were employed to keep Ken Livingstone from winning the Labour nomination for London mayor. The culture of control in New

Labour lies too deep to be easily jettisoned and thrown in the Volga. Ron Davies does not believe the Labour leadership style has fundamentally changed, although he says: 'I think fingers were badly burned over the Alun Michael affair.' Davies says he genuinely does not know whether Blair now considers his whole approach to Welsh devolution was wrong, or whether he simply misjudged the personal qualities of the candidates.

Paul Flynn, the relentlessly off-message Labour MP for Newport West, describes Blair as 'a slow learner on the subject of devolution':

He seems to be saying Rhodri has improved – he is obviously a late developer at the age of 59. Why he opposed Rhodri has to be one of the great mysteries of life. He sets up devolved institutions and then has to decide who runs them. He is a devolutionist because he inherited it from John Smith, not by conviction.

THE END OF THE BEGINNING

As with Scotland, the verdict on the Welsh Assembly has to be a provisional one, but there is no doubt that the fall of Alun Michael was a political watershed, not just for Wales but for the Blair government, despite Blair's somewhat dismissive description of it in the Commons as 'fun and games'. In the words of Plaid Cymru's Dafydd Elis Thomas when I spoke to him the day afterwards: 'Yesterday was the first day of devolution.' Alun Michael was in his view not so much Tony Blair's puppet in Wales but a product of the old Welsh Labour way of doing things, 'the old Cardiff South politics, a very tight way of running the party, populist but with no political ideas'.

The new agenda means that the government in London has to begin to treat Wales as more than just a territorial department. 'The UK is struggling towards a kind of federal state, a century after everybody else. What we are going to have is a reinvented UK federation as part of a European federation. That's fine as far as Wales is concerned. The Liberals are firmly federalist. Some in my party still have to grasp the UK dimension properly.' Unlike the SNP in Scotland, Plaid Cymru tends to avoid using the word 'independence', preferring 'full national status', a less clear-cut concept linked to Europe. But for this to come about, the flawed constitutional settlement passed by Westminster in 1998 will inevitably have to be revisited to give the Assembly more powers. At some point in the coming decade, the government of Wales will force itself back on to the Westminster agenda.

Meanwhile, as the Swansea Labour MP Donald Anderson prophesied, the people of Wales are in the driving seat in the devolution mystery tour. Although public support for the Assembly as an institution has grown since the 1997 referendum, particularly among young people, it is far from certain that the Labour party, now seen as the voice of the establishment in Wales, will always be the one that reaps the benefit. As in Scotland, it appears that devolution, like revolution, can devour its children.

NOTES

[1] Speech on 12 November 1998 at Strathclyde University.

[2] Morgan, Kevin and Mungham, Geoff (2000) *Redesigning Democracy. The Making of the Welsh Assembly*, Bridgend, Seren Press, p 21.

[3] Thatcher, Margaret (1993) *The Downing Street Years*, London, HarperCollins, p 618.

[4] Taylor, Brian (1999) *The Scottish Parliament*, Edinburgh, Polygon, p 38.

[5] Taylor, op. cit., p 38.

[6] Mitchell, James (1999) 'The creation of the Scottish Parliament. Journey without end' in *Parliamentary Affairs*, October, Oxford, OUP.

[7] Mitchell, op. cit.

[8] Taylor, op. cit., p 57.

[9] Taylor, op. cit., p 97.

[10] Hassan, Gerry (1999) *A Guide to the Scottish Parliament. The Shape of Things to Come*, Edinburgh, The Stationery Office, p 31.

[11] Devolution to Scotland, Wales and the Regions. Later the reference to the Regions disappeared.

[12] A reference to the fact that Dewar's wife Alison left him for Irvine.

[13] *The Scotsman*, 10 May 1999.

[14] Hassan, Gerry and Warhurst, Christopher (eds) (1999) *A Different Future: a modernisers' guide to Scotland*, Glasgow, Big Issue and The Centre for Scottish Public Policy, p 16.

[15] Hassan, Gerry and Warhurst, Christopher (eds) (2000) *The New Scottish Politics. The first year of the Scottish Parliament and beyond*, Norwich, The Stationery Office, p 21.

[16] Foreword by Gordon Brewer in Hassan and Warhurst, 2000.

[17] Hassan and Warhurst, 2000.

[18] Hassan and Warhurst, 2000.

[19] Catherine MacLeod in Hassan and Warhurst, 2000.

[20] Edwards, Owen Dudley (ed.) (1989) *A Claim of Right for Scotland*, Edinburgh, Polygon, p 173.

[21] Nairn, Tom (2000) *After Britain. New Labour and the return of Scotland*, London, Granta Books, p 4.

[22] Hassan and Warhurst, 1999, p 47.

[23] Nairn, Tom (2000) *'Let's Get it Down in Black and White'* in *The New Statesman*, 24 January.

[24] Hassan and Warhurst, 1999, p 44.

[25] Interview with Fintan O'Toole in *The Irish Times*, 15 January 2000.

[26] Morgan and Mungham, op. cit., p 13.

[27] See Anthony D. Smith's *National Identity*, p 59 for a summary of the classic explanation of how 'the state created the nation' in early modern Europe. For a particular interpretation of how Scottish national identity was formed, see Neil Davidson's *Scotsman* essay 'Birth of a Nation', 26 March 2000.

[28] Jones, J. Barry and Balsom, Denis (eds) (2000) *The Road to the National Assembly for Wales*, Cardiff, University of Wales Press, p 1.

[29] Morgan and Mungham, op. cit., p 15.

[30] Morgan and Mungham, op. cit., p 88.

[31] From a seminar talk by Ron Davies to the Constitution Unit, University College London, on 3 July 2000.

[32] Morgan and Mungham, op. cit., p 15.

[33] Jones and Balsom, p 181.

[34] Constitution Unit seminar.

[35] Davies, Ron (2000) 'We need a coalition of ideas'. Lecture to the Institute of Welsh Affairs and the Welsh Governance Centre, Cardiff University on 19 January, published in AGENDA, Journal of the IWA, Winter 2000.

[36] Constitution Unit seminar.

[37] Jones and Balsom, op. cit., p 2.

[38] Morgan and Mungham, op. cit., pp 108–19.

[39] Flynn, Paul (1999) *Dragons Led by Poodles. The inside story of a New Labour stitch-up*, London, Politico's, p 127.

[40] *Western Mail*, 8 February 2000.

[41] Morgan, Rhodri (2000) *Variable Geometry UK*, Cardiff, Institute of Welsh Affairs.

[42] Hazell, Robert (ed.) (1999) *Constitutional Futures. A history of the next ten years*, Oxford University Press, p 35.

[43] Davies, 2000.

[44] Constitution Unit seminar, 3 July 2000.

[45] Jones and Balsom, op. cit., p 277.

[46] Davies, Jocelyn (2000) *Developing the Functions of the Assembly*, internal Plaid Cymru policy paper, April, quoted in *Devolution Looks Ahead*, Monitoring Bulletin of the Institute of Welsh Affairs, September 2000.

4

THE ENGLISH QUESTION

'The general rule is governments centralize; oppositions call for power to be decentralized' – IPPR director Matthew Taylor

'England is the hole in the devolution settlement' – Robert Hazell

'Labour, the party that fathered devolution, is now of all the parties potentially the least comfortable with what it has done'– Ron Davies, former Secretary of State for Wales

BEFORE EXAMINING HOW ENGLAND IS AFFECTED by devolution, we need to take a closer look at the implications of the third settlement, the one affecting Northern Ireland. As in Scotland and Wales, the Belfast Agreement of April 1998 involved devolving powers from Westminster to an assembly and executive. But this was only one element in a much wider package designed to end 30 years of violent conflict. The agreement was a prize to which Tony Blair devoted countless hours of detailed negotiation, and became a landmark achievement of his first year in office.

Unlike the rest of Labour's constitutional reforms, this one built on the foundations laid by his predecessor John Major, but the bipartisan atmosphere at Westminster did not make agreement in Belfast much easier. The hostility and mistrust between the Northern Irish parties meant that some key elements of the Belfast Agreement, notably the question of arms decommissioning, had to be fudged, with the real problems postponed until later. By the autumn of 2000 most elements of the agreement were being implemented, although the ultimate stability of the deal was far from guaranteed. This followed two years of argument over arms decommissioning and a series of false starts, including the unilateral suspension of the devolved institutions by the Westminster parliament in early 2000. The suspension appeared to prove that Enoch Powell's maxim 'power devolved is power retained' still held good, at least in the eyes of Westminster, if not in the eyes of a highly critical Irish government. The episode illustrated the underlying tension between the quasi-federal system created by devolution, and buttressed by popular referendums, and the traditional Diceyan doctrine of parliamentary sovereignty under the Westminster model.

GLADSTONE AND THE IRISH QUESTION

The struggle to reconcile these ideas in a manner which makes sense not just in constitutional law but also in terms of practical politics has been going on since the days when Gladstone began trying to solve the Irish question, as Professor Vernon Bogdanor has outlined.[1] Gladstone wrestled with his own version of the West Lothian question in considering 'in and out' solutions for the voting rights of Irish MPs at Westminster. Federalism and quasi-federalism were hotly debated as concepts in the period of 'Home Rule All Round', as devolution was termed in the early years of the last century. The failure to find a solution led to the partition of Ireland in 1920–22. This brought to an end the relatively brief 120-year period during which the British Isles had been governed as a unitary state by one parliament.

After partition, six mainly Protestant Northern Irish counties remained part of the United Kingdom under the Act of Union of 1800, but were reluctantly persuaded to accept a devolved parliament rather than full integration. Home Rule was applied in the only part of Ireland which had not sought it. This is only one of a series of paradoxes outlined in Bogdanor's account; the initial aim in London was that the parliament would be a stepping stone to Irish unity rather than to permanent partition. This proved a miscalculation, as the Protestant Unionists entrenched their control over the province by abolishing proportional representation, which had been introduced to safeguard the rights of the Catholic minority. Northern Ireland became a one-party state in which Westminster by convention did not intervene until the civil rights unrest of the late 1960s forced it to. 'Through the years of devolved government, Westminster devoted on average two hours a year to Northern Ireland.'[2] Devolved government was suspended in 1972 and replaced the following year by direct rule, a system which set Northern Ireland apart from the rest of the United Kingdom and turned it into 'a dependency incapable of self-government'.[3] Until the 1998 agreement, this situation persisted, with only one brief and unsuccessful attempt to introduce power sharing in 1974.

The structures of devolved government established by the Belfast Agreement were bold and imaginative, following the examples of what political science jargon describes as 'consociational' settlements in divided societies. The agreement also recognized an Irish dimension in the politics of Northern Ireland with a North-South ministerial council, and a British-Irish Council. A cross-party consensus at Westminster and the absence of any direct link between the fortunes of UK mainland political parties and the electoral outcomes in the Northern Ireland Assembly helped to make these innovations possible. In this sense Northern Ireland was different from Scotland and Wales, where the Labour party had a huge stake of its own in who controlled the new devolved bodies.

NORTHERN IRELAND – THE KEY FACTS

Stormont and direct rule

Since the abolition of the Stormont parliament in 1972, Northern Ireland had been effectively under direct rule by a Secretary of State in London, governing by Order in Council. Self-determination for Northern Ireland was built into the post-partition Government of Ireland Act 1920. The 1985 Anglo-Irish Agreement underlined the principle of consent by the majority of the Northern Ireland population as the condition of any change in the province's status. In the 1993 Downing Street Declaration the British government declared it had 'no selfish strategic or economic interest in Northern Ireland'. Other factors making devolution in Northern Ireland different from Scotland and Wales include the 30-year guerrilla conflict, the social and political division of the province, and the close involvement of the Irish government.

The Good Friday Agreement

The multiparty agreement reached on 10 April 1978 has three strands, dealing with the internal government of Northern Ireland, with North/South relations, and with relations between the UK and the Republic. Within Northern Ireland it provides for a 108-member Assembly elected by the proportional single transferable vote

(STV), with the executive formed on a proportional basis. Some decisions can be taken by simple majority but important votes require the backing of representatives of both unionist and nationalist sides. Other elements include a Bill of Rights, a Human Rights Commission and an Equality Commission. There is a North/South Ministerial Council and a new British-Irish Council to include representatives from Scotland, Wales and from the territories of the Isle of Man and the Channel Islands, which are not formally part of the UK.

Referendum and elections

The agreement was endorsed by separate referendums in Northern Ireland and the Irish Republic on 22 May 1998. The 'yes' vote in Northern Ireland was 71.2 per cent, in the Republic 94 per cent. The Irish Republic subsequently revised its constitution to drop its claim over the North. In elections to the Assembly on 25 June 1998, the Ulster Unionist party (UUP) won 28 seats, the Social Democratic and Labour party (SDLP) 24, the Democratic Unionist party 20 and Sinn Fein 18. Full implementation of the agreement was held up by disagreement over arms decommissioning and power was not transferred to the cross-party executive headed by UUP leader David Trimble and the SDLP's Seamus Mallon until 2 December 1999.

DICEY STILL RULES

Power was transferred to Northern Ireland's new cross-party executive in December 1999 but was taken back by the UK parliament in February 2000, returning Northern Ireland to direct rule until the end of May that year. For Professor Brendan O'Leary of the London School of Economics, this unilateral move was an illustration of how parliamentary sovereignty, whatever academics and constitutional reformers might think, was still the operating code of Westminster politics, with important implications for Scotland and Wales:

That was a direct breach of the treaty with the Irish government, which required consultation before any action would be taken by either government in the event of a failure of the institutions to operate. It was a direct breach of the will of the people of Ireland, North and South, who had set up a set of arrangements which did *not* give the Secretary of State the power to suspend the Assembly ... Parliament and the parties who negotiated it explicitly agreed the Secretary of State should not have the power of dissolution. They wanted to take responsibility for themselves. Now that action tore up years of constitutional negotiating, because what it meant was that Westminster could expressly override a set of institutional arrangements set up at great cost and great pain, which were subject to consent, North and South, to be compatible with what the Irish wanted, a notion of the Irish people exercising their self-determination to set up these institutional arrangements. That was done with almost no thought. It was a pragmatic response: 'Oh, we need to do this.' When it was pointed out that they were breaking all these constitutional traditions they simply said, 'Oh, Northern Ireland is part of the United Kingdom, and people who voted for the agreement must have known that.'

Nobody who voted for the agreement thought that they were voting to endorse parliamentary sovereignty. If they were, that would mean parliament could unwind any part of the agreement at any time, including the provision that Northern Ireland could become part of the Republic by consent. So the doctrine of parliamentary sovereignty remains a very strong operational code for politicians, and it is academics who are foolish not to notice that it is still the dominant code.

It has interesting repercussions for Scotland and Wales. It was interesting how quiet they were on the suspension of the Assembly, they treated it as a separate case. But nothing can stop Westminster doing the same to the Scottish Parliament or to the Welsh Assembly.

O'Leary's point is that there is an inherent conflict between popular sovereignty and self-determination, which are explicitly endorsed by the Good Friday Agreement, and parliamentary sovereignty under the Westminster model. If the agreement works it could, he believes, lead to a federal or confederal Ireland, with Northern Ireland retaining its devolved institutions but as part of the Irish Republic rather than the UK. 'Plainly that is what Irish nationalists would like to see happen. And it is secretly what quite a significant proportion of the British political establishment would like to see happen.'

Another scenario is that the province remains where it is, and there is a deepening confederal relationship between Ireland and the UK, with the other devolved governments playing a full part. The third possibility is 'an institutional mess' if the arrangements do not work, with renewed suspensions of devolved government.

The twice-yearly summit meetings of the British-Irish Council (sometimes called the Council of the Isles) make it a body comparable to the Nordic Council, which includes not just sovereign governments but territories such as Greenland and the Faroe Islands as well. The new council brings together the governments of the United Kingdom, the Irish Republic, the devolved governments of Wales and Scotland, and the Crown territories of the Isle of Man and the Channel Islands in a radically new forum. Tom Nairn sees the council as the embryo of a 'restructured archipelago' based on a future loose relationship or confederation, a view which O'Leary believes is interesting but premature. The new forum may turn out to be little more than a worthy talking shop, but by placing Scotland and Wales alongside Ireland in a forum where they have equal status, it gives them a whiff of sovereignty.

Donald Dewar told me it was too soon to predict how important the new body would become:

I don't think anyone can say at the moment. It is a very useful getting together. I have enjoyed getting to know colleagues from other parts of the United Kingdom. I think they value it and I do too. But it is not decision making ... At this stage, inevitably, we are not going to take decisions round that table which can be enforced by the various parties taking part in the discussion. We may learn a great deal from their experience, how to combat drugs, how to look at IT instruction in schools, how you manage broadband technology and so on. I think you start at that level and then you just see how it develops.

A more important side-effect may be to highlight the anomalous position of England, shown to lack any political institutions of its own after devolution. The United Kingdom government will become the *de facto* government of England for the day. There are other innovations in the Northern Irish settlement which have implications for the rest of the United Kingdom, such as the creation of a Bill of Rights and a Human Rights Commission, an Equality Commission, and a reform of the judiciary and the police. O'Leary believes minority groups in Britain could latch on to these innovations and press for their wider introduction: 'They will have a role model for recommending constitutional change to improve their rights as they see it.'

The Belfast Agreement's strictly proportional election system could also become an example for wider use, though the cross-community nature of the governing institutions is unlikely to be duplicated elsewhere. O'Leary does not believe Northern Ireland will point the UK in the direction of federalism, although developments in Scotland could lead that way. In the long run, the Good Friday Agreement could influence the British constitutional debate by the radicalism of its departure from the 'Crown-in-Parliament' Westminster model and from the British tradition of unwritten constitutionalism. Popular sovereignty and self-determination are explicitly endorsed in a way that Scottish and Welsh nationalists will see as applicable to their ambitions. Why should the much-quoted 'principle of consent' be valid for the population of Northern Ireland but not elsewhere?

The Belfast Agreement also contains an interesting annex which could set a precedent for widening the normal franchise in a future referendum on Scottish independence. It gives the right to vote in a referendum on the province's status not just to those on the Northern Ireland electoral roll but to the first-generation diaspora as well:

The British and Irish governments declare that it is their joint understanding that the term 'the people of Northern Ireland' in paragraph (vi) of Article 1 of this Agreement means, for the purposes of giving effect to this provision, all persons born in Northern Ireland and having, at the time of their birth, at least one parent who is a British citizen, an Irish citizen or is otherwise entitled to reside in Northern Ireland without any restriction on their period of residence.

If the Belfast Agreement works, it may be that a much closer relationship is forged over time between the UK and the Irish Republic. This is clearly what Tony Blair has in mind. In a speech to the Irish parliament in Dublin on 26 November 1998 he stressed the theme of shared history, including the contribution of Daniel O'Connell and Charles Stuart Parnell to 19th-century Westminster politics. Blair sought to point the way to a changed relationship between London and Dublin, achieved through a more stable framework for politics in Northern Ireland: 'It is all about belonging. The wish of unionists to belong to the UK. The wish of nationalists to belong to Ireland. Both traditions are reasonable. There are no absolutes.'

Coexistence between the two communities would be easier if Dublin and London moved closer together as well, he argued, highlighting the symbolic importance of a joint ceremony which had taken place in Flanders to honour the dead of World War One: 'Our army bands played together. Our heads of state stood together. With our other European neighbours, such a ceremony would be commonplace. For us it was a first. It shows how far we have come. But it also shows we still have far to go.'

Blair's tactful speech clearly showed that he understood how 'the politics of identity' matter in Ireland, even if he would not concede the same for Scotland. The implicit long-term goal of this kind of reconciliation is that British and Irish identities will eventually cease to become mutually exclusive. This would allow a more 'Irish' version of the 'British' identity of Northern Irish Protestants, less based on hostility to the Republic. Not only would the 'British' start to feel partly Irish, but, as relations improve, the Irish diaspora living in the UK might be able to feel they were part of a redefined multicultural British nation.[4]

CAUTION REIGNS IN ENGLAND

By comparison with the boldness and innovation of its devolution package for Northern Ireland, Labour's approach to devolution for England has been at best cautious, at worst confused. The whole subject has shown Tony Blair at his most hesitant and risk-averse. His one personal contribution has been to push through the idea of a directly elected London mayor, a policy which turned into an unmitigated disaster for his own party with the election of Ken Livingstone. As a Charter88 analysis in September 1999 concluded: 'Given the amount of attention the government devoted to developing coherent proposals for Scotland and Wales, it is astonishing how little thought appears to have been given, let alone agreement achieved, on the future shape of elected English regional government.'[5]

Historian Linda Colley, in a millennium lecture delivered at Blair's invitation in Downing Street in 1999, made the same point. 'Any notion that devolution can occur in Wales, Scotland and Northern Ireland, while the 80 per cent plus of the British population who live in England go on exactly as before, is plainly unrealistic. This is not to raise again the weary West Lothian question, nor is it to have any truck with nightmare scenarios of a new, embittered English nationalism, or a fully fledged English parliament. But there will need to be more imagination and more change.'

Robert Hazell, head of the Constitution Unit, has written of England as being the 'black hole' at the centre of the devolution project, while Labour MP Tony Wright, introducing a Fabian Society pamphlet on *The English Question*, listed a series of questions which needed answering, involving not just governance but identity as well: 'The English propensity for muddling through is an exhausted option.'

RUSSIA AS ROLE MODEL?

The Russians, like the English, had got along fine for the last few hundred years without asking too many questions about who they were and where they belonged. But when the Soviet Union, the inheritor state of the Russian empire, began to fragment in 1990, they suddenly had to redefine themselves and how they would be governed. From a shadowy existence with only weak political institutions of its own, Russia emerged with bewildering speed as a national state and an alternative focus of identity. That kind of debate appears to be starting in England, with the white and red symbol of the cross of St George starting to muscle in alongside the Union Jack, just as the Russian tricolour emerged from nowhere to push aside the Soviet red banner. Another parallel between England and Russia in the age of *perestroika* is the appearance of a spate of what might be called 'national backlash' books, such as Simon Heffer's *Nor Shall My Sword* and John Redwood's *The Death of Britain?*

It is amusing to speculate about future parallels between the way Boris Yeltsin's Russia precipitated the collapse of the Soviet Union and the rise of English nationalism, but there is no reason to believe that such a crisis is imminent. There were other factors driving the Soviet collapse, notably an economic crisis of extraordinary proportions and the sudden introduction of free democratic elections. Unlike the Soviet Union, the United Kingdom is not trying simultaneously to dismantle a multi-national empire, a state-controlled economy and 70 years of totalitarian one-party rule. Nor, despite the efforts of fuel protesters, are its citizens yet queuing for hours in the snow to buy non-existent sausage with a worthless currency.

Complaints about English budgetary resources being siphoned off under the Barnett formula to subsidize ungrateful nations on the periphery carry strong echoes of the debates that took place in Russia under Gorbachev. There is, however, a crucial difference: while Russia under Soviet rule had very weak political institutions, England as part of the United Kingdom finds it has none at all. Some would like to create an English parliament to even out the score with Scotland, Wales and Northern Ireland and establish a fully federal system. Cyning Meadowcroft, who waves his English flag outside the Houses of Parliament on most Wednesdays, is the best known of such campaigners. Most advocates of an English parliament, such as the Conservative MP Teresa Gorman, do not envisage a separate institution to rival Westminster. Gorman's plan is for the House of Commons to revert to being a purely English parliament, with the representatives of the unruly Celtic fringes banished to a 'British' second chamber. Any such scheme would probably bring about the disintegration of the United Kingdom. Robert Hazell's blunt view is that a separate English parliament is 'not an option'. And as Sir Malcolm Rifkind argues, most people in Dorset or Yorkshire believe there is an English parliament already – the one at Westminster.

LABOUR'S ENGLISH DILEMMA

The problem remains that, as Tony Wright puts it, 'The English have been the silent and uninvited guests at the devolutionary feast. Scotland has a parliament, Wales an assembly, while England only gets some regional quangos. When Rover collapsed, who was there to speak (and act) for the West Midlands? A striking feature of the devolution legislation has been its total neglect of the union (and English) dimension.'[6] Even if there is no Soviet-style political crisis, there will have to be changes at Westminster and decentralization of government within England if the potential English backlash against devolution is to be warded off. Wright complains that in the government's response, 'what is missing is a vision (and a strategy) for a serious local democracy'.

> 66 The lack of a clear devolution policy for England, as for Wales, is a product of unresolved divisions within the Labour party in opposition and subsequently in Tony Blair's cabinet. 99

The lack of a clear devolution policy for England, as for Wales, is a product of unresolved divisions within the Labour party in opposition and subsequently in Tony Blair's cabinet. Robert Hazell describes how '... the difficulties lie not in Whitehall but in the Labour party itself'. Under the authoritarian culture of New Labour, an absence of open party debate has hampered the search for a solution. Blair's self-proclaimed interest is not in structures but in outcomes, under the slogan 'whatever works best'. The advantage of this approach is that the government has avoided being too rigid and prescriptive; but the ultra-pragmatic approach can easily drift into incoherence and lack of a clear sense of purpose.

Before 1997 Labour's regional policy in opposition had two strands, one political and one economic, entrusted to different members of Blair's shadow cabinet. Under Jack Straw, party policymakers looked at devolution for England, where the Conservatives had set up government offices for the regions and a variety of regional quangos. The policy that emerged proposed the creation of indirectly elected regional chambers of local authority representatives; at a later stage regions could set up directly elected assemblies, but only if a series of tight conditions were met. This was a dilution of the much firmer commitment to regional government made under John Smith. Meanwhile, John Prescott pushed the idea of regional development agencies (RDAs) in the English regions to attract inward investment and help small businesses, copying similar bodies in Scotland and Wales. The 1997 manifesto failed to weld these two policies together, so that they appeared in separate chapters. On devolution, the wording was ultra-cautious:

Demand for directly elected regional government so varies across England that it would be wrong to impose a uniform system. In time we will introduce legislation to allow the people, region by region, to decide in a referendum whether they want directly elected regional government. Only where clear popular consent is established will arrangements be made for elected regional assemblies.

But the manifesto's stringent conditions did not stop there. As well as a referendum, there would have to be a predominantly unitary system of local government in any region wishing to qualify, thus ruling out any region composed mostly of shire counties and districts; parliament would have to approve in each case; and there would have to be confirmation by independent auditors that no additional public expenditure would be involved. There could be no question of adding a new tier of government to the existing English system, the manifesto said, hoisting the drawbridge to fend off possible Conservative attacks.

These conditions were so tightly drawn as to effectively rule out any real hope of devolution in the sense that it was applied to Scotland and Wales, with powers transferred downwards to the English regions from central government. Instead regional issues became downgraded to part of the agenda for local government reform, becoming hopelessly entwined with the issue of city mayors and the delivery of central services under John Prescott's Department of the Environment, Transport and the Regions (DETR). Professor Brendan O'Leary comments:

It is an institutional politics story, in that regional government is somehow the responsibility of John Prescott and that is nothing to do with devolutionary settlements. It is quite extraordinary and they were plainly disconnected organizationally; they have not been thought through as a coherent constitutional package.

YES TO RDAS, NO TO ASSEMBLIES

Soon after the general election the government decided to legislate to set up the RDAs but left the regional chambers out of the package, supposedly because of lack of parliamentary time. Robert Hazell sees it differently: 'This was nonsense: the real reason was a failure of political will.' The government did not want the business-led RDAs to be hindered by chambers 'full of deadbeat local councillors'. The RDAs have been in business since 1999, with a third of their members from local government, reporting to central government; the chambers exist but are non-statutory voluntary bodies – 'mere appendages' in Hazell's phrase. And the RDAs are less powerful than Prescott wanted them to be because Whitehall departments other than his own DETR were reluctant to let go of some of their regional functions. The only RDA that reports not to central government but to a regionally elected authority is the one in London.

There has been little or no movement towards what many see as the logical next step, the creation of directly elected assemblies in the eight English regions outside London. The uncomfortable fact is that England is by far the largest single national unit of population in Europe with no democratic regional government. Those who want to change that can point to a variety of European models, starting with Germany's full-scale federalism. France, with a strong tradition of centralization, began introducing regional government in 1982 under a decentralization law that created 22 regions in metropolitan France and four overseas. The most likely model for the UK to follow if it ever moves on to devolution for England would be the Spanish programme of asymmetric rolling devolution in which regions have acquired different powers at different times under a plan known popularly as *café para todos*.[7] Advocates of regional government see much to learn from the 'variable geometry' approach adopted in Spain, although the government has been reluctant to cite it as an example to follow.

> **The uncomfortable fact is that England is by far the largest single national unit of population in Europe with no democratic regional government.**

One of the main enthusiasts for regional policy, Prescott's lieutenant Richard Caborn, was moved to the Department of Trade and Industry in Blair's July 1999 reshuffle in what many saw as a setback for the regional cause. His successor, Hilary Armstrong, was initially seen as less enthusiastic. According to Liberal Democrat spokesman Don Foster:

Caborn was more enthusiastic about regional government but his enthusiasm stemmed from the power base he had with the RDAs who were reporting to him. It's important to always remember the regional structures all report directly up to the minister rather than down. It is frankly crazy that we have all these quangos, which have no responsibility for linking in to and with their local government counterparts within their areas. There is nothing on the statute book requiring it … We need to find a whole new constitutional settlement where the democratic deficit is ended and where there is also a relationship between the various tiers of government, which we currently don't have.

BISHOPS JOIN THE CAMPAIGN

With the example of the Scottish Constitutional Convention before them, several English regions are now busy trying to follow the route map that led to a Scottish parliament, but they have a long way to go. Robert Hazell's view is that none of them has got beyond sloganizing and into the detailed policy work which the Scottish Constitutional Convention undertook: 'I try to tell them as tactfully as I can how much work went on in endless committees and subcommittees. The Scots were really gritty about it, but I see no signs of such grit or determination or the hard, detailed spade work.'

Where the Scots had Canon Kenyon Wright as their chair, the North West has the Bishop of Liverpool, the North East the Bishop of Durham, and the South West the Bishop of Exeter. Campaigners are also busy in the West Midlands and in Yorkshire and Humberside, though in some other areas, notably the prosperous South East, barely a flicker of public interest has registered. By the autumn of 2000 local campaigners had joined to form the Campaign for the English Regions, a lobby group targeting not so much the government as the Labour party, hoping to influence its next manifesto. Liberal Democrats have long advocated regional government, while the Conservatives under William Hague are implacably opposed; they are now promising to abolish not only the RDAs but the government offices for the regions which they themselves created in the early 1990s.

So lobbying the Labour party has been the only game in town. The campaigners want the government to publish legislation in the first year of the next parliament, though this timetable may be too ambitious. Legislation would set the rules under which regions could hold referendums, following the Scottish and Welsh patterns. Don Foster believes the campaigns will eventually get somewhere because a powerful alliance is building up, especially in the North. 'It's obvious that the different regional campaigns are at different stages of development,' says Steve Machin of the North West Regional Assembly, which despite its title is not a directly elected body but a regional chamber of local authorities. By general consent, the North East, where campaigning began as far back as 1992, is furthest advanced.

The exact shape and proposed functions of regional elected bodies are still up for discussion, though there is a general consensus that the powers should be taken downwards from central government rather than upwards from local authorities. Machin says bodies with around 30 members might be acceptable to government – a slimmed-down size comparable to the Greater London Authority with its 25 members and smaller than the Welsh, Northern Ireland or Scottish bodies. There is also a consensus that such bodies could operate in tandem with directly elected big city mayors, the first of whom may well be in office by the time Labour legislates in a second term. 'We will be offered a hybrid version of what happened in London, with a committee structure,' predicts Machin, though he is not sure Hilary Armstrong has yet been converted from her initial scepticism.

Don Foster says government policy is 'all over the place' and although the exact model of regional government should be left to the regions themselves, there should be a Spanish-style 'pick and mix' menu of powers from which the regions can choose. Meanwhile, the government has a clear responsibility to set the ground rules:

There is a need for clear decisions by government about how you get from a desire for regional government to how you actually then get it to be in existence. Do you have a referendum? If so how is the question worded? How do you go about electing people, what should the powers be and so on? A lot of the powers should be taken down from central government, so it is not unreasonable for central government to have a clear say in how they think that should all work, as they are the ones giving up the powers. I don't think you can have a total free-for-all.

There are numerous problems to be resolved. If you look at the boundaries of the various regional quangos, they are by no terms all coterminous with a regional boundary … Where do you actually draw these boundaries? There is a very strong argument that the South West should not include Devon and Cornwall, that they should be treated as a separate entity in their own right, because the South West region is too big.

NORTH EAST LEADS THE WAY

The reason for the disparity in enthusiasm between regions is not hard to find; it is no accident that the biggest resonance for the campaign is in the economically lagging North East, which looks enviously northwards to see how public expenditure levels in Scotland are far higher per head even though every economic and social indicator shows the Scots are better off. 'The argument over shares of the cake is a political struggle and the North must be empowered to fight it,' is the view of Grimsby MP Austin Mitchell.[8]

There is also the fact of geographical remoteness, which makes Newcastle aware it is closer to Edinburgh than London. Frustration is heightened in the North East by the knowledge that the region sends a large number of senior Labour MPs to Westminster, including Tony Blair, Mo Mowlam, Stephen Byers and Peter Mandelson. According to a Cabinet Office study prepared for Tony Blair in December 1999, the region has the highest unemployment rate and the highest percentage of benefit claimants, a poor health record, one of the lowest levels of car ownership in the UK and in Europe, and the lowest home computer ownership in England. Austin Mitchell believes the regions are potentially better equipped to tackle these problems than Whitehall:

A government that wants to motivate the poor to work so that they can solve their own problems can hardly deny the case for letting regions do the same. That means giving them the power to improve their own lot, to take their own initiatives and respond to their own needs. People in the regions know best. They will make mistakes, but at least regional leaders will be accountable to the people for them.

Professor Iain McLean of Oxford University believes there is a good case for a total overhaul of the way the UK government divides up national spending. Currently, he argues, Scottish spending per head is around 25 per cent higher than the average in England, a product of historical fear in London of the threat of an upsurge of nationalism if Scotland's interests are not protected.[9] In the late 1970s the Treasury devised a formula that was supposed to produce a gradual convergence, which became known as the Barnett formula after James Callaghan's Chief Secretary to the Treasury, Joel Barnett. But the magic formula has not worked as expected. Scotland's advantage over England has widened since 1979, despite the fact that Scottish income per head is now at the UK average. Under current arrangements, as McLean shows, Scotland and Northern Ireland are the winners, while Wales and the North lose out. 'Why have Scotland and Northern Ireland always done so well? Essentially, because politicians fear for the Union, they have shovelled money at both of these territories.'

The fairness or unfairness of this formula is of vital importance because of the extraordinary degree of centralization of state finances in the UK, which means local and devolved government are almost completely dependent on Treasury grants. Local government raises a small part of its revenue from council tax, while the three devolved governments, in the absence of any decision by the Scottish Parliament to use its power to raise the standard rate of income tax, have no resources of their own. 'In the short to medium term, we can assume that the dominance of the centre in tax-raising will not change,' concludes McLean, pointing out the difference between the UK system and the more transparent redistribution system under a Grants Commission that operates in Australia. Another alternative but unlikely path would be to follow the example of Spain, where devolved governments have increasingly acquired tax-raising powers from the centre over the past 20 years. Such a reform in the UK would not only weaken the powers of the Treasury but mark a fundamental shift in the traditional way central government shares out resources around the country, seeking to ensure equal provision of services.

BLAIR AND THE LABOUR 'HEARTLANDS'

The Blair government's response to these issues has been cautious, although the approach of the next general election and nervousness about problems in the party's core electoral areas have prompted a desire to appear responsive. The government's dilemma is that it has pigeon-holed regional and local government issues in John Prescott's giant department and has seen them largely in terms of service delivery. Within this framework it has seen local accountability and democracy as less important than equalizing and improving standards nationwide. It is therefore not surprising that the government has been unable to give a clear reply to the case presented by Austin Mitchell and other English devolution advocates.

Tony Blair himself has blown hot and cold on the issue, and it is hard to detect a coherent set of views, apart from a preference for elected mayors over regional assemblies. Unlike some members of his cabinet, Blair has no experience in politics outside London, apart from his background as an MP with a constituency in the North East. Speaking to regional newspaper editors at the end of March 2000, he acknowledged growing pressure for regional change in England and said the logical conclusion was to create more accountable regional government: 'More regional decentralization in England makes sense, city mayors with real power have their place.' The government was 'moving us from a centralized Britain, where power flowed top-down, to a devolved and plural state'. In an interview with *The Newcastle Journal*,[10] which has campaigned vigorously for a better deal for the North East, Blair said decentralization was 'an idea whose time has come' and 'we've always made it clear that where there is support we favour moving to regional government'. But Blair's verbal gestures towards decentralization have never carried the force of real conviction. As Jonathan Freedland noted perceptively in *The Guardian*, government rhetoric no longer speaks of spreading out power: 'Instead, they want the voters to trust them, and in return, they will spend lots of money.'[11]

KILFOYLE WAS HERE

Blair's trip to the North East and his meeting with regional editors in March 2000 came shortly after the shock resignation from the government of junior defence minister and Liverpool MP Peter Kilfoyle. He was not a household name, but like John Prescott and Ian McCartney, he was one of a small group of key Labour figures who glued the New Labour project together, combining an impeccable working-class background with loyalty to the Prime Minister's modernizing agenda.

Kilfoyle rose to prominence as a rightwing scourge of the Trotskyite Militant Tendency in Liverpool and played a prominent part in Blair's campaign for the Labour leadership. He is among the MPs least likely to be accused of being a member of the chattering classes. In what amounted to a resignation statement during the debate on Gordon Brown's Budget at the end of March 2000, Kilfoyle said he had quit 'because he believed that "heartland issues" and policy towards the English regions were becoming more important'. He and others were wondering what devolution would mean for England outside the wealthy metropolis. 'We wonder when we will be afforded the flexibility that a degree of regional autonomy would bring.' He accused the existing government offices for the regions of a 'colonial Raj mentality' and called for a new financial settlement for the

English regions. 'The current view from the provinces is that key decisions are taken by a very small number of people sitting in Whitehall at the apex of a highly centralized government. They operate through a civil service machine that mirrors that rigid hierarchy, which stamps its will on the regions, and whose practice is based on what many believe are highly discriminatory financial arrangements.'

Kilfoyle's attack resonated more widely in Labour ranks than a hundred seminars at the Constitution Unit or pamphlets by Charter88. His well-publicized exit from the government and his raising of the 'heartlands' issue made the links explicit between devolution, electoral politics and bread-and-butter economics. Other Labour figures such as Peter Hain had warned in 1999 in the wake of the party's poor election results in Wales that the 'heartlands' voters were being neglected in favour of Middle England and the readers of the *Daily Mail*. This argument has always been strongly rejected by Blair, who argues passionately that his policies are designed to benefit all kinds of voters. 'The whole country is our core constituency,' Blair told Labour's local government conference in February 2000:

I reject the politics of division – those who want to see England fight Scotland, those who want to see North fight South. I say the politics of division have damaged the country for far too long and are not the answer to the problems our country faces … I was never able to do anything for the unemployed or the poor in my constituency until we were capable of winning in the South as well as the North. So don't let us ever be pushed back into the position of saying, 'Here is one part of the country we represent, and some parts we don't represent.' We represent all of Britain.

Visiting Wales in April for a meeting of the post-devolution Joint Ministerial Committee with Donald Dewar, Rhodri Morgan and Peter Mandelson, Blair said it was a 'Tory trap' to suggest that different areas had different needs. It was 'nonsense' to suggest a choice between the so-called 'heartlands' and middle Britain, he said, arguing that the whole country wanted decent schools and healthcare. 'Don't let anyone divide this country up,' he said. 'We all want the same things. We all have the same hopes and fears.' Only when addressing a northern regional audience directly has Blair wavered from this position, telling *The Newcastle Journal*: 'The North–South divide exists, and I never said it didn't.'

Behind the New Labour language lurks the traditional Bevanite Labour case for centralization of government. Blair's problem is that he is unclear what he really wants. His defence of 'one size fits all' government does not address either regional economic imbalances or the political problem of the remoteness of central government. A belief in the importance of uniform national policies on education, health and crime is understandable; but to a diverse regional audience the implication is that the man in Whitehall really does know best – hardly a decentralizing message. Blair's instinctive hostility to regional divisions in the Labour party is based on his formative memory of the left-right splits of the early 1980s. He told Robert Harris in an interview published in the US magazine *Talk* in April 2000: 'Sometimes I think the experiences in the Labour party in the early 1980s almost sort of scarred me too much in terms of the Labour party and how it had to be.'

> ❝ Blair's instinctive hostility to regional divisions in the Labour party is based on his formative memory of the left-right splits of the early 1980s. ❞

A RETURN TO TERRITORIAL POLITICS?

Professor John Tomaney of Newcastle University describes regional government as the Cinderella of Labour's constitutional reform plans, and warns it is making a big mistake by giving it such a low priority. 'The People's party has traditionally had a centralizing instinct which is deeply embedded in its political culture and may perhaps have found new life under the highly centralized approach of New Labour. What the regions need is not narrowly focused RDAs to improve business competitiveness but the emergence of strong regional political cultures and institutions,' he argues.[12] His view is that Labour risks losing the plot. 'Labour is refusing to acknowledge a fundamental shift in politics to regional rather than class issues,' he says. People in the North East are increasingly disenchanted with London and find Labour is increasingly irrelevant to their identity. 'People are not miners any more. What do they replace that with? The Labour party seems completely unable to grasp this. People do identify with their regions and the Labour party is well off the pace.'

Blair has led the way in calling for Labour to throw its old class loyalties and identities on the scrap heap, and is now alarmed by the emergence of new territorial loyalties and identities which, given the right circumstances, can prove more powerful than Blairite 'values'. At the next general election Labour voters in the North East will stay at home, Tomaney predicts, though unlike Scotland and Wales there is no strong nationalist party to sweep up protest votes. There are signs, however, that the signals on the line to regional government are no longer fixed at red: 'They are on amber at the moment, but not yet on green,' he told me in October 2000, shortly after Labour's annual conference. 'For a variety of reasons the government is moving, or at least beginning to think.'

REGIONAL IDENTITIES

A poll conducted by MORI for *The Economist* in September 1999 threw up some fascinating data supporting the rise of regional identities. In England, 49 per cent of people identified with their region, compared with 41 per cent identifying with England and 43 per cent with Britain.

Which two or three of these, if any, would you say you most identify with?

	GB %	England %	Scotland %	Wales %
This local community	41	42	39	32
This region	50	49	62	50
England/Scotland/Wales	45	41	72	81
Britain	40	43	18	27
Europe	16	17	11	16
The Commonwealth	9	10	5	3
The global community	8	9	5	2

Which of these flags, if any, do you identify with?

	GB %	England %	Scotland %	Wales %
United Kingdom (Union Jack)	83	88	49	55
England (Cross of St George)	33	38	2	3
Scotland (Cross of St Andrew)	23	18	75	8
Wales (Welsh Dragon)	26	24	12	85
European Union (12 Stars)	21	23	5	7
United States (Stars and Stripes)	23	26	7	*

In 20 years' time, which of these bodies, if any, do you expect to have most influence over your life and the lives of your children?

	GB %	England %	Scotland %	Wales %
My local council	13	14	5	7
Scottish Parliament/Welsh Assembly/ my regional assembly	13	9	46	26
The Westminster Parliament	22	23	8	25
European Parliament/European Union	44	46	31	37

FUTURE LABOUR POLICY

Labour's conference endorsed a policy document which sounded more enthusiastic about regional government; although there was no firm pledge to introduce directly elected assemblies, some of the obstacles were removed. Jane Thomas, who chairs the campaign for regional government in Yorkshire, told a fringe meeting at the conference in Brighton she was 'incredibly pleased' by the Labour response. The party said it wanted 'not more government but better government' and stuck to the condition that regional assemblies could only happen if there was a predominantly unitary structure at the local government level. However, it dropped the requirement in the 1997 manifesto that there should be no extra costs, and said the new structures should be 'inclusive' – a code word pointing in the direction of proportional representation.

The clearest pointer to a desire to move beyond a policy of 'wait and see' was the pledge to request regional chambers to put forward their own proposals, and the commitment to publish a Green or White Paper. But no timescale for action or firm promise to legislate was given, with the party committing itself only 'as soon as practicable, to move to directly elected regional government where and when there is a clear demand for it'. According to Liverpool MP Louise Ellmann, regional government is now 'an idea whose time has come' in the Labour party, though obstacles still remain.

LABOUR'S NATIONAL POLICY FORUM PROPOSAL ON REGIONAL GOVERNMENT

Despite devolution in Scotland and Wales, Britain remains the only large state in the EU with no comprehensive structure of regional government. We strongly believe that:

- decentralized government is better government;
- government power exercised at regional level should be responsive to the people of that region;
- regions need their own voice to get the best out of Europe;
- regions need effective coordination in order to promote economic development;
- democratic regional structures must be based on consent and develop at the pace most appropriate to each region;

- new powers assumed by regional government should principally be by devolution downwards from the centre.

Devolving power can not only provide greater autonomy and accountability at regional level, but also enable better strategic planning and joined-up policy delivery. Labour believes that regional governance should not be about more government but better government – and should be inclusive and extend democratic participation.

* * *

Labour recognizes the legitimate aspirations of the English regions and believes that the essential next step for those regions which wish to do so should be facilitated towards fully fledged, directly elected regional authorities which could help renew democracy, modernize the constitution and empower citizens.

Those with reservations about regional assemblies have stated that careful consideration will need to be given to ensuring that elected assemblies do not create additional tiers of bureaucracy; to the responsibilities, powers, size and type of assembly; to the appropriate test of public consent; to the type of voting system; and to the relationship between assemblies and the other democratic institutions, including local government and Westminster.

Labour intends, as soon as practicable, to move to directly elected regional government where and when there is a clear demand for it. The way forward will include proposals to:

- request that the existing regional assemblies and chambers, working closely with the regional partners, develop detailed proposals for elected assemblies in their respective regions;

- publish a government Green or White Paper on regional governance.

Development of regional governance structures should not result in adding a new tier of government to the English system and would require a move to a predominantly unitary system of local government, as presently exists in Scotland and Wales.

LOCAL GOVERNMENT AND ELECTED MAYORS

While progress towards regional assemblies has stalled, directly elected mayors have been the government's favoured alternative. Blair's idea was that instead of deadbeat local councillors, a wave of dynamic young managers rather like himself would usher in a wave of American-style city government. The Local Government Act 2000 was designed to

> ❝ But critics say the real problem of local government in many areas of England is prolonged one-party rule, for which the obvious cure, a dose of proportional representation instead of first-past-the-post, is not on offer. ❞

replace the 19th-century committee system in local government with a choice of different structures, including a cabinet system and a mayor. The hope is that this will not only make government better, but will break the cycle of apathy and low participation in local elections by arousing public interest. But critics say the real problem of local government in many areas of England is prolonged one-party rule, for which the obvious cure, a dose of proportional representation instead of first-past-the-post, is not on offer. John Prescott, the man in charge for local government, is the cabinet's leading opponent of PR and of the Liberal Democrats, who are its strongest supporters.

Tony Wright MP believes local electoral reform 'is still a real no-go area inside the Labour party because it is too unsettling to things as they are'. This is an area where he believes party policy will have to change eventually. However, a precedent has been set with the use of the additional member system to elect the Greater London Assembly, and the Labour-Liberal Democrat coalition in Scotland is pledged to introduce a proportional system of voting for local government there, despite a rearguard action from Labour's central belt strongholds. Similar moves towards PR in local government are likely in Wales under a Labour-Liberal Democrat coalition. But electoral experts say PR is not a panacea for the ills of local government; whatever its structure and however it is elected, it is bound to remain weak and unloved as long as it controls a mere fraction of its own finances, relying on council tax for only £10 billion out of a UK annual total of approximately £75 billion in spending. This will be the case even in London, where there is a mismatch between the mayor's huge mandate and his minimal level of powers.

As Professor Paul Peterson of Harvard University pointed out in a lecture to the Public Management Association in London in March 2000, what the government has created is a pale shadow of the mayoral system in big US cities, which raise around 80 per cent of their own funding and are forced to be financially responsible, not by central government but by the bond market. According to Peterson, the only mayoralty in the United States which resembles the model being adopted in London is that of Washington D.C., which became a byword for incompetence under mayor Marion Barry and is still heavily dependent on cash handouts and supervision from central government.

THE GREATER LONDON AUTHORITY

The mayor and assembly are elected for four years. Specific powers cover transport, planning, economic development, police, fire and emergency planning, environment and culture. Other powers such as education remain with the London boroughs. The mayor sets the budget and makes strategic decisions but can be overruled by a two-thirds majority in the assembly.

THE LONDON ELECTIONS FOR MAYOR AND ASSEMBLY

The turnout on 4 May 2000 was 34 per cent. Under the SV system, second preference votes for the top two candidates were added to ensure the winning candidate got more than 50 per cent of the vote.

Name	Party	1st Pref	%	2nd Pref	%	Final
Ken Livingstone	Independent	667,877	39.0	178,809	12.6	776,427
Steven Norris	Conservative	464,434	27.1	188,041	13.2	564,137
Frank Dobson	Labour	223,884	13.1	228,095	16.0	
Susan Kramer	Liberal Democrat	203,452	11.9	404,815	28.5	

The assembly has 25 members, 14 elected from constituencies and topped up by 11 London-wide members. Under the AMS system, each voter could vote twice.

Party	Constituency seats	List seats	Total
Conservative	8	1	9
Labour	6	3	9
Liberal Democrat	–	4	4
Green	–	3	3

LOCAL GOVERNMENT REFORM UNDER LABOUR

The 1999 Local Government Act sets out performance standards and targets for 'best value' to replace compulsory competitive tendering; it sets rules for inspections, audits and Whitehall supervision, and for control of Council Tax.

The 2000 Local Government Act gives local authorities a general power to promote the well-being of their communities. It allows councils to move to new constitutions based on mayors or cabinets, sets ethical standards and rules for referendums. Councils will be obliged to ensure that copies of their constitution are available to the public.

A LONDON NATIONALIST

Directly elected mayors have turned out to be a risky venture for Labour, as demonstrated by the party's disastrous defeat at the hands of Ken Livingstone in London in May 2000. Nowhere in the government's long catalogue of constitutional reforms has there been such a dramatic example of the Labour party scoring an own goal. If Blair and his team had anticipated the possibility of Livingstone running and winning as an independent, they might have treated the search for a suitable Labour candidate with greater urgency. When Health Secretary Frank Dobson finally joined the race barely six months before the vote, after earlier proclaiming his lack of interest in the job, it looked as though he had given in to Downing Street pressure. Livingstone, standing as an independent, humiliated the official candidate after losing the Labour nomination in an electoral college deliberately designed to deprive him of victory. Ordinary party members and trade unions made him their first choice, while MPs, MEPs and assembly candidates mostly voted for his rival. Dobson won the same sort of tainted victory as Alun Michael did in Wales, but to his credit was genuinely embarrassed by the way the contest had been conducted. The result was what Austin Mitchell MP described as 'a heartrending mess' and 'our worst cock-up since *In Place of Strife*'.[13]

Blair had dithered for months about finding a suitable 'Stop Livingstone' candidate as the former Greater London Council (GLC) leader began his campaign. By the time Livingstone decided to run as an independent and was expelled from the party, he held an unassailable lead over all other candidates. Blair told voters Livingstone would return the capital to the far-left policies of the 1980s' GLC, but his warnings fell on deaf ears. Livingstone won comfortably under the supplementary vote system, with Dobson trailing in third place behind Conservative candidate Steven Norris, and only just ahead of the Liberal Democrat Susan Kramer.

Livingstone's victory was full of ironies. Not only had the Labour party contrived to lose an election it should easily have won, having swept 49.5 per cent of the general election vote in London, it had lost to a

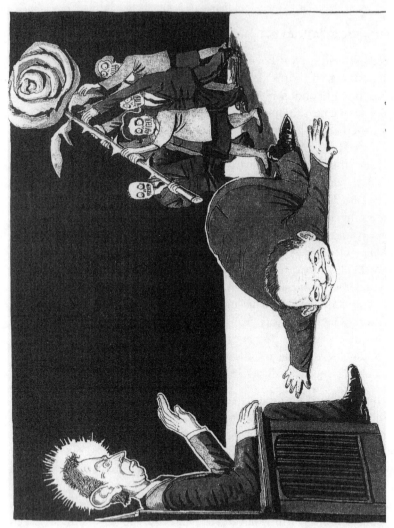

Ken Livingstone prostrates himself before Tony Blair to stay in the race to become official Labour candidate for London mayor. After losing narrowly to Frank Dobson, Livingstone denounced the result as a fix, stood as an independent and won by a wide margin. Dobson came a poor third. Copyright © Steve Bell, 1999.

candidate who used its own methods against it. The new business-friendly Livingstone ran on a positively Blairite 'third way' platform stripped of ideology, opening up a Big Tent for all residents of the capital from tycoons to Trotskyites; essentially his victory was that of an underdog London nationalist campaigning for the capital city against central government. His triumph was a personal defeat for Blair, whose entire career in the party was founded on driving a stake through the heart of the 1980s 'loony leftism' that had made Labour unelectable. If Blair had not created the very job that was tailormade for his talents, Livingstone would have continued to moulder away on the government backbenches as the MP for Brent East, a marginalized figure. For Livingstone to be proved eminently electable after all overturned not only one of the central tenets of New Labour belief but a much older truth of British politics, which is that nobody can defy the party machine and win. Livingstone managed it by turning the black arts of New Labour against it. As Andrew Rawnsley summed it up: 'There is nothing more disorienting for a politician than being thrashed at his own game.'[14]

> ❝ Essentially his victory was that of an underdog London nationalist campaigning for the capital city against central government. ❞

WHY BLAIR VOTED FOR MAYORS

Matthew Taylor of the IPPR told me his explanation for why Blair added directly elected mayors to the constitutional agenda he inherited from John Smith:

I think where it came from was desperation over the state of Labour local government. It was driven, and still is driven, by the need to improve the talent and quality of decision making in local government. So I think the commitment to mayors was in a sense a negative reaction. There has always been in New Labour a pretty profound disdain for local government, for the current quality of local government. Part of that is rooted in the fact that throughout the 1980s the Conservatives were able to get quick wins out of loony leftism and all that stuff. So Labour's message on local government couldn't be hostile to local government because that is a big constituency for Labour, especially among activists, but on the other hand they couldn't just say, we are giving more money to it, it had to be a modernizing and reforming agenda.

Taylor says Labour saw devolution for Scotland and Wales in terms of cooperation with the Liberal Democrats and the pursuit of a more consensual, progressive majority – hence the introduction of proportional representation. But in local government, its motivation was quite different, producing the 'winner-takes-all' mayoral system:

Local government has always been about service delivery. Labour doesn't see local government as being a constitutional issue. It sees it as being a public service modernization issue. Which I think is a mistake, to be honest.

Taylor sees a conflict between Labour's 'radical decentralizing agenda' for Scotland and Wales and the 'dirigiste centralizing agenda' on public services. He believes Blair's advisers are well aware of this contradiction, but believe local government has to reform before it can be granted wider powers. 'What is driving them round the bend is that nobody would want to give local authorities power now because they are seen as being so second rate.' The result is over-centralization and a prescriptive approach. He says it is 'absolutely mad' for the Department of Education in Whitehall to overrule head teachers by telling them how to allocate teacher resources in their schools and which classes should be over or under 30.

Taylor, in an IPPR paper written in 1999,[15] argues: 'With the benefit of hindsight it is clear that the promises in Labour's manifesto would require the centralization of power over public services.' But the party's approach was based on 'pragmatism and opportunism rather than any deeply embedded ideological conviction'. He points out that the Conservatives, who under Thatcher took away most of the powers of local government, are now promising to restore them. By promising to cut class sizes and hospital waiting lists, and end 'postcode rationing' in the NHS, Labour made centralization inevitable. Because of adverse publicity over leftwing councils in the 1980s, continuing problems with corruption and conflict in local government, and huge variations in service quality, the party's leaders were 'deeply sceptical about the virtues of democratic decentralization'. This shows up in the government's 1999 'Modernising Government' White Paper, which says nothing about decentralization, dispersing decision making to local communities or frontline managers. 'New Labour's agenda is about making local government more effective, not about making councils more powerful or more autonomous,' says Taylor.

Local Education Authorities are now increasingly being bypassed as a channel for funding schools in a campaign to 'cut out the middle man', a trend which has infuriated many in local government. Local

Government Association chairman Sir Jeremy Beecham has warned the government that '40,000 schools across the length and breadth of England and Wales cannot be run from Whitehall'. According to Peter Smith (Lord Smith of Leigh), leader of Wigan Metropolitan Borough Council and a leading figure in the campaign for an elected assembly in the North West, there is 'increased prescription' by Whitehall towards local authorities, telling them not just what they are supposed to do but how. 'The price is a loss of local innovation, questionable efficiency, and increased public perception that local government is merely local administration.'[16] The government has set up Education Action Zones, Health Action Zones and Employment Zones, where it can test out its ideas without council interference, but as *Reaching Out*, a Cabinet Office report, reported in February 2000, the results have often been chaotic.

Taylor detects the growth of a 'regulatory state' to enforce 'best practice' in health and education, reducing scope for local variations. Government increasingly sets performance targets monitored by the Treasury and releases 'money for modernization'. In the long run there will be greater freedom for those who modernize successfully, but in the short term the lines of control are to be tightened. 'Thus far, New Labour, unlike the old left or the new right, lacks a theory of government,' Taylor argues, seeing a contradiction in the short-term embrace of centralization as a necessary evil. 'When the government says, as in the case of education, that its initial centralization will create a framework for subsequently handing back freedoms and responsibilities, it is likely to face a problem of credibility.' Another drawback is that risk taking and innovation may be penalized if there is an overriding fear of failure to meet targets.

If Matthew Taylor's theory is correct, and the government sees devolution in England merely as part of its agenda of service delivery modernization, it is clear why it is so lukewarm about creating any alternative centres of power, whether in regional or local government. Peter Riddell of *The Times* says both Conservative and Labour governments have been equally incapable of reconciling localist rhetoric and centralist practice:

Blairite ministers, many of them former council leaders themselves, have been impatient with local authorities. To achieve the improvements they want in public services, ministers are increasingly bypassing town and county halls to run new initiatives from the centre. We have seen a proliferation of centrally appointed zones for education, employment, health and so on, and the direct payment of money to headteachers for books and equipment. This is partly to ensure that the

Blair government gets the political and electoral credit. Local councils have already lost control over water, ambulances, the old polytechnics and further education, and could lose control over most of school funding, care of the elderly, possibly housing benefit and council housing (to voluntary housing associations).[17]

WEST LOTHIAN AND WESTMINSTER

The government's fudging of the English question has tended to obscure the effects of devolution on Westminster. For the time being, Labour's huge majority of around 180 has enabled it to play for time, but the transfer of power to Edinburgh means the way the Commons works can never quite be the same again. One question has already been settled and seems unlikely to be reopened: there will be a cut in the number of Scottish MPs from 72 to 58, to bring the average size of constituency to the same level as England. This change has been written into the Scotland Act, but because of the delay in the work of the Boundary Commission it will not take place for another parliament.

Because the National Assembly for Wales has no primary legislative powers, the issue of the role and numbers of Welsh MPs does not arise in the same way. If the Assembly does eventually gain primary legislative powers, there would be a case for cutting the number of Welsh constituencies from 40 to 33.

What remains is the tangle of issues generally known as the 'West Lothian question'. Now that areas such as health and education are the business of the Scottish Parliament, why should Scottish MPs be able to vote on education and health policy for England? Their English counterparts have no equivalent right to vote on health and education in Scotland. This has led to a Conservative campaign for 'English votes on English laws', outlined by William Hague in a speech to the Centre for Policy Studies on 15 July 1999. This speech committed the Conservatives to accept devolution for Scotland and Wales but said the people of England were now the losers in a political system which was 'manifestly unfair' to them:

We now have a situation where the MPs for Stirling and Banff vote on schools, hospitals, transport and policing in Sheffield and Bournemouth but cannot vote on those issues in their own constituencies; nor, of course, can the MPs for Sheffield and Bournemouth have a say over these things in Stirling or Banff.

❝ What would happen if a government that relied on Scottish MPs for its Commons majority decided to impose a deeply unpopular education or transport law in England? ❞

Hague described this as a 'ticking time-bomb under the British constitution'. What would happen if a government that relied on Scottish MPs for its Commons majority decided to impose a deeply unpopular education or transport law in England? The danger would be an upsurge of English nationalism without a legitimate political outlet. Hague's solution was to dismiss the alternative of English regional assemblies, which he described as 'an expensive exercise in fantasy politics'. He also said he was 'unpersuaded' of the case for an English parliament because it would overshadow Westminster and provide a focus for English nationalism, though he hedged his bets by calling the argument 'wholly respectable'. Instead, he called for 'English votes on English laws', a solution under which the Speaker would designate bills affecting England only and Scottish MPs would not vote.

A more detailed proposal was set out in a report to Hague in July 2000 by a commission on parliamentary reform headed by the Conservative political scientist Professor Philip Norton (Lord Norton of Louth). This recommended that Bills affecting only England, or England and Wales, should be considered by a committee of all 529 English MPs at which Scottish MPs would have the right to speak but not to vote. At third reading, the final stage, all MPs would have the right to vote but Scottish MPs would by convention not take part.[18]

If implemented in a situation where Labour formed a government with a small overall majority but the Conservatives held a majority of English seats, this would effectively make cabinet government unworkable, unless some sort of new convention was agreed. This might create a problem far worse than the original anomaly, and constitutional experts mostly take the view that when considered alongside all the other anomalies in the British constitution, the issue has been overdramatized. Professor Bogdanor told a House of Commons committee the West Lothian question was 'a non-problem', referring to other countries in Europe with asymmetrical devolution. Professor Brendan O'Leary also makes the point that the problem occurs elsewhere:

If you have asymmetrical autonomy under a federal or a unitary state you will always have the equivalent of West Lothian questions. When some regions have more powers than others it means you have an issue of what you do with members of parliament at the centre who have in principle the same voting rights as any other. This problem has arisen in Spain, it arises in countries like Finland where the Åland islands have their own separate statute of autonomy, an MP voting on all-Finnish questions even though Finnish MPs can't vote on Åland island questions.

The intelligent way for Labour to handle this is to say, yes, there is a West Lothian question, but it arises because the English have chosen not to create their own parliament or not to create their own regional assemblies. Now of course Labour occasionally says something like this but then puts formidable obstacles in the path of anybody wanting to create English regions or an English parliament.

The Liberal Democrats also believe that the question will eventually find an answer in regional government. Don Foster says: 'There isn't an answer to the West Lothian question. There doesn't need to be, it's a question that doesn't need answering.'

The government has dismissed the idea of 'English votes on English laws' out of hand; this is hardly surprising, given Labour's historic reliance on the votes of Scottish MPs at Westminster and the prominent role of Scots within the Cabinet. It has, however, announced the creation, or more precisely the revival, of a Standing Committee on Regional Affairs to look at English matters. Leader of the House of Commons Margaret Beckett told MPs on 11 April 2000 that the committee would have 13 members from English constituencies, with all other English members having the right to attend but not to vote:

The government recognize that, in the aftermath of devolution to Scotland and Wales, which is an issue that has been debated extensively in the House and has long been decided, there is a call for a forum specifically for members who sit for English constituencies. The government recognize the validity of such a call.

Conservatives described the proposal as a sop, with Sir George Young arguing that because it would be a standing committee rather than a select committee, the government would effectively set the agenda; crucially, the balance of members would reflect that of the Commons as a whole, rather than of English MPs alone.

HORSES FOR COURSES

Labour's devolution menu has so far produced a bewildering variety of institutional models and electoral systems, ranging from the 'consociational' power sharing of Northern Ireland, through the more-or-less inclusive Welsh model, to the more Westminster-style Scottish variant, and finally to the US-style winner-takes-all model of the London mayor. Almost all of these are elected by different systems, with varying degrees of proportionality. Although Labour's reluctance to be prescriptive and set out uniform models can be seen as a plus, there is a sense in which its ultra-pragmatic 'horses for courses' approach reflects an absence of clear priorities. No doubt there is a strong case for arguing that imposing a rigid uniform pattern on regional and local government would be worse, but often the solution chosen seems to reflect little more than the preferences of the minister in charge. It is a fair bet that if Robin Cook or Mo Mowlam rather than John Prescott had been put in charge of local government, we would by now have seen proposals to elect English local councillors by a proportional system, or at least a few pilot schemes.

Efforts to improve local government have been vigorously pursued, but the effects of Labour's changes are likely to be very limited without electoral reform and a real commitment to devolve power from London and give lower-level bodies real spending and tax-raising authority. Compared with other countries, there is a yawning political space outside central government, with little or nothing to fill it. Undoubtedly the close result of the Welsh referendum on devolution has made Labour even more cautious about trying the same kind of experiment in the English regions. This 'wait and see' policy over regional government has contrasted sharply with other areas of policy where Labour has shown no bashfulness in pushing ahead with pet projects such as the Millennium Dome without waiting for clearly demonstrated public demand. If Labour still believes there is a real 'democratic deficit' in the English regions, then there is no excuse for waiting for demand to emerge.

> ❝ If Labour still believes there is a real 'democratic deficit' in the English regions, then there is no excuse for waiting for demand to emerge. ❞

Tony Wright MP defends the 'horses for courses' approach Labour has adopted, arguing that different political structures have to be tried out to see how they work. Overall, however, he feels Labour has failed so far to get a grip on the 'English question':

England is the big unanswered question and we don't yet know how things are going to work out there. It is clear there is a vacuum and something has to happen in England. I suspect we will see some movement there. We know there is a mess in terms of trying to deliver all these programmes at a local and regional level because of the way in which you have got all these agencies operating. So yes, England is a difficulty, local government is a difficulty. There is the beginnings of some kind of approach coming: we are not prepared to give powers to local authorities as they are, but we are prepared to give more powers to reformed local authorities. This is an undeveloped approach so far, but it seems to be one that is coming through on a variety of fronts, which says when you have proved yourself, more power and more autonomy will come with that. That is not an entirely silly approach because even those of us who are prepared to sign up to the virtues of local democracy, which I am, should not confuse that with the existing structure of local government.

Regional government might not fully answer the 'English question' but it would be a start. So far Labour's thinking on the issue appears to have become heavily compartmentalized, with no real attempt to reverse the trend towards over-centralization in government. Trusting people more to take their own decisions without interfering is a hard lesson, and it is doubtful whether even after the disastrous election of the London mayor New Labour has really learnt it. The goals of shorter hospital waiting lists, better school exam results and fewer crimes all seem to demand greater centralization, not less. Every NHS bedpan that is dropped – at least in England – lands at the feet of central government, because no other accountable institution exists. Wright argues that centralization 'does produce a brute form of accountability, because there is nowhere else to point the finger at':

So decentralization is a way of diffusing responsibility, quite properly. If you seek to run everything from Whitehall, then I am afraid it is only Whitehall that can take the can. Everyone knows this. So this is why people say Blunkett's job is on the line if we don't deliver performance measures in schools. Similarly, we have got a national plan for health which is going to be delivered from the centre ... I think whatever you say about centralism, there is a kind of brute accountability that comes with it. You can't wriggle around and say, it wasn't me guv, because it *was* you.

ENGLAND THE LOSER?

It may take several years before England's real place in the devolution jigsaw becomes clear. A hung parliament in which the Liberal Democrats hold leverage, or a collapse of the Labour vote in its northern heartlands, could galvanize Blair's party into moving decisively on regional government. The House of Commons may become more and more a *de facto* English parliament, even if this is not decided formally. English identity may become more pronounced, as English people celebrate St George's Day and begin to follow the Scots and the Welsh in making the distinction between Britain and England, instead of using the words interchangeably.

None of this is inevitable and it is all hard to predict. In essence, devolution is a gamble not just for the UK but also for the Labour party, which shaped its plans partly for its own political ends, and now finds after the London experience that they can go spectacularly wrong. 'Labour, the party that fathered devolution, is now of all the parties potentially the least comfortable with what it has done,' says Ron Davies.[19]

Slowly but surely, the party may have to federalize itself to reflect the changing institutions it has created. The true test of the devolution legislation will come in a few years' time when governments of a different political colour are in power in Westminster, Edinburgh and Cardiff. That will be the moment to see whether Ron Davies is right in interpreting the creation of the National Assembly as a move of sovereignty to Wales, or whether Enoch Powell's maxim that 'power devolved is power retained' still holds good. In this sense all we have seen so far has been a test drive of the model around the factory circuit at half speed, rather than on the open road. But the early evidence is that wherever the devolution mystery tour ends up, politicians at Westminster are no longer fully in control.

NOTES

[1] Bogdanor, Vernon (1999) *Devolution in the United Kingdom*, Oxford University Press.

[2] Bogdanor, 1999, p 79.

[3] Bogdanor, 1999, p 101.

[4] See Hickman, Mary (2000) 'A new England through Irish eyes?' in *The English Question*, London, Fabian Society.

[5] Tomaney, John and Mitchell, Michelle (1999) *Empowering the English Regions*, London, Charter88.

[6] Wright, Tony (2000) England, whose England? in *The English Question*, London, Fabian Society.

[7] Brightly, David (1999) *State and Region: the Spanish experience*, London, Royal Institute of International Affairs Briefing Paper No. 3, June.

[8] Mitchell, Austin (2000) 'A manifesto for the North' in *The English Question*, London, Fabian Society.

[9] McLean, Iain (2000) 'A fiscal constitution for the UK' in *The English Question*, London, Fabian Society.

[10] 3 March 2000.

[11] *Guardian*, 28 September 2000.

[12] Tomaney, John (1999) 'New Labour and the English Question' in *The Political Quarterly*, Vol. 70 No. 1, Oxford, B.H. Blackwell, Jan–Mar.

[13] The title of the White Paper setting out the Wilson government's unsuccessful attempt in 1969 to reform the law affecting trade unions.

[14] Rawnsley, Andrew (2000) *Servants of the People*, London, Hamish Hamilton, p 368.

[15] Taylor, Matthew with Joseph, Ella (1999) *Freedom for Modernisation. Combining Central Targets with Local Autonomy*, London, Institute for Public Policy Research research paper.

[16] *Local Government First* (LGA newsletter), March 2000.

[17] *The Times*, 21 August 2000.

[18] Norton, Philip (2000) *Strengthening Parliament. The Report of the Commission to Strengthen Parliament*, p 53.

[19] Constitution Unit seminar, 3 July 2000.

Raising the flag: Labour Party activists are invited inside the gates of Downing Street and issued with union jacks to welcome Tony Blair on 2 May 1997, the day after the general election

REUTERS: DAN CHUNG

The John Smith legacy: Tony Blair outlines Labour's constitutional reform plans in his John Smith memorial lecture on 7 February 1996. At this point he had been Labour Party leader for nearly two years and the general election was looming

REUTERS: SIMON KREITEM

Timely arrival: Donald Dewar, the father of the nation, outside the Scottish Parliament in Edinburgh before being voted in as First Minister on 13 May 1999

REUTERS: JEFF J. MITCHELL

The new Welsh team: Rhodri Morgan (L), Alun Michael's successor as first secretary of the National Assembly for Wales, celebrates Welsh night at the Labour conference in Brighton on 27 September 2000. Secretary of State for Wales Paul Murphy flanks Blair on the other side

The Council of the Isles: The British–Irish Council including the devolved institutions holds its first meeting at Lancaster House in London on 17 December 1999. Pictured (L to R) are Senator Pierre Horsfall of Jersey; Irish Taoiseach Bertie Ahern; Northern Ireland's First Minister David Trimble and his deputy Seamus Mallon; First Secretary of the National Assembly for Wales Alun Michael; Scotland's First Minister Donald Dewar; and Tony Blair. The forum effectively puts the prime minister of the UK in the position representing England

Blair's nightmare returns: Ken Livingstone, the man Tony Blair vainly tried to stop, mounts the stage to be declared the winner of the London Mayoral Election on 5 May 2000. Livingstone ran as an independent after narrowly losing the Labour nomination in an internal election which he denounced as a fix. Labour's official candidate, Frank Dobson, came a poor third

REUTERS: DYLAN MARTINEZ

Tony's cronies: Demonstrators from the constitutional reform campaign Charter88 protest outside the House of Lords on 20 January 2000, the day the Wakeham Report on the Second Chamber was published. In line with its mandate from Prime Minister Tony Blair, it recommended a largely appointed membership which critics said would preserve the patronage powers of 10 Downing Street

CHARTER88

Pushing the "project": Tony Blair, Robin Cook and Paddy Ashdown at the first meeting in the Cabinet Room of 10 Downing Street of a joint consultative committee with the Liberal Democrats on constitutional reform. The committee fizzled out after Ashdown resigned as party leader and was replaced by the more sceptical Charles Kennedy

REUTERS: IAN WALDIE

5

THE HOUSE OF PLOTS

'*Lords reform has been a disaster*' – Tony Wright MP

'*If there had been an easy answer, someone would have found it long ago*' – Lord Wakeham

'*Unlike almost every other country, we have no vote over the head of state. We have no vote over the second chamber. If my right hon. friend the Prime Minister reintroduces Edward I's method of appointing peers – when peers began in 1295, they were not hereditary – we will be modernizing ourselves back to the feudal period*' – Tony Benn MP

'*I don't want to say a word against brains – I've a great respect for brains, I often wish I had some myself – but with a House of Peers composed exclusively of people of intellect, what's to become of the House of Commons?*' – The Earl of Mountararat in *Iolanthe*

COMETH THE HOUR, COMETH THE MAN. The 26th of October 1999 was the day for which Francis Topham de Vere Beauclerk, Earl of Burford and heir to the 14th Duke of St Albans, had been waiting. It was the final stage of the government's campaign to deprive hereditary peers of their right to sit and vote in the House of Lords. Within a few hours, the Lords themselves would bow the knee to the inevitable and give a third and last reading to the Bill expelling the hereditaries by 221 votes to 81.

From the packed press gallery overlooking the red leather benches I saw a sudden disturbance at the far end of the chamber, just to the right of the throne. The 34-year-old bearded aristocrat jumped on to the Woolsack and secured his place in history. 'My Lords, this Bill drafted in Brussels is treason! What we are witnessing is the abolition of Britain!' The earl, who as the heir to a peerage was not a member of the Lords himself, was quickly bundled outside and the incident was over in a few seconds. He explained to journalists that Tony Blair was part of a world-wide conspiracy to abolish Britain and absorb it into a European super-state. Two days later, Blair repaid the compliment in the Commons, saying he hoped everybody in the country had witnessed the earl's actions. 'They show exactly why we were right to pursue this policy. We should never expect the Tories to be ready for the 21st century, but I thought at least they might have left the 17th!' he declared.

> If Blair had wanted a dotty hereditary peer from central casting to illustrate the case for removing them from parliament, then the Earl of Burford fitted the bill perfectly.

If Blair had wanted a dotty hereditary peer from central casting to illustrate the case for removing them from parliament, then the Earl of Burford fitted the bill perfectly. Not only was he in Labour eyes a rightwing conspiracy theorist, but the title he would inherit was originally awarded to the illegitimate son of Charles II and his mistress Nell Gwyn. With such unmodernized relics of the past on display, what could more clearly illustrate the Labour government's case for reforming the second chamber?

THE STAINS OF BLUE BLOOD

When climbing the red-carpeted stairs to the Lords press gallery, I am always tempted to hum the lines from *Iolanthe* in which Earl Tolloller defends the peerage:

> Spurn not the nobly born
> With love affected,
> Nor treat with virtuous scorn
> The well-connected.
> High rank involves no shame –
> We boast an equal claim
> With him of humble name
> To be respected!
> Blue Blood! Blue Blood!

After the dreariness of most Commons debates, the Lords offers a feast of under-appreciated theatrical treasures just waiting for Sullivan to set them to music. There is an unrivalled cast of characters, headed by the bewigged Lord Chancellor, the Pooh-Bah of Tony Blair's government, Derry Irvine. Gilbert and Sullivan are not quite the cultural icons of New Labour, but one can easily imagine how they would have relished moving on from *Iolanthe* to turn the story of Irvine's expensive Victorian wallpaper into another successful comic opera.

One of my favourite moments was in November 1998 when I watched Irvine emerge victorious in a battle over his reluctance to wear wig and black tights, overcoming a rearguard action by Conservative peers who opposed his desire to slip into something more comfortable for routine debates. The 13th Earl Ferrers (recreations: shooting, music, travel; clubs: Beefsteak) moved an amendment to block the change, saying the switch from tights and breeches to trousers would be a 'retrograde step'. What would happen, asked the former Coldstream Guards officer, if guardsmen declined to parade in their bearskins on the grounds that they were uncomfortable and out of date like the Lord Chancellor's horsehair wig? Eventually, warned that they risked making themselves a laughing stock, the peers approved the sartorial change by 145 votes to 115.

> ❝ As Bagehot observed, the best cure for admiring the House of Lords is to go and watch it in action. ❞

As Bagehot observed, the best cure for admiring the House of Lords is to go and watch it in action. But his dismissal of it is deeply misleading. Things in the Lords are rarely exactly what they seem. Earl Ferrers, despite his old-bufferish manner, is among the cleverest and best respected of Conservative peers, topping the ballot among fellow hereditaries in November 1999 when they chose who would escape expulsion.

Behind the Savoy opera of Lords reform since 1997 a real political and constitutional drama has been unfolding, the outcome of which is still uncertain. If the plot has on occasion seemed hard for outsiders to follow, those at the centre have sometimes been equally out of the loop. The chief scriptwriter in 10 Downing Street, unable to decide how the story should end, has thrown away his revisions more than once in order to start with a blank sheet of paper. So far there have been several dramatic highpoints, such as the day when several hundred hereditary peers found themselves written out of the script in November 1999. They left the neo-Gothic backdrop of the Palace of Westminster, clutching their possessions in cardboard boxes in what the Downing Street producers had described as stage one of modernization.

TORY OR WHIG

As we shall see in Chapter 11, the real debate over Westminster government is not so much over its failure to be 'modern' as over the respective powers of executive and legislature – whether the two chambers of parliament can hope to influence or make accountable the government of the day. Behind the sound and fury of its attacks on the evils of the hereditary peerage, Labour has executed a neat 180-degree turn away from the radical-sounding language of its time in opposition towards maintaining the untrammelled power of the executive – the 'elective dictatorship' which Lord Hailsham denounced. Douglas Hurd (Lord Hurd of Westwell) describes the traditional argument as follows:

Parliament in this country has to embody both the Whig and the Tory concepts of government. The Tory concept is that the Queen's government has to be carried on. And what most people want in the traditional Tory view is an efficient government, a government that can do things, a Peel-type government or a Thatcher-type government which can get on with doing things. They don't want a government which is completely hamstrung, like an Italian government, with endless committees and bureaucracies and procedures. The Whig theory, which also has to be accommodated, is that you have got to control the government, otherwise the government becomes Stuart and exceeds the proper place of the prerogative.

I asked the former Conservative minister where he would put Tony Blair between the Whigs and the Tories:

I think on Mondays, Wednesdays and Fridays he is one and on Tuesdays, Thursdays and Saturdays he is the other. I don't think he really sits down … He is interested in ideas, but I think he has both elements in him. And obviously when you are actually prime minister the tendency is to get on with things.

Blair's problems over the Lords have stemmed from this basic indecision; the only way he has found to modernize it while keeping it too weak to challenge the executive has been to turn his party's original policy of creating a democratically elected upper house on its head and seek an appointed chamber instead. In the view of Labour MP Tony Wright, the result so far has been a total disaster: 'We haven't really known what we wanted. We've known what we've not wanted, at least what some people have not wanted. They haven't wanted an elected second chamber. But they haven't known what they have wanted.'

To date the battle over the future of the Lords has proved a severe test for all three major parties, and a final settlement is not in sight. The political casualties have included the Labour and Conservative leaders in the upper house, Ivor Richard and Robert Cranborne, both of whom were sacked after falling out with their party leaders. It has been a game of bluff and counter-bluff, in which Labour's uncertainty about the final goal of its reform has forced it into tactical retreats. Blair's party, which as recently as the mid-1990s advocated a directly elected House of Lords, has now embraced the Orwellian argument that asking the voters to pick the upper house would undermine democracy. By the time of the Wakeham report in early 2000, Labour had become the least enthusiastic of the three major parties about direct elections.

As we shall discover, there is no great mystery about this transformation. A close analysis of Blair's evolving policy on the Lords shows a move away from the idea of *democratizing* the upper house to the more ambiguous goal of *modernizing* it. *Modernization* in New Labour language has nothing to do with accountability or democracy. Nor does it mean systematically replacing the old with the new. Instead it means clearing obstacles out of the path of the executive, enabling it to concentrate on delivery of its manifesto policies. This is no far-fetched interpretation of party policy; it was laid down in so many words by Margaret Beckett in a speech at the Labour party conference in Brighton in September 2000.

INFLUENCE WITHOUT POWER

This is the point to stand back from the political battlefield and look at the Lords as an institution. What is its part in Britain's unwritten constitution and what was Labour trying to achieve in reforming it? John Wells' entertaining anecdotal history of the House of Lords quotes the words of 82-year-old Lord Esher in a debate in 1963:

Because it is obvious that the House of Lords has influence without power, it is accepted by everybody who has ever examined the question, and tried to consider how to replace it, as the best second chamber in the world. We are fortunate to have an institution which we should never have had the intelligence to create.

With its origins in the early Middle Ages or even earlier, the House of Lords predates the Commons and did not lose its role as the pre-eminent chamber until well into the 19th century. Despite a brief eclipse under Cromwell, its prestige and power continued until the Victorian reform era, largely because of the influence that peers wielded over elections to the Commons. From the Great Reform Bill of 1832, the Commons not only retained its traditional power over finance but supplanted the upper house as the franchise was gradually widened. Only the extraordinary neo-Gothic grandeur of the current Lords chamber in which the state opening of parliament takes place reminds us of the upper house's past power. During the Queen's Speech, the prime minister – who writes it – and his Commons colleagues have to stand at the back of the chamber, pressed together as if queuing for Wimbledon tickets, while the peers are seated in their red robes trimmed with ermine. For the architect of the rebuilt Palace of Westminster, Sir Charles Barry, and even more for his Gothicizing designer Augustus Welby Pugin, the Lords chamber was far more than a place of business. As Charles Barry (son of Sir Charles) described it, Pugin visualized it as 'the Chamber in which the Sovereign, surrounded by the Court, summoned to the Royal presence the three estates of the realm.'[1]

What changed the House of Lords as a political institution and reduced its power from 1832 was not so much deliberate reform as the rise of mass democracy, which left it marginalized and incapable of using the powers it theoretically possessed. Only in 1911 were its powers limited by statute, the price the peers paid for violating convention and throwing out Lloyd George's tax-raising 'People's Budget' in 1909. Under the Parliament Act the Lords formally lost their power over taxation and spending in any measure certified by the Commons Speaker as a 'money bill'. The power to stop other legislation became the power to delay for a maximum period of two parliamentary sessions. The only exception on which the Lords retained a veto was over Bills to prolong the life of a parliament. The Parliament Act said in a preamble: 'It is intended to substitute for the House of Lords as presently constituted a second chamber constituted on a popular instead of a hereditary basis.'

The two-year delay was cut to one year in 1949 under the post-war Labour government, which saw the formalization of what became known as the 'Salisbury convention'. Named after Cranborne's grandfather, the Marquess of Salisbury, an earlier member of the Cecil dynasty, this convention obliges the Lords not to block Bills implementing election manifesto commitments. Though its origins can be traced back to the 19th century, the convention was dreamed up largely to enable the Attlee government to put through its nationalization plans despite an overwhelming Conservative majority in the Lords.

Both the Parliament Acts and the Salisbury convention can be said to have made the Lords weaker, although the other big reform of the mid-century, the creation of life peers, undoubtedly strengthened the upper house in its composition and reversed its slow decline. In 1958 the Macmillan Conservative government extended the idea of peerages for life, invented in the 19th century to give senior judges membership of the upper house. Instead of hereditary peerages, the creation of which had slowed to a trickle, there entered the chamber a constant flow of life peers, dubbed 'day boys' by the hereditaries, who saw themselves as 'boarders'. For the first time, women became eligible for membership as well, and it also became usual for the prime minister of the day to spread his power of patronage around the opposition parties. By January 1999 there were just over 500 life peers, still outnumbered by more than 600 hereditaries.

For historical reasons, Conservatives have always had a huge majority, though independent cross-benchers have made up the second largest group. As well as the Law Lords, who sit *ex officio* but retain their seats when they retire, there are 26 Anglican bishops who leave and are replaced when they take their pensions. As the government's 1999 White Paper pointed out, the Conservatives' strength in the Lords before the removal of the hereditaries was 66 per cent, almost double their 1997 general election share of 34 per cent of the popular vote. The arrival of the life peers, many of them part-timers with eminent careers elsewhere, reinforced the Lords' reputation as a revising chamber whose scrutiny of legislation was often superior to that of the Commons. Manners in the Lords chamber, which is self-regulating, are much superior to those in the Commons, and debates are often of a higher intellectual quality. Donnish speakers such as the historian Conrad Russell (Earl Russell), who would never survive in the rough and tumble of the Commons, come into their element in the Lords. In the words of the veteran Labour peer Lord Longford, the Lords has 'good manners, civilized style and inherent decency' – a seductive combination of a gentleman's club and an Oxbridge senior common room. It is the very popularity of the club lifestyle and the lure of a title rather than any financial reward that makes the award of a peerage so desirable. 'Speaking for myself, I have not found that being a Lord lost one friends,' says Lord Longford in his history of the Lords, without a trace of irony.

The real strengths of the Lords emerge not so much in the chamber but in committee rooms overlooking the Thames, where peers often seem to make a more thorough job of their investigations than the Commons. This is particularly true in European affairs and in science and technology. But there is a real question whether any of this intellectual firepower hits a useful target. A recently created Labour life peer, David Lipsey, says it is true that Lords debates are often very good and much better informed than in the Commons:

But to absolutely no purpose. Nobody is listening to this, it is just a dialogue between them … I think there is a genuine expertise, but it is exercised to too little purpose. The trouble is, apart from those who have retired, most of the experts would spend their time more fruitfully applying their expertise in other ways. Given how rarely it is that the government accepts amendments here, I don't think it is a very good use of good quality people's time.

There is little reason to quarrel with Professor Vernon Bogdanor's assessment of the British parliament as a disguised unicameral system, with the Lords as an appendix to the body politic.

THE SOMALI WAY

The hereditary basis of the House of Lords links Britain to its pre-modern history and divides it from other modern democracies; for a foreign equivalent one has to look not to France or Germany but to African tribal or clan-based societies, as Irish political scientist Professor Brendan O'Leary discovered to his amusement when he was called in to help constitutional reconstruction in Somalia:

All the people who were not British – I was silent – were saying, we can't possibly have a second chamber built around a House of Elders. It's entirely inconsistent with democracy. So I just had a moment of joy. I said: 'We know this is the Somali system of operating. If we don't have a role for the elders, these proposals will go nowhere. And we do have an example of a functioning democracy where we do have a House of Elders, and it's the House of Lords in the United Kingdom.' And everybody smiled and the Somalis recognized it for themselves and that was fine.

While unique in its size and its hereditary composition, the House of Lords has enough in common with other second chambers abroad for comparisons to be made – as Meg Russell of London University's Constitution Unit points out, other chambers have also wrestled with the lack of legitimacy caused by being appointed rather than elected. Blatant political patronage has made Canada's Senate particularly unpopular, while the Irish Senate is full of 'young politicians on the way up, old politicians on the way down, or mid-level politicians whose careers have received a temporary setback'.[2] More successful foreign examples, such as West Germany's Bundesrat, are inconceivable outside a fully federal system. Other countries which are not federal states, such as Spain, have also tried to use second chambers of parliament to bind the political structures created by regional and national devolution.

LABOUR AS A UNICAMERALIST PARTY

Because of the Lords' lack of legitimacy, reforming the upper house was not much of a priority for the Labour governments of the 1960s and 1970s. The Wilson government's attempt to remove the voting rights of hereditary peers won the assent of the Lords but was torpedoed in the Commons in 1968 by an alliance of backbench Conservative and Labour MPs hostile to the measure for different reasons.

Labour's position was essentially unicameralist, a policy formalized during its swing to the left after losing power in 1979. The 1983 'suicide note' manifesto committed the party to abolition of the Lords. By 1989, Neil Kinnock's policy review had changed this to an elected second chamber, a policy influenced by the role of the Lords as a thorn in the side of the Thatcher government. After the 1992 election defeat, Labour began to advocate a two-stage reform, with the removal of hereditary peers to be followed by a transition to a directly elected house. This was the policy which was approved under the label 'A New Agenda for Democracy' when Blair was shadow Home Secretary in 1993. 'Today, the executive is immensely powerful. Parliament is easily overwhelmed,' it proclaimed. Two years later, Blair's party conference speech as leader promised 'an end to hereditary peers sitting in the House of Lords as the first step to a proper, directly elected second chamber'. But a few months later, there were signs that the second element of this commitment was becoming vague. In his John Smith Memorial Lecture in February 1996, Blair simply said (somewhat inaccurately) that: 'We have always favoured an elected second chamber' and went on to note that some people, like Ivor Richard, had suggested there might also be room for 'people of a particularly distinguished position or record'.

Dismissing criticism that a chamber without hereditary peers would be just an unelected quango, Blair's comments indicated that a rethink was under way on the relative merits of election and appointment. 'Whatever the final balance between election and merit,' he said, there was a need to make the upper house 'a genuine body of the distinguished and meritorious'. There should be 'a more open and independent means of establishing membership' to be followed by a debate on 'how we incorporate democratic accountability'. By the time of the election manifesto, the drift away from the commitment to direct elections was nearly complete, masked by the radical language used about the removal of the hereditaries. Austin Mitchell MP summed up the thinking in opposition as follows:

> 66 By the time of the election manifesto, the drift away from the commitment to direct elections was nearly complete, masked by the radical language used about the removal of the hereditaries. 99

What could be more modern than to scrap hereditary privilege, and what could be easier than to modernize by mugging the easiest victim in the country, one very few would or could defend? This was the kind of fight New Labour liked.[3]

Richard, who was Labour leader in the Lords before and after the election, told me party policy in opposition was still essentially unicameral – 'a unicameral legislature with two chambers'. The House of Lords was seen as useful 'because it dots the i's and crosses the t's and is good at looking at the details of legislation'. Policy before the election had elements of ambiguity, he acknowledged:

It never actually said it would support a wholly elected House. The phrase we kept using in opposition was 'predominantly but not exclusively' elected. That was the phrase the Prime Minister used. Certainly that was the view I had. I thought the policy was very clear when we went into the election. The manifesto was a bit fuzzy round the edges; it talked of making the House more 'democratic' without actually saying that meant direct elections. So there were undoubtedly a number of people who didn't want a substantially elected element. The Chief Whip in opposition, Donald Dewar, was not in favour of an elected House, Margaret Beckett was not in favour of it. It was the old argument about the House of Commons being the predominant House, and wishing it to remain so.

LABOUR'S 1997 MANIFESTO COMMITMENT ON LORDS REFORM

The House of Lords must be reformed. As an initial, self-contained reform, not dependent on further reform in the future, the right of hereditary peers to sit and vote in the House of Lords will be ended by statute. This will be the first stage in a process of reform to make the House of Lords more democratic and representative. The legislative powers of the House of Lords will remain unaltered.

The system of appointment of life peers to the House of Lords will be reviewed. Our objective will be to ensure that over time party appointees as life peers more accurately reflect the proportion of votes cast at the previous general election. We are committed to maintaining an independent cross-bench presence of life peers. No one political party should seek a majority in the House of Lords. A committee of both Houses of Parliament will be appointed to undertake a wide-ranging review of possible further change and then to bring forward proposals for reform.

The word 'democratic' survived in qualified form along with 'representative' as a description of the ultimate reform goal, but it was seriously undermined by the commitment to control the overall balance of the membership. The vagueness over the ultimate end of reform did not prevent Labour reaching agreement with the Liberal Democrats before the election. Robert Maclennan recalled his discussions on the Lords with Robin Cook:

To be honest we had not really given it a great deal of thought. One of the things that the talks did was bring us round to the view that there was much merit in having it in two stages. We embraced that suggestion with some enthusiasm. I had witnessed earlier attempts to reform the House of Lords in the 1960s led by Dick Crossman come unstuck, largely because of confusion over what to do about the hereditaries, and the fact that the upper house as constituted really had no legitimacy to take part in a serious debate about what should replace it. So I thought it would simplify matters. One thing everybody was agreed on was that there was no place for hereditaries, so we could get that out of the way. Of course we had much more developed views than the Labour party about what should take its place. We believed firmly in the principle of election. On that issue the Labour party was less clear. We thought the two-stage approach would allow us to come further down the road than any other way that we could devise.

'Unfinished business' was the phrase on Labour lips when the party returned to power in 1997, but the phrase disguised the complexity of the task. What began as a plan for a neat appendectomy turned into something much more difficult, as Austin Mitchell describes:

Labour should have thought this through before proposing the abolition of the hereditaries. It didn't. Lingering folk-memories of the way Labour governments had been frustrated by the Lords, and the inferiority complex of opposition sustaining a fear that the same might happen again with a small majority, prompted action. Abolition of the last remaining class enemy offered a nicely radical touch to a manifesto otherwise cautious to the point of conservatism. It looked easy. It was modernizing. It wrongfooted the Tories, since the hereditary principle is impossible to defend. So no one thought beyond abolition.[4]

STAGE ONE

This set the scene for the early post-election skirmishes over 'stage one' and 'stage two'. Lords reform was left off the agenda for the first parliamentary session, though clear hints were dropped that the removal of the hereditaries would happen in 1998–99. According to Ivor Richard:

We then started trying to flesh the policy out. We had a cabinet committee. We decided not to do it in the first year, which was right. We were doing the two devolution Bills. I think to do the Lords as well would probably have been too big a chunk. We started trying to produce a White Paper.

The delay left room for more than a year of phoney war as both parties skirmished in public while putting out discreet feelers to each other behind the scenes. While both Labour and the Conservatives appeared united in public, there were strains beneath the surface on both sides. The best account so far of this period is that published by Janet Jones, Richard's wife.[5] Readers of this entertaining memoir will learn about the Richard family's epic struggles with errant Welsh sheep, collapsing central heating systems and failing schools in south London. But behind this innocent camouflage the core of the book is Richard's jaundiced diary-by-proxy of his frustrating year as a member of Tony Blair's cabinet, culminating in his sacking in July 1998.

Tony Blair was widely accused of putting the cart before the horse in expelling the hereditary peers before deciding on how to reform the House of Lords. Copyright © Daily Telegraph, 1998.

In a cabinet with virtually no experience of government, Richard stood out as an exception, having entered the Commons in 1964 as a QC and served under Harold Wilson and James Callaghan as Britain's ambassador to the United Nations from 1974 to 1979. From 1981 to 1985 he was a member of the European Commission in Brussels. His election by Labour peers as leader in the Lords dated from the time of John Smith, another veteran of the Callaghan era. Richard was a veteran of Labour's Old Right and was never part of Blair's close circle, as his wife's diary makes clear. Blair emerges from the book as a Hamlet-like figure who can never make up his mind, at least on the subject of the House of Lords, which is not one of his political priorities.

The pantomime villain of the story is the wallpaper-loving Derry Irvine, whom Richard clearly blames for his sacking. Irvine makes his first appearance before the 1997 election, having mortally offended the wife of Maurice Peston, a fellow Labour peer, at dinner in a restaurant. 'Apparently he was tired,' writes Jones The Diary. In the first week after the election, Irvine emerges – at least in his own estimation – as the Prime Minister's right-hand man. '... he can't go on as he is. He talked for an hour and a half.' A few weeks later Irvine is still chairing cabinet committees like a High Court judge and bullying his colleagues. 'You should have heard him at Donald Dewar today ... as if he were some junior barrister who had not read his brief.'

BLUFF AND COUNTER-BLUFF

Labour, because of its minority position in the Lords, was nervous that an all-out confrontation with the Conservatives could lead to filibustering and legislative chaos, threatening other government Bills. But the occasional tactical defeat at the hands of Conservative hereditary peers was welcome, as it proved the case for reform. Meanwhile, on the Conservative side, Cranborne was publicly threatening a guerrilla war unless Labour provided more details of its proposed stage two reform and a guarantee that the interim chamber, shorn of hereditary peers, would not end up being permanent. In fact, Cranborne was doing his best to restrict his side to occasional victories, not wanting to overplay his hand. Jones The Diary summed up the state of play after two months of Labour government:

Denis Carter and Tommy Strathclyde (the Labour and Conservative Chief Whips) are in cahoots. This suits everybody. The Tories are trying hard not to win. New

Labour doesn't want to win too much either. If the Tories win they draw attention to the fact that they should not be there. If New Labour win they lose the argument for reforming the Lords. Denis and Tommy are meeting and sharing out the unwanted victories in advance. 'I don't know how,' says Ivor, 'Tommy is stopping his people voting.'

This cooperative game of bluff and double bluff was aimed partly at the respective party leaderships on each side. William Hague was particularly tempted to use the Lords to inflict maximum disruption on Blair's legislative programme. As Cranborne confessed to Austin Mitchell:

The shadow cabinet suddenly discovers the only people who can cause trouble for the government are the Tories in the House of Lords. So they start trying to micro-manage you. They are peeved about the House of Lords. They're only thinking about tomorrow's political advantage and they don't realize that we have to think a little bit longer and how would it look if we managed to make an alliance with the cross-benchers, which is not difficult, and roll over the government about 40 times a week? It would not only devalue the currency, but the public, quite rightly, would be slightly irritated. So we've got to walk this tightrope here of not devaluing the currency but at the same time not letting your muscles atrophy because people are going to say, what's the point of it? So you have to box clever.[6]

In fact, as Cranborne freely admitted later, the Conservatives never had any intention of totally disrupting Labour's legislative programme; the idea was to inflict just enough defeats to make a deal of some kind involving the departure of the hereditary peers look attractive to the Labour cabinet. The doomed Conservative hereditaries were of course looking to Cranborne to protect their interests while shadow cabinet spokesmen in the Commons such as Dr Liam Fox were scorning the idea of 'dying in the ditch' for the right of unelected peers to stay in the Lords. Cranborne is widely credited with a talent for plotting, inherited from his famous ancestors. It is a reputation he does little to discourage. He may be a Dorset pig-breeder, but unlike most hereditary peers he does not spring from the world of Gilbert and Sullivan. A faintly exotic character with a taste for wearing bright red socks, his ruthless intelligence led William Rees-Mogg to compare him to Sherlock Holmes, with the amiable Strathclyde as his Dr Watson.

Labour too had its internal problems. Richard had to fend off attempts by Irvine to go behind his back to Blair with plans for a single-stage reform which would remove the hereditaries and leave the upper house as an entirely nominated chamber. In January 1998 the first of a series of secret meetings took place between the four front bench leaders – Cranborne and Richard, accompanied by Strathclyde and Carter. They met for lunch at Cranborne's house in Chelsea, and the first contact seemed promising. Both sides were thinking of a chamber that after the removal of the hereditaries would be two-thirds elected, one-third nominated. At a meeting in Downing Street on 3 February Blair agreed to this package deal, but other members of the cabinet committee on Lords reform, Peter Mandelson, Jack Straw and Commons Chief Whip Nick Brown, kept pressing for a nominated upper house. By March, news of the secret talks had leaked to the newspapers, a sign to Labour that Cranborne had been unable to win the agreement of his party leadership to the proposed deal. Blair told Richard to keep talking and 'flush out' the Tories. Richard drew the conclusion that Blair was not too worried what was in the agreement as long as there was one, but he started to get contradictory messages from Downing Street. Blair's obsession with tactics caused Carter to explode: 'Tactics! Tactics! All he thinks about are tactics! He's got no policy at all.' Richard began to find his task more and more difficult, complaining to Jones The Diary on 11 March: 'Blair's wobbling. I'm not getting clear messages. He seems to be changing his mind. And I'm negotiating with Cranborne with two hands tied behind my back – one is fighting my own people, the other has no policy.'

Minutes of the deadlocked cabinet committee began to be altered and Richard began to feel that Downing Street staffers were muddying the waters: 'The real problem is that Blair's constitutional adviser – Pat McFadden – doesn't want a reformed chamber. He just wants to get rid of the hereditaries … this does not look good for the future … if Blair insists on making all the decisions himself.' Finally, in early April, it was agreed that the negotiations with Cranborne had collapsed. In the next few weeks it became clear that Richard's plan for a two-thirds elected house was losing favour, although his plan for a royal commission rather than a joint committee of both houses – on which Labour would not have commanded a majority – survived. With no prospect of a deal with the Conservatives, by June Blair was suffering 'a distinct chilling of the feet' about pressing ahead with legislation in the November Queen's Speech. Told by Richard that the only possible deal with the Tories would be for a two-thirds elected house, Blair replied: 'We would have to think about that.' Blair finally sacked Richard in his first reshuffle at the end of July, replacing him with Margaret Jay, daughter of the former Labour Prime Minister Lord Callaghan, and a figure much closer to New Labour. In retrospect, it is clear that Richard's favoured solution of a two-thirds elected chamber was not what Blair wanted. As Cranborne told Austin Mitchell:

Poor Ivor Richard has proved to be a man too honourable and honest to be a member of this government. Ivor made it very clear that he believed, as I do, in a stronger second chamber and I suspect for exactly the same reasons as I do. He said that in public and no doubt said it in private to the government. Now a stronger second chamber is just what Mr Blair doesn't want because a stronger second chamber would be a chamber that performs its proper function, which is to act as a check on the House of Commons, and, therefore, make the House of Commons perform better. Mr Blair doesn't want that. To have a leader of the House of Lords who is promoting a sensible constitutional solution for the second chamber doesn't suit him at all.[7]

When I interviewed Richard some two years later he described Blair's position as equivocal:

When you talked to him … at times he seemed to be in favour of a substantial elected element, at other times he was not in favour … I think we would have been all right on this if what we had agreed in opposition had been the policy we decided to implement. I think that was sufficiently thought out. But that was not how it worked out in practice. There was a sufficient rearguard action down the other end, together with the activities of Pat McFadden. Pat's view was always against an elected House. He wanted a wholly nominated House. The other great question mark was what the Lord Chancellor wanted. At one time he wanted a wholly elected House. At one time he wanted a wholly nominated House. I don't think he had any serious views about it.

A LIFEBOAT FOR THE HEREDITARIES

What only emerged much later was that even before Richard was sacked, Blair had gone behind his back. Without Richard's knowledge he sanctioned a second round of secret discussions between Irvine and Cranborne. Richard told me the talks that led to the deal struck a few months after his departure, under which 92 hereditary peers would survive, were nothing to do with him: 'I knew nothing about it at all … For a long time I thought it had started after I had left. But I am not sure about that. I think it may have begun long before.' Cranborne confirmed to me more than two years later that this was indeed the case: 'If my memory serves me right I was approached directly by the Lord Chancellor in June. He made it perfectly clear the only two people who knew about the approach were himself and the Prime Minister.'

> 66 It casts an extraordinary light on Blair's methods of cabinet government that he was prepared to use Irvine to negotiate secretly with Cranborne for several weeks behind the back of Ivor Richard. 99

It casts an extraordinary light on Blair's methods of cabinet government that he was prepared to use Irvine to negotiate secretly with Cranborne for several weeks behind the back of Ivor Richard, who was not sacked as Labour leader in the Lords until 27 July. That Irvine was prepared to cooperate with this plotting casts his behaviour in an equally interesting light. Irvine proudly told the BBC's Michael Cockerell for a *Panorama* documentary: 'Radio silence was maintained. It must have been the best kept secret for a very long time in politics.'

Despite the collapse of the earlier talks, Cranborne was still keen for some sort of deal, as he told Austin Mitchell:

I don't want the battle of the second chamber. It may blow up in our face and make us extremely unpopular with the public. But I think I may get halfway to it. My troops are full of fight. And I hope and believe that Blair now realizes that we have the ability to cause serious trouble for him. It would be much more sensible to come to a deal. That deal is not on anything except the transitional arrangements. There needs to be a deal that guarantees that stage two will happen and happen fast. If I can get that, I will be happy. And the hereditaries will go. That's fine. Not a problem.[8]

Cranborne later described to Cockerell how he had persuaded Irvine that the government's entire legislative programme would be destroyed. 'It is not proper for the Lords to disrupt the legislative programme of an elected government. What *is* on, is to kid the government that we would.' Irvine, a relative political novice, seems to have swallowed the bait completely. Irvine told Cockerell:

He wasn't issuing a formal threat, he was just describing what he no doubt genuinely believed would have occurred. He used the expression Somme and Passchendaele.

According to Cranborne, Irvine began by offering him a lifebelt for a token 15 hereditary peers:

I said, don't be so ridiculous, I'm not in the business of bargaining … I said I want 100, the minimum I can get away with. He laughed and said, don't be so silly. I said, I will ruin your legislative programme next year.

Then, Irvine increased his offer.

He said, what about 50? I reported this to Hague. By July we had got as far as 75, or one in ten.

Cranborne asked for the 75 to be topped up with a further 15 hereditary peers who held office in the Lords, plus the Earl Marshal and the Lord Chamberlain. Irvine breathed a sigh of relief and the deal was done. Instead of 100, Cranborne was to get 92. Later, several more Tory hereditary peers were made life peers, leaving Cranborne to savour the fact that he had obtained more than he had originally asked for. When I asked him about this successful game of bluff at Irvine's expense he beamed a beatific smile: 'I asked for 100 and settled for 116 … It sounds unattractively immodest but you know, it's okay as far as it goes.' Perhaps not surprisingly in the light of the way he took his negotiating partner to the cleaners, Cranborne was very complimentary about him:

I have a confession: I am very fond of Derry Irvine. He is bright as hell and it sounds awfully patronizing, for which I apologize, but he is very shy and the great world is something he has never met before. So it's almost as though in everyday dealings in and out of politics he has got only one skin. Which makes him rather farouche. But he is very clever and entirely honourable as far as I am concerned. He does a deal and he sticks to it, whether it is to his advantage or not. I think he is basically an old Tory, actually – look at the way he wants to hang on to the present status of the Lord Chancellor.

Ivor Richard was not surprised by this positive verdict: 'He (Cranborne) got what he wanted.' He still believes the deal to allow the hereditary peers to survive was unnecessary from Labour's point of view:

It was the wrong way of doing it. I thought we had got a deal inside the government that the way with which you dealt with the Tories was to offer them a

Former Conservative leader in the Lords Robert Cranborne, assisted by his successor Tom Strathclyde, celebrates his entrapment of Derry Irvine. Copyright © Richard Willson, 1999.

certain number of life peerages. And I think they would have accepted that. It was a perfectly reasonable way of dealing with it. But to perpetuate the hereditary peerage in the way that they have done, so that they will go on and on and on … All the government has to do is what I think the government really wants to do – which is nothing at all – and the 92 stay.

Cranborne himself was only to survive a few months longer than Richard, as tensions increased between him and William Hague's shadow cabinet over tactics in the Lords. Cranborne was pushed against his better judgement into leading the Conservative peers to repeatedly vote down the government's proposed voting system for European elections at the very end of the 1997–98 parliamentary session, a move which broke with precedent and caused widespread unease. As Bernard Weatherill, former Speaker of the Commons and convenor of the independent cross-benchers, told his fellow peers: 'I was a Whip for some 12 years and I know something about parliamentary tactics; I can see a trap when it is being set for us.' This incident was followed a few days later at the beginning of December 1998 by Cranborne's spectacular sacking, which provided Hague with his worst ever day as opposition leader.

Cranborne's problem was that while the deal he had negotiated in secret with Irvine had been approved by Blair, the shadow cabinet had told him it was unacceptable. Authorized to go back and seek better terms, Cranborne instead embarked on a risky strategy; behind Hague's back he secretly finalized the deal, gambling correctly on the fact that once it was made public and supported by Tory peers, the shadow cabinet would be faced with a *fait accompli* and would have to put up with it. Hague was furious when he learned what had happened. He brushed aside a warning from Cranborne and revealed the secret contacts himself during Prime Minister's Questions. Hague was hoping to embarrass Blair with his own backbenchers by disclosing that he was playing fast and loose with Labour's manifesto pledge to get rid of the hereditaries altogether. But the Tory leader had spectacularly miscalculated. He found himself being taunted by Blair who revealed that Cranborne had actually finalized the deal without him knowing. Hague immediately sacked Cranborne, who confessed to having run in to Downing Street 'like an ill-trained spaniel' but told Hague he would do it again. 'He said he would rather sack me. I said in his place I would have done the same.'

Labour's glee at the turmoil in Conservative ranks disguised the fact that Cranborne, whatever his motives, had bluffed his way to a negotiating triumph. In the view of Liberal Democrat leader Bill Rodgers (Lord Rodgers of Quarrybank): 'He (Cranborne) got a very good deal. A huge deal.' In exchange for the paper concession of a promise to refrain from disrupting the government's legislative programme, he had gained an indefinite reprieve for the key hereditary members of the Conservative team in the Lords. Not everyone in Hague's party saw it that way, and many still view Cranborne as a traitor. Andrew Tyrie MP, a constitutional reformer on the Tory back benches, told me Cranborne was 'taken to the cleaners' by Blair. The deal was done at far too high a price because it could be presented as a piece of constitutional gerrymandering at the expense of the British people for the benefit of a hereditary clique, Tyrie argued. 'It greatly weakened the opportunities to exploit Labour's gerry-mandering of the second chamber.'

Cranborne's defence is that his intention was not just to save the skins of himself and his fellow hereditaries but to give Labour an incentive to proceed to an eventual stage two reform, partly by building into the Bill absurd elements which would cause the government embarrassment. When the deal was finally approved as a cross-bench amendment in the name of Lord Weatherill, it included complex provisions for internal elections among peers to choose the survivors, and even by-elections among the survivors to pick replacements for those who died. It remains to be seen whether Cranborne's theory will eventually prove correct. New Labour politicians are not easily embarrassed.

THANK YOU AND GOODBYE

The House of Lords Bill to remove the hereditaries was finally intro-duced into the upper house at the end of March 1999 by Margaret Jay, who told the luckless barons, viscounts and earls: 'In this chamber we still confront an ossified system whose days were numbered in the 1900s. In this, the last few months of the 20th century, the government believes we must finally close the political chapter of the 19th.' Modernization, she argued, was nothing more sinister than allowing our institutions to develop to reflect the changes in society. The govern-ment's plans were not ideological but pragmatic, with the goal of achieving 'relevance and contemporary authority for our institutions of government'. She made no apologies for tackling reform in two stages, saying the hereditary peers were a 'wild card' that had to be removed because they might 'join with those who think an elected House is the only solution to defeat a nominated or mixed House'. There was a touch of steel as the baroness declared: 'My Lords, we do not intend to play the game that way again.'

Some hereditary peers denounced the Bill as an act of political vandalism and an insult. 'To remove hereditary peers will break for ever strong historical links and threaten the traditions, pageantry and mystique of a 700-year-old institution that is part of the fabric of this country. It will also expose to threat the hereditary principle of the monarchy,' said the angry Lord Cobbold, a cross-bencher. Lord Ponsonby, one of the small number of Labour hereditary peers, supported the Bill by describing what happened when he tried to explain his membership of the British parliament to legislators from the former Soviet bloc at the Council of Europe:

They laugh out loud and think it is extremely funny. There are light-hearted exchanges about why I am a member of parliament. But there is a more serious side to that because they believe that democracy applies to them as members of the Council of Europe, but that we have found some clever way of circumnavigating democracy in the House of Lords. And of course that is true.

The debates on the Bill were long and repetitive. By mid-October 1999, with the end of the marathon in sight, Baroness Jay told the hereditaries it was time to say 'thank you and goodbye'. The problem with them, she admitted frankly, was not that they were unelected, it was just that too many of them were 'of one political persuasion'. Democracy, according to what became known as the Jay doctrine, required not the involvement of the voters but the correction of the political imbalance in the chamber. 'Any change which produces a fairer balance, as our proposals will, makes this House more democratic,' the baroness declared. 'I have no hesitation in asserting the transitional chamber will be more legitimate than that we have today.'

> 66 Democracy, according to what became known as the Jay doctrine, required not the involvement of the voters but the correction of the political imbalance in the chamber. 99

In early November, a round of internal elections by peers picked the lucky names of those who would survive, with the results announced on Guy Fawkes Day. The 92 included 17 office holders, and 75 chosen by election – 52 of them Conservatives. Earl Ferrers, 70, topped the poll with 190 votes out of the 204 of his peers who cast their ballots. Others who survived were the Earl of Onslow, who once threatened to go out fighting like a football hooligan, and the eyepatched World War Two veteran Baron Mowbray, whose title goes back to 1283. The expelled peers finally departed in mid-November at the end of the session.

The final shape of the transitional chamber still left the Conservatives with a majority over Labour, a hangover from the unequal number of life peers created under Thatcher. Blair tried to redress the balance, nominating a record number of new peers of all parties to bring his total in three years to 202, not much below the 216 created by Margaret Thatcher in a whole decade. Half of these were Labour peers, but the reluctance of some of them to spend time in the House of Lords trudging through the voting lobbies, and the transitional chamber's new mood of self-confidence, meant that it proved if anything less pliant than the old, with the Liberal Democrats holding the whip hand. Emboldened by Margaret Jay's tributes to their new legitimacy,* the Lords defeated the government in the 1999–2000 session on just under 30 per cent of votes, barely fewer than in the previous session when the hereditary peers were present.

Without the 92 surviving hereditaries, it is certain Labour would have had a much more comfortable time. By the start of the summer recess at the end of July 2000, the government had lost 24 votes in the Lords, and in around half of these the result would have been different had hereditaries been excluded, as Labour promised in its manifesto.[9] Lord Cranborne's negotiations had paid off better than he dared hope, even though he lost his job in the process. The lifeboat Labour had negotiated for the hereditary peers was a tactical short-term triumph in the way it divided the Conservative party, but a costly and unnecessary self-inflicted wound and a diversion from real reform of the Lords.

THE TRANSITIONAL HOUSE OF LORDS

On 31 July 2000 there were 694 members, the vast majority of them life peers, compared with around 40 per cent before the reform of 1999.

Peer type	
Life	576
Elected hereditaries	90
Archbishops and bishops	26
Hereditary royal office holders	2
Total	694

Within this total, 108 life peers and four elected hereditary peers were women. The average age had risen to 67 from 65 in 1998 and 58 per cent were aged 65 or over.

In the unreformed House, the Conservatives had 41 per cent of potential members, though not all took their seats. Cross-benchers had 29 per cent, Labour 15 per cent and the Liberal Democrats 6 per cent. The new balance on 31 July 2000 was:

Party	Life peers	Hereditaries	Total
Conservative	181	52	233
Labour	196	4	200
Cross-benchers	133	31	164
Liberal Democrats	58	5	63
Bishops and others	34	–	34
Total	602	92	694

STAGE TWO –THE WHITE PAPER AND WAKEHAM

Removing the hereditary peers was by far the easiest part of the government's task in reforming the Lords. Producing a design for a reformed second chamber was always going to be a more difficult exercise than creating a Scottish parliament or a Welsh assembly; it was the difference between reconstructing an old building and starting from scratch on a greenfield site. Reforming the Lords meant reshaping an institution several hundred years old while it continued to function. In stage one, Labour's team of architects had already got themselves into enormous difficulties by trying to demolish part of the existing structure without having a plan for what would be built in its place. Ivor Richard had favoured a two-thirds elected House of Lords, but he had been sacked.

The government's inability to decide its long-term goals emerged even more clearly as it moved into stage two. Cranborne told Michael Cockerell that Blair assured him privately that he wanted a wholly appointed second chamber – a policy that had never been debated, let alone approved by a Labour conference. Because this contradicted the party's manifesto, it was not a policy which Blair could avow publicly. Blair's plan was to allow the idea of an entirely or mostly nominated upper chamber to emerge through a royal commission of the great and the good, which would carry all-party support and enable the government to swiftly wrap up stage two before the next general election. Unfortunately, the plan misfired.

After the drama of Cranborne's sacking and the embarrassing divisions between the front bench Conservative teams in the Commons and the Lords at the end of 1998, the government appeared to have seized the initiative. Despite Cranborne's removal, the plan to preserve 92 hereditary peers that he had worked out with Irvine survived intact; his successor, Tom Strathclyde, and the rest of the Conservative front bench in the Lords refused to allow Hague to scrap it. This meant that the way ahead was clear for the House of Lords Bill implementing stage one to become law. The government finally published its White Paper on Lords reform in January 1999 and announced a royal commission to map the way ahead.

Much loved by Harold Wilson, royal commissions are a traditional device for kicking political issues into the long grass; they fell out of favour with Margaret Thatcher. Not surprisingly, it was Ivor Richard, a veteran of the Wilson era, who suggested a royal commission rather than a Joint Committee of the two houses, as proposed in Labour's manifesto and agreed with the Liberal Democrats. He envisaged that the commission would take at least two years to report. But the government was suddenly in a hurry and keen to make up for lost time – it instructed the commission to report by the end of 1999, a deadline which gave it only a few months to do its work. This left no time for foreign travel, opinion research, public consultation or creative thinking.

The man chosen to chair it was a Conservative life peer, John Wakeham, an ex-Chief Whip, a former leader of the Commons and of the Lords, and a legendary political fixer. In the rest of the team, former Conservative Foreign Secretary Douglas Hurd and senior Labour MP Gerald Kaufman were the political heavy hitters, while constitutional reformers were conspicuous by their absence. Wakeham explained to me that he was allowed significant influence over the choice of his fellow members:

I had to be satisfied that members of the commission whom the Prime Minister would choose would be the sort of team who would help produce that result … Of course, the fact that he had announced my name before the team had been organized gave me – though I didn't have to use it – a de facto veto over who was in the thing, because if they put up some people who were unacceptable, I'd say 'Good day to you, thank you very much'. In fact, we did have a little debate or two about it, but you will have to wait for a few years to know the story of that.

A WHITE PAPER WITH LARGE PRINT

The government's drift towards a nominated upper house and away from the idea of democratic elections became even clearer when Labour published its White Paper on the next stage of Lords reform. Blair wrote in his introduction that 'many of the key institutions of Britain are among the best in the world'. Hereditary peers 'with no democratic legitimacy' were a blot on this happy picture, making the upper house 'less good than it could be'. After their removal, Labour would carry out a 'careful and considered reform'.

The arguments in the White Paper showed the distance the party had travelled under Blair since the radical days of opposition, when it fretted over the excessive power of the executive and the problems of elective dictatorship and the royal prerogative. Instead of a discussion of separation of powers and the role of the legislature in holding the executive to account, it offered an old-fashioned Tory definition of the role of parliament:

Parliament is the core of political accountability in Britain, where the decision of the electorate to support a published programme of policies is transformed into legislation, into consideration of the opportunities and difficulties facing the nation, and into leadership in government.

This confused back-of-the-envelope definition would restrict parliament's role to ensuring that the government was sustained in office and its manifesto promises were implemented. In the White Paper's tortuous phrasing, it is not clear who is being made accountable to whom; possibly parliament is accountable to the electorate, but it does not look much as though the executive is accountable to parliament. The next paragraph sidestepped the longstanding problem of parliament's subordination to the executive altogether, implying that any decline in its authority was solely attributable to the legacy of Tory sleaze, which Labour was putting right:

In recent years, both the authority and integrity of parliament have been questioned, and its representativeness subject to ever-closer scrutiny. Parliament itself has taken steps to respond to this challenge to its role and performance, by improving its standards and examining its practices.

The White Paper mentioned devolution and what it described as a 'significant' programme to modernize the procedures of the House of

Commons, which had 'already' debated the report of the commission headed by Lord Jenkins on electoral reform. It endorsed the idea of a two-chamber legislature but quickly insisted that the second chamber 'must neither usurp, nor threaten, the supremacy of the first chamber'. Parliament's role was not to scrutinize the executive or hold it accountable – perish the thought – but to 'perform properly' by not interfering with the delivery of its contract with the voters:

The ability of the elected government to fulfil its electoral contract with the British people and deliver what they have asked it to do primarily depends on the proper performance of the House of Commons, but it rests too on an effective and balanced second chamber – the House of Lords.

The role of the Lords in the legislative process was described as 'significant' but it was told that it needed to 'adapt and modernize'. The notion of balance was to apply not between the executive and the two houses of the legislature, but within the second chamber itself. The flaw in the Lords was identified as a lack of legitimacy, attributable not to the fact that it was unelected but '... because the presence of the hereditary peers creates a permanent, inbuilt majority for a single party'. The White Paper went on to argue that 'a place in the legislature should be reserved for those who achieve it on their own merits', a definition which left open the question of who should decide on such merits. Removing the hereditary peers would 'in itself amount to a marked improvement of the House, removing much of the cause of its deficit in both effectiveness and balance'. However, the government rejected accusations that the removal of the hereditary peers would create 'a transitional house of unfettered patronage solely at the disposal of the government of the day'.

The White Paper proposed an appointments commission, which would reduce the prime minister's power of patronage by taking over responsibility for choosing all non-political or cross-bench candidates for the transitional upper house. 'There is no truth to the assertion that we wish to create a "house of patronage" as an abuse of the appointments system,' it argued. The commission, an advisory government body without a statutory basis, would include representatives of the three main parties and a majority of independent figures, one of whom would be chairman. But although the prime minister would lose the right to pick cross-bench peers, he would retain his most important power of patronage – control over his own party's nominations and the overall numbers of new life peers.

Moving on from transitional to longer-term arrangements, the White Paper set the goal of turning the House of Lords into a chamber that was 'modern, fit and effective'. While Labour's manifesto had promised to make the Lords 'more democratic and representative', the White Paper dropped the first part of the pledge and promised only 'a chamber which is more representative of the country as a whole'.

NO MORE DEMOCRACY PLEASE, WE'RE BRITISH

In line with this strategy, the terms of reference for Lord Wakeham and his fellow commission members were carefully crafted to avoid any suggestion of extending democracy:

Having regard to the need to maintain the position of the House of Commons as the pre-eminent chamber of parliament and taking particular account of the present nature of the constitutional settlement, including the newly devolved institutions, the impact of the Human Rights Act and developing relations with the European Union:

- to consider and make recommendations on the role and functions of a second chamber; and

- to make recommendations on the method or combination of methods of composition required to constitute a second chamber fit for that role and those functions;

- to report by 31 December 1999.

The White Paper made it clear that the royal commission would have to observe certain 'no-go' areas; money bills would remain the preserve of the Commons alone, as would the making and unmaking of governments; and the executive would have to retain the right to secure passage of its legislation with the consent of the Commons alone, except for a Bill to extend the life of parliament. This restriction effectively ruled out any role for the new chamber as a constitutional 'long stop', an idea much canvassed by reformers. It was clear from the White Paper that any increase in powers for the Lords would be unacceptable to the government, as would any radical rethinking of the position of the Anglican bishops and the Law Lords. After listing the chamber's existing functions as legislative, deliberative, interrogative and judicial, the White Paper floated the idea that these might be reduced: 'A key question for the royal commission on the future of the Lords, therefore, is whether all of these are necessary to make the second chamber a proper complement to the House of Commons.'

> ❝ It is hardly surprising that Ivor Richard got the sack, in view of his clearly expressed opinion – not so far away from that of Robert Cranborne – that the second chamber's powers should be increased. ❞

Reading the White Paper, it is hardly surprising that Ivor Richard got the sack, in view of his clearly expressed opinion – not so far away from that of Robert Cranborne – that the second chamber's powers should be increased. After discussing what should happen to the Salisbury convention, the White Paper suggested that it might be better to reduce the Lords' formal powers to balance the fact that they might be used more frequently.

Stressing the need for 'stable government', another way of saying the legislature should not rock the boat, the White Paper then considered the case for democratic elections: 'Some will argue that a system which contains no element of election, even indirect election, cannot be democratic or even properly representative of society as a whole.' It was clear that the government did not agree; a directly elected chamber would have a significant impact on the relationship with the Commons, risking conflict and constitutional instability. 'Extreme care' would have to be taken to make sure an elected house did not challenge the supremacy of the Commons on the strength of its separate electoral mandate. A chamber that consisted of two-thirds elected members – Richard's preference – had 'nothing particularly compelling' to recommend it, the White Paper said, in a broad hint to Wakeham of the government's preferred outcome. Such a chamber would 'share many of the disadvantages of a wholly elected second chamber'.

Wakeham and his team would have to be suffering from extreme myopia not to see the signposts leading to what the government wanted. As Cranborne commented in *The Times*: 'Mr Blair does not like to appoint inquiries without telling them what their answer will be.'[10] As Cranborne himself recognized, the choice of Wakeham as chairman blunted the risk of any Conservative criticism of the commission: 'The Tories would not attack one of their own and all Chief Whips, both serving and emeritus, deplore the idea of a more powerful House of Lords. It makes their own job more difficult.' He went on to predict that Wakeham, while acknowledged to be a fixer, would not prove to be a 'stitch-up merchant'.

A RACE FOR THE FINISH

How accurate was this prediction? Did the Wakeham commission deliver exactly what Blair wanted? With one notable exception – its proposals for an appointments commission far more powerful than the government wanted – the answer has to be yes. It was clear from the report's introduction that Wakeham did not want his work to be kicked into the long grass like the Jenkins report on the voting system. 'We were determined to produce recommendations which were not only coherent and intellectually persuasive but also realistic, workable and politically achievable.' Wakeham and his team said they wanted their report to find consensus and have a good chance of being implemented in the near future. 'We did not wish to spend months compiling a report that would gather dust in a pigeonhole.'

THE WAKEHAM REPORT

The report's 131 recommendations included many that would keep the status quo. The principal changes were:

- establishment of a constitutional committee and a human rights subcommittee;

- a proportion of members should represent the UK's nations and regions but devolved institutions such as the Scottish Parliament should not be represented directly;

- Commons ministers should answer questions from the upper house;

- a reformed second chamber should be authoritative but should not challenge the Commons; it should be broadly representative of British society as a whole;

- it should be open to part-time figures from outside politics;

- it should not be dominated by one political party;

- members should mostly be nominated, with overall membership reflecting the most recent general election result;

- an independent appointments commission set up by statute should name all new members, ensuring at least 20 per cent independents; it should decide on party nominees and vet all potential members for propriety, and decide the level of total membership;

- it should ensure a minimum of 30 per cent of new members should be women and 30 per cent men and do its best to introduce more members from ethnic minorites;

- regional members should serve for three electoral cycles and appointed members for 15 years; all members would have equal status, there should be no minimum age, and members would be free to retire but not to seek election to the Commons for ten years;

- regional members should be chosen under one of three schemes by proportional representation:

  - A: 65 members would be chosen according to a regional calculation of general election votes, with one-third chosen at each election;

  - B: 87 members would be elected in thirds at the same time as European parliamentary elections on similar regional lists;

  - C: 195 regional members would be elected, one-third at each European Parliament election to serve for three terms;

- existing life peers would remain members but would be able to retire;

- the Church of England would lose ten of its 26 members, with the places going to other Christian denominations in England, Scotland, Wales and Northern Ireland;

- members should be paid for attendance and committee chairmen should be salaried;

- membership should no longer bring a peerage and a peerage should no longer guarantee membership;

- the question of the name of the second chamber and the titles of its members should be left to evolve.

The report that emerged at the end of 1999 from the 12-member panel was cautious, conservative and unadventurous, although it went further than the White Paper in at least alluding to the problem of 'elective dictatorship' and the need for checks and balances on the executive. Naive ideas about creating a totally non-political 'council of tribal elders' to decide dispassionately about the country's best interests were dismissed as fantasy, on the grounds that political parties would inevitably have a central role to play. However, the idea of a more powerful second chamber was quickly dismissed as out of date, using the convenient pretext that devolution was already reducing the power of Westminster. The commission interpreted its remit to keep the Commons pre-eminent in the narrowest possible sense. The idea of giving the second chamber a major constitutional role was rejected on the grounds that this would 'alter the balance of power between the two chambers and could be exploited to bring the two chambers into conflict'. It rejected the idea of the second chamber giving access to members of the new devolved institutions on the grounds that members of the Scottish and Welsh Assemblies already had full-time jobs and did not want to be co-opted back to Westminster, while English regional assemblies had yet to be created. For similar reasons, the idea of European Parliament members joining the Lords was seen as a non-starter. It recommended that government ministers should continue to sit in the Lords because ministers from the Commons would lack 'a full understanding of the ambience, conventions and style' of the upper house – an argument that suggested the cultural gap between the two chambers should be preserved.

Ever cautious about creating more problems for the government, the commission rejected the idea of confirmation hearings for public appointments, but accepted a suggestion that the Lords set up a select committee to scrutinize treaties, another area covered by the royal prerogative. It saw no bar to the Law Lords remaining members of the upper house, combining the roles of legislators and judges, and ducked the issue of the multiple roles of the Lord Chancellor as judge and cabinet minister, saying this was a matter for the prime minister.

The core of the report was in chapters 10 and 11, which dealt with the character of the upper house and how it should be composed. 'Authoritative, confident and broadly representative' was the ideal for the new upper house, but its authority should 'not be such as to challenge the ultimate authority of the House of Commons which derives directly from the electorate, through popular elections'. Wakeham and his team did not question the government's argument that conflict between the two chambers could only be avoided by keeping democracy at bay: 'The greater the "democratic legitimacy" of the second chamber, the greater the risk of damaging constitutional conflicts arising between the two Houses of Parliament.'

However, there was an answer in sight to the awkward conundrum posed by the need to avoid the risk of consulting the voters: 'It is, however, an error to suppose that the second chamber's authority can only stem from democratic election.' The upper house could create its own authority through the high quality of its members if they were experienced, representative, unpartisan, personally distinguished and had good quality arguments. The new chamber should be confident and 'free of debilitating inhibitions' and cohesive. It should be representative of all the United Kingdom's regions and not contain too many white males. 'There should be steady progress towards gender balance and a more substantial representation of minority ethnic groups.' Expertise should be inside the chamber, not just called in from outside. Part-time members with outside experience, particularly lawyers and those with human rights knowledge, should be facilitated and encouraged. There should be no minimum attendance requirement. The yardstick should not be past services but the future contribution to the legislature, and the House should preserve a strong independent element of cross-benchers. It should not be a career stepping stone to a seat in the Commons.

The commission acknowledged in passing that the replies to its public consultation exercise favoured the one option it dismissed out of hand – an elected chamber: 'In a democracy there is a natural presumption in favour of election as the appropriate way of constituting the second chamber. There was considerable support for direct election among respondents to our consultation exercise. Election implies direct accountability to the electorate.' But it insisted that a chamber with the authority of the ballot box behind it 'could bring it into direct conflict with the House of Commons'. Divergence between the two Houses, rather than leading to negotiation and compromise, would be bound to give rise to constitutional conflicts:

> Regardless of its political complexion, the central objection to a directly elected second chamber is that it would, by its very nature, represent a challenge to the pre-eminence of the House of Commons and make it difficult to strike the balance between the powers of the two Houses that our terms of reference require and that we have recommended … We would be strongly opposed to a situation in which the two Houses of Parliament had equivalent electoral legitimacy. It would represent a substantial change in the present constitutional settlement in the United Kingdom and would almost certainly be a recipe for damaging conflict.

The report warned that too many invitations to the polling booth might lead to voter fatigue: 'Any increase in the number or variety of elections would be a recipe for voter alienation as well as confusion.' It rejected indirect elections through vocational and interest groups because of 'insuperable practical obstacles as well as difficulties of principle' and also dismissed the idea of selecting members as if for jury service, by random selection.

The one area where the Wakeham report departed from the White Paper was in the powerful role it proposed for the appointments commission, which would effectively strip the prime minister of all his direct powers of patronage: 'We consider that leaving the prime minister with the power to determine the political balance in the second chamber by deciding the number of nominations each party should make would be inconsistent with the need to establish the reformed second chamber's independence and its freedom from undue political influence.' With the prime minister excluded from a role in appointing members of the second chamber, the way would be clear to break the link between membership and the peerage. The Crown should no longer issue a writ for membership. 'Precluding any scope for political patronage is a basic element of our scheme.' The appointments commission would be the gatekeeper for all members, including bishops, Law Lords and regionally elected members, but it would have no discretion over these three groups. The commission would be independent and established by primary legislation, on a similar basis to the government's proposed Electoral Commission.

A BAD PRESS

Wakeham's report ran into scathing press criticism, partly for ducking difficult issues such as the name of the second chamber, which it said should be left to 'evolve'. Most of the critics accused the committee of supine loyalty to the government, the accusation made by Simon Jenkins: 'It needed only a faint twitch of a Downing Street eyebrow for Lord Wakeham to get the message.' Magnus Linklater in *Scotland on Sunday* described the report as a classic fudge but predicted that Blair would not like the recommendation for a totally independent appointments commission. 'It is the worst way of going about constitutional change,' he commented. 'It was obvious that the main aim of devolution was to give Scotland a parliament. But no one had a clue what was wanted from the Lords once the hereditary peers were abolished.' Instead of a strong, robust house to stand up to a government with a steamroller majority, Wakeham's proposals would produce a weaker one.

The Scotsman described the report as 'a report drafted by the establishment for the establishment'. An upper house with only a minority of elected members and stuffed with appointees would offer the worst of all worlds. 'It is now Wakeham or nothing. We have difficulty in deciding which is worse.' Lords reform was supposed to be about more than just ending the hereditary principle: 'It was intended to involve the creation of a genuine check on the executive. Lord Wakeham has banished that disturbing possibility from Mr Blair's mind. He has done obedient service to the state, not to the people.'

Some constitutional experts took a more measured view, pointing out that the lack of time at the royal commission's disposal meant it was unable to get to grips with the workings of the devolution settlement, and that some of its secondary proposals were quite sensible. Meg Russell and Robert Hazell of the Constitution Unit pointed out that neither the Welsh Assembly nor the Scottish Parliament got down to work until the autumn of 1999, when Wakeham was already starting to write his report. The commission was also unable to assess the impact of the expulsion of hereditary peers, which happened only in November 1999. 'Given the enormity of the task, and the brevity of the timescale, it is not surprising that the royal commission ducked many of the difficult issues, and made only tentative suggestions about what part the Lords might play in underpinning our new constitutional arrangements.'[11]

Russell and Hazell, after looking at the experience of second chambers abroad, were not convinced by the argument that too many elected members would lead to a clash with the Commons: 'The commission were concerned that an elected chamber would be too legitimate. However, the other danger is that the chamber under their proposals would have *insufficient* legitimacy. This is a potential problem with a chamber which remains dominated by appointees.' They suggested keeping the 195 elected members but cutting the number of appointees to 100, making a much smaller chamber of around 300. They also criticized Wakeham for failing to recommend the removal of the Law Lords from parliament: 'This is one issue on which Wakeham should have taken a stronger constitutional stand. No other democracy allows its highest judges to sit in the legislature. The Law Lords should have been rescued before their position becomes untenable.'

Professor Robert Blackburn of King's College London described the report as 'a major disappointment' because it had failed to follow the logic of the UK's emerging constitutional settlement, with more entrenched rights and codification of basic laws. Professor Brendan O'Leary denounced it as 'second rate, intellectually insular, and uninformed by serious comparative analysis'. The commission was undemocratic not only in its conclusions but in the way it reached them. 'Why was there no proper survey of citizens' views on what kind of second chamber they would prefer? Canvassing the wit and wisdom of Gerald Kaufman is no substitute for democracy or social science.' O'Leary said the proposals for regional representation were 'a canine breakfast' and its proposals for elections every 15 years were risible: 'Rousseau once said that the English were free only once every seven years; it is the singular cognitive achievement of the Wakeham commission to extend that period, to make the English and the rest partly free every 15 years.'[12]

MORE HASTE LESS SPEED

In the White Paper the tight deadline set for Wakeham to report was justified by the need 'to enable the government to make every effort to ensure that the second stage of reform has been approved by parliament by the time of the general election'. The idea was that a Joint Committee of both houses would ratify the results and enable swift progress. But the course of events after Wakeham reported showed that any real intention to legislate before the next general election had evaporated. Though Wakeham reported at the end of December 1999, the first debate on the report in the Lords took place only on 7 March 2000, and the Commons did not debate it until 19 June that year; there was no sign of the Joint Committee being appointed, and the urgency of moving to stage two seemed to have disappeared.

In the Lords debate Margaret Jay praised the report for being evolutionary and said the government would not 'confine it to a dusty top shelf'. Her response was carefully worded; the government would ignore 'siren voices' telling it to reject the proposals and it accepted 'the principles underlying the main elements of the royal commission's proposals' – a phrase that allowed a large space for future manoeuvre. It was no surprise that the government agreed with Wakeham that electing the second chamber would undermine British democracy:

It is an unassailable principle that the right to govern depends on maintaining the confidence of the House of Commons. If the representatives of the people withhold their consent in a vote of confidence in another place, the people are deemed to have withdrawn their consent. The government falls and another general election follows. This is clear; it is democratic; and, so far, it is unchallenged. If a second body of people were also elected, perhaps on a different franchise, the clear voice of the people through the present system must, necessarily, be obscured and perhaps, paradoxically, democratic responsibility weakened ... The challenge to those who press the case for a totally elected second chamber is to explain how they respond to that fundamental point. It may be said that the people should only be governed by those they have elected. That is true, but it does not support the case of advocates of a totally elected second chamber. The second chamber does not, and should not, govern us. We are not a federal government but a unitary parliamentary democracy.

Jay's final phrase was a revealing gaffe. It drew a sharp retort from the Conservative spokesman John MacKay: 'I have news for her – we are no longer a unitary parliamentary democracy. We have a devolved parliament in Scotland, a devolved assembly in Wales, and I hope we are going to have again a devolved assembly in Northern Ireland.' Jay was much less enthusiastic about the powerful independent appointments commission, saying the government would want to consider the proposal carefully, while accepting that a statutory commission would have to come in the long term. The government agreed with the idea of letting in 'a small elected element', which would not be numerous enough to undermine the 'distinctive character' of the upper house.

The debate revealed little enthusiasm for Wakeham's report from any quarter; one Liberal Democrat peer described it as 'a regurgitated dog's breakfast', while many Conservatives made it clear that they opposed introducing any elected members. Norman St John Stevas (Lord St John of Fawsley), a former Conservative minister, described the limited contingent of elected members as '... the fetlocks of the backend of a pantomime horse. They would be merely a complicating factor. They would merely undermine the legitimacy of those appointed here.' Lord Longford, a veteran Labour hereditary peer, said anyone elected to the second chamber would be second rate: 'We would get the dregs.'

It took more than three months before the government risked a debate in the Commons; anyone who was hoping for clarity about what it would do next was disappointed, and it was clear that nothing would happen until after the next general election.

Wakeham's report came in for blistering criticism not just from the Liberal Democrats but from former Conservative Chancellor Kenneth Clarke for failing to recommend a directly elected second chamber. Leader of the Commons Margaret Beckett attacked 'whingeing about the so-called delay' on stage two, pointing out that it had taken the best part of a century – since 1911 – to reach stage one. The promise to act before the next election had not been a promise at all, it turned out. The government was 'minded to accept the broad outlines' of Wakeham – a largely nominated second chamber with a minority elected element representing the regions, and a statutory appointments commission. On everything else the government had yet to make any decisions. Beckett's speech made it clear that the government's determination to keep the second chamber subordinate had if anything hardened; it was, she said, no part of its function to hold the government to account:

It has been suggested that the primary purpose of the second chamber should be not to scrutinize legislation and to ask the government and this House to think again about individual proposals, but rather to hold the government to account. That is the function of this House. It must be done by the chamber that has the power to dismiss the government. To have two chambers, each with an identical role in that respect, would be bound to lead to conflict and confusion.

An elected second chamber would be a recipe for conflict, she warned. Beckett endorsed the view of one of the Wakeham commission's senior members, Gerald Kaufman, who warned of the dangers to MPs' corporate interests; if the second chamber was elected, members of the Commons 'would find there was an alternative member of parliament for their constituencies who would claim to represent them as much as they did and take up the same cases and claim to deal with them better'.

The debate revealed a gulf between the government and Labour backbenchers. Even Kaufman, a veteran loyalist, said the second chamber should be given new ways to hold the government to account, and spoke in favour of a total end to the prime ministerial powers of patronage. Mark Fisher, a former minister, asked Beckett if she was really saying that democracy had no role to play in the second chamber:

Where does that leave the people of this country? Surely they have a right to elect people who sit in half of our parliament and it is not for whoever does the selecting – whether the government, or we in the chamber – to determine who should sit; it is for the people of this country to decide who sits in the legislature over them.

Labour MP Gordon Prentice described the Wakeham proposals as risible, and predicted that in the next election Labour would be outflanked not only by the Liberal Democrats but also by the Conservatives on the issue of elections:

In the nation's consciousness there is an understanding that New Labour is associated with fixes. There was a fix in Scotland, as we all know ... there was a fix in Wales. There was manifestly a fix in London. Are we seriously suggesting that we should go into the next election with our political opponents being able to point the finger at us and say, 'This is another New Labour fix'?

WAKEHAM UNMOVED BY CRITICISM

When I interviewed John Wakeham he was unimpressed by criticism of his report by journalists and academics, whom he dismissed as '... the Blackburns and the Hazells and the Peter Riddells':

It was predictable, absolutely predictable, all written by people who hadn't read the report, who had preconceived notions of what they were going to say, who told me before we wrote the report what they were going to say, and they said it all. It was rubbish from beginning to end, in my view, because they did not understand what we were trying to do ... The first thing about all of these people, all of them, who say all this stuff, is: absolutely nothing would have happened if I had written a report in the terms they wanted. Nothing would have happened. Nobody would have taken any notice of it, it wouldn't have happened. I'm not in that business. I'm in the business of doing something practical. So I dismiss most of them who present policies – whether they are right, wrong or indifferent. If nothing is going to happen, what's the point of me spending a year of my time writing a report? I actually wanted to achieve something, to move the thing forward, and I think it will happen. And most of the criticisms are by people who have put forward proposals. There was no prospect whatsoever of their ideas being adopted. So I think they're daft.

Wakeham was quite clear in his own mind that his job was to concentrate on the House of Lords rather than link up with the government's other constitutional reform plans. 'I said, that's nothing to do with me, I'm not part of that. I'm reforming the House of Lords and making a plan for the future. I'm not part of any great scheme for devolution or anything else.' He explained why he felt the government had 'missed a trick' by failing to embrace his idea of an independent appointments commission which would make it easier and less controversial for Blair to increase the number of Labour members. He told me that he, like Tony Blair, had originally favoured a totally appointed chamber:

What we really wanted – what I wanted, anyway – was an appointed House, a totally appointed House. But what we have produced is in effect still an appointed House, but the regional representatives are appointed by the people in the regions. Because they never can go back to be re-elected … We thought these problems through. And in the same way Tony Blair said to me: 'You have convinced me. I wanted a totally appointed House but your proposal I think is right, and you have changed my mind.' I told him before I took the job I wanted a wholly appointed House. But I did not believe it was a sustainable way of finding representatives of the regions.

Even those commission members who originally wanted direct elections became convinced by Wakeham's argument that those who got in would be 'the fourth eleven' and would lack the necessary expertise. 'What good are they as advisers and wise people? They would be a bunch of berks.' Electing the second chamber 'would damage democracy very substantially'. Wakeham told me he had also pointed out to Blair that introducing a small dose of regional members elected by proportional representation to the second chamber would provide a tailor-made pretext for not introducing PR for the Commons.

Despite widespread predictions to the contrary, Wakeham was convinced that his report could be implemented after the election, provided the government pushed ahead without waiting for all-party agreement and a Joint Commission of both houses:

In my view I think the first thing the government has to do is to recognize that all-party agreement is not something you get these days on issues of this sort, because the agenda for opposition parties is different from the agenda for government parties … Now it's a simple approach, but I'm an ex-Chief Whip, and I'm a pretty good cynic. So they are all looking at it as to how they garner a few votes. The government has to look at it and say, 'What are we actually going to do? We're in charge. The buck has stopped with us.' So the first thing the government has to do is recognize that the test which some of them would like to apply, the possibility of all-party agreement, is a nonsense. Forget it. What they have to do is decide what they think is right.

Douglas Hurd, the other senior Conservative on the commission, was more sympathetic to direct elections than Wakeham. He told me he thought the report had 'staying power'. If stage two ever did come about, he predicted, the result would be something like Wakeham's plan. The core of the proposal, he explained, was the separation of appointment to the second chamber from prime ministerial patronage, which was the element the government had most difficulty with: 'I think the Wakeham report stands or falls by the extent to which the independent appointments commission can be made to work. That is the heart.' Hurd, as a member of the Honours Scrutiny Committee, was well aware of the sensitivity of these issues, having finally given the green light to the controversial nomination for a peerage of Conservative treasurer Michael Ashcroft on condition that he returned to the UK from Belize. 'Working peers have to be available to work, which is not compatible with being a tax exile or being employed by a Commonwealth government. We took a stand on that and enforced that view.' He explained that under the Wakeham proposals there would still be a place for patronage and honours for past services, including services to political parties, but in future these should be quite separate from membership of the second chamber.

Ivor Richard believes the scheme is unworkable:

The idea that you get over the democratic deficit by having an independent commission which will decide on who comes to the Lords, which parties they come from, the sort of people, the personalities ... I just can't see any prime minister being prepared to give up that power. It's a fig leaf to cover up the fact that Wakeham really ends up with a nominated House. The idea that an independent commission is really going to produce the personnel for one of the two Houses of Parliament irrespective of what the government wants is really fanciful.

A DEAD DUCK?

Wakeham's view that the government will implement his recommendations after the election is, to say the least, not universally shared. 'Pigs might fly,' was Cranborne's acid comment. He told me: 'I think Wakeham is a dead duck.' His alternative way forward would be to start a Joint Committee of both houses and admit that all three parties were divided:

All the parties are divided on what to do about stage two. The Tories are divided, even the Liberals are divided, particularly members of this House. They all love the idea of appointed peers. Former MPs think a peerage is a reward for a distinguished career in the House of Commons and so appointment is important to them and to those who will follow them … It suits them very well at the moment. They have effectively a nominated House. All the poor darlings who have become New Labour peers love being called Lord and Lady Snooks. They love the idea of being appointed. They don't want anything to do with an electorate, thank you very much. And it suits the Prime Minister very well indeed.

Cranborne's preference is for a 50 per cent elected upper house. He argues that the present interim second chamber is no more legitimate than the old one, and he is scathing about Dennis Stevenson, the Scottish-born businessman chosen by Blair to head the new Appointments Commission. Since being made a life peer, Stevenson, who is technically a cross-bencher but is regarded by senior cross-bench peers as a fellow traveller for New Labour, has rarely attended the Lords: 'Nobody has ever heard of Lord Stevenson for a start. They said he was a Scot and John MacKay said, "He may be a Scot but I've never heard of him." I am sure he is extremely distinguished and a very great and good man.'

PEOPLE'S PEERS

The Appointments Commission set up by Tony Blair in 2000 was headed by Dennis Stevenson (Lord Stevenson of Coddenham) and included representatives of the three main parties from the interim House of Lords, plus three non-party outsiders. The commission will pick a small number of cross-bench peers each year. The Prime Minister chooses how many slots will be filled, but not the names. In addition, the commission will vet all nominations for membership of the Lords by the political parties to ensure propriety.

The commission advertised in September 2000 for nominations for an initial batch of 'outstanding individuals' to be appointed early in 2001, inviting applications from British, Irish or Commonwealth citizens over 21 'who will broaden the expertise and experience of the House as well as reflect greater representation of the diversity of the people of the United Kingdom'. It added: 'The Appointment Commission will assess nominations against its stated criteria as to the qualities and experience of nominees; their independence and personal integrity; the highest standards of propriety; and their ability to contribute to the work of the House. To make an active and effective contribution, the commission considers that it is likely that your main home will be in the United Kingdom. You should also be resident in the United

Kingdom for tax purposes … The commission is committed to independent and fair assessment of nominations. Its recommendations will be made on individual merit and not on the basis of age, disability, gender, marital status, sexual orientation, background, religion, race, colour, ethnic or national origin.'

The commission said it was looking for candidates:

- who are able to demonstrate outstanding personal qualities, in particular integrity and independence;

- with a strong and personal commitment to the principles and highest standards of public life;

- with a record of significant achievement within their chosen way of life that demonstrates a range of experience, skills and competencies;

- who are able to make an effective and significant contribution to the work of the House of Lords, not only in their areas of particular interest and special expertise but to the wide range of other issues coming before the House;

- with some understanding of the constitutional framework, including the place of the House of Lords, and the skills and qualities needed to be an effective member of the House – for example, nominees should be able to speak with independence and authority;

- with the time available to ensure they can make an effective contribution within the procedures and working practices of the House of Lords. This does not necessarily mean the same amount of time expected of 'working peers'. However, nominees should be prepared to spend the time necessary to become familiar and comfortable with the workings of the House and thereafter, when they have a contribution to make, to participate in its business. The commission recognizes that many active members continue with their professional and other working interests and this can help maintain expertise and experience;

- who are independent of any political party. Nominees and the commission will need to feel confident of their ability to be independent of party political considerations whatever their past political- party involvement. For this reason, all nominees are asked to respond to the standard questions on political involvement and activities that are used for most public appointments.

Successful candidates will be unpaid but will be able to claim expenses of £36 per day or £81.50 if this includes an overnight stay. Peers may also claim travel expenses. When the House is sitting, peers may claim £35 per day for office and secretarial assistance.

Charter88 said any system of appointing peers was inferior to a democratic system of election and the commission 'seems particularly self-serving'. It said under-represented groups would be discouraged from applying and all but those wealthy enough to finance themselves would be excluded. 'Furthermore, the notion of "people's peers" is somewhat disingenuous as, where an individual or organization nominates someone for a peerage, the nominee is then sent an application form to complete. It is a fig leaf for self promotion by the already "great and good".'

Andrew Tyrie MP believes that the interim House knows that if it causes serious trouble for the government as opposed to 'minor ping pong and annoyance', then that will be the day the government will move on to stage two of reform and finally remove the hereditary peers:

I think the government set off with a mixture of bright-eyed, bushy-tailed enthusiasm for a revitalized second chamber as well as getting rid of the hereditaries, quickly realized that it was going to be a political hassle and decided to go for the least hassled option like many executives do, and that transformation was reflected in the switch from Lord Richard to Lord Irvine. So the second question is, what are they going to do now? I think they are engaged in trying to prevent there ever being a second Bill. They have not abolished the hereditary peers but they have convinced the public and even some of their own backbenchers that they have, which shows the level of ignorance and lack of interest in it. I have even met people who voted to keep the hereditary peers, that is the 300 or so Labour backbenchers who were whipped to do this, some of whom think the hereditary peers have gone. As part of that Bill there was a measure to enable them to renew themselves in perpetuity by by-elections ... This is an outrage, in the legislature of a major country ... It is a reflection of the lack of interest in these issues that this has not been more a matter of widespread public debate.

Tom Strathclyde, Cranborne's successor as leader of the Conservative peers, predicts the interim House 'is the one we will have for a very long time'. Superficially, nothing appears to have changed since the hereditary peers left, but the Lords has become more political because of the influx of more than 200 life peers since 1997. He accuses the government of trying to 'modernize' the House's working practices in ways that would make life easier for the executive. Some of the less controversial suggestions in the Wakeham report will be implemented, such as the establishment of a constitutional committee, but the government is 'not serious' about doing anything on its core recommendations, at least until after the next election:

The worst way forward, and if this happens Wakeham will be culpable of this, would be take Wakeham's option B, remove the 90-odd hereditary peers and replace them with 87 elected in some sort of vague way in a house of 600 or 700, wipe your hands and say, stage two is done. I don't think anybody should be fooled by that. That would not be a proper reform worthy of such a name.

He argues that the government's initial aim was to improve its control of the Lords by removing the hereditary peers, but it had failed to crush dissent in the way it had hoped:

They also did not think through what they were trying to do in terms of the role, power and functions of the second chamber. If they go on to stage two they will need to put their own base motives right at the end of the queue, work out for themselves what they want a second chamber to do, what powers it should have, what its relationship should be with the first chamber, and then decide on its composition. But there seems to me to be no thought whatsoever to this process at all. It is an empty vessel. Even before, when we tried to tease out what was in their minds about a second chamber, they came out with the argument that if we don't do stage one, we will never get to stage two. Well, I don't agree with that, but even if you take that at face value, there should still be an answer to the question: 'All right, but then what vision do you have of this second stage?' Answer there came none. It might have been because they did not want that to upset stage one. But now stage one has gone, why can't they tell us? And they are not telling us just because it is a deep secret clutched to the bosom of New Labour. The fact is they don't know the answer. They haven't the faintest idea how to take this whole debate on. It is an outrage.

Bill Rodgers, the Liberal Democrat leader in the Lords, takes the Tory expressions of outrage with a large pinch of salt: 'I don't really think that Cranborne is to be believed. The idea that he wants to get rid of the hereditaries is just not true. The idea that the Tory party can be seen as a reform party in the Lords – that is standing things on its head.'

In the view of Robert Hazell of the Constitution Unit, Labour is unlikely to be bounced into a stage two reform by embarrassment over the continuing role of the hereditaries. But exasperation over lost votes in the interim House might force it into action:

The irony is that any version of stage two will give the government an infinitely harder time. If the government is rational and it is simply interested in having a second chamber that will present it with the minimum obstacles to its legislation, then it should stick with what it has got and bite its lip.

Part of Labour's problem with the Lords is the strength of its unicameralist tradition, which makes it hard for the party to create any credible and legitimate second chamber. The lessons the party learned in the Thatcher period about the need to build in constitutional checks and balances on the executive appear to have been quickly forgotten.

A PEER'S NIGHTMARE

For some recently created Labour life peers, the problem of how the House of Lords is composed pales in comparison with the practical problems of trying to work there. David Lipsey admits to a certain frustration:

I feel quite a lot of affection, quite a lot of anger with how it works at the moment. It is pretty ineffective and inefficient. It produces very little and requires a lot of able people's time and energy … I don't have a desk in my own name. I don't have a telephone and that is extremely hard because I can never be rung up here. All people can do is leave a message on my bleeper and ask me to ring them. I do have an e-mail provided but unfortunately not a modem plug so I can't use it to get messages. There are few working photocopiers and no working faxes. There are fewer meeting rooms than you need to make sure of getting one if you need to have a meeting here of any size. As you see, you can't receive visitors and you can't offer them a cup of tea. The worst thing actually which I hadn't appreciated before I came here is the lack of times for votes. And the fact that the committee stages are on the floor means that you are running a three-line Whip. You are virtually imprisoned here from 2.30 until when you go home. The result is that most of the time we only speak to fellow members of the House. And that is very bad for amateurs with contacts outside.

Lipsey sees a contradiction between the Conservatives' opposition to changing the working practices of the Lords and their insistence on keeping it as a chamber of amateurs:

The Tories at the moment are very reluctant to move away from having committee stages on the floor of the House because they think their purpose is to block legislation and keep people up half the night, which is the other problem with the way we operate. Last week we were up until two in the morning one day on the Financial Services and Markets Bill and until one in the morning for a crucial vote the next day. This is an amateur unpaid house where people have to be up at eight o'clock in the morning because they have got to earn their living by three o'clock. You can't, as the Tories do, argue that we want an amateur house where people aren't paid and have outside jobs – which on the whole I agree with – and on the other say we have got to behave like professional politicians and have all-out opposition, keep everyone up till two in the morning and avoid anything that makes it easy for the government to get its way. You can have either one of those propositions but not both simultaneously.

The problem is that the working practices, style and ethos of the Lords are largely created by the hereditary peers, whose presence Labour has now legitimized for the foreseeable future by agreeing to the Weatherill amendment. The true costs of the Irvine-Cranborne deal for Labour are now starting to emerge. Lipsey says Labour newcomers are fed up with being patronized by the surviving hereditaries:

Unless you change the composition, you will never change the style. Because the real diehards, those who don't want any change at all and think this place is perfect, are disproportionately hereditaries … I think the anomaly of having 92 hereditaries is very great and very offensive to people in the Labour party on principle, and being taunted with it the whole time is very unpleasant.

Labour has no majority in the Lords and if the Conservatives are opposed, it needs the support of the Liberal Democrats and most of the cross-bench peers to get its way. Although on the surface not much has changed, the number of new life peers arriving who dislike being treated as ignorant interlopers by Conservative hereditaries has led to some exchanges of unprecedented acrimony. In a debate on procedures in May 2000 there were accusations of 'ancestor worship'. Norman Warner, a Labour peer since 1998, said he was 'deeply underwhelmed' by the way the chamber operated: 'My perception of this place after 18 months is that it is excessively introspective and rather self-satisfied, with some deeply held social prejudices. It needs to open itself up far more to external influences on its working practices and bring in outside help and expertise to modernize its arrangements.'

His complaints drew a patronizing reply from Cranborne, who referred with sarcasm to Warner's 'long experience of this House' and the 'perennial difficulty for newcomers to parliament' who confused efficiency with effectiveness. An even more aristocratic sneer came from Earl Ferrers, who dismissed Warner's proposals for change out of hand: 'I am sorry that the noble lord is so dissatisfied. Perhaps he is a slow learner and needs more than 18 months. He reminded me of the schoolmaster who wrote a half-term report on a child and said that he was "trying". The parents said that they were so pleased. The end-of-term report arrived. It said, "very trying".'

Other new life peers have complained about their working conditions. One said he was not looking for a luxurious office, but 'I think that half a chair leg is as much as I can expect in terms of accommodation in the next five years'. John Tomlinson, who arrived in 1998, said many members of the Lords did not even have a locker. 'Many aspire not to a whole desk, but to the opportunity to share one and have somewhere where they can put down their papers and have a telephone. There are even extremely ambitious members who are looking for a half-share in a filing cabinet ... for the first time in my life, when I arrived here I felt like a gypsy.'

But it is not just hereditary peers who are a barrier to change. The overwhelmingly elderly life peers, who cannot be asked to retire, are now just as strong an influence. Lipsey says a reform that would remove the life peers would be 'a much tougher nut to crack' than getting rid of most of the hereditaries: 'Which is why Wakeham strategically decided not to force anybody to retire.'

LIBERAL DEMOCRATS LEFT UNHAPPY

Robert Maclennan MP, the Liberal Democrat constitutional spokesman in the Commons, says Labour's basically unicameralist view of the Lords has been the problem all along, a hangover from the days when it wanted to abolish the second chamber. He now finds it very hard to predict what will happen to government policy:

The government hasn't got a very clear view about anything except that it is not a terribly important issue to them. I think they would like to avoid embarrassment and turbulence in the other place. The House of Lords has been turbulent throughout this parliament. …My own view is that what has been done cannot be stable. It has no legitimacy of any kind. It hasn't got rid of the hereditaries. It is inflated by recent appointments. Its moral authority is almost entirely lacking, but if the government of the day is unpopular, and the House of Lords voices views that are hostile to the government, then it could be a bloody nuisance.

I asked Maclennan whether with the benefit of hindsight the Liberal Democrats now regretted not pinning Labour down in more detail on what would happen to the Lords after stage one:

It was presented in the Cook-Maclennan Agreement as a commitment to a democratic upper house. And Tony Blair was on record prior to the election as having supported a democratically elected upper house. But the remit of Wakeham was not agreed with the Liberal Democrats. The White Paper we did have some input into, significantly on the issue of appointments being made on a proportional basis, which reflected the agreement we made prior to the election. We agreed to a royal commission but we did not actually agree the precise terms, nor the membership, I have to say. And the membership was perhaps more important than the terms of reference. That is not just unfinished business, it is a slight unravelling of the agreement.

Maclennan says he is not surprised that Blair had to be persuaded by Wakeham to accept the idea that some members of the second chamber should be elected:

My own judgement is that the Prime Minister is not very deeply entrenched on any position vis-à-vis the House of Lords. If somebody had been able to come up with a respectable case for an appointed House, he probably would have bought it. But I don't feel that he regarded it as an issue of very high importance. He hasn't seen the House of Lords as an effective operative part of the constitution, just as a kind of adjacent assembly of notables whose opinions might prove to be interesting.

A LACK OF CLEAR GOALS

After three years of indecision and intrigue over Lords reform, Labour now finds it has far fewer choices than when it came to power; after the Cranborne-Irvine deal on the hereditaries, the White Paper and the Wakeham report, it no longer has a wide range of options. In the view of Tony Wright MP, the government could have had an agreed settlement on the basis of some kind of mixed-membership chamber long ago if it had had a clear idea of its goals:

We could have run with that system fairly easily a couple of years ago. But we didn't know really what we wanted, and so it all became messy. We started playing games with it. Now the government is having to accept what it did not want to accept when Wakeham was set up, a kind of mixed arrangement. We don't know the nature of the mix, but I think it is pretty clear that you could get broad agreement for something of that kind. And the government now needs to lead on it. It's been a dreadfully messy and unnecessary business. And it's an issue where instead of looking strong, we have begun to look weak.

The largely nominated chamber recommended by Wakeham has not won universal support in Labour ranks. At the party's National Policy Forum in Exeter in July 2000, a minority position calling for at least 50 per cent of the second chamber to be elected won enough support to ensure an open debate at the Brighton party conference in September. But this attempt to return party policy to a predominantly elected second chamber was unsuccessful, despite poll evidence that four out of five Labour voters supported it. The majority policy document approved in Brighton as the basis for the next manifesto claimed somewhat inaccurately that Labour had fulfilled its 'historic' pledge to end the automatic right of hereditary peers to sit in the Lords. The Cranborne-Irvine deal was portrayed as a minor concession which had been essential to prevent Labour's entire programme of government from being wrecked:

A small number of hereditary peers have been elected from those remaining to stay until further reform is enacted, as part of an arrangement to ensure that the House of Lords did not wreck the extensive programme of the Labour government to deliver on our promises.

It said Labour would support a number of elected members 'not less than' the options listed in Wakeham; this could mean as few as 65 under option A.

The debate leading up to the vote was illuminating, not just because open debating and voting on policy are rare at Labour conferences. Behind the fuzzy rhetoric of modernization, it revealed in stark terms the party leadership's insecurity and fear of any constitutional reform that might increase the power of the voters and make the government's job more difficult. With the big trade unions ranged against them, pro-democracy campaigners had little chance of swaying the conference. Arguing the case for electing at least half of the second chamber, Fiona Mactaggart MP told the conference this was not just 'a kind of luvvie position' without relevance to problems in schools and hospitals. 'What this has got to do with that, is our relationship with the electorate. It's our sense of trust and representativeness. I think there is a growing worry amongst British people that we are not listening to them.' Giving the voters the chance to elect the second chamber was a way of showing them that Labour's belief in democracy was more than an empty slogan, she argued. 'I fear that if you don't respect their right to vote, if we don't keep our promise that we made in our last manifesto, that we would have a more democratic second chamber, that they will say, you're all the same, why does my vote make a difference? Why bother to come out? And if they do that, that is the way to hand victory at the next general election to the Tories.'

The rest of the debate showed that such appeals to democracy cut little ice. David Boyle of the GMB union said the upper house was a 'chamber of horrors' which should be abolished rather than reformed. Other delegates warned that a largely elected upper house would 'abuse its author-ity' by obstructing Labour policies such as the minimum wage. Mike Foster MP, originator of the unsuccessful attempt to ban fox-hunting in the first session of the 1997 parliament, called on the conference not to be fooled by arguments about democracy:

A wholly elected second chamber will have the right to block, block and block again measures such as a ban on fox-hunting. The fight for change is hard enough already. Don't strengthen the role of the upper house. Don't tie our hands behind our backs. Give the Commons the right to push through change. Years of deadlock between two houses will find us no friends and only play into the hands of our enemies. And if you want change, conference, don't go for a wholly elected upper house.

Michael Duggan of the AEEU union, a self-proclaimed 'suspicious guy' and conspiracy theorist, said he had discovered that the campaign for an elected second chamber was being directed by the same people who sup-ported the hated Roy Jenkins and his report on proportional representation for the Commons. His message, unspoken but clear to all, was that these people were self-indulgent, middle-class intellectuals:

It sounds very appealing, I can understand the logic. But this isn't some sort of student union, this isn't a Fabian fringe where we are going to indulge ourselves in these debates, we are trying to build for a second term.

People on the Doncaster working-class estate where Duggan was born were not interested in such fancy questions, they wanted to hear about schools and jobs and the health service – 'real issues that matter to real people'. The amendment was the work of a minority and was backed by nobody except student unions, Liberal Democrats and Welsh and Scottish nationalists, he argued: 'I say that is a good reason to vote against.'

Sharon George from Hartlepool, Peter Mandelson's constituency, warned that in an election for the upper house, Labour voters would probably stay at home because of their 'natural abhorrence of privilege' and the result would be a chamber full of Tories: 'Conference, don't let our love for democracy give the Tories a gift.' Brenda Dean, a member of the

Wakeham commission, produced the clinching argument. She warned that the Conservatives were now supporting an elected upper house: 'I don't know about you, but if they support it, there must be something wrong with it when it comes to democracy.'

The government *coup de grâce* was delivered by Margaret Beckett, who neatly knifed the pro-democracy campaigners by bracketing them with the Tories. An elected upper house was deliberately designed to make life more difficult for the government, she argued. Reform of the Lords was only a means to an end, which was to 'lay the groundwork for our party's and our country's objectives to be secured'. Did anybody at the conference actually want to make that harder to achieve? If so, they should own up. An elected second chamber would mean two houses of equal legitimacy and consequent gridlock. This would mean 'a profound and dramatic change both in our party's policy and in our country's constitution,' she warned. Only 'academic and media commentators' favoured such an outcome. Beckett knew exactly what the British people wanted without asking them; they wanted to give the government an easy life: 'I see no evidence they want to make it harder for the governments they elect to make the change for which they elected them. Yet that is, I believe, the inescapable outcome of a second chamber in which the majority is elected.' Labour party members wanted 'a better parliament, a more modern parliament. A parliament better able to pursue reform because it itself has been reformed'.

> 66 Beckett knew exactly what the British people wanted without asking them; they wanted to give the government an easy life. 99

After what pro-democracy campaigners claimed was heavy arm-twisting by the leadership, the result of the vote was a clear defeat for the minority amendment, leaving Labour committed to a policy fully reflecting the Blair-Jay-Beckett doctrine of constitutional modernization; creating a 'better parliament, a more modern parliament' had nothing to do with extending democracy or accountability, but everything to do with making life easier for the government to get its way. It sounded like an argument for elective dictatorship.

NOTES

[1] Cooke, Sir Robert (1987) *The Palace of Westminister*, London, Burton Skira, p 127.

[2] Russell, Meg (2000) *Reforming the House of Lords. Lessons from overseas*, Oxford University Press, p 91.

[3] Mitchell, Austin (1999) *Farewell my Lords*, London, Politico's, p 9.

[4] Mitchell, p 183.

[5] Jones, Janet (1999) *Labour of Love. The 'party-political' diary of a cabinet minister's wife*, Politico's Publishing, London.

[6] Mitchell, p 135.

[7] Mitchell, p 165.

[8] Mitchell, p 176.

[9] Lords Information Office; House of Commons Library Research Paper 00/61 June 2000.

[10] 4 February 1999.

[11] Hazell, Robert and Russell, Meg (2000) *Commentary on the Wakeham Report on Reform of the House of Lords*, Constitution Unit, London.

[12] Conference papers. 'The future of the House of Lords,' 8 March 2000, Constitution Unit, London.

6

A NEW SET OF RULES

'At the next election, all parties will at last compete on a level playing field' –
Tony Blair, speaking to Labour's 1997 conference

'Voting is the only political act most British citizens undertake' – Stuart Weir
and David Beetham

AT THE BEGINNING, IT ALL LOOKED so simple. When Labour drafted its 1997
manifesto commitment to clean up British politics, the wording was
brief and to the point:

We will oblige parties to declare the source of all donations above a minimum figure:
Labour does this voluntarily and all parties should do so. Foreign funding will be
banned. We will ask the Nolan Committee to consider how the funding of political
parties should be regulated and reformed.

What could be easier? Yet this one-paragraph commitment has set in
train a series of reforms so far-reaching that British politics will never be
the same again. Political parties, once free to run their own financial
affairs as they chose, will now find the way they raise money and the
way they spend it under tight legal controls. The referendum, once
spurned as an exotic foreign import for occasional use, is set to become a
native British institution with its own rules of the game. The old certainties of election day – the ballot paper, the blunt pencil, the voting booth
in the local primary school – may be swept away. And this radically new

framework will no longer be supervised by the government, but by an independent body whose members will be chosen because they have no experience of party politics. Remarkably, these reforms have largely been agreed by consensus between the major parties.

Sounds hard to believe? Perhaps. Taken one by one, the Labour government's reforms do not seem very dramatic; taken together, they amount to the biggest changes since the 1880s, when Victorian legislators imposed strict laws to stop the buying and selling of votes in constituencies. A century late, the law is finally being updated to reflect the role of national parties, the big-spending beasts of the political world, just at the moment when their dominance of the landscape may be coming under threat. The impact of this upheaval is uncertain: it is possible that British democracy will be given a shot in the arm, voter turnout will increase and politics will become more transparent; it is also possible that the reverse will happen, leaving politics to become more and more the affair of a narrow elite who will manipulate the rules for their own advantage; perhaps, as the Labour MP Frank Field predicted, the new laws will be workable only if people are sent to jail. Whatever happens, they will require a lot of extra work by all the political parties if they are to comply.

THE GREAT AND THE GOOD

This chapter will examine how Labour has reformed the political system, introducing an independent Electoral Commission, capping spending on national election campaigns, and setting complex rules for referendums that are likely to prove crucially important to the government's chances of winning a vote on the European single currency. Here we stumble upon another paradox: the intellectual spadework for the changes Labour has introduced has been done by outside bodies rather than the party itself. The government has based most of its legislation on the work of the Committee on Standards in Public Life, a body of the great and the good headed not by politicians but by lawyers.

It is interesting to compare the fate of the committee's work with that of the commissions led by those two wily political veterans Roy Jenkins (Lord Jenkins of Hillhead) and John Wakeham (Lord Wakeham of Maldon) on electoral reform and the future of the House of Lords. Despite their strenuous efforts to produce recommendations acceptable to Downing Street, both their reports have been left to gather dust in the government's pending tray until after the next election. Meanwhile, the Committee on Standards in Public Life, the weakest of the three bodies in formal status, has shown itself to be the one most genuinely independent of government. Despite this, most of its recommendations have been accepted, not just by the government but by the other political parties too. Up and down the country, there are probably dozens of political scientists already plotting doctoral dissertations on the extraordinary influence on the British system of government wielded by the committee, headed by two eminent Oxford-educated lawyers well past retirement age. They were the Law Lord Michael Nolan (Lord Nolan of Brasted) and his successor from 1997, Sir Patrick Neill (Lord Neill of Bladen), a barrister and academic who had previously chaired the Press Council and been Warden of All Souls College, Oxford.

PLATONIC GUARDIANS

The role of the committee is worth serious analysis in its own right as an example of the British improvizational style in constitutional design. It was invented by John Major in 1994 as a flood of sleaze accusations threatened to engulf his government. When the internal procedures of his own party, of the government and of the House of Commons proved inadequate to clear the air, Major in desperation created an outside body to do the job. In the view of its critics around Westminster, the Committee on Standards in Public Life has proved a mixed blessing. 'A disaster, a complete disaster,' is the blunt verdict of Robert Cranborne (Lord Cranborne), the former Conservative leader in the House of Lords. 'The political class must feel they have created a monster,' says Brendan O'Leary of the London School of Economics. But Sir George Young, Conservative shadow Leader of the House of Commons and constitutional spokesman until October 2000, says his party is on the whole in favour of the committee: 'It has helped clean up this place … I think on the whole, it's healthy.'

THE COMMITTEE ON STANDARDS IN PUBLIC LIFE

The original terms of reference given by John Major were: 'To examine current concerns about standards of conduct of all holders of public office, including arrangements relating to financial and commercial activities, and make recommendations as to any changes in present arrangements which might be required to ensure the highest standards of propriety in public life.'

In 1997 Tony Blair added new terms of reference: 'To review issues in relation to the funding of political parties, and to make recommendations as to any changes in present arrangements.'

Under Lord Nolan it agreed 'The seven principles of public life':

- **Selflessness** – holders of public office should act solely in terms of the public interest. They should not do so in order to gain financial or other material benefits for themselves, their family, or their friends.

- **Integrity** – holders of public office should not place themselves under any financial or other obligation to outside individuals or organizations that might seek to influence them in the performance of their official duties.

- **Objectivity** – in carrying out public business, including making public appointments, awarding contracts, or recommending individuals for rewards and benefits, holders of public office should make choices on merit.

- **Accountability** – holders of public office are accountable for their decisions and actions to the public and must submit themselves to whatever scrutiny is appropriate to their office.

- **Openness** – holders of public office should be as open as possible about all the decisions and actions that they take. They should give reasons for their decisions and restrict information only when the wider public interest clearly demands.

- **Honesty** – holders of public office have a duty to declare any private interests relating to their public duties and to take steps to resolve any conflicts arising in a way that protects the public interest.

- **Leadership** – holders of public office should promote and support these principles by leadership and example.

Like the Jenkins and Wakeham commissions, this committee of the great and the good is a creation of Downing Street, not of parliament, and has no statutory base. But unlike them it has no finite lifespan; it can go on working indefinitely at the pleasure of the prime minister of the day. Rather than producing a single report to gather dust on the shelf with no follow-up, the committee is permanently open for business and can issue forceful reminders if its recommendations are ignored. Its remit is that of an ethical watchdog rather than a constitutional body, but because the UK has no written constitution, it cannot avoid straying into territory that in any other country would be covered by a constitutional court. 'We inevitably get sucked in a bit ... We are touching the constitution at many points,' Neill told me.

From the point of view of government, the committee is something of an unguided missile. It can effectively decide itself what it wants to look at, rather than waiting to have subjects referred to it, and it has made recommendations on issues such as the proper conduct of referendums which it was not asked to look into at all. After investigating the ethics of MPs and local government, it decided in 2000 to investigate standards in the Lords, a move that provoked angry protests from some of Neill's fellow peers. The committee includes senior figures from the three main political parties but has managed to proceed almost entirely by consensus, giving its reports extra weight. Only a political system in a state of transition could have produced such a unique body, a reflection of the breakdown of the old constitutional culture based on unwritten conventions.

As an ad hoc body created out of nowhere by a prime minister in political trouble, the committee could be seen as a typical product of that culture. But its work has given the British constitution a powerful push towards a quite different political culture, in which implicit conventions between 'good chaps' are replaced by explicit written codes and rules. Now part of the political landscape despite its lack of legal status, it is hard to see any future government abolishing the committee, although some of its functions will be transferred to the new Electoral Commission. Neill acknowledged when I interviewed him in June 2000 that Tony Blair could scrap the committee at any time: 'Tomorrow. Later today.' But he sounded moderately confident that the axe would not fall, at least not just yet:

> **❝ Now part of the political landscape despite its lack of legal status, it is hard to see any future government abolishing the committee. ❞**

I am not sure if you asked the Prime Minister, 'How do you see our committee five years down the road?' you would get a very clear answer. It seems to me that the committee should survive as long as it has a useful role to perform, in looking at areas of public life where things are not as they ought to be. If you get to the point where things are pretty good, or there has been a report written to say how it ought to be, then you might get to a stage of 'What are these guys doing now? This is a waste of public money.' I don't think we have got to it. I think there are issues that still need to be addressed. But I think we have a specific role of being the standards committee and if there is no proper work to be done then we should be folded up. I don't think we should be converted into a constitutional committee. That would be completely different, you would probably pick people on a different basis, and the terms of reference would be different. We are here to do one task, the crudest word is to rectify sleaze.

The committee's usefulness to the government of the day as a kind of all-purpose ethical lightning conductor was highlighted in November 1997 when Tony Blair used it to find an escape route from the severe embarrassment of what became known as the Ecclestone affair. On Neill's advice, the Labour party returned a donation of £1 million from motor racing tycoon Bernie Ecclestone after it emerged that he subsequently met Blair to discuss watering down government plans to curb tobacco advertising.

Neill's view is that however much politicians fulminate against 'unelected Platonic guardians', the man in the street believes the committee is doing a good job. Politicians at Westminster are acutely aware of their low public reputation, so when Neill and his colleagues say the tide of sleaze is ebbing, they are happy to bite their lips and put up with what has become an unofficial 'Ofpol' alongside Ofsted, Ofgas and Ofwat. Inevitably, though, the committee's work creates more trouble for the government than for the opposition. Neill acknowledges that as the public memory of the scandal-hit Major years fades, it is now easier for the Blair government to pick and choose which of the committee's recommendations it will accept and which it will politely turn down, though the public still tends to believe the worst of its political masters:

Our evidence is that the prevalence of sleaze has diminished and therefore the opinion is that there is less of it around. But I still think the public is as cynical as ever about politicians ... They are all a bunch of hypocrites, is the line, feathering their own nests. So I don't think with the public you have got a big change, but possibly you have in Whitehall and Westminster.

FUNDAMENTAL, BUT NOT TOO FUNDAMENTAL

After the 1997 election the first tranche of Labour's constitutional reform plans, including devolution to Scotland and Wales and the Human Rights Act, began their passage through parliament within a few months. Other problems on which the intellectual preparation had not been done were handed over to a variety of commissions, working parties and study groups of varying degrees of independence. Thus the Neill committee investigated party funding at Blair's request, while Roy Jenkins was appointed to head an 'independent' commission on alternatives to first-past-the-post. Out of the public eye, a third group began looking at a more limited package of reforms to make voting easier by updating the Representation of the People Act. The problem to be addressed was not so much corruption or sleaze as evidence of rising voter apathy, particularly in local government elections. But the trend was also clear in the general election that brought Labour to power, when nearly 30 per cent of electors did not vote.

In 1997, Home Secretary Jack Straw set up an internal working party chaired by junior minister George Howarth to consider why 'interest in the democratic process, as measured in part by participation in elections at all levels, had shown a steady decline over a number of years'. Straw wanted recommendations for changes 'which will lead to more open and fairer electoral procedures, command the trust of the electorate and contribute to the democratic renewal of the United Kingdom'. Howarth's report described the working party's work as 'a fundamental re-examination of our electoral process'. But despite this ambitious language the group, mostly composed of civil servants and party representatives, showed few signs of radical thinking about the workings of British democracy:

The strength of our electoral law and procedures is that they have developed with the consent of the electorate over a lengthy period. But in many ways their longevity is also their weakness. We have seen no evidence from the work we have undertaken that we should be seriously concerned about the legitimacy or fairness of elections.[1]

66 The working party did not go out and ask people why they were not voting; in fact, it conducted no original research. 99

The working party did not go out and ask people why they were not voting; in fact, it conducted no original research. Its final report was notable for its narrow focus on the technical side of the voting process and the electoral register. Not only did it deliberately avoid the tricky subject of proportional representation, but also such potentially controversial ideas as Australian-style compulsory voting. Another taboo left unexamined was the case for a fixed-term parliament, a reform which Labour promised to deliver in 1992 but subsequently dropped from its constitutional agenda.

As Professor Robert Blackburn of King's College, London points out, the convention of allowing the prime minister to pick the general election date gives a huge tactical advantage to the governing party, and with the introduction of referendums the original purpose of allowing the government to seek electoral approval for a specific piece of legislation is no longer valid:

The Queen carries out the legal ceremonies involved in dissolving parliament and causing election writs to be issued to constituency returning officers simply whenever the prime minister requests her to do so. So long as the prime minister retains his majority in the House of Commons (or if a minority administration, can ward off any no confidence motion), he is free to call a general election whenever he likes. No law or convention exists to require the prime minister to obtain the consent of MPs to a dissolution, nor even to oblige him to consult or notify them in the House of Commons. The general election date is cursorily announced to the world in the form of a press notice issued direct to the media by the prime minister's staff.[2]

This longstanding Westminster convention has been altered for the Scottish Parliament, where it is the Presiding Officer, not the head of the executive, who advises the monarch if there has to be an early dissolution. Jack Straw's view is that switching to a fixed-term parliament is 'a bit of a chimera'. The only party in favour are the Liberal Democrats, whose spokesman Robert Maclennan told the Commons in January 2000 it was a nonsense to allow the prime minister, 'who is a competitor in the race, to fire the starting gun'.

Another area left untouched was the archaic muddle of discriminatory laws barring priests and ex-priests from taking their seats in the House of Commons. In 1998, the Commons Home Affairs committee had recommended that all eligibility restrictions on the clergy, with the exception of Church of England bishops, should be lifted. According to Blackburn, 'reading the legal sources on the subject requires burrowing away in collections of parliamentary statutes to find at least nine separate legislative acts on the subject stretching back to the 16th century'. Blackburn argues that it should be for individual churches to decide whether their clergy should have the right to stand for parliament, and the voters should have the right to choose: 'There are basic principles of political liberty involved here, about which British public policy as enshrined in its law is muddled and which the government and parliament seem reluctant to confront and prefer to ignore.'

Within the tight limitations of its approach, the Howarth working party managed to make progress on a series of second-order issues, most of which involved updating Victorian voting law to cope with the demands of a far more mobile society. Chief among these was the way the electoral register was compiled once a year, making it difficult for anyone who moved house in the year before an election to vote. It was estimated that as many as three or four million people were effectively barred from voting through not being on the register. Because of strict rules on residence, homeless people were also denied the right to vote, while voluntary psychiatric patients were in the same position. Under the Representation of the People Act 2000 which followed the working party's recommendations, there will be a rolling register updated all year round. Homeless people will be able to make a 'declaration of local connection' to enable them to vote, while psychiatric patients detained in a mental hospital who have not committed a crime will also be able to register. Polling stations will have more aids for blind and disabled people. Service voters and remand prisoners will be able to register at their home addresses, but there will be no change in the longstanding rule that convicted prisoners cannot vote.[3] A statistical effect of increasing the number of voters who are registered may be that although in absolute terms more people may vote, the headline figure for percentage turnout is likely to fall even further.

VOTE EARLY, BUT NOT TOO OFTEN

The most eye-catching feature of the legislation was the green light it gave for the Home Office to experiment with ways of making voting easier by changing polling hours and times, using mobile polling stations, electronic voting, telephone voting and postal voting. As Jack Straw told the House of Commons:

We all have pet theories as to what might improve turnouts, such as weekend voting, all-postal ballots, mobile polling stations, electronic voting and other wheezes. The simple truth is that none of us knows what, if anything, will make a difference.

But he acknowledged that the problem of apathy among the electorate probably had deeper causes:

I do not believe, and I am sure that no member of the House believes, that the Bill will arrest and reverse the decline in turnout at all levels of election. Whatever the electoral procedures are, people will vote only if they are interested in the body being elected and feel that it is worthwhile to vote. So long as we do not have compulsory voting, people in our democracy have the right not to vote as much as they have the right to vote.

Tony Blair, William Hague and Paddy Ashdown provoke a big slump in turnout at the European Elections.
Copyright ©Steve Bell, 1999.

Simon Hughes of the Liberal Democrats told him the Bill failed to address the real problem of matching votes to seats through proportional representation:

The key question that the government are rightly asking is how British people are best represented. How can they vote most easily, how can they participate most fully, and – the government's unasked question – how can their wishes be reflected most accurately?

Hughes said the distortions of first-past-the-post meant that in the 1998 council elections in the London borough of Newham, Labour won 57 per cent of the vote but secured all 60 seats. In Cheltenham, one of his own party's strongholds, the Liberal Democrats won 49 per cent of the vote in 1995 and got 93 per cent of the seats:

We will not persuade people that voting matters unless outcomes reflect what they want when they go to the ballot box …The reality is that people will vote most if they think that they have a chance of influencing something most. If parliament is more powerful, people will vote more often in parliamentary elections. If local government has its chains taken away, people will vote more often in local elections. If those institutions are restricted, 'cabin'd, cribb'd, confin'd, bound in', people will ask, 'Why bother? It won't change anything.' That is why in so many parts of Britain the voting culture reflects that of the one-party state. We have all heard people say, 'It doesn't matter whom you put up. Nothing will change.' That culture has to be changed and the one-party state mentality has to go.

In the House of Lords the Conservative peer and Hull University political scientist Philip Norton dismissed the idea that low turnouts were caused by the difficulty of voting, and said changes to the system were not a panacea for current weaknesses in local government: 'People do not usually stay at home in local elections because of problems with the process of voting.' Norton cited a MORI poll in 1998 showing only 4 per cent of electors in local elections did not know where they were supposed to vote or found it too inconvenient:

People were more likely to say that they did not believe that voting made a difference. If people do not believe that voting makes a difference, there is little incentive to vote, regardless of how convenient or efficient the method of voting.

Most electoral experts remain sceptical about whether the updated Representation of the People Act will achieve its goal of persuading more people to vote. Pilot schemes were conducted in 32 local authorities for the May 2000 local elections, but they provided little evidence of any improvement in voter turnout. The only exception was a big increase shown in a few wards which experimented with all-postal voting. In Doncaster's Conisborough ward, for example, turnout rose from 24.5 per cent in May 1999 to 44.0 per cent in May 2000. Electoral expert Professor John Curtice told me he believed the postal voting results had 'caught the government in a bind'. If the government were to extend the pilot and abolish polling stations, allowing everyone to vote by post, then the secrecy of the ballot would no longer be guaranteed. Turnout might rise, but there would be no way of controlling whether family members had voted on each other's behalf. Curtice's view is that it is hard to see any government introducing postal voting for a general election. Another factor is that postal voting is far more costly to organize than normal balloting, costing 2.5 times as much.

A Local Government Association research report on the pilot projects found that there was no positive evidence of increased fraud, but noted that 'the easier it is to cast a postal vote, the more attention must be paid to security'. Turnout more than doubled in all-postal ballots where no declaration of identity was required. The research found that postal voting did not appear to help or hinder any particular party. The least successful pilot appeared to be the one involving weekend voting, which led to a decline in turnout.

ELECTION PROCEDURES

The Representation of the People Act 2000 keeps unchanged most of the rules on who is eligible to vote and run for office. It introduces a rolling electoral register updated all year round.

■ Detained psychiatric patients cannot vote but voluntary patients can register using their hospital address.

■ A declaration of local connection by homeless persons qualifies them as residents for registration.

■ Members of the armed forces can register at their home addresses.

■ New rules for the sale of the electoral register lay down that an edited version will be offered for sale and voters can remove their names from it.

■ Local authorities can apply to the Home Secretary for permission to use new procedures such as extended voting, postal voting and electronic voting in England and Wales. The Home Secretary can use secondary legislation to extend use of these schemes at local elections in England and Wales.

■ People with disabilities will find it easier to vote.

THE NEILL PACKAGE

The Neill committee published its package of recommendations on political funding in October 1998 after a year in which it took evidence from a wide range of sources. The second volume of the committee's Fifth Report contains more than 600 closely printed pages of evidence, not just from the UK but also from Canada, Sweden, the United States, Ireland and Germany. It made 100 recommendations, of which the most important on funding were:

■ compulsory disclosure of annual donations over £5,000 nationally and £1,000 per constituency;

■ an end to blind trusts, a device Labour had used in opposition;

■ donations only to be allowed from a legally defined 'permissible source'; this would bar foreign donations, allowing them only from those entitled to register as UK voters and from companies incorporated in the UK;

■ a ban on anonymous donations over £50;

■ no upper limit on donations;

■ a spending limit of £20 million in a general election for each party;

■ clear rules for auditing campaign spending;

■ no fresh state funding, but tax relief on donations up to £500 to encourage small donations;

■ wider scrutiny by an honours committee of possible links between political donors and honours;

■ more money for opposition parties at Westminster and an independently run policy development fund;

■ controls on election spending by third parties over £25,000, with registration and reporting requirements, a ban on foreign donations, and local and national limits;

■ continued free television and radio broadcasts for parties;

■ continued ban on television and radio political advertising;

■ shareholder consent for company donations.

The committee also recommended creation of an independent Electoral Commission with wide executive and investigative powers. This body would take over responsibility for the registration of political parties but it would not be able to bring prosecutions itself. Failure to report donations would mean a party surrendering the money in question, and would leave its officers facing criminal charges.

Its final recommendation was a surprise – it strayed into an area which Tony Blair had not asked it to investigate, that of the rules for referendums. Neill argued that referendums had to be considered along with elections in its overall examination of political funding and the role of the Electoral Commission. The committee was worried by the one-sided nature of the September 1997 devolution referendum in Wales, where the government campaigned heavily for a 'yes', but still only won by around 6,000 votes. It recommended more of a level playing field for future referendums, giving each side a fair opportunity to put its case and access to a minimum level of funding to enable a UK-wide campaign. It recommended that the government of the day should remain neutral and refrain from distributing material promoting its case. Third parties spending more than £25,000 in a referendum would have to register. All this was of more than a little interest to campaigners for and against British entry into the European single currency, which the Blair government has said will be determined by a referendum.

GOVERNMENT SAYS YES TO MOST RECOMMENDATIONS

The government's reply to Neill's report came in July 1999. It accepted most of the recommendations, with a few important exceptions:

■ there would be no tax-free deductions for donations;

■ the provision for complete government neutrality in referendums should be limited to 28 days before polling day;

- donors would have to be actually registered to vote in the UK rather than just entitled to do so;

- in order to comply with European law, the right to make donations would be extended not just to companies incorporated in the UK but to all EU companies carrying on business in the UK;

- election campaign spending would be measured from one year before polling day;

- there would be set limits for spending by third parties in referendums;

- there would be a much wider role for the Electoral Commission, which would advise the government on electoral law, encourage people to vote, and eventually take over responsibility for the Boundary Commissions which decide the size of constituencies. It would be responsible not to the government but to parliament.

Many elements of the package were widely seen as long overdue, filling a legal vacuum around the role of political parties. Since the 1880s there had been strict rules on election spending at constituency level, but no provisions to control what political parties spent nationally. They were not required to register, and the Conservative party did not exist as a national legal entity. This changed only in 1998 when the government's introduction of proportional representation for Scottish, Welsh and European elections obliged it to introduce legislation to register party names for the first time.

LABOUR'S TURN TO LEGISLATE

Labour's enthusiasm for a reform of party funding did not mean that it had thought seriously about the issues in opposition, even less that it had done detailed advance planning for legislation. Its desire to change the law was motivated not by any abstract commitment to constitutional reform, but more by a desire to remove what the party saw as a historic injustice of which it was the victim. The absence of a ban on foreign political funding, like the existence of hereditary peers, was a huge bump in the playing field that favoured the Conservatives, and Labour wanted it ironed out. Foreign donors had given the Conservatives £10 million before the 1997 election, enabling them to outspend Labour. Historically outgunned by the Conservatives in the 'arms race' of election spending, Labour leaders were determined to even up the score. They had no way of monitoring, let alone halting the flood of corporate donations to the Conservatives under Margaret Thatcher, some of them from foreign tycoons, solicited by her self-styled 'jolly bagman' Robert McAlpine (Lord McAlpine). According to the Liberal Democrat peer Christopher Rennard, speaking in a Lords debate:

In each of the 1974 elections the Conservative party was calculated to have spent less than £100,000 on its national campaigns. By 1979, with the services for the first time of the noble lord, Lord Saatchi, in charge of advertising, the Conservative party is estimated to have spent £2 million nationally. By 1983 the sum was £4 million; by 1987 it was £9 million; by 1992 it was £11 million; and by 1997 it was a staggering £28 million.

But by the 1997 election Labour's own fundraisers had learned to reduce their reliance on the trade unions, the party's traditional paymasters, and to tap new sources of funds among the rich and powerful. After the electoral landslide, with the Conservatives looking as though they would be out of power for a decade, the balance of advantage tipped even further towards Labour. Conservative chairman Cecil Parkinson (Lord Parkinson) ruefully told the Neill Committee in April 1998 that the party's financial position was 'very, very difficult', with donors scared off through fear of disclosure of their names. These financial problems and the party's need to shake off the 'sleaze' tag acquired under Major appear to have persuaded the Conservatives that they would be best advised to cooperate with Labour over reform, rather than resist.

The party's potential vulnerability over funding has been highlighted by its heavy reliance since 1997 on donations of around £1 million a year from its own treasurer, the Belize-based businessman Michael Ashcroft, now Lord Ashcroft. Sensitive about the Ecclestone affair and about the need to protect its own millionaire donors, Labour has treated Ashcroft with kid gloves, although some heavyhanded attacks on the Tory treasurer by Labour backbencher Peter Bradley in the Commons must have left the Conservatives with no illusions about the damage they might suffer should the government 'cut up nasty'. Labour says 40 per cent of its income comes from membership and small donations, 30 per cent from trade unions and 20 per cent from major donors – enough to ensure a mutual interest in avoiding too much mudslinging on the subject of millionaires. This explains the decorous mood of

❝Sensitive about the Ecclestone affair and about the need to protect its own millionaire donors, Labour has treated Ashcroft with kid gloves.❞

consensus and cross-party agreement between Labour and the Conservatives in which the Political Parties, Elections and Referendums Bill passed through the Commons in the first half of 2000. The Liberal Democrats, who have always had difficulty attracting large donors and keeping up with the other parties in the spending 'arms race', were also strongly in favour of new rules, though they were disappointed that Labour had dropped its earlier acceptance of the idea of state funding.

But consensus on the floor of the House of Commons also has its risks – when all three parties agree, there is little incentive to examine the wording of legislation too closely or probe it with amendments. Memories of the Dangerous Dogs Act and the Child Support Agency, both of which proved disastrous despite the all-party backing they received, have not yet faded at Westminster.

FAREWELL TO THE 1880s

Jack Straw, introducing the Bill's second reading in January 2000, presented it not as a measure designed to cure the abuses of the Conservative party but as a bipartisan attempt to plug a legislative gap left by the Victorians:

For the first time, how political parties conduct themselves will be the subject of statutory regulation. Political groupings have been a feature of our parliamentary system of government for more than 300 years, and it has been well over 100 years since Disraeli led the way with the development of mass party organizations to parallel his 1867 extension of the franchise. It is something of a paradox, then, that so little statutory recognition has so far been given to the central role played by political parties in the political life of this country ... Given every other change that has taken place in our national life over the past 120 years, it is astonishing that we still conduct our elections according to rules laid down at the end of the 19th century. They tightly regulate spending by candidates and third parties at a constituency level, but do not recognize even the existence of political parties and third parties at the national level. That is plainly absurd, and the Bill puts the situation right.

Straw argued that the Bill would be in the interests of all the major parties and would strengthen rather than weaken them:

At the heart of the Bill's provisions is the need to ensure that the funding of political parties is open and transparent. Greater transparency will not only strengthen the accountability of political parties but help to buttress their financial standing. The secrecy that has hitherto been permitted to political parties in their funding, and the scandals to which such secrecy has given rise in recent years, have undoubtedly left a sour taste. In contrast, all political parties – and the reputation of our political system as a whole – will benefit from the Bill.

Straw noted that election spending by the two main parties had mushroomed from an average of £5 million each in 1983 to £27 million in 1997. 'If we took no action, those sums could easily exceed £30 million for each party at the next general election.'

The Bill cleared the Commons with all-party support in March 2000. The government offered some concessions, though it refused to budge on its refusal to allow tax relief for political donations, saying this would cost the Exchequer several million pounds a year and would amount to an extra subsidy from the taxpayer to political parties. By the time it reached the House of Lords, however, weaknesses began to emerge more clearly as the government introduced more and more amendments. It became apparent that the attempt to turn the Neill committee's recommendations into watertight legal language was making the Bill more and more complex, with even the government uncertain about how it would work in practice. After a second reading debate in April in the Lords and the first day of its committee stage in May, the Bill vanished from the parliamentary timetable, a sign that the government had decided on a major rethink. 'I think the government has just twigged that under the provisions of the Bill Labour is going to be hard hit by the national campaign limits. They have probably realized that they are going to get more than we are,' Philip Norton told me.

Sir George Young believes the Bill will help restore the reputation of the political class:

I think the cap on election spending makes sense, we agree with that, 20 million or wherever. I think that will curtail massive advertising campaigns. I hope it won't have an impact on people coming forward to be officers of political parties. When I spoke on second reading I said I was slightly worried. We do need more volunteers. I hope that by implementing what Neill/Nolan suggested it will help clean up British politics by a ban on overseas funding and the transparency of major donations. I think on balance it will help raise the esteem in which we are held.

But Brendan O'Leary of the LSE is sceptical about the wisdom of subjecting political parties to comprehensive state control:

It is too legalistic, trying to regulate things that should not be regulated. It is trying to turn parties into animals which are partly in the state and partly outside it. It is very problematic. In a great number of European countries, when the state became the supporter of political parties, we saw deep levels of corruption, even in Germany. I think there is a very strong case for keeping parties free from the state … Money is much more powerful than the individual voters and there are issues of freedom of organization and so on. But what was nice was that the whole period of the Major government did create a fright for the political class, it was looking cheap and rather easily corruptible. My own views are old-fashioned, I would like to see a smaller political elite paid a lot more to be incorruptible. If we want a very high quality political class, we should pay for it.

Another doubter is the independent MP Martin Bell, who said he detected 'an undemocratic element at the Bill's heart'. While the kind of sleaze represented by cash in brown envelopes had been dealt with, there was still a problem of the relationship between political donations and the award of honours. Signing a large cheque to a political party was still a pathway to honours, he argued, citing testimony to the Neill Committee by the outgoing chairman of the Honours Scrutiny Committee, Francis Pym (Lord Pym), who said such donations were a bonus rather than a minus for candidates. 'The chairman might as well have provided us with a rate card. How much for a peerage? How much for a knighthood, or for a humble MBE? What will £50,000 a year for five years buy?' Political donations should be of zero significance in the award of honours or should even be enough to disqualify candidates, Bell argued.

Critics in the Lords, where the Bill had a much rougher passage than in the Commons, argued that it would be a bureaucratic nightmare for party treasurers, replacing a free-for-all with a web of onerous regulation. Conservative spokesman John MacKay (Lord MacKay of Ardbrecknish) described it as complex and hard to understand:

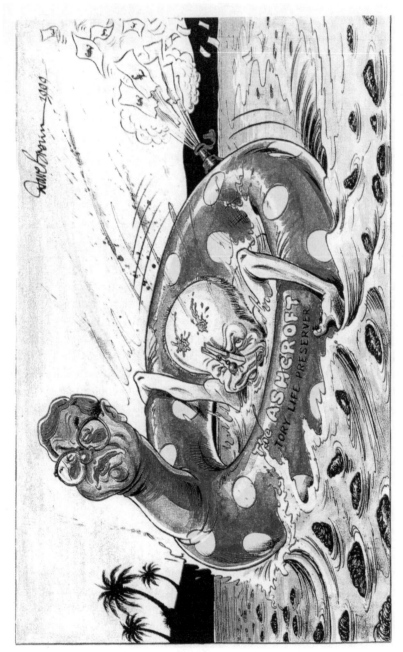

Belize-based millionaire Michael Ashcroft, the Conservative party treasurer, helps keep William Hague's party afloat with around £3 million of his own money. Labour, with its own friendly millionaires to protect, leaves the attacks on Ashcroft largely to the newspapers. Copyright © Dave Brown, 1999.

What at first sight would seem to be a few simple, easily understood propositions in the Fifth Report of the Committee on Standards in Public Life have been turned into a long, complicated and, in many places, pretty impenetrable legalese which no ordinary person could be expected to follow. If ever a Bill needed to be written in plain English, it is this one, affecting as it does the very building blocks of our parliamentary democracy. This Bill will need to be understood not just by the treasurers of our parties nationally – they may have access to legal opinions – but by the treasurers of every constituency association of every political party up and down the land. Frankly, if a potential candidate for the office of treasurer – it is never the easiest office to fill in any organization – finds that he has to read, mark and inwardly digest the stuff in this Bill, he will pass up the chance of being constituency treasurer; and, worse, he will advise all his friends to do likewise – and we are supposed to be encouraging people to participate in the political process!

Liberal Democrat Tom McNally (Lord McNally) said the system should be '… simple, understandable and useable by people, many of whom are amateurs. It is not just professional politicians that will make the system work, but thousands and thousands of volunteers. And if the system becomes too complicated, it will become extremely difficult'.

Sir Geoffrey Howe (Lord Howe of Aberavon) said the Bill was a legislative mountain whose 'over-intrusiveness, over-prescription and over-detail' reminded him of his own legislative mistakes as a Conservative minister:

I am concerned that in the strategic sense the scope, intrusiveness and detail of this legislation go beyond what is sensibly manageable. It was difficult, even in those unregulated days, to find anyone able or willing to act as treasurer. How much more difficult will it now be when this legislation will be judged not simply by the particular provisions brought to bear on any action, but by the fact that it is contained in a Bill of 180 pages with 19 schedules, one of which is five pages long, listing 75 possible offences, 30 of which are punishable by up to one year in prison? It is that overwhelming, comprehensive set of provisions which will be the worry when the legislation comes to be applied. It will be seen as a serious legislative intrusion into the arteries, and indeed the capillary tubes, of democratic life, at a time when the lifeblood of democracy seems to be coursing ever more slowly and in ever shorter supply. I am deeply concerned about legislation, however well considered, on that scale, passed at such speed.

Philip Norton said the Bill would create a 'phenomenal compliance burden' on local party officials, and former Conservative minister Michael Jopling (Lord Jopling), said parties would employ lawyers to hunt for loopholes:

The Bill as it stands will inevitably lead to a new science of keeping the campaign legal and within the law but at the same time taking advantage of all the loopholes in election law that appear as a result of the Bill. The complexity of the Bill and the raft of new offences, running into pages and pages, make it inevitable that not only will parties at local and national level need accountants to look after their finances, but those accountants and those organizers will need a lawyer at their elbow as well in order to ensure that they are kept within this new complexity of election law. The science, which I believe will grow, of finding loopholes in election law will be comparable to that of finding tax loopholes which has proved so profitable to so many professional people. Parties will be forced into trying to find such loopholes. I can hear them now saying, 'If we don't take advantage of every loophole, the other parties will, and they will trample all over our backs.'

Janet Fookes (Baroness Fookes) said she feared the Bill would create the same kind of bureaucratic nightmare as the Child Support Agency, which proved unworkable although it was a product of all-party agreement. Jack Straw told me these complaints were exaggerated; he said the risk of jail for party treasurers was no worse than that faced already by constituency agents, who have been legally liable since the 1880s for staying within the spending rules: 'The courts and prosecutors exercise common sense.' He said the Bill would mean some extra administrative burdens for parties but this would be more than offset by an end to the 'arms race' because spending would now be capped.

> ❝ She feared the Bill would create the same kind of bureaucratic nightmare as the Child Support Agency, which proved unworkable although it was a product of all-party agreement. ❞

THE POLITICAL PARTIES, ELECTIONS AND REFERENDUMS ACT

The Political Parties, Elections and Referendums Act establishes an Electoral Commission of between five and nine members which will be independent of government, reporting to a committee headed by the Speaker of the Commons. The committee includes the Home Secretary, a local government minister, the chairman of the Home Affairs Select Committee, and five backbenchers appointed by the Speaker. Members of the Electoral Commission cannot be members of a political party or have held any party office or have been donors to party funds in the past ten years. The commission has extensive functions, and will eventually take over the work of the Boundary Commissions which decide the size of constituencies, although it is not responsible for the work of returning officers in individual constituencies. It maintains a registration scheme for political parties, supervises their finances and their spending, promotes public awareness of electoral systems and EU institutions, and reviews election law and practice. It gives out up to £2 million a year in policy development grants. Parties register separately either in Northern Ireland or in the rest of the UK because Northern Ireland has been exempted from the ban on foreign donations for at least four years. In the rest of the UK foreign donations are banned, but 'permissible donors' include anyone who is registered to vote. This means UK residents from around 80 Commonwealth countries and 14 EU states are included, as are registered companies incorporated in the EU which do business in the UK. Parties are responsible for ensuring their donors are 'permissible' by checking the electoral register. There are no tax breaks for political donations, and illegal donations can be forfeited by a court order. Parties have to report their donations every three months, and every week during a general election campaign.

There is no upper limit on campaign donations but there is a lower threshold for reporting of £200; any donations over £5,000 (£1,000 at constituency level) must be reported to the Electoral Commission (though not in Northern Ireland) and the identity of the donors will be made public. Parties have to file accounts with the Electoral Commission and follow tight rules on book-keeping. Parties are given grants of up to £700,000 to cope with the initial costs of compliance. Maximum spending by national parties in a general election is held to £30,000 per constituency, giving the big parties an upper limit of around £20 million to spend in the year preceding the poll. This is in addition to a theoretical maximum of £5.6 million spent in individual constituencies. Lower limits apply in Scottish, Welsh and Northern Irish elections and elections for the European Parliament. Items of campaign spending over £200 have to be recorded and invoiced. Third parties such as trade unions and pressure groups have to notify the Electoral Commission if they spend more than £10,000, and are allowed to spend a maximum of £800,000 each in a general election.

Referendum campaigns are not subject to any overall limit on spending, but 'permitted participants' who spend more than £10,000 must register with the Electoral Commission. Political parties have to keep within spending limits determined by their percentage of the general election vote, from £500,000 to £5 million. Designated umbrella organizations for 'yes' and 'no' campaigns get up to £600,000 in financial help from the Electoral Commission and the right to send a free mailshot to all voters. Each campaign can spend up to £5 million while other 'permitted participants' can spend up to £500,000 each.

The government has to observe a 28-day 'purdah' before the vote. The Electoral Commission does not have the right to approve the referendum question but can give its opinion on whether it is intelligible. Individual referendums and their questions will still have to be authorized by separate parliamentary legislation on each occasion. Overseas voters will be able to go on voting in UK elections for 15 years (previously 20). Penalties for violating the terms of the Act include fines or up to a year in prison.

NO POLITICAL EUNUCHS

Many peers were worried about the way the government followed the Neill committee's recommendation in excluding from the Electoral Commission anyone with an active past career in party politics. Seasoned election campaigners in all parties warned that this was a big mistake. Tom McNally said it was wrong to insist on the appointment of 'political eunuchs' and a veteran elections organizer, Labour's Joyce Gould (Lady Gould of Potternewton), said: 'I have great difficulty in believing that it is possible to form a commission of people with no basic experience of the job that they are meant to supervise or regulate.' The government took account of these objections by creating a panel of parliamentary parties to give advice to the Electoral Commission. Neill took issue with the government for expanding the duties of the Electoral Commission beyond what his committee had recommended, by giving it the additional task of political education:

My opinion is that it is a wholly inappropriate role to give to the Electoral Commission as we conceived it. I cannot see how it could carry out the duties conscientiously under Clause 12 without being drawn into political controversy. How does one explain the electoral systems of this country in a wholly neutral way? If one thinks of a clause which says that people can be employed to run programmes, who does one invite to run such a programme? Obviously the natural place to go would be to the politics departments in universities. Let us imagine a professor of politics having to give a completely neutral lecture about the electoral system; any professor who accepts the burden of neutrality should not be in his job at all. He should have a clear view.

The government resisted pressure from Conservatives and Liberal Democrats to allow tax relief on political donations up to £500. An amendment was passed in the House of Lords but was thrown out by the Commons on the grounds that the second chamber had exceeded its powers by approving a measure that would affect government revenues. Another target of criticism was the Bill's definition of the accounting period for election campaign expenses as one year before the date of the poll. As Philip Norton pointed out, this would make sense only if the House of Commons was elected for a fixed term and the election date was known in advance. With the government free to decide the date at short notice, all parties would be in the dark as to when to start counting. The Lords debates produced some moments of government embarrassment, as when the Conservatives' John MacKay (Lord MacKay of Ardbrecknish) spotted that the Bill would oblige the Prime Minister to handle the paperwork personally every time a Labour party constituency treasurer died or resigned:

Is he aware that every now and then – and I suspect in reality quite often – somebody will be trotting up to Downing Street and popping into his red box a form which he will be expected to sign stating that Joe Bloggs has been replaced by Jeanie Bloggs in the Any Town Labour party?

Steve Bassam, the Home Office minister piloting the Bill through the Lords, acknowledged frankly that it was cumbersome and bureaucratic. The most significant change in the Bill as it went through parliament concerned Northern Ireland. All parties acknowledged that for reasons of personal security there was a good case for keeping the identities of political donors secret in the province. But the Neill committee's recommendation to allow anyone in the Irish Republic to be a permissible donor, on the grounds that Sinn Fein operated as a single party on both sides of the border, was unworkable. This would not prevent funding coming in from donors in the United States through the Republic, which would not contravene Irish law. The government then decided that the only way to solve the problem was to exempt Northern Ireland parties completely from the ban on foreign donations. This inevitably meant the creation of a separate register of Northern Ireland parties, and a 'firewall' in party funding between the province and the rest of the UK. This left all parties uneasy. The Conservatives portrayed the measure as a sop to Sinn Fein, allowing it and other Irish nationalist parties freedom to receive unlimited funds from sympathizers across the Atlantic that they could use not only to fight elections but also for referendum campaigns in Northern Ireland and the UK. MacKay outlined the problem:

All of a sudden, the Scottish National party will not be able to obtain money from abroad. If an American citizen of Scottish descent becomes besotted with the 'old country' and thinks that we all want independence and decides to give some of his money to the Scottish National party, he will not be allowed to do that. However, his Irish-American neighbour will be allowed to do that. I just do not understand the fairness of that proposition. It is not at all fair; in fact, it constitutes a reward for violence and a penalty for being non-violent. That cannot be right.

Before the amended Bill was passed by the Commons, Ulster Unionist party leader David Trimble complained bitterly: 'In terms of party organization, a barrier has been put up across the Irish Sea. We are being treated as if we are not part of the United Kingdom. That is fundamentally wrong and deeply offensive to us.'

Eurosceptics in both Houses were deeply suspicious that the referendum provisions would be used to rig a referendum on the single currency. They pointed out that the spending limits would favour the pro-euro parties and handicap the Conservatives. MacKay told the Lords:

In a referendum on the euro, if one were to be called, the Labour party, the Liberal Democrat party, Plaid Cymru in Wales and the SNP in Scotland would be able to spend a combined total of £9 million to run their campaign to abolish the pound, whereas the Conservative party would be able to spend only £5 million to save the pound. Whatever noble Lords may think of the arguments, that is not a level playing field.

Meanwhile, third-party anti-euro campaigners such as the Yorkshire businessman Paul Sykes would be able to spend only £500,000. But as MacKay explained, he would probably find a loophole:

In any referendum campaign, if a rich person wants to go abroad, base himself in Brussels, Paris or wherever, and spend his money trying to influence one side or the other, there is absolutely nothing that can be done about it ... We can forget about limits. I know that the government are terrified about a Mr Sykes, whom I have never met. Frankly, Mr Sykes can simply move from Yorkshire to Brussels and get on with spending all the money that the government fear he might spend in a campaign on the euro on what they see to be the wrong side. So all their efforts to put limits on campaigning will be totally set aside – they will be just nonsense.

MacKay pointed out that because the 'purdah' provision in a referendum campaign would be limited to one month – a departure from the Neill committee's recommendation – the government would still have ample time to influence the result: 'I consider it grossly unfair and yet another attempt to rig future referendums.'

FROM ZERO TO TOTAL REGULATION

The Bill, 175 pages of dense text in its initial version, had swollen to nearly 250 pages by the time it received royal assent. 'We have gone from zero to total regulation of political parties in one Bill,' explained Bassam. There was much talk of Pandora's boxes and coaches and horses being driven through loopholes. Each day of debate appeared to turn up new problems, which were quickly plugged by fresh government amendments. There were predictions that the Act might be successfully challenged in court under the European Convention on Human Rights. Joyce Gould told me the final version of the legislation, though longer, had become simpler and was much improved thanks to the long scrutiny in the Lords, which contrasted sharply with the perfunctory way it had been handled in the Commons. 'If ever there was a case for having a House of Lords, this Bill is it,' she claimed. 'I think this Bill has been examined minutely, every single dot and comma.' She played down the pessimists' predictions: 'All party treasurers, if they are doing their jobs, should be able to do the things required in the Bill.'

> ❝ There was much talk of Pandora's boxes and coaches and horses being driven through loopholes. Each day of debate appeared to turn up new problems, which were quickly plugged by fresh government amendments. ❞

But Gould acknowledged that it was still a leap in the dark. Christopher Rennard of the Liberal Democrats said the law was still flawed in many respects and would not produce a true level playing field. He told me that the approach of the larger parties to capping general election campaign spending had changed since Labour had become by far the wealthier of the two:

You only had to see their conference with a massive amount of exhibition space, heavily oversubscribed. They are the governing party. At an earlier stage the Labour party suggested a £15 million limit, in its evidence to Neill. The government followed Neill in going for £20 million. It looked a pretty tall order at one point but now Labour think they can raise that. So it suits them. The Conservatives started off saying £20 million is fine, but have now done a volte-face on this issue and decided to argue actually for £15 million. Lord Ashcroft, the Conservative treasurer, voted for an amendment that wanted it cut to £13 million. That indicates the Conservatives may struggle to get to £20 million.

Ironically, the uneven playing field that Labour wanted to make level in its own electoral interests is now tilted in its favour; if any party will be handicapped by the end of the 'arms race' in general election spending, it will be Labour, not the Conservatives. In a future referendum on the single currency, the playing field will not be level at all, but wealthy third parties will find their freedom to spend curbed, and are likely to be marginalized by political parties. Rennard commented:

It has highlighted the impossibility of having a fair referendum. The Neill committee thought it was impossible to have spending limits at all, and the government thought the eurosceptics might raise huge amounts of money and that would hardly be fair.

He criticized the Act for ducking the issues of state funding – a long-standing Liberal Democrat goal – and of a maximum limit on single donations, pointing out that in the US presidential campaign nobody was allowed to give either candidate directly more than $1,000.

LIVINGSTONE'S LAW

The legislation could produce unexpected winners and losers. Only the experience of several elections will reveal whether it will tighten or loosen the vice-like grip on political power which large national parties have exerted for the past century. In the words of Tony Wright: 'Politics in Britain is a bleak place for those who eschew party. Those who have broken with or been rejected by their parties and have gone on to ask the electorate for their continued support have all failed, usually immediately, always eventually.'[4] But this conventional wisdom has already been challenged by Ken Livingstone's runaway victory over the Labour party machine in the contest to be mayor of London. Even the campaign experts in the major parties are uncertain what the long-term effects of the new law will be. Gould predicted that the Act might help parties win greater public acceptance: 'I don't think they are going to be changed but I think they are going to become more acceptable. The public can see what the political parties are doing. The whole sleaze episode has got to be put behind us, and I think that will be appreciated.'

Others are more critical. Alex Salmond of the SNP said the way the Bill dealt with Northern Ireland meant there was no longer any consensus. Independent MP Martin Bell said: 'In many respects it is profoundly un-democratic and militates against the independent and independent-minded. It will allow vast sums of money to be thrown at the electoral process and it will take us further down the American path.' The same fear was expressed by Robert Cranborne in the Lords, that the Act would encourage a *de facto* 'closed shop' of larger parties enjoying a privileged position:

One of the great difficulties in the constitutional arrangements of our country is that there is an ill-defined relationship between parties, which are an essential part of our system, and the more carefully defined constitutional elements of our system. We agree that parties are necessary to make the system work and yet, up until now, parties have not been clearly constitutionally defined. One of the effects of the Bill is that parties will be much more clearly defined as part of the constitutional arrangements of this country. Although that may be an inevitable consequence of a number of things which have occurred, particularly in the past three years, what is also happening is that the flexibility which allowed the Labour party to come into being as the dominating party against the Conservatives in the last century will become a thing of the past. In a curious way, the Labour party, having taken advantage of that flexibility, is, perhaps rather belatedly in its view, beginning to pull the ladder up behind it … We should not begin to incorporate the position of the two dominant parties into the constitution in the way in which they have across the Atlantic with the Democrats and Republicans.

There are other uncertainties on the horizon. Will party treasurers resign *en masse* out of fear of going to jail for mistakes in accounting? Will donations to parties continue or will the certainty of disclosure encourage the new generation of millionaires to spend their money on another yacht instead? How will the new rules affect the likely outcome of a referendum on the euro? Will political parties increasingly be overshadowed by single-issue campaigns such as the Scottish 'Keep the Clause' campaign?

A CONSTITUTIONAL 'SLEEPER'

Labour's party funding reforms have not usually been counted among the most important of its constitutional changes. The passage through parliament of the Political Parties, Elections and Referendums Bill attracted virtually no interest in the national press. But there is a strong case for arguing that the changes outlined in this chapter will have as significant an effect on the future of British politics as any other reform passed since 1997. In Martin Bell's words: 'This is not a technical or non-controversial Bill.' A legal free-for-all has been replaced by comprehensive legislation and regulation, with unpredictable consequences. Although Labour has refrained from fitting the reform into any overall constitutional jigsaw, it is easy to trace links to other parts of its agenda:

- the new Electoral Commission will be responsible directly to the House of Commons rather than the Home Office, opening a new dimension in relations between executive and legislature;

- the commission's task will include promoting citizenship and democracy, a subject which the government has already put on the national curriculum with the aim of boosting voter turnout;

- the reform fits in with Tony Blair's determination to preserve party-political patronage in the House of Lords, where despite the creation of a new appointments system for independents, a large record of donations is still the fastest route to becoming a Labour or a Conservative peer;

- the rules under which companies make political donations to parties and sponsor their activities will also influence the increasingly cosy relationship between government and the private sector;

- the new rules for referendums will help determine whether the government will risk a popular vote on the euro and a referendum on voting reform at Westminster in a second term;

- the legislation will offer fertile ground for challenges under the Human Rights Act, with lawyers likely to argue that freedom of expression is threatened by definitions of permitted participants and discriminatory spending limits.

A simple measure designed to tip the electoral balance away from the Conservatives and towards Labour has turned into a major constitutional reform, almost by accident. The road to Downing Street is paved with good intentions.

NOTES

[1] Final report of the Working Party on Electoral Procedures (Home Office 1999), paragraph 1.5.

[2] Blackburn, Robert and Plant, Raymond (eds) (1999) *Constitutional Reform. The Labour government's constitutional reform agenda*, London, Longman, p 84.

[3] Hereditary peers were given the right to vote and stand for the Commons when they lost their places in the House of Lords in 1999. So the longstanding rule of thumb that in British elections 'peers and lunatics cannot vote' no longer applies.

[4] Wright, Tony (ed.) (2000) *The British Political Process: an introduction*, London, Routledge, p 95.

7

THE ONE THAT GOT AWAY

'I heard it said by one cynic that the Labour party is so loyal that, if chimney boys were brought back in the name of modernization, we would all go through the lobby; but turkeys do not vote for Christmas. I do not honestly think that this is a serious plan' – Tony Benn

'I have one great question about you. Are you a pluralist or are you a control freak? Your decision on fair votes will tell us which. It will reveal what kind of government yours will be' – Paddy Ashdown

'All this debate is about fear ... The bottom line is, we are scared of ourselves, we are scared of losing an argument, we are scared our politics aren't strong enough' – Lorna Fitzsimons MP

WHEN JOHN WAKEHAM INTRODUCED HIS royal commission findings on Lords reform by saying he did not see the point of spending months compiling a report that would gather dust in a pigeonhole, there were no prizes for guessing which example of a pigeonholed report he had in mind. The Independent Commission on the Voting System created by Tony Blair and chaired by Roy Jenkins announced its findings in November 1998. Since then, although Jenkins continued for nearly two years to say he was 'not unhopeful' that something might happen after the next election, the prospect of electoral reform for the House of Commons has receded. Since

Jenkins reported, Labour's internal policymaking process has watered down John Smith's original pledge to hold a referendum, further reducing the slim chance that the Jenkins recommendations will ever be on the ballot as an alternative to first-past-the-post.

However, it would be wrong to conclude that debate on electoral reform for the House of Commons is over for good; of all constitutional questions, this is the one on which Labour suffers from serious and long-standing divisions at all levels. It is the pivotal issue for Labour's relations with the Liberal Democrats and for Blair's 'project', his long-term aim of creating a dominant centre-left partnership for the 21st century; it directly affects the vital interests of individual Labour MPs, many of whom would see their parliamentary careers ended by reform. However far it is pushed away into the long grass for tactical reasons, the ups and downs of Labour's electoral fortunes at Westminster will ensure that the issue eventually returns. The pigeonholing of Jenkins is thus just one episode in a long story.

FROM KEIR HARDIE TO ROBIN COOK

Those in the Labour party who want electoral reform can look back to the party's early years and the bearded figure of founding father Keir Hardie, who was first elected in a dual-member seat in Merthyr and Aberdare. 'It's not the first-past-the-post campaigners who represent the original tradition of the Labour party,' Robin Cook told a fringe meeting of reformers at the Scottish Labour conference in March 2000. Hardie's views were of course shaped by the experiences of Labour's early years trying to break into a two-party system. 'No system of election can be satisfactory which does not give opportunity to all parties to obtain representation in proportion to their voting strength,' he once said. As Welsh First Secretary Rhodri Morgan reminded a Labour conference fringe meeting in Brighton in September 2000:

Let it never be said that Labour never benefits from a proportional system. Only people who know nothing about Labour history say that. This party would never have got off the ground without proportional representation.

The first-past-the-post system, now seen as an age-old pillar of British constitutional tradition, in fact dates in its present form (single-member constituencies) to 1885 when the Redistribution of Seats Act abolished most multiple-member constituencies. Labour's breakthrough into the House of Commons in the early years of the 20th century was assisted by a secret pact with the Liberals in the 1906 election, which allowed the party to win 29 seats in constituencies where there was no Liberal candidate. Proportional representation remained on the party agenda despite the opposition of Ramsay MacDonald and Fabian intellectuals, and only disagreement between the Commons and the Lords led to the collapse of an attempt to reform the voting system in 1918. In the 1920s, Labour's enthusiasm for reform faded as it began to supplant the Liberals as the main alternative to the Conservatives, just at the time that the Liberals began to worry about their long-term survival. Labour support for PR was overturned at the party conference of 1926, though it continued to support the introduction of the alternative vote – not a proportional system – until it was blocked by the Lords in 1930.

VOTING SYSTEMS – THE ANORAK'S GUIDE

First-past-the-post (FPTP)

Used for the House of Commons in single-member constituencies, it allows voters a single cross on the ballot paper and obliges the winning candidate to win a plurality of votes (more than any other candidate) rather than a majority. Supporters say it ensures stable, coalition-free government, quick and decisive general election results, and close links between MPs and their constituencies. Critics say it works only in a two-party system and exaggerates voting swings, producing landslide majorities and squeezing minority parties. It tends to divide the country geographically, gives the voters only a single choice, narrows the election contest to 100 marginal seats and leaves millions of votes wasted. It also has a tendency to bias against one or other of the major parties because of boundary factors. Also used in the United States, Canada and India.

Alternative vote (AV)

Like FPTP it is based on single-member constituencies, but gives the voter the chance to pick candidates in order of preference. A winning candidate has to achieve 50 per cent of first-preference votes to win outright on the first count, otherwise the bottom candidates are eliminated one at a time and their second-preference votes are redistributed. Supporters say it allows more voter choice, but critics say the use of second-preference votes distorts the result and can lead to even more disproportionate results than FPTP. Used to elect Australia's House of Representatives, it is not a true proportional system. Favoured by some in the Labour party, including Peter Mandelson.

Supplementary vote (SV)

Similar to AV but voters are limited to a first and second preference. Supporters say the elimination of third, fourth and fifth preferences is fairer. Was recommended by Labour's Plant working party in 1993 for the House of Commons and was used for the first time in Britain to elect the London mayor in 2000.

Second ballot

Based on single-member constituencies, it uses the same principle as AV and SV, requiring the winning candidate to gain 50 per cent of the vote in a second ballot after elimination or voluntary withdrawal of trailing candidates. Widely used in France.

List system

Voters choose party lists allowing an exact relationship between each party's share of the vote and its number of seats. Lists can be either closed, allowing voters only a choice of party, or open, allowing a choice of candidate. Minimum thresholds can be used to eliminate minority parties. There can be single national lists (Israel, South Africa, some continental European countries), a limited number of regional lists, or a large number of sub-regional voting areas with three or four seats in each. Supporters say it can be the fairest system because it is fully proportional and can allow a greater representation of women and minorities. Critics say it removes the constituency link, gives too much power to party machines and encourages instability, fragmentation and the election of extremist parties.

Single transferable vote (STV)

Long preferred by the Liberal Democrats, it allows voters to mark preferences (as with AV) but in multi-member constituencies. A numerical quota based on the number of seats decides the election, which involves a series of counts in which votes are redistributed according to preferences until sufficient candidates reach the quota. Used to elect the Irish Dail, the Australian Senate, and in Northern Ireland for the European Parliament and local government. Supporters say it is the fairest truly proportional system. Critics say it is over-complex and encourages rivalry between candidates of the same party.

Additional member system (AMS)

A combination of single constituency and list, with voters casting two ballots for a constituency member (through FPTP, SV or AV) and for a party on a regional or national list. The system can be used to correct the disproportional effect of the constituency vote through the list. A party whose candidates tend to come second in the constituencies will do better in the list vote. Used in Germany, Italy, Japan and New Zealand, for the Scottish Parliament and Welsh Assembly. Supporters say it combines the constituency link with a 'top-up' proportional system that is fair. Critics say it creates turf wars between two classes of members and can give too much power to small parties.

The Jenkins formula (AV plus)

This is a variant of the AMS system, adapted to ensure where possible majority rather than coalition government and maintaining strong constituency links at the expense of pure proportionality. Between 80 per cent and 85 per cent of MPs would still be elected in individual constituencies under AV rather than FPTP as in Scotland and Wales. The remaining seats would be filled by between 98 and 132 top-up MPs, making up between 15 per cent and 20 per cent of the Commons. They would be elected from county-sized constituencies – 65 in England, eight in Scotland, five in Wales and two in Northern Ireland. Of these, 44 would elect a single top-up MP and the remaining 36 would elect two.

THE HEYDAY OF THE TWO-PARTY SYSTEM

'For the best part of a century change has been frustrated because only one of the three main parties has supported it. Until the 1920s it was the Labour party. Since then it has been the Liberals. Unfortunately the Liberals converted to it just as Labour was losing interest.'[1] Martin Linton MP wonders whether it was poetic justice that the Labour party lost only six percentage points of the vote in 1931 but said goodbye to all but 52 of its 287 seats. Labour's hopes of reversing the tide and reaping the benefits of the winner-takes-all system were finally fulfilled in 1945 with a landslide that 'put the issue of electoral reform to the very bottom of the political agenda where it stayed for the next 30 years'. The outright majority won under Attlee ushered in a period of two-party politics. More than 96 per cent of voters supported the two main parties in 1951 and 1955 – conditions under which there was little pressure to change the first-past-the-post system. However, the 1951 election was famous for the fact that Labour lost power despite polling 230,000 more votes than the Conservatives, who won 321 seats to Labour's 295.

The Liberal vote slumped for a decade after the war, partly because the party was unable to afford the deposits to field candidates throughout the country, but showed signs of recovery in the late 1950s, culminating in a famous by-election win in Orpington in 1962. In 1974, the Conservatives suffered the same experience as Labour in 1951, winning a majority of votes but not of seats, leading to an untypical flutter of interest in electoral reform in the party while it remained in opposition, and the celebrated attack on 'elective dictatorship' by Lord Hailsham in 1976. Since Margaret Thatcher's rise to power, the Conservatives have consistently opposed electoral reform, despite the fact that in 1999 it enabled them to overcome their general election catastrophe in Scotland and Wales and win list seats in the new Scottish and Welsh devolved bodies.

Historically, the Conservatives have done very well out of first-past-the-post and remain committed to opposing PR for Westminster, although Jenkins thinks they are 'absolutely crazy' because the present system is now seriously biased against them. Largely because of Labour's success in influencing the last round of boundary changes, the Conservatives can at present win the same number of votes as Labour in a general election but finish with

> ❝ The Conservatives can at present win the same number of votes as Labour in a general election but finish with 81 fewer seats. ❞

81 fewer seats. Jenkins points out that this means that even with a lead of 7 per cent over Labour, the Conservatives would still not have an overall majority. The Liberal Democrats remain fully committed to proportional representation, their flagship policy; their internal dilemma is over how far to compromise their beliefs in bargaining with Labour over other less purist systems such as AV.

It is hard to see Charles Kennedy or any leader of the party abandoning the goal of a proportional electoral system for the Commons as the party's price for entering a coalition government. From the Liberal Democrat point of view, cooperation with Labour has helped deliver proportional voting in elections for Scotland, Wales, the European Parliament and the Greater London Assembly. In Edinburgh, Scottish Liberal Democrat leader Jim Wallace filled the role of acting First Minister while Donald Dewar was recovering from heart surgery. Liberal Democrats in Wales followed the Scottish pattern in October 2000, agreeing a coalition pact with Labour which included a promise to review the operation of the voting system. But John Prescott has blocked any discussion of proportional representation for local government in England.

Paddy Ashdown awakening the Spirit of Proportional Representation

Ashdown has this cartoon hanging in his office. Copyright © Steve Bell, 1997.

FROM COOK-MACLENNAN TO JENKINS

The commitment to a referendum on electoral reform made by John Smith was not only useful to Tony Blair as a way of papering over his party's internal divisions over electoral reform. It was also a tasty carrot to dangle before Paddy Ashdown and the Liberal Democrats in talks about a partnership between the two parties. Thanks to the publication of the first volume of Ashdown's diaries in October 2000, we now know his side of the secret 'project' talks with Blair, which began even before he succeeded John Smith in 1994. Going behind the back of his shadow cabinet, Blair went perilously far in discussing a possible coalition or even a merger of the two parties. Ashdown said no to a merger but was certainly interested in a coalition. Blair gave private assurances that he favoured electoral reform but was unable to promise it publicly. On 21 January 1997, less than four months before the election, there was a tense meeting between the two men. Ashdown told Blair it was 'very disturbing' to find he could not deliver on an important private verbal agreement. Blair explained that he had real problems with his colleagues. Agreeing to put PR on the election agenda would only help the Tories, he told Ashdown. All he could offer was the idea of a post-election commission on voting systems that would provide cover for him to change position.

This was the secret background to the Cook-Maclennan talks which agreed that in a referendum on PR for Westminster, the choice would be between first-past-the-post and a single proportional alternative, rather than a range of options. Cook was a longstanding supporter of PR and the Liberal Democrats saw the agreement as another step towards their goal of electoral reform. Blair, keen to keep the issue off the election agenda as far as possible, maintained a publicly neutral position, saying he was unpersuaded of the case for PR because it would give too much power to smaller parties. This is the argument about 'proportionality of power' which is used by opponents of PR to argue that while allocating seats in line with the number of votes may look fair on paper, it leads to smaller parties holding a disproportionate share of power.

In the event, the scale of Labour's election victory made a coalition impossible, though Blair tried to revive the idea in October 1997. But his plan to offer two cabinet seats to the Liberal Democrats foundered when John Prescott made clear the price would be his resignation, and possibly that of other cabinet colleagues. According to Andrew Rawnsley's account, Prescott made clear to Blair that he would quit the moment Ashdown was brought into a coalition. 'The day that man walks through the door is the day I walk out of it'.[2] It was not a price that Blair was prepared to pay, whatever the long-term attractions of the centre-left 'project'.

When Blair announced in December 1997 that Roy Jenkins would chair the Independent Commission on the Voting System it was a gesture towards the Liberal Democrats, and a choice that was seen as highly provocative by many in his own party. Not only was Jenkins a Liberal Democrat elder statesman and a confidant and adviser to Blair, but he was also regarded with deep loathing by many Labour traditionalists for his role in splitting the party in the early 1980s by forming the SDP. As Labour MP Jimmy Hood complained to a rally at the Scottish Labour conference in March 2000 in defence of first-past-the-post: 'What do we expect when we put Jenkins in charge of a commission? This was the guy who wanted to destroy the Labour party in 1981.'

Other members of the commission were a former senior civil servant, Sir John Chilcot, a longtime Labour party and trade union stalwart, Joyce Gould (Baroness Gould), Labour journalist and former Whitehall special adviser David Lipsey (later to become Lord Lipsey), and Conservative barrister and banker Robert Alexander (Lord Alexander of Weedon). Alexander was to dissent from one of the main recommendations of the report. It is instructive to compare the composition of the group with that of the royal commission on the Lords two years later. For this body Blair chose not a constitutional reformer in the Jenkins mould but a veteran Conservative fixer and self-proclaimed cynic in the person of John Wakeham. This appeared to reflect not only a difference in political tactics but also a cooling in Blair's appetite for constitutional reform between 1997 and 1999. As a royal commission, Wakeham's group had a higher profile, but in practice both groups had a similar task: to deliver reforms that would be politically feasible rather than radical constitutional blueprints.

Apart from some characteristic literary flourishes from the pen of Lord Jenkins, the commission did what it was asked to do by sticking closely to its terms of reference:

The commission shall be free to consider and recommend any appropriate system or combination of systems in recommending an alternative to the present system for parliamentary elections to be put before the people in the government's referendum. The commission shall observe the requirement for broad proportionality, the need for stable government, an extension of voter choice and the maintenance of a link between MPs and geographical constituencies.

These four criteria were described by Jenkins himself as 'not entirely compatible'. It was clear that the commission was expected to take an instrumental view of electoral reform; in other words a proportional outcome to an election was not to be seen as an absolute end in itself, but only a possible means of achieving a number of goals, one of them being stable government. Charter88 described the requirement for stable government as curious, adding that accountable government would have been preferable. As Jenkins remarked with a touch of acidity in his introduction, the only real way of ensuring stable government is to avoid elections altogether, 'which would make our enquiry otiose'.

The commission saw itself as seeking 'relative virtue in an imperfect world'. Despite the presence of Robert Alexander on the group, the Conservative party took the view that the Jenkins commission was no more than a front to pave the way for a Labour-Liberal Democrat pact. Conservative constitutional affairs spokesman Dr Liam Fox told the Commons after the report was issued:

It was a rigged commission – a sham process – which might as well have begun with its conclusions and worked backwards towards its remit. That is effectively what it did. It was a plan for an arranged marriage between a minority party and a section of the governing party, a relationship in which neither side knows the outcome.

The Conservative faith in first-past-the-post appears to be solid. Sir George Young acknowledged to me that other systems than first-past-the-post would allow the Conservatives to win more seats, but maintained that his party 'doesn't look at it in that self-interested way'.

We actually have asked, what is the best system for the country, and the answer is first-past-the-post. There are other systems, certainly, which would have given us more seats at the last election. Nonetheless we have taken a rather detached view and we genuinely believe the present system, with single members and, nine times out of ten, clear results, is the right one. We don't believe these other systems which might work in other countries would work here. So that is a very clear commitment as far as Westminster is concerned.

BRIDGING THE LABOUR-LIBERAL DEMOCRAT GAP

Despite the Cook-Maclennan agreement and the post-election cosy chats between Tony Blair and Paddy Ashdown, there was still a yawning gap to be bridged between Labour and the Liberal Democrats over electoral reform. This was evident when Jenkins and his team read their submissions to the commission. Labour stressed the 'horses for courses' view, endorsed several years earlier by the Plant working party, that there was no need for a uniform electoral system in the UK and there were 'specific factors' involved in picking a system for the Commons. Without formally endorsing first-past-the-post, the party argued that any alternative might undermine the role of general elections in producing a clear mandate for a change of government.

These elections determine the composition of the dominant chamber in parliament and decide which party will form the executive. They are an opportunity for the people to reaffirm their support for or to change their leaders. General elections such as those in 1945, 1979 or 1997 were crucial moments which defined the direction the country wished to take for the future.

The Labour submission advised the commission to seek 'a system which sustains open, stable and accountable government' and described the constituency link as the bedrock of the parliamentary system, which was 'widely understood and is deeply embedded in Britain's parliamentary history and culture'. It sang the praises of stable single-party government as superior to coalitions:

We do not believe the electoral system should result in perpetual coalition. Nor do we believe that a government is illegitimate because it has won less than 50 per cent of the vote. The existing system produces a clear 'winner' and 'loser' in accordance with the broad national mood.

It argued that Jenkins and his colleagues should consider 'both proportionality of representation and proportionality of power' – in other words, the excessive power wielded by small parties in coalitions – and dismissed evidence of falling election turnouts in Britain as 'in line with most European countries'.

By contrast, the Liberal Democrat evidence opened with a classic statement of the case for proportional representation by John Stuart Mill and followed it with a sharp denunciation of the status quo: 'We deplore the existing, crude 'winner-takes-all' system in dislocated, single-member constituencies drawn on boundaries that are often highly contrived.' First-past-the-post had failed to represent adequately the views of voters in parliament, delivering overwhelming majorities to parties backed by only a third of those entitled to vote. While accepting that no electoral system was perfect and different systems could be appropriate in different circumstances, it argued that all proportional systems were better both in principle and in practice than first-past-the-post or AV. Liberal Democrats believed PR would encourage people to vote, would reduce the regional polarization of the electorate, and help pluralism by giving wider expression to the views of minorities. The submission argued for the introduction of STV, under which 'no party would be likely to secure a Commons majority without the support of nearly half the popular vote'. STV would maximize voter choice, encourage parties to present a broader range of candidates and make the Commons more representative. It pointed out that AV could produce a result even less proportional than first-past-the-post, a drawback shared by SV.

HOW TO PLEASE TONY BLAIR

With the two key parties so far apart, Jenkins and his team faced a delicate task in squaring the circle and producing a report attractive enough to Tony Blair to have a chance of being implemented. In the view of Professor Vernon Bogdanor, Blair has always been strictly a pragmatist about electoral reform:

I suspect the Prime Minister's view is that this is a means to an end. His project is to unite the progressive forces of British politics around one party, the Labour party ideally, and if proportional representation would help with that, he is in favour of it, but if it wouldn't, he isn't.

As Jenkins noted in his report: 'There has been an element of 'the devil was sick, the devil a monk would be, the devil was well, the devil a devil he'd be' about the attitude of all parties to electoral reform. Their desire to improve the electoral system has tended to vary in inverse proportion to their ability to do anything about it.'[3] Analyzing the perverse effects of first-past-the-post on the Conservatives in 1997, he noted that the party had won 31 per cent of the vote but only 25 per cent of seats. The Labour party, by contrast, had benefited from 'a cornucopia of luscious psephological fruit emptied over its head', winning 63.6 per cent of the seats with 43.2 per cent of the vote. With hindsight, one can see a note of well-founded scepticism about Labour's eagerness for electoral reform in Jenkins' comments:

If this disposition persists, this Labour government will have the unique distinction of having broken the spell under which parties when they want to reform do not have the power and when they have the power do not want to reform. As a result of this knot the existing electoral system, in many ways irrational and, to judge from most opinion polls on the subject, not particularly loved either, has persisted.[4]

The commission listed the faults of first-past-the-post: its tendency to create landslide majorities, its tendency to squeeze out third parties, its creation of regional 'electoral deserts' of single-party rule, and the lack of real voter choice. Labour had successfully played the system in 1997 by concentrating its campaigning in key seats 'with all the clinical precision of the German general staff going for weak points in their 1870 or 1940 advances'. Other voters were ignored and those in safe seats voted with no hope of influencing the overall outcome. The built-in bias against the Conservatives caused by boundary inequalities could be cured by a proportional system.

A SEARCH FOR COMPROMISE

The search was for a compromise rather than for perfection. 'I am a relativist on electoral matters,' Jenkins says. The commission rejected AV because it offered little prospect of a move towards greater proportionality, and because expert calculations showed it would have accentuated still further the outcome of the 1997 general election. One estimate showed that instead of 419 Commons seats Labour would have won 452, the Liberal Democrats 82 instead of 46, and the Conservatives would have been reduced to 96 seats instead of 165. As Jenkins pointed out, an injustice to the Liberal Democrats would have been corrected at the price of a still greater injustice to the Conservatives. The system would be 'unacceptably unfair' to the Conservatives and would exaggerate big electoral swings, as would the related SV system.

The next decision was to reject STV, the preferred choice of the Liberal Democrats and of PR purists such as the Electoral Reform Society, on the grounds that it would be 'too big a leap from that to which we have become used, and it would be a leap in a confusingly different direction from the other electoral changes which are currently being made in Britain'. It would also weaken the link between MPs and geographical constituencies. Having decided to reject STV, it was inevitable that a mixed system would be recommended, and the remainder of the report was devoted to narrowing down the best option, concluding that a top-up of between 15 per cent and 20 per cent would be enough to secure a broadly proportional outcome.

With the exception of Robert Alexander, the Jenkins Commission argued for the introduction of AV in constituency voting, on the grounds that it would lead to more consensual politics. Because of the need to accommodate top-up seats, a review of constituency boundaries and a reduction in the number of constituencies would be needed. This in turn ruled out any implementation before the next election in 2002. For the election of top-up members, Jenkins recommended an open list system in 80 top-up areas, of which 65 would be in England, mostly based on metropolitan areas and counties. This would be better than creating members with no area ties – 'a flock of unattached birds clouding the sky and wheeling under central party directions'.[5]

Using the Jenkins system of 'AV top-up' with 17.5 per cent of seats decided on sub-regional lists, Labour's landslide victory in 1997 would have been reduced. Instead of 419 seats, the party would have won 368. The Conservatives would have seen little change, winning 168 instead of 165, while the Liberal Democrats would have been the real winners, with 89 instead of 46. Scottish and Welsh nationalists would have won 15 seats instead of 10. Labour's majority would have been cut from 179 seats to 77. Liberal Democrats would have gained more under a fully proportional system, which would have given them 111 seats. According to the commission's calculations, largely the work of London University researchers, the system would have produced a hung parliament in 1992 instead of a narrow Conservative majority, but would have delivered single party government in 1983 and 1987. 'It is therefore difficult to argue that what we propose is a recipe either for a predominance of coalitions or for producing a weakness of government authority, except when it springs out of a hesitancy of national mood which may rightly show itself through any electoral system.'[6]

Robert Alexander's note of reservation opposed the use of AV in constituency elections, warning that it could heighten the use of tactical voting

Tony Blair is disturbed by the outcome of Roy Jenkins' report on reforming the voting system for Westminster. Copyright © Daily Telegraph, 1998.

and encourage attempts by two parties to marshal their supporters to gang up on a third. Using AV, he argued, would be inconsistent with the electoral system used in Scotland and Wales. Alexander also criticized AV as inherently unfair because of the way it used preference votes cast for the least successful candidates, producing unpredictable and illogical results.

A NON-COMMITTAL REACTION FROM LABOUR

The reaction to Jenkins was non-committal from the government, hostile from the Conservatives and supportive from the Liberal Democrats. This reflected longstanding political differences. The report won a much more favourable reception from the press than Wakeham's plan for the House of Lords, though it was clearly a compromise. The three pro-PR academics whose calculations underpinned the Jenkins report, Patrick Dunleavy, Helen Margetts and Stuart Weir, found too much fudge in the Jenkins recipe. They described the report as 'clearly anxious to appease pro-first-past-the-post sentiment' and said this undermined the case for AV-plus, presented as a compromise between the status quo and a more pluralist and proportional alternative.[7]

The commission's desire to split the difference understated the major structural faults of first-past-the-post and the obsolescence of the current system. Jenkins, they argued, should not have taken at face value the conventional Westminster wisdom about the closeness of the link between MPs and their constituencies: 'The idea that MPs are dependent on their constituents rather than on their parties is a political myth. Loyalty by MPs to their party, in government or opposition, is the keystone of their political role and determines all or most of their conduct.' Dunleavy, Margetts and Weir also took Jenkins to task for failing to subject to rigorous analysis the idea that coalition government is weaker and less desirable than single-party government.[8] Jenkins, they argued, failed to properly nail the myth that first-past-the-post 'enables the electorate sharply and cleanly to rid itself of unwanted government'. The real decision to sack a government under the British system is taken by a small minority of voters in marginal seats, and the evidence is that the party with most votes can still lose the election. The three academics acknowledged that first-past-the-post produced a reasonably proportional result in countries like the United States, which

> 66 The real decision to sack a government under the British system is taken by a small minority of voters in marginal seats, and the evidence is that the party with most votes can still lose the election. 99

has a two-party system. But, they said, Jenkins failed to grasp the slow structural shift under way in British politics to a more pluralist system: 'Since 1972, thousands of opinion polls, 26 years of municipal elections, and seven successive general elections have shown one-fifth of the vote going to third and fourth parties – to the Liberal Democrats, to the SNP in Scotland and Plaid Cymru in Wales, or to the Greens (notably in the 1989 Euro elections).' In 1997 even fifth and sixth parties such as the Referendum party and the UK Independence party won a record 4.4 per cent. In Northern Ireland elections 12 parties all won seats in 1998. 'Most media commentators and many academics are blind to the new structure of British politics. In their minds politics is still a two-party affair. Like first-past-the-post itself, they treat all the voters for third parties with contempt. Liberal Democrat arguments for fairness for their voters and party are dismissed as special pleading.'

Dunleavy and his colleagues argued that there would be no return to the orderly two-party system: 'The consistent voting patterns and trends of the last 28 years will not suddenly go into reverse.' They questioned the theory that coalition government was inevitably weak and that first-past-the-post enabled the fulfilment of an electoral mandate by a single party. 'The full operation of the mandate really demands that parliament be totally subordinate to the government formed by the majority party. All opposition parties can or should do is try to rally popular support for alternative programmes in light of the next election.' Dunleavy and his colleagues argued that coalition government did not rule out parties agreeing to govern together under a clear mandate: 'British voters have little to fear from coalition governments and something to gain.'

Meanwhile, academics have been going over the lessons to be learned from the 1999 voting in Scotland and Wales, which took place several months after Jenkins reported. Professor John Curtice and other researchers for the Constitution Unit found that voters were generally positive about PR, with a firmer endorsement in Scotland than in Wales. 'The idea that PR is too complicated receives little support,' Curtice wrote.[9] In Scotland, 54 per cent of those asked found PR was 'much fairer', while 23 per cent disagreed; the equivalent figures for Wales were 39 per cent and 12 per cent; 62 per cent in Scotland and 54 per cent in Wales felt there was more point in voting under a PR system. Only 16 per cent in both countries thought PR gave small parties too much power, the key argument used by Labour opponents of change. There was resistance to PR closed lists, used for the Edinburgh and Cardiff bodies but not recommended by Jenkins for Westminster. However, the survey showed that voters still thought it was important for elections to give a clear result – one of the main virtues of first-past-the-post.

INTO THE LONG GRASS

When the Commons debated the Jenkins report on 5 November 1998, Labour opponents of reform set the tone. Home Secretary Jack Straw, without actually opposing the report, used a tone of light mockery which implied that as far as he was concerned, it could and would be ignored:

In all the debates about the appropriate electoral system for Westminster, I have personally taken one side of the argument – in favour of first-past-the-post. That will come as no great surprise to hon. members on either side. I therefore remain unpersuaded of the case for change, although I am always open to higher argument.

Straw said the government had always envisaged a referendum before the next election, and 'that remains an option'. But the new system could not be introduced until the election after next and there was no need for the government to come to an early view on the report. He went on to explain that a decision would not only have to wait until the new systems adopted for Scotland, Wales and the European Parliament had settled down, but more importantly until stage two of reform of the Lords had been decided: 'It would not be wise to embark on reform to the House of Commons electoral system until we are more certain of the changes that will take place in the other place.'

For the Conservatives, Dr Liam Fox congratulated Straw on 'a kicking into the long grass of Olympic standard', attributing Labour's new coolness to reform as the product of the realism of government. 'Decision making in government is a first-past-the-post activity. I think that ministers are increasingly understanding that.' Meanwhile, the Liberal Democrat spokesman Robert Maclennan insisted somewhat forlornly that the referendum should go ahead as promised before the next election, even if the changes themselves would have to wait. The subsequent debate laid bare the huge gulf between the two camps in the Labour party over electoral reform. Veteran Manchester MP Gerald Kaufman, in a deliberate parody of Lord Jenkins' orotund prose style, described his report as 'glutinously euphuistic as well as being intellectually shoddy'. Denouncing its proposals as hopelessly complicated, he defended first-past-the-post as clear and comprehensible and said the proposed changes were biased against Labour:

I have been elected to the House eight times, sometimes during periods of immense electoral adversity. I have sat here for 28 years. I have not sought election ten times and been elected eight times in order to support a system that is definitely intended to reduce the number of members of parliament from my own party. That may be regarded as self-interest, but I must tell my honourable friends in marginal seats who floated in here that they will not be here for 28 years with this system. The report is deliberately aimed at reducing the number of Labour members of parliament through a referendum. I offer my right honourable and honourable friends on the front bench a serious warning based on the past. They ought not to support this system when the referendum comes because, if they do, the Labour party will be split in a referendum campaign against a Conservative party that is united.

The *Financial Times* reported today that my right honourable friend the Prime Minister will allow cabinet ministers to take either side of the argument in a referendum campaign. We had that in 1975 and the direct result was the split that developed in the party right through to 1980; it was Lord Jenkins who split the Labour party in 1980. In 1980, Lord Jenkins nearly inflicted a terminal split on my party and he is now trying to do that in another way. I recommend to my right honourable and honourable friends that they should have nothing to do with the report, because it is a poisoned chalice being offered by our ex-colleague.

Labour's longest serving MP Tony Benn said he did not think the report had a cat in hell's chance of succeeding:

The idea that the parliamentary Labour party would go through the lobby to destroy 50 of its own members, to redraw all the constituencies and to introduce a new group of piggy-back members is ludicrous. I heard it said by one cynic that the Labour party is so loyal that, if chimney boys were brought back in the name of modernization, we would all go through the lobby; but turkeys do not vote for Christmas. I do not honestly think that this is a serious plan.

Benn, on other subjects a constitutional radical, explained why he was a strong supporter of first-past-the-post on the grounds that it enables a direct relationship between the member and his voters:

Direct representation is the delicate thread that links the people with their Government and the basis of it is that they elect a man or woman they know, can argue with and can get rid of.

Labour MP Martin Salter, echoing Kaufman, described the Jenkins proposal as '... a recipe for civil war inside the Labour party. The constituencies of many Labour members are surrounded by those of other Labour members. Will we spend the next three, four, five or eight years deciding which of our number will be chopped? I think not. This system is not a recipe for a cohesive parliamentary party.' Tony Wright, a Labour supporter of electoral reform, tried to inject some realism into the argument:

Members of parliament go through the lobbies night after night, voting with their party. If they were representing their constituents, they would vote for the views of the majority of their constituents who have supported other parties, but they do not do that. Under our system, with all its merits, we first get ourselves selected – the selection is far more important than the election – by a very few people. We are not selected by first-past-the-post but by some other system. We then get ourselves elected, often by a minority of the electorate, and we then claim that we represent everybody, even though by our behaviour we do not. Then we invent conventions that tell everybody else to keep off our patch. That is an interesting system, but we need to be honest when we describe it.

Gordon Prentice, on the left of the party, challenged Blair to explain how electoral reform fitted into the wider picture of constitutional change:

There is no coherence there. Commentators rightly say that we do not have the faintest idea of where the dismantling of the British state is taking us. The Prime Minister has an obligation to start painting the big constitutional picture. I have no idea yet what that big constitutional picture is. I want to know whether changing the voting system is part of the project, because I do not yet have a clear idea what the project is. If we are turning completely on its head the way in which this country is governed, members of parliament, members of the Labour party and people in the community must have a vision of where those changes are taking us.

Prentice is one of the Labour MPs who is deeply suspicious of Blair's centrist flirtations with the Liberal Democrats, as he made clear when I interviewed him shortly before the 2000 summer parliamentary recess:

I think Blair wants some kind of rapprochement with the Liberal Democrats but he can't say so publicly. It's all hints, nods, winks, although over the years it has got more and more explicit. But I think it would split the party if he were to say that he wants electoral reform for Westminster, he wants to go for a proportional system … Blair would have to be explicit, he would have to say, this is my vision of the future, the only way to win is to have a rapprochement with the Liberal Democrats.

PADDY, TONY AND THE 'FORCES OF TRIBALISM'

Ashdown told me in July 2000 that he and Blair had fought an unsuccessful battle against the 'forces of tribalism' in their own parties:

In the end, the forces of tribalism beat us. Tribalism in his party, but don't underestimate the tribalism in mine. I've got tribalists too. I've got people who hate Labour just as viscerally as Labour hates us.

Here we get closer to the real reason why the Jenkins report never had much chance of being considered on its merits – for the Labour party, electoral reform has never been a question of principle, merely a functional aspect of the struggle for power; for Blair, electoral reform has been a stepping stone to a closer relationship with the Liberal Democrats, rather than a matter of fairness to the voters. To some extent Ashdown was responsible for making the issue the touchstone of the relationship between the two parties, when he addressed Blair directly at the 1998 Liberal Democrat party conference:

I have one great question about you. Are you a pluralist or are you a control freak? Your decision on fair votes will tell us which. It will reveal what kind of government yours will be. It will determine the future course of our work together and it will tell us what kind of country you want Britain to be.

This public challenge reflected the frustrations Ashdown felt after a year or more of dealing with Blair in the Joint Cabinet Committee with the

Liberal Democrats on constitutional matters. The meetings every few weeks in Downing Street formed the centre of an informal network of contacts between the two parties which left many Labour backbenchers seething with envy and many Liberal Democrats deeply suspicious. Despite its exalted title, the committee did not give the Liberal Democrats more than a sniff of real power, as Ashdown acknowledged:

It's very easy to see the JCC as the only event. In a sense it was the centre and it was constructed as centre of a network of contacts. It was the point at which we brought together and coordinated what were the most important and substantive elements of this, which were bilateral discussions between Liberal Democrat senior spokesmen and ministers ... In a sense the JCC was a formal structure and in a sense quite limited in what it could do. We were ranged around two sides of the cabinet table and with the prime minister and ministers there, and us on the other side. It wasn't a trades union negotiation, it was much more friendly than that ... Things that couldn't be solved on a bilateral basis came to the JCC.

I asked Ashdown how much he and his colleagues were listened to:

I think there were a number of drawbacks to it. One of them was the government's reluctance from the first, something we tried to break down, to let us see papers in the early process. I think that was a substantial mistake. It is one of the areas where he and I disagreed quite strongly. We went into bat after a year saying, this isn't working. What happened was, we actually began to discuss things after the government's view had been formulated rather than in the formative stage. The second problem with it was that inevitably in an hour it was quite short and quite stylized and limited in its discussions ... It was a problem-solving and early warning mechanism. For instance, on the Lords, we said to them, look, if you go ahead on this basis we're not going to be able to vote with you on that clause, that clause and that clause. So that when it came to the Lords we weren't seen to be acting capriciously.

Ashdown believes the meetings helped make changes in the government's Freedom of Information Bill and its White Paper on the House of Lords, and prevented a Blair cave-in to the Conservatives who wanted to drop proportional voting for the European Parliament elections and return to the first-past-the-post system:

I suppose our greatest success in the ambit of the JCC was getting PR for Europe. I had to threaten him that I would blow up the whole thing if he wouldn't carry that through. In the Christmas of 1998 he was going to give in to the Tories and go back to first-past-the-post. We had to step in as a result or we would have lost that.

Robert Maclennan told me there were also disagreements about the scope of the Greater London Authority, which the Liberal Democrats wanted to have wider powers. He recalls the rows over voting for the European Parliament as 'a sticky period' in which there were serious arguments with Labour. The government agreed to proportional voting, but with closed lists rather than open lists, thus ensuring that parties, rather than voters, would rank candidates in order of preference. 'We felt it gave too much control to political parties and not enough to the electors. That wasn't simply a compromise, that was candidly a defeat.' Ashdown believes that overall, the joint committee helped ensure Labour implemented a constitutional reform programme for which many of its leaders had little real enthusiasm:

I am convinced that however unhappy one might be with the constitutional programme of this government, it would have been one hell of a lot less had it not been for the Liberal Democrats. Not just P. Ashdown and T. Blair, but Jim Wallace's work with George Robertson in the Scottish Convention and so on. We have nailed Labour's colours to its mast for it.

But the partnership in the first two years of government failed to develop into something more solid. Ashdown acknowledged that the lack of movement on electoral reform was the biggest disappointment of his experience dealing with Labour. I asked him if he ever felt Blair was just stringing the Liberal Democrats along with a promise of a fairer voting system that he never intended to deliver:

Was Blair stringing us along? No, I think he was sincere, but consistently underestimated the strength of the forces within his own cabinet that he had to overcome. I do not accuse him in any sense of a deliberate attempt to deceive, but when we struck agreements between us, they were agreements he subsequently found he could not keep because of the pressures he had to overcome as leader of his government.

Moving to a more solid agreement between the two parties proved more difficult for Blair than he imagined when he set out, Ashdown believes:

That was *force majeure*. It is also true that he had to deliver his bit before I had to deliver mine and who knows, I might not have been able to deliver mine either in the end.

He believes Blair was sincere in wanting a pact, but the opportunity was missed. In Ashdown's recollections, Blair emerges as more Hamlet than Iago or Macbeth:

What I am clear about is that the Prime Minister was both sincere and determined – that determination is not terribly evident, I must say, that is one of his faults – to reshape British politics on the left in which we are partners. And about that I am completely convinced that he is sincere.

When I asked Ashdown whether Blair simply wanted to swallow up the Liberal Democrats, there was a long pause before he replied:

Yes, of course, just as I want to with him. When we first met I said, you and I both run an equivalent and opposite risk. My risk is that you want to swallow us up, well that's what I would want to do in your position. Your risk is that we are what John Prescott says we are, feckless and unreliable partners when things get tough. And both of us will have to run that risk. My argument to him was: 'You think change is the merger of the two parties, I think change is introducing a pluralist system in which the two parties work together in partnership for ten years, and who knows what happens at the end of that.' My approach to this was organic. People say that is something evil and wrong of him. But if I was in his position I would want to do the same thing. My job was to resist his natural intentions, and his job was to make sure that when we had a partnership together it was one he could rely on.

AN 'ISOLATED BASTION'

So the Jenkins report remained on the shelf, not so much because of any intrinsic flaws but because it formed part of a larger political construction project that never really got off the ground. Jenkins told me in May

2000 he felt Blair was still open to reviving electoral reform, but the project would only come to life if Labour's political fortunes started to fade:

It is increasingly difficult to defend Westminster as a totally isolated bastion, with some form of PR or some form of different representation applying to every other institution in the country and in all neighbouring countries. So I think he will find that difficult to do, and won't be all that keen. But his great enemy from that point of view, or obstacle, is a sense of Labour triumphalism. 'We can do it all on our own for ever.' And though I don't think the election results (in May 2000) cast a serious doubt on Blair's re-election as prime minister, I think they did take a good deal of the edge off Labour triumphalism.

A substantially reduced Labour majority after the next general election would be enough to make a difference in the relationship between the two parties, Jenkins told me:

I think Blair has a strong attachment to an ongoing relationship with the Liberal Democrats, a strong attachment to leaving a different shape of British politics from that which he found. The Liberal Democrats are an important function in that. I think he will find it difficult to do that, probably impossible, without a measure of electoral reform. He and (Charles) Kennedy get on quite well. They don't have as close a relationship as he and Ashdown did. That is a constant in a way. What is a variable is how strong his position is *vis-à-vis* the anti-reformers in the Labour party. And that in turn is a variable according to how much the Labour party seems to be in need of Liberal Democrat support in the future. Clearly if he were in a position where there was no independent Labour majority – but I don't think that myself – then we would certainly have electoral reform.

David Lipsey, a supporter of electoral reform in the Labour party and a member of the Jenkins commission, says the fact that the project is marking time should come as no surprise:

During Jenkins we thought quite a bit about the politics of it, and it was clear it would be a jolly difficult thing to bring off because of the divisions in the ruling party, the threat it would offer to lots of MPs. It was always a long shot. There was then a wave of euphoria because Jenkins was such a wonderful report, beautifully written and all that. But that didn't remove the obstacles and the House of Commons had a very unfavourable debate on it, unnoticed by the press. And when the first elections under PR took place, that was also an immediate hit because there was no overall majority.

A CHANGE IN LIBERAL DEMOCRAT TACTICS?

Paddy Ashdown now believes the Liberal Democrats should adopt a 'softly, softly' approach rather than challenging Labour openly to deliver electoral reform for the Commons:

PR was the big prize for us and I am of course disappointed that we did not get that through. On the other hand I had a suspicion, and I said so to Charles (Kennedy) when I handed over to him, that we ought to become less the importunate impatient bangers on the door for PR, and rather more the patient waiters for the ripeness of the fruit. By which I mean, you've got PR for Europe, you've got PR for Scotland, you've got PR for Wales, you've got PR for London, you will have PR for regional assemblies, and if you can get PR for local government – and it is entirely logical that we should – then PR for Westminster comes in due course and in the fullness of time. So I think from using a battering ram, which I used, the party needs to have a slightly more subtle approach to this. The block of course is Prescott's opposition to PR for local government. But I don't think that can be sustained. It is in Labour's entire interest that it should clean up its own act in local government and the best means to do so is PR.

Robert Maclennan says the Liberal Democrats recognize that the Labour party is deeply divided on electoral reform and has to resolve the issue internally. 'They know exactly where we stand.' He told me it would be a mistake to regard Blair's failure to implement the Jenkins report as a major piece of backsliding on the deal he made with Robin Cook before the election:

It has been a difficult issue for the Prime Minister, always, and it doesn't become any easier. I think at some point he will have to take a stand and say where his judgement is on the issue and that will be all-important. In a curious way, in a parliament with such a large Labour majority it is actually quite difficult for the

Labour party to focus on this issue. Many of them expect to lose their seats on the swing and are bound to focus very much on their own futures. None of us anticipated when we entered this agreement an election result such as we had.

A SCOTTISH BACKLASH

Although the voters in Scotland seem happy with PR, this has not prevented a forceful backlash in the traditional wing of Scottish Labour. The venom between Labour supporters and opponents of electoral reform has been brought to the surface by the prospect of the introduction of proportional representation in local government under Labour's coalition pact with the Liberal Democrats. At a fringe meeting at the Scottish Labour conference in March 2000, Glasgow MP Jimmy Hood described PR as a disaster in Scotland and Wales. 'There is one value that is greater than all the others and that is the preservation of the Labour party. PR is damaging the Labour party,' he argued, calling on his audience to resist its introduction for Scottish local government. 'Defend democracy and, more importantly, defend the Labour party,' he declared. 'It (electoral reform) is not a burning issue. Call me a working-class snob if you like. It is one of those issues the chattering classes like getting hold of.'

In Scotland, opposition to PR is centred in the densely populated central belt, where much of local government has long been a Labour one-party state. In May 1999, Labour secured 94 per cent of the seats in Midlothian on 46 per cent of the vote, while the SNP polled 31 per cent of the vote and won no seats. In Angus, the positions were reversed, with Labour polling 18 per cent and winning 3 per cent of the seats and the SNP polling 47 per cent and taking 72 per cent of the seats. In Scottish Borders, the Liberal Democrats won 42 per cent of the seats on 27 per cent of the vote, while the Conservatives polled 17 per cent and won only 3 per cent of the seats.[10]

Labour MPs and MSPs in Scotland have reacted with hostility to the appearance of SNP list members of the Scottish Parliament campaigning on their home patches and wooing their constituents. Labour MSP Helen Eadie told the same fringe meeting that the party's control over the whole central belt of Scotland was now at stake. Another cause of complaint was the excessive power in the Edinburgh coalition government wielded by Liberal Democrats and in particular by Jim Wallace. Liberal Democrat MSPs were fully consulted on the plans of the executive while 'Labour MSPs turn up and are told what the decisions are,' complained Eadie.

Meanwhile, Labour MSPs from the areas where the party has traditionally been weak support PR because it has enabled them to enter the Scottish Parliament via the list system. At a rival fringe meeting at the Scottish Labour conference, Peter Peacock, elected from the Highlands and Islands, acknowledged that constituency members did not like to see rival candidates whom they had defeated in a constituency contest gaining seats through the list voting. 'Some of them are challenged by the new politics,' he said. Robin Cook told the meeting he had always felt deeply uncomfortable calling on people to vote Labour in areas where because of the electoral system they had no chance of electing a Labour MP. Cook argued that it was even a virtue of the AMS system that it allowed the election of some Conservative MSPs. 'I am personally in favour of keeping a few Tories around to remind us what they are like.' MP and MSP John McAllion told the same meeting: 'We can't run a country on the basis of what suits us as a party. We have to be democratic.'

Looking ahead to the rest of the 21st century, he said it was inevitable that at some point Labour in Scotland would lose power. 'That will be the moment when we need the list members.' Labour's dominance of local government in central Scotland had created a series of virtual one-party states which ruled out effective opposition. 'We need the discipline of knowing we will face strong opposition and if we don't we will be out on our ears.' McAllion argued that if the Labour party was to be truly radical it must commit itself to PR at all levels of government.

The test of the anti-PR backlash in Scotland will be the outcome of the debate over local government, for which a working group set up by the executive has recommended adoption of the proportional STV system, as used in Northen Ireland and the Irish Republic. The change is strongly opposed by most Labour-led councils, though Professor Curtice believes that under STV the party would retain control of some of its fiefdoms such as Glasgow.[11] Elsewhere in Scotland, Labour would lose influence and overall control of councils such as Edinburgh, where it won less than a third of the vote in 1999. The SNP would gain influence, but the Conservatives would be handicapped by the relatively high threshold of 20 per cent of the vote needed to win a seat in a five-member ward. Paradoxically, the Liberal Democrats, who in theory are committed to STV as their preferred system, might also find this threshold too high. Curtice believes the Liberal Democrats may not mind if any change is put off well beyond the next Scottish local elections in 2002.

If Scotland does eventually introduce PR for local government elections, it will mark a further policy divergence from the English pattern laid down by John Prescott. Labour's annual conference in September 2000 approved a National Policy Forum pledge not to change the voting system for councillors in England and Wales, with the exception of directly elected mayors.

ELECTORAL REFORM IN SCOTTISH LOCAL GOVERNMENT

The Renewing Local Democracy Working Group, chaired by Richard Kerley, an Edinburgh academic and former Labour councillor, was asked by the Scottish executive in 1999 to map out a revitalization of Scottish local government. This followed an earlier report by the Commission on Local Government and the Scottish Parliament which had recommended a switch from first-past-the-post to proportional representation for local government elections.

The Kerley working group was asked to consider five criteria: proportionality, the councillor-ward link, fair provision for independents, allowance for geographical diversity, and a close fit between council wards and natural communities. It was asked to look in particular at three systems – AMS, STV and AV top-up.

In June 2000 the group recommended a switch to STV in multi-member wards, with between three and five members in each ward. Three of the ten members of the group, two of them Labour and one Conservative, dissented.

THE DRIVE TO DITCH THE REFERENDUM

Since Jenkins reported in 1998 there has been a vigorous counter-offensive against proportional representation for the Commons by Labour supporters of first-past-the-post, led by Sir Ken Jackson and the AEEU. Their goal has been to drop the John Smith referendum commitment from Labour's next election manifesto. Among Labour MPs there is a hard core of around 100 who are firmly committed to first-past-the-post, with a smaller number who support PR, and the rest somewhere in between. At cabinet level Robin Cook, Clare Short and Mo Mowlam are PR supporters, but the majority of ministers are opposed.

Martin Linton, a leading advocate of PR, told a meeting of the Labour Campaign for Electoral Reform (LCER) in April 2000 that MPs were not the most promising audience for the reformers' gospel. 'They have a vested interest in the system that elected them. Deep down they are thinking, this is the best system because it elected me.' He said anecdotal evidence on lack of voter interest in the subject – 'the Ferret and Firkin theory' – should be disregarded because MPs rarely heard the views of those who did not vote for them. 'I am frankly disappointed in my colleagues. They are very radical about everything else, but the radicalism evaporates when they come to electoral reform.'

MANDELSON AND THE ALTERNATIVE VOTE

The Labour leadership's desire to soften its commitment to putting the Jenkins plan to a referendum while keeping enough options open to avoid a complete break with the Liberal Democrats was clearly evident in a speech by Peter Mandelson at the end of June 2000. Mandelson, addressing the all-party Make Votes Count campaigning group in London, argued that Labour should 'maintain its options' and that the Jenkins formula was 'not the only way forward'. Mandelson made it clear that he advocated a switch to AV, which in the 1997 election would have given Labour not 419 seats but 452, and would have reduced the Conservatives from 165 to 96, with the Liberal Democrats going up from 46 to 82. Labour's majority over all other parties would have soared to more than 200, and it would have translated a 13 per cent poll lead over the Conservatives into a four-to-one superiority in seats.[12]

Despite the caveat that he was expressing his personal views, Mandelson's plea to both sides in the argument to leave the leadership room for manoeuvre reflected the views of 10 Downing Street. Mandelson argued for 'not closing the door on change', while denying that this was 'a classic piece of procrastination and political fudge'. Labour was taking 'the right and principled position' and its constitutional changes were 'a programme fit for Charter88 to applaud'. He went on to outline the case for Labour's 'horses for courses' approach to change: 'We have not sought to roll out a pre-ordained blueprint, to counterpose a uniform model of constitutional reform to the rigid uniformity of our once over-centralized state.' Arguing that constitutional choices did not have to conform to a 'rigid grand plan', Mandelson said his experience in Northern Ireland showed the historic weakness of first-past-the-post and the essential role of proportional representation in overcoming the province's communal divide. But this was a matter of particular circumstances and not a lesson that applied automatically to the House of Commons.

'Let me say that I have never been a passionate advocate of constitutional reform,' Mandelson admitted. What people wanted from Labour, he argued in a revealing phrase, was a new political style. 'People didn't want things uprooted, but liked the idea that we were going to throw open the shutters and blow away a few cobwebs.' Inclusiveness was 'the defining characteristic of New Labour', he declared, describing the party's approach to constitutional reform as bespoke rather than off-the-peg. This was not the approach of those 'whose preference is for the grand constitutional design, in which tidiness and consistency are more prized than functionality'. Proportional voting had been an essential step in Scotland and Wales, he reminded the champions of first-past-the-post: 'The idea that a Labour government could have pushed through devolution without touching electoral reform is serious self-delusion. PR was vital to the success of the Scottish and Welsh devolution referenda.' But the arguments over a voting system for Westminster were different, he insisted.

Making an essentially conservative argument for the Westminster model, Mandelson argued that the swing of the electoral pendulum and the self-restraint of the major parties ensured that nobody was ever permanently excluded from power. 'Political parties have observed self-imposed restraint on the 'winner-takes-all' abuses that our voting system and lack of written constitution theoretically make possible.' He called on supporters of electoral reform to acknowledge a range of options and the strength of the arguments for first-past-the-post, including the constituency link, the clarity of the election result and the lack of European-style coalitions. Acknowledging some of the arguments for reform, he argued that AV would meet some of these requirements.

FUDGE IN THE WEST COUNTRY

Mandelson's speech pointed the way towards a compromise on electoral reform agreed at Labour's National Policy Forum in Exeter in July 2000. It essentially met the Labour leadership's requirements by leaving open as many options as possible. According to participants in the closed-door meeting, reformers managed to stave off an attempt by Sir Ken Jackson's AEEU to ditch the party's referendum commitment completely, a step which would have seriously complicated Blair's relations with the Liberal Democrats. But the final wording largely reflected the AEEU's strong opposition to any change in the status quo. While recalling the 1997 commitment to a referendum on the voting system for the Commons, the new policy text introduced a subtle change of emphasis; instead of actually promising to hold a referendum, the text promised that the voting system for the Commons *would not be altered without one* – a significant watering down of the original pledge. New voting systems already introduced in Scotland, Wales and elsewhere would have to be given time to become familiar and for all their consequences to be felt before any more decisions could be taken on electoral reform, the text said. This was a clear pointer that no decisions would be taken before a second round of elections to devolved bodies in 2003–04.

The second shift of policy was to distance the party decisively from the Jenkins recommendations by saying an internal consultation of members had revealed 'serious concerns' about them. There was no mention of AV, but in the light of Mandelson's speech praising it, there could be little doubt that this was the solution destined to replace the Jenkins formula in a future referendum. David Lipsey pointed out to me that the government had always been careful to avoid committing itself formally to a referendum on the Jenkins plan:

They said firstly, we will establish a commission to find the best alternative to first-past-the-post, and secondly, there will be a referendum. But they did not specifically commit themselves to that referendum being on what that commission recommended. It would fulfil the pledge of the last manifesto to have a vote on AV alone. Obviously Jenkins does not recommend AV alone, and Make Votes Count wants the whole of the Jenkins solution. But from the government point of view it is not Jenkins or nothing.

Pam Giddy of Charter88 takes a highly critical view of Labour's sudden enthusiasm for AV: 'This whole AV thing is a fix. To hold a referendum between first-past-the-post and AV is not fulfilling their pledge and it will split the reform movement because Charter88 would not support AV.' She believes some Liberal Democrats will be tempted to go along with Labour because AV, while not a proportional solution, would win Charles Kennedy's party 'more bums on seats' at Westminster. 'They risk losing the moral high ground and falling into the trap of being accused of favouring reform just for their own ends,' she argues.

Jenkins, whose report described AV as potentially even more unfair in its outcome than first-past-the-post, particularly to the Conservatives, believes Blair will be tempted by this solution.

Conservative spokesman Sir George Young told me his party was well aware of the danger of a Labour attempt to bring in AV:

I think it would be bad news for everybody. By no stretch of the imagination is that proportional. It simply is not PR. Jenkins looked at it and rejected it. The government actually committed themselves, when they hold a referendum, to do it on AV plus. They actually said that in a debate, George Howarth said it. So it would be reneging on the commitment for a vote on AV plus if they held it on AV. They seem to be trying to finesse their way out of a very clear manifesto commitment. They are wondering what on earth they can put in the next manifesto that keeps Charlie Kennedy on board and doesn't wind up too many Labour MPs. It seems they have lighted on AV. I would be amazed if Kennedy would agree to that because it is simply not PR, which is what the Liberals have always wanted. What it would do is stuff the Tory party. You have the centre right, which is us, you have the centre left, which is the two of them, and AV plus makes it even easier for the two of them to knock us out. It is an unhealthy thought that that is the motivation for doing it.

Some Labour reformers argued that they had little alternative but to agree to the compromise text in Exeter. 'The choice was between a form of wording which expressed the AEEU agenda or losing the commitment to the referendum,' one of them told me. Supporters of electoral reform say the formula agreed in Exeter and approved by the Brighton conference keeps their cause alive and kicking. Labour activist Tony Robinson told a fringe meeting at Brighton:

In the face of the most unscrupulous opposition, we have managed to keep electoral reform on the agenda. Given the attack on us, we should really pat ourselves on the back. We have to accept that we have suffered a bit of a defeat as well. People threw mud at us, saying we were a middle-class organization, an organization of obsessives, that we were neurotic, single issue, not engaging in what ordinary Labour supporters really cared about in this country. Some of that mud has undoubtedly stuck. That is not our fault.

However, Labour opponents of electoral reform such as Sir Ken Jackson are confident that they have kicked the whole idea of a referendum into the long grass and that the Jenkins plan is dead and buried.

LABOUR'S NATIONAL POLICY FORUM ON ELECTORAL REFORM

'The 1997 Labour party manifesto promised the British people a referendum on the voting system for the House of Commons between the current first-past-the-post system and a form of electoral reform. Whilst remaining committed to the holding of a referendum before any change to the House of Commons electoral system is introduced, Labour will allow the changes for elections to the European and Scottish Parliament and for the Welsh and London Assemblies to become familiar and allow time for all their consequences to be felt before deciding on any further proposals for electoral reform. Labour has conducted a consultation on the issues raised by the report of the Independent Commission on the Voting System and which is contained in a separate document. There were serious concerns about the acceptability of AV plus. It was strongly felt that the electoral system for the House of Commons needs to maintain the constituency link, encourage stable government and take account of proportionality of power as well as that of representation.'

HEADS I WIN, TAILS YOU LOSE?

The outlook for electoral reform for the Commons depends on several variables. If the Labour manifesto follows the fudge of the National Policy Forum, it will maintain some vague reference to a referendum in the future, but insist that other changes must have time to 'bed down' before any decisions can be taken. There will be no mention of Jenkins and no clear indication of which alternative might be offered to first-past-the-post. Rhodri Morgan's estimate is that it will take another decade for electoral reform to be introduced at Westminster as part of a wider movement to a written constitution. For that to happen, voting reform will have to be linked up with other constitutional changes rather than treated in isolation. Some Labour MPs such as Rochdale's Lorna Fitzsimons see PR as a way of reconnecting with voters in Labour's inner-city heartlands, where the party has clung to first-past-the-post out of fear of the unknown:

The bottom line is, we are scared of ourselves, we are scared of losing an argument, we are scared that our politics aren't strong enough. I think that's not good enough … We have got to stop talking to ourselves and start talking to the people we claim to represent. The Labour party, I am afraid to say, is scared of the voters. It would rather sit in a room with five people than go out and talk to the people we represent. The only way is to go out and have that dialogue; currently, under this system, you don't have to. Perhaps we wouldn't have things like the fuel protest.

The problem with the Labour party's purely instrumentalist approach to the issue is that arguments over electoral reform on grounds of principle have become disconnected from the rest of the party's constitutional measures. Tony Robinson told fellow reformers in Brighton:

The only way to get our argument back into the centre of Labour party politics is to argue that what we are arguing for is the same as the Human Rights Act, the same as the written constitution, the same as our desire to reform the House of Commons and the House of Lords, the same as our struggle for regional assemblies and against racism.

If Labour manages to secure a substantial majority for a second term, the party will not need Liberal Democrat support in the Commons, and it is a fair bet that no referendum on electoral reform will take place. It is clear that given the choice, Blair would much prefer to concentrate his energies on winning a referendum on the single currency instead. The alternative scenario is a slump in the Labour general election vote and a hung parliament, with Liberal Democrats holding the balance of power. David Lipsey told reform supporters at Labour's annual conference a few days after the nationwide fuel blockades in September 2000 that the party's sudden dive in the opinion polls should lead to a rethink by campaigners for first-past-the-post: 'By delaying electoral reform, they have opened the door to the possibility of a Tory government. It could be elected under our present system on well under 40 per cent of the vote.'

By distancing itself from Jenkins, Labour has sought to keep open all its possible options; Blair has now positioned his government so it can still hold a referendum if it needs to, but can avoid offering voters a genuine choice between the status quo and a proportional system. So the constitutional menu for a Labour second term is unlikely to offer the 'luscious cornucopia' of a Jenkins-inspired top-up system, nor Tony Benn's nightmare of Labour MPs lining up like turkeys and voting for their own extinction. If the Liberal Democrats agree, then the choice will be between first-past-the-post and AV, while the prospect of a more substantial change in the voting system for Westminster floats back to the bottom of the seabed – the reform that got away. This lost sea monster will resurface only when Labour finds itself back in opposition again, with plenty of leisure time to re-examine the flaws of first-past-the-post.

NOTES

[1] Linton, Martin and Southcott, Mary (1998) *Making Votes Count. The case for electoral reform*, London, Profile Books, p 90.

[2] Rawnsley, Andrew (2000) *Servants of the People*, London, Hamish Hamilton, p 199.

[3] *Report of the Independent Commission on the Voting System (The Jenkins Report) Cm 4090-1*, The Stationery Office, 1998, p 6.

[4] *The Jenkins Report*, p 7.

[5] *The Jenkins Report*, p 40.

[6] *The Jenkins Report*, p 47.

[7] Dunleavy, Patrick, Margetts, Helen and Weir, Stuart (1993) *The Politico's Guide to Electoral Reform in Britain*, London, Politico's.

[8] Peter Mandelson used this argument in a speech in July 2000 pressing the case for AV: 'When coalitions are largely about buying off small minority parties, they are often at their weakest in times of crisis. We witnessed this in continental governments during the Kosovo campaign.' Blair was the only leader of a major European NATO government based on a single party and had a much wider freedom of manoeuvre in the Kosovo campaign than his counterparts. However, it is arguable that this came not so much from the absence of a coalition as from the wide prerogative powers of the British prime minister, who can send troops into action without the permission of parliament.

[9] *Guardian*, 25 April 2000.

[10] *The Report of the Renewing Local Democracy Working Group (The Kerley Report)*, The Scottish Executive, 2000.

[11] *The Scotsman*, 28 June 2000.

[12] These estimates come from the Jenkins report, not (needless to say) from Mandelson's speech.

8

JOINING UP SIR HUMPHREY

'Command premierships have a terrible tendency to end in tears'
– Professor Peter Hennessy

'Hands-off is the hardest lesson of all for British central government to learn'
– Professor Rod Rhodes

'The first right of a citizen in any mature democracy should be the right to information. It is time to sweep away the cobwebs of secrecy which hang over far too much government activity' – Tony Blair, John Smith Memorial Lecture, 1996

THE SCENE WAS MORE WHITE HOUSE than Whitehall. Rows of plastic chairs covered the lawn in the walled garden behind 10 Downing Street; television cameras pointed at a wooden lectern in front of the flowerbeds and loudspeakers were dotted among the shrubs; anxious officials squinted at the sky looking for rain as the members of Tony Blair's government filed in to take their seats.

It was 30 July 1998, and I had been invited as one of two token members of the written press to witness an event which, if it did not exactly make history, at least qualified as an attempt to create a piece of what historians call invented tradition. Blair had summoned his newly reshuffled cabinet ministers and their deputies to the launch of a glossy report on his government's first year in office. From my seat at the back I watched as Blair

strode down the steps into the garden to polite applause from his colleagues and civil servants and delivered a 15-minute pep-talk. The spots of
rain miraculously stopped after a few seconds as Blair promoted his
favourite theme of the 'third way' in government and told his ministers to
ignore 'froth and nonsense' in the press. 'Every pledge we made we will
deliver. Every line of the contract we will fulfil. Line by line, pledge by
pledge, step by step it is our task to make this country better,' he declared
in a final crescendo. 'It is and remains for me a tremendous privilege and
honour to lead what I hope in retrospect and in history will be seen as one
of the great reforming governments of our time. Thank you.'

I was expecting Blair to stick around on the lawn and mingle with his
colleagues, or even answer questions, but I had forgotten that this was a
typical New Labour made-for-television event, not a real one. Off he
strode again up the steps to another round of applause, leaving a sense
of anticlimax. It was rather like a school prize-giving ceremony somewhere in Middle England, abruptly curtailed with only the headmaster's
speech, and no prizes or refreshments afterwards.

THE ROSE GARDEN STYLE

The event – which was not repeated when the second government
report was published a year later – is worth recalling in detail because it
transmitted several clear messages about
how Blair saw himself and his government.
The model was that of the President of the
United States addressing the nation from the
White House Rose Garden, rather than a
British prime minister accountable to parliament. Blair's quasi-presidential entrance and
exit underlined the fact that here was a
prime minister who was more than just first
among equals in the cabinet. The annual report itself was modelled on a
company annual report, suggesting that government was primarily a
business, with Blair as the dynamic chief executive reporting once a year
to his shareholders and customers. In the document, Blair made the parallel explicit, describing a change of government as being like sweeping
away the entire top management of a company: 'Trust matters. In all
walks of life people act as consumers, not just citizens. They want those
providing a service to justify themselves. How much is it costing me?
Where is the money going? Government is no different.'

> **"The model was that of the President of the United States addressing the nation from the White House Rose Garden, rather than a British prime minister accountable to parliament. "**

Blair promised sweeping changes: 'The truth is that in many areas Britain is not yet equipped to tackle the challenges of the next century – our institutions, our constitution, our attitudes. That is why I have challenged every part of the country to modernize.'

RHETORIC AND CONVENTION

This rhetoric provides the backdrop when we look at Blair's impact on the machinery of British government. In a largely pre-democratic system lacking a written constitution and even a proper legislative framework for the operation of the civil service, the style imposed at the top determines the working practices and conventions of government. But no government starts off with a blank sheet of paper; it has to build on the style and conventions of its predecessors, even if these are not openly acknowledged. Many of these conventions have hardened into a quasi-constitutional set of rules, while others are loose parameters. They have been described as 'the rules of a now half-obsolete club culture'.[1] If a government wants to go outside these parameters or change the conventions, it can be argued that this does not necessarily constitute a constitutional change, or at least not the kind of change represented by the setting up of a Scottish parliament or the removal of hereditary peers from the House of Lords. Reforms such as a Freedom of Information Act or a Human Rights Act clearly come under the definition of constitutional change because they have the potential to fundamentally change the relationship between the citizen and the state. The constitutional effects of other changes in the way government operates are less clear-cut. Rather than seeking to define constitutional change from first principles, the analysis that follows will adopt a simple rule-of-thumb definition: it will look for the kind of changes in the rulebook and operations of Whitehall that a future government would find it hard to reverse.

Using this definition, this chapter will look in turn at a number of aspects of the Blair impact on Whitehall; firstly, the survival or otherwise of cabinet government, held by Bagehot to be the distinguishing feature of his 'English constitution'; secondly, accusations that the civil service has been politicized and its neutrality undermined; thirdly, Blair's modernization agenda and his attempts to make government more like business; fourthly, the reliance on outside task forces to shape policy; and finally, the long saga of the government's attempts to bring in a Freedom of Information Act.

In each of these areas, there are a number of questions to answer. Has the quasi-presidential, quasi-corporate style of the Blair 'Rose Garden' premiership really changed the way the executive functions, or has it remained a matter of style? Is the unique professional ethos of the British civil service, shaped by the Victorian era, still a reality, or is it by now just a historical myth? Should we judge the Blair government solely by the narrow benchmarks it has set for itself, or against broader criteria of good governance such as accountability and openness? To what extent has Blair continued or overturned the policies of his Conservative predecessors? If there have been big changes, then are they likely to be permanent? In other words, has the Labour government just been blowing away a few cobwebs in the Whitehall corridors of power and letting in the fresh air, or has it been tearing out and replacing what Professor Peter Hennessy calls the state's hidden wiring?

AFTER THATCHER

Adopting a 'constitutional' perspective on British government often obscures the complex reality of power relationships in Westminster and Whitehall. As Professor Martin J. Smith of Sheffield University writes: 'Political reality has been masked by constitutional myths which are themselves continually reinforced by ministers, officials and political scientists.'[2] The problem is easily illustrated by examining the paradoxical record of the Thatcher government. While opposed to anything that smacked of constitutional reform in the formal sense, Margaret Thatcher was, at least in her rhetoric, a committed radical when it came to the British state and its institutions. She was deeply suspicious of the civil service as a force for consensus and the status quo, and subjected it to radical change. However, her crusade against bureaucracy and state intervention had paradoxical results; while cutting the size of the state through privatization, in many ways she left it more centralized and more powerful than before by whittling away the power of local government and moving it to Whitehall. When Thatcher entered Downing Street in 1979 she inherited a civil service that had 732,000 staff. When Blair took over from John Major 18 years later, the total had fallen to about 450,000 because of privatization. What was left had been mostly broken up into dozens of 'Next Steps' agencies, still linked to their parent ministries but with the freedom to set their own wages and working conditions and headed by chief executives. Instead of concentrating on policy advice, civil servants became managers. Ministerial accountability to parliament became blurred as civil servants became chief executives of independent agencies, responsible for meeting performance targets.

Under the Conservative reforms the traditional doctrine of ministerial responsibility – that civil servants were anonymous and powerless, and ministers alone took decisions and were accountable to parliament – became undermined, with the government drawing a distinction between policy (for which ministers were responsible) and implementation (for which they were not). That this distinction was impossible to define became clear during the Major government with the sacking of Derek Lewis, head of the Prison Service, by Home Secretary Michael Howard. The aftermath of this row and the even more traumatic investigation by Sir Richard Scott into arms sales to Iraq contributed to a widespread sense of unease in Whitehall in the closing years of Conservative rule. This was reflected in an authoritative report in February 1998 by the House of Lords Select Committee on the Public Service. It concluded after nearly two years of evidence-gathering 'that there has been little or no coherent rationale underlying the changes made in the civil service in recent years'. Even the experts were often baffled, let alone the public. The Lords committee expressed concern that the traditional values of the civil service, dating back to the Victorian reforms that followed the 1853 Northcote-Trevelyan report, might be jeopardized by the Thatcherite stress on emulating the private sector:

The civil service traditions of integrity, loyalty to the Crown, commitment to the task and lack of political bias have been responsible for the high regard in which the civil service has been held. These qualities, together with the principle that civil servants are constitutionally the alter ego of their ministers, with not merely the right but the duty when necessary to proffer unwelcome advice to ministers, mean that a post in the civil service is not merely a job but is genuinely a form of service to the public, so that analogies with the terms and conditions of employees in the private sector must not be pushed too far.

The Lords' unease was partly motivated by the longstanding failure of all successive governments to define the status and role of the civil service in law. Since the 19th-century reforms introduced the principles of impartiality, open recruitment and security of tenure, there has never been a proper Civil Service Act, leaving each successive government to operate the executive under Orders in Council, which are not subject to approval by parliament. It is only by convention, rather than by statute, that the limits of what is 'constitutional' in the internal procedures of the British executive are laid down. In principle, every incoming government has been free to write its own rulebook, though this flexibility has been much reduced over the past decade by the publication of the key documents.

The gradual accretion of quasi-constitutional lore and convention under successive governments has been chronicled by Professor Peter Hennessy, who was instrumental in persuading John Major to make public the previously secret *Questions of Procedure for Ministers* in 1992.[3] This document, now known as the Ministerial Code, has been updated and reissued by the Blair government as a framework for cabinet procedure and a handbook of ethical guidelines for ministers. Conventions and unwritten understandings are gradually being replaced with written codes, eroding the traditional 'back-of-the-envelope' Whitehall culture. The Ministerial Code, originally a private list of 'do's and don'ts', is now a public document of quasi-constitutional status.[4] The change has partly come about because the document is no longer secret, allowing public judgement on how it is being observed in practice, and partly because of the outside involvement of the Nolan/Neill Committee on Standards in Public Life, which has meant the text is no longer solely a matter of prime ministerial discretion. Parliament, too, has become involved, because the current version of the code incorporates an all-party resolution passed in March 1997 governing ministerial accountability to parliament. Although the former Cabinet Secretary Robin Butler (Lord Butler of Brockwell) has argued that it would be theoretically possible for an incoming prime minister to scrap the document and devise new rules, this would pose severe political problems, given the prominence now given to the code. John Major told a Commons committee in June 2000: 'Robin Butler is perfectly right that any incoming government can change it. But it would be very unwise to do so. It's unlikely to happen.'

> 66 Conventions and unwritten understandings are gradually being replaced with written codes, eroding the traditional 'back-of-the-envelope' Whitehall culture. 99

A BLANK SHEET OF PAPER

Tony Blair, in contrast to Margaret Thatcher, entered office with a raft of planned constitutional changes and policies, but without any clear agenda for the processes of government. Freedom of information was an aspiration rather than a worked-out policy, and 'modernization' emerged later in the light of experience. Blair and his team mostly arrived unencumbered by folk memories and preconceptions about the world of Whitehall; they had received extensive civil service briefings before the election, and harboured none of the deep suspicions of the

mandarin class as lackeys of the conservative establishment and sabo-
teurs of socialism which afflicted an earlier generation of Labour
politicians such as Tony Benn. Labour's 1997 manifesto had little to say
about the civil service or the running of the core executive, with the
exception of a promise to introduce a Freedom of Information Act and
give government statisticians more independence:

> Unnecessary secrecy in government leads to arrogance in government and
> defective policy decisions. The Scott report on arms to Iraq revealed Conservative
> abuses of power. We are pledged to a Freedom of Information Act, leading to
> more open government, and an independent National Statistical Service.

There was no commitment to restore the pre-Thatcher status quo.
According to Professor Gavin Drewry: 'On the basis of its own stance in
opposition it is no surprise to find that Labour's approach to civil service-
related issues on taking office was to go with the flow of existing change
rather than to try to put the clock back or radically change direction.'[5]

Professor Rod Rhodes of Newcastle University, noting the long delay in producing the 1999 *Modernising Government* White Paper, told the House of
Commons Public Administration Committee: 'I err on the side of understatement when I infer public sector reform was not a priority.'[6] When the
government did finally issue its White Paper after nearly two years, the continuity with the philosophy of the Conservatives was palpable. But the
'presidential' style of the annual report reflected a determined attempt to
strengthen central control of the executive, moving from a system of
'feudal baronies' to a more powerful, even Napoleonic system based on the
prime minister's office in 10 Downing Street.

THE OVAL OFFICE IN DOWNING STREET?

For Walter Bagehot, cabinet government was the secret of what he called
the 'English' constitution, guaranteeing the close fusion of the executive
to the legislature.

> A Cabinet is a combining committee – a *hyphen* which joins, a *buckle* which
> fastens the legislative part of the State to the executive part of the State.

I asked Robin Butler, who as head of the civil service handled the transition
from the Major government to the Blair government in 1997, whether

cabinet government in this sense was a constitutional norm that prime ministers should observe. He thought for a moment before replying:

I find the word 'constitution' difficult because we haven't got a written constitution, and I find 'should' a difficult word because people run things the way that suits them. But the situation is that the prime minister is not like the president of the United States. He is not elected to an executive position under a constitution. He needs to command the assent of various people in order to continue to hold his office. He has clearly got to have the support of a majority in parliament, and as the experience of Margaret Thatcher showed, he has got to hold the assent of his cabinet. And providing that is done, prime ministers have really got a great deal of latitude in the way in which they run things. Now what has certainly happened with the cabinet over the years is that from being a thing where most of the major decisions were at least formally taken – a lot of them would have been done by cabinet committees beforehand, but most major issues would go to the cabinet to get their formal assent – over a long period that has diminished. There was never a formal requirement for it – it is not like a company board meeting where there are certain resolutions which the board of directors has got to take. The system of government doesn't work like that. And now very few decisions are taken formally in the cabinet. The thing has become more and more informal. It has become rather like it was in the 18th century in that it is a group of the top political figures, colleagues, meeting around the table once a week to discuss whatever they care to discuss. And there were some formal elements of the agenda under Margaret Thatcher and John Major – parliamentary affairs, home affairs, foreign affairs, European affairs, which were the main headings. The Prime Minister has got away from that. And so frankly they meet and discuss for an hour, maybe less, whatever he feels that it would be useful for them to discuss.

> 66 It has become rather like it was in the 18th century in that it is a group of the top political figures, colleagues, meeting around the table once a week to discuss whatever they care to discuss. 99

Butler's views on the demise of cabinet government are widely shared by academics, who believe Blair has merely accelerated a trend towards prime ministerial government that was first spotted some four decades ago. The decline of cabinet government in post-war Britain is a well-chewed academic bone. It was described in the early 1960s by the Labour MP and political scientist John P. Mackintosh and then by the

Labour minister Richard Crossman in a famous essay introducing a new edition of Bagehot's *English Constitution*. Margaret Thatcher's dominance of her cabinet was legendary, as was her tendency to bypass it by taking decisions in small ad hoc groups or bilateral meetings with her ministers. Even Clement Attlee, probably the greatest stickler for procedure among all post-World War Two prime ministers, bypassed most of his cabinet when it came to developing Britain's nuclear weapons.

The ousting of Thatcher in 1991 by her cabinet colleagues and by Conservative MPs, and the more collegiate style of her successor John Major, provides evidence for some that Bagehot's theory of cabinet government is not completely dead. In the words of a current Labour MP and political scientist, Tony Wright: 'The death of the cabinet is regularly announced, but it is resurrected equally regularly. The underlying trends are what matters.'[7] It is also important to remember that in dealing with their cabinet colleagues, prime ministers are constrained less by rules and conventions and more by political circumstances, especially the size of their majority in parliament. Professor Martin Smith writes:

Power within the core executive does not depend on the personality of the prime minister. Thatcher appeared strong in 1987 and John Major appeared weak in 1997, not because Thatcher was a dominant personality and Major was a weak personality but because the circumstances were different. Major had no majority in parliament, the government was divided, and the popular perception was that his government lacked economic competence – circumstance created Major's indecisiveness; it was not indecisiveness that led to the Conservative defeat.

THE THATCHER SCHOOL AND ITS PUPILS

Blair has made it clear that he follows Thatcher in tackling contentious issues in bilateral meetings rather than round the cabinet table in the manner of the Wilson and Callaghan governments. Interviewed by Michael Cockerell[8] for a BBC television documentary, he denied – unprompted – that he never discussed things with his ministerial colleagues: 'Look, I would be pretty shocked if the first time I knew a cabinet minister felt strongly about something was if they raised it at the cabinet table. I would expect them to come and knock on my door and say: "Look Tony, I've got a problem here, I disagree with this or disagree with that." And that happens from time to time, and then you sit down and you work it out. But the old days of Labour governments where cabinet meetings occasionally went on for two days and you had a show of hands at the end of it – I shudder to think what would happen if we were running it like that.'

Peter Hennessy quotes Jack Straw as telling his students: 'The Prime Minister operates as chief executive of ... various subsidiary companies and you are called in to account for yourself.'[9]

The key constitutional aspect of the long-running and somewhat sterile debate over cabinet government is whether any future prime minister would be at liberty to ignore the Blair method and return to an earlier pattern. When I asked Robin Butler to confirm this, he replied: 'Absolutely. Yes. It is precisely the way the prime minister and his colleagues want to run it.' Blair's style was made clear at the start by the way he and Gordon Brown brushed aside Butler's worries and decided to make the Bank of England independent immediately after the 1997 election without even consulting their cabinet colleagues.[10] Some constitutional experts, such as Peter Hennessy, are left very uneasy by Blair's abandonment of the cabinet as a decision-making forum. 'It worries me,' Hennessy said in a lecture, arguing on pragmatic grounds that a sense of the collective was a safeguard against overmightiness at the top and an aid to careful policymaking. 'Command models, Napoleonic or otherwise, have a habit of ending in tears. The temptation to install and operate them is best resisted.'[11] In other words, a wise prime minister is the one who makes sure all his cabinet colleagues have 'hands dipped in the blood' when the going gets rough.[12] Hennessy sees the cabinet under Blair as 'even more peripheral than under Mrs Thatcher at her most tigress-like' and sees a further significant change in Blair's downgrading of cabinet committees, which have mostly ceased to be the place where real policy decisions are taken. The model of British government that has operated since 1945 is since the arrival of Blair 'now effectively at an end', he argues. Hennessy's conclusion is that Blair's failure to operate a collegiate style of government is not so much a constitutional *faux pas* as a political error of judgement that will return to haunt him in a second term, when life gets more difficult and loyalties fray.

While, as Butler argues, a successor to Blair would be free in theory to resurrect the post-1945 system of cabinet government and its committees, in practice such a decision would depend on the depth of civil service institutional memory. Blair's 'strong centre' in 10 Downing Street amounts, in the view of some analysts, to a prime minister's department in all but name. The Cabinet Office now serves 10 Downing Street more than the rest of Whitehall, and some of its key sections, such as the Performance and Innovation Unit (PIU), report not to Cabinet Office ministers but directly to Blair and his staff. This kind of change might be difficult, but certainly not impossible, to reverse in the future.

Some analysts believe the picture of a presidential administration under Blair is grossly exaggerated. Professor Vernon Bogdanor says a strong centre is vital for good cabinet government, but Britain is unusual among Westminster-type systems in that it has a very weak centre: 'Both Australia and Canada have very strong prime ministerial departments ... no one in Australia or Canada believes that these departments make their prime ministers more like presidents or dictators or anything of that kind. A great deal of nonsense has been talked about our own prime minister assuming presidential or dictatorial powers.'[13]

> **❝The 'Rose Garden' presidentialism of the Blair government should not necessarily be taken as a true reflection of reality, but as an aspiration.❞**

The 'Rose Garden' presidentialism of the Blair government should not necessarily be taken as a true reflection of reality, but as an aspiration. Future historians of the 1997 Labour government may well see more significance in the increased powers of the Treasury under Gordon Brown to exert control over other departments by tightening the purse strings and imposing public service agreements and 'money for modernization'. There is a certain visible rivalry between Number 10 and the better-resourced Treasury, with the former sometimes struggling to catch up with Brown's number-crunchers. It would be a mistake to imagine that the 'feudal baronies' of Whitehall, the big departments of state, have become totally subordinate to Blair's office in a new and irreversible way. Some academics believe the barons will sooner or later strike back. The ability of prime ministers to play Napoleon or set up their version of the Oval Office depends not on formal powers, of which 10 Downing Street has very few, but on political authority, which can be quickly eroded, as Margaret Thatcher found to her cost.

POLITICIZATION AND SPECIAL ADVISERS

The traditional model of the British civil service since the reforms of 1870 has preserved intact something that has either been eroded, or has never existed in other countries – the presumption that political neutrality can be maintained at the very highest level of officialdom. Defenders of the traditional model, such as Peter Hennessy, believe Britain is the only country to have preserved what is required for a clean and decent civil service: 'We are not just the world leader, we are the only citadel, and that is the rock on which the civil service should stand. That is the bit where they can actually legitimately say, "The rest of the world is an object lesson in how not to do it. Push off".'[14] The 'neutrality' of top civil servants is of course a constitutional fiction which has proved convenient for all concerned; civil servants are required to go into bat vigorously for their political masters and their policies, but crucially both parties recognize that they will do the same for their opponents in the event of a change of government. Impartiality for civil servants means not Olympian detachment and objectivity, but rather an obligation to be partial to whoever is in government at the time. Under this bargain, civil servants have benefited from long-term career stability, relative anonymity, security of tenure and decent salaries in return for switching loyalties and policies without a murmur on election day. Robin Butler describes the deal:

I think as far as the civil service is concerned, the great protection of the regime put into place in the last century was that civil servants were decently paid, they have security of employment, in the sense that politicians can't arbitrarily get rid of them or exercise their own patronage, and they are given inflation-proofed pensions and so there is no reason, no motivation for them to pursue their own private interests ... I am sure people would like to pay me a great deal of money for my memoirs. I don't think I should write those memoirs, and financially I don't need to because I can survive perfectly decently without doing that. I am not a public figure with a reputation to defend like a politician. So we have created a regime where there is no reason why people shouldn't follow the highest standards and that I think still applies, and that is our best protection.

For politicians, the traditional Whitehall system has drawbacks in that they cannot bring in to government an unlimited number of their political camp-followers. But it also has advantages – the lack of a US-style spoils system or even a French-style *cabinet* system means newly appointed ministers do not have to spend months assembling a team of staff. As soon as they are appointed they have the use of a deferential and experienced civil service team, who will already have been thinking hard about how to turn their ideas into workable policy. One benefit is a strong institutional memory. This delicate balance of interests began to come under strain during the Thatcher period because of her preference for dealing with kindred spirits who shared her ideas; her interrogatory 'Is he one of us?' became legendary. However, fears of permanent politicization of the civil service under the 18 years of Conservative rule proved wide of the mark. In fact, the mandarins were initially enthusiastic about the transition to Labour in 1997. 'Professional neutrality meant that any celebrations had to be private and muted, but the sense of relief throughout Whitehall was almost palpable.'[15]

NEW POWERS FOR POLITICAL APPOINTEES

Under Blair there have been accusations of a different sort of politicization of the civil service; critics charge him not with purging Conservative sympathizers in favour of Labour supporters but of upsetting the delicate Whitehall balance by bringing in too many special advisers, particularly in 10 Downing Street, where posts once filled by civil servants are now occupied by political appointees. When Blair took over in May 1997 he brought with him the three key staffers on whom he had relied in opposition. Chief of staff Jonathan Powell, spokesman Alastair Campbell and chief policy adviser David Miliband formed a 'through train' which enabled him to make a quick start at 10 Downing Street. The most distinctive Blair innovation was to try to make Powell, a former diplomat, his Principal Private Secretary (PPS), the key Downing Street job always held by a civil servant rather than a political appointee. Traditionally the PPS is one of a trio of officials who may have to play a role of critical constitutional importance in advising the Queen on which party leader should be asked to form a government after an election.

Robin Butler described to me the Solomon-like compromise under which he agreed that Powell could be chief of staff, while the PPS job continued in civil service hands:

Tony Blair originally wanted him to be Principal Private Secretary. It was eventually decided and agreed that he shouldn't be PPS. He is called Chief of Staff. But he was in the room that the PPS occupied. It is a shared room with the foreign affairs private secretary. But he was much more in the line of direct access to the prime minister than any previous political appointee had been.

It is clear that although the formalities were preserved, Blair won the essential argument over Powell's appointment, as he was bound to do.

Powell and Campbell, as political appointees, would not normally have had the authority to give instructions to civil servants, but this was amended by Order in Council, a procedure to which Butler gave his assent. Blair's government was far from the first to use special advisers, who were initially brought into government in an organized way by Harold Wilson in the 1960s. The tradition continued under the Conservatives, but they now accuse Blair's government of upsetting the balance by appointing too many political appointees. In fact, civil servants mostly welcome the existence of special advisers as political bag-carriers on behalf of their ministers; they see them as a useful buffer that prevents rather than encourages politicization of the permanent machine. What is at stake is not so much the principle or the cost, but the risk that with too dense a network of advisers, civil servants will end up out of the policy loop altogether.

Professor Robert Hazell of the Constitution Unit, a former civil servant in the Home Office, told the Commons Public Administration Committee in May 2000 that appointment of so many outside advisers had created independent networks within Whitehall and a high degree of resentment among permanent staff: 'The civil service now feels badly demoralized and out of the loop.' He cited as an example of changing practices a letter he had sent to a minister, which had been copied not to the civil servant handling the policy area concerned but only to a special adviser. Hazell believes that the morale problems and the atrophying of old-fashioned policymaking skills within the civil service pre-date the arrival of the Blair government, though they have got worse since 1997. This applies particularly in the Treasury under the secretive Gordon Brown, who has relied heavily on his special adviser Ed Balls for policymaking and has often kept permanent officials in the dark. 'Morale there went very sharply down when it became clear how Gordon Brown works.'

Andrew Tyrie, a Conservative MP who was once a Treasury special adviser, argues that under Blair the position of political appointees in 10 Downing Street has changed, partly because of the extra powers given to Powell and Campbell, but more because of their sheer numbers:

If you took anybody who had been a private secretary to a prime minister since the First World War, or at least since the Second World War, and put him in any Number 10 Downing St before 1997 he would immediately know what he was doing, who was answering to whom, what the chains of command were, who filled the boxes and what he needed to tell the prime minister, who was running the diary, the correspondence, contacting the press. He would know the answer to all of those questions immediately. He could sit down and start running the office. It would be roughly the same as the office he had run 20 or 30 years earlier … basically he would fit in very quickly.

If you put him into Downing Street today I don't think he would have a clue what's going on. He wouldn't be able to start work. For a start, the office is answerable to an outsider. The Principal Private Secretary would find himself answerable to this political appointee. Then he would find the press secretary had acquired powers that with the possible exception of Joe Haines[16] he could not have imagined – certainly Bernard Ingham[17] didn't have remotely the powers that Alastair Campbell has.

When you have 50 or 60 administrative-grade officials at Number 10 who are all civil servants, and then you have a bolt-on group of five or six advisers, basically the official machine is the structure around which other things work, and they always know what is going on. What you have at the moment is: you have 67 of those slots, of which 28 are outside appointees. That is a fundamental shift in power at the heart of government. That is an end of a completely neutral civil service running a machine on behalf of the prime minister and the introduction of something quite different. A *cabinet* system, an American-style system in miniature.

The First Division Association, the trade union representing senior civil servants, told the Commons Public Administration Committee in a letter in July 2000 that it was worried about the lack of controls on the number of special advisers working in 10 Downing Street:

A prime minister could appoint 40 special advisers, or 400 or 4,000; it would not be difficult for a future prime minister to subvert much of the tradition of the civil service by adopting this route.

The union's general secretary Jonathan Baume criticized the ambiguous role being played by some special advisers in civil service appointments, which he described as inappropriate. While neither Powell nor Campbell had abused their positions, it was far from clear that they required the executive powers Blair had given them in order to do their jobs:

On balance therefore the FDA believes that no special adviser should be given executive power over civil servants and that the executive powers currently allocated to these two posts should be withdrawn, certainly by no later than the next general election.

John Major told the Commons Public Administration Committee in June 2000 that special advisers had 'got out of hand', particularly in their dealings with the media: 'They are becoming a significant problem for the government as a whole.' He said that with hindsight he realized that in his own government 'a lot of the terrible spats came from special advisers ... below the salt.' If he had won a second term in office he would have brought the number down sharply. Major said he did not approve of having a political appointee like Campbell as press spokesman at Number 10, because a civil servant would always have greater credibility: 'I would rather live with the drawbacks than with the politicization of the government information machine.'

Major's pragmatic view of Blair's over-reliance on special advisers has much in common with Peter Hennessy's verdict on his neglect of cabinet government; it is not so much a matter of constitutional rights and wrongs as of political wisdom and intelligent self-interest. Robin Butler takes a similar approach, acknowledging the possibility of the government bypassing civil servants:

Yes, they could do. One has to ask oneself, has a government a right to do that? In a sense, they are politicians, they are answerable to parliament and to the electorate, there is a case for saying, they ought to be able to run things however they think best. If they want to set that up, let them. So what one is really doing is asking oneself, when one considers the Neill recommendations, whether there are barriers that we need to put in the way where they would have to take more formal action if they wanted to go beyond. Now I have always felt that what matters with special advisers is that in the minister's own interests, they oughtn't to form a barrier between the minister and the department. The minister should have access to the objective advice of the civil service. A wise minister will do that. It doesn't mean they will take it, but they would be very foolish not to have it. And so I have always been in favour, as a practical, not a constitutional matter, of limiting the number of special advisers in each department so that they don't form a curtain between the minister and the department.

When I interviewed Patrick Neill (Lord Neill of Bladen), chairman of the Committee on Standards in Public Life, he was still awaiting the government's reply to his committee's report recommending a cap on the number of special advisers and a code to regulate their activities. He finds the present situation 'rather a mess' and favours a Civil Service Act to sort it out:

The civil service is a fundamental thing in our constitution. We have a party which said in opposition, when we get into government we will have a Civil Service Act. We think there ought to be one. It should embody things like the code to which ordinary civil servants ought to subscribe, and it ought to have another code for the special advisers. It would be much more efficient to have it all in one place and so parliament would also be in on the act, in the sense of being able to pass legislation and amend it. The civil service would then have a statutory base. I think that would be in accordance with precedents elsewhere. I said to the committee that we hadn't examined them but I believe that is the case across Europe. It's time to do it and I think it might be a good defence for civil servants.

In its reply to the Neill committee, the government accepted the idea of including an overall limit on numbers of special advisers in civil service legislation, and of a code of conduct for them. There has been no sign, however, that such legislation is in the pipeline or even that a consultation process is envisaged until well after the next election. The risk for any government is that putting the operation of the civil service on a statutory basis will inevitably reduce its own discretionary powers. Andrew Tyrie argues that a Civil Service Act should make civil servants ultimately accountable not to the Crown – in practice, the government of the day – but to parliament. Removing the civil service from the grey area of Crown prerogative would make it far easier for MPs to obtain information about how it operates, rather than relying on probing by the media:

That is the basic change. They are acting basically on the royal prerogative. I don't think that is any way to run a modern country. And I think it is a tribute to the fact that we are basically a very well-balanced and sophisticated political nation that such an arrangement could be carried on for so long ... The fact that self-restraint has for so many decades enabled this bizarre arrangement to carry on is not the same as saying we should leave it there for ever. I think that self-restraint on both sides can be buttressed by the creation of a Civil Service Act. This is much more important now we have a cadre of political advisers in Whitehall who are substituting for the roles formerly performed by civil servants. That is a big difference. That was not the case with advisers in the Thatcher era. For example, advisers did not go abroad and take part in meetings – full stop. There have been hundreds and hundreds of such trips, now it is nearly a thousand. Now I don't object to that in principle, but I do object to us not knowing about it. It is back to this question of information.

A QUESTION OF LOYALTY

The question of whether civil servants have ultimate loyalties that go beyond the government of the day is a crucial one; if they do owe a higher loyalty to parliament than to their ministers, then it is hard to maintain the convention that they are anonymous ciphers who exist merely to execute the will of their political masters. Keeping up this useful fiction requires mutual respect and trust on both sides; civil servants, unlike business executives in the private sector, are supposed to show their loyalty and integrity by sometimes saying 'no' to ministers instead of 'yes', but their readiness to do so will be curbed if the government adopts Thatcher's 'one of us?' approach, or the milder Blairite version which, according to Peter Hennessy, is 'helpful or unhelpful?'

Under Blair as under Thatcher, civil servants are more appreciated for their 'can-do' approach than for their traditional role of snag-hunters. Butler's successor as Cabinet Secretary, Sir Richard Wilson, famously told a television interviewer he would be quite happy to say 'bollocks' to the prime minister, but less senior civil servants with mortgages and career ambitions may not take the same risk. A Civil Service Act would have to lay down whether civil servants, who swear an oath of loyalty to the Crown, are bound only to obey the government of the day or to uphold some unspecified ideal of good government instead. The traditional view in Whitehall is that of Butler's predecessor as Cabinet Secretary, Sir Robert Armstrong, who in 1985 argued: 'Civil servants are servants of the Crown. For all practical purposes the Crown in this context means and is represented by the government of the day … The civil service as such has no constitutional personality or responsibility separate from the duly elected government of the day.' The Lords Select Committee made clear that since the publication by John Major of the Ministerial Code this definition had become outdated:

The civil service may have no specific legal status, but its distinctive responsibilities and the manner in which they are carried out play a significant part in our constitutional arrangements. A definable body of people which owes a loyalty to, and has certain duties in relation to, the duly constituted government undeniably has a personality and responsibility of its own …

Sir Richard Wilson told a conference in April 2000 on Whitehall modernization that the civil service represented 'a great force for steadiness, stability and fairness at the heart of the state'. Other top civil servants have used the term 'ballast', suggesting their function is to prevent the ship of state from capsizing. When it comes to financial discipline, the position is clear-cut; every permanent secretary acts as chief accounting officer for his or her department and has a reporting line to the National Audit Office, and thus to parliament. In political and ethical matters, the position is less clear. Permanent secretaries feel deeply uncomfortable when they are obliged to act as a kind of referee or guardian of the Ministerial Code and tell the minister whether he or she is breaking the rules or not. Can the minister take a spouse or partner on a foreign trip at government expense? Can he or she sign a contract for a book of memoirs while still in office? Can he or she accept a holiday invitation from a business contact? There is a risk that top civil servants can be used by ministers as a convenient screen or coat of whitewash for their personal conduct.

Neill's view, which is shared by top civil servants, is that they should not be forced to be ethical shields for the reputations of their political bosses:

My very strong opinion is that it is incredibly unfair on the permanent secretary to put him in the position where the minister can stand up and say, I told my permanent secretary and he said it was okay. Usually in these situations what has happened is that the full truth was not told to the permanent secretary or whoever. If he did say okay, he said it on the basis of incomplete information, or different information from what has subsequently emerged from press inquiries or whatever. The civil servant, the permanent secretary, cannot then step forward and say, well hang on a moment, he said this was done with my advice. What he suppressed was the following … That's impossible, it's completely contrary to the nature of the permanent secretary and very unsatisfactory. The idea of shuffling it off and saying, 'I got advice on this' just won't do.

I asked Robin Butler whether he ever saw himself as a provider of constitutional ballast, being prepared to tell the prime minister of the day 'You cannot do that'. He gave the example of public appointments:

There is the civil service Order in Council, which requires appointments to be made on merit through open competition. So you have to go to the prime minister and say, 'I'm afraid it isn't open to you under the civil service Orders to appoint somebody a civil servant. You can appoint them a special adviser on a limited contract. You can't appoint them a civil servant without due process.'

I asked Butler a hypothetical question: what might happen if Blair were one day to try to appoint Jonathan Powell, a political adviser, as Cabinet Secretary and head of the civil service in succession to Sir Richard Wilson? If a determined prime minister was told this was impossible because of existing Orders in Council, could he or she not just amend the Orders without further ado? Sir Robin agreed that this was the case: 'You have cited an example which I think is rather far-fetched, but it illustrates why it ought to be made more difficult for a prime minister to do that.' He now reluctantly favours proper legislation covering the civil service to limit government freedom to change the rules without reference to parliament:

I think – sadly – the time has probably come when it would be a good thing to have a Civil Service Act, just to protect us all from a new government coming in and saying, we are going to do away with all these things, appointment by merit and so on. And make them go through a rather longer process of debate in the House of Commons before they did so. I say that with some regret, because in general I think the British constitution has worked well.

WHERE THE BUCK STOPS

Where the personal conduct of ministers is concerned, the Ministerial Code still has some ambiguities. The Neill committee has been pressing Blair, so far without success, to revise a key paragraph that leaves it unclear whether or not the prime minister is personally responsible for enforcing it. The current version from 1997 reads as follows:

It will be for individual ministers to judge how best to act in order to uphold the highest standards. They are responsible for justifying their conduct to parliament. And they can only remain in office for so long as they retain the prime minister's confidence.

In its sixth report, the Neill committee suggested the following alternative wording to make it clear that the buck finally stopped with the prime minister:

It will be for individual ministers to judge how best to act in order to uphold the highest standards. They are responsible for justifying their conduct to parliament and retaining its confidence. The prime minister remains the ultimate judge of the requirements of the code and the appropriate consequences of breaches of it.

But the government, replying in July 2000, rejected this version, arguing that the potential loophole the committee was trying to close did not exist. Neill argues that the change would in fact make it easier for a prime minister to sack a minister suspected of misconduct, even if all the facts were not yet available:

The recommendation is that it should be absolutely clear that the prime minister is the master of the code and the judge of whether people in his view have matched the standards. The standard includes retaining the confidence of the prime minister. It is my belief that there may be situations where rough justice has to be done. You haven't got time to investigate it all, things are being said in the media about a high-ranking minister, and you can't run a government with that going on and you may have to say, 'I am sorry, you may have a complete answer to all this, but you have got to go.'

John Major told the Commons Public Administration Committee in June 2000 that if he were still in office he would now accept the Neill committee's recommended text. He agreed that it was for the prime minister to decide whether a rule had been broken: 'Only one person can decide – the prime minister. He promulgates the code.'

Blair, in a Commons debate called by the Conservatives in July 2000 on relations between parliament and the executive, suggested he saw questions about the Ministerial Code as a nit-picking irrelevance:

No one will be better governed through fine-tuning the Ministerial Code. Those are good issues for academics and constitutional experts but they are not the big issues that parliament should debate when we consider our role in the modern society and our relationship with the executive today.

Professor Peter Hennessy, speaking to the Commons Public Administration Committee, described this as 'a deeply unfortunate thing to say', even if Blair was being cross with the leader of the opposition at the time he made the remark:

You can do that without rubbishing the one set of guidelines, of which you are the guardian – the only set of guidelines that we have that covers the essentials of central government, its procedures, practices and decencies.

MODERNIZE OR DIE

The Blair government's early honeymoon with the civil service under Robin Butler has not lasted. There has been growing pressure for change under his successor Sir Richard Wilson, reflecting Blair's sense of frustration at the way he has pulled the levers of government but has obtained only slow and limited results. Part of the reason for the frustration is the lack of experience among cabinet ministers, Blair included, in managing any kind of large organization. Blair's early career experience was gained in barristers' chambers, which is hardly a preparation for management. This lack of first-hand knowledge may account for Blair's enthusiastic idealization of the private sector as a model for the public services. In the view of Conservative MP Andrew Lansley: 'He hasn't got anybody around him who has ever run anything much, which is probably why they are compensating.' Conservative politicians, who often have a business background, are less starry-eyed than Labour about the virtues of bringing in business talent to government. Lansley says:

Blair is definitely of the man-on-horseback persuasion, where somebody rides in and takes control. That is fine in a command-and-control environment as many businesses are. But it is not fine in environments which operate by consent according to democratic principles. There is a difference between business and government. My experience is that businessmen, with honourable exceptions, don't succeed at politics, and politicians don't make the best businessmen.

Civil servants learn how to say yes to Tony Blair. Copyright © Richard Willson, 1999.

The government's White Paper of March 1999 included a preface by Blair which attempted to draw a line under the controversial reforms of the Thatcher era and set a new 'third way' agenda:

The old arguments about government are now outdated – big government against small government, interventionism against *laissez-faire*. The new issues are the right issues: modernizing government, better government, getting government right.

In fact, the basic philosophy continued the Conservative approach. Dr Christopher Pollitt, Professor of Public Management at Rotterdam University, told the Commons Public Administration Committee: 'The continuities with the general lines of management reform under the previous administration are more striking than the discontinuities.'[18]

The stress throughout was on improving delivery to customers and on the need for public services to catch up with private business practice in being available to the public 24 hours a day, seven days a week. Public services should no longer be 'denigrated', the White Paper insisted in a rebuke to the ghost of Thatcherism. But it was clear that emulating private sector culture and performance would still be the goal. What the government wanted was more innovation, more risk taking, more recruitment of women and minorities, more computers, more joined-up work between departments, and more co-operation with business. Significantly, there was no emphasis on the end to unnecessary secrecy and the improved accountability that Labour had promised in its manifesto, nor was there any commitment to decentralize. Peter Hennessy described the White Paper as 'illiterate' and 'appallingly gushy, preachy and acronymia-laden'. He told the Commons Public Administration Committee: 'It is quite the worst written White Paper to come off the most literate civil service's word processors ever.'

Other academic critics also found flaws. Christopher Pollitt commented that '... in many continental countries the idea that central government would measure and control local affairs to the extent now practised by the Labour government would be regarded as extraordinary'. He noted the absence of any discussion of the relationship between administrative change and citizens' rights, despite the planned Freedom of Information Act; the White Paper had little or nothing to say about the European Union and was silent on the issue of accountability: 'Looked at overall, the White Paper does not seem to contain a single, unifying theme or "big idea". Rather, it is a collection of assorted ideas.'

Professor Rod Rhodes noted the government had dropped Conservative 'marketization' reforms but in all other aspects was continuing to promote private sector corporate management. The 'brute reality of everyday life' was tight financial control at the heart of the reform package, under Labour just as under the Conservatives. Labour had continued the Conservative policy of controlling local government, especially its spending. Rhodes summed up the government's approach to the civil service as centralizing rather than decentralizing, though he pointed out that 'the centre has rubber levers; pulling the central policy lever does not necessarily mean something happens at the bottom'. Accountability to citizens had been confused with responsiveness to consumers under both Conservatives and Labour.

Rhodes also highlighted the perception of a general erosion of the sense of public duty, made worse by fragmentation of the civil service. 'Civil servants are no longer socialized into its shared traditions. The principles of the Citizen's Charter replace the public service ethos.'

In Rhodes' view, the White Paper

… pays no heed to the question of political accountability. The government has no proposals to strengthen ministerial accountability to parliament. The emphasis falls on central political control of priorities and managerial control of implementation. *Modernising Government* proposes a technological fix. Devolution apart, political caution pervades the government's distrust of local authorities, the decision to shelve regional assemblies in England and the proposals on 'freedom' of information.

The ultimate conclusion was that 'hands-off is the hardest lesson of all for British central government to learn'.

LET'S JOIN IT UP

The White Paper was followed at the end of 1999 by a report by Sir Richard Wilson to Blair. Despite the business school buzzwords and management jargon, most expert civil service-watchers believe there is nothing very revolutionary in the Labour government's approach. Some of the managerial trends it is continuing can be traced back even further than Thatcher, to the Fulton report of the late 1960s. The distinctive

Blairite novelty is the stress on breaking down departmental barriers to allow horizontal, 'joined-up' or 'holistic' government at all levels. But is this approach really compatible with the target-oriented government-as-business approach?

Writing in February 2000, Sir Richard Mottram, the top civil servant in the Department of Environment, Transport and the Regions, sounded a warning note. In an article in the Public Management and Policy Association Review he predicted a possible conflict between short-term results and long-term goals. 'We need a civil service which is more business-like in its processes and how it works, but we must not fall into the trap of thinking government is a business.'

A more detailed critique was given by Professor Vernon Bogdanor in evidence to the Commons Public Administration Committee. He questioned the case for abandoning the traditional civil service ethos in favour of business practices on several grounds:

> While the British civil service has been the subject of much emulation and admiration, it is doubtful if the same is true of British management. The suggestion, therefore, that the civil service would become more efficient if it adopted the practices of British management seems somewhat bizarre.[19]

Bogdanor said pressure for the civil service to recruit outsiders for senior jobs on short-term contracts rather than promote internal candidates was based on a fundamental misconception of how large private companies operated; most of them followed civil service practice and filled their top jobs from within their own ranks using rolling contracts. Open competition to bring in outsiders was unpopular because it damaged morale:

> Anyone who objects to the infusion of outsiders into the civil service is liable to be met with the rhetorical question, 'Do you want a closed civil service?' It would not, however, be very sensible to suggest to someone who objected to unqualified doctors or lawyers that he or she favoured a 'closed' medical or legal profession.

Jeopardizing the idea of the civil service as a profession and a lifetime career would inevitably call into question its political neutrality, he warned:

The political neutrality of the British civil service flows fundamentally from its career basis, since if one joins the service for life, one will inevitably be called upon to serve successive administrations of different political colours. One is not likely to succeed, therefore, as a civil servant, unless one succeeds in displaying political impartiality.

Bogdanor saw a fundamental contradiction between the Blair government's plans for civil service reform and the idea of joined-up or holistic government; the first implied individual responsibility, while the second implied shared responsibility and cooperative working. Success in dealing with social exclusion and rebuilding communities was not likely to be achieved by maximizing individual incentives and targets, he argued:

There is, then, a deep-seated conflict between the ethos of the new public management, which lies behind the proposals for civil service reform, by which government is broken down into discrete or separate units of accountability, and the idea of holistic government whose central theme is that there is a social context of interdependence to many of our most intractable problems.

The Blairite analogy of a chief executive reporting to his shareholders was a false one because the civil service was a profession, not a business, and was subject to a more fundamental and detailed kind of scrutiny:

There can, in the last resort, be no real analogy between the civil service and private management. For there is no real analogy in the private sector to the central constitutional principle of ministerial accountability to parliament.

Peter Hennessy made a similar point in his evidence to the Neill committee for its sixth report, arguing that the danger was not overt politicization of the civil service under Blair but the growing tendency to bring in outsiders to fill the top jobs. This is why a proper civil service statute was needed for a second Labour term:

If a government won a second term and thought it was time to go for broke, and one of the obstacles in the way was a senior civil service so rooted in tradition and procedure and too old – there is a lot of ageism around in this government on the part of ministers – there would not be overt politicization. The government would go for advertising a very high proportion of the top three ranked jobs.

Recruiting outsiders to fill the top civil service jobs under fixed-term contracts would finally kill off the last vestiges of the Northcote-Trevelyan principles of the civil service, by destroying the idea of a lifetime career. According to Hennessy, the White Paper shows the Blair government still supports the Northcote-Trevelyan ideals, but only 'through gritted teeth'. Hennessy's view is that the value of special advisers compared with experienced civil servants has been grossly overrated under Blair:

> What can a 25-year-old special adviser tell you about the great intractables? They have been career politicians at university, they have been trying to get the kinds of seats you are in and dislodge you since their adolescence. What on earth can they bring to the table at the age of 25 except the beauty of their prejudices?

FROM QUANGO TO TASK FORCE

It is clear that the civil service, in Blair's view, will have to justify its future existence. While the great public/private debate is officially said to be over, the thrust of government policy is increasingly towards private-sector solutions. Private business has been courted as never before by Labour, which has set up hundreds of temporary bodies to help it work out policy. These are not the quangos, the 'flexible friends of central government' (Hennessy) of which Labour was so critical in opposition; as permanent 'non-departmental public bodies' they are now regulated in their appointment procedures by a Commissioner for Public Appointments. The new plant in the Whitehall undergrowth since 1997 is the temporary task force, which has spread like bindweed through the corridors of one department after another. According to *Ruling by Task Force* by Tony Barker of Essex University, there were more than 300 such temporary task forces in operation by 1999, though nobody in Whitehall had bothered to count them, classify them or standardize their existence.[20]

Official estimates of their number are much lower; in July 2000, replying to the Neill committee, the government said there were only 19 task forces operating in April of the same year. According to political scientist Trevor Smith (Lord Smith of Clifton), in the same survey:

> The 'elite participation' of some 2,500 people, mainly from private and public producer interests, in the task forces, however valuable their skills and opinions,

can hardly be acceptable as a substitute for traditional forms of government accountability … Central government has no across-the-board rules for establishing such bodies or co-ordinating their existence.

The Essex University Democratic Audit group, commenting on the issues raised by Barker's research, said it showed the 'informality and ad hockery that characterizes central government in Britain'. It criticized the haphazard way in which membership details were made public, said there was real cause for concern over the representativeness of task forces, and their lack of balance between consumers and producers.

Andrew Lansley told me he was concerned by the spread of task forces for a slightly different reason:

Task forces do worry me because essentially, despite the argument for outside advice – that's all true – the point is that all the mechanisms of consultation with which civil servants are familiar are designed to achieve that, and do so in a more transparent way. Task forces are like a black box. You put a problem in one end and get a solution out of the other. It is much less transparent. There is a choice made at the beginning about the dozen or so people who are going to be the external sources of advice. That often prejudges the nature of the solution.

I asked Robin Butler whether task forces opened the door to conflicts of interest, as the Democratic Audit survey seemed to suggest:

You obviously want to avoid conflict of interest. I think steps do need to be taken to avoid conflict of interest. But that is the main area where there needs to be concern about propriety. Other than that, I think governments ought to be pretty free to do whatever they think fit to try to produce good government and effective delivery of services. And if they want to do it by setting up a whole lot of task forces, provided there isn't a case that this is a waste of public money – in general these aren't paid, so the amount of public money is limited – I take the view that governments ought to be pretty free to do what they think is going to help them most … I always took the view that the civil service should not have a monopoly right to advise government. The wider the area of advice politicians have, the better. But it would be a very foolish politician who went to the point of neglecting the advice of the civil service. I don't think they have the last word, but they have a great deal of experience and expertise and know-how. Although I never took the view that it would be constitutionally improper not to take the advice of the civil service, I thought it would be very foolish.

Most of the bodies listed by Barker were unpaid groups of outside experts called in by government to advise on particular problems, as their names indicate: the Leylandii Working Group, the Hedgerows Regulations Review Group, or the White-headed Duck Task Force; some were relatively high-profile, such as the Football Task Force, headed by former Conservative minister David Mellor, while others, such as the Composting Development Group, toiled away in fragrant obscurity.

A small number were far more significant and carried out executive functions, such as the PFI Task Force, set up in 1997 to provide outside expertise to the public sector in negotiating private finance deals. It was headed by a City banker on an annual salary of £160,000. In July 1999, the government announced it would be transformed into a public-private joint venture under the title Partnerships UK, in which the private sector would have a majority stake and the new chief executive would earn £200,000 plus incentives.

Partnerships UK is an interesting test case of how the old dividing lines between the civil service and the private sector have become so blurred under Labour that the two are barely distinguishable; they are so meshed together that even the idea of a conflict of interest becomes hard to imagine. Chief Secretary to the Treasury Andrew Smith told the Partnerships UK launch conference in December 1999 that arguments over public ownership or privatization were 'for the history books' and even the debate itself was 'a mistaken legacy'.

WHAT WORKS FOR WHOM?

Does this blurring of the lines between public and private matter? According to the government, 'what counts is what works'. But there is an alternative argument, put forward by constitutional reformers who believe the 'how' of government is as important as the outcomes on which the civil service is now supposed to focus. In the words of Democratic Audit, 'The prime ministerial "what works?" test demands the question, "works for whom?"':

The tendency of task forces is to depoliticize issues which are the stuff of representative politics – major divisions in views, moral dilemmas and scientific controversies; and the idea that they can be resolved rationally by chosen cadres of representatives of the private and public interests involved is grossly mistaken.

The same kind of criticism of the trend towards unaccountable 'Platonic guardians' can be heard from traditionalist Conservatives who tend to argue that essentially political decisions should not be hived off to experts but should remain in parliament; the counter-argument is that parliament, because of its partisan character and the dominance of the executive, is the worst of all places for rational decision making.

Before turning to the vexed issue of freedom of information, it is appropriate to come to some tentative conclusions on what has happened to Whitehall under Blair. The picture is inevitably fuzzy, partly because the government has escaped major scandals; with the possible exception of the Millennium Dome, there has been no equivalent of the two *affaires* which spotlighted the failings of government under the Conservatives – arms to Iraq and mad cow disease (BSE). In general, the evidence suggests that Labour has largely continued Conservative policies towards Whitehall, rather than trying to put the clock back or impose radical ideas of its own.

The trend seems to lead inexorably to the erosion of the old Northcote-Trevelyan civil service as a profession in its own right, and into a new managerial world in which the public/private distinction ceases to matter. The Conservatives are not too worried; I asked Andrew Lansley whether, when his party returned to power, it would find the civil service machine wrecked and the Whitehall landscape totally different from 1997:

No. But it will be very bruised and I think there will be quite a lot of scapegoating that will have gone on. I don't think we have seen the half of it yet. Scapegoating of the civil service for government failure has only just begun but will grow in intensity. The government will want to give the impression that they came in and gave them all the money but they couldn't do it.

Robert Hazell believes the UK is following a trend already established in Australia and Canada:

You can push the analogy with the private sector too far and I think Blair has. Blair's admiration for businessmen is bizarre in terms of what they can contribute to public sector management. But it's not just the UK; there is a chilling vision of the future in Australia and Canada, where the civil service has undergone much more marginalization than here, and it leads to politicization … It becomes a vicious circle; politicians want the civil service to deliver quickly, they want alternative sources of advice, which is good, and what happens then is that the civil service loses confidence, feels marginalized, loses its capacity for policymaking and if it is not used, it atrophies.

If Hazell is right and there is a vicious circle in which vital civil service skills are being lost, then the 'modernizing government' drive is likely to fail to meet even the narrow goals set by Blair, of greater efficiency and better service delivery in the front line. There remains the issue of accountability and democratic control. Stuart Weir and David Beetham of Democratic Audit, writing not long after the Blair government took office, argued that:

The structure, organization and operation of this core executive is of crucial importance from a *democratic* point of view, because it determines how far government in Britain can be properly accountable to parliament and the public, how open government decision making is to scrutiny and to alternative points of view, how widely and equally it consults a full range of interests in making policies and laws, how responsive it is to public opinion, how representative it is of a range of political interests and forces, and how far it may be said to be subject to the 'rule of law' in its conduct and use of its wide discretionary powers.[21]

THE ART OF THE U-TURN

If better government is defined not only as more efficient but as more accountable, then freedom of information should have been the central theme of Labour's policy towards Whitehall, as promised in the 1997 manifesto. And if any eager Labour activist had been asked in the aftermath of Blair's election victory what permanent impact the government was likely to leave on Whitehall in its first term, the reply would probably have been, 'freedom of information'. A Bill with that title was indeed introduced into parliament and became law at the end of the 1999–2000

Unlike Manet's Olympia, Jack Straw and Tony Blair make clear they plan to reveal as little as possible in their draft Freedom of Information Bill. Copyright © Steve Bell, 1999.

session. But the story of the legislation throws into sharp focus the difference between Labour's rhetoric in opposition and its conduct in government. As Weir and Beetham presciently noted:

It is the curse of democracy that those in authority must expose themselves to the risk of losing face, prestige, or even authority itself ... A freedom of information law worth its name must be able to bite the hand that drafts it.

While other major reforms reached the statute book in fairly smooth progression, the Freedom of Information Bill showed a radically different pattern, with the original White Paper effectively torn up and its author sacked from the cabinet. A much more restrictive Bill, barely recognizable from the White Paper, followed in May 1999, but underwent a long and gruelling passage through parliament lasting a year and a half. The U-turn from radicalism in opposition to conservatism in office over freedom of information was more dramatic than in any other policy field. As Charter88 concluded in April 2000:

It is now clear, however, that in office Labour has abandoned its much heralded belief in freedom of information. The long awaited Freedom of Information Bill is still with us, but the original proposals have been so watered down that they are hardly worthy of the name.

Labour had been committed to freedom of information legislation since 1974, though the governments of the 1970s did nothing about it. Hugo Young described the process the party went through in opposition:

The longer Labour stayed in opposition, the more dedicated it became to the notion that the entire culture of government had to change. Power, the nectar of which it had been deprived for so long, would finally be diluted when this period in the wilderness was over. When it supped once more from the cup, it would transfer significant amounts of public information into the public realm and create a right to know. [22]

Before the 1992 election the party prepared a draft Bill that was going to be Neil Kinnock's first measure in government. In the wake of Labour's defeat, the commitment to legislation survived but was downgraded in priority among constitutional measures and little attention was paid to it. The draft Bill itself, prepared by Mark Fisher MP and Maurice Frankel of the Campaign for Freedom of Information, was forgotten. Meanwhile, the Major government in 1994 introduced a Code of Practice on Access to Government Information requiring central government bodies to release information on request, subject to various exemptions. It did not cover personal files, the subject matter most frequently requested in other countries under freedom of information legislation. As a code rather than a statute, it had no legal force, but it was still important as a benchmark for supporters and critics of the legislation.

The Major government also moved towards openness by making public the Ministerial Code, and by publishing the minutes of the monthly meeting between the Chancellor of the Exchequer and the Governor of the Bank of England. This brought into the open, with entirely positive results, what had previously been one of the most jealously guarded secrets in government. After the 1997 election, Chancellor of the Exchequer Gordon Brown was to go even further, setting up a transparent arm's-length framework for interest rate policy in the Monetary Policy Committee of the newly independent Bank of England, whose minutes were also published.

However, the Major government was seriously weakened by two scandals in which the twin themes of accountability and freedom of information were crucial – arms sales to Iraq, investigated by the Scott inquiry, and BSE. Both were used by the Labour opposition to bolster the case for a proper Freedom of Information Act which would go much further than the Conservatives' code.

Tony Blair's commitment to freedom of information in opposition could not have been stronger. In March 1996 he was invited to present the annual Freedom of Information awards and delivered a speech singing the praises of access and disclosure as a key to good government. It makes extraordinary reading in the light of what happened once he reached Downing Street. Hugo Young described it as 'an almost messianic performance'. Professor James Cornford, a veteran member of the campaign, recalls: 'It was a very eloquent statement of the case for freedom of information. Whether he believed it or not, I don't know.'

Robert Hazell, writing in *The Guardian* in October 1996, noted prophetically that it was an article of faith among campaigners that the

TONY BLAIR'S 1996 SPEECH (EXTRACTS)

Before I go on to talk about Labour's commitment to the area of freedom of information, I would like if I might just to set this argument in context, because it is not some isolated constitutional reform that we are proposing with a Freedom of Information Act. It is a change that is absolutely fundamental to how we see politics developing in this country over the next few years.

Information is power and any government's attitude about sharing information with the people actually says a great deal about how it views power itself and how it views the relationship between itself and the people who elected it.

The crucial question is, does the government regard people's involvement in politics as being restricted to periodic elections? Or, does it regard itself as in some sense in a genuine partnership with people? And the government's attitude to what it is prepared to tell people and the knowledge it will share with them says a great deal about where it stands on that matter. My argument is that if a government is genuine about wanting a partnership with the people it is governing, then the act of government itself must be seen in some sense as a shared responsibility and the government has to empower the people and give them a say in how that politics is conducted.

I actually believe that if we want to make government effective in the modern world, it simply is not possible to do that on the basis of government just handing down tablets of stone. In fact, you can see, in my view, both with Scott and BSE it would have been far better if government had been more open, far better actually for the proper conduct of government.

The government grants information when it wants to. What is needed is a change in culture and a statutory obligation on government to make it a duty to release information to the people who elect the government.

Our commitment to a Freedom of Information Act is clear, and I reaffirm it here tonight. We want to end the obsessive and unnecessary secrecy which surrounds government activity and make government information available to the public unless there are good reasons not to do so. So the presumption is that information should be, rather than should not be, released. In fact, we want to open up the quango state and the appointed bodies, which will of course exist under any government, but which should operate in a manner which exposes their actions to proper public scrutiny.

A Freedom of Information Act would entitle the public to government information and would leave it to government to justify why information should not be released. I don't believe that its impact would simply be in the pure matter of legislation, in the detail of the legislation. It would also signal a culture change that would make a dramatic difference to the way that Britain is governed. The very fact of its introduction will signal a new relationship between government and people: a relationship which sees the public as legitimate stakeholders in the running of the country and sees election to serve the public as being given on trust.

That is my view of how government should be. I believe in the programme of constitutional change that the Labour party has outlined. I think that a Freedom of Information Act is an important and essential part of that.

I hope you understand from what I have said this evening that I regard it not merely as simply a list of commitments that we give because at some point in time someone got up and agitated for it and party conference passed a resolution. It is genuinely about changing the relationship in politics today.

There is so much disaffection from politics, so much disillusion with it, and one of the very clear and simple reasons is that we live in a modern and far better educated and far more open and far more assertive democracy and country – and it is good that people feel in that way. The irony is that the system of government is about 50, 60, 70 years behind the actual feelings and sentiments of the broad majority of people. A Freedom of Information Act is not just important in itself. It is part of bringing our politics up to date, of letting politics catch up with the aspirations of people and delivering not just more open government but more effective, more efficient government for the future.

government would have to legislate early on FOI before it acquired its own secrets to hide. 'Without a sponsoring minister, freedom of information simply won't happen.' And it needed to be a senior minister, he added. James Cornford recalls: 'They weren't coming in to a sort of *tabula rasa*, but from the point of view of the party they had not made their minds up on all the important issues, or even thought about them.'

CLARK THE IDEALIST

After the election, freedom of information became part of the brief of David Clark, an Old Labour figure who was not part of Blair's inner circle but owed his presence around the cabinet table to Labour's internal shadow cabinet elections. He had not been responsible for freedom of information questions in opposition. Civil servants in the Cabinet Office who had been preparing the ground advised Clark to take the easy option of putting the Conservatives' Code of Practice on a statutory basis, on the grounds that nobody could possibly object. But Clark instead chose the more ambitious goal of a White Paper, to be followed by legislation. A Freedom of Information Bill, it quickly emerged, would not be the subject of early legislation in the first session. There were early battles between Clark and Jack Straw in a cabinet subcommittee chaired by Derry Irvine, according to Cornford, who became an adviser to Clark after what he describes as 'the first crunch' in the summer of 1997, when Clark's early draft was torn up.

What followed, in the words of David Clark, was 'a great deal of debate among ministers' during which the issues were 'argued very forcibly'. Clark told the Commons Public Administration committee in December 1997: 'What seemed so simple in opposition, in government became much more difficult.' Mark Fisher, who sat on the subcommittee as a junior minister, told a Labour conference fringe meeting in September 2000 that the negotiations were very tricky. 'David met a lot of resistance.' Clark and Fisher, greatly helped by Derry Irvine's chairmanship of the committee, mostly got their way. According to Cornford, the initial problems arose because, despite the heady rhetoric from Blair in opposition, the Labour party had done no serious policy work on the issue, and was reluctant to simply adopt a policy drafted by outside campaigners:

The campaign had done lots of work. But you were dealing with very strong party politicians, and they regard the only work that is significant to them to be within the party … At that time the Lord Chancellor was a much more prominent figure, and I think he more or less carried the day for the White Paper as it appeared, with the support of the Prime Minister. If the Prime Minister had been against it at that point, it wouldn't have gone through in the form it did. Irvine was very keen on meeting his timetable, he was very set on the idea that he was going to get constitutional reform through, that it was his programme. He was chair of the committee, and his monument was going to be … the constitutional reform programme delivered. He and Straw were pretty much at loggerheads.

There is no doubt in Cornford's mind that Jack Straw led the Whitehall resistance to the liberal ideas Clark was putting forward with Irvine's support. Other senior ministers, who had often despatched their deputies to the cabinet subcommittee instead of attending in person, were slow to realize the implications of the White Paper when it appeared at the end of 1997. It was very much a product of the government's honeymoon period. It carried a preface by Tony Blair, heralding freedom of information as part of the government's comprehensive programme of constitutional reform. 'We believe it is right to decentralize power; to guarantee individual rights; to open up government; and to reform parliament.' The White Paper would mean more open government: 'The traditional culture of secrecy will only be broken down by giving people in the United Kingdom the legal right to know. This fundamental and vital change in the relationship between government and governed is at the heart of this White Paper.'

Clark described the White Paper as a watershed marking the government's readiness to trust the people with a legal right to information that was central to a mature democracy. It would strike a balance between disclosure and confidentiality 'with the scales now weighted decisively in favour of openness'. The White Paper promised a general statutory right of access comparable to that enjoyed in Sweden since the 18th century, in the United States since 1966, in France since 1978, in Canada, Australia and New Zealand since 1983, and in the Netherlands since 1991. Crucially, it described a future Freedom of Information Act as central to the programme of modernizing government and linked it with the principle of accountability to parliament. It promised that a future Act would apply not just to central government but to a long list of other public bodies. The objective was clearly stated – to open up public authorities and empower people by giving them access by right to the information they wanted to see, and by obliging bodies covered by the Act to make information available as a matter of course. No questions would be asked about the reasons for requests for information or about the purposes for which it would be used. Decisions would be based as far as possible not on blanket exemptions but on a test of 'substantial harm' resulting from disclosure. These covered seven areas: national security, defence and international relations; law enforcement; personal privacy; commercial confidentiality; the safety of the individual, the public and the environment; information supplied in confidence; and government decision making. For the latter, the key factor would be 'harm' rather than 'substantial harm'. But the test would be based on the contents, not the nature, of the documents requested. Policy advice to ministers would stay secret but the raw data and factual material on which it was based would be opened up. The Act would cover all personal files and dovetail with legislation on data protection. Appeals would be made to an Information Commissioner whose decision would be binding and ministers would have no right of veto.

TOO GOOD TO BE TRUE?

The White Paper was widely welcomed by campaigners and was seen as a substantial advance in liberalization over similar laws elsewhere. Maurice Frankel told the Commons Public Administration Committee it would 'provide a fundamental break with Britain's tradition of government secrecy and lead to a Freedom of Information Act comparable to some of the better overseas freedom of information laws'. The committee congratulated Clark on his proposals, which it compared favourably with the existing Code of Practice, although it expressed some concern about the unclear relationship of the proposed Bill to existing privacy and data protection legislation. It also criticized the extent of planned exemptions, for example of information covering law enforcement, and a lack of clarity in several other areas. Clark told the Select Committee: 'I just happen to believe that information is about power and I am very much aware of the jibe that this is seen in many cases as the preserve of the chattering classes ... really this Act will turn the people of Britain from subjects into citizens.' He was backed up by Derry Irvine, who described the White Paper as 'very liberal' and 'as liberal a freedom of information regime ... as any in the world'.

Robert Hazell, an expert on freedom of information legislation in other countries, was one of the few people who took the view that Clark was an idealist and that the White Paper was simply too good to be true: 'I found it hard to believe the other departments had signed up to this and I was given a hard time by other freedom of information enthusiasts.' Hazell was correct in suspecting that a counter-offensive was under way. After the publication of the White Paper, in the words of Cornford, 'the treacle came in'.

We were then working on the text of the Bill and suddenly it became very difficult to get committee meetings. And the whole atmosphere changed. Instead of the Lord Chancellor hurrying on from one meeting to the next, and holding meetings fortnightly and being on a great sort of roll, it began to slow up. And of course throughout this time the idea that David Clark was for the chop was being busily spread abroad, which made it very difficult from his point of view.

Clark was being undermined by his nominal deputy in the Cabinet Office, Peter Mandelson, who appeared keen to take over his boss's job. He was too low in the Whitehall pecking order to be able to resist a counter-offensive against his freedom of information plans by other ministers, notably Jack Straw. The White Paper had gone further than any government had gone before, and a backlash was inevitable. In the words of Hugo Young:

To watch its subsequent dismembering was to witness, in clinical detail, the evolving of the New Labour personality, from opposition idealist into governmental cynic. The spectacle could be used as a graphic case study not just of how governments change their minds – which they're quite entitled to do when they get to grips, say, with the realities of the health service or the tax system – but of how the mind-set of ministerialism itself soon infuses everything they do: the compelling need for power, the aversion to the possibility of embarrassment, and therefore the belief that the slightest risk of these imperatives being compromised, by losing control of information, must always be avoided.

James Cornford's view is slightly different: 'The idea that they came into office and suddenly discovered the realities of life and what it was like having power – I don't think that is very convincing. On freedom of information, I don't think they had thought seriously about it at all. It wasn't about having second thoughts, it was about having first thoughts.'

STRAW ADOPTS A POLICY ORPHAN

When I asked Jack Straw about the background to the policy U-turn, he explained that unlike other constitutional reforms such as devolution and the Human Rights Act, where Labour had worked hard and assembled policy teams to prepare legislation in opposition, freedom of information had been something of an orphan issue, with nobody clearly responsible for it in the shadow cabinet:

For freedom of information there was nothing. There was a series of proselytizing papers from the pressure groups, mainly Maurice Frankel's one, but that was it. It wasn't anybody's particular responsibility in opposition, it wasn't mine and there was no real shadow for the Cabinet Office. It was just one of those things that was left, and I think it was thought to be rather easier than it turned out to be. That meant that David Clark had to start with a clean sheet. And what we ended up with was that the White Paper was very much a (consultative) Green Paper.

Bear in mind, we published in December 1997, we didn't really get started until July 1997, and we had all these other things as well – Scottish devolution, Welsh devolution, human rights – with the same people involved, so that's where we had got to. Some more work was done in the early months of 1998, and then following a reshuffle I was asked to take it on. It had become clear too that the official side needed strengthening.

Straw's account tells only part of the story; the Home Office and other major Whitehall departments mounted an ultimately successful offensive against the draft of Clark's Bill. In July 1998 Maurice Frankel, sensing that the government was going into reverse, wrote that the longer the proposals were delayed, the less likely it was that a real change in culture would take place: 'The more used to office ministers become, the more plausible the case for caution will seem.'[23] Clark, as one of his final acts as Chancellor of the Duchy of Lancaster and Cabinet Office supremo, announced on 22 July that the draft Bill would be published in September. A week later he was clearing his desk. Clark went quietly, though he later angrily accused Blair's officials of trying to blacken him. At this point the Home Office took over responsibility for the Bill from the Cabinet Office. Despite the fact that it was 90 per cent complete, it was sent back to the drawing board by Straw and dropped from the November 1998 Queen's Speech. Hazell believes that Jack Cunningham, Clark's successor, was not personally keen to take the project over, and this is why it passed to the Home Office:

I assume he could see freedom of information was not going to earn him a lot of goodwill, and it was not his subject. Jack Straw was a safe pair of hands, and he was the only minister in 1997 who took Clark's proposals seriously and negotiated a gaping opt-out for police and law enforcement. Jack said, if that's what the government is proposing, count my people out.

Straw denied to me that the original White Paper was effectively discarded, although he acknowledged he had made a major change by dropping the idea of 'substantial harm' and substituting a test of simple prejudice instead:

Well it is big, but it is a gradation. It doesn't mark a departure from the intellectual structure of the White Paper. So that's why we haven't discarded it all.

In that area the White Paper is more restrictive, in other areas such as law enforcement it actually goes further than the White Paper.

Straw also acknowledged that in opposition Labour had failed to engage properly on the difficulties ahead with campaigners for freedom of information, who were only one of the three rival interest groups involved:

What I would say is that you are dealing here with three competing interests, only one of which is represented publicly. You are dealing with the right to know against the right of individual privacy and the right of corporate, including government confidentiality, and that triangular relationship creates a very strong tension. You are trying to balance that in the Bill. It is in the nature of it that the people campaigning for the right to know are most vocal. And so at one level, people have an interest in maintaining corporate confidentiality and so does government, so you are seen as *parti pris*, as you are not in other areas.

Straw argued the need to balance data protection issues with the right to know, and expressed the view that journalists were just as much *parti pris* as governments because of their vested interest in disclosure. He described Robert Hazell's approach to the issue as 'very evangelist':

I think we have got the balance about right. The regime that we establish should be transparent and should be fully complied with. It's all very well people going on about other countries, but what happens in other countries, where they have gone too far, is you then get evasion, as in Australia and in other states. You get the Post-It Note syndrome.

James Cornford says there is no doubt that the Home Office was responsible for the big changes in the Bill, though there was hostility to the Clark White Paper all over Whitehall. As Derry Irvine's influence with Blair faded, enthusiasm in 10 Downing Street for freedom of information also faded:

I think it is a Home Office production. The Home Office was the chief opponent of our version of the Bill, through Straw. As you notice, one of the curious things about the Bill is the class exemptions don't cover the things you would expect them to be most sensitive about, they cover the Home Office, criminal processes and courts and all that … I feel that if the Prime Minister had wanted a strong Bill and felt that was important, an important carry through to deliver on his promises, he could have got what he wanted. In the absence of clear unequivocal support from Number 10, there were a lot of people who did not want it to happen, or who were nervous about it or wanted to protect their department in some particular way. I think Straw would have made more concessions to people who wanted a better Bill if he hadn't had to get it through a large committee of people hostile to it, and if he had any reason to believe he would get support from Number 10 … Their support of the Lord Chancellor in the initial stages, the strength of the relationship of the Prime Minister and the Lord Chancellor in the early stages of government, was the reason the White Paper came out as it did. That simply dissipated.

THE HOME OFFICE VERSION

The new draft Bill written in the Home Office finally surfaced in May 1999. It was clear much earlier that the whole emphasis of government policy had shifted away from freedom of information as a citizen's right and back to the Conservative concept of open government as a top-down policy. Unlike David Clark, Straw was a statist, far more in tune with the views of those holding information than those seeking it. An advisory group chaired by his junior minister Mike O'Brien was packed with government and local authority officials but contained no outside campaigners or representatives of the press, except as observers. Initially dubbed the Advisory Group on Implementing Freedom of Information, it soon became the Advisory Group on Openness in the Public Sector. The solitary independent academic in the group, Robert Hazell, complained in a letter to the Home Office in February 1999:

> **❝ Unlike David Clark, Straw was a statist, far more in tune with the views of those holding information than those seeking it. ❞**

I do have quite serious reservations about the way this exercise is going. The change of title is symptomatic. We were invited to give advice on implementing freedom of information. That is not the same as 'openness'. Open government generally means the government publishing more information on what it thinks people want to know or need to know. Very rarely does that kind of information coincide with the kinds of information which people seek under freedom of information.[24]

Hazell pointed out that the advisory group's stress on changing the working methods of officials would have little result unless politicians led the way:

The lead in changing the culture must come from ministers. Officials are acutely sensitive to the signals given out by ministers. If ministers show a wholehearted commitment themselves to be more open, officials will follow. If (as happened in Canada) ministers are ambivalent about freedom of information, then attempts to change the culture will be seen to be empty rhetoric, and are likely to fail.

Hazell found the experience of the advisory group dispiriting: 'It was like banging your head against a brick wall.' He finally decided that his appointment was a piece of window dressing. As a former Home Office official in the 1980s he had studied freedom of information regimes in other countries and had come to the conclusion that the conceptual distinction between open government and freedom of information was an essential one:

Open government as practised in Britain means the government engaging in widespread consultation before formulating policy or coming to a decision, and publishing Green Papers and White Papers and other discussion documents to that end. The government does this largely for its own purposes … it sharpens up the proposals and softens up public opinion … Freedom of information means entitling the people to ask for what they want to know. The two things are very different. What the people want to know is very rarely what government thinks they want to know.

Hazell described the May 1999 draft Bill as restrictive by international standards and commented that the government 'appears to have made no systematic attempt to learn from overseas experience'. Many of its worst features were home grown. Instead of giving the final decision on the disclosure of information to the Information Commissioner, the Bill left ministers with a veto and reduced the test of 'substantial harm' to just 'prejudice'. The biggest change was the enormous expansion of class exemptions covering whole categories of information, an approach quite different from the White Paper. There was no 'purpose clause' setting out its main thrust, avoiding any presumption in favour of openness. Above all, disclosure was to be essentially voluntary. 'Significant elements in the draft Bill are based on the paternalistic model of open government, with the government deciding what we need to know.'[25] One of the main class exemptions would cover all forms of investigation, not only criminal investigations but health, environmental and safety inquiries. 'This class exemption is unprecedented, both in its scope and duration. There is no equivalent in overseas legislation.' A blanket exemption was also included for commercial information.

The signals in the draft Bill for public servants are all consistently negative ... Civil servants are very astute at reading political messages; the messages in the draft Bill will not encourage them to be more open. The general tenor goes directly against all the messages in the *Modernising Government* White Paper, which is meant to encourage civil servants to be more outward looking, innovative and risk taking.

Hazell described the draft as 'a mess', saying the process of turning the aspirational White Paper into law had degenerated into a downward spiral, with Whitehall departments pleading for extra exemptions. An orderly retreat 'appears to have become a rout', he commented, producing a Bill 'which contains no clear or coherent scheme, and is tortuous and very difficult to understand'.

GOLD INTO LEAD

Straw's draft met with withering criticism from separate committees of the Lords and the Commons which joined forces at the end of July 1999 to produce reports on it. 'We think on fundamental aspects they have got it wrong,' said Tony Wright, chairman of the Commons Public Administration Committee. He criticized the failure to include a clear presumption in favour of disclosure and described the Bill as needing rebalancing. Some changes were made when the Bill was introduced to the Commons in November 1999 for the opening round in a long parliamentary battle to improve the Bill that ended a year later. In the Commons debates, during which Straw made limited concessions, not a single Labour backbencher spoke in his support, a sign that many were deeply unhappy with the Bill. Nearly 40 Labour MPs joined the Liberal Democrats in voting for amendments that would give it more teeth. Liberal Democrat spokesman Robert Maclennan told the Commons: 'Alchemy was the search to transmute lead into gold. We have witnessed the reverse process.' He accused Labour of betrayal:

They are betraying the White Paper produced by the right hon. member for
South Shields (Dr Clark), going back on their undertaking to the electorate in the
Labour party's manifesto and repudiating the agreement entered into with the
Liberal Democrats prior to the election.

MPs complained of the absence of a clause in the Bill explaining its overall purpose, which the government resisted on the grounds that it would
'change the balance of rights and put a gloss on the Bill as a whole' with
results that might be 'unpredictable and uncontrollable'. They complained about the large categories of exempt information and about the
power of veto given to the authorities. Conservative MP Richard
Shepherd summed up the text as 'anally retentive'. Mark Fisher told the
Commons: 'It rings through the Bill like a tocsin that the balance falls in
favour of the owner of information rather than the applicant.' Quentin
Davies, a Conservative, said freedom of information had turned out to
be the 'most strikingly unpredicted disappointment with the new
Labour government', and Blair's pre-election promises about a new relationship between government and people were nothing more than
political hyperbole and eyewash. Nobody on the Labour benches rose to
contradict him. In the view of many speakers, the Bill marked a step
backwards from the Conservative openness code. Fisher denounced
what he described as '... an amazing defensive edifice for the government ... a virtually impregnable fortress; it is a high place, an acropolis':

The provisions are a mound, a rampart, a bailey, a keep to protect the
government – but from what? At one level, they are protecting the information
that the government have at their disposal and wish to share with the rest of us
only by their grace and favour and on their own terms. That is an unacceptable
basis and it is at the heart of the Bill. It is why we have needed such a Bill for the
past 20 years and why some hon. members have been arguing for one for so
long and on such terms. If it maintains that enormous defensive rampart around
government policy, the Bill will cease to be a Freedom of Information Bill, and will
become instead a Protection of Information Bill.

Mike O'Brien put forward a bizarre argument to justify the government's
right to veto decisions of the Information Commissioner and to be judge
and jury in its own cause. To let the Commissioner have the final say
would be undemocratic, he said, accusing Liberal Democrat Simon

Hughes of 'trying to shift power away from those, like him or me, who are democratically elected to do our job in this place to those who are not democratically elected. There is a danger of enhancing an unfortunate democratic deficit'. This was described in the Lords as 'absolutely breathtaking' by the Labour peer Peter Archer, who had been Solicitor-General in James Callaghan's government. 'In a constitutional law paper, a student who came up with that would not even be allowed to continue the course ... It is not a democratic deficit. It is called the executive being subject to the rule of law.'

The Bill included a long series of blanket exemptions, one of which would ensure that information and policy advice given to ministers would remain secret. Tony Wright told the Commons:

Nothing that crosses the desks of ministers or their advisers in connection with policy would have to be disclosed, even after decisions had been made, announced and implemented. Factual information on which decisions are based and scientific advice, for instance, would be edited out. Submissions from lobbyists, enabling us to see what representations had been made to government, would similarly be covered. The provision ignores the fact that more scrutiny may increase the rigour of the analysis. It even ignores the fact that when we have moved in that direction – as with publication of the minutes of meetings between the Chancellor and the Governor of the Bank of England – it has, on the whole, proved to be beneficial. When we have gone even further, by publishing the minutes of meetings of the Monetary Policy Committee, the sky has not fallen in. Such action has even been thought to be an act of strengthening generally helpful to policymaking.

The official who would have to help implement the Bill, Elizabeth France, the Data Protection Commissioner, who was destined to combine her existing job with that of Information Commissioner, described the Bill as over complex and drafted back to front. She told newspaper editors in May 2000 that even her own lawyers found it difficult and criticized the absence of a purpose clause.

Meanwhile, there were signs that the government's ramparts might be undermined by its allies in Scotland and Wales, the Labour-led devolved administrations. Scotland had the right to draft its own FOI legislation, and according to proposals published in November 1999, authorities there would have to prove 'substantial prejudice' to stop disclosure. This was more in line with the original White Paper than the version which Jack Straw drew up for England, Wales and Northern Ireland. Scotland's Information Commissioner would in some cases, though not in all, have the final say. In Wales, Rhodri Morgan, Wright's predecessor as chair of the Commons Public Administration Committee, announced a startling breach with the tradition of government secrecy by putting the minutes of cabinet meetings on the Assembly website after a six-week delay. The use of a six-week timelapse followed the practice laid down for the Bank of England Monetary Policy Committee's meetings on interest rates. Maurice Frankel commented that his initiative 'shatters the taboo that revealing cabinet proceedings before 30 years have passed will fatally undermine decision making'.

ENDGAME

At the very end of an overcrowded legislative session, the Freedom of Information Bill was finally examined by the House of Lords only in October and November 2000. Campaigners were confident that they would find a majority of peers to outvote the government, ensuring that an amended version would be sent back to the Commons, with a good prospect of securing concessions from Jack Straw in the last hectic days of the session. But their hopes were dashed when Liberal Democrat peers, led by Anthony Lester and William Goodhart, negotiated a surprise deal with the government. Leaders of the Campaign for Freedom of Information were outraged, believing the concessions which the two eminent QCs had secured from the government in exchange for their support were insignificant. 'It was not just a political error of judgement, they got it wrong in law as well,' one commented. Liberal Democrats in the Commons were equally unhappy when they saw the fine print of what had been negotiated.[26] Lester and Goodhart, the sharpshooters in the forward trenches, had thrown away their muskets and sided with the enemy. In *The Guardian*, Hugo Young accused them of joining 'a conspiracy to gut true reform'.

> ❝ Lester and Goodhart, the sharpshooters in the forward trenches, had thrown away their muskets and sided with the enemy. ❞

A meeting of campaigners which I witnessed in a Commons committee room took on something of the air of a court martial, with Goodhart sitting in the dock. Maurice Frankel, who had campaigned for the legislation since 1983, said the Act would reach the statute book with substantial defects still in place. 'The opportunity we had to get rid of those defects has been whisked away from us.' The campaigners' disappointment was all the greater because they believed their case had been reinforced by the publication of the results of the BSE public inquiry. 'Rather than a call to arms, this is something of a wake,' Frankel told the meeting. Richard Shepherd, a lone campaigner for freedom of information in the Conservative ranks, said he had wanted a clear and simple law that any lay person could understand. 'We don't have it. We have a wondrously complex Bill with references to clauses here and sub-sections there. It's a very difficult Bill as it stands now.' Simon Hughes pointedly declined to say anything in defence of the four compromise amendments negotiated by his party colleagues in the Lords. Goodhart, looking like a defiant man about to be taken out and shot at dawn for desertion, refused to apologize and said the deal was a good one. 'It is the best deal we could have expected to get, and I think we could have ended in a worse position than we are now.' He said it was unlikely that Conservative peers would have turned up in sufficient numbers to ensure a defeat for the government. 'We see the present Bill not as an end in itself but as a first step towards a wider freedom of information law for which we will continue to campaign,' he declared.

THE FREEDOM OF INFORMATION ACT 2000

The Act creates a statutory right to information and a process under which public authorities handle its release. It also amends the Data Protection Act 1998 governing access to personal information. A very wide range of public authorities is covered, including central and local government, police, NHS hospitals, state schools, universities, art galleries, quangos and agencies.

Anyone making a request has a general right to be told whether the authority holds the information, subject to certain exemptions. No reason has to be given for a request and applicants do not have to be UK residents or British citizens. A fee has to be paid and authorities must initially respond within 20 working days.

The Act creates an Information Commissioner and an Information Tribunal, which take the place of the existing Data Protection Commissioner and Tribunal.

The first stage in the process is a decision whether the information is exempt. Exemptions, which are absolute or non-absolute, cover:

■ any information about the intelligence services, special forces, security bodies and the National Criminal Intelligence Service;

■ any information certified by a minister as exempt for the purpose of safeguarding national security;

- information which would prejudice national defence or the armed forces of the UK and its allies, or the UK's foreign relations or interests abroad;

- information given in confidence by other states or international bodies;

- information which would prejudice relations between the UK government and devolved administrations in Scotland, Wales and Northern Ireland;

- information which would prejudice UK financial or economic interests;

- information held by a public authority for investigation of crimes;

- information for other investigations which has been obtained in confidence;

- information that would prejudice crime prevention, prosecution, administration of justice, tax, immigration, prisons and other inquiries including health and safety investigations;

- court, inquiry or tribunal documents;

- information exempted for parliamentary privilege;

- information relating to the formulation or development of government policy, ministerial communications, advice from law officers and the operation of any ministerial private office. But statistical information used to provide an informed background to the taking of a decision is not exempt;

- information held by government which in the reasonable opinion of a qualified person would prejudice collective responsibility or inhibit the free and frank provision of advice, or would otherwise prejudice the effective conduct of public affairs. This does not include statistics;

- information about the royal family or the honours system;

- information that would endanger the health or safety of any individual;

- personal data;

- information obtained in confidence or covered by legal professional privilege, trade secrets or likely to prejudice commercial interests.

Security matters, parliamentary privilege, personal data, court records, and information provided in confidence are covered by absolute exemptions. Where exemptions are non-absolute, the public authority has to apply a public interest test to decide whether to release the information. If the outcome is equally balanced, the test favours disclosure.

The Information Commissioner can overrule an authority about the scope of exemptions and can require it to reconsider the public interest test. The Commissioner can serve an enforcement notice on an authority to release information after an appeal, but cabinet ministers can exercise a veto. They will be told to consult their colleagues first, and will have to inform parliament.

The Act will come into force stage by stage within a maximum limit of five years. April 2002 is the expected date when most public authorities will start to comply.

UNDER THE GUILLOTINE

The final stage of the Freedom of Information Bill in the Commons took place under a guillotine motion whose effect was to allow only three-and-a-half-hours to pass some 120 amendments. Only a fraction were debated. O'Brien said the government wanted 'a new culture of open-ness in the public sector' in place of Whitehall secrecy:

We are introducing the Bill because we want to change that. The question is how to achieve the necessary balance between opening up the public sector and recognizing that openness does not always have a monopoly on righteousness. It needs to be balanced against the need for personal privacy, commercial confidentiality and effective government. We do not want a similar situation to that in America, where commercial companies make 60 per cent of applications under freedom of information legislation. Nor do we want to remove the right to ensure that government operates effectively.

O'Brien argued that with the amended public interest test, there could now be no repetition of the secrecy which prevented information about BSE from being disclosed in the 1980s and early 1990s:

Where public health is seriously at risk and information is held by the government, it is difficult to see, on any reading of the Bill, how it could be justified for a minister to take the view that the public interest was in favour of secrecy, unless a criminal investigation were about to be undertaken, in which case the public interest would have to be weighed very carefully. In circumstances where there is a clear view that public health would be at risk – particularly in the sort of situation in which BSE arose – under the Bill, it would always be in the public interest for that information to be in the public domain.

Government concessions during the Bill's year-long passage through parliament included an increase in the powers of the Information Commissioner, who initially would only have been able to recommend disclosure of information rather than order it. The government agreed that statistical information could be treated differently from other information held by government, but refused to extend this to analysis or to the broader category of all factual information. It also accepted that public authorities would have a duty, not just a discretionary power, to consider the public interest in disclosure. The public interest test was reversed to favour disclosure in cases where the outcome was finely balanced, and the executive override or veto was limited to cabinet ministers, government law officers and heads of devolved administrations in Cardiff and Belfast. Jack Straw said any cabinet minister who ordered a veto without consulting his cabinet colleagues would be extremely unwise. The government agreed to drop a provision that would have allowed it to add new exemptions, and accepted a clause obliging public authorities not just to advise applicants for information but to assist them.

TOO MANY EXEMPTIONS

Campaigners say that despite these changes, the Act is still flawed by the extent of the exemptions, the lack of a strong general test of harm or prejudice, and by the ministerial veto. 'Really all the significant problems come from that particular phenomenon of class exemptions,' says Maurice Frankel. There is particular controversy over the exemptions covering health and safety inspections and investigations. Critics say routine safety information about rail and air travel, food and agriculture, nuclear installations, drinking water and environmental health will stay under wraps. Mark Fisher finds the government's reluctance to rely on a simple harm test in this area baffling:

When you see the tragedy of things like the Paddington crash or the Clapham rail disaster or the Marchioness ferry, whenever you have a public horror like that, the first thing any human being wants to know is, tell us what went wrong, so we can be reassured that it is understood and accepted what went wrong, so we can judge if the authority is putting those things right. But if you don't know what the facts of the case are, it is terribly difficult to put right.

Louise Christian, solicitor for victims of the 1999 Ladbroke Grove rail crash, says information about rail safety, such as reports on signals passed at danger and Health and Safety Executive investigations, are hard to obtain, and the lack of transparency in the industry has led to substantial mismanagement:

What has happened to this Bill is terribly sad. It was one of the main things we all believed a Labour government would deliver. It's also very sad for the Liberal Democrats who appear to have sold out the campaign in the House of Lords.

In some respects, the Act appears to be a step backwards from the 1994 code of practice, particularly in its exemption not just of policy advice to ministers but of factual information and analysis as well. The Conservative peer Lord Lucas described this as the absolute heart of the Bill:

Here we have a government who say that they want much more openness in public affairs, but when we reach the part of the Bill where their own affairs are concerned, they are quite clearly determined to stay rooted to the spot and even to go backwards.

Maurice Frankel's view is that 'No freedom of information law in the world that I know of adopts that approach to the formulation of policy.' He told me there was nothing in the Act that would make it easier to uncover any repetition of the arms-to-Iraq affair, which Labour had used in opposition as evidence of the need for freedom of information legislation:

The bad things which are still in there are the very large number of class exemptions where, although the exemptions are not absolute, information can be withheld without any evidence of harm, especially for policy formulation where that concerns facts, or ministerial communications, or a minister's private office; there is a class exemption for investigations by authorities with a power to bring proceedings which covers not just the police and Crown Prosecution Service but also the Health and Safety Executive and environmental safety officers.

There is this very dubious exemption for information which 'in the opinion of a qualified person' would have various effects, including prejudicing effective conduct of public affairs, which I think will be used not so much in its own right but as a backup to all other claims. That is because the 'reasonable opinion of a qualified person' makes it a subjective test where you can't overturn a decision unless the opinion is unreasonable in the sense of irrational and perverse, which is a very difficult test to overturn. That means that if the Ministry of Defence claim this disclosure is going to be harmful to defence, that is an objective test which the commissioner can overturn on the merits. If they then say, it would also prejudice the conduct of public affairs, they reinforce their claim by a much broader, more difficult claim. I think this exemption will be used to back up all kinds of other exemptions which appear to be reasonable in their own right. It will be used to make all claims unreasonable.

This catch-all provision gives legal weight to the opinion of a minister, which is placed outside the scope of review by the Information Commissioner. Mike O'Brien told the Commons:

The government consider that only a qualified person can have a full understanding of the issues involved in the decision-making process of a public authority … we do not consider that it would be right for the prejudice caused by that sort of information to be determined by the Commissioner.

Paradoxically, like many other liberal rights activists, Maurice Frankel gives full marks to Jack Straw and his civil servants for keeping up a dialogue with their critics, even while resisting changes in the Bill:

They have been very good on a personal level. I deal with the officials on good terms and with the ministers on good terms as well. Straw has spoken on a number of our platforms, he has always been quite friendly and amenable, and they asked me to serve on their advisory group on openness in the public sector … I went along not as a member but as an observer. Straw has clearly said to the officials they can be reasonably frank in letting me know what is going on, and they have been. Relations with them have been good. I have absolutely no complaints. Oddly enough it has been better under Straw, despite the fact we have been so unhappy with the proposals, than it has been in many other areas. Straw is not the only player in the game – that is part of the problem. There is a whole collective thinking, collective decision-taking process going on here. Every small change has literally got to be put around the whole of Whitehall. It's not like dealing with a normal departmental Bill where you have to persuade the officials, the ministers, and then they take it up with an outside interest group or with another department and try to square it. There is also Number 10, which no doubt has its own fears about all of this. So progress is very, very difficult. It has been fantastically uphill.

Robert Hazell told me he was 'very gloomy' about the final result, which he said was similar to Canada's freedom of information legislation:

It will be the worst of both worlds – highly restrictive legislation but a lot of pain and discomfort and workload processing freedom of information requests. That is what we are heading for. It is going to be highly restrictive legislation, which will give very little satisfaction to requesters, particularly in your business. It's unintelligent, and it won't stop the flow of requests.

He said the Liberal Democrats had missed the chance to simplify and strengthen the public interest test in the House of Lords:

The basic point is that for hard-pressed (and mostly fairly low-level) officials dealing with freedom of information requests, this is like theologians dancing on the head of a pin. They are not lawyers, let alone high-powered lawyers. They want a simple, strong, basic steer.

One person I interviewed who was not worried by the risk of the new Act disturbing the Whitehall status quo was the retired mandarin's mandarin, Robin Butler, who told me:

I think it will be very unimportant, because I doubt whether it will be used all that much. I certainly don't think it will be used all that much at the centre of government … Politicians and senior civil servants will always find a way of protecting the confidentiality of deliberations about policy – and should. I think the public have the right to know the basis on which governments take decisions, and in general it is possible to find that out. From the inside it never seemed as if people were concealing a lot. But if you are going to have frank discussions, you have got to have a certain amount of privacy about them. I think the danger of a Freedom of Information Act is that where people want to speak frankly to each other, they might have done it on paper in a pretty uninhibited way before. Now they won't. They just won't put that down on paper. And that's a pity because when something goes wrong and you need a chain of accountability, as for the Scott inquiry, you ought to be able to find all the bits of paper. So I regard freedom of information legislation as something that is a fashion of the times. It will do some good, people will be able to get access to information the government holds about them, or about contracts, but I don't think it will be huge.

Mark Fisher sees an important link between freedom of information and other constitutional reforms, because access to facts is crucial to the way citizens can hold government to account and scrutinize public affairs:

Both of these things turn on being able to know on what basis the government has made a decision. You can only actually have a serious grown-up dialogue with the government on any issue if you know what the facts are. And the whole point of politics is the way you interpret those facts and the conclusions you draw … It is perfectly proper that government should make the decisions because they have a lot of competing things to balance. But at least you should know what the facts are, and at the moment we are not going to be able to, and that seems to completely undermine the democratic side of freedom of information.[27]

Fisher says the tortuous history of Labour's legislation has illustrated one of the government's growing vices, its desire to maintain centralized control:

We are doing so many good things, but I think the underlying vice of this government is an obsessive desire to hold control centrally, to control everything themselves, whether it is spending or almost anything else. There is a desire by our government to have central control, and this goes to the heart of it. If we cannot get information it is very difficult to see if we are being controlled fairly. We are seeing signs that at the moment the government are not enthusiastic about trusting the public or the party or the unions or local government, about trusting democracy. They want to keep control in their own hands. This is where freedom of information comes in. It is a key that could unlock that desire not to let go. It would improve this area of weakness at the centre of government.

NOTES

[1] Weir, Stuart and Beetham, David (1999) *Political Power and Democratic Control in Britain*, London, Routledge, p 303.

[2] Smith, Martin J. (1999) 'The Institutions of Central Government' in Holliday, Ian, Gamble, Andrew and Parry, Geraint (eds) *Fundamentals in British Politics*, London, Macmillan.

[3] Hennessy, Peter (1996) *The Hidden Wiring. Unearthing the British constitution*, London, Indigo.

[4] Baker, Amy (2000) *Prime Ministers and the Rule Book,* London, Politico's, p 101.

[5] Drewry, Gavin (1999) 'The Civil Service' in Blackburn, Robert and Plant, Raymond (eds) *Constitutional Reform. The Labour government's constitutional reform agenda*, London, Longman.

[6] Rhodes R.A.W. (2000) *New Labour's Civil Service; summing-up joining-up*, evidence to House of Commons Public Administration Committee.

[7] Wright, Tony (ed.) (2000) *The British Political Process: an introduction*, London, Routledge, p 264.

[8] Quoted in Cockerell's *New Statesman* article on the programme, 14 February 2000.

[9] Hennessy, Peter (2000) *Patterns of Premiership: the Blair style in historical perspective*, The Mishcon Lecture, University College London.

[10] Rawnsley, Andrew (2000) *Servants of the People*, London, Hamish Hamilton, p 33.

[11] Hennessy, Peter (1999) *The Blair Centre: a question of command and control?* Public Management Foundation Lecture.

[12] The phrase used by Kenneth Clarke in BBC television's *The Major Years* (1999) about the ERM debacle in 1992 when he and other senior ministers stayed with John Major and Norman Lamont.

[13] Bogdanor, Vernon (2000) *Civil Service Reform: a critique*, evidence to House of Commons Public Administration Committee.

[14] *Report of the Select Committee on the Public Service*, House of Lords, 1998, p 86.

[15] Drewry, Gavin (1999) 'The Civil Service' in Blackburn, Robert and Plant, Raymond (eds) op. cit., p 156.

[16] A political appointee, Haines was Harold Wilson's press secretary. Like Campbell, he also insisted that major announcements had to be cleared with his office.

[17] Margaret Thatcher's powerful press secretary was a career civil servant rather than a political appointee, though he began life as a journalist.

[18] Pollitt, Christopher (2000) *Modernising Government: four points and four proposals*, evidence to House of Commons Public Administration Committee.

[19] Bogdanor, Vernon op. cit.

[20] Barker, Tony, Byrne, Iain and Veall, Anjuli (1999) *Ruling by Task Force. Politico's guide to Labour's new elite*, London, Politico's.

[21] Weir, Stuart and Beetham, David, op. cit., p 119.

[22] Young, Hugo (2000) *The Right to Secrecy*, lecture to British Institute for Human Rights, Kings College, London.

[23] *Independent on Sunday*, 26 July 1998.

[24] This letter appeared on the Home Office website – a small victory for openness in government.

[25] Hazell, Robert (1999) *Commentary on Draft Freedom of Information Bill*, Constitution Unit.

[26] Of the four amendments negotiated by Lester and Goodhart, the most important reversed the public interest test, so that the public interest in keeping information secret would have to outweigh the interest in disclosure before it could be withheld. Lester argued that this would create a *de facto* 'harm test' throughout the Bill and that under the European Convention on Human Rights authorities would be forced to prove the case for secrecy. 'The burden of proof ... is placed upon the public authority to show that there is some pressing need for non-disclosure and that the restriction on the public right of access is necessary in the sense of being a proportionate way of meeting that need.' The government gave no support to this interpretation. In the Commons, Mike O'Brien said: 'In the case of a fine decision about the balance of the public interest and where it lies, the way in which the decision is reached errs on the side of openness. As far as I can see, that constitutes a strengthening of the Bill, although some might seek to claim that the strengthening was greater than it is.' The Campaign for Freedom of Information, backed up by other experts such as Robert Hazell, took the view that Lester, despite his reputation as the UK's leading expert on the ECHR, was simply wrong in his interpretation because the amendment would apply only in case of a finely balanced 'dead heat' and the public interest test did not require a legal burden of proof either way. Authorities would still be able to argue there was a general public interest in keeping secret *all* information in a particular class, such as cabinet papers. Other human rights lawyers say the ECHR's Article 10 guaranteeing the right to free expression does *not* guarantee any right of access to government information in the way Lester claims.

[27] Remarks at a Freedom of Information Campaign fringe meeting at the Labour party conference in September 2000.

CHASING THE DRAGON

'Be you ever so high, yet the law is above you' – Lord Denning

'Of all my experience of Western countries, the British seem to have the most inconsistent democracy' – Chinese dissident Wei Jinsheng

'I distrust the government's instinctive attitude to questions of human liberty. On the whole raft of Home Office issues, it has no bedrock of libertarianism on which to rest. There is a dangerous tendency to snatch at quick-fix, populist solutions, which generally turn out to be no solutions at all, rather than to look askance at anything that puts the individual more at the mercy of authority' – Roy Jenkins[1]

IT WAS THE LORD CHANCELLOR Derry Irvine who quoted the famous dictum of Lord Denning in a lecture to Beijing University law faculty in September 1999, a few weeks before President Jiang Zemin's state visit to London. Irvine was explaining why under the rule of law it was essential that executive action had to be subject to review by the courts: 'If a country is to be governed under the rule of law, the law must be consistently applied and the executive, the government, must be subject to it,' he told his audience, explaining how judges had to be independent of the legislature and the executive to ensure that governments did not bend the law. 'In the British constitution, the influence of the executive over the legislature is strong, and the judiciary is commensurately weak, but the judiciary must still ensure that government does not go beyond the powers conferred on it by parliament and remains subject to the law.' Irvine went on to tell his Chinese audience about new powers that the government's 1998 Human Rights Act would give to judges and 'the potential for controversy between the judiciary and government which their exercise will bring'.

Irvine's prediction in Beijing of controversy ahead was to be proved true much quicker than he imagined. Irony of ironies, it was Jiang Zemin's visit to London that was to highlight in dramatic fashion the impact of the new Human Rights Act on the law, showing the truth of Lord Denning's words. And the government whose denial of human rights was to come under scrutiny in court was not China but the United Kingdom. Because the Human Rights Act has such constitutional importance, and because the story illustrates so well the contradictions of the Labour government's policies, it is worth telling in detail.

> 66 The government whose denial of human rights was to come under scrutiny in court was not China but the United Kingdom. 99

DON'T WAVE THAT FLAG

Joe Ruhland, a 76-year-old pensioner from Ruislip, first became interested in Tibet 40 years ago. He was in India when the Dalai Lama fled there into exile during the Chinese takeover of Tibet. On 19 October 1999, the second day of Jiang Zemin's state visit to Britain, Ruhland, a former British Rail employee, had gone to central London to demonstrate with a Tibetan flag against the Chinese president who was to drive past in a horse-drawn carriage with the Queen. 'I was going towards the Mall and two police horses tried to nudge me out of the way but I wasn't having that and I carried on,' he told me. 'As I was unfurling the flag three policemen came up behind me and snatched it from me. I was very annoyed. I said, it's private property, give it back, and I was asked to give my name and address.' The flag was taken to Charing Cross police station where Ruhland tried in vain to recover it from police, who accused him of a possible breach of the peace. 'I said that was rubbish. I was very annoyed. I said, I am a ratepayer, a taxpayer and a responsible citizen and a soldier of the last war, I don't have to put up with this rubbish. I slapped a piece of paper on the desk with a forwarding address and they later sent the flag back to me.'

Other demonstrators had similar stories. While police didn't bother people waving Chinese flags and Union Jacks, they systematically removed any flags and banners from anti-Chinese protesters. Sonam

Dugdak, a Tibetan exile who lives in London, fared little better when he walked down the Mall towards Buckingham Palace a little later the same day. His two protest placards, wrapped in a black bin-liner, were confiscated by police, who told him they would upset the Queen. 'They then took my name and address and asked me for my ID as though I had committed some crime. I felt humiliated and quite angry.' Dugdak never got his placards back. In his sworn statement used in a court action by the Free Tibet Campaign against the police he said:

I do not know how easy it is to understand how distressing this sort of behaviour is. Our country has been occupied and colonized by other people and our entire way of life destroyed. To come across bullying tactics of this kind which prevent reasonable protest about what has happened to our country is very disturbing.

Sue Byrne, a 57-year-old marketing consultant and longtime supporter of the Free Tibet Campaign, was taken aback by the change from the way the movement's usual demonstrations were policed:

It's always been smile, smile, smile, we hardly had any police protection, it's always been jolly and friendly. We've got used to demonstrating and cooperating with the police very straightforwardly. This time I felt the whole thing was beyond control, they had rictus grins on their faces, smiling at us, doing the tolerant speech but at the same time ruthlessly going to suppress what we were trying to do.

Byrne stood with a friend who had brought a banner calling on China to free the Panchen Lama and get out of Tibet:

We stood there – I am not a young person, I am a respectable lady. Suddenly there were four policemen at the back of us and they said, 'You won't be able to have those.' I said, 'What about freedom of speech?' Two policemen on horses came and we were sort of surrounded.

Then a senior police officer ordered them to hand over the banner, which was put on the ground on the other side of the police barrier. Police said that flags, banners and protests were forbidden by law inside the royal parks – London's equivalent of Tiananmen Square. But outside the royal parks, the treatment they gave to demonstrators was the same.

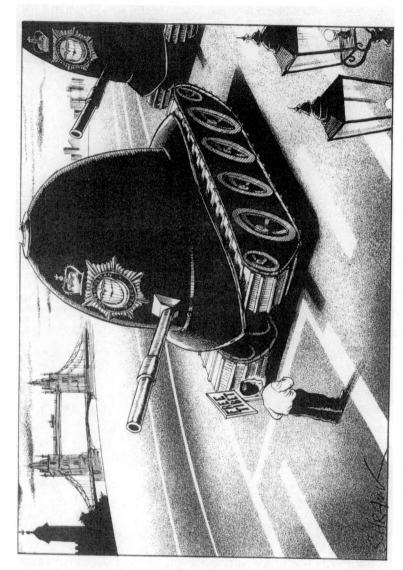

The Metropolitan Police, after meetings with Foreign Office and Chinese officials, cracks down on peaceful protesters during President Jiang Zemin's visit to London, but later has to admit it broke the law. Copyright © Peter Schrank, 1999.

Lucy Jing, a British citizen, tried to protest by waving a banner on Tower Bridge as a boat carrying the Chinese head of state passed underneath. Police, acting in tight coordination with Chinese security men, grabbed her. 'They twisted my arms hard behind my back and pushed me all the way from the middle of the bridge to the end and off to the side. I screamed. "You are hurting me." Stop it but they would not. This is just like fascism,' she told the *Daily Telegraph*.

The police had clear instructions to make sure that Jiang Zemin would not see any protests, and they went to extraordinary lengths. Outside Buckingham Palace and near the Chinese embassy they parked vans bumper to bumper to hide the demonstrators. 'Several people told the police that it was just like it was in China,' Dalha Tsering, another Tibetan exile, said in a sworn statement.

INTERRUPTIVE FACTORS

The handling of the visit proved highly controversial at home and generated a harvest of bad headlines in the world press about Britain's human rights policies. China's official press, of course, was the exception. The Foreign Office received between 600 and 700 letters from the public about how the visit was handled and the Metropolitan Police received 127 complaints. The affair was raised repeatedly in parliament, where Conservatives accused the government of 'kowtowing obsequiously' to the Chinese while bullying and lecturing less powerful foreign countries on human rights. Home Secretary Jack Straw was questioned for 20 minutes by the Home Affairs Select Committee and backed the police to the hilt, saying they had carried out a difficult balancing act. 'There was no restraint exercised over these demonstrations whatsoever,' he argued, rejecting as hyperbole any comparison with the Tiananmen Square massacre in Beijing in 1989. Straw stressed that his department had not been directly involved in preparations for Jiang's visit, which were handled in a series of nine preparatory meetings between the Foreign Office, the Metropolitan Police and Chinese officials.

The critics argued that by imposing Chinese-style restrictions on public dissent the government missed an opportunity to show Jiang democratic freedom in action. Liberal Democrat peer Conrad Russell wrote in *The Independent*: 'To let the Chinese go home not knowing that Britain is a country in which things happen that its government does not like, is to do them no service. If they are to do business with us, they must know us as we are.' Unfortunately, in Chinese eyes, the repression was not thorough enough, as Jiang's spokesman Zhu Bangzhao made clear to journalists: 'During the visit, there have been some interruptions. We have taken note of the fact that the British side have taken necessary measures in addressing these issues. It is our view that some of these interruptive factors should have been avoided.'

Most press comment in Britain was highly critical, with even *The Times*, which had carried an obsequious pre-visit interview with Jiang, attacking the police. The handling of the visit in a country supposed to be the home of free speech was described in *The Scotsman* by Iain Macwhirter as gut-wrenching. 'A British soldier rushing a demonstrator with bayonet fixed. Peaceful protesters roughed up and denied the right even to display the Tibetan flag. It was as if a little of the spirit of Tiananmen had been brought to the heart of Britain.' In *The Washington Post*, veteran foreign policy commentator Jim Hoagland described Tony Blair's welcome for the Chinese 'hardened despot' as somewhere between distasteful and harmful. *The Bangkok Post* accused Blair in an editorial of rolling out a red carpet trimmed with razor wire. 'At a stroke, the British government has compromised its claims to an ethical foreign policy and has shown it attaches more importance to business deals than to a tradition of tolerance and freedom of expression that has long been admired throughout the world. If the British authorities had wanted to make Mr Jiang feel as though he were at home, they could not have tried harder.' In India, *The Hindustan Times* summed up Jiang's visit, which included a state banquet with the Queen, as 'Britain's great crawl'. Exiled Chinese dissident Wei Jinsheng, who had his banner taken away by police outside Buckingham Palace, said he was surprised to see British police behaving in this way: 'I had not thought it possible in a democratic country. Of all my experience of Western countries, the British seem to have the most inconsistent democracy.'

SEE YOU IN COURT

The story of the Free Tibet Campaign and its banners and posters had a sequel in court a few months later. The Human Rights Act incorporating the European Convention on Human Rights (ECHR) into British law may not have been in force at the time of Jiang's visit, but the courts were already bearing it in mind. So when Alison Reynolds and her fellow campaigners decided to seek a judicial review of the police tactics, their barrister Keir Starmer used the Human Rights Act as a lever. He cited Articles 10 and 11 of the ECHR covering freedom of expression and the right of peaceful assembly, and Article 14 barring discrimination on political grounds by public authorities. Rather than defend the case, the Metropolitan Police caved in; they abandoned the conclusions of their internal review rejecting the protesters' complaints, and admitted their policing had been illegal. Starmer described the outcome to me as 'a complete volte-face' by the police and said it underlined the importance of the ECHR in strengthening the weak protection of freedom of speech and assembly under English common law. He explained how the police backed down:

It ended with the police conceding that they had acted unlawfully in a number of respects. That was hugely important for a whole variety of reasons. It was the first time the police have accepted in operational terms that they have acted unlawfully. They obviously have accepted individual cases that have gone wrong. Secondly, it demonstrates the importance of bringing a group action in court. Up until then individual complaints had been made by those that had their flags swiped and an internal police inquiry had taken place. That internal police inquiry had said there was nothing unlawful about anything that anybody did that day, and it was all the fault of the press for whipping up anti-police sentiment. Had the Free Tibet Campaign not brought the case, we would never have got an admission out of the police that anything they did was unlawful. Equally significantly, the police accepted not only that taking the flags was unlawful, but that moving vans in front of the protesters was unlawful. They accepted in principle it was wrong to do that if the purpose was to stifle free speech. Therefore they were unusually binding themselves to a yardstick for the future. So it was quite significant in a number of respects.

The reason they caved in was because the evidence of discrimination against them was so compelling. It was absolutely clear from the video evidence and from the statements that what they had done was to go and remove all the flags and banners from anybody who was anti-Chinese and leave those who were pro-Chinese or waving Union Jacks exactly where they were, doing what they wanted, and they knew they were in real trouble on that. Had it not been for the Human Rights Act, we would have had one less argument, but I think on bald discrimination they would still have gone down. We would have said it was arbitrary. What the Human Rights Act does is sharpen the focus on all of this and to put it into everyday language.

Some of the Free Tibet Campaign protesters felt the victory was only a partial one, because the case failed to reveal on whose orders the police had been acting and how the instructions were given. Joe Ruhland told me he was not satisfied and had written to his MP:

To me it is obvious that the police were instructed, I suspect by the Foreign Office and the Home Office. All these officers acting uniformly, all snatching Tibetan flags and banners and so on – that is just too much of a fib. There is no doubt there was government involvement. The police say all the officers acted independently. We have a traditional British desire to work with the police but we can't do this unless there is openness and honesty on their part.

Sue Byrne said she felt it was a hollow victory and the government would probably behave in exactly the same way the next time it wanted to avoid embarrassing demonstrations during a sensitive state visit:

The police backed down because if we had gone to court and we had got the right man in the dock it would all have come out, all these conversations with the Foreign Office. I think they just got imbued with the sense of panic that the Foreign Office were in about President Jiang Zemin throwing a wobbly. So somehow President Jiang throwing a wobbly overtook all the stuff about peaceful protest.

She told me she felt sorry for the police at the bottom taking the blame for orders they had been given from on high, and said she felt revolted by the partial nature of the police climbdown:

The police said to me, I am sure Tony Blair is perfectly happy with what happened. I feel really annoyed that the foot soldiers are being blamed for carrying out instructions.

TO THE FORBIDDEN CITY

Was it all just a bureaucratic muddle by over-zealous policemen and officials? Or did the orders to break the law come from the top, as Sue Byrne believed? Unlike Wei Jinsheng, I cannot say I was surprised at the way the protesters were dealt with, after travelling to China with Blair a year earlier in October 1998 and seeing his flash of irritation whenever the 'interruptive factor' of human rights came up. The previous week, at the

Labour party conference in Blackpool, Foreign Secretary Robin Cook had boasted that the British Labour government was now 'recognized around the world as a champion of democracy and human rights'. Blair had announced in a preface to the 1997 White Paper *Rights Brought Home* that his government had decided 'to put the promotion of human rights at the forefront of our foreign policy'.

Before Blair left for the week-long trip to Beijing, Shanghai and Hong Kong, his spokesman told journalists human rights constituted 'a problem area, but it's not one we wish to exaggerate, because there are other parts of the relationship which are more important'. China was already making 'very considerable progress' on human rights and Blair thought more could be achieved by dialogue than by 'hectoring from the sidelines'. Blair would encourage Chinese leaders to welcome, rather than resist, political change, an argument that seemed to reflect an element of wishful thinking, given the lessons learned by the Communist party politburo in Beijing from Mikhail Gorbachev's ill-fated experiments with political change in Moscow a decade earlier. The spokesman explained to journalists that Blair's experiences in Northern Ireland had led him to believe that 'it is possible through dialogue to reconcile the seemingly irreconcilable' and he wanted to apply this principle to human rights in China. There would be no 'table-thumping and grandstanding' during the visit, which would coincide with a programme of seminars by top lawyers including Blair's wife Cherie Booth QC, and a mock trial designed to showcase for the Chinese the way the law operated in Britain.

When we got to Beijing, it seemed to me that Blair, briefed beforehand by Sir Percy Cradock, a retired 'old China hand' from the Foreign Office, had seriously overestimated the extent to which speaking publicly about human rights would be regarded as offensive by his hosts. As China experts from Amnesty International in London had predicted to me, the Chinese leaders were not going to march out of the talks in a huff; they were quite used to the 'dialogue' game and regarded it as a useful way of deflecting criticism while continuing to act towards dissidents exactly as they pleased. At formal talks in the Great Hall of the People, the travelling journalists were ushered in to hear Prime Minister Zhu Rongji tell Blair: 'You can feel at home in China. Feel free to talk about anything you like with us. Nothing will offend us.' Blair failed to respond to the invitation during this semi-public part of the meeting. Fifteen-love to the Chinese, I thought.

> ❝ They were quite used to the 'dialogue' game and regarded it as a useful way of deflecting criticism while continuing to act towards dissidents exactly as they pleased. ❞

There seemed to be a world of difference between Blair's approach and the tough but diplomatic way most Western leaders handled human rights issues on visits to the Soviet Union in the 1970s and 1980s. Most of them not only made a point of discussing the subject publicly but also met dissidents personally in Moscow, a practice their hosts accepted through gritted teeth.

JUST MARVELLOUS TO BE BACK

Later Blair recorded an interview with Chinese state television against the backdrop of the Forbidden City. Being back in China after ten years away and seeing so many changes was 'just marvellous', he said.

I think what was good about the meeting this morning was that of course there will be differences, for example over the human rights issue, but I think that there is an acknowledgement on the Chinese side that there is progress to be made, and there is an acknowledgement on our side that progress is being made, and we want to try to continue that dialogue, not in a sort of grandstanding hectoring way, but in a way that makes genuine progress.

The interviewer asked a question about modernization in Britain and in China. Blair needed no prompting:

I would say that Premier Zhu Rongji is himself a real modernizer ... I have a very great admiration for the way he is tackling the problems of change, of economic change in China. And I think what is interesting today is that the new millennium will mark a sideways shift in political ideas and political attitudes. The battle between extreme forms of socialism, extreme forms of capitalism, that marked the 20th century, I think that is over, and I think that fundamentalist ideology has gone.

Britain and China were tackling the same problems in modernizing their industries and public services and shared the same objectives and a common language, he told his interviewer. It seemed to me a waste of a unique opportunity; Blair was throwing away the once-in-a-lifetime chance to tell hundreds of millions of Chinese something about the way democracy worked in Britain. While sticking to his policy of not criticizing China in public, Blair could easily have dropped in a few phrases about Britain's multi-party democracy and the fact that as prime minister, he might – unlike his Beijing counterparts – be removed by the voters at the ballot box. This kind of message would have sounded banal to a television audience familiar with democracy but would have resonated widely in a totalitarian one-party state such as China.

Margaret Thatcher famously used the opportunity of an interview with Soviet television during a visit to Moscow in 1987 to tell her audience some facts about human rights and arms control that they would not find in *Pravda*. By contrast, Blair seemed to be bending over backwards to tell his official hosts what they wanted to hear. This was more than just the result of being poorly briefed or being reluctant to offend his hosts; he seemed to believe quite sincerely that the big ideological disputes in the world were now over and all societies, Britain and China included, were heading in the same direction and facing the same challenges. Blair's readiness to minimize the essential difference between democracy and totalitarianism suggested that he did not really see it as important. It was just another tedious old 20th century ideological dispute, superseded by the 21st century challenges of globalization and modernization. China's widespread denial of human rights amounted merely to a difference of view to be resolved through dialogue, rather than a fundamental pillar of one-party rule.

> ❝ Blair's readiness to minimize the essential difference between democracy and totalitarianism suggested that he did not really see it as important. It was just another tedious old 20th century ideological dispute. ❞

Before Blair left Beijing, any hope he had that dialogue was paying dividends was punctured when it emerged that Chinese authorities had detained Xu Wenli, a veteran dissident. Xu was released after seven hours when Blair's officials raised the issue with China's ambassador to London, but the incident sent a clear message. Blair mentioned it in a speech to a British-Chinese business dinner, drawing the upbeat conclusion that 'there is at least a process of dialogue in which (such incidents) can be addressed and resolved'. He did, however, come closer than before to a hint of criticism: 'Much remains to be done on civil and political rights. Such rights are universal: to be applied to each and every one of us.'

Blair rounded off his trip in Shanghai by praising Zhu Rongji and Jiang Zemin for their 'tremendous imagination and real commitment' to liberalizing their country. He urged them to expand freedom, predicting that the result would be 'a China that is stronger, rather than weaker'. In Hong Kong, Blair met one of his most outspoken critics, pro-democracy politician Martin Lee, who accused him of sacrificing democracy for the sake of British contracts with China. Britain's foreign policy had more to do with economics than ethics, he complained. Blair dismissed his views as 'simply wrong' and responded with a note of irritation: 'If people want me to say that I want to wreck Britain's relations with China, well, I'm not in for that, I'm afraid.'

CYNICISM OR NAIVETY?

The story of Blair's handling of his visit to China and of Jiang Zemin's visit to London is important not because it showed hard-bitten cynicism over human rights – rather the reverse. Blair if anything suffers from an excess of naivety and goodwill, and a touching belief in his ability to influence others by the power of his personality. Hugo Young described the Blair approach in a commentary on his enthusiasm for dialogue with the 'butcher of Chechnya', Russian leader Vladimir Putin:

Dialogue, in all and any circumstances, has become the hallmark of his foreign policy ... Moral protest, such as Putin generated in Whitehall and elsewhere, will cut no ice. This contrast between the theory and practice of Blair presents a startling spectacle. He's a fervent believer in his powers of persuasion.[2]

The problem is that often the powers of persuasion do not work, at least on human rights issues. Given Blair's tentative approach in China, that may be hardly surprising. The visit had a postscript. Less than three months after Blair's departure from Beijing, Xu Wenli was sentenced to 13 years in jail for trying to set up the banned Chinese Democratic party. There was no comment from Downing Street.

At the end of 1999 the House of Commons Foreign Affairs Committee, reviewing the government's annual human rights report, underlined the continuing need for 'clear and consistent principles' to prop up the policy of constructive engagement with countries such as China and Saudi Arabia. 'The principles do not appear to have the solid ethical foundations we would like to see,' the committee commented.

The recent visit of the President of China to the United Kingdom placed the government's policy of constructive engagement towards China under the spotlight. In our view it did not withstand the glare. The consensus is that there has been some slippage in human rights performance in China over the past year.

Human rights in China had deteriorated in the year since Blair's visit, according to the committee, which challenged the government to come up with some results to show for its policy of critical dialogue. Foreign Secretary Robin Cook, replying to the report in March 2000, acknowledged that things in China were getting worse but added: 'The government has never claimed that the dialogue would prevent the kind of deterioration that occurred in 1999. There is no quick solution to the human rights situation in China.'

The Select Committee challenged the government to make public the principles on which it based its decision to pursue dialogue and constructive engagement with some countries but not with others:

The failure to make these principles explicit lays the government open to the accusation that it is strong with the weak and weak with the mighty. Government human rights policy can then be portrayed as unprincipled and insignificant when confronted by the UK's trade interests. Such a picture of government human rights policy would significantly undermine the UK's ability to negotiate effectively with other states for human rights improvements.

The point the Select Committee was making was that human rights policy, like economic policy and environmental policy, has to be a seamless whole at home and abroad. To be logical and consistent, a government has to indulge in 'joined-up thinking' on the subject or appear incoherent:

Joined-up government is a sensible objective. If the government is serious about furthering the human rights agenda internationally, it cannot afford to allow the concept to become a rhetorical fashion accessory; it must be translated into tangible policies and practices that range across departments.

A lengthy audit of UK human rights policies by Amnesty International in September 2000 made uncomfortable reading for Labour. Top of the list of shortcomings was the export of arms to authoritarian regimes, which it described as the acid test of the government's principles. It recommended 'clear leadership' by the Prime Minister in implementing human rights policies across Whitehall, saying the lead had to come from Downing Street:

The protection of human rights and fundamental freedoms is an imperative that should override others, even if the means for achieving that goal necessarily vary from one situation to another … If the UK's authority in influencing human rights internationally is not to be undermined, the government needs to ensure that it is applying the same standards at home as abroad, and that a commitment to human rights is demonstrated across the different parts of government.

The report singled out the visits to London by the leaders of China and Russia, both countries 'with a recent egregious record of human rights violations'. Blair had failed to seize the opportunity of Jiang Zemin's visit by making a public statement about human rights violations in China, which included the heaviest crackdown on peaceful dissent for a decade and more than 1,000 executions, Amnesty said, concluding with a withering assessment of his policies:

The principal objectives of the UK's China policy appear to be to enhance the visibility of the UK as a trading partner and to improve the penetration of British products in the Chinese market. The strategy appears to be highly vulnerable to threats of retaliation if the UK government speaks out about human rights. As far as human rights is concerned, the UK is playing a game on terms set in Beijing.

A CULTURE OF CRACKDOWNS

The goal of a joined-up human rights policy at home and abroad has been endorsed by the government. In a speech in December 1997 Irvine quoted Cook as saying: 'If Britain is to carry credibility when we talk to other governments about their observance of human rights, we must command respect for our own human rights record.'[3] Irvine added: 'The government believes it is as important to safeguard human rights at home as it is abroad.'

But while recognizing the connection in theory, the Blair government seems to have experienced considerable difficulty in practice. Part of the problem is its exaggerated love and fear of tabloid headlines and reverence for focus groups; the evidence is clear from Blair's leaked memo written in April 2000[4] that this characteristic cannot be blamed on subordinates and advisers – it comes from the top. When the desire to appear tough on law and order conflicts with human rights policy, it is normally the first that wins out. As Hugo Young wrote after the leaking of the Blair memo:

Running through these law and order attitudes is Mr Blair's own most consistent defect as a progressive politician: his indifference to civil liberties. I've never heard him giving them priority. At the last party conference he spat on the very concept.[5]

This explains the obsession with 'crackdowns' on bogus asylum seekers, noisy neighbours, football hooligans, squeegee merchants and other undesirables; in domestic and foreign affairs alike, 'joined-upness' on human rights appears to be out of the government's grasp. Analyzing Labour policy would be easier if the government *were* to follow a policy of pure cynicism, based on a narrow conservative view of the British national interest abroad and indifference to human rights at home. But Blair's government, in its stress on ethics and values, is different from John Major's government, which took the view that most human rights abuses committed abroad were not its business, and that Britain had no need for a Human Rights Act because the country already enjoyed domestic freedom. Such *realpolitik* doctrines have a long pedigree on the right, from Metternich and Bismarck to Henry Kissinger. Blair's refusal to contemplate 'wrecking' relations with China over human rights suggests that at least some of the time he sees himself trapped in a zero-sum game where he has to put the national interest first and human rights second. This has been his approach to Russia's bloody post-colonial war in Chechnya, which Blair has justified as a crackdown on 'extremists and terrorists' and has treated as no more than a minor 'interruptive factor' in his desire to forge a bond with the Kremlin's new master Vladimir Putin. But the Kosovo conflict in 1999 – which cost far fewer civilian lives than Chechnya – suggested a more complex zigzagging between idealism and pragmatism that was not entirely cynical. It revealed Blair to be genuinely appalled by ethnic cleansing, but struggling to frame a coherent intellectual framework for his hawkish response.

THE BLAIR DOCTRINE

Halfway through the air campaign against Serbia, journalists who travelled to the United States with Blair for a NATO summit in April 1999 got a revealing insight into the confusion of the prime ministerial mind. Blair made a detour to Chicago for a speech that attempted to put the case for moral intervention into context. 'Unspeakable things are happening in Europe,' he told his audience. 'Awful crimes that we never thought we would see again have reappeared – ethnic cleansing, systematic rape, mass murder.' Blair went on to make the liberal case against cynicism and *realpolitik*, dismissing Bismarck's famous remark that the Balkans were not worth the bones of one Pomeranian grenadier. 'Anyone who has seen the tearstained faces of the hundreds of thousands of refugees streaming across the border, heard their heart-rending tales of cruelty or contemplated the unknown fates of those left behind, knows that Bismarck was wrong.' NATO's war in Kosovo was a just war, based on human values, he argued. But it was also a reflection of globalization: 'We are all internationalists now, whether we like it or not ...We cannot turn our backs on conflicts and the violation of human rights within other countries if we want still to be secure.'

Blair declared: 'We are witnessing the beginnings of a new doctrine of international community.' This applied not only in economics but in international security too, where 'our actions are guided by a more subtle blend of mutual self-interest and moral purpose in defending the values we cherish.' Blair appeared to be demolishing the logic of his own China policy – no longer was there a zero-sum choice between defending human rights and 'wrecking' wider national interests:

In the end, values and interests merge. If we can establish and spread the values of liberty, the rule of law, human rights and an open society, then that is in our national interest too. The spread of our values makes us safer. As John Kennedy put it: 'Freedom is indivisible and when one man is enslaved, who is free?'

Listening to this in the ornate Chicago hotel ballroom where Blair was speaking, I felt it might be useful to introduce Kosovo Blair to Beijing Blair. They would have an interesting Socratic dialogue. What came next, however, was a lurch away from the ringing idealism of John Kennedy into back-of-the-envelope territory. In trying to frame his grandiose new 'Doctrine of International Community', Blair was clearly wrestling for the first time with the concepts of intervention and national sovereignty, which have been common currency in world politics for half a century. Non-interference, Blair acknowledged, had long been considered an important principle of international order. 'And it is not one we would want to jettison too readily.' But however important, the principle should be qualified, he argued. Acts of genocide could never be a purely internal matter, while refugee flows could threaten international peace, and minority regimes such as South Africa under apartheid were illegitimate. I imagined Blair scratching away with his fountain pen in the first-class cabin of his plane on the way to Chicago, rather like a first-year international relations student with an essay to write: 'Humanitarian intervention in the affairs of other countries can never be justified. Discuss.' The speech was starting to sound like a 'Blair doctrine' justifying widespread and frequent intervention against human rights abuses, and I was reminded of the 'Brezhnev doctrine' of limited sovereignty used by the Soviet Union to justify the 1968 Warsaw Pact invasion of Czechoslovakia. But the argument trickled away to be replaced by its opposite:

Looking around the world there are many regimes that are undemocratic and engaged in barbarous acts. If we wanted to right every wrong that we see in the modern world then we would do little else than intervene in the affairs of other countries. We would not be able to cope.

Blair then outlined what he called five tests for international intervention, all of them framed with Kosovo in mind. Are we sure of our case? Have we exhausted all diplomatic options? Are there military operations we can prudently and sensibly undertake? Are we prepared for the long term? And do we have national interests involved? These were not absolute tests, Blair added apologetically, just 'the kind of issues we need to think about in deciding in the future when and whether we will intervene'. What was striking was the absence from the list of what should perhaps have been the most important question of all for a prime minister trained as a lawyer: *'Is it legal?'*

> 66 What was striking was the absence from the list of what should perhaps have been the most important question of all for a prime minister trained as a lawyer: *'Is it legal?'* 99

As a ringing new doctrine, the speech left a lot to be desired. After we left Chicago for Washington, the new 'Doctrine of International Community' vanished as quickly as it had arrived, though the phrase resurfaced briefly in a much less controversial form in a speech Blair made to the Global Ethics Foundation in Germany, in June 2000.

THE HUMAN RIGHTS ACT

Unlike the new 'Blair doctrine', the 1998 Human Rights Act is not going to go away. It stands along with devolution as the biggest constitutional landmark of the 1997 parliament. Like devolution, it was awarded pride of place at the head of the legislative timetable after the election victory, thanks to the vigorous advocacy of Jack Straw and Derry Irvine. Its importance stems not only from the way it subtly shifts the balance between the executive and the judges but from the fact that it is likely to be irreversible. Anthony Lester QC, a Liberal Democrat life peer and human rights expert who campaigned for years for this measure, describes it as 'the most significant constitutional measure since the Bill of Rights of 1688–89 (apart from the European Communities Act in the areas where it reigns supreme)'.[6] Some lawyers have described it as the most significant document since the Magna Carta. Paradoxically, the government has appeared keen to minimize its significance. After the case of the Free Tibet Campaign demonstrators, one can see why.

Legal scholar Francesca Klug of King's College London, who advised the government on the Act, told me the Tibet judgement pointed the way ahead:

The Tibet judgement is an optimistic judgement of what the changes may be, and I think there is very little doubt that they (the police) responded the way they did because of the Human Rights Act, because they knew how it would go. They accepted the right to demonstrate.

John Wadham of the human rights pressure group Liberty explained to me what would change:

We haven't ever really had a Bill of Rights in this country. There was one in 1688, but that did not really describe the rights of individuals. For the first time, from October 2000, we will have a set of positive rights. The way the constitution has worked in the past has been that your freedoms exist 'in the silence of the law'. In other words, you can do what isn't actually prohibited. What that means, of course, is that over hundreds of years and perhaps the last 20 or so years, there have been a whole series of encroachments by parliament in legislation on the rights we have. So they have been sliced away, slice by slice, from the freedoms that we had some time ago. And so therefore having a series of positive rights is a very important thing.

The truth is that after a long string of judgements from the European Court in Strasbourg against the United Kingdom, the new Labour government had little choice but to incorporate the Convention, if only to bring the embarrassing run of government defeats to an end. The Strasbourg court's long list of verdicts against the UK – more than 50 by the late 1990s – involved such issues as the restriction of prisoners' civil rights, corporal punishment in state schools, ministerial control of the release of prisoners, telephone tapping by employers, refusal of access to social security records, restrictions on legal aid, inadequate protection for journalists, unfair court martial procedures, retrospective criminal penalties and failure to guarantee respect for human life.

The UK, whose lawyers had played a leading part in drafting the ECHR and was the first country to ratify it, did not incorporate it into its own law because of the traditional Diceyan suspicion of 'foreign constitution makers' and their declarations of rights. 'Victorian commentators naturally took it for granted that, once again, England had got things entirely right while all foreigners had got them completely wrong.'[7] An entrenched Bill of Rights on the American pattern would inevitably place limits on the sovereignty of parliament. The Labour Chancellor of the Exchequer under Attlee, Sir Stafford Cripps, opposed ratification on the grounds that the ECHR might make Labour's nationalization policies more difficult. But the result of sticking to what Professor Rodney Brazier calls 'the old Victorian certainties' was to isolate Britain and make it infinitely harder for its citizens to use the ECHR to protect their rights. As Derry Irvine said in a lecture soon after the 1997 election: 'At present, Britain is virtually alone among the major nations of Western Europe in failing to give its citizens a direct means of asserting their Convention rights through their national courts. As more and more countries in Eastern Europe ratify the Convention, we have become increasingly isolated.'[8]

Like devolution for Scotland, incorporation of the ECHR was a long-standing Labour party commitment dating back to 1993. The party's traditional suspicion of judges and the courts and its belief in the primacy of parliament had begun to change in the 1980s under the impact of the Thatcher government. By the time Tony Blair came along, incorporation of the Convention counted among the issues on which policy was well developed. There was a crucial conundrum to be solved, however. Would the sovereignty of parliament be unaffected, or would the ECHR's incorporation give judges the same right as their US counterparts to strike down old or new parliamentary legislation that they found to be incompatible with fundamental freedoms?

Labour initially favoured a variant similar to the law in Canada, which allows the judges to overturn laws, but also allows parliament to overrule the judges by passing laws that apply 'notwithstanding' the Canadian Charter of Rights. John Wadham told me that Liberty helped persuade Labour to adopt this policy. Finally, after the 1997 election, the party

opted for a legal formula similar to that used in New Zealand, which pre-
serves parliamentary sovereignty more clearly; the Human Rights Act
therefore allows the courts to issue a 'declaration of incompatibility'
regarding primary legislation from Westminster that conflicts with the
ECHR. It will then be up to the government and parliament to take reme-
dial action. Francesca Klug, who helped devise this formula, believes it is
important to leave parliament and the government room to manoeuvre
and take decisions, rather than just make them submit to the courts:

If you let the judges decide whether fox-hunting should be banned or whether
tobacco is acceptable, it would lead to the most enormous backlash ... I think there
is a culture here of saying these kinds of decisions should be made by politicians.
What this kind of model does is to allow those decisions to be made by politicians. If
the courts make a declaration of incompatibility, then I think the government of the
day feel they have the legal and moral authority to say, one minute, we are not just
going to do what you say here, this is a big philosophical and political issue ... On
philosophical and social issues the political debate will rule. I think that's an
appropriate model for the UK. I don't think the judges have any more legitimacy.

Despite the fact that the ECHR is 50 years old and has some important
omissions, such as an absence of any reference to children's rights and a
paucity of social and economic rights, the choices made by the government
on the way it would be incorporated were radical. Francesca Klug describes
the final version as 'formidable' in its impact. For example, courts will be
able to go beyond the jurisprudence of the Strasbourg court and range more
widely around the world for models. Judges will be able to do their best to
interpret existing legislation in line with the spirit of the ECHR, rather than
just the letter. 'It is broader than the narrowest possible interpretation. It
could have been much more limited.' She told me the radicalism of Straw
and Irvine 'wasn't universally popular' in the government. 'Jack Straw and
Derry Irvine pushed this at the very first cabinet meeting. It would never
happen now. All credit to them that they pushed it through ... It's a very
difficult thing for a government to do, to give away power.'

A FLOOR NOT A CEILING

The ECHR, Irvine has argued, will be a floor for human rights, not a ceil-
ing. 'This government's position is that we should be leading in the
development of human rights in Europe, not grudgingly driven to swal-

low the medicine prescribed for us by the court in Strasbourg when we are found in breach of the Convention.'[9]

Irvine, a past critic of excessive judicial activism while in opposition, dismissed Conservative fears that incorporation would give too much political power to judges. The British constitution was firmly based on the separation of powers, he argued, and incorporation would not change that. 'It is for parliament to pass laws, not the judges. It is for the judges to interpret these laws and to develop the common law, not for parliament or the executive.' Incorporation, he promised, would enhance the judges' powers to protect the individual against the abuse of power by the state. While judicial review to hold the executive to account for its actions was in itself nothing new, the innovation lay in the framework given to the judges to interpret the law.

Derry Irvine's speeches on the Human Rights Act show a reforming zeal that reveals him to be a true heir of his close friend John Smith. Anthony Barnett, a co-founder of Charter88, told me: 'I know it sounds paradoxical, but he is a constitutional radical.' He referred to Irvine's role in bulldozing through the Scottish and Welsh devolution Bills and the Human Rights Act. 'Those are remarkable pieces of legislation. He doesn't really believe in parliamentary sovereignty. He is a judge. And he knows that the Human Rights Act in reality means sovereignty is now shared with the judiciary. The old sovereignty of parliament has been broken by the Human Rights Act.' Barnett may be exaggerating somewhat, but Irvine certainly sounds more radical in his gloss on the Human Rights Act than Jack Straw, the other minister closely associated with it. Here is Irvine explaining in a lecture at the end of 1997 how the Act will change the law to give the citizen more protection against the state:

This negative approach means that 'the starting point of our domestic law is that every citizen has a right to do what he likes, unless restrained by the common law or by statute'. The liberty of the subject is therefore the 'negative' right of what is left over when all the prohibitions have limited the area of lawful conduct … By proposing this law the government has decisively demonstrated its view that the more serious threat to liberty is an absence of written guarantees of freedom. For the negative approach offers little protection against a creeping erosion of freedom by a legislature willing to countenance infringement of liberty or simply blind to the effect of an otherwise well-intentioned piece of law. As Professor Dworkin, Professor of Jurisprudence at the University of Oxford, argued in an important article in 1988, the challenge to liberty is not only from despots. A government may show 'a more mundane but still corrupting insensitivity to liberty, a failure to grasp its force and place in democratic ideals'. The Human Rights Bill is our bulwark against that danger.[10]

In the words of the Lord Chancellor: 'The Convention rights are the magnetic north and the needle of judicial interpretation will swing towards them.' Irvine has promised that in future, because ministers will have to certify that new laws put before parliament conform to the ECHR, 'human rights will not be a matter of fudge'. This applies particularly to the articles such as freedom of expression, where the ECHR states the limitations that can be placed on grounds of national security, territorial integrity or public safety, to prevent crime, to protect health or morals and other grounds. All this will ensure parliament 'knows exactly what it is doing in a human rights context'. As a result of the Act, the courts will have to abandon what Irvine has called 'the old Diceyan approach' to interpreting the law: 'It will not be necessary to find an ambiguity. On the contrary, the courts will be required to interpret legislation so as to uphold the Convention rights unless the legislation itself is so clearly incompatible with the Convention that it is impossible to do so.' Court decisions 'will be based on a more overtly principled, indeed moral, basis. The court will look at the positive right. It will only accept an interference with that right where a justification, allowed under the Convention, is made out'. This means the spirit, not just the words of the ECHR, will count. 'As we move from the traditional Diceyan model of the common law to a rights-based system, the effects will be felt throughout the common law and in the very process of judicial decision making.'

FREEDOM OF SPEECH AND ASSEMBLY

I asked Keir Starmer to explain in detail how the Human Rights Act affected the outcome of the case brought by the Free Tibet protesters against the Metropolitan Police:

The major difference is this: up until now we have had this concept of negative liberty, you can do anything that isn't prohibited. And therefore there hasn't been any proper protection of freedom of speech or assembly. As legislation has progressively restricted the freedom of people to demonstrate, they have got nothing to put into the balance, and in particular in public spaces and on highways it has always been deemed as civil trespass to hold an assembly. And that means that potentially peaceful assemblers could always be moved. The only reason they are not moved is because the police exercise their discretion not to. And that obviously causes problems, because there is the potential for discrimination and there is nothing legal for a peaceful assembler to hang on to if they want to protest.

What the Convention does through the Human Rights Act is to set up for the first time a positive right of peaceful assembly that people can assert. And the way they assert it primarily is to say that all legislation that restricts their right of freedom of assembly has to be interpreted in such a way as to be compliant with the Convention. So it is quite a powerful tool for re-examining all of the old case law about the rights of protesters.

Equally importantly, the Human Rights Act puts a duty on all public authorities to act compatibly with Convention rights. Therefore the police as a public authority will be acting unlawfully if they disregard the right of peaceful assembly. Now this doesn't mean that the right of peaceful assembly has in any way become absolute. It's not a trump card that any protester can use. But it does mean that it has got positive value and that if the police or anyone else are going to restrict it, it's for them to justify why they are doing it, and to do it according to a much stricter test under Convention law: is it necessary and proportionate?

The other thing is, the European Court of Human Rights has developed what it calls a concept of positive obligations. What that means is it recognizes that state authorities are sometimes under a duty to protect one individual or a group of individuals from the actions of another. And in the public order/peaceful assembly context, what that can mean is a duty on the police or others to protect those who want to protest peacefully from those who want to break up their protest. So it is quite a radical shift in emphasis.

Starmer explained that the positive right to peaceful assembly, like the right to privacy under the ECHR, was new in British law. Other articles of the Convention, such as the one guaranteeing the right to a fair trial, already had their equivalents in domestic law and so the impact would be less dramatic.

INCORPORATION OF THE ECHR

The UK played a major part in drafting the post-war Convention and was the first country to ratify it in March 1951. In 1966, the Wilson government made it possible for individuals to bring cases against the UK government at the Court of Human Rights in Strasbourg. But because the Convention was not part of UK domestic law, it was not binding on the courts. Cases could only be brought in Strasbourg after all domestic remedies had been exhausted and anyone bringing a case faced a costly wait of several years. By 1999 more than 50 landmark judgements had been handed down from Strasbourg against the UK, which was found to have breached the Convention on such issues as corporal punishment in state schools, the rights of homosexuals in the armed forces, telephone tapping, denial of legal aid, inadequate legal protection for journalists, and discriminatory immigration rules.

The ECHR guarantees the right to life, liberty, security and a fair trial, freedom from torture, slavery, forced labour, illegal punishment, the right to privacy and family life, the right to freedom of thought, conscience and religion and to freedom of expression, freedom of assembly and association. It guarantees the right to marry and prohibits discrimination on grounds of sex, race, colour, language, religion, political or other opinion, national or social origin, association with a national minority, property, birth or other status.

Under the Human Rights Act, the ECHR is binding not only on government but on all public authorities and private bodies carrying out functions of a public nature. The precise scope will be determined by the courts. It requires the courts to interpret all laws as far as is possible in a way compatible with the ECHR. Courts will not be able to strike down legislation that clashes with the ECHR. In order to preserve parliamentary sovereignty, they will instead be able to make a formal 'declaration of incompatibility', leaving government and parliament to change the law. Any person who believes his or her rights have been violated can seek redress in the courts and sue the body involved for damages.

PARLIAMENT STILL RULES OK

Will the Act inevitably lead to friction between parliament and the courts? Jack Straw is on record as claiming that 'parliament still rules OK'.[11] Ann Owers, director of the legal reform group Justice, was among those closely consulted by the Home Office as the reform went through:

I think a lot will depend on the seriousness with which parliament, the government and other executive bodies take their human rights obligations. The notion of the Act is very much a partnership. It is for government to look at its legislation to see if it is compliant, and it is for government and all other public authorities to make sure that what they are going to do is human rights compliant. It is for parliament to examine legislation in the light of the Human Rights Act, scrutinize it and if necessary revise it if the courts find it incompatible, and it is for the courts to have this overall role. Now that's a nice and well-balanced scheme which gives roles and responsibilities to all those partners. If it works, that will be very good. The danger will be that governments do what governments have done before, which is to carry on regardless and then blame the courts when their actions are overturned or their laws are declared incompatible. We have seen this before with previous governments' attitude to the Strasbourg court – 'We don't want foreigners telling us what to do.' There has been a hint of this with this government, as with other governments, in terms of decisions in our own courts that they don't much like, saying that the judges are out of touch or unrealistic or they don't really understand how government needs to operate. And similarly with parliament.

Owers told me she felt the House of Commons had a very poor record on examining human rights issues when processing legislation:

The interest in civil rights is extremely low. It is much better in the Lords. It's a knee-jerk thing … We get very bad legislation, there are far too many which are coathanger Bills, they go through parliament, they are not properly scrutinized and you get bad law. The process is dire. Parliament's ability to exercise its part of the three-legged stool of human rights compliance is limited by its own limitations.

Francesca Klug shares this view, blaming the traditional left–right adversarial system for parliament's failure to develop a common culture sensitive to civil liberties: 'So you had the left's civil liberties such as the right to strike, and the right's civil liberties such as the right to property.' John Wadham also told me he was hoping more legislators at Westminster would now start to take a serious interest in human rights:

I don't think there is a culture amongst many MPs and Lords to look at the human rights provisions in any significant way. That has got to change, because MPs have got to understand that they are the other part of the protection process, it is not just lawyers and the courts.

In view of this, there has been disappointment at the government's slowness in setting up the parliamentary Human Rights Committee promised when the Act became law at the end of 1998. First steps to create it were announced just before the summer recess in July 2000, ensuring that the Committee would not be in place until well after the Act came into force the following October.

NO HUMAN RIGHTS COMMISSION

The government also disappointed human rights advocates by failing to create a Human Rights Commission to prepare the way for incorporation on 2 October 2000 and educate the public. John Wadham believes there are still a number of tasks for such a body:

There are number of roles for a Human Rights Commission: promoting an understanding of human rights to the public, providing information to public authorities, codes of practice, providing sources of information about the Convention; providing detailed advice to individuals who come to it, saying, I've got this problem; taking some cases, maybe doing some inquiries, in other ways saying, there is a human rights problem in a particular part of government and actually launching an inquiry with teeth, so they could find out what is actually going on and write reports; and providing advice to ministers and to parliament itself, to the committee on any particular provision. So it would be a source of expert advice.

Sarah Spencer, human rights expert at the centre-left think tank IPPR, says: 'The perception of a Human Rights Commission in the senior ranks of government is that this is a body that will make life more difficult for them. My argument is exactly the opposite – this is a body that will help manage the process for them because its primary task will be going out to public authorities, promoting good practice on how not to end up in court.'

Francesca Klug says the failure to create a Human Rights Commission is potentially 'a terrible mistake'. She believes Labour was anxious that it might simply criticize the government and lead to an 'own goal', but the absence of a commission has left the field open for *Daily Mail* criticism of the HRA as a 'thieves' charter'. Ann Owers believes that 'the government was worried about setting up a body that was going to be an active litigator against the government. I think there were a lot of cautious voices'. She points out that Northern Ireland's new Human Rights Commission, established under the Good Friday Agreement, will fill exactly this role. Scotland may also set up its own Human Rights Commission, a move that would highlight the anomalous position of England and Wales. The government's main reason for hesitation was because it feared problems with the existing bodies such as the Commission for Racial Equality and the Equal Opportunities Commission, some of which felt they would be marginalized: 'There were a lot of turf arguments which they felt would be too difficult to deal with and which might hold up the progress of the Human Rights Act. It was too problematic an issue to tackle. It think now the feeling is much more positive from them and I hope the government will look again at it.'

Jack Straw told me: 'We don't rule it out at all ... but we felt in the early stages it was better to make the responsibility for implementing this a matter for government. It cuts both ways. It could come eventually, we will have to see ... I am not opposed to setting it up but it is a second order issue.'

AN ACT NOT JUST FOR LAWYERS

The lack of a Human Rights Commission to handle educational work on the Human Rights Act has paradoxically meant that the government has relied on the expertise of people like John Wadham – who apart from his role at Liberty is also solicitor for former MI5 agent David Shayler – to help ensure the courts are prepared for how the Human Rights Act will work. There has been what Wadham describes as an explosion in the need to train thousands of lawyers in human rights law. 'I and somebody else have trained 250 magistrates' court clerks, who have trained 1,700 other magistrates' court clerks, who are going to train 32,000 magistrates.' As far as the judiciary is concerned, Francesca Klug says incorporating the ECHR is 'kicking at an open door' because British judges have felt uncomfortable being excluded from the international development of human rights law. John Wadham highlights the role of a number of prominent human rights lawyers with experience of taking cases to Strasbourg over the past 20 years, who are now senior judges. 'There is an understanding among a very small group of judges, but those judges are significant and influential and intelligent, therefore there is a small division of the courts where people understand a great deal about the Convention.' He points out that Lord Bingham, appointed this year to be the senior Law Lord, and Lord Woolf, the new Lord Chief Justice, were both advocates of incorporation of the ECHR and have a strong interest in human rights.

Keir Starmer predicts that the impact of incorporation will come in two stages: in the first the courts will be asked to clarify a host of mismatches between the provisions of the Convention and existing law, most of which will be trivial. 'Because the government hasn't taken it seriously so far, there will be a series of irritating cases that will clog things up for a while.' But the real deeper impact will be that under the Act all public authorities will have to go about their decision making in a different way.

They will have to think, are we interfering with the Convention rights, and if we are, is what we are doing justifiable under the Convention and in particular can we show that what we are doing is necessary and proportionate? Now that is a new framework in which decisions are going to have to be taken. Forget litigation – that is the real change, the culture change, and when we look back after five or ten years we will say, that was the real difference.

Sarah Spencer also believes the long-term impact of the Human Rights Act will be much wider than generally imagined; it will require a new culture from public authorities such as schools, hospitals and prisons, and the government has not been vigorous enough in promoting this:

The Human Rights Act started life as a legal tidying-up measure in a way. It was 'Bringing Rights Home', it was a sort of lawyers' Bill and not seen as something that was going to have a broad effect on education, health, and the environment. As the lawyers have gone through it, there has been a process of realizing that this is bigger than any of us had first realized because of the profound impact. It is actually about a cultural shift, first of all in public authorities who have to think convention principles in everything they do.

Spencer wants the Human Rights Act to go further, creating a new atmosphere in which young people will be encouraged to see human rights as part of citizenship. But she feels the Labour government has undersold one of its most radical achievements:

It is a shift away from the communitarian anti-rights agenda they had before they came into power. But the message has not got across to the rest of government.

The Home Secretary makes speeches, but you don't hear the Prime Minister saying, this is one of the proudest things we have done, this is at the heart of our agenda. You are not yet hearing the Health Secretary saying, this is important for people in psychiatric care.

A LISTENING MINISTER?

The legal and human rights experts whom I interviewed praise Jack Straw for his readiness to listen to their concerns, but they all have reservations about his approach to human rights. Firstly, they are dubious about his strong emphasis on linking rights in the ECHR with responsibilities and duties. Secondly, they feel Straw has undermined civil liberties with a whole range of new anti-crime laws, some of which they predict will turn out to be incompatible with the ECHR, despite his assurances to the contrary. These include attempts to limit the right to trial by jury in certain cases, anti-terrorism laws, new powers to snoop on use of the Internet, legislation to stop football hooligans travelling abroad, and anti-social behaviour orders against noisy neighbours. The government has tended to gloss over the potential problems with such laws in parliament by arguing that the police and the courts will have to interpret them in the light of the convention. But John Wadham says: 'This is missing a trick. Parliament should be safeguarding our rights too. We shouldn't be relying on police officers or the courts or the prosecution to protect our rights.'[12] Wadham told me the Labour government's eagerness to consult outside groups was in sharp contrast to the habits of its Conservative predecessor:

The new Labour government had a different approach to NGOs and pressure groups and was much more transparent in its workings, much more open to talking to people. It was very significant. I went to the Home Office more times in the first six months than in the last six years of the previous administration. And at the beginning they and civil servants and police officers were desperate to know about the European Convention because of the new policy on human rights. So we had access, not just to government directly but to many other people who wanted to know where we thought Labour would be going on human rights. And there were some Bills going through at that stage where we had a significant influence, including the Human Rights Act. Although we didn't get everything we wanted, we did influence its make-up quite considerably at the edges. Now as civil servants have got more up to speed and have had more contact with ministers themselves, we have had less contact and that is inevitable. That is no surprise.

Wadham sees the Human Rights Act as the most important development in protecting human rights for hundreds of years, but he knows very well that Labour has other fish to fry:

But separately the Labour government has a tough-on-crime agenda and these two things clash, and for Jack Straw and others often the tough-on-crime approach wins, for a variety of reasons, including just not wanting to be outflanked by the Tories and not wanting to lose the next election. So it is about votes. It is not *only* about votes, they are not *that* cynical. There are things which I just don't understand, like the erosion of the right to jury trial, because Straw opposed that on two occasions, once when he was in opposition and once when he was in government. He has changed his mind... The flagship approach of this government was really the Crime and Disorder Act where they wanted to change the nature of disorder generally, to noisy neighbours and 'neighbours from hell'. Even there they bent the rules on human rights. We told them before the election, and we had seminars before the election saying, 'We think you have got it wrong.'

Wadham points out that Straw's controversial anti-social behaviour orders, which require only a civil standard of proof against hooligans and louts, have been hardly used by local authorities; he says he is 'surprised and disappointed' by the plans to limit trial by jury, and by the 'unnecessary and draconian' provisions of Straw's new Prevention of Terrorism Act 2000. This measure followed an earlier anti-terrorism Bill rushed through parliament in 1998 after the Omagh bombing, at a time when virtually none of the MPs recalled from their summer holidays would take the political risk of speaking out against it:

That was the nadir. That was when we realized how bad this government was going to be. One provision relates to convicting people, virtually on the evidence of a police officer, that they were members of a proscribed group. It's wrong in principle to believe the evidence of a police officer alone, and proscription has had virtually no effect in Northern Ireland. We have always said it is wrong in principle. If people have done things or committed criminal offences or

Home Secretary Jack Straw lines up with the police against liberals who criticise his attitude to civil rights. Copyright © Steve Bell, 2000.

attempted to do so, they should be prosecuted for those. Membership of an organization, if they haven't done anything, shouldn't be an offence. Already the law allows people who are aiding and abetting someone else to be committing the offence itself. So it is unnecessary, it is not used, and the evidential change was draconian. But they slipped in the same Bill something entirely unconnected, to make it an offence to conspire here to do things abroad. This was nothing to do with Omagh, didn't have to be discussed then, and it was rushed through. I came back from holiday and it was all happening. It was just unbelievable. And we didn't have any ability to lobby people and they didn't have any ability to talk to us or anyone else about what it meant. And when people say to me, parliamentary sovereignty is important, parliament is the guardian of our rights, I say, look at that, because that is the example where it is most difficult, where there is a bomb, and we need people to sit back and say, 'What are we doing here?' And parliamentarians, I am afraid, won't do that.

Under the new anti-terrorism laws people involved in protests against genetically modified crops or new roads could be treated as terrorists, according to Wadham, who is also unhappy about possible plans to detain people diagnosed with untreatable serious personality disorders, even if they have committed no crime. He believes the Human Rights Act will help prevent the worst excesses of such measures by providing a floor for basic rights:

Personally I like Jack Straw a lot, he gives me time to listen to what I have got to say and he can then make his own decision. As a pressure group you can't ask for more than that. So I have got a lot of time for him. But he has a view about what is right and wrong, and he won't be told that there are certain principles in the Convention.

Ann Owers of Justice sees a historic problem in the structure of the Home Office, with its law-and-order priorities as well as its responsibility for civil rights:

There is a problem always with the Home Office. So much of the Home Office's remit is a policing/enforcement remit – police, prisons, immigration, public order, all of those things which are essentially negative. Yet out of the Home Office also comes the race relations stuff, the Roy Jenkins reforms, that all came out of the

Home Office, so there is always more than slight schizophrenia. Like all home secretaries he (Straw) is subject to an immense number of conflicts and some very high-profile decisions which can go wrong very publicly and very dramatically, probably very much more so than other ministers. But I do think there is an unresolved conflict within the Home Office in terms of the Human Rights Act. I think there are certainly a large number of civil servants within the Home Office who would not have advised the government to pass this Act at all, and who are very aware that it can restrict what the government wants to do. They are aware from their own history as civil servants that we have in the UK a very robust legal profession, very robust public lawyers who are very good at using the law to their advantage … There are a number of recent laws where we would have clear question marks as to whether they will in the end be seen to be compliant with the Human Rights Act … I think two things could happen when those laws come before the courts. One is that the courts could declare that the legislation is incompatible with the Human Rights Act, and that just throws the thing back to government, and government then has to do something about it. It can just say, 'Tough, see you in Strasbourg, we disagree.' The other thing that could happen is that the Human Rights Act places on the courts a very strong duty to try if they possibly can to interpret legislation in the light of the Act. Legislation comes before parliament with a little stamp from the Home Secretary saying it is compatible with the Human Rights Act, and the courts are entitled to say, well, he meant it to be. How can we strain the meaning of these words to try to make it compliant? On the face of it they don't seem to be, but we are assuming that he meant them to be. So in the end they could interpret the law in a different way from what the Home Secretary thought when he was putting it to parliament.

THE STRAW DOCTRINE: RIGHTS AND RESPONSIBILITIES

Jack Straw's speeches on the human rights issue have a particular slant which is quite different from Derry Irvine's. At times he sounds like a fully paid-up Hampstead liberal: 'The test in a democracy is not whether one accords rights to people with whom one agrees, but to those with whom one profoundly disagrees. I defend their rights,' he remarked during the Commons debate on the second reading of the Prevention of

Terrorism Bill, which he said had been subject to 'wilful misunderstanding' by its critics. On the Human Rights Act, Straw sounds less radical than Irvine; his speeches show him to be a communitarian rather than a liberal, and a strong believer in the power of the state to do good. Like Tony Blair, he always stresses that rights cannot be divorced from responsibilities and duties. This emphasis on duties as the source of rights is reflected in the Labour party's constitution and is a key part of New Labour doctrine. But it also has a pedigree. It was one of the principles in Stalin's 1936 Soviet Constitution which Sidney and Beatrice Webb most admired.

The Webbs were particularly impressed with the constitutional principle that 'he who does not work shall not eat' which they described as the duty *not to be a parasite.* They also liked the tough language against spies, deserters and traitors, noting approvingly that after the Nazi invasion there were no quislings or fifth column in the Soviet Union, because all undesirable citizens had been 'dealt with in the much abused Moscow trials of the Thirties'. The Webbs commented: 'Perhaps it is this unique emphasis on the *Duties of Man* as a necessary complement to the *Rights of Man* which is the peculiar characteristic of the Soviet Constitution of 1936. It explains why the defeated, starving, illiterate inhabitants of Tsarist Russia became in the course of 20 years the relatively comfortable and cultured, healthy and skilled, courageous and adventurous Soviet people of 1941–42; who alone among the inhabitants of the European continent have been able to resist and beat back the mighty military machine of Hitler's Germany, intent on the conquest and enslavement of the world.'[13]

Straw set out the broadest statement of his beliefs in a lecture in October 1999.[14] He said the government's constitutional reforms were designed to create a new relationship between the citizen and the state. But the reasons he gave had nothing in common with the goals of constitutional reformers such as John Smith, who in 1993 proclaimed in his lecture to Charter88 that the rights Labour was seeking to protect through a Human Rights Act were 'those of the individual against the state'. The Act 'is not designed to alter existing legal relations between individuals, but to protect individuals from state power,' Smith said. Irvine's speeches four years later gave much the same message.

> ❝ It was the selfish and ungrateful citizens who needed reforming, not the state. ❞

Straw, by contrast, proclaimed that the goal of constitutional reform was not to protect individuals or to expand their civic liberties; it was the selfish and ungrateful citizens who needed reforming, not the state:

We wanted to change the culture of a society where people have been encouraged to take what they can for themselves without contributing to the common good. Some people trace the roots of that culture selfishness back to the so-called 'me' generation of the 1960s. I think that's a fair point. But part of the poison also came from the Conservatives during the 1980s. They kept on telling us that the state and all its works was a bad thing; that the state was inimical to personal freedom and rights; that the only thing that mattered was individuals and their families.

'Rights don't exist in a vacuum,' Straw said, quoting a sentence from Tom Paine's *Rights of Man* to prove his point: 'Whatever is my right as a man is also the right of another, and it becomes my duty to guarantee as well as to possess.' He said the Human Rights Act 'defines and legitimizes responsibilities', arguing that '… the balances and limitations in the ECHR amount to a statement of duties and responsibilities'. Duties and rights should go together, Straw argued. People brawling in the streets on Saturday nights and shouting obscenities were the legacy of 'selfish, dutiless rights' without responsibilities, he said. Such rights formed no part of any coherent moral or social order. Straw seemed to be suggesting that those looking for extra rights from the ECHR would be disappointed:

When the Human Rights Act was going through parliament, I referred several times to building a culture of rights and responsibilities. Some people misheard me. They didn't hear the word 'responsibilities'. They just heard the 'rights' bit. They thought I was making some kind of government pledge to mint new rights. The Human Rights Act isn't about minting new rights in any case. We have had the ECHR for 50 years.

Speaking to civil servants a few weeks later, Straw seemed keen to dampen down expectations of the Human Rights Act as a major constitutional change: 'It's ridiculous to talk about incorporating the ECHR as if it's going to lead the UK out of the dark ages into some glorious European enlightenment.'[15] Far from lagging behind other countries, the English had been ahead of the field, he argued, contrasting England's Glorious Revolution of 1688 and Scotland's Claim of Right in 1689 with later bloody upheavals in France and Russia and America, which were 'reactionary in effect, if not intention'. Straw argued that where human rights were concerned, Britain had always been 'top nation'. 'This is the country of *habeas corpus*,' he declared, proclaiming that the United Kingdom had abolished slavery a century before the United States. The ECHR was a British export to Europe and our ideas had been copied all over the world. There was not a word in the speech about the long run of embarrassing defeats for the British government in Strasbourg which had left it isolated (Irvine's argument) and led to the decision to incorporate.

Straw poured scorn on lawyers who were planning to 'use the Human Rights Act like a bottle of gin – the best of all possible pick-me-ups. But too much gin can give you a nasty headache'. He also took aim at what he called 'wannabe rights' such as 'slavery and forced labour is unlawful so the council can't make me put my wheelie bin on the pavement'. Violation of a right and legitimate interference with a right were not the same thing, he argued: 'The culture of rights and responsibilities we need to build is not about giving the citizen a new cudgel with which to beat the state. That's the old-fashioned, individualistic, libertarian idea that gave the whole rights movement a bad and selfish name.' The goal of the Act was not to create 'a litigious collection of individuals and interest groups who see rights as a free good and the Human Rights Act simply as a means of enforcing the rights of individuals against public authorities. The culture we need is one which is *not* always soft when an individual's rights are in play'.

MOTHER'S MILK

I asked Straw if it was not somewhat tricky to make rights contingent on duties and responsibilities. He dismissed the argument, saying this was something which he had been '... taught with my mother's milk when I did first-year jurisprudence at Leeds ... The most obvious example is, you lose your right to liberty the moment you stop respecting other people's rights and damage their property. Your liberty is taken away from you ... If you are saying responsibilities should not be used to diminish people's rights, then I entirely agree with you.'

All the human rights experts to whom I spoke were uneasy about Straw's interpretation. As John Wadham put it: 'I'm not saying that responsibilities aren't important, but the Convention has nothing to do with responsibilities. All the responsibilities that the Convention produces are the responsibilities of public authorities, of the state. It doesn't go beyond that.' He linked Straw's somewhat defensive interpretation of the Human Rights Act to the government's fear of being accused by rightwing newspapers of introducing a charter for criminals:

That is precisely not what the Convention is about. That is the subtext of the argument, but in fact it has got nothing to do with the Convention. Take the two boys who killed Jamie Bulger. Some people think that they are the wickedest people in the country. Even those people have the same rights as I have, as somebody accused of shoplifting, because that is what the Convention means. Human rights are universal and apply to everyone, irrespective of what they have done or haven't done … The issues for human rights are the hard issues. You don't need a Human Rights Act if it is just respectable criminals you are dealing with, because they will be treated properly by the police, they will be treated properly by the courts. It is the people like sex offenders. There is no group in this country apart from us and maybe NACRO[16] who will get up and say sex offenders should have rights too.

Sarah Spencer is equally worried by Straw's emphasis on duties: 'If you murder someone you lose your right to liberty, but very importantly you don't lose *all* of your rights. You still shouldn't be subject to degrading treatment. What I mean by rights and responsibilities is that for us to enjoy our rights it imposes responsibilities on others.'

Straw's minimalist approach to the Human Rights Act now seems to be official government policy; Irvine's more radical view of the law protecting newly empowered citizens against the government no longer seems to be flavour of the month in Downing Street, if it ever was. The Straw approach is reflected in much current legislation, notably the Prevention of Terrorism Act, which Amnesty International has warned will create a twin-track system of justice in which people suspected of terrorist offences will have fewer rights than criminals. Human rights advocates such as Ann Owers and Francesca Klug still believe there is a case for following up the Human Rights Act with a home-grown British Bill of Rights when the time is ripe. Straw disagrees; when I asked him about the possibility, he replied: 'You've got one. It is called the Human Rights Act.' It is hard to escape the conclusion that after marching in step over the introduction of the Human Rights Act, New Labour and old-fashioned Hampstead liberals appear to be drifting further apart. One small symptom of this was an attack on the 'extreme politics' of liberals and their 'slavish devotion to the European Convention on Human Rights' by David Lipsey.[17] Anthony Lester, the Liberal Democrat peer who led the long campaign to incorporate the Convention, pleaded guilty as charged to being a 'Hampstead liberal':

The political values of most members of Tony Blair's cabinet, which Lipsey expresses, embody moral populism and a weak and confused commitment to personal liberty and to accountable government. Those have been enduring characteristics of the Labour party, both 'old' and 'new' … My fear is that the government's manifest lack of liberalism (except for homosexual law reform) is undermining basic civil liberties of the individual and of minorities in this country. Mr Blair's 'project' to unite the centre left in British politics will fail if he and his government continue to reject liberal democratic principles.[18]

The evidence from Blair's leaked April 2000 memo backs up Lester's diagnosis of a prime minister suffering from 'moral populism'. Blair's main fear was revealed as appearing to be out of touch with 'gut British instincts', and his main desire was to be personally associated with 'eye-catching initiatives' to persuade people of the opposite. These initiatives were left undefined, but appeared to involve lowering sentences for those convicted of vigilante justice (the Tony Martin case), sending home as many asylum seekers as possible, jailing more burglars, confiscating criminal assets, locking up street muggers, boosting the family, and increasing defence spending. Human rights were omitted, presumably because they were not seen as relevant to 'gut British instincts'.

Blair's annual party conference speech at the end of September 2000, just a week before the Human Rights Act came into force, also failed to mention it, though he called at length for sweeping new powers for the police and the abandonment of what he called the 'Queensberry rules' against organized crime. Whether Sidney and Beatrice Webb would have applauded is unclear, but the Chinese politburo would certainly have smiled their approval.

NOTES

[1] *Independent*, 12 July 2000.

[2] *Guardian*, 18 April 2000.

[3] Speech to the Law Society, 10 December 1997.

[4] See *The Times* of 28 July 2000 for the Blair-Gould memos.

[5] *Guardian*, 18 July 2000.

[6] *Counsel*, December 1999.

[7] Brazier, Rodney (1998) *Constitutional Reform. Reshaping the British political system*, Oxford University Press, 2nd edition, p 144.

[8] Speech to conference on a Bill of Rights for the United Kingdom, University College London, 4 July 1997.

[9] Speech to conference on a Bill of Rights for the United Kingdom, University College London, 4 July 1997.

[10] 'The development of human rights in Britain under an incorporated convention on human rights,' The Tom Sargant Memorial Lecture, 16 December 1997, Law Society Hall, London.

[11] Speech to Civil Service College, 9 December 1999.

[12] From remarks at a Labour party conference fringe meeting, September 2000.

[13] Webb, Beatrice and Webb, Sidney (1944) *Soviet Communism: A New Civilisation*, London, Longmans, 3rd edition, p 437.

[14] Speech to the Constitution Unit, University College London, 27 October 1999.

[15] Speech to Civil Service College, 9 December 1999.

[16] National Association for the Care and Resettlement of Offenders.

[17] *The Times*, 27 July 2000.

[18] *The Times*, 3 August 2000.

Blair's first team: The new Labour cabinet meets for the first time on 8 May 1997. On the right of Tony Blair is Cabinet Secretary Sir Robin Butler, who eventually knuckled under to Blair's insistence on appointing Jonathan Powell as his Chief of Staff. this set a new precedent by making a political appointee rather than a civil servant the top official in Downing Street

REUTERS

The rose garden style: Tony Blair addresses his cabinet on the lawn of 10 Downing Street on 30 July 1998 after publication of his government's first annual report

REUTERS: KIERAN DOHERTY

A safe pair of hands: Home Secretary Jack Straw outside Wormwood Scrubs prison in London on
6 September 1999. Straw's department had played a crucial role in constitutional reform, taking charge of
human rights legislation, freedom of information, political party funding and other issues   REUTERS

You can't wave that banner here: police prevent campaigners for a free Tibet from demonstrating peacefully outside Greenwich Royal Observatory during a visit by Chinese president Jiang Zemin on 20 October 1999. The police subsequently admitted they had acted unlawfully after lawyers for the protesters invoked the government's human rights act

REUTERS: PAUL HACKETT

Great to be here: Tony Blair sticks mostly to pleasantries during an interview with Chinese television in Beijing's forbidden city on October 1998, saying ideological disputes are over and praising Chinese leaders as fellow modernisers

REUTERS: NATALIE BEHRING

Lords and commons: The Lord Chancellor, Lord Irvine of Lairg, and Speaker of the House of Commons Betty Boothroyd addressing delegates to an international conference in the Palace of Westminister on 5 May 1999 to mark the 50th anniversary of the Council of Europe. Irvine has always strongly defended his combined roles as a member of the cabinet, head of the judiciary in England and Wales and presiding officer of the Lords   REUTERS

Dignified or efficient? The Queen reads out the government's programme for the year ahead on 17 November 1999 in the House of Lords, a few days after the departure of the bulk of the hereditary peers. Under Blair, Labour has switched to wanting a largely appointed upper house, arguing that electing its members would undermine democracy   REUTERS

Save the pound: a protester reminds Tony Blair during a by-election campaign trip to Eddisbury on 21 July 1999 that his goal of taking Britain into the European single currency is still widely unpopular   REUTERS: DAN CHUNG

Not In the coronation oath: The Queen, dutiful as ever, joins hands with Tony Blair and Prince Philip to sing Auld Lang Syne at midnight on 31 December 1999 for the opening of the Millennium Dome

Reuters

10

A RATHER SUSCEPTIBLE
CHANCELLOR

'The British constitution, largely unwritten, is firmly based upon the separation of powers' – Lord Irvine, speech in House of Lords, 5 June 1996

'In this country, our constitution does not embody a full separation of powers' – Lord Irvine, speech to Third Worldwide Common Law Judiciary Conference, 5 July 1999

'Ah, my Lords, it is indeed painful to have to sit upon a woolsack which is stuffed with such thorns as these!' – W.S. Gilbert, *Iolanthe*

IT BEGAN AS AN OBSCURE PLANNING dispute about a shed on the Channel Island of Guernsey. Flower grower Richard 'Rosie' McGonnell had bought the Calais Vinery glasshouses in 1982. By the mid-1980s, facing business difficulties, he began living in a packing shed in the middle of the site. When he asked the Island Development Committee to give him permission for change of use, 'I got a letter back saying, effectively, "Get lost".' He was taken to the magistrates' court and fined and his final appeal in Guernsey's Royal Court failed in 1995. Then a local lawyer suggested he take his case to the European Court of Human Rights in Strasbourg on the grounds that he had not had a fair trial. 'I felt I had been harassed,' he said. 'All I wanted was to be left alone.' By the time the European Court of Human Rights found in his favour in a judgement on 8 February 2000, the Guernsey flower grower had long ago left his uncomfortable shed and was working for a Dutch company in Kenya.[1]

The real importance of the outcome was not in its impact on the fate of McGonnell or his packing shed but in its implications for the constitutional position of Tony Blair's Lord Chancellor, Derry Irvine. McGonnell's lawyers argued successfully that he had been denied a hearing before an independent and impartial tribunal because the Guernsey Bailiff, Sir Graham Dorey, who turned down his appeal, had earlier presided over the island's legislature, the States, when it approved the zoning plan that reserved the Calais Vinery site for horticulture. Because of the close parallels between the position of the Bailiff and the Lord Chancellor, the Strasbourg decision could prove a catalyst for reform of an office that dates back almost 1,000 years.

It is a recent twist in a long-running battle over the future of the senior judiciary, in which the Labour government has so far lined up with the forces of conservatism against radical reform. The controversy, which has so far been confined to the legal world, involves a key constitutional principle – separation of powers. But politicians would be unwise to dismiss it for good as a 'chattering classes' issue that will never be discussed in the bar of the Dog and Duck. As the case of General Augusto Pinochet showed, legal arguments can quickly become political. Already the waves of change are starting to lap around the buckled and stockinged feet of the Lord High Chancellor of Great Britain, who combines legislative, executive and judicial roles in a way which many senior lawyers now regard as indefensible. The retired Master of the Rolls Lord Donaldson, in evidence in 1999 to the Royal Commission on the House of Lords, dismissed the case for the present arrangements in blunt terms:

> 66 Already the waves of change are starting to lap around the buckled and stockinged feet of the Lord High Chancellor of Great Britain, who combines legislative, executive and judicial roles in a way which many senior lawyers now regard as indefensible. 99

> Such an extraordinary aggregation, as contrasted with separation, of powers could never have lasted so long unless it was known only to a politically conscious few, who accepted that Lord Chancellors could and did wear three hats divided from each other by lightweight Chinese walls. I do not believe that that situation any longer exists either factually or as a matter of public belief.

In the view of Donaldson, the McGonnell case is crucial to the future of the office now held by Irvine: 'The similarity between the position of the Bailiff and the Lord Chancellor is obvious.' He argues that the conflict of interest is inherent in the job and will not be solved by Irvine picking and choosing carefully the cases on which he will exercise his right to sit as a judge: 'I think that the real vice of the situation is not the occasional involvement of the Lord Chancellor in the hearing of an appeal but that the nature of his office necessarily involves a breach of the basic principle of a separation of powers.' Donaldson believes that the Lord Chancellor should divest himself of any judicial role, actual or titular, and become a Secretary of State for Justice, with the Lord Chief Justice becoming head of the judiciary in England and Wales.

CHANGE IN THE COURTS

Pressure for change at the top of the judicial system in the United Kingdom has been building slowly, as courts and judges have gradually assumed a more prominent political role over the past 30 years. Legislation on race and sex discrimination, and the development of employment law have brought the judges more and more into the forefront of social change. Judicial review of the actions of the executive has become more and more commonplace. In the view of legal scholar Robert Stevens, Master of Pembroke College, Oxford: 'Perhaps nothing changed the judges more than the long period of Conservative rule between 1979 and 1997.' The weakness of opposition in parliament left a gap in control of the executive. 'It was into that vacuum that the judges increasingly stepped, as some of them even hinted that they would help "remedy the democratic deficit".'[2] Gradually the old perception, dating back to the days of the reactionary Lord Goddard, of judges as a bulwark of the conservative status quo has become obsolete; it is now the courts, not parliament, which are seen as the best protection for rights and liberties. Some of these changes since the 1950s have been attributed to the way activist judges such as Lord Denning, Lord Reid, Lord Wilberforce and Lord Diplock stuck their necks out in a series of landmark judgements. The old maxim that judges would never tread on the toes of the executive no longer holds good. Perhaps the largest single factor in this shift to a more activist and political judiciary was British entry to the European Community, which led to the courts being obliged to uphold European legislation over UK domestic law, thus driving another nail into the coffin of the Diceyan doctrine of the supremacy of parliament. As Stevens explains it: '... the judges found that they were, *de facto*, making decisions about the constitutionality of British statutes.' One prominent judge, Sir Stephen Sedley, even argued controversially that Diceyan parliamentary sovereignty was gradually being replaced by a new kind of 'bipolar sovereignty' of the Crown-in-Parliament and the Crown in the courts, making ministers answerable to both.

Even without such a doctrine, judges during the 1990s regularly used the process of judicial review to hold the government to account when it exceeded its powers. Courts rapped the Conservative Home Secretary over the knuckles for his policies on sentencing, immigration and prisons, while the Foreign Secretary suffered the same fate over foreign aid.

Since 1997 pressures for change have intensified, largely as a result of the Labour government's constitutional changes, although the high-octane public rows between ministers and judges which marked the Conservative years have been missing. The absence of such disputes should not be taken as evidence that all has gone quiet, however. Devolution has brought a new role for senior judges, as yet untested, in settling disputes over the powers of the new devolved assemblies through the little-known Judicial Committee of the Privy Council, which up to now has mostly judged appeals from the Commonwealth. The Human Rights Act, as explained in the previous chapter, has greatly expanded the political role of the courts, which will now be able to declare laws incompatible with the ECHR and flag them up for parliament to change them. Meanwhile, the long-postponed process of reforming the House of Lords has opened up a debate on whether the upper chamber should continue its role as the ultimate court of appeal or be replaced by a properly constituted supreme court. Finally, the high-profile battle of former Chilean head of state General Augusto Pinochet for immunity from extradition to Spain in 1998–99 has shone an unwelcome spotlight on the institutional inadequacies of the Lords as a final appeal court.

FORCES OF CONSERVATISM

> **Far from leading the campaign to modernize the United Kingdom's antiquated judicial arrangements, Tony Blair's Labour government – so quick to tell the rest of the country to modernize itself – has been staking out the trenches to defend the 19th-century status quo.**

What is intriguing in this debate is that far from leading the campaign to modernize the United Kingdom's antiquated judicial arrangements, Tony Blair's Labour government – so quick to tell the rest of the country to modernize itself – has been staking out the trenches to defend the 19th-century status quo. 'Tony Blair attacks the forces of conservatism and it seems to me that in the reorganization of the judiciary the chief conservative force is his Lord Chancellor,' Robert Stevens told me. This paradox is worth exploring in greater detail.

The present incumbent of the Lord Chancellor's office, Lord Irvine of Lairg, who once famously compared himself to his predecessor Cardinal Wolsey, is the most powerful Lord Chancellor of modern times. Alexander 'Derry' Irvine, son of a modest Scottish builder, not only chairs several cabinet committees and steers the government's constitutional reform agenda but is personally close to Tony Blair, having given the future Labour party leader his first toehold in the legal profession as a pupil barrister. The story of how Tony Blair met and married his fellow pupil Cherie Booth under the stern gaze of the man who later dubbed himself 'Cupid QC' is too well known to need retelling. Once overheard by Roy Jenkins addressing the Prime Minister as 'Young Blair' to his face,[3] Irvine's personal authority has stamped itself on most, but not all, of the areas of government for which he has been responsible. Only his lack of political experience and his unelected status have acted as curbs on the role in government of this 'brusque, arrogant and irascible' barrister.[4]

Bill Rodgers, leader of the Liberal Democrat peers, told me that Irvine was the real Labour leader in the Lords rather than Margaret Jay:

> He has been a much more integrated Lord Chancellor. Lord Chancellors normally stand on the outside of government and make very little contribution. Irvine has been much more a party figure and integrated with policymaking. Clearly the Weatherill amendment was negotiated by him and not by the Leader of the House. The personal relationship he has to Blair is quite unlike that of any prime minister I can think of or any Lord Chancellor I can think of. Personal relations matter. I would more readily go to him than to Margaret Jay. And I think Margaret Jay knows that the Lord Chancellor is the big boss really. Although there are areas that the Lord Chancellor doesn't want anything to do with. On a crucial constitutional issue Margaret Jay's advice would be taken, but it would be the Lord Chancellor who decided, not her.

WALLPAPER WARS

Unlike most Lord Chancellors, who have glided through the legal and political corridors of power largely unnoticed by the press, Irvine has frequently found himself in the newspapers, in whose columns his name has become indelibly linked with expensive Victorian wallpaper. I remember sitting in a Commons committee room in March 1998 listening to him defend the £650,000 refurbishment of the Lord Chancellor's apartments, around one-tenth of it on wallpaper. As a fellow admirer of that wonderfully dotty Victorian Augustus Welby Pugin, who designed

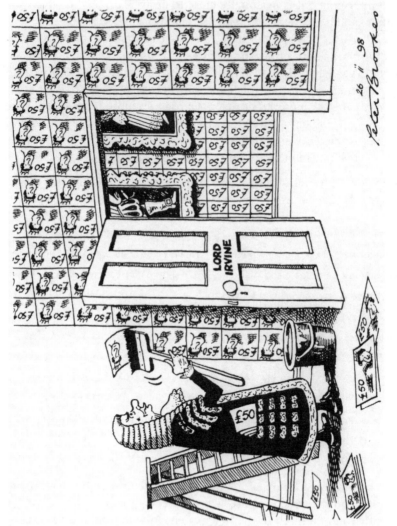

The Lord Chancellor Derry Irvine is immortalised not for his role in the Human Rights Act but for his expensive taste in wallpaper. Copyright © Peter Brooks, 1998.

the interiors of the Palace of Westminster, I had a sneaking sympathy for Irvine's case. But the hearing before the Commons Public Administration Committee gave convincing evidence of his lack of political guile. He offered to 'seize the wallpaper charge straight on the chin' and told the committee: 'We are not talking about something down in a DIY store which may collapse after a year or two.'

> **In the House of Commons it is quite in order never to have heard of Augustus Welby Pugin, but never to have heard of B&Q is a capital offence.**

When one MP asked sarcastically for advice on what to avoid when shopping at B&Q, Irvine looked flummoxed. In the House of Commons it is quite in order never to have heard of Augustus Welby Pugin, but never to have heard of B&Q is a capital offence. Irvine's disastrous press coverage the next day reflected his ignorance of this well-established constitutional convention.

A LEGAL REFORMER?

Irvine's wallpaper wars have tended to distract attention from his desire to go down in history as a legal reformer for his role in changing the legal aid system and in incorporating the European Convention on Human Rights into United Kingdom law. The first of these lies outside the scope of this book, but as we have seen in an earlier chapter, he was one of the architects of the government's radical Human Rights Act. This major Bill, although introduced by Irvine in the Lords, was largely drafted by the Home Office and Jack Straw. Irvine's close ties with his Glasgow University friend John Smith and his successor Tony Blair gave him a large input on policy while in opposition, although he was the only shadow minister with a constitutional brief who could not find time to meet the Constitution Unit think tank at University College London before the 1997 election. 'Derry was not interested in what they were going to do if they got in. He was busy making a pile at the Bar,' according to one well-placed witness.

But the Irvine reform agenda, as was clear even before the 1997 election, was carefully designed to rule out any threat to the position of the Lord Chancellor himself. The idea of replacing the office with a continental-style Minister of Legal Administration responsible to the House of Commons had been Labour policy in the early 1990s, but dropped off the agenda as soon as Irvine took over the job of shadow Lord Chancellor. Irvine's pre-election speeches were notable less for their radicalism than for the way in which he reminded judges they should not challenge the supremacy of parliament. As David Pannick QC noted drily in *The Times* in November 1995: 'To paraphrase Dr Johnson, when a man knows that he is soon to be a minister, it concentrates his mind wonderfully ... No government welcomes scrutiny of its activities by an independent judiciary.'

What has become apparent since 1997 is that while life in the courts after Irvine is going to be different in many ways because of reforms in the legal aid system, in civil law and in criminal law, his reforming zeal has carefully bypassed the bodies at the apex of the legal pyramid, particularly the House of Lords. This is because any questioning of its role would inevitably open up a discussion about Irvine's own three jobs as a cabinet minister, head of the judiciary in England and Wales, and Speaker of the House of Lords. While it would theoretically be possible to reform the office of Lord Chancellor while leaving the judicial role of the House of Lords intact, it is widely accepted that the reverse operation would not be possible. Any reform of the Law Lords' membership of the upper house would leave the Lord Chancellor isolated as the only person remaining as a judge and a legislator.

THREE HATS

Before considering the rising pressures for change, an explanation is required of the three roles which Irvine combines. The Lord Chancellor is at his most visible in the first of his three jobs, as a legislator. For half an hour or so after lunch he presides most days over questions in the House of Lords, sitting in his full-bottomed wig on the red Woolsack, sometimes donning and doffing a black tricorn hat at formal moments. He also presides over votes. This job, quite unlike that of Speaker of the House of Commons, is non-controversial and largely ceremonial – in Bagehot's terms, more dignified than efficient. Because the House of Lords organizes and disciplines itself, the Lord Chancellor plays no role in selecting speakers, interpreting the rules of procedure or deciding the order of business. The sight of him shuffling between the government front bench and the Woolsack to announce the result of a vote between 'contents' and 'not contents' can be placed among the many harmless historical anomalies of the British constitutional system. Those who want to see a greater separation of powers and believe that in a modern democracy symbols should reflect reality will disagree. Those who look at the Lord Chancellor's annual salary of more than £140,000 will argue that presiding over the Lords is a waste of his highly paid time.

Irvine wears his second and most important hat as a member of the executive. In formal precedence as well as in pay, the Lord Chancellor ranks above the Prime Minister as the senior member of the government. On state occasions he comes just after the Archbishop of Canterbury but before the Archbishop of York. Despite holding a title that goes back to the 11th century, he is not the only government minister responsible for legal matters. While the Attorney-General and Solicitor-General are the government's legal advisers, the Lord Chancellor operates an uneasy division of executive responsibility with the Home Secretary, an arrangement which Professor Rodney Brazier of Manchester University says would not be acceptable abroad: 'No modern state which wished to establish responsibility for such things as the administration of justice, public order, the treatment of offenders, law reform and the appointment of the judiciary would follow the British pattern and allocate those and related matters almost haphazardly between two ministers. Nor would it place each of those ministers in different chambers of the legislature, with one minister ... having for good measure judicial and parliamentary duties as well.' He describes the system as chaotic, noting that civil law reform is the business of the Lord Chancellor while criminal law reform falls to the Home Secretary, who has to balance responsibilities for law and order with the protection of minorities and civil rights: 'These ministerial dispositions have resulted in a complete lack of ministerial responsibility and accountability in a number of areas.' The split between Lord Chancellor and Home Secretary means that no one minister has clear responsibility for constitutional affairs. 'As is so often the case, ad hockery reigns: whenever a government decides to embark on a constitutional change, it makes ministerial dispositions especially for the purpose, and winds them up when that purpose has been achieved.'[5]

Even before Irvine's appointment in 1997, the role of the Lord Chancellor had been changing, with his judicial functions becoming less prominent and his executive responsibilities increasing. This was evident under his Conservative predecessor James Mackay (Lord Mackay of Clashfern), whose relations with the judiciary were often uneasy. The Lord Chancellor's Department has moved under Labour more and more into the Whitehall mainstream, and is now headed for the first time by a non-lawyer civil servant as Permanent Secretary. Irvine has played a prominent and unprecedented political role in the Blair government, sitting on ten cabinet committees and chairing several of them, although his influence has undoubtedly waned since 1997. He is a minister responsible for a large-spending department with 11,000 employees, and accountable to parliament for the administration of justice, including magistrates' courts. Although as a peer he cannot be questioned in the Commons, he now has two MPs as parliamentary secretaries to back him up and answer questions on his behalf.

THE LORD CHANCELLOR

He (the office has never been held by a woman) is head of the judiciary in England and Wales but not in Scotland and Northern Ireland. He is technically President of the Supreme Court of England and Wales, an *ex officio* judge of the Court of Appeal, and President of the Chancery Division. He is ultimately responsible for organizing judicial business in both the House of Lords and the Privy Council, but normally delegates the task of deciding who should sit on which cases to the senior Law Lord. When he sits in either court, he presides. He is also Speaker of the House of Lords, a largely ceremonial role, and carries out most of the responsibilities of a minister of justice. He sits in the cabinet and takes precedence over all other ministers, including the prime minister.

SECRET SOUNDINGS

Controversy over the role of the Lord Chancellor focuses mostly on the third of his three hats – his role as a judge. We shall look at this in more detail, but he has another critical function which is also under challenge – appointing judges and Queen's Counsel, the high-earning officer corps of the barristers' profession. At the highest level, judicial appointments are in the gift of the prime minister rather than the Lord Chancellor, but the process of 'secret soundings' is essentially the same. This traditional system has been much criticized for arranging 'jobs for the boys' under a system favouring white males from an elite group of barristers' chambers. Reformers have long advocated an independent Judicial Appointments Commission to increase the number of women and lawyers from ethnic minorities. Irvine has rejected these arguments, saying appointments are and must be made on merit rather than on any other criteria. 'I am resolutely opposed to any proposition that our courts should be sculpted to conform to any notion of social, political, gender or any other balance,' he declared in a speech to an international audience of judges in Edinburgh in July 1999.

Irvine seems for the time being to have fended off pressure for change, thanks to a report in December 1999 by Sir Leonard Peach, a former Commissioner for Public Appointments. Rather than recommending removing the power of appointment from the Lord Chancellor, the report suggested an independent commissioner to monitor the assessment and selection process and act as an ombudsman for candidates with unresolved grievances. The essential debate, however, has less to do with fairness or unfairness to individual candidates than with the Lord Chancellor's power of patronage. As Rodney Brazier says, such concentration of power in one set of hands is unhealthy. 'The patronage system at the disposal of Lord Chancellors, to put it bluntly, looks bad.'

> ❝The essential debate, however, has less to do with fairness or unfairness to individual candidates than with the Lord Chancellor's power of patronage.❞

The Human Rights Act may soon tip the balance in favour of reform, thanks to a court decision in Scotland which could be reproduced in England and Wales now the Act is fully in force. The Court of Session ruled in *Starrs and Chalmers v Procurator Fiscal* that the appointment of one-year temporary sheriffs (judges) infringed the ECHR Article 6 (1) guaranteeing the right to trial by an impartial and independent tribunal. According to David Pannick QC, the case will have important consequences for judicial appointment procedures throughout the UK. This is because the Convention jurisprudence looks at the manner of appointment, the term of office and the appearance of independence, which must be guaranteed against any legitimate doubt. Judges who are appointed directly by the executive, rather than by an intermediate body such as a Judicial Appointments Commission, must have security of tenure if they are appointed directly by the executive. According to Pannick: 'Other categories of temporary judge carrying short-term appointments and no security of tenure such as tribunal members, assistant recorders, and deputy High Court judges might find themselves challenged ... The judgement ... demonstrates how conventional British practices may fail to withstand scrutiny when tested against the standards of the European Convention.'[6]

John Wadham of the human rights group Liberty says the UK needs a system of judicial appointments which is transparent, open and advertised. He notes that the crucial factor in the case of the Scottish sheriffs was not that they were temporary but the method by which they were appointed:

It's the same in England; if you had a Judicial Appointments Commission that objection would disappear. There is no way it can be right for the Lord Chancellor to make decisions about who is a QC or who is a judge. For instance, the senior Law Lord, Lord Bingham, and the Lord Chief Justice, Lord Woolf, are appointments that I support because of their human rights record, but a different government could have thought, 'We have a Human Rights Act coming in, we don't want anybody who is too human rights, let's not promote those people.' That seems to me unacceptable. You should choose people on the basis of who is the best. Now Derry says he does that, and perhaps he genuinely does, but structurally it can't withstand the test of time.

The choice may be between abandoning the system of part-time judges or taking the appointments out of the hands of the executive and handing them over to an independent body. It may be that the government's hand will be forced if the courts rule that the existing system is incompatible with the ECHR.

THE LAST HAT

Thanks to the McGonnell case, the Lord Chancellor's third role as a judge has become extremely sensitive, raising questions over how long he will be able to follow in the footsteps of his predecessors and preside over the Appellate Committee of the House of Lords and the Judicial Committee of the Privy Council. Irvine considers the McGonnell case to be irrelevant to his position, according to his aides. The record shows that Irvine, while robustly defending his right to continue sitting, has in fact done so far less frequently than his predecessors. Since 1997 he has presided over one case in the Privy Council involving Gibraltar, and four in the House of Lords. The first of these, *Boddington v British Transport Police*, in April 1998, involved the right to smoke on a train. The smoker lost. The second, *Director of Public Prosecutions v Jones*, in March 1999, involved the right to peaceful assembly on a public road. Irvine helped decide the case in favour of demonstrators at Stonehenge who had been prosecuted for trespass. The third case, *Murray and Another v Foyle Meats*, in July 1999, involved redundancies in a Northern Ireland slaughterhouse and issues of employment law. The sacked men lost their case. In January 2000 he presided in *B v. Director of Public Prosecutions*, which involved an accusation of indecency between teenagers on a bus in Harrow. Irvine was due to sit in another case involving a death in custody but stood down in March 1999 after objections from lawyers for one of the parties – an illustration of the difficulties of his position. He told a fringe meeting at the Labour party conference in September 2000: 'Obviously I will be enormously careful never to sit in the chair in a case where the interests of the government, of the executive, are directly engaged.' This follows the practice of most modern Lord Chancellors, who have generally accepted the need to steer clear of cases where there is a direct government interest or a party political element.

But there is still a controversial grey area where the government's interests are indirectly involved. Irvine's predecessor, Mackay, drew criticism for sitting in two such cases and in particular for presiding over the landmark case of *Pepper v Hart* in 1993, an Inland Revenue case in which the House of Lords ruled – with Mackay dissenting – that judges should be able to interpret the law by referring to debates in *Hansard*. Irvine gave a spirited defence of his right to sit as a judge in a House of Lords debate in February 1999 in which the Liberal Democrat peers Anthony Lester and William Goodhart, both well-known QCs, called on him to stick to his role as a minister. Goodhart told the Lords:

I believe that the Lord Chancellor could not sit in a judicial review case involving a government department, in many cases under the Human Rights Act and certainly not in a devolution case. Plainly, it would have been wrong for him to have sat in the Pinochet case. It is strongly arguable that he should not sit in a criminal case. Maybe a Lord Chancellor would be seen as impartial in a commercial case involving two independent corporate bodies but, frankly, in my view, sitting in such a case would be a waste of his time. The problems of having a senior member of the Government sitting as a judge are so serious that I believe it is much better for the Lord Chancellor not to sit at all.

In reply, Irvine argued:

Sitting gives the Lord Chancellor a practical awareness of the development of the common law at the highest level. It enables him to assess the quality of the most senior advocates. And it is just possible that the Lord Chancellor may himself have a contribution to make. Many Lord Chancellors across the centuries have done so. I am unwilling to lay down any detailed rules because it is ever a question of judgement combined with a need to ensure that no party to an appeal could reasonably believe or suspect that the Lord Chancellor might, because of his other roles, have an interest in a specific outcome. Examples might be where the lawfulness of a decision or action by any minister or department might be at issue. In my view, however, there is no category of cases that could be labelled 'constitutional' which should be 'no-go areas' for the Lord Chancellor.

Speaking to an international law conference in Edinburgh in July 1999, Irvine explained:

Like my predecessors, I exercise my discretion not to sit where I consider it would be improper to do so. I have no doubt that any future Lord Chancellor would do likewise. Provided that the Lord Chancellor has abstained from expressing considered views on an issue coming before him judicially, and he does not sit in any case where the interests of the executive are directly engaged, there is no reason at all why he should not sit and preside judicially.[7]

Professor Diana Woodhouse of Oxford Brookes University notes that, given the choice of cases on which Irvine has presided, his definition of issues where the government has a stake is a narrow one. There are other principles at stake here than merely the choice of cases. Though the Lord Chancellor's security of tenure as a judge is guaranteed in that he can remain a Law Lord after leaving the government, some lawyers believe he is still vulnerable under the European Convention on Human Rights. Ann Owers of the legal reform group Justice says Irvine is likely to be challenged under the ECHR if he continues to sit as a judge, whatever the subject matter of the case:

He is also a member of the executive with his own government department, which is now a much more active and policy-driven government department than it was years ago. He is also an active legislator and Speaker of the House of Lords … Should he sit post 2 October, I feel there will be a challenge to it. It will be interesting to see whether he does.[8]

Inevitable questions have been raised about whether the Lord Chancellor will eventually waive his right to sit in practice while defending it in theory. Ann Owers believes it is too soon to conclude that the Lord Chancellor has heard his last case, although she believes Irvine is being very cautious, particularly in view of the McGonnell judgement. She thinks change is inevitable sooner or later, although Irvine is unlikely ever to climb down publicly:

One possibility is that it simply falls into disuse, it becomes one of those archaic practices that you look back on and say, 'My God, 100 years ago Lord Chancellors used to sit as judges, isn't that strange?' So that could happen; it simply won't be exercised and therefore it won't be an issue and won't be challenged. It is a bit like the powers the Queen theoretically has, but to use them would throw things into complete disarray.

There is pressure for change not just from legal ginger groups but from the heart of the judiciary itself, though the controversy mostly bubbles along out of public view. It appears that the Law Lords past and present are divided on the issue, with some sharing the view of Lord Donaldson that it is time for change and others happy with the status quo. It would be a mistake to imagine that all today's top judges are impatient to expel the Lord Chancellor from their midst. Lord Woolf, writing in 1998, two years before Irvine moved him from Master of the Rolls to Lord Chief Justice, gave an eloquent defence of the status quo:

As a member of the cabinet, he (the Lord Chancellor) can act as an advocate on behalf of the courts and the justice system. He can explain to his colleagues in the cabinet the proper significance of a decision which they regard as being distasteful in consequence of an application for judicial review. He can, as a member of the government, ensure that the courts are properly resourced. On the other hand, on behalf of the government he can explain to the judiciary the realities of the political situation and the constraints on the resources which they must inevitably accept. As long as the Lord Chancellor is punctilious in keeping his separate roles distinct, the separation of powers is not undermined and the justice system benefits immeasurably. The justice system is better served by having the head of the judiciary at the centre of government than it would be by having its interests represented by a Minister of Justice who would lack these other roles.[9]

Among those who have said publicly they want to change the status quo is South African-born Lord Steyn, who wrote in 1997:

On balance it seems to me that little of value would be lost if the Lord Chancellor ceased to be head of the judiciary in England ... A Lord Chancellor gives the appearance to the public of speaking as the head of the judiciary with the neutrality and impartiality so involved. The truth is quite different ... (The) Lord Chancellor is always a spokesman for the government in furtherance of its party political agenda.[10]

Lord Lloyd of Berwick, in his evidence to Wakeham, cited Irvine's leading role in promoting the Human Rights Act and the Scotland Act as reason for him not to sit in cases where judges will have to consider their meaning. He cited one past Lord Chancellor as telling his fellows: 'My Lords, I am responsible for drafting this Act, so I know what I intended; therefore I am the very last person to say what it means.' Lloyd went on to say that even in cases where the Lord Chancellor had not been involved in legislation, 'there is a strong argument for saying that a member of the executive, like the Lord Chancellor, should not also sit in judgement'. Writing before the outcome of the McGonnell case in Strasbourg, he predicted that the Lord Chancellor would be in an increasingly difficult position if the court found in favour of the Guernsey flower grower:

He is in an equally peculiar position. Clearly, as a member of the cabinet, he is part of the executive just as much as the Bailiff. Clearly, as a member of the House of Lords, he is a member of the legislature. How then can it be said that he is sufficiently impartial (in an objective sense) to sit on appeals in judicial hearings in the House of Lords?

The retired Law Lord, Lord Scarman, was one of seven prominent lawyers who argued in a submission to Wakeham on behalf of Justice that the Lord Chancellor should no longer sit as a judge, and should hand over his position as head of the judiciary in England and Wales to the Lord Chief Justice.[11] Similar views have been expressed by a number of Labour MPs, and by Ivor Richard, Labour's former leader in the Lords. He told me:

I think the time has come. The Lord Chancellor's position is totally anomalous. He straddles the three branches of government; that is too much for any man, even Cardinal Wolsey. And the idea that you have to have your senior judges sitting in the legislature is again slightly odd. I personally would be in favour of taking the judges out of the House of Lords and making a supreme court. If you want to bring retired judges in, you do it in the usual way and bring them in as crossbenchers, and they are very useful .

Professor Rodney Brazier, like Lord Steyn, argues that the Lord Chancellor's judicial and parliamentary duties 'should not obscure the fact that he is as much a departmental minister as any other member of the cabinet'. Compared with many countries, under the present system judges in the United Kingdom are relatively free of political pressures from the government. But Professor Diana Woodhouse points out that there are different definitions of judicial independence. While some judges argue it means that they should have a bigger role in running the court system, Irvine follows his predecessor Mackay in arguing that it merely means no government interference in how judges apply the law. 'Such disagreement has seriously weakened the Lord Chancellor's constitutional role as a bulwark or buffer between the judiciary and the executive and protector of judicial independence,' Woodhouse believes. Irvine argues that he is able to act as a bridge between the government and the judiciary, but for his critics this fails to answer the question of how he would act in a real crisis between the executive and the courts. When the crunch comes, can a minister bound by cabinet responsibility do anything other than protect the interests of the government of which he is a member?

For Woodhouse, the conclusion is that the Lord Chancellor 'no longer adequately fulfils his constitutional role' and his job should be handed to a proper secretary of state accountable to the House of Commons. 'The position of Lord Chancellor should therefore be abolished. His constitutional role should transfer to the Lord Chief Justice, his executive responsibilities should be undertaken by a Minister of Justice or Legal Affairs, and his appointment role by a Judicial Commission.'[12] Such a reform would of course spell the end of Derry Irvine's unelected political career as Tony Blair's Cardinal Wolsey.

A WIDER DEBATE

The arguments over whether or not Irvine should sit as a judge and whether he should still control judicial appointments have nothing to do with his personal conduct in the job;[13] they go to the heart of a wider constitutional debate over judicial independence, separation of powers, and accountability to parliament. John Wadham describes Labour's failure to consider reforming the Lord Chancellor's office as a disappointment:

Derry Irvine seems to have his heart in the right place in a lot of areas, including a case we had about the right to protest, which was decided by three votes to two in the House of Lords and Derry was in the majority for us. But nevertheless it is wrong for him to take that kind of a role. The Minister of Justice should be busy getting on with other things. So far as I understand it, he has already decided not to sit in any case where the government or public authorities are involved ... And obviously we should have a Minister of Justice responsible to the Commons, not the Lords; the Speaker of the House of Lords should be a separate person, and we should have a Judicial Appointments Commission which should be transparent and open and advertised.

With some of the Law Lords and most leading academic lawyers lining up in favour of reform, Irvine has presented historical arguments for preserving the status quo and keeping his job. At times, as in the House of Lords debate in February 1999, he seems to be putting forward a High Tory view of the British constitution which echoes 17th-century arguments for monarchical authority:

It is the nature of great offices, and the values which historically inhere in them, that they provide at least as sure a guarantee of our traditional rights and liberties as any transient constitutional text. It is the unique position which the Lord Chancellor occupies in our constitutional arrangements which provides a strong and contemporary, as well as a historic, justification for both the office itself and for the Lord Chancellor to be a professional. In our country, the legislative, the executive and the judicial branches are not equal and coordinate as in the United States of America. Parliament is the senior partner in principle and the executive is very powerful in practice. The office of Lord Chancellor has evolved as the means of ensuring judicial independence within a constitution which both concentrates supreme power in an elected legislature dominated by fierce party political warfare, and at the same time permits a powerful executive to govern day by day.

After approaching two years in office, my belief which I brought to the office of Lord Chancellor, that it stands at a critical cusp in the separation of powers, is even stronger. Through the office, the judiciary has a representative in the cabinet and the cabinet in the judiciary. Lord Chancellors must have the confidence both of their judicial and cabinet colleagues. They promote mutual understanding in order to avoid collisions at a major intersection in the separation of the powers. The protection of the judiciary from executive interference is, in my view, a high-order duty – perhaps the highest-order duty – of any Lord Chancellor. The office is a buffer between the judiciary and the executive which protects judicial independence. The executive cannot tell the judges how to decide cases, civil or criminal, nor what sentences in criminal cases to impose within the discretion conferred by parliament. Any executive is capable of being tempted, but executive interference with judicial independence must never be allowed. Freedom under the law and judicial independence are two sides of the same coin.

Irvine returned to the fray in his Edinburgh lecture in July 1999, defending his office in terms rather similar to those used by elderly Conservative peers to justify their hereditary membership of the House of Lords. The Lord Chancellorship was 'older than our parliament, older than our democratic system', he said, arguing that the ECHR's guarantee of the right to a fair trial should not be used to overturn 'long-held constitutional arrangements'. Article 6 of the Convention required a fair and impartial hearing, not a full separation of powers, Irvine said. The office of Lord Chancellor was the 'English solution' to the problem of balancing judicial independence and accountability. 'It holds the different parts together, and withstands pressure from all sides,' he argued. 'There are those who think that the time has come to dismantle the office of Lord Chancellor. They base themselves in part on a purist view of the separation of powers, which if pursued with purity would lead them to drive every cabinet minister from the House of Commons or the House of Lords,' Irvine declared. 'I am not persuaded this view is correct and I am reinforced by my experience in office. The role of the Lord Chancellor is to compensate for the fusion of powers elsewhere.'

He acknowledged that the Human Rights Act and devolution would increase the potential for controversy, but drew the opposite conclusion from his critics: 'I am clear that the only effect these changes will have on the office of Lord Chancellor is to make it more valuable and necessary than ever, as a buffer between executive and judiciary; and as a bulwark of our constitution.'

SEPARATION OF POWERS

Experts on the separation of powers agree that the principle is much less entrenched in Britain than in the United States, where the division of functions between the three branches of government – executive,

> 66 In Britain, separation of powers, applies on Mondays, Wednesdays and Fridays, but not on Tuesdays, Thursdays and Saturdays. 99

legislative and judicial – is fundamental to the constitution. In Britain separation of powers, as can be seen from the two quotations from Derry Irvine at the head of this chapter, applies on Mondays, Wednesdays and Fridays, but not on Tuesdays, Thursdays and Saturdays. The legal scholar Eric Barendt argues that Montesquieu's famous principle 'has never really been taken seriously in the United Kingdom'.[14] Because British ministers sit in the legislature, as they do in Germany and Ireland though not in France or the Netherlands, there is an effective fusion of the legislature and executive, the phenomenon of the 'buckle' described by Walter Bagehot. When it comes to the judiciary, however, it is generally acknowledged that there is a reasonably effective mixture of laws and conventions to ensure the independence of the courts as the weakest of the three branches of government. Judges cannot sit in the House of Commons, and standing orders prohibit both criticism of judges and debate on issues that are before the courts. This is why the Commons never debated the case of General Pinochet. Judges can only be sacked by a joint address to the Crown by both Houses, a procedure last used in 1830. Their salaries are protected.

When I asked Douglas Hurd, a key member of the Wakeham commission, about separation of powers, he gave a traditionally British pragmatic view:

We don't have it. Our executive grows out of the legislature. It's part of it. Lord Chancellor is a funny old position, because he is all three – he is judiciary and legislature and executive. But I don't think that actually does anybody any harm. We looked at it. The Lord Chancellor was defiant in defending his own patch. And we didn't think there were compelling reasons to take him on. We don't operate on the basis of separation of powers. That's an American concept … I think Lord Chancellors slightly exaggerate the importance of their position. I have never in cabinet felt that the Lord Chancellor should be playing the kind of pivotal role which sometimes some occupants of the office describe. But equally I have never felt any harm to our liberties or the way the system works by having a Lord Chancellor.

The academic view is more critical, according to Robert Stevens:

In modern Britain, the concept of the separation of powers is cloudy and the notion of the independence of the judiciary remains primarily a term of constitutional rhetoric. Certainly its penumbra, and perhaps even its core, are vague. No general theory exists, although practically the English have developed surprisingly effective informal systems for the separation of powers.[15]

Stevens believes it is political culture – in other words, conventions – rather than the law that protects judicial independence in the United Kingdom. He says there is a case for a clearer separation of powers but this will require 'a dramatic rethinking of responsible government and parliamentary sovereignty if it is to occur'. Dicey's doctrine of parliamentary sovereignty, in other words, rules out the establishment of the judiciary as an independent and co-equal branch of government, the formula advocated by the famous 18th-century jurist Sir William Blackstone and developed across the Atlantic after the American Revolution. Stevens quotes Blackstone's advocacy of the separation of the judicial from the executive and legislative powers in his *Commentaries* of 1765:

Were such functions joined with the legislative, the life, liberty and property of the subject would be in the hands of arbitrary judges, whose decisions would not be based by any fundamental principles of law: which though legislators might depart from, yet judges are bound to observe. Were it joined with the executive, this union might soon be an overbalance for the legislative ... Nothing is more to be avoided, in a free constitution, than uniting the province of a judge with that of a minister of state.

The argument for separation of powers put forward by Blackstone is really about a balance between different institutions. In the 18th century this meant a system of checks and balances between the Lords, the Commons and the monarch, all three of them taking a share of responsibility for different functions such as legislation. The balance was undone in the 19th century by the pre-eminent rise of the Commons and the party-dominated system in which the executive controlled the legislature, with few remaining checks and balances applied by the Lords and none from the Crown. According to Professor Eric Barendt: 'The United Kingdom not only lacks a clear separation of legislative and executive institutions but has lost the balance of powers which characterized the traditional constitution of the 18th and 19th centuries ... It is in fact hard to reconcile the legislative supremacy of parliament with any strong commitment to the separation-of-powers principle.'

AN ABSENCE OF JOINED-UP THINKING

This intellectual fuzziness over separation of powers in relation to the Lord Chancellor forms the backdrop to the parallel debate over the position of the House of Lords as the supreme appeal court. Unlike the Lord Chancellor, the 12 Law Lords who make up the Appellate Committee are not part of the executive, but they straddle the legislative and judicial branches in a way which is hard to justify. Even defenders of this Victorian institution say it would never be created today.

THE JUDICIAL ROLE OF THE HOUSE OF LORDS

Its role in handling appeals dates back to medieval times but in its present form only to the time of Gladstone and Disraeli and the Appellate Jurisdiction Act of 1876. The judicial function of the Lords came within a whisker of abolition in 1874 and only a change of government from Liberal to Conservative rescued it. The Appellate Committee of the House of Lords is not part of the judiciary in a formal sense, being an arm of the legislature. Judicial business is sometimes taken on the floor of the house where judgements are read out. Until 1948 all appeals were held in the chamber but now mostly take place in a committee room. There is no right of appeal in criminal cases from Scotland.

Since 1887 the Law Lords have been life peers, though unlike the bishops of the Church of England they do not lose their seats in the House of Lords when they retire. As such they sit as legislators with the right to speak and vote and chair committees. The present number is 12. In the Appellate Committee they normally sit as a bench of five but sometimes as seven. After retirement they can still be called in to make up numbers. This is necessary when Law Lords are away chairing long judicial inquiries such as those into Bloody Sunday and BSE. The Law Lords are properly called Lords of Appeal, who come in two categories: the 12 Lords of Appeal in Ordinary, and other peers who have held high judicial office. Of the 12, two are normally from Scotland. At the moment one is from Northern Ireland. The other Lords of Appeal can include non-UK judges such as Lord Cooke of Thorndon, former President of the Court of Appeal of New Zealand. Those over 75 can speak and vote in Lords debates but not sit as judges. Legal expertise in the Lords also comes from eminent lawyers who have been given life peerages but who have never been judges, such as Patrick Neill and Robert Alexander.

THE JUDICIAL COMMITTEE OF THE PRIVY COUNCIL

The Judicial Committee of the Privy Council, created in its present form in 1833, mostly hears appeals from Commonwealth countries that have kept its jurisdiction, such as New Zealand. Judges sit four days a week in Number 1 Downing Street in panels of three or five. Judges from elsewhere in the Commonwealth can be members of the Privy Council and can sit to hear Commonwealth appeals. It is not an entirely UK body. The Lord Chancellor is also a member and can sit as a member of the Judicial Committee. When he sits, he presides over the panel. The Judicial Committee includes non-members of the House of Lords from the English Court of Appeal and the Scottish Court of Session, and the Northern Ireland Court of Appeal. It can hear appeals from the Channel Islands and the Isle of Man, from professional bodies such as the General Medical Council, and on church matters.

Under the Scotland, Wales and Northern Ireland Acts the Judicial Committee is the final court of appeal for disputes over devolution powers, including some human rights issues but not all. This is because the Appellate Committee of the House of Lords is perceived as being too much of an English body. No set rules have been established for who should sit in a devolution case.

Two academics who have made a detailed study of the cases which the Appellate Committee and the Judicial Committee of the Privy Council handle see mostly an old-fashioned British muddle: 'Anyone searching for an example of a field of governance in which institutional boundaries encourage an absence of joined-up thinking need look no further than the top courts.'[16] The United Kingdom has two courts of final appeal, the House of Lords and the Privy Council, one being a committee of parliament and the other a committee of a department of state. Neither top court is the responsibility of the Lord Chancellor's department and confusingly, neither is part of the Supreme Court, a body which exists only in England and Wales. 'Recent reforms and proposals for reform have bypassed the Law Lords,' Andrew Le Sueur and Richard Cornes say, drawing attention to the particular obscurity of the Judicial Committee of the Privy Council, which unlike most official bodies had no website giving its judgements until August 2000. Professor Rodney Brazier is also unimpressed by the current system, noting that 'England already has a Supreme Court, although I doubt whether many non-lawyers (and even some lawyers) know what it is'.

According to the letter of the law, the Court of Appeal, the High Court and the Crown Court make up the Supreme Court, which confusingly does *not* include the Appellate Committee of the House of Lords or the Judicial Committee of the Privy Council.

THE LORDS AND PINOCHET

The inadequacies of the House of Lords Appellate Committee as a proper supreme court judging cases with political and constitutional implications were cruelly exposed by the Pinochet case. The former Chilean dictator was arrested in London in October 1998 on an international warrant from a Spanish judge who wanted him to answer charges of crimes against humanity. The role of the Law Lords in this saga was to decide on his claim to immunity from prosecution as a former head of state.

Lord Bingham, the Lord Chief Justice, initially upheld Pinochet's immunity in the Divisional Court, but when the case reached the Lords on appeal, a panel of five Law Lords overturned this decision by a narrow margin of three to two. The decision was hailed internationally as a major advance for human rights, but at this point the problems began. It emerged that Lord Hoffmann, one of the three Law Lords who had ruled against Pinochet, had failed to disclose a link with Amnesty International, which was a party to the case. Amid deepening embarrassment, a different panel headed by Lord Browne-Wilkinson agreed that the Lords should go back to square one and examine the case again. A third panel of seven finally ruled that Pinochet could have immunity only for the early period of his rule in Chile, before the United Kingdom adhered to the International Convention against Torture in 1988. As Robert Stevens described it: 'The bungling had caused acute embarrassment to a judiciary which liked to pride itself on the respect in which it is held in other countries.' Lord Irvine rapped the Law Lords over their collective knuckles and told them to make sure it never happened again. In the words of David Robertson of St Hugh's College Oxford: 'If it showed one single thing, it was that they had not ever thought seriously about their role as a constitutional court. They were so used to dealing with constitutional matters just as if they were routine bits of law. They hadn't thought out any of the aspects of what it takes to be the national political court.'

Robertson argues that the Pinochet case 'demonstrated how inadequately the Law Lords perform when judged against a primary function

The Law Lords come clean before rehearing the Pinochet case

The Law Lords are forced to be purer than pure after their ruling on General Pinochet's immunity was overturned on appeal because one of them had undisclosed links with Amnesty International. Copyright © Express Newspapers plc, 1999.

of a nation's supreme court, if that court is viewed, as political scientists must view it, as a major component of the national political system'. The bungling went beyond the failure of Hoffmann to disclose his Amnesty link, he told me:

I think it was broader than that. The first thing about Hoffman is that they should have been organized enough to spot that. Having had to redo it, the analysis they gave of that situation, the way they accounted for why it was necessary, was completely inadequate. It was unfair to Hoffmann. They didn't face up to a whole set of issues about when judges can and cannot sit in major political cases. They trivialized it. There are real issues that a constitutional court has to work out. They have to accept that top judges do have political ideas – how do they not? – and work out a serious doctrine on when their ideas do or don't make them fit to hear a case. My other objection is the multiplicity of different opinions. I'm not saying they should be unanimous, but they really need a clear opinion of the court. The majority need to get together and make a clear statement of what the law is. A lawyer asking what is the constitutional position now doesn't really know.

Robertson argues that the way the Law Lords function, with random panels of five, produces results that are too much of a lottery:

That is the biggest structural problem. They sit in randomly selected panels of five or seven. If you add up the votes cast in the Pinochet case, you can see just how easily that very first case could have gone the other way round. If Hoffmann had stood down and been replaced by one specific other judge, then the decision would have been the other way around and we would never have known there was any doubt. It is the clearest case I have ever seen demonstrating just how much the random panel matters.

The problem of inconsistency is worse, he argues, in the Judicial Committee of the Privy Council, where normally only three judges sit out of a much larger pool of qualified members, and dissenting judgements are rare. Robertson does not believe the Lord Chancellor has much appetite for the real changes that are necessary:

The route out is really root and branch reform. They need to sit *en banc* for really serious cases, with nine of them. They will then tell you they can't do this because of the workload. The answer is that they need to cut down the huge amount of time they spend on oral argument. The reason other supreme courts can get through a caseload twice as large sitting *en banc* is that they don't spend three days listening to oral argument. They need to use more briefs, and employ research clerks, but they don't really want it. They say, 'What would I do with him?' The judge is there to craft the opinion, he doesn't need to do the research himself. He can have a bright new law graduate to do that.

LEGAL LEAPFROG

Robertson argues that instead of these horse-and-buggy arrangements there should be a separate constitutional court that would specialize in the kind of public law that is at present the background of only a minority of the Law Lords. But he detects some recognition of the need for change in the Lord Chancellor's unusual appointment of Lord Bingham as senior Law Lord from June 2000. Under past precedent, the top job was allocated by seniority, but on this occasion Lord Bingham was plucked from his job as Lord Chief Justice of England and Wales and parachuted in above the heir apparent Lord Slynn when Lord Browne-Wilkinson, the outgoing senior Law Lord, retired. 'Bingham's appointment is unprecedented – leapfrogging him up is tantamount to creating an American-style Chief Justice of the Supreme Court.' Aides to the Lord Chancellor, however, say this interpretation is wrong and Bingham's appointment was not intended as any real change in the previous arrangements.

Bingham himself made clear in 1999 in his evidence to the royal commission that he was sympathetic to reform. He told Wakeham that having the supreme court as a committee of the legislature was an anomaly that existed for historical reasons. But he added: 'There are ... powerful reasons for thinking that the standing and authority of the Appellate Committee will be best served in future by its reconstitution, entirely separate from the legislature, as a supreme court, properly equipped for the very important tasks it has to discharge.'

As the submissions to Wakeham make clear, the issue of reform divides the Law Lords themselves, with some reluctant to leave the familiar surroundings of the Palace of Westminster for an unknown existence elsewhere. There appears to be a general mood of 'if it ain't broke, don't fix it' and a perverse pride in the lack of pomp and ceremony attached to their operations as a court. Writing on behalf of his colleagues to

Wakeham, Lord Slynn summed up their views as follows: 'It is an accepted convention among the Law Lords that they do not participate, whether by way of speaking or voting, on matters which are controversial in a party political way ... The boundary line is not always easy to discern with precision, but occasions when, with the benefit of hindsight, it might be better if a Law Lord had not participated in a particular debate are few and far between. In no case has participation given rise to serious embarrassment subsequently. In most cases, debates in which Law Lords participate have a close connection with the legal and judicial expertise of the particular Law Lord.'

The Law Lords, according to Lord Slynn, say they 'benefit from the wider perspective derived from this closer contact with the legislative process and also from their awareness of debates in the House on matters of current interest. They believe their judicial work would be the poorer without this'. They say the issue of the court of final appeal for the United Kingdom is 'a particularly complex question'. On balance they are against change because 'existing arrangements by and large function satisfactorily'.

Lord Woolf told Wakeham that he supported the idea of Law Lords being able to 'speak directly to the upper house' and 'this aspect' of the relationship worked well – a somewhat cautious endorsement of the status quo. But he added that the present accommodation arrangements at Westminster 'are such that, because of an absence of space, the final court of appeal does not operate in the way that it should. This has been a disadvantage in the past, and will in the future be an immense impediment to the proper workings of what should be our supreme court.'

Lord Lloyd of Berwick, opposing the creation of a separate supreme court, pointed out to Wakeham that the US Supreme Court used to sit in the old Senate Chamber until the 1930s. With only eight legal staff and eight secretaries packed into 12 small rooms and one conference room, the Appellate Committee was, he argued, 'the most cost-efficient supreme court in the world'. On grounds of cost and practicality, the Law Lords should stay put at Westminster, where they had access to the House of Lords library and could keep in touch better with the 'real world' than in a purpose-built ivory tower. Lord Lloyd, while acknowledging the implications of the McGonnell case for the Lord Chancellor, saw no such problem for the Law Lords, because they were not part of the executive and did not promote legislation:

Whereas the position of the Lord Chancellor as head of the judiciary would raise questions of considerable difficulty if his position were ever challenged in the ECHR, I cannot envisage such a challenge in the case of the Law Lords. The risk is so small it can be safely ignored. The theoretical objection to the Law Lords sitting as members of the reformed chamber is not one to which I would attach any weight. It works in practice.

Lord Hope of Craighead, one of the two Scottish Law Lords, drew attention in his evidence to Wakeham to the fact that any reorganization of the top courts could become a political minefield in Scotland, which at present sends only civil, not criminal, appeals to the House of Lords. Hope's reading of the Scotland Act was that the Scottish Parliament would be acting within its powers if it decided at some future date that it would no longer send civil appeals to the House of Lords. It would be possible for parliament at Westminster to set up a supreme court for the United Kingdom, but the extent of its jurisdiction over Scotland would be a matter for the Scottish Parliament to decide. Any reform would require simultaneous legislation in Westminster and Edinburgh, and such a measure would raise so many sensitive issues about sovereignty it would be preferable to leave matters well alone for the time being. Lord Hope warned that any changes affecting the Privy Council would also have to be agreed with the Commonwealth countries which used it as their final court of appeal, such as Brunei, Trinidad, New Zealand and British overseas territories such as Gibraltar.

Lord Donaldson told Wakeham: 'No designer of constitutions who had any respect for the separation of powers would for one moment have considered using one part of a bicameral legislature as a substitute for a supreme court. But, of course, there never was a designer of our unwritten constitution. It just evolved. And given the fact that by and large it works well, I personally regard its eccentricities as part of its charm.'

Lord Goff, like Lord Lloyd, stressed the stripped-down 'economy-class' nature of the Law Lords' work environment compared with foreign supreme courts. Visitors, he told Wakeham, were struck by the small scale of the room and the 'extreme informality and indeed intimacy of the proceedings'. While the Law Lords researched and wrote all their judgements themselves, Germany's Federal Supreme Court had 123 judges and a staff of 300. 'Your lordships' House may justly be said to provide a most cost-effective service ... The reason why we have 12 Law

Lords is to enable two committees of five to sit regularly hearing appeals, while others write judgements or perform other functions directly related to our judicial work. Obviously, nobody is allowed to be ill.'

WAKEHAM SIDESTEPS THE ISSUE

John Wakeham told me that he and his fellow members of the royal commission felt the Law Lords wanted to have their cake and eat it: 'The Law Lords were divided, of course. Broadly speaking, what they said was, we would like a separate supreme court but we would like to remain members of the House of Lords ... So we thought that was a lot of rubbish.' In the end the royal commission largely sidestepped the issue of the Law Lords' future, though it recommended that they should issue a joint statement clarifying their ground rules for taking part in debates and votes, and considering their eligibility to sit on related cases. This finally came about in June 2000, after Lord Bingham's appointment as senior Law Lord. Bingham read out a statement agreed with his 11 colleagues and with the Lord Chancellor, which essentially reaffirmed the status quo and stopped short of laying down any binding rules. The Law Lords, it said, had a right to participate in the business of the second chamber, but 'do not think it appropriate to engage in matters where there is a strong element of party political controversy'. They would also bear in mind that they might render themselves ineligible to sit judicially if they were to express an opinion on a matter which might later be relevant to an appeal. 'They stress that it is impossible to frame rules which cover every eventuality. In the end it must be for the judgement of each individual Lord of Appeal to decide how to conduct himself in any particular situation.'

Wakeham told me his commission felt the creation of a proper supreme court would not have prevented the conflict of interest involving Lord Hoffmann, and it was in any case clear that 'it (a supreme court) wasn't going to happen, whatever we said':

Nobody who started from scratch would say, we've got a wonderful idea for a supreme court of the United Kingdom, we'll make it a committee of the House of Lords. Nobody would do that. But that's what we've got. There was actually no way it was going to be changed. The question is, how do you make it better ... Of course, it would be intolerable if you had judges in there banging on about the merits or demerits of the legislation, whether they liked it, and then they sat to interpret it in a judicial figure. I think they've got to be very careful that they don't do that. But what happens in practice is, the judges sit there and they hear the debate about some particular aspect of some criminal justice Bill or something, and one of them will say: 'No my lords, the issue that will come before the judges will not be *that* issue, it will be *this* issue that we have to decide. So if you are looking at this part of the legislation I think you need to think in terms of whether you think that is satisfactory or you don't. Because that is how it will be presented to us by counsel for either side in order to reach a verdict.' So it is valuable expertise, but of course they have to be careful they are not involved in conflicts of interest.

Outside experts are less complacent; Robert Stevens says the continued presence of the Law Lords in the upper chamber is 'ultimately very corrupting', explaining: 'This assumption that there are legal issues and non-legal issues is a very English assumption. I think it is quite disgraceful that the Law Lords are sitting there.' Legal scholars point out that while some Law Lords have deliberately avoided political controversy, such as Lord Steyn who has deliberately never spoken nor voted, others have shown no hesitation in speaking out in debates on controversial legal/political measures on which they might later have to pass judgement.

Robert Alexander QC (Lord Alexander of Weedon), writing at the end of 1999, takes a similar view. He says the Law Lords are largely victims of their own success because of the increased role of the judiciary over the past few decades. 'Our anomalous position is regarded with a mix of bemusement and incredulity elsewhere in Europe. Indeed, the Charter of the European Magistracy stipulates that an independent judiciary must have no executive or legislative power. How in the future can Law Lords rule on the human rights compliance of legislation passed by the very parliament of which they are technically members?'[17] He urges the adoption of a more formal procedure, post-Pinochet, on declarations of interest, and predicts a continuing public interest in how panels are chosen. This applies in particular to the Judicial Committee of the Privy Council's role in solving devolution disputes. Should there automatically be a Scottish judge on the panel? And if so, should the same apply to Northern Ireland? 'Any informal permutation will be open to criticism and ... the spotlight will be relentless.'

Lord Alexander points the Law Lords in the direction of the example of transparency given by the Bank of England's Monetary Policy Committee, a body set up with clear goals, procedure and accountability: 'Pinochet was sadly damaging to the standing of the Law Lords and we do not want to risk another embarrassing muddle. One lesson is that informal ways of choosing which judges sit, and whether they disclose a conflict of interest, will no longer do. It is also time to recognize that the same people cannot be both judges and legislators. Sooner or later this has got to change.'

In the submission to Wakeham on behalf of Justice, Alexander and his colleagues make a case for setting up a separate supreme court whose members would only be eligible for membership of the upper house after retirement. Such a court would take over devolution issues from the Privy Council and have its own building and better resources: 'The source and strength of the convention that serving Law Lords do not become involved in political issues is obscure; and it is difficult to draw a clear line between what are and are not political issues, where law and politics intersect.' Alexander lists a long series of cases on which Law Lords intervened in debates on sensitive issues under the Conservatives. 'The merits of these politically controversial issues are irrelevant. What matters is that serving Law Lords have become involved as legislators in debating such matters, some of which have become, and may in future become, matters to be decided by the senior judges in their judicial capacity.' The valuable role of the Law Lords in scrutinizing legislation is acknowledged, but the present arrangements are 'inherently flawed' and reform is 'not a luxury but an urgent practical necessity'.

A PECULIAR SYSTEM

Ann Owers of Justice says the Pinochet case, even without the embarrassment over Lord Hoffmann, highlighted the fact that Britain's peculiar top courts are not easy for foreign lawyers to understand:

I think the notion of setting up a supreme court isn't all that radical. I think there would be the task of physically removing the Law Lords from the House of Lords, and having them sit for example in the Royal Courts of Justice or where they sit as the Privy Council at the moment. I think it would be a signal more than it would be a change in the way that they operate. I was at a conference of international human rights lawyers when Pinochet was going on. These were people who were very up to speed on international human rights issues, and they were very pleased that the Pinochet case was being decided in the UK; they thought the UK was taking a very good and brave and principled stance in this. But one of them did say to me, we do think it is really good, but we slightly worry that in the UK you let these fundamental matters of international law be decided by your hereditary peers! And we had to explain at that point that this was not just any old hereditary peer casting a view on whether international law said torturers should be prosecuted.

But perception is important … and the perception does mask a reality. There is virtually no proper clerical and administrative support for this important court. We compare it to the resources that go into the Supreme Court in the US. That is an extreme example, but constitutional courts all over the place have proper assistance. There is an enormous amount of expertise, and judgements are rightly considered and are very good, but it does sort of creak along in a rather strange way. And I think the perception internally is important too. You have got the House of Lords now in a much more exposed position not only in terms of the Human Rights Act but also in terms of devolution. It will be the first time ever that Scots criminal law can be overturned by an English court. They really have got to be perceived to be squeaky clean, which they are in all material senses, but they have got to be perceived to be completely independent, and they have also got to have the resources they need to do this new job.

It is clear that Irvine, mindful of the threat posed to his own position by any reform of the Law Lords, wants them to remain indefinitely in the legislature, of which he says they are 'an organic part'. Lord Bingham's statement of the status quo represents the limit of reform. Irvine, in his Edinburgh speech in July 1999, gave a robustly negative response to the reformers: 'To the question whether the House of Lords in its legislative capacity must lose the benefits the Law Lords confer because of the doctrine of separation of powers, I say "no" for two reasons: firstly, because we do not apply the doctrine strictly; and secondly, provided their role in the legislature does not prejudice their primary role as our final appellate judges, there is no need to change a beneficial system.' In Blair's

Britain, the 'whole country' has to modernize, but at the summit of the judiciary, the interests of the Lord Chancellor require that everything shall remain as it is. Aides to Irvine strongly discourage any idea that the appointment of Lord Bingham as Senior Law Lord might mean that the Lord Chancellor is going to take a back seat in organizing the work of the top courts.

It remains to be seen, however, for how much longer the status quo can be preserved. By 2001 it is likely to become clear whether Irvine has in practice given up sitting as a judge, while maintaining intact his *droit de seigneur* to do so. The catalyst could be a government decision to go ahead with a second stage of reform of the Lords. If this happens, it is unlikely that the position of the Law Lords and the Lord Chancellor can be given the same kind of cursory treatment applied by Wakeham. A more thorough reform of the top courts will be essential, though it looks unlikely to happen unless Blair decides to separate Derry Irvine from his Pugin wallpaper. Until that point is reached, the words of the 'rather susceptible' Lord Chancellor in *Iolanthe* will continue to hold good:

The Law is the true embodiment
Of everything that's excellent.
It has no kind of fault or flaw,
And I, my Lords, embody the Law.

NOTES

[1] *Rosie: a thorn in the establishment's side* by James Falla, *Guernsey Press*, 26 October 1999.

[2] Stevens, Robert (1999) 'A Loss of Innocence? Judicial Independence and the Separation of Powers', *Oxford Journal of Legal Studies*, Vol. 19.

[3] Extracts from the diaries of Walter Runciman (Viscount Runciman of Doxford), *Sunday Telegraph*, 7 June 1998.

[4] Egan, Dominic (1999) *Irvine. Politically correct?*, Edinburgh, Mainstream Publishing Projects.

[5] Brazier, Rodney (1998) *Constitutional Reform. Reshaping the British political system*, Oxford University Press, 2nd edition, p 162.

[6] *The Times*, 30 November 1999.

[7] Speech to Third Worldwide Common Law Judiciary Conference, 5 July 1999.

[8] The Human Rights Act came into force on 2 October 2000.

[9] Quoted in Stevens, Robert (1999), op. cit.

[10] Lord Steyn (1997) 'The weakest and least dangerous department of government', *Public Law*, pp 84, 90–91.

[11] The other signatories were Justice chairman Robert Alexander QC, Peter Archer QC, Professor Jeffrey Jowell of London University, Helena Kennedy QC, Anthony Lester QC and William Goodhart QC.

[12] Woodhouse, Diana (2000) unpublished research summary.

[13] Ivor Richard's view is that Irvine's long spell without sitting in the Appellate Committee may be a result of the fact that '… you know, one gets a bit out of one's depth. I mean, Derry is quite a good lawyer but I don't think he would have ended up in the House of Lords by his own legal abilities. He is not a natural supreme court justice.' He points out that Harold Wilson's Lord Chancellor Gerald Gardiner also sat very infrequently as a judge.

[14] Barendt, Eric (1998) *An Introduction to Constitutional Law*, Oxford University Press, p 35.

[15] Stevens, Robert (1999), op. cit.

[16] Le Sueur, Andrew and Cornes, Richard (2000) draft seminar paper, the Constitution Unit.

[17] *Counsel*, December 1999.

11

HOGWARTS-ON-THAMES

'I've seen it (Houses of Parliament) somewhere, like on the news or something, is it? London, is it? ... I've seen the clock on the news. I've seen it before but I don't know what it is ... Is it a hotel? People go on holiday there' (male, 15 years, indifferent)

'When you see it on telly though it just looks like a big joke. I mean like the way they carry on in the House of Commons ... You wouldn't even get kids in a school carrying on like that ... with them screaming, and folks sitting on the benches sleeping' (female, 23 years, cynically uninterested)[1]

'This is a brutal place. It destroys more people than it creates'
– Gwyneth Dunwoody MP

'I detest it. I think it is a dreadful place' – Paddy Ashdown MP

WITH ITS COMPLEX RULES AND HIERARCHIES, its neo-Gothic vaults and corridors, its old-fashioned food and its air of muscular Christianity, the House of Commons is often compared with a Victorian public school. One day sitting in the Commons press gallery watching Prime Minister's Questions, it suddenly dawned on me that I was sitting in the real model for J.K. Rowling's fictional Hogwarts School of Witchcraft and Wizardry. It all made perfect sense at last. I imagined Rowling's hero, Harry Potter, as a new young Labour MP arriving for his first term at Hogwarts in 1997, keen to try out flying on his broomstick for the first time. Like Harry, he wonders if he will ever find his way around:

There were a hundred and forty-two staircases at Hogwarts: wide, sweeping ones; narrow, rickety ones; some that led somewhere different on a Friday; some with a vanishing step halfway up that you had to remember to jump. Then there were the doors that wouldn't open until you asked politely, or tickled them in exactly the right place, and doors that weren't really doors at all, but solid walls just pretending. It was also very hard to remember where anything was, because it all seemed to move around a lot. The people in the portraits kept going to visit each other and Harry was sure the coats of armour could walk.

Harry himself is obviously modelled on Stephen Twigg, the Labour MP for Enfield Southgate, whose magical powers won a famous upset victory over Michael Portillo in 1997. Look closely at young Twigg from the press gallery and you may just see the trace of a Potterish lightning flash on his forehead. Enfield Southgate is of course the suburb where Harry spent his early years in Privet Drive with his dreadful Muggle relatives, the Dursleys. Stephen Twigg is New Labour to the core, but Harry's red-haired best friend Ron Weasley, from a modest family with more children than they can afford, is clearly an Old Labour holdover – perhaps a distant nephew of the retired Welsh wizard Neil Kinnock. Then there is Harry's friend Hermione Granger ('a bossy sort of voice, lots of bushy brown hair and rather large front teeth') whose air of slightly priggish self-importance marks her down as a Liberal Democrat.

The Conservative benches provided Rowling with her raw material for the untrustworthy wizards of Slytherin House, such as Harry's enemy Draco Malfoy ('a pale, pointed face and a bored, drawling voice'). Malfoy, son of Lucius Malfoy, a great supporter of 'You Know Who', is modelled on one of those bright young Tories who cut their teeth as political advisers under Mrs Thatcher, and whose father served in cabinet under the great 'You Know Who' herself. Severus Snape, Harry's least favourite teacher, is probably John Redwood, and Albus Dumbledore, the headmaster, could be the Sergeant at Arms. Margaret Beckett is the model for Minerva McGonagall, while the former Madam Speaker Betty Boothroyd appears as Madam Hooch, briskly refereeing games of Quidditch on her broomstick. This complex seven-a-side game involving Beaters, Chasers and Bludgers, played with a Quaffle and a Golden Snitch, has strong similarities with the arcane rules of Commons debating procedure laid down in Erskine May. There are, Rowling tells us, 700 ways of committing a Quidditch foul and all of them happened in a match in 1473.

But the parallels go further. Like Hogwarts, the Commons until quite recently had a magic black hat which was used by MPs at crucial moments when they needed to catch the Speaker's attention during a vote. The menu at Harry Potter's school resembles the old-fashioned English nosh produced by the House of Commons catering department. There is 'roast beef, roast chicken, pork chops, bacon and steak, boiled potatoes, roast potatoes, chips, Yorkshire pudding, peas, carrots, gravy, ketchup and for some reason mint humbugs ...' Even the rock cakes are hard enough to break a tooth on, just like the ones at Westminster.

LETTING IN THE MUGGLES

Unlike Hogwarts, the House of Commons allows the Muggles (voters) to come in on sufferance for a few minutes to sit in the public gallery. If they are lucky, they catch the circus knockabout of Prime Minister's Questions on a Wednesday afternoon. If they are less fortunate, they may stumble on a long and incomprehensible debate on reforming limited liability partnerships, involving just a handful of MPs. They will probably be not much wiser about the British system of government when they leave with a look of anti-climax on their faces. Is this really the Mother of Parliaments, the place where Gladstone, Disraeli, Lloyd George and Winston Churchill performed? The magic seems to have deserted the green leather benches which Churchill called 'the shrine of the world's liberties'. At Hogwarts-on-Thames, the parliamentary wizards wave their wands at each other, but the spells no longer work.

Most recent analyses of the woes of the House of Commons begin with the complaints of MPs about how they are marginalized by the executive, by the media, by the courts, by Brussels, and viewed with contempt by the public. In the words of Peter Riddell of *The Times*: 'The real malaise at Westminster is a sense of exclusion, a belief that the real political debate and decision making are elsewhere ...' Many MPs are disillusioned, though few confess it openly. But we should turn the problem round and look at parliament for a moment from the point of view of the ordinary voter. Let us take a Muggle's eye view of Westminster.

Television journalist Jackie Ashley recently examined how Parliament treats visitors and was not impressed by what she found. Entitling her Hansard Society pamphlet 'I Spy Strangers',[2] she pointed out that the phrase, symbolizing the arcane procedure of the Commons, was no longer used but its legacy lingered. 'At a symbolic level, it sums up the attitude to anyone who is not a member of that most exclusive of Britain's clubs, the

House of Commons.' The people who elect the Commons are treated as strangers, not as owners of the political process, and the impression given to visitors is 'cold, ritualized, unwelcoming and stuffy'. The unwelcoming atmosphere is particularly striking to visitors who have been to the new Scottish Parliament and to the National Assembly for Wales, whose modest foyer has a children's play area with toys.

Ashley believes parliament is 'too remote from the British people, in style, in tradition, in language and in atmosphere'. She describes the struggle a visitor has to go through to queue for a seat in the public gallery: 'From time to time, rude officials will order her to shove up the bench a bit until she reaches the top. Then Mrs Vote will be escorted by more rude officials, dressed in tails and a white bow tie, to the gallery where she'll be "shushed" and ordered into a seat – to look down on, and try to fathom out the proceedings below.' Afterwards there is no chance of a cup of tea and no easy way of finding a lavatory. Except for the summer recess, when parliament is not sitting, there are no organized tours except for those lucky enough to be invited by an MP. 'For the main assembly of a modern, plural nation which prides itself on its vigorous democratic traditions, this is nothing short of a scandal.'

Even those at the top are worried. Betty Boothroyd, in her farewell speech as Speaker in July 2000, told MPs: 'The level of cynicism about parliament, and the accompanying alienation of many of the young from the democratic process, is troubling.' Social research carried out by the Joseph Rowntree Foundation among young people makes bleak reading for anyone concerned about parliamentary government. It makes clear that the main image of parliament is that of Prime Minister's Questions, and the impact is wholly negative.

The predominant image of parliament was of politicians arguing and shouting at each other during parliamentary debates seen on television. They described this in various terms such as politicians 'blabbering on', 'huffing and puffing', 'ripping and digging', 'slagging each other off', 'back biting' and 'bickering'. Some of the participants felt that the general public is only given a limited impression of parliament, as only one room is ever shown on television, leaving the public with a stereotypical image of the arguing …

References were also made to the traditional and ceremonial aspects of the proceedings in parliament. For those with the least interest in politics, this reinforced the unfamiliarity and strangeness of parliamentary proceedings; amusement was expressed at seeing a politician 'flinging a mace round his head', and a vision of a woman shouting 'order' and banging a hammer. Those who were more interested also commented on the 'pomp and ceremony' of parliament, which they found difficult to understand, irrelevant, old-fashioned and a waste of money. Only a small minority felt the ceremony and 'fancy dress' gave the proceedings a sense of dignity and tradition.[3]

Jackie Ashley's pamphlet describes an institution that Walter Bagehot would still recognize, a holdover from the pre-democratic era of deference and hierarchy when the Palace of Westminster was built. The ethos is overwhelmingly white and male, something which has begun to change only marginally since 1997. Fiona Mactaggart, elected for Labour in 1997, believes the arrival of more women MPs has made some changes, but not enough:

I think you have to understand how oppressive tradition is here. It all works by precedent and tradition and consensus. No one tells you what that is. On my first day here I looked down these benches and there was no room, so I went and sat there by the Liberal Democrats. You can imagine what happened. A Whip got up and shot across and pulled me off the seat. 'What's wrong, what have I done?' 'You can't sit there!' I said, 'Why not? I want to sit down.'

Mactaggart believes Labour's women have been handicapped in acting collectively because of the 'Blair Babes' tag that was attached to them after they were photographed with Tony Blair after the 1997 election:

Ever since then we have been trying to live it down. That's part of the problem. That oik Nicholas Soames comes up to me the other day and says, 'Waw, waw, what are you going to do about the Speaker? Can you make sure that the Babes vote for Gwyneth?' I said, 'Nicholas, have you thought how offensive that remark is?' He said, 'Oh you're not a Babe, Fiona, but you have got influence over the Babes.' I said, 'You are just digging yourself deeper.' There is a kind of currency of denigration of women, which by calling us Babes has made us so much less able to be effective ... It is an oppressive place. These stone floors make your

Labour's 419 MPs are not expected to think for themselves. Tony Blair makes it clear he expects them to stay on message.
Copyright © Steve Bell, 1997.

feet hurt like hell. Most women's shoes have thin leather soles. The evenings are dominated by smoke and alcohol, which is ghastly. It isn't only the sort of place you don't want to be in, but it is the sort of place where men behave in inappropriate ways towards you. The food is food for boys.

Technically and culturally, Westminster still lives in an age in which messages are passed around by white-tied footmen rather than by e-mail. Labour MP Joan Ruddock complains that it is typical of the Commons that MPs have pink ribbons for their swords but no computers and no childcare facilities. Writing in the Hansard Society publication *Under Pressure*, her colleague Anne Campbell echoes this view:

It is far easier to buy a drink at Westminster at 2 am than it is to send a fax to a constituent. Messages from constituents waiting to see an MP are carried by a messenger round the building until the MP is located. On average it takes such messages four hours to reach me, by which time the constituent has, of course, long departed … There are no computers in committee rooms and the use of one's own laptop is forbidden. Information, which might be needed to inform a particular debate, has to be carried in one's head or on a mass of paper … I was told that it was because MPs might be tempted to do their own work and not pay attention to the committee if they had a computer to work on. I regard this as gratuitously offensive to members' intelligence and commitment. There is a sharp contrast between a complete lack of direction for most procedures and petty restrictions, which undermine MPs' independence. Life at Westminster is often very frustrating, time wasting and inefficient.

Information tends to be mostly circulated on paper; there is no e-mail directory of MPs, and parliament's websites are old-fashioned and difficult to use. Hansard reports of debates appear only after an overnight delay, while most transcripts of Select Committee hearings are not published for months. Only recently were tape recorders allowed in the Commons press gallery, and they are still not permitted in Select Committee hearings. While 10 Downing Street offers streamed audio and video clips of the Prime Minister on its website, the legislature has done nothing comparable to make itself transparent and comprehensible to a wider audience. Television broadcasts of debates in the Commons chamber have been allowed since the 1980s, but the restrictions on what can be shown are so tight that less and less material is used. Despite minor relaxations by the Broadcasting Committee in July 2000, which allow 'reaction shots' of MPs, the Commons is still able to restrict how its operations are shown to the outside world.

Ashley, a television journalist, describes the sanitized feed of pictures that comes out of the Commons as 'virtually unwatchable and unintelligible to the average viewer'. The end product 'can make a Japanese Noh play or a modernist opera seem positively accessible'. In the corridors outside the chamber, the sort of mobile television and radio reporting that could make the workings of parliament come alive is banned. So is photography. Is it any wonder that what happens in parliament rarely seems to make the main news bulletins? As Charter88 said in its strategy document *Unlocking Democracy*:

The fact that the customs and traditions of the UK parliament are based on those of a 19th-century gentleman's club sends a very clear message to the public: we are not like you and you are not welcome here.

NEITHER DIGNIFIED NOR EFFICIENT

The problem for the Commons is that in Bagehot's language it is now neither dignified nor efficient; like the royal family, it is its own worst enemy, lagging even behind the House of Lords in public relations skills.

Tony Benn, first elected to the Commons in 1950, told MPs on the day they met to choose Boothroyd's successor as Speaker:

The people who elect us to parliament ask us certain questions. They ask, 'When we go to war, do you have a say in it?' and the answer is that we do not. We were not consulted, in terms of a vote, about the bombing in Iraq or Kosovo … That is a royal prerogative. We could not even start electing a Speaker without instructions from the Queen, so the royal prerogative is very strong. Then we come to the laws made in Brussels. I have been on the Council of Ministers, and was its president once. When ministers go to Brussels and agree to laws in secret, they repeal the laws that we have made and we have no say, either before the minister goes or when he comes back.

Patronage is on a massive scale. Every prime minister has done it – almost 1,000 peers have been made by prime ministers since the war. There is no consultation with the House of Commons about the patronage exercised by the prime minister of the day. We must face the fact that we are, to a large extent, an impotent House of Commons. I can give a practical example of that. We have been in recess since July, and during that time there has been a fuel crisis, a Danish 'no' vote, the collapse of the euro, and a war in the Middle East, but what is our business tomorrow? The Insolvency Bill *[Lords]*. It ought to be called the Bankruptcy Bill *[Commons]*, because we play no role.

The brutal truth is that despite its theoretical position as the keystone of the British constitution, supreme over all other authorities, the Commons in fact wields very little power. 'The House of Commons deceives itself into thinking it is important and powerful,' says one member of the Labour government team who acknowledges his original hopes of democratic change under Blair have been dashed.

Paddy Ashdown, who decided to retire as an MP after handing over leadership of the Liberal Democrats, is among those who have never been seduced by Westminster:

I detest it. I think it is a dreadful place. I shall be very sad to cease to be an MP. I come here because it is a place where I have to do my work, unfortunately. I think as an institution for governing a modern democracy it is about as ludicrous as you can get. I think it would have delighted Kafka. It would get nought marks in any A-level politics exam where you asked someone to design a democratic institution for governing a country. I think it doesn't respond to the needs of its people. I think it doesn't hold the executive to account. I think the only function it performs tolerably well is that of providing bread and circuses for people to watch on television. The theatre here is excellent, but there it finishes. It is also in my view Britain's most powerful job preservation conspiracy. It would knock any trade union into a cocked hat. Because the one thing we mustn't do is change the nature of members of parliament's jobs. Give people fair votes? Certainly not. Transfer power to Europe if there is a transfer to a lower level? Certainly not. The one thing that this place fights absolutely tooth and nail for is the preservation of MPs' jobs as they currently are, totally unchanged, wigs and all if they can.

For most of the time, the House of Commons functions as an electoral college which sustains a government between elections, and a theatrical backdrop for that government's announcements. The malaise goes far beyond poor communications, and it has no single cause. Some problems can be traced to the impossibility of adapting Sir Charles Barry's grade one listed building into a modern parliament for the 21st century. Ashdown told me with a glint in his eye that he took 'a sort of Guy Fawkes' approach to the building: 'I would love to turn that place into a tourist attraction and build a modern one in Milton Keynes or somewhere. I am not entirely serious about that.' Ashdown told me that if Labour and the Liberal Democrats had formed a coalition after 1997, his party would have insisted on a redesign of the Commons chamber: 'We would have had to move in my view to a semi-circular system.' This was the solution advocated by Labour's Graham Allen in the mid-1990s, when he called for a semi-circular chamber, a seat for every member and electronic voting: 'The carpenter and electrician will help contribute to Britain's democratic revival.'[4]

It is widely accepted that parliament, an essentially amateur institution, has failed to keep pace with the huge growth in the complexity and scope of government and with the wider social and political changes of the last half-century. The power of the executive over the legislature has grown and grown, for a variety of reasons. Since 1972 there has been a slow shift of power to European institutions in Brussels with which government has learned to cope, but which has left the legislature floundering. Globalization has had similar effects. The centre of domestic political debate has moved elsewhere, mostly to radio and television studios, and every government minister knows there are few less effective ways of attracting publicity than announcing something in the House of Commons. Power has also slipped away to the courts, a trend that will increase under the Human Rights Act. There may still be some MPs who, against all the evidence, think the Westminster model of parliamentary government works as it should do, but they are heavily outnumbered by those who see it as increasingly dysfunctional.

> 66 Every government minister knows there are few less effective ways of attracting publicity than announcing something in the House of Commons. 99

Not all the discontent is voiced by recent arrivals. Norman Godman, a Labour MP first elected in 1983, admits: 'I am thoroughly disaffected with this kind of political system.' He believes the archaism of the Commons has an immensely seductive effect on many newcomers: 'They love it, it becomes a bloody fix of some kind.' But the place remains intimidating, especially for the dwindling minority of MPs from a working-class background. It is not just women who find the atmosphere oppressive. Godman tells the story of a former miner who became an MP: 'He said to me: "I don't know how you've got the nerve to get up in that place and speak." I said; "I've got no choice. I've got to get up and speak." He said he found it so intimidating he just couldn't get to his feet in the place.'

NO GOLDEN AGE

Some trace the Westminster malaise to the declining individual quality of MPs and the professionalization of the political class, which has led to a decline in the authority, independence and experience of those who get elected. The former Conservative minister Douglas Hurd sympathizes with this argument:

What the House of Commons now lacks is not democratic authority. What it lacks is independence and experience. I don't see much chance of the House of Commons going back to the days when it contained a large element of independent-minded people, quite a large element of people who had practical experience outside politics, in many cases continuing experience because they were in many respects part-time members of parliament who spent part of their time doing other things in other professions on both sides. That has almost gone from the House of Commons, to the great weakening, I think, of our parliamentary system.

Another veteran of the Commons and the Lords, Roy Jenkins, believes the quality of debate has deteriorated and the days when the chamber was packed for wind-up speeches have gone for ever. But he is sceptical about nostalgia for some lost parliamentary golden age: 'It has been a constant feature of British political life that things have never been as good as they were 30 years before. And unless one believes in the theory of biological degeneration it is difficult to believe this has always been the case.'

Sneering at full-time career politicians and implying that gifted amateurs and part-timers will always be preferable seems to be a questionable approach to the ills of parliament, although the Wakeham report on the House of Lords echoes this kind of argument. Parliament's shortcomings lie not in the faults of its individual members, though women and ethnic minorities are still seriously under-represented, but in how it works as an institution. Not many MPs, dashing around Westminster from meeting to meeting and from vote to vote during 14-hour days, their pagers at the ready, have much time to reflect on such questions. Most of them spend a large part of the week on constituency business, answering mountains of correspondence. This explains why the Commons chamber is so often nearly empty. Fiona Mactaggart wishes she could cast the same spell as Harry Potter's friend Hermione, and be in two places at once:

I think the fact that we can't have our papers in the chamber means we aren't in the chamber enough. In most legislatures people can write and contribute at the same time … We are not ignoring it when we are in our rooms with the monitors on. You can't be an MP and *not* do two things at once. That is why women are so good at it. You absolutely can't afford to sit listening to oratory. If you had a desk you could, you could sign letters … The hours were constructed for a completely different life, so you could be at the Inns of Court in the morning and come here in the afternoon. There are still a few MPs who do that, the two-dinners guys. They can go to hell, frankly. What we want is full-time MPs who put their constituents first. That is what people want and we should change our hours in order to reflect that … It's like (hospital) consultants – 'I had to work all night, why shouldn't you.' They can go to hell. I think it's offensive. I think children would still be up chimneys if we stuck with that. 'I had to go up a chimney, why shouldn't you.' Well, the world has moved on.

SOCIAL WORKERS

Greg Power of Charter88 analyzed the constituency role of MPs and found that before 1945 many MPs visited their constituencies only once a year. They received two or three letters a day and replied in longhand. Today, because of the weakness of the ombudsman system, many MPs have become social workers and problem-solvers for their constituents. Liberal Democrat MP for Winchester Mark Oaten, for example, gets 500 or 600 letters a week, while Power cites the absurd example of an MP who was asked by a constituent to update him on the British Antarctic Survey, a subject on which he knew nothing. He nonetheless complied. Many of these MPs are struggling to cope, but are unwilling to adopt the robust approach of former Speaker Bernard Weatherill, who once replied to a constituent asking for help with council housing by telling him: 'If it was called parliamentary housing, I would be delighted to help you.'

The Labour party initially encouraged its large number of MPs, many of whom have no real job in parliament if they are not on a Select Committee, to spend regular weeks away from Westminster, holding extended constituency surgeries. Power quotes research from 1990 revealing that MPs spent 40 per cent of their time – the largest slice – on constituency work. Labour's Paul Flynn had one constituent who complained about the dustmen leaving a bin in the middle of his drive, forcing him to get out of his car and move it to one side. 'The MP politely enquired why he had contacted him about this, and the constituent replied: "Well, I've already phoned 10 Downing Street and they told me to call you."' Power suggests many MPs are afraid of becoming known as bad constituency members and suffering the fate of Michael Portillo in 1997.

The leftwing Labour MP Gordon Prentice described to me his multiple roles:

The classic division of the job is you are part social worker, you are part legislator, you are part advocate, because this place is like a gigantic soap box. You can stand up and get publicity for a cause you want to believe in, a cause you want to support. And you just move the argument along … It is up to individual MPs how they divide the time. Certainly as far as I am concerned, constituency work is important, but it doesn't submerge me … But on the political side, doing your surgeries is immensely important for giving you a political feel for what's happening.

Fiona Mactaggart also believes the constituency link and the representative function is vital for MPs:

The most important is to make parliament make sense to the people. I believe in democracy and I am terrified that democracy is sort of going out of fashion, that there is some faint sense that somehow a business oligarchy would be better. Actually it wouldn't. The wonderful, the gorgeous, the splendid thing about MPs is that however stupid, venal, whatever we are, any MP who does any work, and even those who don't, has to know what a quite wide cross-section of people think, a wide cross-section whom they would never think of going to a dinner party with … Because they knock on their doors, because they come to their surgeries, because they get bumped into in the supermarket. And that is such a powerful tool, which is underused by all parties. What we have to do as well as recognizing and celebrating the role of MPs as people's tribune is to make sure that people can see themselves here in parliament. To a lot of people, having someone like Dennis Skinner who used to be down a pit is actually a significant motivator to vote. It is not just the toffs, the nobs. For a lot of women, having more women in parliament is significant.

THE AWKWARD SQUAD

> 66 Some MPs manage to carve out a distinctive niche as parliamentary sharpshooters. It is possible to make a distinctive career out of asking awkward questions. 99

Some MPs manage to carve out a distinctive niche as parliamentary sharpshooters. It is possible, as the veteran Labour member Tam Dalyell has shown, to make a distinctive career out of asking awkward questions. Gordon Prentice has many of the same qualities of sheer cussedness and persistence that can get a backbencher quite a long way. Labour's Ann Clwyd, who has been in the Commons for 16 years and has also been a member of the European Parliament, believes individual MPs can still make a difference, but only if they are prepared to work at an issue for a number of years. In May 2000 I watched Clwyd introduce a 90-minute debate in Westminster Hall, a new Commons 'alternative' chamber created as an experiment in 1999, on the need to regulate cosmetic surgery. Although I saw only two or three other MPs present, and even fewer journalists, she was not wasting her breath. Her speech led the radio news bulletins that day because she used parliamentary privilege to name a particular cosmetic surgeon as responsible for a whole string of botched operations. I asked her afterwards if she had been surprised by the level of media interest:

I was a bit surprised by the coverage, but also not that surprised – I have been a journalist myself. So if you name somebody and call him a butcher and say other people are calling him a psychopath, it's not surprising that you get that kind of reaction. But you have to consider also that I have been campaigning for six years. That is the thing in this place. If you are campaigning for somebody, you just don't do a one-off. You have got to be persistent ... There came a time when I was getting so many letters I really couldn't handle them any more, it was a full-time job just replying.

Clwyd chairs the all-party group on human rights, campaigning on issues such as the rights of Iraqi Kurds, arms sales to Indonesia, and the abolition of landmines. She is also prepared to defy the Labour Whips when she feels it is the right thing to do. Her recalcitrance in opposition over a Bill to privatize Felixstowe docks led directly to a reform in the way the Commons deals with private (i.e. non-governmental) legislation. Clwyd wishes some of her colleagues were equally prepared to use their freedom to ask the government questions: 'Obviously I would prefer people to be a bit more robust, rather than asking their honourable friend if their honourable friend agrees with them or not.'

Another avenue for an industrious backbench MP is to sponsor a private member's Bill to promote a particular cause, but the mathematical chances of such Bills reaching the statute book are tiny because of lack of parliamentary time. When it comes to government legislation, individual backbench MPs can filibuster and delay legislation in the Commons chamber, but only rarely can they force big changes if the government has a large majority. One who succeeded was Gordon Prentice, who in 2000 managed, by lining up Labour backbenchers to support an amendment of his own, to extract a promise from the government to introduce its own Bill to ban fox-hunting:

The Countryside and Rights of Way Bill had three sections: access to the open countryside, improving the right of way network, and wildlife protection. In my second reading debate I realized it was possibly amendable to ban fox-hunting because of section three. I said to the Whips, if you put me on this Bill, I am going to move an amendment in committee to stop people hunting with hounds within a certain distance of a public right of way. The whole country is criss-crossed with public rights of way, so the net effect of that would be to ban fox-hunting. It was an open secret that I was thinking of doing this ... I spoke to the RSPCA and they got a QC to draft a new clause for me so I knew that legally it was watertight, and I spoke extensively to the Clerks here to make sure that it was in order ... So Kevin Hughes, the Whip, would sort of chide me about it and say, you are not going to do this, are you? Then as we got to the end of the committee stage, I actually put it in and that is when the shit hit the fan. There was tremendous pressure on me to withdraw it ... It was really very difficult. I was accused of being a dilettante. 'You're not helping the government, you are letting colleagues down.' I said, what I want to do is, I will withdraw my amendment if you say publicly on the record that the government will bring in its own Bill. And that was a Blairite third way that was staring everyone in the face.

The other thing is, you have to get people behind you. So I wrote to all members of the parliamentary Labour party including the Prime Minister, and said, here is my amendment, I want you to sign it, and the first couple of days I got 60 names back, and it just kept going up and the Whips tried to collar people. Three people withdrew their names, only three. Eventually it got to the 100 mark and it was up to about 105, 106. Also I said to the Whips, unless I get this public statement, when the Bill returns to the floor of the House … I will press it to a division. It is just going to be Armageddon. I lose, the government loses, the Prime Minister loses, you alienate the animal welfare lobby and it is just lose, lose, lose. And do what I am suggesting and it is win, win.

Such successful arm-twisting is rare, but the essential point is that the power of the party managers is not as great as popularly believed, even under Blair. Fiona Mactaggart, who as Parliamentary Private Secretary to Culture Secretary Chris Smith has a toehold on the lowest rung of the government ladder, agrees:

You tell me what powers the Whips have. Actually, it's all complete nonsense. They don't have any. They have the power you give them. You have to take responsibility … The Whips work by making you think they can do terrible things to you. I believe in a party system and so I accept the responsibilities of the Whip and if I had a fundamental objection I would vote against.

DOUBLE POTIONS

Philip Norton, the Conservative political scientist from Hull University who keeps a professional eye on the Commons from his seat in the House of Lords, believes the clock cannot be put back:

You can't deratchet it, you can't stop MPs having offices. You give them offices, they will go and sit in them, you give them TVs, they will watch the chamber. You can't stop televising parliament. There is a ratchet effect, you can't simply reverse the changes; you have to look to other ways of correcting the situation.

Norton believes it is too simplistic to blame the decline of parliament on the rise of the party Whips: 'The Whips have always been there. At the turn of the century they were issuing four- and five-line Whips. That is just being reinforced by giving people pagers.'

His solution, set out in a report written for William Hague under the title *Strengthening Parliament*, assumes that parliament is the answer rather than the problem; the Westminster model has to be restored to health and strength rather than have its powers devolved elsewhere:

Failure on the part of parliament to carry out its tasks effectively is not an argument for looking to other bodies to carry out those tasks … To strengthen parliament in fulfilling its functions is to boost the health of the political system. That is our starting point … We accept the basic attributes of the Westminster model … Our task therefore is not to create a new constitutional framework for the United Kingdom but rather to ensure that the balance within the Westminster system is achieved.

The ineffectiveness of the Commons in giving proper scrutiny to new laws has been commonly acknowledged at Westminster for years. 'It is a scandal,' admits one senior Labour backbencher. One of the weakest links in the chain is the system of ad hoc Standing Committees, which are supposed to scrutinize Bills clause by clause. Such committees are the equivalent of Harry Potter's 'double potions' class and attract even less press attention than debates in the chamber. 'Standing Committees absorb huge amounts of parliamentarians' time and energy, limiting the amount available for more useful forms of executive scrutiny – just what the government Whips want.'[5] Government backbenchers are required to attend Standing Committees in order to vote, but are not otherwise expected to prolong the proceedings. In the process, as Liberal Democrat Robert Maclennan explains, items as important as the government's annual tax changes in the Budget do not get properly examined:

As they are at present operated they are largely useless. I have served now on more than I care to remember. It has got worse and worse. Governments are less and less inclined to listen to suggestions, however constructive, however broadly supported outside of the committee. They seem to take the opportunity to display machismo, to turn down everything that is proposed, and the result of that is that the government members just sit there like *tricoteuses*. While they don't do their knitting they do their constituency correspondence, while two or three deputed members of the opposition speak for all the lobbying interests and groups and just get swatted aside. I think the whole thing has become a sham. And because it is an adversarial process, it is not the best way to extract from the government the case for what they are doing. It remains a system that is wedded to the past and not to present needs, which are to allow those who are affected by legislation or potentially affected by legislation to have an opportunity seriously to consider its impact and to make recommendations during the process of legislation.

It is at its worst no doubt in the area of the Finance Acts, where there is a failure to distinguish between what is necessary to enable the government to manage the macro economy, and changes which are being brought forward to fine-tune the tax system. And I think we should be separating these and giving the legislature much greater *ex-ante* consideration of fiscal measures than they have. Parliament is at present virtually powerless in respect of taxation proposals, and we have specifically proposed changes in this area to allow the Commons to substitute its view as to where funding should go, subject to overall totals and subject to an overriding veto from the Chancellor if he felt it would have some untoward effect. There hasn't been any change in a tax proposal of a government, I think, since there was a successful attempt to reduce expenditure on the Lord Chancellor's apartment in 1919. So there is a huge issue here.

Tony Wright confesses his experience as a Standing Committee member: 'At first I was shocked to see some government members writing their Christmas cards. Now I understand and write my Christmas cards too.' A more productive avenue for MPs is to win a coveted place on a prominent Select Committee dealing with education, health or foreign affairs. But the performance of these committees is patchy, partly because the high turnover of membership at the behest of the Whips does not allow MPs to build up the kind of expertise they would need to provide really effective scrutiny. Standing Committees can be used as the equivalent of a punishment battalion for dissident MPs, while appointment to a Select Committee is generally a reward for good behaviour. In the words of Gordon Prentice:

The way the whole thing works is the bestowal or the withdrawal of favours. If you want to get on a particular committee, if you want to get off a particular committee, if you want to get on a Select Committee, it's bestowing favours or withholding favours … The whole thing is about managing and manipulating.

And that only happens where everything is opaque and people don't know the processes. Once you start explaining clearly what processes are, how you get on committees, how you do this, how you do that, then obviously the kind of clout of the Whips will diminish.

If offered the chance, most MPs want to advance their careers by joining the government. 'One whiff of the greasy pole and they are off to be bag-carrier for a minister,' as one Select Committee chairman ruefully remarked. Sometimes even Select Committee chairmen take the government shilling, as Chris Mullin did when he swapped the Home Affairs committee leadership for a junior job at the Department of the Environment, Transport and the Regions in 1999.

A LUXURY PRISON

> 66 Many start to compare Westminster with a luxury prison and wonder why they fought so hard to get the Muggles to elect them. 'What am I doing here?' is the obvious question. 99

At busy times of the year, the 14-hour day becomes an 18-hour day and exhausted MPs sit around waiting to vote at two in the morning on a Bill they have not read after a debate they have not attended. Many start to compare Westminster with a luxury prison and wonder why they fought so hard to get the Muggles to elect them. 'What am I doing here?' is the obvious question. The case for modernizing parliament's working hours and practices starts to seem overwhelming. But this is the point at which the argument becomes complicated, as Tony Wright explains:

There are two kinds of modernization. One is, can we make the place slightly more efficient, can we stop engaging in funny practices, can we get home at reasonable times? It's an antique club, and it needs sorting out. But the second and more fundamental kind of modernization is about altering the balance between parliament and the executive. That would be the test you would apply at the end of a period of modernization: have you altered the balance between parliament and the executive? The answer so far on the modernization programme is no. It's not been intended to do that.

Labour's 1997 election manifesto promised a modest menu of changes to the Commons – the creation of a Modernization Committee, a change to Prime

Minister's Questions to make it more effective, a review of ministerial accountability 'so as to remove recent abuses', and better procedures for dealing with European legislation. Much of this modernization agenda has come about and further moves are due, but the malaise in parliament has got worse. 'Modernization' has turned out to mean cautious changes in working hours and in the legislative process, most of which make life easier for the executive. 'Reviewing' accountability has not meant increasing it. The result has been frustration, accentuated by Labour's big 179-seat majority which has left many Labour MPs without a clear role. Robert Maclennan of the Liberal Democrats believes the balance between legislature and executive could be altered by making the government payroll smaller:

It is an inflated administration, and it is inflated not because there is an administrative need to have this many ministers. It is inflated because it is helpful to the government to get its way. A third of its membership is very closely tied to it, and about half lives in expectation of favours or offices or emoluments. That has resulted, in my opinion, in an excessive deference on the part of the government benches towards the executive. Now I do think this has got worse.

The Commons is more marginalized under Blair than under John Major, who told the Commons Public Administration Committee in July 2000:

What has happened over a long period of a quarter of a century is that the power and authority of the executive has grown, the power and authority of the House of Commons has weakened. That needs redressing. That was masked by the lack of a majority. If you have a majority of 21 and 30 people who disagree with you on every issue, then there is no lack of accountability. Giving more power to the chamber, that is whistling in the wind. There is no way back to the days when 600 members crowded in and made up their minds at the end of a debate. Or you can go down the road of increasing scrutiny through a committee system. I don't think that is perfect, but it is less imperfect than the other alternative.[6]

Major, who defended the constitutional status quo when he was in office, now sounds rather more radical than Blair. The really big questions about the role of parliament in Labour's 'new constitutional settlement' have been sidestepped in favour of institutional tinkering on a narrow front. Tony Wright admitted in a Hansard Society discussion in May 2000 that the results of Labour's modernization of parliament were meagre compared with the effort it had expended on modernizing government:

We didn't say we were just going to improve the hours, tidy the place up and stop people wearing funny hats ... Have we made progress? No, we haven't. Has the balance shifted one jot from the executive towards the legislature? I would say it hasn't.

Wright's verdict to the Hansard Society audience was fairly bleak; he quoted a 30-year-old definition of parliament by Enoch Powell as 'simply the place where government and opposition come together and do battle, the site of a permanent election campaign'. The inevitable conclusion is that parliament *as parliament* does not really exist, except as a backdrop.

BLAIR AND PARLIAMENT

While Tony Blair has denounced the 'forces of conservatism' elsewhere in Britain, telling institutions such as the civil service, the teaching profession and the NHS to adapt or die, the truth is that he has proved the opposite of a reformer in his own Westminster backyard. Conservative MP Andrew Tyrie, in a recent pamphlet, blames Blair personally for accelerating the decline of parliament. He argues that Blair stands alone in the infrequency with which he takes part in debates and turns up to vote, making it to the division lobby only 6 per cent of the time in his first year and only 8 per cent in his second: 'What distinguishes Tony Blair even from the Lloyd George and Churchill comparisons, born of the unique pressures of war, is the current Prime Minister's neglect of, even disdain for, parliament.'[7] Tyrie says Blair's attitude to parliament is 'tokenism'. This may be seen as a partisan view, but two academics who recently analyzed Blair's record came to a similar conclusion: 'Both Lloyd George and Bonar Law were ten or 20 times more likely than Blair to make a major speech in a debate or intervene to correct or defend a point at issue.' They concluded on a downbeat note: 'Pessimists might wonder whether perhaps Blair is right to stay away from an anachronistic parliament, doomed to be replaced by focus groups and websites.'[8]

When the independent MP Martin Bell questioned him in March 1999 about giving backbenchers more freedom and making parliament 'rather more the free parliament of a free people, and rather less a rubber-stamp assembly', Blair was dismissive, saying he believed his government was entitled to put through its programme on which it was elected. As things stand, Blair appears in parliament mostly to report on his foreign travels and on EU summits, occasions where supplementary questions are not allowed. With the exception of the announcement of the government's plan for the NHS, he has avoided taking the lead in debates on significant policy issues, as his predecessors might have done. Blair's rustiness in routine parliamentary debate was cruelly exposed in July 2000 when he repeatedly addressed one of Betty Boothroyd's deputies, Sir Alan Haselhurst, as 'Madam Speaker'. The mistake revealed that Blair had lost the habit of attending the Commons after the initial two-hour period devoted to questions and ministerial statements, presided over by Boothroyd in person.

ORDER, ORDER

Immediately after taking office, Blair unilaterally announced that Prime Minister's Questions would in future be held for half an hour on Wednesdays rather than a quarter of an hour each on Tuesdays and Thursdays. The change was announced as a *fait accompli*, with no discussion with the opposition through normal Commons channels, or in the Modernization Committee. Roy Jenkins believes Blair genuinely wanted to change the atmosphere of the session by slowing down the pace and going back to a genuine exchange. 'Exactly the reverse has happened ... It has become more and more a Punch and Judy show.' The weekly attempt by Blair and William Hague to produce a killer soundbite for the evening news has begun to look increasingly desperate. Blair has acknowledged that the raucous partisanship of the occasion is hardly a good advertisement for parliament.[9] John Major, speaking to the Commons Public Administration Committee, described Prime Minister's Questions as:

... a bit of a bear garden, it is as much a test of memory as policy. Can he remember that there is a shortage of bedpans in Basingstoke hospital and who is responsible? Prime Minister's Questions is wonderful entertainment, but no forum for constructive debate.

Blair has, however, rejected the alternative idea that he might occasionally appear before the Commons Liaison Committee, which groups together the 30 or so senior legislators who chair the Select Committees. Those who favour it say this would produce proper scrutiny of government business in a much calmer atmosphere, and Major now favours the idea:

Appearing before the Liaison Committee would be of use to the Prime Minister, to parliament and to the public. Not every month, but once or twice a year. Would I have accepted? If it was serious, yes. The Cabinet Secretary would probably have argued against it on grounds of precedent. I am not trying to open a bear trap under the Prime Minister's foot. I am trying to find the forum for detailed examination. There is no reason not to invite the leader of the opposition either.

Tony Wright's Public Administration Committee has tried unsuccessfully to invite Blair to come and answer questions about the Ministerial Code, an issue for which the Prime Minister has sole responsibility. In reply to two letters from Wright, Blair cited 'long-standing convention' as a reason for his refusal. Blair's chief of staff Jonathan Powell has also refused to be questioned by the committee about his own role in 10 Downing Street.

THE GOLDEN PAGER

66 Prime Minister's Questions provides an instant litmus test to distinguish those MPs on the Labour benches who are still trying to climb the career ladder and those who have given up. 99

One of the few good things to be said about Prime Minister's Questions is that it provides an instant litmus test to distinguish those MPs on the Labour benches who are still trying to climb the career ladder and those who have given up. In 1999 at Bournemouth I attended an unusual award ceremony during the Labour conference, organized by the self-styled 'Old Testament Prophets', a curmudgeonly group of off-message Labour MPs including Robert Marshall-Andrews, a raffish and gravel-voiced barrister, and veteran professional Yorkshireman Austin Mitchell. The party was to announce their annual 'golden pager' award to one of their colleagues for the most sycophantic question posed to Blair. There was hot competition for the award, which finally went to Labour loyalist Barry Sheerman. The pager, golden or just plain black, has become a symbol of the discipline imposed by the Labour Whips' office. What is intriguing about Blair is that the more 'helpful' (sycophantic) the question from his own backbenchers, the more groans it provokes in the press gallery, the more he seems to like it.

Andrew Mackinlay, another one of Labour's awkward squad, challenged Blair directly on 3 June 1998, pressing him to give up the 'fawning, obsequious, softball, well-rehearsed and planted questions'. Blair's put-down was elegantly phrased to indicate that people who asked such questions might have a chance of getting on the government payroll, but free thinkers like Mackinlay would not. 'I fully respect my honourable friend's independence of mind, and shall do my very best to ensure that he retains it.'

THE USES OF MODERNITY

Labour loyalists, however, are just as gloomy about the state of the Commons as Labour dissidents. In a debate in November 2000, Barry Sheerman complained:

Those who have been members of parliament for some time know that this place is dying on its feet. If we do not find a proper role for parliament, we shall become merely subservient to ministers and the executive.

Talking to MPs one soon realizes there is no such thing as a simple division between 'modernizers' and 'conservatives'. There are tensions which criss-cross party lines, not only between generations but between London-based MPs and those who try to split their week between Westminster and their far-flung constituencies, and between those whose whole life revolves around their existence as an MP and those who are trying to juggle Westminster with their family commitments. Although the party divide runs the deepest, there is also an important division between frontbenchers and backbenchers on both sides. The adversarial culture and design of the Commons disguises the fact that for the institution to function at all, government and opposition front benches have to talk. In practice, they communicate regularly behind the scenes through what are known as the 'usual channels' to agree the calendar of business, though the process is not transparent. Without such agreement, the opposition would not get the chance to hold debates on issues of its choice. Under the Blair government, with its packed legislative programme, cooperation between the two front benches has often gone further, with the opposition agreeing to speed up the progress of Bills by cutting off debate. The move towards what are known euphemistically as 'programme motions', or guillotines-by-agreement, leaves some Conservative and Labour backbenchers fuming. These MPs, such as the Conservative Eric Forth, seek to defend a long tradition of backbench filibustering and use of Commons procedure to deprive the government of time, the only real weapon the opposition has. The problem for backbenchers is that the executive dominates the

Commons not just through the Whips but through its control of the legislative timetable, something which dates back to the 1880s when the major parties agreed on a major reform of standing orders to block filibustering by Irish nationalist MPs.

Late-night sittings have angered younger Labour MPs from the 1997 intake, who are seen by their older colleagues, veterans of similar guerrilla ambushes in opposition against the Thatcher government, as wet behind the ears. A leading advocate of the view that family-friendly modernization is just a smokescreen for making life easier for the executive is veteran Labour MP Gwyneth Dunwoody, who chairs the Commons Select Committee on Transport. 'I am devastated when I hear members speak about the need to modernize, by which they mean to timetable and to reorganize the House of Commons,' she complained in a debate in June 1998. She lamented the fact that many new MPs did not understand that they had the right to hold the government to account and ask awkward questions. 'This is rather an unfashionable view, but we as individual members have a responsibility not only to our constituents but to a number of basic principles, one of which concerns the desire of the people of the United Kingdom to be governed by responsible and open government that is accountable at every level.' Dunwoody warned against altering the rules of the Commons just to make things convenient for the current government. 'It is sometimes assumed that we shall have Labour governments in perpetuity. That may be the case, but we should never alter the rules of the House on that assumption. That would be extremely dangerous.'

In May 2000 Tess Kingham, one of the very few among the 1997 intake of Labour MPs with an interest and expertise in foreign affairs, announced she was standing down at the next election, partly out of frustration at the hours. The former Oxfam worker complained that the Commons never got the chance to debate serious matters because it was being kept up all night by the opposition's 'silly games'. Kingham, who spent four months away from the Commons having twins, told her fellow MPs: 'This should be a modern parliament that can accommodate women members having children as well as serving their constituents.' Veteran Conservative Sir Patrick Cormack replied in patronizing terms that by expecting 'fixed hours and clocking on and off' she had 'failed to understand what being a member of parliament is all about.' Cormack's view was, good riddance to the woman. 'I believe very strongly that it is not the job of parliament to adjust its procedures for the convenience of individual members.' Cormack was supported by Dunwoody, who acknowledged that her views on modernization would not make her popular either with the government or with newer members, 'who will only too readily write off the views of anyone who does not believe that our role in parliament is to be a salaried employee of particular parties, answerable not to those who send us here and perhaps not even, in a wider sense, to the constituencies that are, to me, the final and most important arbiter of my life'.

Dunwoody described as dangerous the idea that 'if we were somehow to reorganize the hours of parliament and go home at 5pm – like well brought up office personnel – and if we were not to sit through the night, we would produce better legislation.' Parliament was not a rubber stamp for the executive and MPs should recognize that they would not be able to get away to see their families whenever they wanted. 'I had three children when I first entered the house, aged 12, 10 and 8. I therefore know what tremendous costs family life has to bear. That is the same for males and females. This is a brutal place. It destroys more people than it creates. Those of us who come here do so because we believe that democracy and the expression of the views of ordinary voters are of fundamental importance.'

A similar message was given by arch-traditionalist Speaker Betty Boothroyd in her retirement speech, which reminded MPs that the function and 'core task' of parliament was to hold the executive to account:

The House must be prepared to put in the hours necessary to carry out effective examination of the government's legislative programme. If that means long days, or rearrangement of the parliamentary year, so be it. Of course, I have been here long enough to recognize the importance of enabling parliamentarians to enjoy a domestic life; it should not be impossible to meet both objectives. But where there is a clash, the requirements of effective scrutiny and the democratic process must take priority over the convenience of members.

The election of Boothroyd's successor in October 2000 provided ample evidence of the Commons' collective inability to embrace reform. An unprecedented field of 12 candidates led many MPs to seek to alter the traditional procedure under which they vote on candidates one after the other by means of amendments to a motion. But the push for change proved unsuccessful; Sir Edward Heath, chairing proceedings as the longest-serving MP, turned down a request by fellow veteran Tony Benn for a ballot and a runoff between the two leading candidates. The debate which followed left many MPs deeply uneasy about what the Conservative MP and Public Accounts Committee chairman David Davis described as an antiquated procedure that would bring the House into disrepute. Gordon Prentice, who helped organize unofficial hustings with candidates before the session, expressed the view of many when he said: 'People do not want to elect the new Speaker using a discredited system that would not have been out of place in Eastern Europe before the (Berlin) wall came down.'

Heath told MPs he had considerable sympathy with their anxieties but did not believe he had the power under Commons standing orders to open a debate on changing the method of election. As a result the election took an entire day, ending with the victory of one of Boothroyd's deputies, Labour MP Michael Martin, a Glasgow trade unionist and the first Catholic to hold the job since the Reformation. Unlike most of the candidates, Martin failed to attract cross-party support and owed his victory to Labour's large majority. His first decision was to follow Boothroyd in dispensing with the traditional Speaker's wig, a small gesture in the direction of modernization.

Despite the prestige of the Speaker's historic office, the holder of the post has only limited powers. These were summarized by Tony Benn in the 1992 debate which led to Boothroyd's election:

Apart from keeping order, which is not as difficult as it might appear, the Speaker can allow or disallow parliamentary questions to ministers, and thus expose or protect them; accept or refuse closure motions, which can prolong or stop debates; select or reject backbench motions or amendments, and thus deny a minority view in the House from ever being put in the lobbies; permit or deny private notice questions or emergency debates; call or not call individual members; and give or withhold precedence to Privy Councillors, which is the source of much anger. He can determine which Bills are hybrid and which are not; use a casting vote if there is a tie; recall the Commons in a recess – a formidable power – in the event of some international crisis; certify a money Bill; and rule on matters of privilege.

This list of functions sounds impressive, but the real power in the Commons lies elsewhere, as Ken Livingstone wrote in *The Independent* after Martin's election:

As I sat through the interminable voting on Monday, I was struck by the number of MPs who bemoaned the decline in their power and prestige over the past 30 years and seemed to feel that, somehow, one particular candidate or another might reverse the trend. That is nonsense. The Speaker is both bound by the precedents established by the rulings of previous Speakers and a prisoner of the brutal reality that most MPs are more concerned about getting a job as a minister than building a strong parliament capable of holding the executive to account. Even in my relatively brief parliamentary career of 13 years, things have become considerably worse. Each new election brings in more fresh, eager young puppies to be contained in the holding-pen until the Prime Minister puts them on the first rung of the ministerial ladder.

Livingstone said neither a new Speaker nor the government would rescue MPs from their impotence; they would have to do it themselves. Real change would happen only with a change in the voting system to PR, which would deny governments an automatic majority.

MODERNIZATION – THE CASE AGAINST

One Labour and one Conservative backbencher argue against modernization during a debate on 4 July 2000 on whether to cut short debate on the report stage of the Local Government Bill:

Mrs Gwyneth Dunwoody (Crewe and Nantwich): If both frontbench teams agree a timetable – I am not talking about any particular type of legislation, but about all legislation – the right of backbenchers to move amendments and the right of constituents to ask their individual members to move an amendment that may not be agreed by their particular party will be, if not grossly circumscribed, then, even worse, lost.

As a democrat, I happen to think that the reason why the House of Commons works – indeed, the reason why our extraordinary system of government in the United Kingdom works – is because it is sufficiently flexible to allow any person who wants to write, to telephone or to visit an individual member of parliament to raise a matter that could form the basis of an amendment to legislation. If that is lost because of an agreement by both frontbench teams to get legislation through, irrespective of how many individual members of parliament have the right to take part in the debate, we are moving towards a juggernaut system that will destroy many of the rights of individuals in this place and in the UK generally. I am almost coming to dread the words 'programme motion' and 'usual channels' because I have been here long enough to know that power always resides in the Whips' offices and with those who agree on the general programming of the material.

Mr Richard Shepherd (Aldridge-Brownhills): In this session so far – not even counting what the Home Secretary has in store for us – there have been 2,537 pages of legislation. That is putting not a quart but a gallon into a pint pot ... The system is breaking down. The government write legislation as it goes through the House, as the hon. member for Crewe and Nantwich made admirably clear. The practice is improper, but yet again the House is being marched to the guillotine.

Modernization – the case for

Male Members by Bethnal Green Labour MP Oona King in the *Guardian*, 19 May 2000.

I first saw Tess Kingham at the Commons during a vote. Her short, peroxide-blonde hair stood out in a sea of establishment grey. I almost fell over in my hurry to reach her. 'I just wanted to say hello because [subtext: you look like a normal person who I would go out with in normal circumstances, and I haven't got any mates to vote with] . . . I don't think we've met.' 'Yes we have,' she replied, 'but that was before I got elected. The day after, I dyed my hair blonde.' Good woman, I thought, and was thrilled when we were both nominated to the Select Committee on International Development. Over the past three years she's become my closest friend at Westminster. She is well balanced, witty, highly intelligent (she excels in the scrutiny role of an MP), immensely sympathetic and very human. In essence, everything Westminster demands you are not. Now Tess is standing down as a Labour MP at the general election. The media pounce on her decision as proof that women with young children can't cope with the rigours of Westminster. In fact, it highlights the more significant point that Westminster can't cope with well-balanced human beings. The attitude of many senior politicians and hacks is 'if you can't stand the heat get out of the kitchen'. They don't appreciate that this kitchen flouts modern employment and health and safety standards; and it churns out low-grade slop.

Important legislation affecting millions of lives is routinely discussed in the middle of the night. How awake are you at 4am? Is it a good time to consider equality legislation, public procurement, or military attack (issues we've been asked to consider in the early hours)? The concept of 24 hours on call infects the lives of backbenchers and ministers alike. Yvette Cooper, minister for public health, at 31 with a ten-month-old baby, says: 'The whole ministerial system is predicated on the idea that all decisions are taken between 10pm [after the vote] and 8am when your day at the office begins.' True, a breastfeeding mother would have problems with this. But so too would anyone – unless they are institutionalized or socially maladjusted. The British public should have a problem with it too, because this is the system that governs the people who govern them.

People complain that MPs are out of touch with the real world. Is that a surprise, if they aren't allowed to leave the rarefied environs of the House of Commons – the world's most luxurious prison – until after 10pm? If you create an environment where only those with no regard for their family and their relationships can survive, then you shouldn't be surprised if those same politicians do not push hard enough for radical legislation needed to tackle the pressures British people face at work. We work the longest hours in Europe. But MPs are taught that a 14-hour day is normal. Our current democracy is decidedly unrepresentative. On the whole, Westminster is not a place women want to hang around. 'It's set up to suit 19th-century men,' protests Tess. 'Everything about it is a gentleman's club – the atmosphere, the bars, the restaurants, the appointments on to committees. I'm not interested in soaking up a culture of Commons living. I'm interested in doing my job efficiently, but the rules make it impossible.' Tess complains that 'it's like a public school fagging system. Certain people have the power to decide, on a whim, what your working hours are. The same rules don't apply to everyone. You can't ever understand until you've been an MP, the reality of the whipping system. It's not the fault of the individual Whips themselves, but the whole system stinks.' She is right. Even though my own Whip has gone out of his way to make my life easier, I don't see why I have to discuss details of my marriage if I want an evening off. It should be like any other business, with clear rules and procedures.

So what has to change? Firstly, the hours. That means switching the average parliamentary day from 2.30pm–10pm, to say, 9am–7pm (with the exception of Mondays so that the needs of those MPs outside London are taken into account). We need some predictability. We have to change the rules around the timetabling and programming of Bills so that one or two individuals do not hold the rest of their colleagues hostage. The most notorious parliamentary guerrilla is Eric Forth, a Tory MP who delights in gratuitous warfare (he's currently in full swing over the Royal Parks Trading Bill, which among other things considers the crucial importance of ice-cream vans outside parks).

We need to change the culture of the place and its facilities. Why do we still have a shooting gallery and no creche? Why can an MP still buy scrambled eggs at any time of the day or night, but can't access a word processor in the library? Saner MPs – male and female, with children and without – want some answers. The government says it is moving as quickly as it can. We have been told it is very difficult to change the standing orders of the House. But I just don't buy it. The fact is, there are conservatives among both the government and the opposition who don't want change. That's why Tess is leaving. She believes the cost to her private life isn't worth the thrill of listening to debates on ice-cream cones at 2am. But equally significant is the commitment of Labour MPs who stay behind to change this system for the good.

DIVIDE AND RULE

These sharp divisions among MPs form the background to the Labour government's cautious attempts to nudge through a series of piecemeal changes in Commons working procedures since 1997. Change has gone too fast for some and too slowly for others, allowing the government to divide and rule, pursuing its own priorities. As Peter Riddell of *The Times* puts it, modernization of the Commons 'has been one of the most slippery of the Blair government's pledges'. The government's instrument has been the Commons Modernization Committee, chaired for the 1997–98 session by Ann Taylor, who then became Chief Whip, and since then by her successor as Leader of the House Margaret Beckett. Many MPs now believe it was a fatal flaw to have the Select Committee run by a minister. Sir George Young, who was shadow Leader of the House for most of this period and also a member of the committee, told the Commons in November 2000:

The chairman of the Modernization Committee is the Leader of the House, whose task as a member of the Cabinet is to deliver the Queen's Speech – she is its midwife. She winds up the debate on the Loyal Address and, every Thursday, she announces the business, which is inevitably dominated by the political imperative of getting the Bills through. Is it right to entrust to a committee under the chairmanship of the Leader of the House the responsibility for changing our rules? Has not the House traditionally done that? Does not the concept of a Select Committee chaired by a cabinet minister sit uneasily with the rationale of establishing Select Committees: to strengthen the House's ability to hold the government to account?

The committee has built on earlier reforms initiated by Tony Newton, the Leader of the House under John Major, aimed at improving parliament's notoriously poor scrutiny of legislation. The magic black opera hat, kept in the Commons for MPs to put on to catch the Speaker's attention during a vote, has finally been banished to a museum. More significant changes have included the early publication of Bills in draft form to be chewed over by committees before they begin their formal passage through parliament. In some cases, such as the Freedom of Information Bill and the Financial Services and Markets Bill, this has proved a lengthy and painful process for the government. Bills can now be carried over by agreement between government and opposition from one annual session to the next, rather than falling completely at the end of a session. Sitting times on Thursdays have been brought forward to 11.30 am. to enable members to leave for their constituencies at 7 pm. Adjournment debates without a vote, in which MPs raise their issues of concern, have been increased in number and moved out of the Commons chamber to the new Westminster Hall chamber, a continental-style semicircle in a previously little-used committee room. In the Commons chamber the Speaker now has the discretion to limit the length of speeches by backbenchers. Other mooted changes, such as the introduction of electronic voting to replace the system of filing through lobbies, have failed to win widespread support and have been shelved for the time being.

Tony Wright believes Beckett's Modernization Committee was flawed because it ignored the example set by Leader of the House Richard Crossman in the 1960s and began work without agreeing a clear goal and identifying what parliament should be doing:

The better thing would have been for it to have started off with some position statement setting out how it saw parliament. Then you measure the modernization measures against the template that you have got. It explicitly didn't do that. It just went off looking at particular issues. So it never had a frame of reference.

Much of the problem in parliament stems from the sheer volume of legislation produced by the government, much of it poorly drafted and managed, and the Commons' inability to digest it. There are times when the machine seems overloaded, not only with legislation but with matters that in most countries of comparable size would never be debated in the national parliament; the lack of devolution in ultra-centralized England explains why week after week MPs have to take up the time of the national legislature with complaints about bypass roads, casualty units, local train timetables and bus routes in their constituencies. On 11 July 2000 it was the turn of Conservative MP Christopher

Gill, who used Westminster Hall to discuss the number of fire engines in Shropshire in mind-boggling detail:

As a result of reducing the number of fire appliances at Bridgnorth from two to one, calls on the single engine at Cleobury Mortimer are almost bound to increase. However, difficulties in recruiting suitable fire fighters in that town are already causing major headaches.

These are what Robert Maclennan calls 'easily devolvable issues' without which Westminster might have more time to spend on truly national questions. But the majority of MPs relish their role as constituency advocates and would strongly resist the idea that some matters are too local to be raised in parliament.

A BREAKDOWN IN CONSENSUS

In July 2000 the Modernization Committee's all-party consensus broke down over the issue of timetabling of legislation, with Conservative members issuing a minority report. The Labour and Liberal Democrat majority proposed changes that would mean an end to all-night sittings, with main Commons business ending at 10 p.m. on Mondays, Tuesdays and Wednesdays, with votes shortly afterwards. Votes on secondary legislation, instead of taking place at the end of the evening, would be deferred until a set time of the week such as Wednesday afternoon. The Conservative minority rejected the timetabling plans and the idea of a once-a-week 'vote-in' on statutory instruments. It voiced less serious objections to ending late-night sittings but said the government, not the opposition, was to blame for them. Sir George Young told me:

Everything on the table really came from the opposition and the backbenchers, with no undertaking by the government to reduce the sheer volume of Bills or to draft them better, so we saw it as a rather one-sided deal. We always made it clear that the terms of trade have shifted from parliament to the executive, and they need to be tilted back towards parliament ... On this particular item we just saw it as tilting the terms of trade the wrong way, making it even easier for the executive to get its programme through and reducing the opposition's opportunities for scrutiny. Which is why we didn't go along with it.

Beckett told a Hansard Society meeting in November 2000 that she rather regretted the shift towards universal programming of Commons business, which was made necessary by 'a phenomenon of working to rule' among some backbenchers. This was a reference to the filibustering habits of Conservatives such as Eric Forth. She predicted that the shift towards timetabling of parliamentary business might actually make life harder for the government, rather than easier. When I asked Sir George Young about his dealings with Beckett, his reply suggested a large area of consensus:

I think Margaret does have a rather traditional approach, and as Leader of the House she is actually quite conscious of the rights of opposition, and is aware that she is not just a member of the cabinet, she has a responsibility to the House as a whole. And I have certainly found her very aware of the difficulties that some of these proposals pose for us, not least if she was doing my job. And I think she is very aware that there has to be a balance and if possible you try and do things by agreement. I am sure she wouldn't say she was more conservative than me. But I think she is very conscious of the need for balance. She has come under enormous pressure from her own newer members to make faster progress than the committee has made.

Under Beckett there has been no shift towards the daytime working hours that many younger Labour MPs would like to introduce, and which are now the norm in Edinburgh and Cardiff. She told me that it was ludicrous for modernization to be defined solely as a demand for civilized working hours, which she described as 'if you are not sitting between 9 and 5.30 and then everybody goes home, it's not modernization'. Beckett said there had to be an opportunity for backbenchers to 'let off steam' but added:

I have never, as far as I can recall, been an advocate of this notion that it is a jolly clever wheeze to keep everybody up all night talking about something completely irrelevant when actually you could be discussing issues of real substance.

When I asked Beckett whether she agreed that Tess Kingham's decision to leave parliament was worrying for the Labour party, she replied:

It's not just worrying for the Labour party ... She doesn't object to the hours at all. What she objects to is being kept here until two o'clock in the morning while somebody talks about how you license hot dog trolleys in the royal parks. That is what she objects to.

There is another issue with which the Modernization Committee has yet to get to grips. Should the Commons, like the Scottish Parliament and the Welsh Assembly, spend less time in plenary debates? As Peter Riddell says, many MPs now question the value of debates in the Commons chamber, whatever time of day or night they take place. 'For most people, particularly under 40, standing up and making a speech is a strange way of communicating in the age of e-mails and the Internet.'[10]

ACCOUNTABILITY

Modernization of the Commons' internal workings may be worthwhile, but it is essentially a secondary issue. The real problem is accountability of the executive to parliament, where the government's dogged resistance to any tampering with the status quo has emerged with striking clarity. Tony Wright argues that the Commons chamber is no good at controlling the government in a sustained way: 'This chamber is good at many things, but awfully bad at accountability. It is good at raw political accountability, but bad at serious scrutiny and serious, continuous accountability.'

The Liaison Committee, which brings together the 33 senior back-benchers (31 men and two women) who chair Commons committees, proposed in March 2000 a series of modest changes to make the 20-year-old Select Committee system more effective. Its report, *Shifting the Balance: Select Committees and the Executive*, attracted almost no publicity, but its bipartisan authorship made it a significant document. In the words of David Davis, Conservative chairman of the powerful Public Accounts Committee:

To understand this battle, it is important to understand the Liaison Committee. It is not a bunch of young radicals, and it is certainly not a Tory front organization trying to undermine the government. It is the committee of chairmen of Select Committees, the senior parliamentarians of the day. Most are very senior Labour party members, who in a different age would have been ministers.[11]

The report began by noting that over the centuries, governmental power had always outstripped parliamentary control. The key recommendation was that party Whips should no longer make the key decisions over the membership and chairmanship of Select Committees. 'Members have undoubtedly been kept off committees, or removed from them, on account of their views. Oppositions as well as governments have been guilty of this, but of course if committees are to be effective scrutineers of government it is the influence of the governing party that causes us the greater concern.' Instead of the present system, which Gordon Prentice describes as 'the big fix', nominations to Select Committees should be handled by an independent panel of three senior back-benchers. The committee recommended that the government should stop looking at the work of Select Committees 'as a threat rather than an opportunity' and proposed a wider role for them in several respects, including scrutiny of appointments. The chairmen also sought extra resources for their committees and the creation of an alternative career path that would give ambitious MPs a choice other than joining the lowest rung of the government ladder. One possibility might be to pay Select Committee chairmen or to give them higher expenses. The report also recommended weekly half-hour 'prime time' debates in the Commons on Select Committee investigations.

In May these proposals drew a negative response from the government, which dismissed virtually all of them on the grounds that they might harm the rights of opposition parties, cost too much or waste parliamentary time. The authors of the report were particularly annoyed by a misleading press release from the government claiming it had 'welcomed' the report and supported the Liaison Committee's aims. Peter Riddell, abandoning his usual understatement in *The Times*, described the response as brutal, evasive, mendacious, and hypocritical:

The report was a challenge to ministers. If they believed what they said about 'modernizing' the Commons, the government would agree to allow the committees to become more independent and influential. Some hope, given that the Leader of the Commons is Margaret Beckett. She is a highly competent manager, as she showed during the John Smith era, but she epitomizes the executive-minded politician, the woman of government, without a fibre of pluralism in her being.

In July there was a frosty public exchange between the Liaison Committee and Beckett. The chairman, the veteran Labour MP Robert Sheldon, asked her directly: 'You have rejected every one of our major recommendations and yet nevertheless you say that you support our aims. What are you going to do about strengthening the system?' Beckett's stonewalling was followed by a second Liaison Committee report describing the government attitude as both disappointing and surprising:

We found it surprising that a government which has made so much of its policy of modernizing parliament should apparently take so different a view when its own accountability and freedom of action are at issue.

The Liaison Committee concluded:

We believe that in its reply the government has missed an opportunity of reforms which would have been greatly to its credit. It is strange that the expressions of support for increasing the effectiveness of Select Committees are not matched by things that might make a real difference – not even by Select Committees at Westminster having some of the powers which the government has been happy to see in Edinburgh, Cardiff and Belfast. There has been much discussion about shorter sitting hours, and more family-friendly scheduling of business in the House. This may be all very well; but any real modernization of parliament must provide better accountability and tougher scrutiny of the government of the day. This is our aim. We believe it is the test by which the public will judge the effectiveness and value of parliament. This is not something that will go away.

When I suggested to Beckett that in the argument with the Liaison Committee she was revealing herself to be on the side of the forces of conservatism, she dismissed this as 'a rather glib conclusion'. She said the committee's suggestion of a three-person panel to pick Select Committee members would give them 'enormous power and patronage'. She had been asked by Tony Wright whether she accepted the basic goal of shifting the balance between executive and legislature. 'Yes ... but not in the way that you suggest,' she replied. I asked her what she meant. Beckett told me she was worried that Select Committees might go beyond scrutinizing the work of government and 'substitute their judgement for that of government'. She described this as 'very difficult and dangerous territory to be in'. The idea of the prime minister being questioned by the Liaison Committee or the Public Administration Committee was 'completely unprecedented', she said. As Donald Macintyre commented in the *Independent*: 'Shorn of some sophistry, the government is merely saying that if previous governments haven't reformed the system, why should it?'

Tony Wright described Beckett's reasoning to me as 'very revealing':

It's a way of saying, you know and I know how we do politics here. Don't make demands on us that have never been made on anybody else before. And that I think is the most revealing thing of all, because it does highlight the issue of whether you really do want to shift the balance or not.

When the Commons finally debated the Liaison Committee report on 9 November, it became clear that the government was more determined than ever to kick it into touch. It was helped by the fact that many of the senior Select Committee chairmen who had prepared the report failed to turn up for the debate. Despite explicit promises by Blair and Beckett during an earlier debate on 13 July that there would be a free vote on the proposals, there was no motion and no chance to vote. Beckett, pressed to repeat Blair's promise of a free vote, denied that it had ever been made: 'I do not accept that there is any implication for when the debate may be carried forward, when it may be concluded, and when or whether a vote may be taken.' MPs were elected to parliament purely to be representatives of their parties, Beckett declared: 'Only in this country is it considered somehow ignoble to be a party representative, and to be above parties is considered to be the highest accolade that a politician can receive.' The veteran Conservative Peter Brooke summed this up as 'Let them eat cake'.

After more than three years of Labour government, Tony Wright's view is that the Commons is still trying to do too much and not doing anything particularly well:

The only thing it does well is the party battle. You can argue that in terms of raw political accountability it does work. You have the government clearly identified, the opposition clearly identified, constantly engaged in battle. People can see it.

The arguments about reforming parliament have been around for years and there is no lack of foreign models from which Westminster could learn some lessons, if it was prepared to do so:

The question you have to ask is, why, knowing all this, having the reform agenda there, it's never been done. It's never been done because of the way in which we do politics here. Then the question is, can you really make any substantial reform while we do politics in the same way? If you had a separation of powers, it would be entirely different. If you had a kind of electoral reform which meant that governments did not routinely have the ability to control the House of Commons, it would clearly become a different institution. But there is no appetite for changes of that kind. The real argument is that we have a system of strong government. You can explain historically how that happened, the transfer of power from Crown to executive, the modern party system. There are many virtues in that. And people seem to like a system of strong government, it is much envied elsewhere. But if you have that, it has to be balanced by a system of strong accountability.

From the government's allergic reaction to the Liaison Committee proposals, it appears that Tony Blair is deeply opposed to this kind of thinking. In the Commons as in the Lords, Labour is now the most hostile of the three major parties to any kind of democratization and reform. The unwillingness to change the status quo goes beyond the natural tendency of government to seek control. Labour's ideas fall well short of the modest

> **❝ In the Commons as in the Lords, Labour is now the most hostile of the three major parties to any kind of democratization and reform. ❞**

reformism of the proposals prepared by the Norton committee for William Hague on ways to strengthen parliament. Though individual MPs cannot shrug off responsibility, the fact remains that real reform of the Commons will not happen unless the government wants it to. In the opinion of Alex Brazier, a former Commons Committee clerk, the signs are not encouraging:

It is often said that change in the House of Commons should be incremental and evolutionary. This is understandable, in that all organizations wish to cherish their long-established procedures. But too frequently the incremental approach can be an excuse for delay and obstruction. Furthermore it is never fully explained why the House of Commons should be changed in an evolutionary, incremental way when the rest of society has to change at a rapid, often dramatic pace. The City had its 'big bang', the civil service has been transformed, and industry and the trades unions have had to modernize massively to reflect a changing market. None of this was easy or comfortable, but all concerned would now accept that it was necessary. The need to change, to adapt and be flexible is considered essential in any modern success. The lack of change in the House of Commons explains why it seems at odds with so much of a fast-moving society.[12]

The Blair-Beckett approach is that past precedent is a good enough argument for resisting the kind of change among the wizards at Westminster which the Muggles in the rest of the country are supposed to embrace.

NOTES

[1] Quoted in White, Clarissa, Bruce, Sara and Ritchie, Jane (2000) *Young People's Politics. Political interest and engagement amongst 14- to 24-year-olds*, London, Joseph Rowntree Foundation.

[2] Ashley, Jackie (2000) *I Spy Strangers: Improving access to parliament*, London, Hansard Society.

[3] White, Bruce and Ritchie., op. cit., p 25.

[4] Allen, Graham (1995) *Reinventing Democracy. Labour's mission for the new century*, London, Features Unlimited.

[5] Tyrie, Andrew (2000) *Mr Blair's Poodle*, London, Centre for Policy Studies, p 51.

[6] 18 June 2000.

[7] Tyrie, op. cit.

[8] Burnham, June and Jones, George (2000) *Accounting to Parliament by British Prime Ministers: trends and discontinuities; illusions and realities*, paper for the Political Studies Association UK 50th Annual Conference, London, April.

[9] BBC *Question Time*, 6 July 2000.

[10] *The Times*, 7 July 2000.

[11] *Independent*, 30 July 2000.

[12] Brazier, Alex (2000) *Systematic Scrutiny. Reforming the Select Committees*, London, Hansard Society.

12

SUBJECTS, CUSTOMERS
OR CITIZENS?

'At present, if an ordinary man, woman or child in these islands enquires "What are my rights as a citizen here? What defines me?", only expert, constitutional lawyers – and not always they – can supply answers' – Linda Colley

'Under the old constitution we were subjects. Under New Labour's we are customers. It is time we became citizens' – Unlocking Democracy (Charter88)

'We have no plans to replace the monarchy' – Labour party election manifesto 1997

'In the end, there is no solution to Britain's European problem that does not begin at home, with Britain's British problem' – Andrew Marr

DAN GRAHAM LIKES TO KICK OFF the A-level politics syllabus by giving his pupils an assignment. He tells them to go to a bookshop and come back with a copy of the British constitution. When the sixth formers return to Preston Manor High School in Wembley, they are crestfallen – no such constitution is to be found. Graham, who comes from New England, has made his point, just as Tom Paine did more than 200 years ago in *Rights of Man*, his polemic with Edmund Burke:

Can then Mr Burke produce the English Constitution? If he cannot, we may fairly conclude, that though it has been so much talked about, no such thing as a constitution exists, or ever did exist, and consequently that the people have yet a constitution to form.

My visit to Preston Manor High School with Debbie Chay, a lecturer from Charter88, showed how constitutional matters can be brought alive for teenagers. She asked them to imagine themselves as survivors of an air crash on a desert island. How would they run society? Who would have votes? Who would take decisions and by what sort of majority? Dan Graham's A-level students needed no lessons in the distinction between the dignified and the efficient parts of the constitution when they were asked who wielded power in the government. Back came the quick reply: 'It's Alastair Campbell. He takes the decisions. Tony Blair just carries them out.'

POLITICAL EXCLUSION

Most young people have none of this level of knowledge and interest; a real sense of citizenship appears to be on the decline. Political exclusion, like social exclusion, seems to be on the rise. Alienation of young people from politics is noticeable in many countries but seems particularly marked here. Professor Brendan O'Leary of the London School of Economics told me:

I think the alienation of the young is a normal phenomenon in mature democracies. But I think a great deal could be done to make the citizens of this country better educated in the law, in rights, in the core institutions of government. It always strikes me as remarkable how ill-informed most citizens of this country are who haven't done courses in political science about how their institutions operate.

The truth is that Britain, for historical reasons, starts from a low base in citizenship education and has a lot of ground to make up in all areas, including political literacy. Campaigners for the rights of the child say Britain is out of line with the rest of Europe in its lack of pupil democracy in schools. According to the latest British Social Attitudes Survey:

One in three teenagers (34 per cent) have no interest whatever in politics, a rise of seven percentage points since 1994, compared to only one in ten adults (11 per cent). And although interest in politics does grow with age, young people nowadays seem to be entering adult life with even lower levels of engagement than in the past – making it harder for them than it was for previous generations to 'catch up'. More than one in three teenagers (37 per cent) do not identify with any political party, again a rise of seven percentage points since 1994, compared to only one in seven adults (14 per cent). This rise in indifference is most marked among younger teenagers (12 to 15 year olds) – from 31 per cent who identified with no party four years ago, to 44 per cent now.[1]

A study for the Joseph Rowntree Foundation among 14- to 24-year-olds found that young people 'have depressingly low levels of political interest and knowledge'. Most saw politics as boring, dull and not relevant to their lives.[2]

There is no sign that the arrival of a Labour government has changed this picture, and the low turnouts in recent elections are worrying politicians. Despite the excitement of the 1997 election, the percentage of those who could not be bothered to vote rose to 29, the highest in half a century. In the 1999 European elections, the United Kingdom got less than one in four of its electors to the polls, less than half the number in Ireland and even further behind some other European states such as Belgium. In the Leeds Central by-election in 1999, less than one in five electors voted, and at one polling station in Sunderland the turnout for the European election was 1.5 per cent.

A report by the Adam Smith Institute in 2000 based on opinion research by MORI found that only 60 per cent of 18- to 24-year-olds were registered to vote, compared with 92 per cent of the wider population. More than half described themselves as 'not interested in politics' and only 6 per cent said it was inconvenience that stopped them from voting. Asked about proportional representation, 88 per cent said they knew little or nothing about it, including 30 per cent who had never heard of it. Most of the young people interviewed saw citizenship in terms of how to treat other people and in terms of their entitlements, rather than as something in which they could participate. The report came to a gloomy conclusion:

The institutions and attitudes which young people reject are ones which evolved in a different time to meet different circumstances. It could be that young people regard them as no longer relevant and decline to participate because they are no longer seen to matter … The efforts of governments and parties to encourage people to become involved might be misconceived, and doomed to failure … Today's young people say they are not interested in politics, and do not regard political activity as worthwhile. They know little about the institutions of government at various levels, and feel little loyalties (sic) to the communities of which they are part. They reject community activism, and do not participate. They regard citizenship only as a way of behaving, and of having regard for others. The young people could be right.[3]

DON'T WORRY ABOUT THE MACE

Since Labour came to power in 1997 it has recognized the need to do something to reverse these trends. But promoting citizenship in a country without a written constitution is a tricky business. How should teachers approach such subjects as human rights, the monarchy and Britain's membership of the European Union? The British constitution and old-fashioned civics used to be among the fustiest of subjects taught in schools. Professor Bernard Crick, the government's leading adviser on citizenship education, now pokes fun at the sort of courses which used to ask students to list the 11 reasons for parliamentary reform, and why the House of Commons mace was not in its usual place on Fridays. Crick argues that:

... knowledge of constitutional rules, real or imagined, is a very poor beginning for a genuine political education. In countries with written constitutions we find that some citizenship education, far from seeking to encourage active citizenship, too often takes refuge in the safe-haven of learning the articles of the constitution, federal and state.[4]

Now a revamped type of 'active citizenship' teaching is on its way back, not just for bright A-level students but for everybody. Schoolchildren will not only learn about citizenship but will be encouraged to go out and practise it, a potential minefield. 'I thought there might be trouble,' Crick told a local government education conference in London in July 2000. 'People are quick to cry political indoctrination.' As it happened, the professor's recommendations seem to have been mostly accepted, thanks largely to the relationship between Education Secretary David Blunkett and his old university teacher. According to those in the know, it was not Crick who had difficulty persuading Blunkett but Blunkett who found it hard to persuade a nervous Tony Blair of the need to put citizenship on the National Curriculum from September 2002 as a foundation subject for secondary pupils in England. No doubt he was worried about the kind of polemic unleashed by *Sunday Times* commentator Melanie Phillips, who warned that Crick's ideas were causing 'consternation in Whitehall' where sharp minds had detected 'a rampant agenda of rights that would erode still further the duties essential for citizenship'.[5] Phillips argued that human rights were too deeply contested to be taught in the classroom.

Educational researchers recognize that teaching 'active citizenship' can be tricky, given the lack of a written constitution, a history of citizenship rights and a civic republican tradition of active self-government. As one study put it: 'With the lack of support in this country around the notion of "citizenship" and the lack of clarity about the distinction between being a "citizen" and a "subject", there are difficulties about defining citizenship in general.'[6] This study for a local government audience distinguishes between three models of citizenship: the traditional passive model which understands the concept as a set of rights and obligations, the 'consumer' model which underpinned the Conservative government's Citizen's Charter, and the model of 'active citizenship' which the Labour government has now embraced. The authors warn that this model 'represents a radical shift in the way that the majority of people see their relationship to the rest of society'.

Scottish academic Lindsay Paterson argues that real citizenship education means encouraging not just support for the status quo but radical dissent:

A full understanding of citizenship and the barriers to full citizenship would have to include an understanding of the economic and social inequalities that leave millions of people shut out from politics because they are shut out from virtually everything else ... But encouraging radical dissent is not usually what the enthusiasts for citizenship education have in mind. What they want is moral responsibility. So here's a simple test for any proposed citizenship curriculum: will it make people less satisfied – and even angry – with our society's economic organization, political power, and relationship to the rest of the globe? If the answer is no, then it will be hardly worth having at all.[7]

Crick and Blunkett are well aware of these arguments, and realize that a deep change in political culture is needed. Blunkett has spoken in terms of 'bringing alive democracy at a time when cynicism and apathy are rife', while Crick has called for 'informed scepticism' to replace cynicism. There is a sense in which something will have to change in the wider picture of the ill-defined British constitution if the goals of citizenship education are to be met. In the view of Michael Jacobs of the Fabian Society:

In a sense the government is taking the classic road of liberals of saying 'Let's educate more and that will solve the problem', rather than changing structures. And liberals from time immemorial have thought that education was the answer to any problem. They are quite right that the education system needs to teach citizenship principles and so on, and that that will be part of the answer. But you have to change the structures. Education on its own isn't sufficient.

The risk is that too much participation for teenagers and too much teaching of equality in schools will lead to disillusionment later in adult life when 'active citizens' discover the reality of the British constitution and their expectations are dashed. 'For too long in England we have been basically a deferential, subject culture, not a citizen culture,' is how Crick puts it. For Tony Wright MP, the mere fact of citizenship education being introduced into schools means a catalyst for constitutional change:

I don't think you should devalue the importance of what has been achieved there. I think those of us who have been campaigning for 20 or 30 years to get some sort of proper citizenship education should recognize and rejoice in the fact that it came about only because we had David Blunkett in post, and only because David Blunkett knew Bernard Crick and was committed to the whole enterprise and understood the argument. That is a real achievement, to get citizenship education after all these years into schools. I don't think it is fair to say, Oh God, because we have still got a monarchy, we have still got a royal prerogative, it doesn't matter. This is a process and it leads to people – hopefully – having a more critical engagement with the political system. It's a dynamic thing and I think it is wrong to see it as undercut by the fact that we have a certain kind of political arrangement here. That arrangement is changing anyway.

Labour MP Fiona Mactaggart, a former teacher, believes the absence of a written constitution does not mean that schools cannot successfully teach children about citizenship:

Of course you can, children are cleverer than that. There are strong themes in our constitution, even if we have some nonsenses going on ... I don't think children need everything set out like a sum. They can understand a set of balances. It is good to live in a society where citizens have rights, where there is a judicial process. I don't think it has to be like America, with us swearing allegiance to the flag every morning. I am in favour of a written constitution, but the absence of one is not a bar to teaching children. It is not a matter of teaching children, here are the rules, stick with them.

A MORE RADICAL VIEW

A number of writers on constitutional matters take a much more radical view of what is needed, arguing that the archaism of Britain's constitutional arrangements makes true democratic citizenship impossible. Anthony Barnett, writing in late 1997 in the aftermath of the death of Princess Diana, argued in his book *This Time* that the whole point of the British constitution was that 'it is not owned, let alone controlled, by the people. It does not belong to us as citizens and we do not have democratic rights'. However, Barnett detected a sea-change in popular attitudes in the discontent with the monarchy in the week after Diana's death, opening the way forward to a 'lasting emancipation from deference'. Jonathan Freedland's *Bring Home the Revolution*, picking up where Tom Paine left off, contrasted the fog of British constitutional ignorance with the way the Americans know their way around their own system:

They learn their Constitution in school, and venerate it thereafter. It inspires a near-religious reverence, its authors accorded similar status to the writers of the gospels. The major amendments are known by almost everyone and even the obscure ones have a following … The US Constitution lends an unusual clarity and coherence to the American national conversation. Any new proposal or policy can be instantly measured against the original goals of the nation … The result is a great leveller. With no hidden body of knowledge decipherable only by experts, all Americans can take part in their collective discussion. Everyone can see what is in the Constitution; it is there in black and white. [8]

This is essentially the argument of Charter88 for a written constitution. Full citizenship demands that a clear knowledge of rights and authority should be accessible to all, not just to lawyers and scholars. The UK's constitution fails this 'Tom Paine test'. As Pam Giddy says in the introduction to Charter88's policy document *Unlocking Democracy*, writing down the constitution 'is one of the means – although only one – whereby voters become citizens and take possession of their country'. According to Ann Dummett, an expert on immigration and nationality law:

In most countries, the concept of citizenship can be clearly explained by reference to a written constitution and subsequent legislation. The former will say what a citizen's rights and duties are; the latter will draw a line between citizens and non-citizens. In the United Kingdom we have no such clarity.[9]

Dummett contrasts the vagueness of British nationality, originating in the ancient common law idea of subjecthood, with the more clear-cut civic definition in France and the strictly ethnic basis enshrined in Germany. This vagueness has been only partly clarified by the British Nationality Act of 1981, which created five categories of nationality, four of which did not guarantee entry to the UK. For historical reasons, Irish and Commonwealth citizens share many of the rights of British citizens, as do citizens of member states of the European Union. Out of this muddle, the Labour government has tried to find a new sense of British identity based on shared values, but it is hard to find values that are distinctively British rather than European. Dummett argues that this is barking up the wrong tree:

Britishness is partly a matter of culture, values and national character, but perhaps the most obvious feature of Britishness is to be suspicious of any attempt to lay down what our culture, values and character are or should be. We like to be different. We do not have a single set of values.

Like Blunkett, Home Secretary Jack Straw is an enthusiast for citizenship education, but his vision of the relationship between the citizen and the state is a conservative one, placing the accent on responsibilities as well as rights. Straw's explanation to me suggested that he was seeking a return to the past, a way to persuade young people to replicate the attitudes of their parents and grandparents:

People had a better developed sense of citizenship when they had a better developed sense of what the role of the state in the most benign sense was. That was there for the first 60 years of the last century when we were recovering from conflict. National Service and war make very explicit what the power of the state is, not least because your young men between the ages of 16 and 40 are invited to have themselves killed on behalf of other people. So that leads to people saying, who is making these decisions and why? We should never ignore the huge effect the Army Education Corps had on two generations of people. Now that has all gone and you have to replace it.

Charter88 sees a large gap between its own view of citizenship and the model being promoted by the government. Its strategy document issued in July 2000 says that the government's definition will stress community action, participation in local and charitable organizations, and other worthy causes:

In this guise, citizenship is no threat to established power and cannot call those in authority to account. Charter88 is committed to a different definition in which to be a citizen carries a degree of power. It means a capacity to influence outcomes and arrive at one's own view. It involves complex identities and assertions. It is a challenge to authority, not a convenience. Above all, it is a claim on one's country, to a right to a livelihood within it, a degree of autonomy from it, a stake in the direction over it. How can this stake be realized? Above all, through accountability.[10]

Charter88 asks how people can hold themselves to be full citizens if they do not own their own constitution.

Longtime constitutional reformers such as Tony Benn, who once introduced a 'Commonwealth of Britain' Bill in the House of Commons, argue that unless people can be motivated to vote by feeling it will bring results and change their lives, no amount of tinkering with the system will help. Benn says democracy 'is very controversial – more controversial than socialism' and encourages his fellow citizens to put five democratic questions to all those in authority: 'What power do you have, where did you get it from, in whose interests are you exercising it, to whom are you accountable and how can we get rid of you?'

I mention Tony Benn at this point because there is no figure in the Labour party whose ideas are more out of fashion in the Blair government. Even more than Ken Livingstone, Benn is identified with the 'loony left' ascendancy of the early 1980s from which Blair and his immediate predecessors have struggled to rescue their party.

CITIZENSHIP, NOT IDENTITY

There is nonetheless a more moderate and pragmatic way of tying together the threads of citizenship, constitutional reform and the vexed subject of British identity, one with which Tony Blair has wrestled publicly (and not very successfully) in his speeches. The historian Linda Colley was invited to Downing Street in late 1999 to give one of a series of millennium lectures, later to be published on the Downing Street website. Colley, whose classic book *Britons* describes the forging of British identity in the 18th century, was asked to speak on 'Britishness in the 21st century'. After surveying the decline of older props of British identity such as Protestantism, the empire, the monarchy and the two world wars, Colley added another three factors – the sharing of sovereignty with the European Union, Britain's ethnic diversity, and the privatization of the old 'British' nationalized industries under the Conservatives. Labour had followed these changes with its own constitutional reforms, altering the 'customary institutional components of Britishness'. Meanwhile, old-fashioned all-British class politics was giving way to more sectional, territorial and identity-based politics.

Colley said she did not regard either the breakup of Britain or its absorption by a European superstate as inevitable. But instead of agonizing over Britishness, politicians should leave such issues to look after themselves and focus on an area where they could bring more influence to bear – the renewal of British citizenship. Reinforcing British citizenship might paradoxically make people more relaxed about being citizens of the European Union. 'So think hard about the distinction between identity and citizenship and focus on the latter.' Colley said she was unsure about the need for a comprehensive written constitution, but advocated a more limited 'contract of citizen rights' summarizing European, English and Scots law, which would also be available in a much briefer, more accessible version:

At present, if an ordinary man, woman or child in these islands enquires 'What are my rights as a citizen here? What defines me?', only expert, constitutional lawyers – and not always they – can supply answers. If citizenship is to function well and to excite and unite, then citizens themselves must feel they have direct access to some of the answers to these questions.

Colley said a new citizen nation would have to have symbols that acknowledged far more than at present the 'essential equality of the people of these islands'. Did this mean a republic? 'Again, I don't think so, though it may happen.'

Monarchs can serve as extremely useful and reassuring symbols of stability, especially in periods of massive cultural, economic and political flux like this one. But if there is to be a 21st-century citizen's monarchy in this country capable of attracting broad, enduring support, it will require far more than a face-lift in image. Its public presentation will have to continue changing, but so must its avowed rationale. The crown jewels, together with the gorgeous robes, the golden coaches and the ermine, should be consigned to museums. At their coronations, future monarchs should not only undertake to protect the faiths of each and all of their subjects, they should also swear a new oath of service to the majesty of the people. Members of all parliaments and assemblies in these islands should also swear oaths of service to the majesty of the people. If all this sounds excessively radical, I must point out that Denmark implemented similar reforms to the ones I've just outlined after 1848, yet the Danish monarchy remains – as you know – one of the most dignified and popular in Europe. The notion that monarchs must either be surrounded by pomp, circumstance, rank and traditional glitter, or be reduced to riding bicycles, sets up a thoroughly false dichotomy. We need in the next millennium to move beyond it.

Colley went on to argue for the abolition of titles suggestive of rank, including lords and ladies, and a reform of the state opening of parliament, which she described as 'an affair littered with coronets, white tights, long dresses, Ruritanian uniforms, and assorted jewels and staffs'. Active citizenship would require a real diffusion of power away from the centre of the state, restoring local authorities' tax-raising powers and restoring local patriotism. Whether Tony Blair and his guests shifted uneasily in their chairs at this point is not recorded. Colley said there would have to be more imagination and more change. 'Any notion that devolution can occur in Wales, Scotland and Northern Ireland, while the 80 per cent plus of the British population who live in England go on exactly as before, is plainly unrealistic.' Giving a qualified endorsement to Jonathan Freedland's ideas on the liveliness of American grass roots political activism, Colley argued that improving the position of ethnic minorities and women was a powerful argument for the continuing usefulness of Britishness.

TOTEM AND TABOO

The essence of Colley's powerful plea for clear thinking is that constitutional change does not have to be revolutionary or reject the past; but to make a new and revived citizenship possible, it will have to embrace taboo areas which the Blair government has so far avoided. The first of these is the monarchy.

The Labour party's tone towards the monarchy is set by Tony Blair, who publicly describes himself as an 'ardent monarchist'. While closet republicanism in the Labour party is now widespread, too open an expression of such views brings down the wrath of Downing Street on the head of those responsible. This was the fate before the 1997 election of shadow Welsh Secretary Ron Davies, who was forced to apologize after suggesting Prince Charles was unfit to be king. Before the election Blair, writing on the Queen's 70th birthday, said the country had a choice about whether it should retain a constitutional monarchy, adding: 'I believe that it should.' But the preservation of its legitimacy depended on a willingness to adapt and change.[11] Labour's election manifesto promised that the party had no plans to 'replace' the monarchy, a choice of language that fell well short of full endorsement of the status quo and left open the idea of reform. Since the election, outbursts of republicanism in the cabinet have been strongly discouraged; Mo Mowlam had to say sorry for suggesting the royal family should move out of Buckingham Palace.

Deference to royalty has a long tradition in Labour ranks, and the monarchy has not been up for debate at an annual conference of the party since the early 1920s. Open republicanism has generally been seen as a vote-loser, a conclusion that recent opinion polls suggest is still the case, though public views are slowly changing. A MORI poll in June 2000 showed only 19 per cent of voters would back a republic in a referendum, with 70 per cent voting to keep the monarchy. But there are signs of growing indifference; another MORI poll in the same month found that while 50 per cent thought Britain would be worse off without the monarchy, 37 per cent thought it would make no difference. Asked to look into the future, a large majority thought the monarchy would still be there in ten years' time, but only a minority expected it to last 50 years, and only 22 per cent expected it to be there in 100 years. Those questioned thought by a majority of nearly two to one that Mo Mowlam was right to speak out. Asked what should happen to the monarchy, 65 per cent felt it should be 'modernized to reflect changes in British life'.

From the viewpoint of ardent royalists, the long-term trend of public opinion is worrying. In 1984, as many as 77 per cent thought Britain would be worse off without the monarchy, with only 5 per cent thinking it would be better off. Vernon Bogdanor, writing in the mid-1990s before the death of Princess Diana, detected signs that the period of 'magical monarchy' was coming to an end and traced this to the cumulative effects of the Thatcher era.

HOW TO BE A REPUBLIC

With the benefit of hindsight, the decisive shift in attitudes to monarchy which Anthony Barnett detected in September 1997 appears to have been a mirage. The public anger at the monarchy's perceived indifference to Diana's death was real, but it was itself a monarchist reflex, not a republican one. A truly republican nation of citizens would have reacted with indifference. As Tim Hames and Mark Leonard wrote the following year: 'An allegedly symbolic monarchy that could not symbolize national sentiment at the death of one of its own members did not seem a very effective institution.'

Not many in the Labour party are prepared to sign up to the outright abolition of the monarchy, advocated openly by the campaigning group Republic, led by Professor Stephen Haseler. They argue that the monarchy cannot be modernized and the only solution is to do away with it by a referendum at the end of the present Queen's reign. Republicans argue that the *subjects-or-citizens?* conundrum cannot be resolved under a monarch, and that only an elected head of state will allow the creation of true equality and democratic citizenship. *The Observer*, in an editorial arguing for abolition of the monarchy in July 2000, dismissed the case for historical continuity as 'ancestor worship, at which we would smile if it were practised by a native tribe'. This type of rationalist sneering ignores the fact that all constitutions, democratic or not, depend on historical legitimacy, not to mention a dose of magic and ceremonial, for their survival. There are good reasons for regarding as mistaken the idea that removing the monarchy would be 'a simple seamless transition', as Stephen Haseler believes.[12]

Far from being a crowned republic in the sense that Bagehot believed, the United Kingdom is a country where the monarchy is an essential tool of government. Far from an irrelevance, it has to be taken seriously, as Tom Nairn was the first to make clear, in 1988, in *The Enchanted Glass*, a prophetic book which saw the malaise of the House of Windsor less in terms of its personal shortcomings and failed marriages, and more in terms of its role as a prop for an archaic political system. 'Contrary to many appearances, the United Kingdom monarchy is not decorative icing on the socio-political cake. It is an important ingredient of the whole mixture ...' One does not have to agree with all of Nairn's denunciation of 'Ukania' to accept his analysis of the ideology of 'Crown-in-Parliament' and what he calls 'Parliamentary Divine Right'. Nairn's argument is that British parliamentary democracy in the post-1688 version has little in common with republican democracy and popular sovereignty in the sense in which they are understood elsewhere. 'It is a transmuted version of Monarchy – the collective Monarch that replaced individual Sovereigns after 1688. It was built up as a barrier against democracy and popular sovereignty.'[13]

Nairn regards the upheavals of the mid-17th century as premature. 'The old British Monarchy was decapitated too soon. This is why it was able to creep back into the void left by its departure, head under its arm, to find permanent lodgement in the compromise of a quasi-regal power structure.' Parliament's victory was of one absolutism over another. 'The Parliamentary class seized sovereignty, and legitimized the transfer with a myth of the Crown-in-Parliament.' Nairn provides a perceptive quote from Friedrich Engels, writing in 1844: 'Nevertheless – and in this, fear reaches its climax – the English Constitution cannot exist without the monarchy. Remove the Crown, the "subjective apex", and the whole artificial structure comes tumbling down.'[14] According to a pamphlet written by Tim Hames and Mark Leonard in 1998 for the Demos think-tank, not much has changed since the days of Engels:

In constitutional terms, the concept of the Crown in Parliament is the central doctrine around which the governance of Britain operates. The Crown is the essence of the executive, an element of the legislature, the spine of the judicial system and the employer of the bureaucracy. In this country, the terms 'crown' and 'state' are almost interchangeable. A government committed to constitutional reform but indifferent to questions concerning the Crown would have a very confused sense of priorities.[15]

Hames and Leonard's curious pamphlet (one author is a Tory journalist and *Times* leader-writer, the other runs a New Labour foreign policy think-tank) looked at monarchies around the world. It found three basic models – monarchies that *are* in effect the state, such as those in the Arab world, monarchies that are *above* the state, such as those in Japan and East Asia, and *secular* monarchies such as those in Northern Europe. Britain has a monarchy that is a strange hybrid of the three models, and this lies at the root of its problems. Hames and Leonard argued that:

It is only a mild overstatement to claim that in formal terms the Queen of the United Kingdom runs the state in the same fashion in which the King of Jordan determines the course of that country, except that in Britain the monarch acts according to the advice of ministers … In a sense, the core problem for the monarchy is its schizophrenic identity. In its current position it is trying to embody three radically different models that are often in conflict with each other: part Morocco, part Nepal and part Norway.

The pamphlet suggested that the next monarch should be approved in a referendum by popular vote between accession and coronation, which would 'revolutionize the constitutional standing of the sovereign'. If the heir to the throne got the thumbs down from the electorate, the next in line would be put to a vote, and so on. Hames and Leonard also recommended that royal children should be educated in state schools and have their medical treatment on the NHS, a suggestion that would lead to the fantasies of Sue Townsend's *The Queen and I* becoming reality. Such suggestions seem unlikely to find favour in Downing Street.

RITUALS FOR ANTHROPOLOGISTS

Ilse Hayden, an American anthropologist who analyzed the role of royalty in Britain, also dismissed the widespread idea that it was irrelevant, or just a façade. She pointed out in 1987 that the Queen had two roles, one constitutional and the other ceremonial. The iconography of royalty and its public ceremonial, Hayden concluded, were more than just cosmetic, they amounted to 'instruments of rule' by a small governing class:

The governance of Britain, then, is an aristocratic undertaking; the aristocratic ethic of silence and exclusion is made manifest by not publishing the workings of government as they are in the United States. Yet Britain is also a democratic nation – and the principle of democracy is that the workings of government should be publicized so that citizens can be familiar with both the structure and function of that government. This collision of values presents a dilemma: the desire to conceal, the need to reveal. The Queen's role in government is an example of the problem; it is also part of the solution, reconciling as it does the contradictory demands of government in Britain.[16]

The eye of the anthropologist is essential to understand such extraordinary political rituals as the annual state opening of parliament, at which the Queen, like a ventriloquist's dummy, reads out a speech written entirely by her prime minister. He meanwhile is forced to stand at the back of the House of Lords with other members of the Commons like gatecrashers at an aristocratic party. The contrast between the regal pomp and dress of the crowned monarch and the mundanity of the civil service prose she utters is a perfect expression of the post-1688 bargain that brought William and Mary and their Hanoverian successors to the throne as hired monarchs. As Linda Colley describes it:

> The Hanoverian kings were still powerful. But they did not rule primarily because of who they were. Nor because of who their ancestors had been. Parliament had brought them to the throne, and Protestantism kept them there. They were essentially serviceable kings, occupying their office because they catered to the religious bias of the bulk of their subjects ...[17]

Colley's book reminds us of the utilitarian view of the monarchy as the servant of the political class by quoting from Henry St John, Viscount Bolingbroke's *The Idea of A Patriot King* written in 1738, which compares the monarch not to the captain or the owner but to the pilot of a ship who is 'made for the sake of the ship, her lading, and her crew, who are always the owners in the political vessel'. Colley also notes an important shift in attitudes in the late 18th century when George III was caricatured and ridiculed in the age of Gillray:

> Laughing at royal individuals led in practice very easily to amused tolerance for royalty itself. Those who satirize the British Royal Family today, lampooning their corgis, their reputed philistinism, their funny clothes and their even funnier accents, may imagine they are being subversive, but, of course, they are not. The shift in criticism of the monarchy which first became apparent in the 1780s, a shift away from anger at the institution to mockery of individual royals and their foibles, helped – as it may still help – to preserve it.[18]

This paradox still holds good today; while the press can criticize and lampoon the royal family to its heart's content, political debate over the role of the constitutional role of the Crown has become much more difficult than 300 years ago. No subject is more taboo in parliament than the monarchy, a rule that exists for perfectly valid historical reasons but that prevents any serious discussion of its role at a time of constitutional change. In 1996, Tony Wright MP tried to hold an adjournment debate on the monarchy, but was prevented by the Speaker on the grounds that it did not fall under any ministerial responsibility. 'We all feel frustrated that this is a traditional no-go area, and discussion on a major part of our constitution is out of bounds,' Wright said.[19]

GOOD QUEEN LIZ

Since 1997, when Tony Blair helped rescue the royals from their self-inflicted post-Diana sticky patch, the relationship between Buckingham Palace and Downing Street has been, on the surface at least, all smiles. With the Royal Yacht now safely at anchor as a tourist attraction in Leith, and Windsor Castle rebuilt, the heat has gone out of the arguments over royal finances. The announcement over the Civil List and the cost of the monarchy in July 2000 passed without a breath of controversy. Rather than modernizing the monarchy or downsizing it, Blair has tried to give it a populist New Labour makeover.

In November 1997 he hosted a 'people's banquet' to mark the Queen's 50th wedding anniversary. As a one-time Kremlinogist I scanned the guest list looking for political clues, finding that Blair had invited precisely two trade unionists to the party of 300, who lunched on trio of Scottish salmon, roast saddle of lamb and caramelized pear tart (*caterer:* Mosimann's). The event took place in the Banqueting House, just a few feet away from where the Queen's distant ancestor Charles I was beheaded in 1649. No such unhappy fate threatened the current monarch, though thoughts of biting corgis may have crossed her mind after the pear tart as she heard Blair hail her in demotic mockney as the 'simply the best of British'. Blair's effusive speech recalled how as a boy in short trousers in Durham in the 1960s he enthusiastically waved his flag at his first sight of the Queen. He described his weekly meetings with her as 'a little awesome' and added: 'There are only two people in the world to whom a prime minister can say what he likes about his cabinet colleagues. One's the wife, the other's the Queen.'

This populist reinvention of the monarch as a much-loved character from *EastEnders*, symbolized by the Queen's visit to a pub, reached new heights at the end of December 1999 when the Queen and her husband attended the opening of the Millennium Dome in Greenwich. The evening climaxed in a unique moment, captured by the television cameras, when Her Majesty and consort linked hands with the Blairs for a rousing chorus of *Auld Lang Syne*. Less than a decade earlier, Australian Prime Minister Paul Keating had sparked a press furore and been dubbed the 'Lizard of Oz' for momentarily touching the Queen. Here was the British Prime Minister grabbing the royal hand and pumping it up and down as if it belonged to the barmaid in the Trimdon Working Men's Club. The anthropologists are still arguing about the true meaning of this new ritual for the future of the monarchy, but one thing seems certain – the distinction between Queen and Pearly Queen has become more blurred.

> 66 Here was the British Prime Minister grabbing the royal hand and pumping it up and down as if it belonged to the barmaid in the Trimdon Working Men's Club. 99

PREROGATIVE POWERS

Beyond such moments of populist bathos, it is hard to detect any real innovation in the Blair government's attitude to the monarchy. In political terms, this is hardly surprising. Every prime minister soon discovers that it is the historic prerogatives of the Crown, dating back to before the 1688 settlement, that underpin his or her powers. Tony Blair is no exception. There are other royal powers that no prime minister would ever voluntarily surrender, notably the right to choose the date of a general election by asking the monarch to dissolve parliament. As Tony Benn never tires of pointing out, no British parliament has to approve a prime ministerial decision to drop bombs on Iraq or the Balkans, to deploy troops to Bosnia or Sierra Leone. Of course, all governments have to give an account of their decisions to parliament, but legally prime ministers have powers of which US presidents can only dream. Unlike his European counterparts, the British prime minister can use the powers of the monarch to declare war, sign and ratify treaties, change the coinage of the realm, appoint bishops, judges and generals and members of the upper house, all without reference to the Commons. These huge powers of patronage and the operation of the armed forces, the Foreign Office and the security services are exercised in the name of the Crown. Like the organization of the civil service, they do not rest on any statutory power granted by parliament.

What Haseler and other supporters of a republic tend to gloss over is the amount of legislation that would be needed to fill the gaps left by the end of the royal prerogative. There was a time in opposition when Labour was enthusiastic about reforming the prerogative powers, but the ambition faded as the 1997 election came closer. Home Secretary Jack Straw told me he would not wish to argue the case against reform of the prerogative on principle, but there was no way Labour could have made it a priority in its first term:

I certainly would not have started from here. There is a case that can be made for a Government of Britain Act that would describe the powers of government departments, the powers that are currently exercised by prerogative, that are currently exercised by the prime minister … I don't argue with the case and down the track we may get to it … In 1989–90, people had not really thought it through. They never thought we were going to be in government, and it concentrates the mind. That is true. At any point you have to make a choice: do you have an Act on the royal prerogative which involves the position of the Crown, and all the rest of it, which is a very, very big undertaking, or do you go for race relations or human rights? At an intellectual level I don't rule it out, but it could not have been on the agenda unless people thought we had lost our sense of priorities. Assuming that government operates to high standards of probity and very high standards of accountability to parliament, which it does, it wouldn't make that much difference. It would make a bit. I am in favour of transparency. On parliamentary accountability, for all the guff you hear about it, my responsibility *is* to parliament. In the last three weeks I have been there nine times explaining myself, quite rightly.

The point Jack Straw was making was that as Home Secretary, virtually all his powers and duties are based on laws passed by parliament; the same is true for most ministers running home departments in Whitehall. But there are still backwaters of government that operate exclusively under powers borrowed from the monarch. This whole area is something of a trade secret; attentive readers of the Court Circular in *The Times* will spot once a month or so a notice describing how Her Majesty has held a meeting of her Privy Council. Occasionally, as with the unscheduled Privy Council meeting at Balmoral in September 2000 to approve emergency powers to deal with the fuel crisis, the occasion makes headlines, but this is the exception. The President of the Council, currently Margaret Beckett, and four other ministers usually drive to Buckingham Palace. 'The quorum is three and we always invite four to make sure in case one gets held up in traffic,' said a senior civil servant who explained the intricacies of the system to me. The prime minister never attends and unlike his weekly meeting with the Queen, the Privy Council sessions are purely formal, like those at which the Queen gives her assent to legislation. All cabinet ministers have to be members of the Privy Council, and formally they retain membership and the 'Right Honourable' tag for life. But in practice their membership lapses when they leave government. 'The idea that Ted Heath or Tony Benn are still having a say in these matters because they happen to be Privy Councillors is as ludicrous as it sounds,' I was told. Nonetheless, the whole Privy Council meets to proclaim the accession of a new monarch and to approve the marriage of a reigning sovereign.

The Privy Council handles mainstream government business, much of it involving bodies governed by royal charter such as the BBC, universities and self-regulating medical and professional councils. Some of the business is statutory, but is handled through the Privy Council rather than normal government channels for administrative convenience because the procedure covers not just the United Kingdom but also the Channel Islands and the Isle of Man. This is why the Privy Council is used to pass Orders complying with United Nations sanctions. As we have seen, the Privy Council also has a Judicial Committee that handles appeals from some Commonwealth countries and disputes over devolved powers. Does it work? As a piece of bureaucratic machinery, undoubtedly it does; but it is neither transparent nor accountable, and more importantly it fails the constitutional test of being understood by the Muggles outside.

KEEPING THE STATUS QUO

The reasons for Blair's 'ardent' royalism should now be clearer. How does his stout defence of the monarchy fit in with the rest of Labour's constitutional reforms, such as the abolition of hereditary peers? Blair says there is no contradiction between maintaining the one and scrapping the other. Even most Conservatives, such as Robert Cranborne, agree:

I don't agree with those who say there is a link between the preservation of the hereditary peers and the preservation of the monarchy. You could argue the other way actually. Scandinavian monarchies are perfectly safe and they don't have hereditary peerages.

But maintaining the royal status quo may not be an option for ever. Royal issues have a habit of forcing themselves onto the agenda of prime ministers whose interest in constitutional change is non-existent, as John Major discovered with the separation and divorce of the heir to the throne. Blair, after the hysteria following Diana's death, needs no reminding of the way a royal crisis can push everything else off the political agenda. While Prince Charles has removed one potential area of controversy by declaring he does not plan to remarry, there is still a big question mark over whether the 300-year-old relationship between the Crown and the Protestant religion can remain unaltered in a new century. Should the monarch remain Supreme Governor of the Church of England, a position that does not exist in the Church of Scotland? The Bishop of Woolwich, Colin Buchanan, argues that the Church of England should be disestablished, ending the bizarre situation in which it depends on the prime minister of the day, who may be an atheist, to appoint its bishops.

There are signs on the horizon indicating that however much the government may hope such issues will go away, they will keep resurfacing. Already there have been moves both in the Scottish Parliament and the House of Lords to repeal the 300-year-old Act of Settlement, which bars the heir to the throne from marrying a Roman Catholic. The historic royal pledge to uphold the Protestant religion, one of the pillars of the 1688 settlement, now looks discriminatory and in the words of Vernon Bogdanor 'deeply offensive'. Though not linked directly to the issue of church establishment, the position of the 26 Anglican bishops in the House of Lords is already up for discussion, with the Wakeham commission recommending a reduction to 16 to make way for representatives of other faiths. Prince Charles has said he would prefer to be crowned not as Defender of the Faith but as Defender of Faith, implying an end to the Anglican monopoly of ceremonial. Even the most dyed-in-the-wool traditionalist would find it hard to advocate a coronation ceremony for a new monarch that followed the pattern of the last one in 1953, which emphasized the pre-eminence of court and aristocracy.

> 66 Even the most dyed-in-the-wool traditionalist would find it hard to advocate a coronation ceremony for a new monarch that followed the pattern of the last one in 1953. 99

Reinventing tradition in a way that is acceptable both to the new monarch and whatever government is in office at the time will require a common vision of tradition and modernity which is spectacularly lacking between Prince Charles and the Blair government. Not only has Charles made clear his deep contempt for the Millennium Dome and his opposition to genetically modified food, but, unlike his mother, he shows every sign of wanting to carve out a role in which he will do more as monarch than just take the advice of ministers. In October 1999 he delivered what amounted to a calculated snub to Downing Street by declining to attend a Chinese Embassy dinner during the state visit of President Jiang Zemin. What would happen if a future government wanted him to follow in his mother's footsteps and visit China to be entertained by Blair's fellow modernizers? Charles might well try to refuse, opening the way for a real constitutional crisis.

Another imponderable factor on the horizon is the debate on the future of the monarchy in Australia and New Zealand. A rerun of the November 1999 referendum in Australia would almost certainly produce a vote for a republic. This would have no direct legal or constitutional consequences for the UK, but it would be bound to have a huge public impact and spark a fresh debate. Closer to home, a referendum on independence for Scotland would inevitably involve a debate on the future role of the monarchy north of the border and a possible return to a pre-1707 Union of the Crowns.

No doubt each inhabitant of 10 Downing Street prays that these thorny issues can safely be left to his or her successor. If the Queen has inherited her mother's longevity, her reign might last another 25 years, but it is doubtful that radical change can be postponed that long. The real enemy of the monarchy is likely to be not open republicanism but indifference. The fact remains that the Blair government, beyond its experiments with matey royalist populism, does not have a convincing story to tell about the long-term future of the monarchy that links up with its other constitutional reforms and its goal of promoting more active citizenship.

Linda Colley's call for a Danish-style monarchy taken out of politics and a renewed British citizenship is a less radical agenda than that of the republicans, but it may still be a modernization too far for the Blair government. There are, however, some clear signposts to the future if the government wishes to follow them. The devolution settlements in Scotland and Northern Ireland point the way to removing the potentially controversial role of the monarch in picking prime ministers at Westminster. Proportional representation at Westminster, if it ever happens, will make hung parliaments more frequent, and provide an extra argument for a newly elected parliament and its Speaker, rather than the monarch, to choose the prime minister. This would have the advantage of a slight post-election delay in changing governments, avoiding the unnecessary and undignified scramble of furniture vans in Downing Street on the day after an election.

EUROPE AND ITS CITIZENS

The third element in the constitutional agenda sketched out in Linda Colley's lecture is Britain's relationship with Europe. Since 1973 membership of what was then called the Common Market has exerted profound changes over British sovereignty, undermining the Westminster model and the legal pre-eminence of parliament. It is easy to forget, in the light of current Conservative divisions over Europe, just how rancorously the Labour party was divided a generation ago over the very same issues. Labour's splits over European Community membership led in 1975 to the huge constitutional innovation of a referendum, originally proposed by Tony Benn. The pro-European wing of Labour was less than 20 years ago a marginalized rump, whose key figures such as David Owen and Roy Jenkins left the party to form the SDP. Meanwhile, the Conservatives, once the pro-European party, have swung round to an increasingly hostile posture, leaving pro-Europeans such as Sir Edward Heath, Michael Heseltine and Kenneth Clarke isolated. No single subject in British politics has destroyed so many political careers as Europe in the last two decades, as both Margaret Thatcher and John Major can testify.

Ferdinand Mount quotes Richard Crossman, speaking less than three years before Britain finally entered the Community, as telling a Harvard audience:

To enter Europe is for us, in terms of constitutional methods, almost as difficult as making ourselves an extra state in the USA ... It might be true that in our local British problems we could retain our British ways. But we couldn't possibly retain our fusion of executive and legislature in our relations with the rest of Europe.[20]

Crossman told his audience that he could not predict that the British political system would last for ever: 'If we go into Europe, it probably won't.'

Other EU countries have had moments of constitutional indigestion over Europe, but none have experienced the repeated agonies chronicled by Hugo Young in *This Blessed Plot*:

Entry was meant to settle Britain's national destiny, but in politics it settled nothing. It was immediately an agent of fracture, not of healing, a propensity it has never shaken off.[21]

This reflects the difficulty the two main parties have had in reconciling their traditional constitutional belief in the unchanging sovereignty of parliament with the reality that European law now takes precedence over UK law. This contradiction was glossed over by the campaign for a 'yes' vote in the 1975 referendum, which stressed that English common law would be unaffected. There was what Hugo Young described as a 'golden thread of deceptive reassurance' in the promise that nothing important in the British political system would change. The reality that emerged was different, as the courts recognized, even if the politicians preferred not to. As Lord Denning famously said: 'The Treaty is like an incoming tide. It flows into the estuaries and up the rivers. It cannot be held back.'

FOLLOWING THE TIDE

Large areas of government business such as trade, industrial and environmental policy and agriculture are now conducted wholly or partially through Brussels. Justice, policing, immigration, foreign policy and defence are following the same route. Although the trend of the last decade has been away from increasing the powers of the supranational Commission in favour of government-to-government cooperation, the long-term trend towards greater political integration continues. Robin Cook asserted soon after the government took office that the high tide of integration had peaked, but this is true only if integration is taken narrowly to mean the powers of the Commission.

By the time Labour returned to power in 1997, its European policy was unrecognizable from the early 1980s, when the party was committed to withdrawal from the hated Common Market. This hostility was upheld only by veterans of an earlier era such as Tony Benn and Peter Shore. In Hugo Young's phrase, the conversion happened not because the party saw the light but because it tired of the darkness. It was not a fundamental change of heart or a new vision of a European future, more a tactical shift driven by the chance to open up a successful avenue of opposition to Thatcherism. 'Largely, though not entirely, because Mrs Thatcher was anti-Europe, Labour became pro-Europe.'[22] Trade union opinion underwent a sea-change, symbolized by the speech of Commission president Jacques Delors to the TUC congress in 1988. In Hugo Young's account, Delors was received as if he were a prophet and serenaded as *Frère Jacques* when he lifted the union delegates' morale by offering them a European alternative to Thatcherism.

Under Neil Kinnock and John Smith, Labour began to see Europe as a stronghold of the social model which the Conservatives were trying to destroy in Britain. Under Blair, the pro-European trend intensified, even though the admiration for the European social model faded. Europe, for Tony Blair and Gordon Brown, was increasingly seen as inflexible in its labour markets and its old-fashioned social democratic 'tax-and-spend' habits. Labour, in a policy that had echoes of Thatcher, would champion an alternative 'Anglo-Saxon' economic model whose credibility was enhanced by the Clinton administration's successes. Nonetheless, Labour promised constructive engagement that would put Britain at the centre of Europe rather than at the fringes. Without that place at the heart of Europe, the country would not be a global player. But the party was always careful to play the 'patriotic' card as well, with an eye on readers of the *Sun* and the *Daily Mail*. Not for nothing did the party stage a photocall with a British bulldog in the 1997 election campaign.

Another Blair innovation in the years of opposition was a promise to hold a referendum on taking Britain into the single currency. The 1997 manifesto reflected this cautious balance between a desire to strike a contrast with the Conservatives and fear of being seen as insufficiently resolute in defending British interests and sovereignty:

Our vision of Europe is of an alliance of independent nations choosing to cooperate to achieve the goals they cannot achieve alone. We oppose a European federal superstate.

The manifesto rejected the idea of staying in the EU 'on the sidelines' and promised a fresh start with a reform agenda that included greater openness and democracy. The national veto should be retained in key matters of national interest such as taxation, defence and security, immigration, budget decisions and treaty changes, while majority voting could be extended 'in limited areas where that is in Britain's interests'. Britain would sign the Social Chapter, but a decision on the single currency would be determined by 'a hard-headed assessment of Britain's economic interests'. This amounted to a 'wait-and-see' stand that was fundamentally not very different from that of the Major government.

TONE AND SUBSTANCE

After the election Blair tried energetically to change the tone and the atmosphere of Britain's relations in Europe, but this disguised the fact that there was no wholesale change of policy. The UK remained outside the Schengen pact on frontier controls, and until Blair decided on a switch of policy in 1998, it opposed moves towards European defence. On the single currency, the key decision came in October 1997; despite many warm words, there would be no entry during the current parliament, a policy that Conservative Eurosceptics had unsuccessfully tried to push John Major into adopting before the election.

When Tony Blair talks about the European single currency, he often complains that the press misreports him as blowing either hot or cold on the subject. 'Day in, day out, there are stories in the press about our changing our position on it. Warming up, cooling down ... If the policy changes, I'll tell you,' he said in a speech at the London Business School on 27 July 1999.

In terms of tone and atmospherics, the Blair message varies, but essentially the line has followed the parameters of the announcement to parliament on 27 October 1997 by Chancellor of the Exchequer Gordon Brown. The formula, a tortuous compromise agreed after several weeks of damaging confusion, was to favour entry 'in principle' while postponing a decision until after the next election and making it subject to five economic tests and approval in a referendum. The effect of this was essentially to keep the government sitting on the fence with its options open, but to narrow down the criteria on which it would take a decision to a matter of economics. By ensuring that political arguments were taken out of the equation, Brown was assured in advance of victory in a future Whitehall turf war; the formula guaranteed that any eventual decision would be taken on the basis of an assessment conducted in the Treasury, not in 10 Downing Street or the Foreign Office. In its insistence that the only questions that needed answering were economic, the government was sending the message that the political and constitutional aspects of the single currency were of secondary importance.

NO CONSTITUTIONAL BAR

Brown's statement dealt briefly with constitutional issues of sovereignty, narrowing them down in a way that reduced them almost to vanishing point. After declaring that the potential benefits of a successful single currency were obvious, he added:

It must be clearly recognized that to share a common monetary policy with other states does represent a major pooling of economic sovereignty. There are those who argue that this should be a constitutional bar to British participation in a single currency, regardless of the economic benefits it could bring to the people of this country. In other words, they would rule out a single currency in principle, even if it were in the best economic interests of the country. That is an understandable objection and one argued from principle. But in our view it is wrong. If a single currency would be good for British jobs, business and future prosperity, it is right, in principle, to join. The constitutional issue is a factor in the decision, but it is not an overriding one. Rather it signifies that in order for monetary union to be right for Britain, the economic benefit should be clear and unambiguous.

Strictly speaking, there is no such thing as a 'constitutional bar' to anything in the Westminster model of parliamentary sovereignty, under which laws are not entrenched. Brown's statement was therefore technically correct, but essentially meaningless. The government's intention was to shut down debate on the political and constitutional pros and cons of the single currency by declaring that these questions had all been 'resolved', a word Blair frequently uses in this context. The problem with this approach is that it effectively muzzles the single currency's supporters while failing to silence its critics. Michael Jacobs of the Fabian Society describes the attempt to present the single currency as purely an economic issue as 'palpable nonsense' and says the only result is 'you grant the constitutional question to your opponent while trying to maintain a fiction in which nobody believes'.

This has led to a lopsided public debate in which single currency opponents have been free to dwell on political and constitutional arguments, while the government and its policy outriders, such as the Britain in Europe movement, have been operating with both hands behind their backs. Not allowed by Treasury fiat to give a running commentary on the economic tests, they have also been hampered by the government's nervousness about publicly arguing the case for the pooling of sovereignty inherent in adopting the single currency. The only way the government has been able to reply to constitutional and political critics of the euro has been to move the goalposts by suggesting that their hidden agenda is withdrawal from the European Union itself. Such a charge can well be levelled against Conservative Eurosceptics, but not against such bodies as New Europe, led by lifelong pro-Europeans such as David Owen and James Prior. Those most enthusiastic for the single currency argue that it is impossible to be pro-European and stay out of

".. SHEDDING A LITTLE EXCESS BAGGAGE .."

Tony Blair runs to catch the European train as it leaves the station with Chirac and Schröder on board, dropping the pound sterling, the union jack, the crown, the Magna Carta and parliament in the process.
Copyright © Richard Willson, 1999.

the euro. But the government, keen to keep its options open, is reluctant to climb so decisively off the fence. It looks at the opinion polls, remembers the debacle of the 1992 expulsion of the pound from the European Exchange Rate Mechanism, and fears being boxed into a corner without an escape route.

LIVING OUTSIDE EUROLAND

The government's first problem is that life in Europe does not stand still, making the 1997 policy framework more and more difficult to maintain. Since 1997 the euro has confounded sceptics by transforming itself smoothly from a blueprint to a real currency. It was launched with 11 members in 1999, with Greece joining two years later. As the euro group consolidates, the meetings of finance ministers from which Britain is excluded have started to become more influential than the formal 15-member ECOFIN meetings in which it takes part. While the Treasury insists it will give no running commentaries on how much progress has been made in meeting the five economic tests, other commentators are free to make their judgements. But since its launch the euro has embarrassed its creators with a prolonged slump on the foreign exchange markets, leading to a painfully high exchange rate for the pound. Meanwhile, the British economy has performed well, undermining the arguments of those single currency supporters who predicted that foreign investment would dry up and the City of London would suffer.

The Blair government's second problem is that opinion surveys in Britain have shown rising public hostility to the single currency. A MORI poll for the *News of the World* in June 2000 showed 64 per cent would vote against replacing the pound with the euro in a referendum, with only 24 per cent in favour. Labour supporters would vote 51–35 against, with Liberal Democrat voters saying no by an even larger margin of 56–28, despite the pro-euro stance of their party leadership. Most significantly, asked to cite the main arguments against joining, 29 per cent cited a political reason – the loss of national identity. Asked whether joining the euro would involve giving up Britain's national identity, 41 per cent strongly agreed and a further 21 per cent agreed. More than half agreed with the statements that the government was trying to hide the real facts from the public, and that the government was divided on the issue. But at the same time, there was less evidence of anti-European views. Two-thirds of those questioned supported Blair's wish to see Britain playing a role 'at the heart of Europe'.

Faced with this kind of polling evidence, and the way Denmark voted against joining the euro in its September 2000 referendum, any hopes the government may have had that the single currency might be a vote-winning issue have evaporated; instead, the emphasis has been on keeping the whole issue out of the next general election, and limiting the potential gains for the Conservatives. Supporters of the single currency, such as Robin Cook and Peter Mandelson, have argued that a referendum in favour of the euro cannot be won in the next parliament unless the government climbs off the fence and starts campaigning well before the election. But this has been fiercely resisted by Gordon Brown, who has insisted the government stick to the letter of its 1997 compromise. Tony Blair has appeared to hover between the two camps, with his room for manoeuvre narrowing. The government has boxed itself into a Catch-22 dilemma: the case for surrendering national control of interest rates to the unaccountable European Central Bank and embracing the idea of European economic government can only be made convincing if the existing British policymaking framework can be shown to be inferior to the alternative on offer in the single currency zone. To succeed in making the single currency look attractive, the government has to make the case that its own economic policy has failed. But the longer it reaps a successful harvest in low inflation and stable growth from the arrangements which Brown created in 1997 for an independent Bank of England, the harder it is to argue that they should be abandoned.

> ❝ To succeed in making the single currency look attractive, the government has to make the case that its own economic policy has failed. ❞

While the Bank's Monetary Policy Committee operates transparently, follows an inflation target set by the Chancellor and is accountable to parliament, the European Central Bank is constitutionally independent of governments in its judgement of what interest rate to set to maintain price stability. According to two respected former Chancellors, Labour's Denis Healey and the Conservative Nigel Lawson, this is an unacceptable surrender of democratic control: 'The elimination of a national currency involves a major reduction in our ability to control our own affairs and thus a serious and permanent erosion of self-government.'[23]

MORTGAGE OR MARRIAGE?

Paddy Ashdown, who supports entry into the single currency, agrees that it is a question too important to be left to the economists and central bankers:

The people with whom I get most angry … are the ones who say they are all pro-European but they all pretend that monetary union is not a constitutional issue. It's a *massive* constitutional issue. My view is that the crisis for the euro is not that it goes up and down, all major tradable currencies do that. The crisis for the euro is coming, it is that we have created a hugely powerful economic institution set within a hugely weak political one. And when the euro faces the challenge of the asynchronization of the rate at which economies are growing, and we have to take some very tough political decisions about the transfer of resources between the richer parts of Europe and the poorer, we haven't got political institutions capable of doing that. That is the challenge that is coming, and it will force, in my view, a political reform of Europe that is inevitable.

The problem for Blair is that by stripping out the politics and concentrating on Brown's five economic tests, he has made the decision on the single currency sound like taking out a mortgage; Britain will sign on the dotted line if and when the figures look right. But a more convincing comparison would be with the permanent commitment of getting married or having a baby. In the rest of Europe, the single currency has long been seen above all as a political marriage, a staging post on the road to European integration. Bank of England governor Eddie George, while careful not to take sides in the political argument for or against entry, gives no help to the government in this area, saying monetary union is 'fundamentally a political rather than an economic issue'.

> ❝ He has made the decision on the single currency sound like taking out a mortgage. But a more convincing comparison would be with the permanent commitment of getting married or having a baby. ❞

It necessarily involves the deliberate pooling of national sovereignty over important aspects of public policy, in the interest not just of collective economic advantage but of a perceived wider political harmony within Europe.[24]

German Foreign Minister Joschka Fischer described the new currency in a speech to the European Parliament in January 1999 as 'a historic, possibly even a revolutionary, step which will bring a new quality to the work of European integration'. For the first time a core element of national sovereignty, the power to issue currency, had been ceded to a European institution, Fischer declared:

This act creates a new political quality. Currency, security and constitution are the three spheres where modern nation states exercise sovereignty, and with the introduction of the euro a first step has been taken towards exercising them in common in the EU. It will take some time before the full significance of this step for Europe and international politics can be grasped. The introduction of a common money is not first and foremost an economic act, but above all a sovereign one, and thus an eminently political one.

Fischer went on to predict that this step towards common sovereignty would create tensions within the EU's present inadequate political and democratic structures and make the current institutional status quo untenable. The risk would be that the member states would lack the vision to take further bold steps on the path to complete political union, a process which Fischer described as *Vergemeinschaftung*, or pooling of sovereignty. The EU's constitution would have to change to reflect the new goal of an enlarged political union, which he argued was the logical consequence of economic and monetary union, the final destination of the European train.

Fischer's ideas may not be universally accepted even by member states of the euro group, but even when watered down or dismissed as rhetoric for domestic consumption, they present a powerful challenge to the Labour government's approach. If the leading member state of the euro zone defines the single currency as a constitutional watershed, it makes it hard to say that British voters should be encouraged not to worry their heads too much about such arguments. The options for Blair and Brown after the next election are unpalatable: to argue in favour of entry on narrow economic grounds, leaving the political argument in a referendum campaign to be dominated by their opponents; to accept the same logic as Joschka Fischer and make an enthusiastic political case for pooling sovereignty, risking a suicidal battle with public opinion and Britain's anti-European newspapers; or to continue to opt out and risk relegation to the sidelines of the EU's economic decision making. In the words of former Conservative Chancellor Kenneth Clarke, a 'secondary and subordinate' role for Britain would be the inevitable consequence 'if we sit dithering on the edge'. This would put in jeopardy Blair's vision of Britain's destiny, which is 'to be a major European nation and to be happy and active in that role'. For the UK to stay outside economic and monetary union indefinitely would mean acquiescing in the creation of a two-speed Europe, with Britain in the slow lane.

FROM AMSTERDAM TO NICE

While Britain has dithered on the single currency, the EU's constitutional agenda has moved ahead on other fronts. The Blair government's pragmatic approach to European institutions has not been so different in practice from that of its Conservative predecessors; the motto has been 'integrate where necessary, decentralize where possible'. Britain wanted Europe to change its ways, but was wary of any major institutional upheaval. While leading the drive for reform of the Brussels Commission after the 1999 crisis and the resignation of its president Jacques Santer, Blair gave no sign at that point of seeking any wider institutional change. In his London Business School speech he called for a Europe that was 'accountable, democratic and efficient' but avoided spelling out in detail what he meant. It was clear that like the Conservatives, he was opposed to any increase in the powers of the European Parliament, which he once described as 'sometimes better known for its buildings than its achievements'. But he also resisted talk of turning the Commission into a government for Europe with its own democratic legitimacy, preferring to see it as a subordinate institution responsible to member governments. The attitude to political integration remained cautious, summed up by soundbites about 'a united Europe of states, not a United States of Europe'. Blair, interviewed by *The Economist* in February 2000, was asked about the goal of 'ever closer union' and replied: 'We seek ways of cooperating ever more closely because that's what's going to happen in the world, as we move to a single market and a single currency in Europe.' Had the high tide of supranational European integration passed? 'In relation to European integration I think there is a very clear sense in Europe that we cooperate as nation states, but that in a modern world states are going to move closer together ... I don't think that we need to be frightened of the prospect of ever closer union, provided we're clear about our own nation-state and national identity.'

The Intergovernmental Conference (IGC) completed in Nice in December 2000 was supposed to tidy up the unfinished business of the 1997 Treaty of Amsterdam and prepare the EU's institutions for the challenge of eastward expansion. Blair's government, strongly in favour of enlargement, argued early on for a limited agenda that would make it possible, rather than opening up a wider 'Whither Europe?' debate. It opposed a major reorganization of the European Treaties, as proposed by the Commission. A government White Paper in February 2000 dismissed Eurosceptic warnings of a European 'superstate' lurking at the end of the trail. 'There is not going to be a superstate,' the document declared, adding as proof that there would 'always be arguments between member states'. It acknowledged that political changes were on the way in Europe, but added: 'We should not fall into the trap of reading more into these changes than is really the case.' Europe would integrate where it made sense to do so, but coordination between member states would continue to be the norm.

Luckily for Blair, the outcome of the Nice summit largely followed this minimalist agenda. Blair agreed to extend majority voting on a series of issues but refused to compromise on key subjects such as taxation and social security, which would remain subject to unanimity. The horse-trading over the shape and size of the Commission and over national voting strengths went on for five days and left idealistic supporters of European unity outraged. The sharpest arguments were between France and Germany, the two countries whose traditional alliance had always led the way towards integration and created problems for Britain. The disarray between Paris and Bonn meant an easier summit than expected for Blair, anxious to keep the EU out of the headlines until the general election. On his return, he acknowledged that the IGC negotiation had not worked properly. 'We cannot continue to take decisions as important as this in this way,' he told the Commons. Reform of the EU was essential to create a more rational system of decision making, he said. 'That means on the one hand, making common decisions at a European level, where that makes sense, and on the other hand, making decisions on a national, or indeed regional, level, where that makes sense.'

Blair was referring to the agreement in Nice to hold a fresh and potentially far more important IGC in 2004 on the EU's future shape. Overcoming Foreign Office reservations, Blair swung his weight behind Germany's proposal for a simplification of the treaties and a delimitation of competences between the EU, national governments and regions. Germany saw the task of the IGC as constitutional: the preparation of a 'basic law' for Europe, which would settle once and for all the arguments about who did what between Brussels, national governments and regional authorities. Germany, it was clear, wanted a legally binding document, while constitution-shy Britain wanted no more than a political declaration. This was a high-risk game, with huge potential implications for the British domestic debate on constitutional matters.

A HA'PENNY WORTH OF BEANS?

British fear of entanglement in European constitution-building was highlighted by the drafting of a European Charter of Fundamental Rights.

This proposal, launched at the Berlin summit in June 1999, was an ambitious plan to give Europe's citizens new rights, going further on the economic and social front than the 50-year-old European Convention on Human Rights devised by the Council of Europe. It was drafted by a convention of government representatives and parliamentarians, chaired by Germany's former President Roman Herzog. The idea was to not only expand rights but to incorporate the charter in the European treaties and thus make them justiciable, or enforceable in court. The UK government strongly resisted this approach, saying the Charter should be no more than a summary of existing rights and should not have legal force. Europe Minister Keith Vaz told the House of Commons Foreign Affairs Committee in March 2000: 'What the Charter will not be doing is to be giving out new rights to people, rights that they do not have at the moment. I think we have a pretty sufficient list of rights already without the need to add anything more.' Andrew Mackinlay, a Labour member, asked him if this meant the government intended that the Charter was 'not going to amount to a ha'penny worth of beans'. Vaz insisted: 'We are not going to have any new tiers of law, any new methods of enforcement, any new ways in which people can prosecute. It is a declaration, a codification, a simplification, a communication of existing rights.'

A high-powered House of Lords subcommittee packed with top lawyers delved much more deeply into the Charter project than the Commons. It was told by Vaz that the Charter was 'more political than legal, and it is certainly not constitutional'. He insisted that the document was neither a Bill of Rights nor a European constitution. The Lords committee report concluded by warning the government it risked appearing 'excessively negative' and missing a major opportunity to give more effective protection to individuals in their dealings with European institutions. Lord Hope of Craighead, the Scottish Law Lord who chaired the committee, pointed out that the Charter would involve only rights applicable at EU level, and the process was 'primarily one of consolidation'. However, he acknowledged that the proposal 'was, and still is, an extremely sensitive one, both in this country and throughout the EU'. Lord Hope, speaking in a Lords debate on 16 June 2000, noted drily that it might have been better to 'put the horse before the cart' and decide the status of the proposed document before working out its contents. He said the Charter was unlikely to end up as insignificant as the government appeared to hope: 'However much some may wish that the document should be accorded as little by way of status as possible ... the reality is likely to be quite different.'

Whatever the formal status of the Charter, the European Court of Justice would find itself using it as a guide in developing its jurisprudence. Lord Hope said it would be unsatisfactory for the document to be no more than a showcase, as the government wished, because there were significant gaps in rights protection in the EU, notably in the areas of crime fighting, visa control, immigration and asylum. 'It would be better to take a more positive stance on this issue,' Lord Hope suggested. 'We suggest that it should be recognized that the time has come for the provision of effective remedies for the infringement of existing rights at EU level.' However, the committee backed the government's worries about including social and economic rights: 'If the Charter is to include such rights, great care needs to be taken to ensure that their inclusion does not enlarge the competence of the EU or the Community by the back door.'

Anthony Lester QC, another member of the committee, told the Lords that the complex legal, political and constitutional issues raised by the charter 'go to the heart of the debate about the nature and future of Europe'. The charter was 'a major opportunity to give more effective protection to the individual in relation to the activities of the EU's institutions'. To introduce protection against misuse of power by the EU was not to extend EU competence but to limit it under the rule of law, he argued. 'The government's present line, we think, runs the risk of appearing to be extremely negative when it comes to the practical protection of the individual against the infringement of rights by the EU institutions.'

As the negotiations progressed, the government's lack of enthusiasm for the whole project became more and more evident. At one point Vaz said the document would have no more legal significance than *The Beano* or *The Sun*. Government nervousness appeared to be partly motivated by concerns about a new document appearing just at the time the European Convention on Human Rights was incorporated into UK law, leading to legal confusion. But there were wider political worries that Germany in particular wanted the document to serve as the legal underpinning for a new federalist stage of European institutional reform. This aspect was highlighted by *The Times*, which at the beginning of June forcibly reminded the government of its problems with Eurosceptic opposition at home with a barrage of attacks on the whole project. 'This Charter has far less to do with human rights than it does with building the legal basis for a federal Europe,' the newspaper complained. It suggested that if the document became EU law, automatically enforceable in British courts, it would lead to workers suing their employers for shorter hours and other social rights.

The Nice summit left the document's legal status to be resolved in 2004, but the debate clearly marked out Britain as being in the European slow lane on human rights and consitutional issues.

ONWARDS AND UPWARDS

A fresh round of constitutional debate – highly unwelcome in London – was triggered by another Joschka Fischer speech, delivered on 12 May 2000 at the Humboldt University, Berlin. Although Fischer described it as his personal views, most commentators saw it as a trial balloon for official policy, delivered with the backing of Chancellor Gerhard Schröder. Deliberately going beyond the December 2000 Nice summit and the current IGC, Fischer looked over the horizon to what he called the 'finality' of the process of European union. Answering his own 'whither Europe?' question, Fischer declared: 'Onwards until European integration is complete.' Standing still or retreating would mean paying a high price, he warned. Drawing the opposite conclusion from those who maintained that a wider Europe would have to be a looser body, Fischer said enlargement to the east meant placing the last block in the European building – political integration. This task would have to be led by France and Germany, whose common interests had underpinned earlier phases of integration under Robert Schuman and Jean Monnet. Not only a single currency but a common legal sphere and a common defence were now on the agenda, in addition to enlargement, which would place the existing EU institutions under intolerable strain.

Looking beyond the IGC, Fischer said he was putting aside his foreign minister's hat to give his personal vision of what might come next, while warning 'Eurosceptics on both sides of the Channel' not to produce their biggest headlines. The only answer to an enlarged European Union with 30 member states was a federation, with a European parliament and government exercising legislative and executive power, based on a treaty setting up a constitution. This would be difficult, not least because of the role of nation states to which people would cling for security. Such national state traditions would have to be built in to the new federation, leading not to the abolition of national sovereignty but to a shared sovereignty. A new two-chamber European parliament would have to be created to represent both states and citizens, including representatives of national parliaments. Executive power would be wielded either by the existing Council of Ministers, or by a Commission whose president would be directly elected, not appointed by governments.

Rather than making Europe more complicated, a constitution setting out the respective powers of the federation and national states would clear up misunderstandings and leave the former with only what was absolutely necessary. 'It would be a federation which was transparent and comprehensible to its citizens, because it would overcome their democratic deficit,' he argued. Fischer half-apologized to British opponents of a federal system for using the word, but said he could think of no other term that fitted. 'In this final European phase we will still be Britons and Germans and French and Poles. The nation states will continue to exist and maintain a much stronger role than the German federal states,' he predicted.

Fischer then reviewed suggestions for 'variable geometry' from European elder statesmen such as Jacques Delors, Helmut Schmidt and Valéry Giscard d'Estaing, recalling plans by two German Christian Democrats in 1994 for a 'hard core' of EU states which would pursue closer integration on their own. If not all EU states could move together to a federal system, a smaller group could lead the way, following the models of the Schengen group and the single currency zone. Such a group with its own constitution and government would create a centre of gravity in the EU which would be open to all states that wished to join. A new constitutional treaty would form the basis for 'a deliberate political act of refoundation' for Europe.

A few weeks after Fischer's speech, it was the turn of French President Jacques Chirac to use an official visit to Berlin to pick up the ball and run with it. Chirac proposed a 'pioneer group' of EU states, led by France and Germany, which would forge ahead of the others, backed up by their own secretariat. 'Neither you nor we envisage the creation of a European superstate which would substitute itself for our nation states and mark the end of their existence as actors in international life,' he declared. The EU had to increase democracy and settle 'who does what' between institutions at different levels. Those countries that wished to go further in integration should not be held back by the others, he said. Unlike Fischer, Chirac said it would be wrong for the inner group to sign a special treaty of their own. Other post-IGC questions on which he called for further debate and study included the potential geographical limits of the EU, the final status of the Charter of Fundamental Rights, and further changes in the role of the Commission and the European Parliament. All this would take several years, and the final stage would be for everyone in the EU to vote on the proposed European constitution.

AN UNAVOIDABLE DEBATE

Chirac's speech provoked a rift with the Socialist-led government, unexpectedly outflanked on the pro-European front by a man whose long and opportunistic political career had mostly been marked by the nationalist legacy of Gaullism. But French commentators saw Chirac's intervention as much more than an episode in domestic 'cohabitation' politics in the run-up to the next presidential election, or the work of a maverick. As André Fontaine noted in *Le Monde*, the debate on 'who does what' and the next stage of European integration was unavoidable. 'Whether or not one calls it a constitution, one can't avoid it.'

Beyond the speeches by Fischer and Chirac, a wider Franco-German debate has been developing on future political integration in the European Union, focusing on that long-term British nightmare – a two-speed Europe in which London is excluded from the inner group, led by Paris and Berlin. François Bayrou, leader of the pro-European centre-right UDF party, has suggested a directly elected president of Europe, an idea supported by the Greens; two of Chirac's closest political allies, Alain Juppé and Jacques Toubon, have argued for the creation of a European government responsible to the European Parliament; former Commission president Jacques Delors has also proposed his vision of an inner group of states; and support for the idea of a European constitution has come from the presidents of Italy and Germany. Policy documents prepared by the French Socialist party push in the same direction. According to *Le Monde*, the groundwork for the current debate has been laid by the policy planning staffs of the French and German foreign ministries, who have been working since 1998 on a 100-page document about the future of Europe. The diplomats, according to *Le Monde*, have suggested strengthening the role of the Commission by making its president either directly elected in a Europe-wide vote, or chosen by the European Parliament. The EU's foreign policy supremo would also become part of the Commission rather than reporting to governments, as Javier Solana does at present. A tighter coordination of foreign and security policies led by the Commission could lead to a joint EU seat on the United Nations Security Council.

BACK TO GAULLISM?

Where has this debate on the constitutional future of post-Nice Europe left the Blair government? Between a rock and a hard place. Blair's reply to Fischer and Chirac came in a speech in Warsaw in October 2000, in which he tried desperately to reconcile the conflicting pressures. With an eye to the British domestic audience, he tried to make a coherent case for Britain being at the centre of influence in Europe: 'We can choose not to be there; but no one should doubt the consequences of that choice, and it is wildly unrealistic to pretend those consequences are not serious.' But in the debate about Europe's political future, Blair said, it would be wrong to 'plunge in to the thicket of institutional change' without first asking the basic question of what direction Europe should take. The need for change was driven by the fact that with the prospect of enlargement, Europe was widening and deepening simultaneously. Blair, following his usual 'third way' approach, presented the argument as a choice between two over-simplified stereotypes – the Conservative model of a simple free trade zone or a 'classic federalist model' in which the Commission President would be elected and the European Parliament would become the main legislative European body and democratic checking mechanism. The first was too limited, the second would lead to a superstate: 'It too fails the test of the people,' Blair declared. The question of democratic accountability could not be answered on a European level, only through national parliaments and governments. The aim should be to square this circle and turn Europe into 'a superpower, but not a superstate'.

Blair argued that instead of 'an abstract discussion of institutional change' the debate should be more practical and focus on how best to achieve a series of policy goals. His proposal was to use the European Council – the periodic summits of leaders – as the body that should set an annual agenda for Europe and give clear political direction. But he appeared sceptical about the idea of giving Europe a formal constitution:

In practice I suspect that, given the sheer diversity and complexity of the EU, its constitution, like the British constitution, will continue to be found in a number of different treaties, laws and precedents. It is perhaps easier for the British than for others to recognize that a constitutional debate must not necessarily end with a single, legally binding document called a constitution for an entity as dynamic as the EU. What I think is both desirable and realistic is to draw up a statement of the principles according to which we should decide what is best done at the European level and what should be done at the national level, a kind of charter of competences. This would allow countries too to define clearly what is then done at a regional level. This statement of principles would be a political, not a legal, document. It could therefore be much simpler and more accessible to Europe's citizens.

Blair went on to adapt one of Fischer's proposals, calling for a second chamber of the European Parliament, composed of representatives of national parliaments, to review the implementation of this statement of principles and keep an eye on the common foreign and security policy.

He then addressed the most sensitive issue arising from the speeches by Fischer and Chirac – the idea of a two-speed Europe. While appearing to soften Britain's earlier suspicion of moves towards greater flexibility, he warned that this 'must not lead to a hard core, a Europe in which some member states create their own set of shared policies and institutions from which others are in practice excluded'. 'Enhanced co-operation' between groups of states could go ahead, but there must be no multi-tier Europe with different sets of rules. Blair concluded by saying that the political foundations of Europe were 'rooted in the democratic nation state'. Coining another 'third way' slogan, he proclaimed that 'democracy and efficiency go together'.

Blair's Warsaw speech left many questions unanswered; although he went out of his way not to say that the role of the Commission and the European Parliament should be downgraded, his proposals for a greater role for the European Council clearly implied that the path forward for the EU lay in intergovernmental cooperation, a view closer to Chirac than to Schröder and the Commission President, Romano Prodi. Supporters of integration saw the five days of wrangling at Nice as proof that the Council, composed of 15 heads of state and government, was not an effective decision-making forum for the future. As Dutch EU Commissioner Frits Bolkestein put it in a speech in January 2001:

What would meetings be like with twice that number? The efficiency of intergovernmental decision making is in inverse proportion to the number of member states around the table. The bigger the group, the more limited its decision-making powers become. With the system it applies at present, the European Council is running the risk of turning into a sort of Congress of Vienna.

Blair's belief in a Europe run by national governments appeared to conflict with his enthusiasm for joining the single currency, run by a supranational and unaccountable central bank. The Warsaw speech, with its bow in the direction of *L'Europe des patries*, was an embrace of Gaullism just at the moment when the General's ideas were being cast aside by the Gaullists themselves. It was only a partial and superficial answer to the questions raised by the approach of a new IGC devoted to constitutional matters, in which it was possible that France and Germany, overcoming their differences, would agree a common approach.

A VIEW OF THE FUTURE

In his book *Democracy in Europe*, Professor Larry Siedentop of Oxford University sees deep-seated reasons for the peripheral role in the debate on Europe's future played by Britain, the country that invented representative government and the culture of consent. 'Would it not be reasonable to expect Britain to take the lead in any further development of representative government in Europe? Should not Britain, with its remarkable constitutional history, take the principal part in creating a federal Europe? But that has not been the case.' Instead Britain has largely taken over the Gaullist position, insisting on a Europe of nation states. Siedentop sees an essential link between the symptoms of constitutional uncertainty at home and in Europe: 'For the nature of the British state explains why Britain finds it so difficult today to make a constructive contribution to the creation of Europe. The truth is, that it cannot.' Britain is handicapped in the European constitutional debate because it is lagging behind its partners in such areas as civil liberties, social guarantees and representative government. Siedentop also noted 'the traditional embarrassment of the British when faced with general ideas'.[25]

> 66 Britain is handicapped in the European constitutional debate because it is lagging behind its partners in such areas as civil liberties, social guarantees and representative government. 99

Paddy Ashdown argues that the UK, to take part properly in the European debate, has to look seriously at the traditionally taboo concepts of federalism and power sharing:

I first called for this three years ago and now this is quite a big issue amongst leaders. My view is very simple. We are creating for better or worse a 'federal' institution, and that word is not for me to use since I am English and the word is

English and I know its true meaning is a dirty word – it means power to the lowest levels, not the opposite. If you are creating a federal institution you cannot leave unanswered the absolutely central question about federalism which is, what power resides with the federal institutions and what resides with the component elements. For as long as we leave that unanswered and hide behind a word like subsidiarity which nobody means, we should not be surprised that people get frightened about the encroachment of Europe or politicians believe it is a threat to their parliaments. In the end, you can call it anything you like, a constitution, a statute of limitations if you wish, my view is that you have to define again by exception those powers that are going to be held by Europe, leaving all other powers with the nation state. We have to face up to that.

It is difficult to escape the conclusion that within the next few years any British government is going to face some hard choices between the United Kingdom's future as a nation state and its future at the heart of a more politically integrated European Union. Michael Jacobs of the Fabian Society says he is worried about the process of 'ever-closer union' in Europe because it has no defined end. 'I don't think this has been properly debated. If we don't get into this debate it will be decided for us. This is part of the constitution … it is a debate about how we are governed. It isn't debated, except by those people who reject the whole thing.'

The history of recent decades suggests that France and Germany may start with widely differing visions of the European future. But as with the creation of the single currency, sooner or later they will reach some kind of joint view. At that point, preparatory work is likely to begin on drawing up some kind of European constitution, either by a group of 'wise men' or in some kind of Convention of the European great and good. But without any national constitution of its own as a starting point and with no clear ideas to guide it except for the tattered principle of parliamentary sovereignty, and a generalized pragmatism, Britain is at a huge disadvantage. Blair has often spoken of the need to overcome the historic British ambivalence about Europe, but it is an ambivalence he cannot escape; it pervades his own speeches in such trite formulas as 'a superpower not a superstate'. It reflects British domestic constitutional uncertainty and Blair's lack of joined-up thinking. Larry Siedentop says: 'The British are held back by the task of completing the destruction of the British *ancien régime* and renewing the British form of the state.' Siedentop worries that a British government will end up acquiescing in

European arrangements of which it does not really approve. Because 'federalism' is a British taboo, being widely misunderstood as a synonym for centralization rather than self-government and balanced power sharing, Britain will side with a French-inspired, bureaucratic vision of Europe instead.

Siedentop's diagnosis of the British inability to enter the debate on either side is a convincing one, and it is shared by the authors of Charter88's long-term strategy paper *Unlocking Democracy*. It is the failure to think clearly about constitutional questions in domestic politics that results in an inability to address them in the European context:

Nowhere is the impact of Britain's failure to draw up a new constitution more disastrous than in relations with the EU. Britain's position *vis-à-vis* Europe is bound to remain evasive and half-hearted until it has the self-respect that accompanies a secure constitution.

Both sides in the argument over the single currency are clinging to different versions of the same old-fashioned myth of the British state, according to Charter88:

The fact is that the familiar British sovereignty – which each wishes in a different way to preserve – is finished. Whether or not Britain joins the euro, this has to be confronted on its own terms. Yet one of the reasons why the argument seems likely to run and run is that it allows both sides to postpone facing up to the terminal condition of the UK's unwritten constitution.

The failure to decide on the single currency puts Britain in the worst of all possible worlds – suspended animation:

With the European Union committed to enlargement and drafting a constitution for itself, British democrats ought to be openly participating in a political process that will apply directly to them. Thanks to the stance of government and opposition, British voices are not shaping the strategic direction of a polity that now generates a quarter of the UK's domestic legislation. Or if they are, they are only doing so by stealth. Britain is being governed by the EU without being fully in the EU – the least democratic outcome of all.

The self-confidence in its own national identity which Blair identified in his *Economist* interview as essential for political integration to succeed is in fact the very quality which Britain is lacking:

In these circumstances, when the UK's own identity and institutions are so weak, ever-closer union and the prospect of joining the euro are bound to frighten. Only a UK self-confident enough to be moving towards defining its own constitution could be sure enough to participate in Europe in the way the Prime Minister suggests.

Anatole Kaletsky of *The Times* predicts that Britain's relationship with Europe will 'act as the lens through which all the contradictions of government policy are focused and intensified'.

Because of Europe, Mr Blair will be forced to engage in a profound and uncomfortable debate on the British constitution, on the meaning of democracy in a modern state, on the balance between government and the market in providing public services, and on the inherent tensions between equality and freedom ... The Blair-Brown policy is to present a potentially revolutionary transformation in Britain's relationship with Europe as a purely economic issue. Can this possibly survive the debate and scrutiny of a general election campaign? The answer must surely be no ... The bedrock of this policy is that joining the single currency is a purely economic matter, with no overriding constitutional implications. This is manifestly untrue.[26]

Kaletsky believes the 'fundamental dishonesty' of the Blair-Brown approach has been exposed by the way Fischer, Chirac and other European leaders have set out their visions for Europe's future:

Whatever their disagreements on detail, almost all continental leaders agree – and say publicly – that one of the most important purposes of the single currency project is to transform the EU from a primarily economic enterprise into a much more coherent political entity, capable of taking major decisions on social, fiscal, diplomatic, defence and legal issues that are now reserved to the member states.

Tony Wright MP is more sceptical about the link between the absence of a written domestic constitution and the lack of a British contribution to the European constitutional debate:

I'm not sure it's because we lack a written constitution here. It's true we haven't made the contribution that we could have and I think we genuinely could do. There is a role for Britain with its own traditions in putting together a group of countries who ask some fairly critical questions about some of the projects for Europe. My sense is that in continental Europe there is a huge gulf between the political classes talking about these things and the populations, who seem to be entirely disengaged from the project while the political class is wholly engaged. Here it is quite different. Here Europe is actually a rather live political argument. It's a good thing. The issue of what kind of Europe we want to see is far more central to the argument here than anywhere else. So there is a kind of irony that because of that, we haven't yet developed a view.

BRITANNIC MINIMALISM

Blair's dilemma is that signing up to a more integrated Europe ('federal' or not) alongside France and Germany will be deeply unpalatable both to British public opinion and to the political class at Westminster, jealous of its privileges. It is far from certain that Blair's idea of a second chamber for the European Parliament composed of national parliamentarians will be enough to connect the UK's increasingly sceptical citizens with a more politically integrated Europe. The alternative, a two-speed Europe with Britain in the slow lane, might appease the eurosceptic tabloids and defuse attacks from the Conservatives, but would lead to a marginalization which Blair would consider a failure. The third alternative, to muddle through pragmatically and maintain the European status quo, is to ignore the reality of EU enlargement. It also means surrendering the initiative of leadership in Europe to which Blair has laid claim. Britannic minimalism over Europe is therefore not a long-term option, and may not even stand the test of a short-term general election campaign.

The point of this chapter's detour into Europe has not been to take sides on whether Britain should opt in or out of a more integrated political union or a single currency. As with the future of the monarchy, there are powerful arguments on both sides, which demand a real political debate on the future of the British nation state. The old elastic doctrine of the sovereign Crown-in-Parliament can no longer be stretched to cover the new realities. Economic tests, however justified in themselves, will not provide satisfactory answers to these questions. There is room for a new constitutional story about Britain, embracing citizenship, the Crown, regional devolution and Europe, but there are few signs that Labour is ready to embrace the challenge of telling it.

NOTES

[1] *Who Shares New Labour Values?* (1999) British Social Attitudes, 16th report, London, National Centre for Social Research/Ashgate Press.

[2] White, Clarissa, Bruce, Sara and Ritchie, Jane (2000) *Young People's Politics. Political interest and engagement amongst 14- to 24-year-olds*, London, Joseph Rowntree Foundation.

[3] Pirie, Dr Madsen and Worcester, Robert (2000) *The Big Turn-Off*, London, Adam Smith Institute.

[4] Crick, Bernard (2000) *Essays on Citizenship*, London, Continuum, p 160.

[5] *Sunday Times*, 7 March 1999.

[6] *Citizenship: Challenges for Councils*, Local Government Information Unit, 2000.

[7] *The Herald*, 7 December 1999.

[8] Freedland, Jonathan (1999) *Bring Home the Revolution. The case for a British republic*, London, Fourth Estate, p 213.

[9] Dummett, Ann (1999) *Citizenship and National Identity* in Hazell (ed.) *Constitutional Futures*, Oxford.

[10] *Unlocking Democracy* (2000) London, Charter88, p 17.

[11] *Daily Telegraph*, 22 April 1996.

[12] *Observer*, 13 August 2000.

[13] Nairn, Tom (1988 and 1994) *The Enchanted Glass. Britain and its monarchy*, London, Vintage, p 155.

[14] Nairn, op. cit., p 204.

[15] Hames, Tim and Leonard, Mark (1998) *Modernising the Monarchy*, London, Demos.

[16] Hayden, Ilse (1987) *Symbol and Privilege. The ritual context of British royalty*, University of Arizona Press, p 164.

[17] Colley, Linda (1997) *Britons. Forging the nation 1707–1837*, London, Vintage, p 49.

[18] Colley, op. cit., p 225.

[19] *Daily Telegraph*, 1 March 1996.

[20] Mount, Ferdinand (1993) *The British Constitution Now*, London, Mandarin, p 219.

[21] Young, Hugo (1998) *This Blessed Plot. Britain and Europe from Churchill to Blair*, London, Macmillan, p 258.

[22] Young, op. cit., p 474.

[23] *A New EU White Paper* (2000) London, New Europe.

[24] Speech to British Swiss Chamber of Commerce Lunch, 12 September 2000.

[25] Siedentop, Larry (2000) *Democracy in Europe*, London, Allen Lane, The Penguin Press.

[26] *The Times*, 8 June 2000.

13

THE D-WORD

'I never met anyone on the doorstep in Hartlepool who claimed to be a convert to New Labour because of constitutional reform' – Peter Mandelson

'There is a profound scepticism about the concept of democracy at the heart of New Labour' – Matthew Taylor, IPPR

'You have seen the greatest constitutional change arguably in a century. Devolution to Scotland and Wales has altered things fundamentally, as the government is now beginning to understand. Britain will never be governed the same again' – Paddy Ashdown

'They have triggered the endgame for a regime that dates back to 1688. Whether this ending will take five or 50 years is not yet clear' – Anthony Barnett

AFTER THREE FULL PARLIAMENTARY SESSIONS SINCE Tony Blair entered Downing Street, it is time to take stock and draw up a balance sheet of Labour's constitutional reforms. But what yardsticks should we use to judge them? The first and narrowest is Labour's own, the 1997 manifesto. Has Labour 'delivered' on its promises? This means following the government's glossy annual report, and ticking the boxes to mark electoral pledges 'kept' or 'on track'. We can also ask some subordinate questions: has Labour kept to the letter and spirit of the Cook-Maclennan agreement with the Liberal Democrats signed in the run-up to the 1997 election? Has it met the broader hopes and aspirations for constitutional change which Labour helped encourage between 1992 and 1997, including the legacy of John Smith and the 'whiners, whingers and wankers' whom the party cultivated in opposition? We can look at the overall coherence of the reforms. Are they joined-up or poorly coordinated? Are they complete or unfinished? Have they worked, or more precisely *for whom* have they worked?

This is perhaps the most important question of all. Mikhail Gorbachev's political reforms were a complete disaster for the Soviet communists whose rule he was trying to preserve, but a huge success in freeing Russia from a totalitarian political system. So reforms that have failed to benefit the Labour party can still be a success for the rest of us. What kind of values can we discern in the Blair constitutional project? What is the relationship, if any, between Blairite 'modernization' and democratization?

A REFORM SCORECARD FOR LABOUR

Scotland: Devolution in Scotland, now accepted by all parties, has to be counted among the most solid of Labour's constitutional achievements. The new parliament looks a robust institution but it has failed to deliver the death blow to Scottish nationalism that Labour hoped. Coalition government with the Liberal Democrats has set a precedent followed later in Wales. Policy divergences between Edinburgh and London have emerged since the death of 'father of the nation' Donald Dewar and the outlook for Labour is uncertain. An SNP election win in 2003 would prove a real test of the devolution settlement, possibly leading to a referendum on independence and the possible breakup of the UK.

Wales: Labour's internal divisions over devolution and the lack of all-party consensus have produced a much shakier outcome. Failure to give the National Assembly primary legislative powers makes it almost certain the devolution settlement will have to be revised within the next ten years. Labour's worst nightmares have already occurred with the disgrace of Ron Davies and the fall of Alun Michael. Under Rhodri Morgan's coalition with the Liberal Democrats, things can only get better.

Northern Ireland: The Good Friday Agreement, Tony Blair's biggest personal achievement in office, was an innovative devolution settlement whose subsequent implementation has been difficult and which could still fall apart, with a collapse in Unionist support for the agreement and a return to direct rule.

England: A political vacuum has emerged as Labour has failed to follow up devolution elsewhere by decentralizing power to the English regions. Regional development agencies and non-elected regional chambers are in place, but there has been no progress towards democratically elected regional government, except in London. The capital's first direct election for mayor turned into a humiliation for Labour, with the election of Ken Livingstone as an independent. The unsolved English question will be on Labour's agenda for a second term.

Party funding, elections and referendums: Some election procedures have been updated to make voting easier, but there are few hopes that the changes will reverse declining turnouts. Complex new rules on party funding are in place, to be supervised by an electoral commission reporting to parliament. This is a major, largely unsung reform, but even the experts do not know how level the playing field will really be in future elections and referendums.

Electoral reform: The UK now has an alphabet soup of proportional new electoral systems: the additional member system for the Scottish Parliament, the Welsh Assembly and the London Assembly; the single transferable vote in Northern Ireland; the supplementary vote for the London mayor; and closed regional lists for European elections. But the government, facing hostility among Labour MPs to reform for the Commons, has pigeonholed the Jenkins commission report. The referendum on PR that John Smith promised the voters has not taken place, and looks unlikely in a second term unless Labour depends on Liberal Democrat support for a Commons majority. Any reform will be dependent on Labour's own electoral interests, which remain paramount.

Whitehall: Labour has seen government above all as a business delivering services and has built on Conservative management reforms aimed at improving value for money rather than democracy or accountability. Cabinet government has declined further, with a strong 10 Downing Street machine making heavy use of political appointees, and a powerful Treasury. Modernization has meant more private finance and more centralized control, despite much talk of decentralization.

Freedom of information: Labour's failure to do its homework in opposition, despite Tony Blair's rousing rhetoric about the right to know, led to a spectacular U-turn in policy in government. A liberal White Paper was followed by restrictive legislation which experts say compares badly with foreign equivalents and is likely to satisfy nobody.

Human rights: The Human Rights Act incorporating the European Convention on Human Rights is a historic constitutional reform which will produce big changes in the relationship between parliament and the courts. Like devolution, its full effects will take decades to emerge. The old doctrine of parliamentary sovereignty has been preserved in theory, but maybe not in practice. The Act has been undersold by a nervous government, whose leader has not seen human rights policy as a priority at home and abroad.

The senior judiciary: Labour has rigidly preserved the constitutional status quo, avoiding reform of judicial appointments, the position of the Law Lords in the upper house and the much criticized triple role of the Lord Chancellor. Changes could happen as a byproduct of stage two of reform of the House of Lords.

Citizenship: Education for citizenship will be on the national curriculum in schools from 2002, but critics say more is needed to turn subjects into real citizens and not just customers.

The monarchy: Labour has shown no sign of wanting to reform the constitutional role of the monarchy or the royal prerogative powers exercised in the name of the Crown by the prime minister. Other constitutional changes may eventually force a rethink.

Europe: Despite pro-European rhetoric, Labour has postponed a decision on joining the single currency, while tying the choice to five economic tests to shut down political and constitutional debate. It has done its best to minimize the EU's new Charter of Rights and has likewise resisted calls to give the EU a legally binding constitution. By agreeing to hold a new conference on reforming the EU in 2004, it has helped ensure that a real constitutional debate in Europe is inevitable.

Parliament: Dither and confusion have reigned over Lords reform, though most hereditary peers have been ejected from the second chamber in a first stage. The government agreed to a questionable deal allowing around 100 hereditary peers to remain and has lost dozens of votes in the Lords as a result. Tony Blair has moved Labour policy away from the idea of an elected second chamber and towards a mostly appointed upper house of notables. The government is uncertain what to do next, but is determined to prevent creation of a chamber that would get in the way of the Commons. In a second term it may – or may not – implement the Wakeham commission report. In the Commons there has been superficial modernization but Labour has strongly resisted attempts to strengthen Select Committees and make the executive more accountable to parliament. The forces of conservatism remain intact, and Westminster still awaits the kind of painful reforms that other British institutions have undergone.

THE BEST AND THE WORST

Labour can claim that the most important boxes in its 1997 election manifesto have been ticked, with the retreat from a referendum on electoral reform as the biggest gap in the list. But there is an extraordinary variation between the best and the worst of the government's reforms. Scottish and Welsh devolution, the Northern Ireland peace agreement, and the Human Rights Act head the list of promises kept. But there has been ambivalence about devolution, seen in a reluctance to surrender control of events. Over the Human Rights Act, there has been the same hesitation; from various sources I heard that 10 Downing Street suffered from cold feet *after* the legislation was passed by parliament, fearing it had created a rod for its own back and seeking to delay its implementation. The government has stalled on creating a Human Rights Commission, delayed setting up a parliamentary Human Rights Committee, and has generally tried to discourage the idea that people will gain new rights that they did not have before. A consistent government message on human rights at home and abroad has been undermined by the illiberal nature of much Home Office legislation and the twisting imperatives of foreign policy. While I have looked in detail at the human rights implications of relations with China, others have singled out policy on asylum seekers or arms sales to find examples of the right hand not knowing what the left hand is up to.

In some fields, such as freedom of information, the letter of the manifesto commitment has been followed, but not the spirit. In others, such as the monarchy and the senior judiciary, reform has been neither promised nor delivered. In one area, the reform of party funding, Labour has actually delivered a far more ambitious package than it promised. It is interesting to note that the two most radical and arguably most successful measures, the Scotland Act and the Human Rights Act, were the ones on which Labour had done most detailed preparation in opposition, both in the Scottish Constitutional Convention and in negotiations with the Liberal Democrats. The devolution settlement in Wales, where Labour did not cooperate with other parties and was hamstrung by internal divisions, has revealed serious flaws. In areas where little or no spadework was done in opposition, such as House of Lords reform, the results have been muddled and unimpressive. Tony Blair's government has often lacked a clear idea of what it was trying to achieve, leaving policy to be driven by the perceived short-term interests of the Labour party. This has been the case with electoral reform, which has been inextricably linked to relations between Tony Blair's party and the Liberal Democrats. The promise of a referendum, originally made by John Smith, survives only in a severely weakened form, with signs that the Jenkins report on voting reform for the Commons will stay firmly in Blair's pigeonhole. Only if Labour needs Charles Kennedy's party in order to command a Commons majority is the juicy dish of electoral reform likely to be taken out of the policy deep freeze and reheated.

Lords reform has been an entertaining story of deviousness and confusion, in which the Blair government has effectively defaulted back to unicameralism, abandoning Labour's goal in opposition of turning the second chamber into a democratically elected legislature. The manifesto pledge to remove hereditary peers from the House of Lords has been met only in part. As a result the statement in the foreword to the Cook-Maclennan agreement that 'Britain is alone in the Western world in allowing some people to take a seat in parliament on the hereditary principle rather than by the democratic process' is as true now as it was in 1997. The deal negotiated by Derry Irvine with Robert Cranborne to preserve 92 hereditary peers initially looked like a big coup by Labour because of the havoc it caused in Conservative ranks. With hindsight, it looks like a major blunder, a huge concession offered to appease a threat of disruption by Tory peers that was just a bluff. The deal showed Tony Blair at his most devious – authorizing one minister (Derry Irvine) to plot in secret with the opposition behind the back of another (Ivor Richard). On stage two of reform, Labour has stalled. The consensus view is that the most important of the Wakeham proposals are unlikely to be implemented. Of the three main parties, Labour is now the most hostile to elections for the upper house, having embraced the Orwellian argument that they would harm democracy. Tony Blair may have been unable to decide exactly what he wanted for the Lords, but he knew what he didn't want – a democratically elected chamber that would complicate life for his government by setting up an alternative centre of legitimacy to the Commons and reducing his powers of patronage. Lords reform has provided the spectacle of a reluctant Labour prime minister having to be persuaded by a Conservative with a deserved reputation as a hardened political cynic, John Wakeham, of the case for allowing in a small number of elected members to sit among his appointees.

In Europe, the government, handicapped by the lack of a proper constitutional framework at home, has lagged behind in the debate on the future of the EU. But the prospect of a full-scale debate on a constitution for Europe at the 2004 Intergovernmental Conference (IGC) will force the government to clarify its ideas. It will be hard to promote a vigorous popular discussion on a written basic law for the EU without the argument spilling over into the need for a similar law for the UK. If the rest of Europe agrees that some powers should belong at regional level, what happens to the country that lacks a proper regional tier of government? And if sovereignty is to be formally pooled at a European level, what happens to the traditional Diceyan formula of the sovereignty of Westminster? It may, after all, be Europe, which has so often proved a catalyst for change in the United Kingdom since 1973, that provokes the next stage of constitutional reform.

Without electoral reform at Westminster, modernization of the Commons has amounted to tinkering around the edges, and has lacked a clear set of agreed goals. The government has fiercely resisted any suggestion that its vice-like control over the legislature should be weakened. Too often, the only reason offered for refusing change has been past historical precedent or the complaint that 'no previous government has been asked to do this' – hardly the argument of a radical reforming administration. Strong government has yet to be matched by strong accountability, and the impact of devolution on Westminster has yet to be properly addressed. It is hard to avoid the conclusion that despite all the reforms at the periphery, the core of the British political system of elective dictatorship, which John Smith wanted to change, has remained intact under his successor. Conservative sleaze has been washed away, leaving the other dysfunctional aspects of Britain's over-centralized government exposed.

A STAKHANOVITE RECORD

Government ministers such as Jack Straw insist that the government has done the maximum in the time available, and point to the unprecedented number of around 20 constitutional Bills passed in three parliamentary sessions. This looks like a Stakhanovite overfulfilment of the norm when one considers the advice from the Constitution Unit before the election that the government should limit itself to just two constitutional Bills in each session. Straw told me his cabinet colleagues felt too much time had been spent on constitutional change, to the exclusion of other issues:

I think when constitutional historians look back on this three-year period they will be staggered by the constitutional change we have put through. As much constitutional change has happened in the last three years as has happened in the whole of the last century, when you think about it. Include Northern Ireland as well ... We could not have done more in this three-year period in terms of constitutional reform than we have done. The criticism I am under from my colleagues is, we have done too much. It is a huge amount.

Parliamentary time is always scarce, but Straw's argument has a certain element of 'never mind the quality, feel the width'. Delays and log-jams over legislation have often been caused by the government's poor drafting of Bills and its frequent changes of mind. A better Freedom of Information Bill than Jack Straw's would have received less of a mauling in parliament, would have attracted fewer amendments and less criticism, and would certainly have reached the statute book sooner. Similar criticisms can be made of other legislation such as the Bill on political party funding. What has been lacking in the 20 pieces of legislation has been a coherent set of guiding principles tying them together. The 'big picture' on constitutional reform is still waiting to be painted. Frequent lip-service has been paid to and bringing politics closer to the citizen, but this has been a centralizing top-down government that has increasingly appeared mistrustful of anything that slips outside its control.

> 66 Delays and log-jams over legislation have often been caused by the government's poor drafting of Bills and its frequent changes of mind. 99

NO COHERENT FRAMEWORK

Roy Jenkins' verdict is that the government has generally got its priorities right, but has lacked a coherent framework for its reforms:

I don't think their priorities have been too bad. I'm not sure they have been very good at fitting the various things they've done, all of which broadly I'm in favour

of, into an overall philosophy and pattern. I think they were quite right to start
with Scotland. The case for Wales is less strong. I think Wales was bound to come
in rather on the coat-tails of Scotland. Obviously one would have liked a stronger
Freedom of Information Act, but taking the whole raft of things, I don't think the
order in which they have done them has been too bad. The reform of the House
of Lords is a bit incoherent, but they have achieved something which nobody
else managed to achieve since the Parliament Act, which said reform was
'urgently necessary'. That was 1911 and it went through to 1998–99. They haven't
done too badly.

Professor Brendan O'Leary sees the lack of coherence as a reflection of
the Labour leadership's lack of real enthusiasm for the whole constitutional agenda, which was not theirs:

In large sections of the party there was no great enthusiasm for constitutional
change, but this was a legacy inherited from John Smith and others, which they
were obliged to deliver on. They didn't have a particular appetite for it. If there
had been another one or two years of the Major government, I suspect certain
people close to the Labour leadership would have sought to prevent the Scottish
Parliament and the Welsh Assembly if they possibly could. But that didn't
happen. To their credit, they very quickly embarked upon devolution to Scotland
and Wales and to Blair's own particular credit they negotiated the Belfast
Agreement. Now, what was clearly evident from then on, was that there was no
thought given to the long-run consequences of the changes they had made. This
was a pattern of asymmetrical devolution, quite distinct arrangements for each
area, and no coherent thinking through of the consequences for England in
particular and for second chamber reform in particular. It wasn't really decided
whether to follow through on the logic of the quasi-federal system that had been
developed, to push it further in the direction of a federation. They thought that
they could retain traditional parliamentary sovereignty and set up a whole series
of quasi-federal arrangements without that ever coming home to roost. In
consequence you have got some fascinating heterogeneity and variety out there.
You have got different electoral systems being used in different parts of the
kingdom, you have different electoral systems for the European Union, different

systems for Scotland and Wales as compared to Northern Ireland. That has put pressure obviously on the House of Commons, which has so far been beaten off.

Paddy Ashdown told me that he and Robert Maclennan had tried unsuccessfully to persuade Blair to link his reforms together in a more comprehensive programme:

Their consistent failure has been not to put together a cohesive framework within which you saw constitutional change. They always saw this as penny packets, a bit here, a bit here, a bit there and patted themselves on the back. Our consistent point was, this is part of a comprehensive programme, it is all interlocking and you have got to see this as a whole. We sought to get over that by means of a constitutional declaration that Blair and I made. But in the end the government could not see it … Bob's case was always that there should be a Great Reform Bill, a 'big bang' approach. They wouldn't do that. I think what we have got instead is a piecemeal approach.

A FAILURE OF WILL

Ashdown told me a lot had been achieved, but he was disappointed by more than the failure to achieve electoral reform. His verdict on Blair's leadership is quite harsh:

I am disappointed by the fact that although we have freedom of information legislation, it is not as strong as I would have wished. Although we have proportional representation for the European Parliament, it is a closed system rather than an open one, which I find offensive. Although we have devolution for Scotland, we have pathetic half-devolution for Wales. It's a step forward, but in the end they will have to move to a complete step. So the argument I have with the government is about timidity. A failure of vision. And a failure, it seems to me, of political will. The argument I always used to make to Blair was: if you will the ends, which you do, a modern British constitution, you must will the means. He consistently refused to do that.

Maclennan is prepared to acknowledge that his original insistence on an all-inclusive 'big bang' reform Bill may have been misguided; he now accepts

> 66 Blair's lack of real interest in constitutional reform is demonstrated by the fact that he has not made a single speech on the subject since he became Prime Minister. 99

that a written constitution, if it ever comes, will happen step by step. Maclennan, like many other observers, notes that Blair's lack of real interest in constitutional reform is demonstrated by the fact that he has not made a single speech on the subject since he became Prime Minister. Those in the know say such a speech was written a few months after he entered Downing Street but was never delivered. Constitutional reforms, in the words of the never-to-be-forgotten Blair secret memo of April 2000, have never been the kind of 'eye-catching initiative' with which the Prime Minister wanted to be personally associated. Even groundbreaking reforms such as the Human Rights Act have been undersold and underspun by Downing Street, while far less substantial policies have been trumpeted from the rooftops. Tony Wright says this is a typically British way of approaching reform:

On any measure, it's been a huge constitutional change, in many respects a constitutional revolution. The only criticism I have is that we haven't always spoken about it like that. And we haven't followed through some of the implications in a systematic way. That is an entirely characteristic British way of approaching these things. You make revolutions and hope nobody notices ... I don't think Tony Blair is engaged by constitutional reform, and he has got all his pollsters telling him it is a pest and an irrelevance to people and that it's not a real issue. And I think he actually believes that. And any appearance of being excessively interested in these things he would regard as politically very damaging. That is not a bizarre view. That simply reflects broadly speaking how people feel about things. They would be absolutely astounded if, when set against crime, jobs, health, education, the government looked as though it was preoccupied with political reform. So that is not a criticism.

I asked Wright if the outcome would have been very different under John Smith. He replied:

You can't say that. John Smith, who was absolutely a pro in terms of politics, would have had exactly the same perception of things now. The only thing I would add, though, is that if you are doing big constitutional change you have to look as though you believe in it, you have to make it sound exciting, you have to communicate that belief in why you are doing it to other people. So you can't just do it and then not talk it up. That's a deficiency if you do that.

NO CENTRAL BRAIN

Raymond Plant, whose now-forgotten working party hacked through the intellectual undergrowth of electoral reform for Neil Kinnock and John Smith in the early 1990s, agreed with my conclusion that there was no point in looking for the cortex of the government's constitutional reforms. There simply wasn't one:

There is nobody who has tried to knit the whole thing together ... The person in Downing Street with all this under his belt was Pat McFadden, who is a very amiable chap, but he is just a fixer. He is not a brain – there isn't one. What I think the optimists expected to happen was that Robert Hazell's Constitution Unit would somehow be taken into government, and that would be a bit like a think-tank in the government. I think Straw didn't like that, partly because of his lack of interest and partly because it would have been a bit of an intrusion into his bailiwick. For whatever reason, it didn't happen. The consequence is, there has not been anybody really at the centre trying to think through these issues. There has been nobody able to do a synthesis.

Plant agreed that the government was probably right to resist the Liberal Democrat idea of an all-embracing constitutional reform Bill, which would have delayed devolution and 'would have drawn in every pressure group known to man'.

They might however have brought together a White Paper, which would have said, 'This is going to happen in a series of stages, but this is our overall scheme.' I don't think Tony had either the interest or the synthesis. I think John (Smith) did. I disagreed with John so much over electoral reform, but I think he saw how it fitted together. When John was alive it was fair to say Tony was utterly uninterested in what we were doing.

The result has been a garment whose pieces do not fit smoothly together; each one has been cut out and stitched by a different ministerial team, leaving some gaping holes. There are many who feel that even if the importance of Tam Dalyell's West Lothian question has been exaggerated, Labour has failed to understand the importance of England in the devolution equation. If the Conservatives do not manage to oust Labour from government but win a majority of English seats, this issue will haunt Blair's party at Westminster. The other failure has been to think coherently about the relationship between the two chambers of parliament, the new devolved bodies and electoral reform. The future of the second chamber was tackled in isolation by the Wakeham commission, while the Jenkins commission looked at voting systems for the Commons without any idea what might happen in the Lords. Elected mayors and regional issues have been handled quite separately from devolution to Edinburgh, Cardiff and Belfast. Pragmatism and ad hockery have been the only guiding principles. Conservative spokesman Sir George Young uses the word 'shambles':

There was a problem in Scotland, so they have a Scottish parliament. They had to keep the left quiet, so they abolish the hereditary peers. They needed the Liberal Democrats before the last election in case it was close, and so they had a commitment to PR. It was a random series of responses which in no way added up, nor was it particularly coherent. For example, if you are going to change the voting system, then that has implications for the role of the second chamber. If you have what we have here, then you need a second chamber. If you have more of a balance in the House of Commons, then that has an impact on the role of the House of Lords. But they never thought of that. They never looked at reform of the second chamber together with changes to the voting system. So we would argue that it has not been joined up at all.

Young's view is that this reflected Blair's lack of personal interest in constitutional matters and the way he farmed out individual reforms to different members of his cabinet, with no single minister in overall charge:

I am not sure he is frightfully interested. I don't think it is number one. It is rather scattered around cabinet. You have got Margaret Jay doing the House of Lords, Lord Irvine a bit everywhere, Jack Straw doing the voting system and he doesn't want to change that, you have got Margaret Beckett doing modernization ... you haven't got one constitutional person ... I don't think there is a serious agenda, and I don't think they sat back and said, 'What is wrong with the British constitution and how do we strengthen it, how do we put things right?' I think it was a series of initiatives that were not thought through, and don't hang together very well. There is quite a lot of instability floating around.

Tony Wright acknowledges that no single minister was ever fully in charge, leaving Labour without a central narrative on constitutional reform:

There hasn't been a part of government, there has not been a minister who has been personally associated with this programme. Nobody felt personally committed to it and led it. It has been diffused across government. But that is an entirely characteristic way of doing it. It is not an immediately sensible way. It is not one that is designed to highlight what you are doing. But in those terms it has been technically very competent …. What there wasn't was the grand plan of how it all fitted together, partly because nobody knew what the grand plan was. And partly because we don't do it like that … It does mean that there is perhaps no compelling story about what we are doing, which there ought to be.

A LAWYER'S DEFENCE

Derry Irvine, in the absence of Blair, has chaired the cabinet committees most concerned with constitutional reform and is the only minister to have set out a substantive defence to the repeated accusations of incoherence from critics. In a speech to the Constitution Unit in 1998 he tried valiantly to square the circle, arguing simultaneously that the reforms were coherent while making a virtue of the fact that the government was muddling through, rather than 'hunting the chimera of constitutional master plans, or ultimate outcomes'. Such an approach could lead to disaster and was, he implied, thoroughly un-British: 'We prefer the empirical genius of our nation: to go, pragmatically, step by step, for change through continuing consent. Principled steps, not absolutist master plans, are the winning route to constitutional renewal in unity and in peace.' Irvine described Labour's reforms as sensibly incremental:

Our aim is to develop a maturer democracy with different centres of power, where individuals enjoy greater rights and where government is carried out closer to the people ... Because we believe that 'what matters is what works' we are not imposing uniformity for uniformity's sake ... Intellectually satisfying neatness and tidiness is not the cement which makes new constitutional arrangements stick. What sticks are arrangements to which people can give their continuing consent because they satisfy their democratic desires for themselves ... I dispute any proposition that our programme lacks coherence. We made conscious choices about precisely which aspects of our constitution needed earliest attention, and on what basis. We are conscious of the way different elements of any constitutional settlement can impact on each other. Nonetheless many elements of the package are not interdependent. Nor is there any reason why they should be ... The strands do not spring from a single master plan, however much that concept might appeal to purists. *Non sequitur* that they are incoherent. There are uniting themes and objectives – modernization; decentralization; openness; accountability; the protection of fundamental human rights; the sharing of authority within a framework of law – all of which will fundamentally change the fabric of our political and administrative culture. In a sentence: our objective is to put in place an integrated programme of measures to decentralize power in the United Kingdom, and to enhance the rights of individuals within a more open society.[1]

The problem with Irvine's list of 'uniting themes and objectives' is that it is very easy to find evidence that some of them – especially openness, accountability and decentralization – have been abandoned or downgraded under the pressure of government. Others are ill-defined; there is no indication whether modernization is supposed to mean a greater separation of powers or not. And does 'the sharing of authority within a framework of law' mean a departure from the Diceyan model of the supremacy of parliament? Conservative constitutional expert Philip Norton believes this question goes to the heart of Labour's incoherence. He, like most Conservatives, wants to preserve the Westminster model, while Liberal Democrats such as Paddy Ashdown and Robert Maclennan want to replace it. But Labour falls somewhere between two stools, according to Professor Norton, who gives Blair and his team low marks:

In terms of reforms, what has happened is that they have taken the Westminster model, the traditional constitution, and modified it, some would say vandalized it, and not actually replaced it with a new form of constitution. So they are moving away from one approach, which I would adhere to, but they have not embraced the other principled approach, the liberal approach to the constitution. They have gone slightly in that direction, but where I would say they have gone too far, someone like Charter88 would say they have not gone far enough. Now the government has changed a lot, but none of it is in an intellectually coherent framework. So it knows what it is moving away from, but has no idea what it is trying to put in its place. I keep putting this to them: what shape, what form do you want the constitution to be in five or ten years' time? What is the approach that underpins these various changes? Answer comes back none … They don't know, or they put it in such bland terms as to be meaningless.

From the Labour side there has been no real thought about the constitution as a constitution. It has all been disparate and discrete. We'll change this and we'll change that. And for reasons which, like devolution, have a lot to do with political expediency, they are committed to it and can't get away from it. Some of the other movements have been largely because they were the 'out' party for so long. So they think, we are not doing well under the present system, perhaps we should do something about it, so electoral reform starts to be more attractive. Of course, when they become the government, these changes seem less attractive.

AMBIGUITIES OF REFORM

The real ambiguity in Labour's constitutional reforms is over democracy, the 'D-word' which was notably absent from Irvine's list of themes and principles. Labour has been ambivalent about whether it really wanted to give power away or hang on to it and use it after 18 years in opposition. Fiona Mactaggart describes the uncertainty in Labour ranks over this issue:

When we were in opposition there was a significant strand in the Labour party which understood modernization as modernization of the state and the constitution, and that strand also supported a number of issues of policy modernization, part of a Third Way project. One of the problems was that some people who bought the package didn't realize how radical things like a Human Rights Act would be, how radical the reforms we were talking about in this place were. I think they got a moment of fear. I think that does happen. There is a sort of pendulum when you have got your hands on the levers of power – we saw that with freedom of information – that you say, why can't I have those oppressive powers that they had? There are all sorts of very good reasons why you can't. I have a sense that the pendulum will actually shift back … What I am concerned about is that in government you have less thinking time by such an enormous amount. It is one of the reasons governments become bad at their job.

Vernon Bogdanor gives the government the benefit of the doubt, on the grounds that all constitutional reforms limit the power of central government and discourage what Lord Hailsham called elective dictatorship:

You have got the dispersal of power to Scotland and Wales, to Northern Ireland of course, you've got the strengthening of local government through elected mayors, a cabinet system, the Human Rights Act which is a further limitation on the power of government, the Freedom of Information Act. It is also fair to say proportional representation systems in Scotland and Wales prevented Labour getting a majority – I think Donald Dewar said it was a case of 'charitable giving'. The one exception to that is the reform of the House of Lords. A fully elected second chamber would limit the power of government but it may be that the removal of the hereditary peers and the large Conservative majority would actually increase the power of government.

Brendan O'Leary, however, takes the view that all Labour's reforms have been designed to favour its own interests and damage the Conservatives, with House of Lords reform being a prime example:

We have seen reform of the House of Lords carried out absolutely ruthlessly out of the logic of party interests and nothing else. There is no way of interpreting what has happened other than a pure party interest-driven – 'reform' I think is too generous a term. It is an appalling thing to say that in some respects it would have been better to leave the House of Lords unreformed than to carry out this particular reform …. Now the obvious point to make is that most of the constitutional changes looked like an attack on those parts of the constitution which primarily benefited the Conservatives – an entirely sensible and smart thing to do as a political party. Plainly, giving Scotland a parliament was essential if the Labour party was to head off the prospect of SNP growth. The model of devolution for Wales was an explicit compromise between serious devolutionists for Wales and that section of the Labour party which was thoroughly hostile to devolution, which is why you have got this bizarre model of executive devolution, you don't have any statutory law-making capacity. Northern Ireland is a separate case, with no clear Labour interests at stake, which is why they acted perhaps more imaginatively than they did in either Scotland or Wales. The absence of a decision on England reflected fears and anxieties within the Labour movement: should England be broken up into different regions, should it have its own parliament, if so, how would that work? In the case of Scotland, issues related to the over-representation of Scotland have been postponed for quite some time, obviously in the interests of the Labour party. The model of London government which they chose was originally considered to be deeply in the interests of the Labour party. So if you look at it with a rather sceptical eye, most of the changes were designed to stabilize Labour's own interests or cement Labour's interests in ways that were at odds with the Conservatives.

In O'Leary's view Blair has damaged Labour by his obvious inability to let go of his party's internal operations in Wales and London after devolution:

It might have looked smart, but I think by insisting on very firm centralization within the party they lost the opportunity to maximize their number of allies, to maximize flexibility, to adopt local political preferences suited to local needs. They could have presided over all that in a rather generous way, and I think they would be looking much prettier today if they had done that.

UNINTENDED CONSEQUENCES

Here we return to what might be called the 'Gorbachev principle' or the law of unintended consequences in politics. The 'charitable giving' that Donald Dewar referred to was an accident, not part of the plan. O'Leary believes Labour failed to anticipate the way voters would turn against it in Scotland and Wales in 1999, leaving it short of a working majority:

The degree of proportionality introduced in Scotland and Wales was in my view finely tuned to maximize the chances that Labour could govern as a single party government or as a minority government. They did not expect to be obliged so quickly to have to govern in coalition with the Liberal Democrats in Scotland, and likewise they did not anticipate what happened in Wales … People tend to interpret this government as very, very smart, full of Machiavellian spin doctors, very intelligent. I think they are getting a great deal of credit for a lot of accidents and they make many more blunders than are often recognized.

Paddy Ashdown claims part of the credit for pushing the ever-indecisive Blair into going much further down the constitutional reform road than he ever intended. He explains how the results are both minimalist and far-reaching at the same time:

I think you can say it was minimalist but will turn out to be far-reaching even if it is not intended to be. I remember once going to see Jacques Delors and asking for his approach. And he said: 'My strategy is progressive constructive destabilization.' I said, 'What do you mean by this?' and he said, 'What I mean is, a change in the European Community that makes it necessary to have another change in the European Community. Each time you have a change it presents a problem you then have to resolve. That is exactly what has happened.' I remember saying to him, 'That is exactly the right strategy I have got to have with Blair.' What I did with Blair is get agreements, which forced him to make a second agreement and a third, and it was progressive constructive destabilization. Now I don't think the government quite understands yet. But they have swallowed sufficient of this pill for this thing to go inside them, which they will have to resolve. The moment you have got Scotland, you have to think about altering the nature of the House of Commons. London too. The government has made changes and said, 'Crumbs, how do we cope with this inconsistency?'

O'Leary wonders how stable the constitutional reforms will be if Labour is no longer in power to maintain them:

I think the only party with a clear self-interest in maintaining this settlement in roughly its current form is Labour. Every other party, including to some extent the Liberal Democrats, has an interest in taking advantage of these changes to push it in a different direction.

Looking ahead, there is no sign that the Conservatives are bent on reversing Labour's key reforms, such as devolution and the Human Rights Act. In my interviews for this book I was struck by the disappearance from Conservative rhetoric of the apocalyptic tone about Labour's constitutional changes which the party used before and immediately after the last election. John Major once warned of Blair 'tearing up the constitution at a terrifying rate' and compared the process to Mao's permanent revolution.[2] These bloodcurdling statements are now forgotten, as is Robert Cranborne's colourful warning: 'Letting Mr Blair loose on the constitution looks increasingly like trusting a first-year physics student with an atom bomb.'[3]

The more considered Conservative view perhaps reflects the way the initial radicalism of Labour's constitutional reform drive in 1997–98 has fizzled out. Labour's instincts as the status quo party have re-emerged with a vengeance as it has spent longer in government, rediscovering the executive-minded pleasures of secrecy and patronage. This is a pattern that Conservatives understand and feel comfortable with. The managerialist, semi-Thatcherite language of public sector reform, of 'what matters is what works', poses no difficulty for the Conservatives. Philip Norton says: 'The Westminster model has been modified, perhaps vandalized but it has not been destroyed.' Sir George Young describes the constitution as 'slightly weakened' by Labour's reforms but quickly adds: 'There is no going back.' The Tory party, if returned to power, would probably bring back first-past-the-post voting for the European Parliament and abolish regional development agencies, but would otherwise leave Labour's reforms untouched.

> 66 Labour's instincts as the status quo party have re-emerged with a vengeance as it has spent longer in government, rediscovering the executive-minded pleasures of secrecy and patronage. This is a pattern that Conservatives understand and feel comfortable with. 99

A PROCESS, OR A MESS?

O'Leary, from a different political perspective, believes the reforms have left the Westminster model exposed to new stresses and strains which will lead in new directions:

We are now in a very interesting institutional mess because we have principles of jurisprudence deriving from the ECHR, we have principles of jurisprudence that flow directly from our membership of the European Union, which affects the way we do our business, our commerce, our trading standards, our notions of what constitutes good values in goods and services, and this has fundamentally a uniform rationalist character, and it sits unhappily with the historic pragmatic common law traditions. The Scots have never shared or bought into the English philosophy of full-scale constitutional organic conservatism. So I think the picture is looking much messier than even someone who is a celebrant of constitutional conservatism might want to suggest …

In the oft-repeated words of Ron Davies about devolution, constitutional reform is 'a process, not an event'. Tony Wright argues that crossing off manifesto pledges does not begin to reflect the dynamic reality of the process of constitutional reform that Labour has set in motion:

If you just tick the boxes, it is actually not to understand the nature of all this. This is absolutely a dynamic process. Everything connects with everything else. You may say they have not done this, they have not done that. The fact is these things become inevitably part of the agenda. Because they are all in there. They all have knock-on effects from somewhere else. A process has started and once that process is started it's okay. As de Tocqueville famously said, the real danger for an unreformed regime is when it starts to reform. Then a dynamic builds up and you can't keep the roadblocks in place. Everything is in the pot. So whatever else has happened, this dynamic process is under way and it will not stop … They may not understand that, although I suspect they are beginning to. But it is inevitable anyway.

Wright acknowledges that in a way, the original Conservative doom-sayers were right to ring the alarm bells:

So those people who said: 'This is the thin end of the wedge, the floodgates are opening' – they were right. They were absolutely right. The John Majors of this world who said, once you start this you don't know where it is going to end – that is precisely the point. You do not know where it is going to end. But you've done it. It is happening. And you now have to go with the flow … I was one of those who knew it was like that in the first place. Those people who were fearful of it were also right. Their instincts were right in thinking that you couldn't just segregate off various things, that it would eventually fundamentally alter the character of British politics. They didn't want that to happen, they wanted it to stay as it was. I wanted it to change, therefore I welcome the process. That seems to me more important than seeing if we have ticked enough boxes yet.

Robin Butler also believes that the process has further to run, though he understands why the government had no advance blueprint:

With all these things, once you throw a pebble in the pool, the ripples spread and with all these things – human rights, judicial review – they are not neatly parcelled little reforms that you just do and stop there. They have other implications. So all of them are going to have further repercussions and they all interact with each other. I don't think those have necessarily been thought out. And to say the whole thing should have been thought out by the government was asking the impossible. You see something you think needs to be changed, like the hereditary principle, then you change it, and you see where you go from there.

Butler, perhaps surprisingly for a former head of the civil service, told me he was increasingly worried by the executive's excessive power over the House of Commons, and by the risk of the United Kingdom eventually disintegrating. The spectre of becoming the government that 'lost' Scotland to independence is of course the ultimate Labour nightmare. It is hard to rule out this scenario, but just as wrong to see it as inevitable.

ASLEEP ON WATCH

Political scientist Michael Foley argues that Labour has failed to articulate properly the constitutional transformation it has unleashed:

In raising the public's awareness of the imminence and scale of a new constitutional order, the government persistently draws back from what this means – what the transformed regime represents in terms of principles, objectives and implications. A constitution – and especially a reformulated constitution – is supposed to provide an alternative dimension of authority, meaning and legitimacy to that of the government. The sign of a constitutional order is one of a normative point of reference, one that is related to an autonomy that is separate and independent from the government of the day.

In other words Labour, despite all the energy it has put into constitutional change, has failed to explain properly what it has been up to:

> … It is no exaggeration to say that the British constitution is in the process of slipping its moorings and developing into quite a different entity to that which it was. I do not have a problem with this. What I do have a problem with is the fact that its chief sponsor appears to be asleep on watch. Great political changes have occurred in the name of constitutional transformation and yet there has been a failure to use that political mobilization to create and legitimize a changed constitutional authority. The result is that what can be termed a constitutional lag has come into existence.

Foley attributes this to the 'narcotic effect' of Dicey's doctrines, which encourage a kind of lazy determinism in which all the bits of the constitutional jigsaw will fit together:

> New Labour's answer to formal set-piece constitutional change has been one of reassuring minimalism. Even sweeping structural reforms have been given Dicey's soft-focus treatment of change suffused in gentle continuity … As we have seen, this disjunction between constitutional reform and political conservatism creates severe problems of adjustment. By looking carefully at the history of the issue within the Labour party, I have to say that the overriding impression is one in which constitutional reform has been conceived as a political solution to a political problem. Far from envisaging the opening up of new dimensions of political engagement, the impetus was to close down issues and especially the issue of the constitution …The British constitution has out-mutated its own traditions. It has out-improvised itself. It is not possible for everything to be traced back to parliamentary sovereignty. The problem is that the conventional arrangements have not been replaced with any discernible conception of an alternative constitution.[4]

So constitutional reform under Labour is far from over. It may be simultaneously far less radical than it promised in opposition, but far more radical than it has pretended in government. In Paddy Ashdown's words, it has been both minimalist and far-reaching at the same time. Michael Jacobs of the Fabian Society distinguishes between what is constitutionally sustainable and what is politically sustainable in the current settlement:

I think in practice, politically it probably is sustainable in that the demand for constitutional reform amongst the public has always been pretty minimal, except for devolution to Scotland ... Constitutionally I don't think it is. Clearly we have got a case of unfinished business. The Lords settlement is thoroughly unsatisfactory. The English question is thoroughly unsatisfactory. There is a clear tension between Blair's desire for more elected mayors and Prescott's desire for regional government ... The other bit of unfinished business is that the powers in Wales are not sufficient. The lack of an independent tax-raising power in Wales and Northern Ireland is very odd. I think there is a fundamental constitutional problem with elected bodies that can't raise their own income. It's not been properly discussed, even in Scotland because Labour refused to use the (tax-raising) powers, so there has not been very much discussion.

Jacobs laments the lack of real debate on fiscal centralization and similar issues:

This is what's missing. We have engaged in this process without a proper public debate about the constitution as a whole. And only in Scotland and Wales where there were referendums have there been proper debates about it. But there hasn't been one about the tax question, there hasn't been one about English government, there hasn't been one about the House of Lords. You have to have proper public debates. The idea that we could change the Lords just by administrative fiat, by a government with a large majority saying this is what we are going for, is monstrous, actually. Although there was a royal commission, there was no sense in which the public have been engaged ...

Charter88, after a decade or more tugging Labour's coat-tails about constitutional reform, now sees a paradox:

New Labour has altered the way our country is governed. But most of us still don't believe it. At the moment, the impact of what is happening has not sunk in.

Tony Blair welcomes everyone into the Labour Big Tent. Copyright © Chris Riddell, 1999.

It is as if the government, media and opposition parties are in a state of shock, unable to accept that the system will not default back to 'normal'.[5]

Without giving up completely on Labour and the Blair government, Charter88 is now shifting its sights away from Westminster as a deliberate strategy for the next decade. Its director, Pam Giddy, says: 'This government's approach is, unless you agree with what we say, you are the enemy. And therefore you are dangerous.' The organization is likely to become more critical in future, rather than biting its lip and hoping to keep a seat inside the New Labour big tent. Giddy believes the government is underselling its own reforms and possibly does not fully understand what it has done:

New Labour's reforms have, some of them, been incredibly powerful, and it is an indication of their lack of understanding of the constitution that actually no cabinet minister stood up at the party conference last year and revelled in the fact they had made all these reforms. The hereditary peers issue gets a good cheer, but that's about it. Nobody wants to think about it, although it is their one big success. When the history of this government is written, that is what people will say: they began the process of recasting the British constitution … I think they have made a big mistake in thinking the population as a whole isn't interested in this. They could have spun this whole agenda incredibly well. If they had a minister for the constitution to coordinate reforms, I think you would have had a more cogent approach.

Charter88's ultimate aim is a 'citizens' constitution' devised not by politicians but by a wider democratic process. The idea sounds utopian, but a decade ago, the same could have been said of the Claim of Right that produced a Scottish Parliament.

BLAIR UNINTERESTED

Robert Hazell says that Lords reform and regional government for England are the two big remaining items of unfinished business, with the possibility of a referendum on electoral reform for the Commons still open. But the Prime Minister is not fully engaged:

Mr Blair's view on all of those? He's not interested. He's never been interested in the constitutional reform agenda. It's not his bag. He took it over. He would not have thought it up himself.

Matthew Taylor believes the government wants to move on to other issues when it seeks a second term, and will downplay constitutional matters in its manifesto:

I certainly think that given the pressure they are under on health and education it would be peculiar to say to people, 'We have got a new constitutional agenda.' People will say, 'Here you are again fannying around with freedom of information or the House of Lords or whatever' when … even more than before 1997, people are going to say, 'Let's focus on the stuff that matters.'

But a second-term Labour government will still have several big constitutional issues to tackle – Lords reform, electoral reform and the single currency, the last two of which involve referendums.

So in a sense the constitutional agenda is out there. If at the end of the second term we've got a semi-elected House of Lords, we have entered the single currency and we have had a referendum on proportional representation, that will be a hell of a lot.

Robert Maclennan has a long wish-list of Liberal Democrat proposals for further constitutional change, but acknowledges that Blair's priorities now lie elsewhere:

I think it is true his mind has moved on to other more pressing and other more immediate issues. I think he thinks that because he has done what he has done, he has shown his good faith to that section of the community that I referred to as the *bien pensants*. I don't think he has much sense that it is unfinished business, though I think he is conscious that there is an irritating problem over the House of Lords, which wasn't wrapped up with the smart footwork over Lord Cranborne's proposed amendment. He is also conscious that there is a large element in his own party that is pressing him hard on regional government, about which something at some point will have to be done … So even although he lacks great enthusiasm at this stage for carrying the process forward, I think he probably does recognize that more will have to be done.

Maclennan believes Blair is unlikely to abandon his efforts to bring about some kind of centre-left partnership between the two parties, which he describes as 'very much part of his historic perception of himself'. He believes that at some point Labour will have to face up to the need to find an alternative to the traditional Diceyan view of parliamentary sovereignty:

It's got to be rooted out. We as a party have consistently referred to the sovereignty of the people, and if sovereignty has any meaning, that is the meaning I would like to give it. It's more of an obstacle to clear thinking than an assistance now. To talk of sovereignty in a world where interdependence and limitations upon power are more evident than the supreme power of parliament … I think it is making headway. It is not something that the members of the Labour party would instinctively recoil from. I do think there is more of an opening for discussion of these things. There has been far more discussion in parliament of these matters on the floor of the House in the last three years than in the rest of my 30 or more years in the House of Commons put together … The whole context of the debate has changed.

TABOO AREAS

The same is true of other taboo areas of the old constitution into which Labour decided before 1997 it would not venture. The logic of reform is that Labour will eventually have to get to grips with some of the most archaic central features of the constitution – the monarchy, the royal prerogative, the establishment of the Church of England, the triple role of the Lord Chancellor, the absence of a proper supreme court and an independent system for appointing judges. The country as a whole has been repeatedly told by Blair that it has to modernize or perish in the hurricane of globalization, but at the very heart of the constitution, he has preserved a large zone where nothing much is allowed to change. Here Bagehot's admired system of elective dictatorship has survived intact and modernization has been a matter of 'don't do as I do, do as I say'. For Brendan O'Leary the reason for Labour's fundamental caution about disturbing these taboo zones is clear:

> 66 The country as a whole has been repeatedly told by Blair that it has to modernize or perish in the hurricane of globalization, but at the very heart of the constitution, he has preserved a large zone where nothing much is allowed to change. 99

I think there is in the Labour leadership, not just in the person of Tony Blair, a deep desire to replace the Tories as the natural party of government. They believe the way to do that is to embrace as many of the traditional institutions as possible, if you can possibly colonize them. The use of patronage on a very large scale is directly comparable to that of the Conservatives. They don't show themselves to have been modernizers in this respect. There is a vast careful placement of individuals who are known to be loyal. That is patently the case in the House of Lords, but it is also true in a whole series of task forces and so on. Most of these people are networked to key leaders. There are clients of clients. It looks courtly. It bears no resemblance to a republican culture of meritocratic appointment. Genuine modernization implies reliance upon merit, not on networks of patronage.

THE MODERNIZATION RIDDLE

The word *modernization*, so crucial to the whole New Labour project, is worth examining in more detail. Taken literally, it could be seen as a ruthless Stalinist determination to impose change for change's sake, to replace the old by the new wherever possible. Or it could be just a matter of a quick spring clean, as outlined by Peter Mandelson:

People were looking for a new political style … our commitment to constitutional reform helped the change of mood. People didn't want things uprooted, but liked the idea that we were going to throw open the shutters and blow away a few cobwebs.[6]

As Brendan O'Leary says, modernizers have to have some kind of template to follow:

If you are modernizing, what are you doing? You are presumably modernizing against some implicit model of what is more modern than you, or else you have absolutely self-confident knowledge about what the future is. Now I presume one of the reasons the rhetoric of modernization was adopted was partly the conviction that things were better elsewhere. Whence the slogan, 'things can only get better'. But it's not clear what the Blairite model of a more modern democratic state is. Is it the United States? If it is, then a much more rationalist constitution and judicial process, separation of powers, all that would follow. If it is continental Europe, if it's France or Germany, many of the same things apply.

Whatever modernization means in the Blair lexicon, it has precious little to do with democratization, as Matthew Taylor explains from his inside knowledge of the Labour party's processes:

There is a profound scepticism about the concept of democracy at the heart of New Labour, I think. That scepticism has got two elements to it, I would say. The first is elitism. New Labour is an elitist set-up. It is a set-up of very clever people. One of its weaknesses is that they do find it quite difficult to empathize with people who are ordinary citizens, to be quite honest. But the second part of it is that they quite rightly recognize that an awful lot of things which claim to be democratic are entirely bogus. The internal democracy of the Labour movement is not internal democracy, it is the capture by a small group of activists who are atypical. The use of democracy is often a rhetorical appeal by people whose mandate is not real at all. They are technocrats as well. I think they are sceptical about democracy, which is one of my complaints about them. It is one of the reasons they have given so little attention to the quality of our political culture. It is one of the things they are now coming to recognize, I think. They have spent two-and-a-half or three years saying we can spin, we can manipulate, because what actually matters is making the lives of poor people a bit better and these are all a means to an end. They are beginning to realize that devaluing political discourse, allowing a state of cynicism to grow out there, is actually damaging to Labour and to the government. It undermines people's willingness to be told anything is getting better. And I think there is a realization now – well, I hope there is a realization – that the quick wins, a phrase in a party conference speech, whether it is 'the giving age' or 'young country' or the 'forces of conservatism', getting good headlines after the Budget for a week because you have managed to con people into thinking there is more money than there really is – this is all counter-productive. I think this is a government which is now asking itself: 'How can we try to tell the people the truth?'

The argument over whether the end justifies the means is hardly a new one; one of Labour's problems is that it entered office promising to fight cynicism and restore faith in politics, while having become quite cynical itself as a result of its narrow 1992 defeat, as Matthew Taylor described in *Prospect* magazine:

We felt cheated – by lying Tories, by lazy journalists, and by stupid, selfish voters. We promised ourselves that it would never happen again. We would never be the suckers who told the truth while the other side peddled smears. We would never trust voters who told pollsters that they wanted higher taxes and better services and then voted for the opposite. In April 1992 we grew an extra skin of cynicism, and now we find it hard to shed.[7]

Modernization of the constitution under Blair has always had more to do with making government more effective than with making it more democratic or accountable. Geoff Mulgan, one of the Downing Street policy unit's best brains, made this explicit shortly before the 1997 election when he was still head of the Demos think-tank. In a newspaper interview he criticized leftist intellectuals for seeing government in terms that would have made sense in the 19th century but no longer did so in the 20th, when the bulk of government activity consisted of running systems of provision:

If a government of the left was to come to power and put its main energies into the formal high constitution and not have a strategy for low government, prosaic government, that would be disastrous. I would turn the priority around, and say the top priority is shifting those big systems of government towards left-of-centre goals and delivering on those, prior to spending enormous amounts of time and energy on things like the monarchy and the House of Lords. There's a real danger that the public would see that as a strange indulgence.[8]

DEMOCRACY, CYNICISM AND MODERNIZATION

Michael Jacobs also sees a link between the absence of democracy in New Labour's 'Third Way' modernization and the growth of cynicism about politics:

The 'third way' theory of the state is managerial rather than democratic. The 'third way' is committed to making the state as effective as possible.

Accountability is not it, frankly. It's crudely arguing that old social democracy was complacent about the state; it failed to acknowledge that the state could be useless and worse than useless. The 'third way' has to be non-complacent about the state, the state has to be in a constant process of improvement, effectiveness, efficiency with all kinds of mechanisms, purchaser/provider splits, best value, performance agreements and all of that stuff. My view is that it needs another dimension as well, which is a democratic agenda. You have to add the extra legitimacy of democracy.

Public confidence in democratic institutions has declined enormously. There is public cynicism about democracy. What you have got here is a wrestling with the attempt to create better government at the same time as the demand for more democratic government. These two things can be seen to conflict. Now the reason they don't want to give greater tax power to local government or the regional level is that they don't believe that these governments are good enough. And giving them more responsibility at a time when they are not good enough is problematic. That's their problem. Seen from a purely constitutional or democratic ideal, we should be expanding the democratic role of government, giving more power, devolving it and so forth. But as long as government is regarded very cynically by the people, and is not actually regarded as very good, that is a risk. And this government is very conscious of how poor government can be, and is often perceived to be, by the public. And it is much more interested in improving the performance of government rather than in making government more accountable and democratic. It's also that until government is better, providing more democracy is a risk.

Genuine constitutional reform involves imposing constraints and limits on government and shifting the balance away from the state, as Michael Foley describes:

The government senses that constitutions worth their salt rarely operate in any government's interest. Far from being effectively managed, effective constitutions are politically unmanageable by governments. Constitutions are about friction, checks, jurisdictional disputes, internal confrontation, and institutional counterweights. A constitutional culture is one of an alternative frame of reference and legitimacy – a fixture of ideals and core principles that generates a moral intelligence and with it a source of ethical challenge and political leverage.

Labour's modernization entails the opposite process. It means *removing* these constraints in order to make government more effective. It is only a short jump from here to believing that parliamentary democracy and accountability are obstacles that get in the way of effective government, which is what the Muggles really want. The ultimate test for Labour is that constitutional change should buttress the 'elective dictatorship' of Westminster rather than weaken it.

Any doubts I might have had about the fairness of this interpretation were dispelled when I heard Margaret Beckett's rejection of proposals by the House of Commons Liaison Committee for stronger Select Committees to shift the balance between executive and legislature. She made the argument for strong executive power even more explicit when she urged Labour's 2000 annual conference not to support an elected second chamber because it might complicate life for the government:

I see no evidence that (the British people) want to make it harder for the governments they elect to make the change for which they elected them.

CORPORATE POPULISM

Stuart Weir of the Democratic Audit, looking behind the rhetoric, sees a lot of continuity with statist Old Labour attitudes in the way Blair has governed:

The executive remains as powerful as ever, if not more powerful. This government has clearly decided not to do anything really that is going to undermine that power or make it more transparent to scrutiny or accountable. That has been clear right the way through. Parliament remains astonishingly weak *vis-à-vis* the government. The modernization of parliament has clearly stopped short of any willingness to make its powers of scrutiny more effective. And the proposals for the Lords are from a democratic perspective utterly unacceptable … New Labour is a smokescreen. Broadly what we have is a pretty Old Labour party in terms of its pragmatism and its acceptance of the status quo politically.

One goes right back to the way Labour's attitude to government was shaped during the 1939–45 war, you have got all of that running right through. It's statist, showing deference to the institutions of the state and the security forces, or panic at what they might do to them. A kind of relish for the power, the idea that strong government and powerful government is an unmitigated good, all that seems to me thoroughly Old Labour. So part of the project is trying to protect all the things that are valuable for you while you are in government, while you are there: 'It's our turn, we are not going to have strong Select Committees, we are not going to have effective freedom of information. We are going to protect the state, which is now our creature.' They are going to be biting their hands in about ten years' time … I think the kind of salutary lessons of Thatcherism, of being on the receiving end and being punched all over the ring, those have disappeared because they are now doing the punching.

Anthony Barnett also detects a feeling, epitomized by such ministers as Peter Mandelson, that after so many years in the wilderness it is now 'Labour's turn' to enjoy the advantages, freedoms and perquisites of government. Barnett defines Blair's style of governance as 'corporate populism' which is different from Old Labour, at least in its aspirations. It sees the country rather like a large company, with 10 Downing Street as the headquarters and Blair as the chief executive:

It manages party, cabinet and civil service as if they were parts of a single giant company whose aim is to persuade voters that they are happy customers who want to return Labour to office … Downing Street has become enamoured with the image of agency provided by big companies. Unlike the free market, the big corporation is a place of order and policy. It creates wealth and jobs, it develops and applies knowledge in a purposive fashion, it innovates, it is a global player competing around the world. It is light on its feet, effective and meritocratic. When it works, it improves living standards. It gets results.[9]

The 'corporate' element reflects a somewhat naive belief in the abilities of risk-taking big corporations to succeed where government has failed. It is subtly different from the Thatcherite belief in the raw power of the market to allocate resources and solve problems. Barnett sees this as the modernization of subjecthood, rather than popular sovereignty; citizens are principally consumers who are sold the New Labour brand. The populism comes in the reliance on 'people's panel' focus groups, marketing and polling, which enable the government to bypass traditional representative institutions and conduct a two-way dialogue with the masses, bypassing representative institutions such as parliament. Law is seen not as a system designed to limit government but as an administrative tool allowing it to achieve its goals.

TWO HARD KNOCKS

As Barnett wrote prophetically in his *Prospect* essay: 'It cannot last.' In the late summer of 2000 the Blairite model received two separate but very powerful jolts. The first of these was the financial meltdown of the ultimate 'eye-catching initiative' and symbol of Blairite corporate populism, the Millennium Dome. Although begun by the Conservatives, the Dome was invested with huge significance by Blair as a showcase for his modernizing project. It was supposed to be the first paragraph of Labour's next election manifesto, a paradigm of New Labour governance. This was a matter not just of the Dome's contents – classless, universal, creative, 'best of British' – but of the way the project was put together and managed. It was supposed to be an illustration of the 'third way' approach, combining the best of public and private sectors, but it managed to waste hundreds of millions of pounds by escaping the disciplines of both. It was a project that, if entrusted to fuddy-duddy, snag-hunting civil servants of the Northcote-Trevelyan tradition, would never have crossed the start line. This was the reason why Sir Humphrey and his Whitehall colleagues were comprehensively bypassed and the project was given to a specially created private company, with a government minister as the single shareholder. This created a zone of commercial confidentiality that lay beyond the detailed scrutiny of parliament. But despite the involvement of leading Blairite businessmen, none of the tough bottom-line financial disciplines that would have been applied to a genuine private sector project were allowed to function. With the Millennium Commission and its National Lottery funds as a cash-cow in the background to ward off insolvency, there was no hard budget constraint, and the ultimate decisions were politically rather than commercially driven.

The second unpleasant jolt to the Blair model of governance came out of the blue with the September 2000 fuel crisis. Like the Dome, it fell outside the traditional parameters of 'constitutional' affairs, but it hit the government's authority with devastating force. What happened can only be understood by reference to the governing style of New Labour. The empty petrol pumps did far more than just dent the government's reputation for managerial competence. Blair and New Labour have always been ambivalent about representative democracy, preferring to bypass parliament in favour of a direct connection to the hearts and minds of the voters of Middle England, mediated through phone-ins, tabloids and TV studios. Being shown to be out of touch with public opinion was therefore a far more serious blow for them than it would have been to a truly Thatcherite conviction government, steeled against unpopularity and seeing itself as a beleaguered minority. A government that always paid more attention to *The Sun* and *The Daily Mail* than to its own backbenchers in the House of Commons was bound to be extra vulnerable to populist anger. Voters who had been carefully led to believe that Blair and his team were 'on their side' were shocked and upset to discover their populist government suddenly scrambling for the high ground of parliamentary authority to resist popular demands for a tax cut on the grounds that they had been elected to govern.

CORE BELIEFS

One of Blair's problems is that many in his own party do not feel they have much in common with him, as Gordon Prentice MP made clear when he gave me his definition of his party leader: 'Nice guy, pretty face, but he is basically a conservative with a small c, or maybe a kind of Christian Democrat.' It was to respond to such concerns that Blair, in a carefully scripted departure from his printed text, told the Labour conference in Brighton in September 2000 that he had an 'irreducible core' of beliefs and values. The attempt was not entirely convincing; the modernizing ultra-pragmatism of 'what matters is what works' often seems nothing more than a desire to please all of the people all of the time, to appear inclusive to widely differing audiences and to tell people what they want to hear.

Robert Maclennan interprets the enthusiasm Blair expressed for constitutional reform before the 1997 election as little more than an attempt to fish for votes among the liberal intelligentsia, while his real objectives for government were different: 'I think he is managerial, and meritocratic in his outlook. He is not instinctively democratic. And that colours his view about the constitution.'

Paddy Ashdown sees a big difference between his own attitude to reform and the fuzzy 'third way', but optimistically sees Blair as a possible liberal in the making:

The difference between us is that reform is an iron in my soul and liberals' soul. It is not for Blair. It is a badge of modernity. It all comes back to this business of him not believing in any single thing. He doesn't have a code of belief. He hasn't arrived at one. At the bottom end you really need that in politics. What you believe in is the sheet anchor that carries you through storms … Now Blair is above all other things a man on a journey. That journey starts from the rejection of socialism, which he has done in the last ten years, to moving towards a different home, and I am convinced that although his steps are faltering and sometimes misguided, the home to which he is heading – whether he acknowledges it or not – is the agenda on which I have stood for a very long time.

For Ashdown, Blair's absence of an ideological sheet anchor is exasperating:

He annoys me enormously, and he knows he annoys me, because I tell him. Here is a prime minister who enjoys a massive majority, unheard of in this century, enjoys a huge lead over a pathetic opposition at the mid-term which is also unheard of, has got a not bad line to the erogenous zones of the British people, and he will risk none of these to achieve things that look perfectly achievable.

The former Liberal Democrat leader's diagnosis makes clear he has not written off Blair altogether:

I have got a theory of the three ages of Blair. Age one is Young Lochinvar Blair out in front of his party, slaying the dragon of Clause Four. Age two is Zen Blair. This is Zen Blairism. He sits there and he waits until all the constellations are in line and the political *feng shui* is correct and then he will do things, but not before, and he won't take any risks. He emerges at the head of what is already the national consensus which he has helped to create. I think we saw it first in Diana's funeral. And then age three which is a Blair we haven't seen, but I think is there. I call him Young Father Blair. When he has at last defeated the demons that sit on his shoulder – the demons are named Conrad Black and Rupert

Murdoch, the rightwing press – and he does that on the issue of the euro, then he becomes something totally different. I think he becomes a much more relaxed prime minister, calmly and benignly presiding over a mildly dissenting party and a nation whose spirit he somehow embodies. And doing quite remarkable things. They used to say of Gladstone he was terrible on the rebound. I am sort of hoping that Blair will be terrible on the rebound.

BELIEVE IN ME

None of the usual political labels seem to fit Blair exactly. He is too modernizing to be a conservative with a small c, too indifferent to human rights and civil liberties to be a liberal, and too hostile to the traditions of his own party to be a social democrat in the Attlee mould. But nor is he just a mouthpiece for his speechwriters, or a cynical ultra-pragmatist who cares nothing for ideas. 'I have always believed that politics is first and foremost about ideas,' he proclaimed in a pamphlet written in 1998 on the 'third way'.[10] His occasional cynicism is outweighed by a sometimes naive enthusiasm. Blair's mostly self-written speeches and his fondness for seminars reveal a man who likes political ideas, even if he cannot quite make up his mind which ones he likes the most. Blair, despite his legal background, does not see life or politics in legalistic terms, and this partly explains his lack of interest in constitutional matters. Theoretical concepts such as 'separation of powers' and 'parliamentary sovereignty' do not set his pulses racing. He is not a member of what Oona King calls the 'anorak brigade' of constitutional reformers. Democracy and human rights do not seem to be part of the 'irreducible core' of Blair's beliefs, at least on the evidence of his trip to China. They, like the environment, are good causes with which he likes to be personally associated only when the populist wind from the focus groups is blowing in the right direction.

> 66 Blair, despite his legal background, does not see life or politics in legalistic terms, and this partly explains his lack of interest in constitutional matters. 99

Professor Norman Fairclough of Lancaster University has made a penetrating analysis of the way Blair loves to reconcile ideas previously thought to be antagonistic. Anyone who listens to Blair's speeches knows that when 'enterprise' is mentioned, 'fairness' will not be far behind. The 'not only but also' message is that two desirable goods previously thought irreconcilable can both be enjoyed without having to make a choice. In foreign policy, Britain does not have to choose between Europe and America. In economic policy, it does not have to choose between low inflation and low unemployment. In Europe, it does not have to choose between national sovereignty and political integration. In social policy, it can have both first-class public services and low taxation. The Labour party does not have to choose between the voters in its heartlands and those in Middle England, because the same policies can appeal to both. 'Contentiously, one might say that the power of rhetoric is used to portray what some commentators see as the potentially fatal contradictions of New Labour as its greatest strengths,' Fairclough writes.[11] He also pinpoints Blair's love of lists – those interminable catalogues of nouns with the verbs left out which pepper his speeches and are so easily parodied.

The factors or elements in such lists are seen as connected only in the sense that they appear together. There is no attempt at explanation that tries to specify deeper relations amongst them (e.g. of cause and effect) which might constitute a system.

Blair's preference for nouns over verbs is no accident; it indicates a reluctance to think in a joined-up way and make connections. The lack of coherence in constitutional reform reflects a well-meaning but not very coherent prime ministerial mind, insecure and reluctant to make choices, trying desperately to be perceived as decisive and 'tough'. This is exactly the picture revealed by the leaked Blair memo on 'touchstone issues'.[12]

THE 'TOUCHSTONE ISSUES' MEMO

There are a clutch of issues – seemingly disparate – that are in fact linked. We need a strategy that is almost discrete, focussed on them. They are roughly combining 'on your side' issues with toughness and standing up for Britain. They range from the family where, partly due to MCA [Married Couples' Allowance] and gay issues, we are perceived as weak; asylum and crime, where we are perceived as soft; and asserting the nation's interests where, because of the unpopularity of Europe, a constant barrage of small stories beginning to add up on defence and even issues like Zimbabwe, we are seen as insufficiently assertive.

All this, of course, is perception. It is bizarre that any government I lead should be seen as anti-family. We are, in fact, taking very tough measures on asylum and crime. Kosovo should have laid to rest any doubts about our strength in defence.

But all these things add up to a sense that the government – and this even applies to me – are somehow out of touch with gut British instincts. The Martin case – and the lack of any response from us that appeared to empathize with public concern and then channel it into the correct course – has only heightened this problem.

We need a thoroughly worked-out strategy stretching over several months to regain the initiative in this area.

Each of these issues should be analyzed and the correct policy response drawn up. Then each should be dealt with, but with a message which ties it all together. This is precisely the sort of thing AC [Alastair Campbell, Tony Blair's press secretary] and CF [Charles Falconer, Lord Falconer of Thoroton, Cabinet Office minister] should do if a new system is put in place which frees up their time.

My thoughts are:

(i)   Possibly on the Martin case, asking a senior judge to look at changing the sentencing law, i.e. to allow lesser sentences than life. We also need a far tougher rebuttal or alternatively action re the allegations that jurors were intimidated.

(ii) On asylum, we need to be highlighting removals and decisions plus if the April figures show a reduction, then a downward trend. Also if the benefits bill really starts to fall, that should be highlighted also. Plus some of the genuine asylum claims being given some publicity.

(iii) On crime, we need to highlight tough measures: compulsory tests for drugs before bail; the PIU [Performance and Innovation Unit] report on the confiscation of assets; the extra number of burglars jailed under the 'three strikes and you're out'.

Above all, we must deal now with street crime, especially in London. When the figures are published for the six months to April, they will show a small – 4 per cent – rise in crime. But this will almost certainly be due to the rise in levels of street crime – mobile phones, bags being snatched. This will be worst in London. The Met Police are putting in place measures to deal with it; but, as ever, we are lacking a tough public message along with the strategy.

We should think now of an initiative, e.g. locking up street muggers. Something tough, with immediate bite which sends a message through the system. Maybe, the driving licence penalty for young offenders. But this should be done soon and I, personally, should be associated with it.

(iv) On defence, we need to make the CSR (Comprehensive Spending Review) work for defence. Big cuts and you can forget any hope of winning back ground on 'standing up for Britain'.

(v) On the family, we need two or three eye-catching initiatives that are entirely conventional in terms of their attitude to the family. Despite the rubbish about gay couples, the adoption issue worked well. We need more.

I should be personally associated with as much of this as possible.

TB, 29 April 2000

The 'touchstone issues' memo is a spine-chilling insight into Blair's mind. The level of defence spending is to be determined not by any objective need but by the Prime Minister's desire to be seen to be standing up for Britain. Sentencing policy and family policy follow the same relentless logic in which public perception is more important than reality. The mixture of caution, indecisiveness and control freakery that have characterized Blair's constitutional reforms are all linked to this sense of political insecurity, what Peter Hennessy calls his 'private squishiness'. This explains the 'not-only-but-also' rhetoric of the 'third way', which rationalizes the inability to make clear choices between different political values by saying the choices are not really necessary. Blair's ideological Holy Grail is what he describes as 'a popular politics reconciling themes which in the past have wrongly been regarded as antagonistic – patriotism *and* internationalism; rights *and* responsibilities; the promotion of enterprise *and* the attack on poverty and discrimination'.[13] One can certainly make a positive case for the open-minded pragmatism of Blair's 'what works' approach over the dogmas and knee-jerk reactions of tribalist party politics, as practised in the Labour party. But somewhere there has to be an 'irreducible core' of political beliefs, what Paddy Ashdown calls the 'sheet anchor that carries you through storms'.

My impression is that Blair's 'irreducible core' of values certainly exists; but his personal sheet anchor is moral and religious, not political. When he talks publicly about his basic beliefs, as in the very personal speech he delivered in Tübingen on 30 June 2000, what emerges are some simple and logical *moral* ideas; that individuals are of equal worth and are created through their relationship to others in families and communities: 'The idea of community resolves the paradox of the modern world: it acknowledges our interdependence; it recognizes our individual worth.' This is a communitarian world of harmonious synthesis in which hard political choices can mostly be avoided. It is not much of a foundation for political action. In the words of Professor David Marquand:

> He dreams of a united and homogeneous people, undifferentiated by class or locality, with which he, as leader, can communicate directly, without the need for intermediaries. In his vision of it, new Labour's vocation is to mobilize the suburbs as well as the inner cities; rich as well as poor; old as well as young; Christians as well as unbelievers; hunters as well as animal rights activists; believers in family values as well as opponents of Clause 28. His warm embrace covers all men and women of goodwill, provided only that they are prepared to enlist in the relentless, never-ending crusade for modernization that he and his colleagues have set in motion.[14]

Only on rare occasions does Blair become Young Lochinvar, throwing away the safety net of caution and allowing himself to be guided by the sheet anchor of his convictions. The two examples that spring to mind are the search for peace in Northern Ireland and the Kosovo conflict. On both these issues he displayed a reckless personal commitment to what he believed was right and threw his personal credibility into what he saw as a moral battle between good and evil. But most political issues do not lend themselves to this kind of approach. Blair's moral vision of community cannot offer much in the way of detailed guidance for reforming the constitution, as Paddy Ashdown points out:

> **On both these issues he displayed a reckless personal commitment to what he believed was right and threw his personal credibility into what he saw as a moral battle between good and evil.**

> It's a sort of democratic view, community, but then you ask him to define it. The real thing he believes in is that Britain will be okay if it is governed by decent people. By which he means 'people like me'. He admires people who do tough things to bring their countries up to date, without necessarily assessing whether the 'up to date' means more democratic or not.

In other words, putting the modernizers in charge is more important than any particular system of government. Ashdown's pithy summary may over-simplify Blair's constitutional thinking, but not by much. Like 'What the Queen in parliament enacts is law', it is a traditionally British top-down formula. It is the 'decent chaps' theory of government, suitably updated for the 21st century. But however inadequate their theory, Blair and his chaps have begun reforming Britain. As Mikhail Gorbachev used to say, *protsess poshol* (the process has started). The final destination is unclear, even to the managers in Downing Street. Perhaps it is time for another seminar at Number 10, this time about the word that New Labour forgot – democracy.

NOTES

[1] Lecture to Constitution Unit, 8 December 1998.

[2] Disraeli Lecture, 29 October 1998.

[3] Cranborne, Robert (1998) *The End of Representative Democracy?*, London, Politeia.

[4] Foley, Michael (2000) *Isaac Newton meets Peter Mandelson: British politics on the turn*, Millennium Public Lecture, University of Wales, Aberystwyth, 30 March.

[5] *Unlocking Democracy*, Charter88, p 4.

[6] Speech to Make Votes Count, July 2000.

[7] *Prospect*, May 2000.

[8] *Irish Times*, 28 February 1997.

[9] *Prospect*, February 1999.

[10] Blair, Tony (1998) *The Third Way. New politics for a new century*, London, Fabian Society.

[11] Fairclough, Norman (2000) *New Labour, New Language*, London, Routledge.

[12] *The Times*, 28 July 2000.

[13] Blair, op. cit.

[14] *New Statesman*, 12 June 2000.

BIBLIOGRAPHY

BIBLIOGRAPHICAL NOTE

In writing this book I have drawn heavily on the wisdom of other journalists and academics who have marked out what Tom Nairn called the constitutional goat-tracks to and from Westminster. With a few exceptions, it is worth noting that the people who have given the subject most thought have come from outside the Labour party. There have been many useful works on specific constitutional matters, but significantly fewer attempts to address the subject as a whole. The most elegant overview in the past decade has come from Ferdinand Mount, who worked for Margaret Thatcher in 10 Downing Street as head of her policy unit. The argument for constitutional reform in his 1992 book *The British Constitution Now* is all the more powerful for being written from a conservative perspective.

Professor Peter Hennessy, a journalist-turned-academic, wrote two influential books in the mid-1990s, *The Hidden Wiring* and *Muddling Through*. Hennessy turned the absence of a written constitution into a treasure hunt, poking around with forensic skill into what Ferdinand Mount described as 'this accumulation of statutes, conventions, customs and historical deposits, written down in a dozen different places and in no place at all'. It is partly thanks to Hennessy that the Ministerial Code, previously *Questions of Procedure for Ministers*, is now a public document rather than a secret cabinet paper. Hennessy took a pragmatic insider's view on the need to reform the constitution 'with the grain', building on changes already under way. The story of his game of hunt-the-slipper around Whitehall and the Public Record Office illustrates better than any theoretical argument the way in which the absence of a written constitution leads to political exclusion. Hennessy's books also shed a great deal of light on Whitehall and its mandarins, and on the backstage constitutional role of the monarchy in the 20th century, including the insight that the Queen is as puzzled by the constitution as most of her citizens.

Vernon Bogdanor, Oxford University Professor of Government and a leading authority on constitutional history, wrote in his 1997 book *Power and the People* that Britain's constitution, once admired and imitated abroad, 'has become a warning of what to avoid'. He singled out as the key feature of the British system of government its concentration of power at the centre and the absence of checks or balances on the executive. His book was moderate, factual and non-partisan, but his conclusions were nonetheless devastating: 'Democracy in Britain today is predicated on the passivity of the vast majority of the country's citizens. The role of the people is limited to that of consenting or withholding its consent to the government of the day at periodic intervals … The British constitution has become a system for selecting, maintaining and dismissing a governing elite, the leaders of the ruling party.' Bogdanor identified proportional representation as the key remedy which would open up the political system and help make the people, not parliament, the source of sovereignty. His *Devolution in the United Kingdom* and *The Monarchy and the Constitution* are equally authoritative.

Andrew Marr's *Ruling Britannia*, published in 1995, is the best recent book by a journalist on constitutional matters. Marr examined the defects of British democracy under the Major government, concluding that there really was something rotten in the state that demanded profound change. A more militant campaigning argument came from Anthony Barnett, one of the founders of Charter88, in *This Time*, published in 1997, a few months after the election that brought Labour to power. The book was a vigorous plea for radical constitutional reform to build on the watershed event of Tony Blair's victory.

A similar radical spirit inspired two formidable, if somewhat indigestible, studies from the Democratic Audit, an academic group based at the University of Essex. Professor Stuart Weir and his colleagues tried to create an accurate snapshot of the state of Britain's rights, freedoms and democracy in two comprehensive volumes, measuring the system not against some historical or ideological norm but against international conventions and agreements. *The Three Pillars of Liberty*, published in 1996, found a 'pattern of systemic weakness' at the heart of Britain's political and constitutional arrangements. 'The British system precisely does not put the onus on government to justify interference with fundamental political rights. Parliamentary sovereignty in practice raises the executive above any systematic legal or political restraint.' The authors warned that neither parliament nor public opinion was strong enough to protect fundamental liberties, arguing that 'there are scarcely any countervailing institutions in this country between the weight of the executive and its coercive powers and the lives of ordinary citizens'.

In a second volume, *Political Power and Democratic Control in Britain*, Weir and co-author David Beetham looked at how the British political system worked, examining the results delivered by the electoral system, decision making in government, accountability to parliament and other issues. Starting from the principles of popular control and political equality, they concluded that although the United Kingdom clearly qualified as a democracy, it had systemic failings. The book included a prescient analysis of Labour's constitutional plans.

A markedly different approach was taken by Professor Robert Hazell of the Constitution Unit at University College London, which deliberately took a Whitehall-friendly line and tried to produce work that would be helpful and useful to an incoming Labour government. Hazell's unit produced a series of 'how to do it' studies on constitutional reform from 1996, many of which influenced Labour policy in opposition. The Unit's book *Constitutional Futures*, completed in late 1998, was predictive rather than polemical, setting out maximum and minimum scenarios for constitutional reform under Labour and drawing international comparisons. Subsequent developments matched almost exactly the minimum scenario, but Hazell predicted that further change would be inevitable: 'Even on the mini scenario ... the cumulative impact will be profound, because the constitutional reforms already set in train will unleash a political and legal dynamic which the government will not be able to rein back.'

Others whose works I have found invaluable in preparing this book include Peter Riddell of *The Times*, Tony Wright MP, and the Institute of Welsh Affairs in Cardiff, headed by John Osmond. Finally, I should add a mention of the Scottish author Tom Nairn, whose books are packed with stimulating insights. He visualizes the United Kingdom as 'Ukania', a term invented as the counterpart to 'Kakania', Robert Musil's vision of the dying Austro-Hungarian empire. At the risk of over-simplifying his views, one can say that Nairn tweaks the tail of the internationalist left by rehabilitating nationalism as a modernizing and democratizing force. Over the years his books and articles have made uncomfortable reading for just about everyone, including the SNP. Scotland, he believes, is halfway to a real constitutional settlement in which it will fully recover the independence it lost in 1707. Nairn at his best is brilliant; at his worst he can be opaque, disguising his meaning in layers of indigestible metaphor. The result is a bit like that famous Scottish delicacy, the deep-fried Mars bar hidden in layers of batter.

BOOKS, LECTURES AND PAMPHLETS

Alexander, Robert: *The Voice of the People. A constitution for tomorrow* (London, Weidenfeld & Nicholson) 1997.

Allen, Graham: *Reinventing Democracy. Labour's mission for the new century* (London, Features Unlimited) 1995.

Anderson, Paul and Mann, Nyta: *Safety First. The making of New Labour* (London, Granta Books) 1997.

Archer, Peter: 'The House of Lords, Past, Present and Future' in *The Political Quarterly*, Vol. 70, No. 4 (Oxford, B.H. Blackwell) Oct–Dec 1999.

Ashley, Jackie: *I Spy Strangers: Improving access to parliament* (London, Hansard Society) 2000.

Bagehot, Walter: *The English Constitution* (Brighton, Sussex Academic Press) 1997.

Baker, Amy: *Prime Ministers and the Rule Book* (London, Politico's) 2000.

Barendt, Eric: *An Introduction to Constitutional Law* (Oxford University Press) 1998.

Barker, Tony, Byrne, Iain and Veall, Anjuli: *Ruling by Task Force. Politico's guide to Labour's new elite* (London, Politico's) 1999.

Barnett, Anthony: *This Time. Our constitutional revolution* (London, Vintage) 1997.

Barnett, Anthony: 'Corporate Control' in *Prospect* magazine, February 1999.

Barnett, Anthony (ed.): *Power and the Throne* (London, Vintage) 1994.

Benn, Tony: *The Speaker, The Commons and Democracy* (Nottingham, Spokesman Books) 2000.

Benn, Anthony and Hood, Andrew: *Common Sense. A new constitution for Britain* (London, Hutchinson) 1993.

Bennie, Lynn, Brand, Jack and Mitchell, James: *How Scotland Votes* (Manchester University Press) 1997.

Biffen, John: *Inside Westminster* (London, André Deutsch) 1996.

Blackburn, Robert (ed.): *Constitutional Studies. Contemporary issues and controversies* (London, Mansell) 1992.

Blackburn, Robert (gen. ed.): *A Written Constitution for the United Kingdom* (London, Institute for Public Policy Research, Mansell) 1995.

Blackburn, Robert and Plant, Raymond (eds): *Constitutional Reform. The Labour government's constitutional reform agenda* (London, Longman) 1999.

Blair, Tony: *New Britain. My vision of a young country* (London, Fourth Estate) 1996.

Blair, Tony: *The Third Way. New politics for a new century* (London, Fabian Society) 1998.

Bogdanor, Vernon: 'Reform of the House of Lords: A sceptical view' in *The Political Quarterly*, Vol. 70, No. 4 (Oxford, B.H. Blackwell) Oct–Dec 1999.

Bogdanor, Vernon: *Devolution in the United Kingdom* (Oxford University Press) 1999.

Bogdanor, Vernon: *The Monarchy and the Constitution* (Oxford University Press) 1997.

Bogdanor, Vernon: *Power and the People. A guide to constitutional reform* (London, Victor Gollancz) 1997

Bogdanor, Vernon: *Civil Service Reform: a critique* (evidence to House of Commons Public Administration Committee) 2000.

Brazier, Rodney: *Constitutional Reform. Reshaping the British political system* (Oxford University Press) 2nd edition, 1998.

Brighty, David: *State and Region: the Spanish experience* (London, Royal Institute of International Affairs Briefing Paper No. 3) June 1999.

Brivati, Brian and Bale, Timothy: *New Labour in Power. Precedents and prospects* (London, Routledge) 1997.

Brown, Gordon and Alexander, Douglas: *New Scotland, New Britain* (London, The Smith Institute) 1999.

Brown, Gordon: *Constitutional Change and the Future of Britain* (London, The Charter88 Trust) 1992.

Burnham, June and Jones, George: *Accounting to Parliament by British Prime Ministers: Trends and discontinuities; illusions and realities* (paper for the Political Studies Association UK 50th Annual Conference, London) April 2000.

Chen, Selina and Wright, Tony (eds): *The English Question* (London, Fabian Society) 2000.

Colley, Linda: *Britons. Forging the nation 1707–1837* (London, Vintage) 1997.

Colley, Linda: *Britishness in the 21st Century* (Downing Street Millennium Lecture) 1999.

Cooke, Sir Robert: *The Palace of Westminster* (London, Burton Skira) 1987.

Cranborne, Robert: *The End of Representative Democracy?* (London, Politeia) 1998.

Crick, Bernard: *Essays on Citizenship* (London, Continuum) 2000.

Davies, Ron: *Devolution. A process not an event* (Cardiff, Institute of Welsh Affairs) 1999.

Dunleavy, Patrick, Margetts, Helen and Weir, Stuart: *The Politico's Guide to Electoral Reform in Britain* (London, Politico's) 1998.

Edwards, Owen Dudley (ed.): *A Claim of Right for Scotland* (Edinburgh, Polygon) 1989.

Egan, Dominic: *Irvine. Politically correct?* (Edinburgh, Mainstream Publishing Projects) 1999.

Evans, Eric J.: *Parliamentary Reform, 1770–1918* (London, Longmans) 2000.

Fairclough, Norman: *New Labour, New Language* (London, Routledge) 2000.

Finlayson, Alan: 'Third Way Theory' in *The Political Quarterly,* Vol. 70, No. 3 (Oxford, B.H. Blackwell) July–Sept 1999.

Flynn, Paul: *Dragons Led by Poodles. The inside story of a New Labour stitch-up* (London, Politico's) 1999.

Foley, Michael: *The Politics of the British Constitution* (Manchester University Press) 1999.

Foley, Michael: *Isaac Newton meets Peter Mandelson: British politics on the turn* (Millennium Public Lecture, University of Wales, Aberystwyth) 2000.

Foote, Geoffrey: *The Labour Party's Political Thought. A history* (London, Macmillan) 3rd edition, 1997.

Freedland, Jonathan: *Bring Home the Revolution. The case for a British republic* (London, Fourth Estate) 1999.

Gamble, Andrew and Wright, Tony: 'Reforming the Lords (Again)' in *The Political Quarterly,* Vol. 70, No. 3 (Oxford, B.H Blackwell) July–Sept 1999.

Gamble, Andrew and Wright, Tony: 'The New Social Democracy' in *The Political Quarterly* (Oxford, B.H. Blackwell) 1999.

Gorman, Teresa: *A Parliament for England* (Cheltenham, This England Books) 1999.

Grant, Charles: *EU 2010: an optimistic vision of the future* (London, Centre for European Reform) 2000.

Hambleton, Robin: *Directly Elected Mayors: reinvigorating the debate* (London, LGA discussion paper) 1999.

Hames, Tim: *The Coming Constitutional Crisis* (London, Politeia) 1998.

Hames, Tim and Leonard, Mark: *Modernising the Monarchy* (London, Demos) 1998.

Hassan, Gerry: *A Guide to the Scottish Parliament. The shape of things to come* (Edinburgh, The Stationery Office) 1999.

Hassan, Gerry and Warhurst, Christopher (eds): *A Different Future: A modernisers' guide to Scotland* (Glasgow, Big Issue and The Centre for Scottish Public Policy) 1999.

Hassan, Gerry and Warhurst, Christopher (eds): *The New Scottish Politics. The first year of the Scottish Parliament and beyond* (Norwich, The Stationery Office) 2000.

Hayden, Ilse: *Symbol and Privilege. The ritual context of British royalty* (University of Arizona Press) 1987.

Hazell, Robert (ed.): *Constitutional Futures. A history of the next ten years* (Oxford University Press) 1999.

Hazell, Robert: *Commentary on the Draft Freedom of Information Bill* (Constitution Unit) 1999.

Hazell, Robert and Russell, Meg: *Commentary on the Wakeham Report on Reform of the House of Lords* (Constitution Unit, London) 2000.

Heffer, Simon: *Nor Shall My Sword. The reinvention of England* (London, Phoenix) 1999.

Hennessy, Peter: *Muddling Through. Power, politics and the quality of government in post-war Britain* (London, Indigo) 1997.

Hennessy, Peter: *Whitehall* (New York, Macmillan) 1989.

Hennessy, Peter: *The Hidden Wiring. Unearthing the British constitution* (London, Indigo) 1996.

Hennessy, Peter: *Re-engineering the State in Flight: A year in the life of the British constitution* (Lloyds TSB Forum Lecture) 1998.

Hennessy, Peter: *The Blair Centre: a question of command and control?* (Public Management Foundation Lecture) 1999.

Hennessy, Peter: *The Blair Revolution in Government?* (Institute for Politics and International Studies, University of Leeds) 2000.

Hennessy, Peter: *Patterns of Premiership: the Blair style in historical perspective* (The Mishcon Lecture, University College London) 2000.

Hilton, Dominic: 'How did the British Labour party come to adopt the proposals for constitutional reform as described in its 1997 General Election Manifesto? (University of Oxford unpublished M. Phil thesis) 2000.

Himsworth, C.M.G and Munro, C.R.: *Devolution and the Scotland Bill* (Edinburgh, W. Green) 1998.

Holliday, Ian, Gamble, Andrew and Parry, Geraint (eds): *Fundamentals in British Politics* (London, Macmillan) 1999.

Jones, Barry and Keating, Michael: *Labour and the British State* (Oxford University Press) 1985.

Jones, Barry and Balsom, Denis (eds): *The Road to the National Assembly for Wales* (Cardiff, University of Wales Press) 2000.

Jones, Janet: *Labour of Love. The 'party-political' diary of a cabinet minister's wife* (London, Politico's) 1999.

Kavanagh, Dennis and Seldon, Anthony: *The Powers Behind the Prime Minister. The hidden influence of Number Ten* (London, HarperCollins) 1999

Kearney, Hugh: 'The Importance of Being British' in *The Political Quarterly*, Vol. 71, No. 1 (Oxford, B.H. Blackwell) Jan–March 2000.

Kishlansky, Mark: *A Monarchy Transformed. Britain 1603–1714* (London, Penguin) 1997.

Klug, Francesca, Starmer, Keir and Weir, Stuart: *The Three Pillars of Liberty. Political rights and freedoms in the United Kingdom* (London, Routledge) 1996.

Linton, Martin, Raymond, Katherine and Whitehead, Alan (eds): *Beyond 2002. Long-term policies for Labour* (London, Profile Books) 1999.

Linton, Martin and Southcott, Mary: *Making Votes Count. The case for electoral reform* (London, Profile Books) 1998.

Longford, Lord: *A History of the House of Lords* (Stroud, Sutton Publishing) 1999.

Mandelson, Peter and Liddle, Roger: *The Blair Revolution. Can New Labour deliver?* (London, Faber & Faber) 1996.

Marquand, David: 'The Blair Paradox' in *Prospect* magazine, May 1998.

Marr, Andrew: *Ruling Britannia. The failure and future of British democracy* (London, Michael Joseph) 1995.

Marr, Andrew: *The Day Britain Died* (London, Profile Books) 2000.

Mclean, Iain: 'Mr. Asquith's Unfinished Business' in *The Political Quarterly*, Vol. 70, No. 4 (Oxford, B.H. Blackwell) Oct-Dec 1999.

Meehan, Elizabeth: 'The Belfast Agreement: Distinctiveness and cross-fertilisation in the UK's devolution programme' in *Parliamentary Affairs*, Vol. 52, No. 1 (Oxford University Press) Jan 1999.

Mitchell, Austin: *Farewell my Lords* (London, Politico's) 1999.

Mitchell, James: 'The creation of the Scottish Parliament. Journey without end' in *Parliamentary Affairs* (Oxford University Press) October 1999.

Morgan, Kevin and Mungham, Geoff: *Redesigning Democracy. The making of the Welsh Assembly* (Bridgend, Seren Press) 2000.

Morgan, Rhodri: *Variable Geometry UK* (Cardiff, Institute of Welsh Affairs) 2000.

Mount, Ferdinand: *The British Constitution Now* (London, Mandarin) 1993.

Nairn, Tom: *The Enchanted Glass. Britain and its monarchy* (London, Vintage) 1988 and 1994.

Nairn, Tom: *After Britain. New Labour and the return of Scotland* (London, Granta Books) 2000.

Osmond, John (ed.): *The National Assembly Agenda. A handbook for the first four years* (Cardiff, Institute of Welsh Affairs) 1998.

Osmond, John (ed.): *A Parliament for Wales* (Llandysul, Gomer Press) 1995.

Paine, Thomas: *Rights of Man* (London, Penguin) 1995.

Parekh, Bhiku: 'Defining British National Identity' in *The Political Quarterly*, Vol. 71, No. 1 (Oxford, B.H. Blackwell) Jan–March 2000.

Paterson, Lindsay: *A Diverse Assembly. The debate on a Scottish Parliament* (Edinburgh University Press) 1998.

Perryman, Mark (ed.): *The Blair Agenda* (London, Lawrence & Wishart) 1996.

Pirie, Dr Madsen and Worcester, Robert: *The Big Turn-Off* (London, Adam Smith Institute) 2000.

Pollitt, Christopher: *Modernising Government: Four points and four proposals* (evidence to House of Commons Public Administration Committee) 2000.

Power, Greg (ed.): *Under Pressure: Are we getting the most from our MPs?* (London, Hansard Society) 2000.

Puttnam, David: 'A Democratic and Expert House' in *The Political Quarterly*, Vol. 70, No. 4 (Oxford, B.H. Blackwell) Oct–Dec 1999.

Rawnsley, Andrew: *Servants of the People* (London, Hamish Hamilton) 2000.

Redwood, John: *The Death of Britain?* (London, Macmillan) 1999.

Rhodes, R.A.W.: *New Labour's Civil Service; summing up joining-up* (evidence to House of Commons Public Administration Committee) 2000.

Richard, Ivor and Welfare, Damien: *Unfinished Business. Reforming the House of Lords* (London, Vintage) 1999.

Riddell, Peter: *Parliament Under Pressure* (London, Victor Gollancz) 1998.

Riddell, Peter: *Parliament Under Blair* (London, Politico's) 2000.

Russell, Conrad: 'Who's Afraid of Tony?', in *Prospect* magazine, October 1998.

Russell, Meg: 'Second Chambers Overseas' in *The Political Quarterly*, Vol. 70, No. 4 (Oxford, B.H. Blackwell) Oct–Dec 1999.

Russell, Meg: *Reforming the House of Lords. Lessons from overseas* (Oxford University Press) 2000.

Scarman, Lord: *Why Britain Needs a Written Constitution* (London, Charter88 Trust) 1992.

Shell, Donald: 'The Future of the Second Chamber' in *The Political Quarterly*, Vol. 70, No. 4 (Oxford, B.H. Blackwell) Oct–Dec. 1999.

Siedentop, Larry: *Democracy in Europe* (London, Allen Lane, The Penguin Press) 2000.

Smith, Anthony D.: *National Identity* (London, Penguin Books) 1991.

Smith, John: *A Citizen's Democracy* (London, Charter88) 1993.

Sutherland, Keith (ed.): *The Rape of the Constitution?* (Exeter, Imprint Academic) 2000.

Taylor, Alan (ed.): *What a State! Is devolution for Scotland the end of Britain?* (London, HarperCollins) 2000.

Taylor, Brian: *The Scottish Parliament* (Edinburgh, Polygon) 1999.

Taylor, Matthew with Joseph, Ella: *Freedom for Modernisation. Combining central targets with local autonomy* (London, Institute for Public Policy Research research paper) 1999.

Thatcher, Margaret: *The Downing Street Years* (London, HarperCollins) 1993.

Tomaney, John: 'New Labour and the English Question' in *The Political Quarterly*, Vol. 70, No. 1 (Oxford, B.H. Blackwell) Jan–Mar 1999.

Tomaney, John and Mitchell, Michelle: *Empowering the English Regions* (London, Charter88) 1999.

Tyrie, Andrew: *Mr Blair's Poodle* (London, Centre for Policy Studies) 2000.

Weir, Stuart and Beetham, David: *Political Power and Democratic Control in Britain* (London, Routledge) 1999.ˈ

Wells, John: *The House of Lords: From Saxon wargods to a modern senate. An anecdotal history* (London, Sceptre) 1998.

White, Clarissa, Bruce, Sara and Ritchie, Jane: *Young People's Politics. Political interest and engagement amongst 14- to 24-year-olds* (London, Joseph Rowntree Foundation) 2000.

Wright, Tony (ed.): *The British Political Process: An introduction* (London, Routledge) 2000.

Young, Hugo: *The Right to Secrecy* (Lecture to British Institute for Human Rights, King's College London) 2000.

Young, Hugo: *This Blessed Plot. Britain and Europe from Churchill to Blair* (London, Macmillan) 1998.

REPORTS AND GOVERNMENT DOCUMENTS

Report of the Independent Commission on the Voting System (The Jenkins Report) Cm 4090-1, The Stationery Office 1998, Vol. 1 and Vol. 2 (evidence on CD-rom only).

The Report of the Renewing Local Democracy Working Group (The Kerley Report) The Scottish Executive 2000.

Modernising Parliament. Reforming the House of Lords (The White Paper) Cm 4183 Cabinet Office 1999.

A House for the Future (The Wakeham Report) Cm 4534, The Royal Commission on the Reform of the House of Lords. The Stationery Office 2000.

Conference papers. The Future of the House of Lords. 8 March 2000 (Constitution Unit, London).

Open Government (Code of Practice on Access to Government Information) Second Edition, The Stationery Office 1997.

Your Right to Know (The Freedom of Information White Paper) Cm 3818, The Stationery Office 1997.

Your Right to Know: The Government's Proposals for a Freedom of Information Act, House of Commons Select Committee on Public Administration 1998.

The Government's Annual Report 97/98 Cm 3969, The Stationery Office.

The Government's Annual Report 98/99 Cm 4401, The Stationery Office.

The Government's Annual Report 99/00, The Stationery Office.

Modernising Government (The White Paper) Cm 4310, The Stationery Office 1999.

Civil Service Reform (Report to the Prime Minister from Sir Richard Wilson, Head of the Home Civil Service), Cabinet Office 1999.

Sharing the Nation's Prosperity. Variation in Economic and Social Conditions across the UK (A Report to the Prime Minister by the Cabinet Office), Cabinet Office 1999.

Reaching Out: The Role of Central Government at Regional and Local Level (A Performance and Innovation Unit Report), Cabinet Office 2000.

Wiring It Up. Whitehall's Management of Cross-Cutting Policies and Services (A Performance and Innovation Unit Report), Cabinet Office 2000.

Report of the Select Committee on the Public Service, House of Lords 1998.

Strengthening Parliament (The Norton Commission Report) Report of the Commission to Strengthen Parliament appointed by William Hague, Leader of the Conservative Party, chaired by Professor The Lord Norton of Louth, July 2000.

IGC: Reform for Enlargement. The British Approach to the European Union Intergovernmental Conference 2000 (The White Paper) Cm 4595, Foreign and Commonwealth Office 2000.

UK Foreign and Asylum Policy Human Rights Audit 2000 (Amnesty International UK).

Unlocking Democracy (Charter88 strategy document) June 2000.

The Funding of Political Parties in the United Kingdom (The Neill Report) Fifth Report of the Committee on Standards in Public Life Cm 4057-1, The Stationery Office 1998.

Reinforcing Standards. Review of the First Report of the Committee on Standards in Public Life Cm 4557-1, The Stationery Office 2000.

INDEX